The OPS Story

by
Adolph Saenz

Robert D. Reed Publishers • San Francisco, CA

Robert D. Reed Publishers

750 La Playa, Suite 647
San Francisco, CA 94121
Phone: 650-994-6570 • Fax: -6579
E-mail: 4bobreed@msn.com
web site: www.rdrpublishers.com

Typesetter: **Barbara Kruger**
Cover Designer: **Julia Gaskill with Mark Shea**

ISBN 1-931741-07-7

Library of Congress Catalog Card Number 2001118496

Manufactured, typeset and printed in the United States of America

Dedication

This book is dedicated to Byron Engle, the Director of the United States Office of Public Safety, and the men and women of OPS who, with unfaltering loyalty and patriotism, served their country in fighting communist aggression in a treacherous Cold War. I include a special tribute and salute for the American public safety advisors who were killed or wounded serving their country with OPS in the Cold War conflict.

Acknowledgments

There are many friends, colleagues and special people who helped make this book a reality. Byron Engle, the Director of OPS before he died, urged many times that one of us write the true story of the United States Office of Public Safety and respond to the communist propaganda. Engle greatly wanted to make known the important contributions and the accomplishments made by OPS to World peace. He once said that he wanted the people of this country to know that the OPS police advisors were the Nation's finest. The police forces of many Free World countries were able to improve their ability to provide police services to their citizens, to combat crime, drug trafficking, transnational terrorists, and to counter communist subversion and insurgency in the Cold War with the assistance of the U.S. OPS.

From the beginning, Bob Reed, the publisher, and I seemed to match up nicely for this book project where others could not. Barbara Kruger, Margaret Dugger, and Dr. Hemming Atterbom were extremely helpful with formatting and editing. Julia Gaskill along with Mark Shea helped to design a beautiful book cover. To all of them I am most grateful.

I am fortunate to have two fine friends who supported me in this project and with their financial help and encouragement the production of the book was possible.

Julian Lindenauer, my friend, former colleague, and veteran of the Drug Enforcement Administration (DEA), helped financially and was the one who convinced me to write **The OPS Story.**

My friend George Adams helped me financially and with excellent suggestions. As a decorated combat veteran of World War II and the Korean War with the 101st Airborne Division, he is an exemplary American and a man I am pleased to call my friend. To both of you, my heartfelt thanks.

There were others who provided moral support, including my cousin Carl Bernal, my daughters Babette and Marie Annette Saenz, and my sons Michael, Eric and Kurt Saenz. My daughter Lauren (Lori) Saenz-Keeley died at a young age of breast cancer, and has always been a great inspiration in my life.

The members of the former OPS program who helped with information and advice were many. I gratefully acknowledge the former Director of OPS, Lauren "Jack" Goin, for his suggestions and for writing a preface, and Herb Hardin, Julian Lindenauer, David Laughlin, Sam Turner, Bill Bartreau, Reg

Davis, Henry James, and others who helped with suggestions and information. I also thank two left-wing friends who prefer to remain anonymous after they told me of individuals they knew who supported communist and left-wing causes in America and Latin America to the detriment of the United States.

Lastly, I thank JoAnn Ortega for her enormous help in typing most of my manuscript and for her patience, and my wife Mary Ellen for her support, encouragement, and for helping in every way possible. I also thank Mr. Jonah.

Contents

Foreword ix

Preface xxiii

1   The United States Office of Public Safety, OPS 1

2   El Salvador, Central America 16

3   The Inter-American Police Academy. 27

4   The School of the Americas 33

5   The CINC 47

6   Bobby Kennedy. 65

7   Panama Explodes. 75

8   Assignment to Uruguay 93

9   Switzerland of the Americas 103

10   The *Tupamaros* 135

11   The Summit 156

12   Americans in Uruguay 176

13   *Ché* Guevara and Bolivia 198

14   The Replacement 222

15   Bogota, Columbia. 257

16   The Country Team 272

17   The Cali Kidnapping Cartel. 285

18   Cali 301

19   Ransom 317

20   El Eden. 335

21   Ley de Fuga. 365

22   Gringo Abduction 383

23   Resolution of a Murder 406

Epilogue 422

Appendix—The Career of Adolph Saenz. 452

Index. 461

Foreword

"The Cold War did not, of course, have the dramatic intensity of, say, World War II. But it was just as real and just as dangerous. Though often clandestine and subtle, it ranged worldwide, cost many lives, evoked much heroism, and lasted what seemed forever."   Charles Krauthammer, 2000

The OPS Story is not another *cri de coeur* about the Cold War. Columnist George Will says we never left the Cold War. But we remain subject to a secret and dangerous terrorist war with linkages to the Cold War. That new war may turn out to be the most evil of all wars. In the Cold War, **The OPS Story** is a singular piece of history that remains untold and is a lesson to be learned by America. In 1962, President John F. Kennedy established the United States Office of Public Safety (OPS), a national security initiative that was intended to provide police assistance to foreign countries. The objective of police assistance was to help other countries maintain a political climate that would support economic progress, democratization and to resist worldwide communist aggression.

America and the rest of the world now face the unprecedented challenge of a fanatical and suicidal hidden enemy. On September 11, 2001, the freedom and security enjoyed by all Americans was shattered to pieces with the cowardly terrorist attacks made on the World Trade Center in New York and on the Pentagon. Now the war that must surely follow will be the most vicious of all wars. It has already been predicted that it will be a long and arduous conflict. The enemies of freedom and democracy will not be easily defeated by conventional means. Americans must unite to use every means at our disposal against those who intend to destroy us. Many sacrifices for Americans loom ahead. But the division that took place in the Cold War conflict must not happen again. **The OPS Story** has a lesson for America as we prepare to fight the deadliest of all wars. The story is true.

The research undertaken to write this book and my own experiences led me to an impressive vista of a special breed of Americans who served with the OPS during the long, dark ideological conflict called the Cold War.

Many OPS Officers were killed in the line of duty. The threat of communist aggression that followed World War II was real for the Americans serving in the Cold War. But the fight against terrorists cannot be fought with one hand tied behind our back.

The OPS Story is a true and important part of history regarding United States police assistance provided to Free World countries in the period of the Cold War to support political and economic progress and to counter communist subversion, insurgency and terrorism. This is the true history of U.S. international police assistance, the operations involved and the numerous police professionals, diplomats, CIA and U.S. military officers who served on the hot front lines of the Cold War to carry out police assistance missions in many countries of the world.

My reason for writing this book was to provide the true story of American police assistance to other countries, the people who served as police advisors and their contribution to the national security interests of the United States during the Cold War. The factual story has never been told.

The OPS Story is also written for the benefit of the children, grandchildren and future generations of all Americans who served their country in the Cold War. That includes my own children and grandchildren. Hopefully it will help them to understand and appreciate the challenges faced by their country in the era of the '60s and '70s and the patriotic contributions made by their fathers and forefathers in a treacherous and thankless Cold War.

Lindy Biggs, an Associate Professor of History at Auburn University, described the importance of history in the National Forum, *Phi Kappa Phi* Journal of the Honor Society in the summer of 1997. **"History matters because it tells us who we are and where we have been. History matters because it reminds us of what we have won and lost. History matters because it teaches us, and if we listen to its lessons, helps correct injustices. History matters because only the rich and powerful have an identity and the status that goes along with it."**

The unraveling of the false communist allegations of torture by Americans and the allegations of **Hidden Terrors** by A.J. Langguth to justify the kidnapping and brutal murder of OPS Officer Dan Mitrione by Marxist guerrillas is overdue. It is fair, and it is just. This is my own perspective of the sad betrayal of Americans by other Americans during the Cold War.

A Historical Context of the Cold War

In the aftermath of the Allied Victory in World War II, Winston Churchill expressed the fear that Joseph Stalin intended to swallow up

Eastern Europe. It was obvious that the Red Army had no intention of retreating back to Russia from occupied territory at the end of the war. In a prophetic outrage made by Adolph Hitler and allegedly overheard by a certain Private "Ivan Nikitin" (a captured German SS trooper), the Führer angrily predicted that the threat to the world was Stalin's Realpolitik and the domination of the world by communism.

The global conflict that eventually followed World War II became known as the Cold War. President Richard Nixon called it World War III. Many believe that the Cold War was a conflict between capitalism and communism or between democracy and totalitarianism. CIA defector Phillip Agee was quoted in a **Playboy Magazine** article as saying that the communist conspiracy of the Cold War was an American façade. Agee believed that "The CIA initiated the conflict to guarantee a favorable foreign-investment climate for U.S. industry." But, like many Americans, Agee is biased.

President Harry Truman presided over the inchoate threat of the Cold War when pro-Communist governments loyal to the Soviet Union were installed in every country occupied by the Russian Army after World War II. European countries liberated by the Allied Armies remained locked geopolitically under the domination of the Red Army.

In 1946, Winston Churchill coined the phrase **Iron Curtain** to describe the blockade imposed by the USSR to close off Europe. After World War II President Franklin Roosevelt had remained positive and optimistic about the Soviet intransigence regarding hegemony and the global balance of power. He apparently believed that Stalin could be tempered by moral principle and would abandon the terms of his aggression. But in reality it was already a Cold War.

In 1948, a *coup d'état* in Czechoslovakia gave the communists control. In 1948, the USSR stopped road and rail traffic between Berlin and the West and isolated millions of people.

As a result, General George C. Marshall, the United States Secretary of State, established the Berlin Airlift to neutralize the Soviet effort of blockade that had lasted until September 1949. Marshall also supported the formation of NATO to stem the tide of communist aggression.

The construction of the Berlin Wall became a monument to Soviet domination and hegemony but communist aggression continued with intransigent resolve. A communist regime established in Hungary in 1949 was aided by Russian troops. In 1956, Russian troops invaded Hungary to ensure continued communist control of that country.

As far back as the administrations of President Theodore Roosevelt and Woodrow Wilson, United States foreign policy had been based on the idea that the security of our country had been inseparable from the security of other countries. That *raison d'état* was ideally suited for the Cold War, an ideological struggle for world domination that began with the Russian Bolshevik revolution. Vladimir Ilyich Lenin had combined Marxist theory with ruthless insurrection tactics in an attempt to form a communist world.

My first glimpse of communist aggression occurred when I was a young U.S. Marine. In 1946, Communist and Nationalist forces were at war to take over China when I was sixteen years of age and my Marine Corps outfit was stationed in Peking (Beijing). For over a year, veterans from the First Marine Division and First Marine Air Wing watched the war between two mammoth armies develop, often from just a few miles away.

U.S. Marine units in China were surrounded by over a million Nationalist Chinese and Communist Chinese troops and in danger of becoming engulfed in the internal war. U.S. Secretary of State Cordell Hull later expressed his concern that the U.S. troops would be annihilated before they could be gotten out of China. The U.S. Marines were evacuated from China in early 1947 as the struggle between the Nationalists and the Communists expanded.

"What the hell is communism?" I posed the question innocuously to a Marine Gunnery Sergeant as we marched out of China loaded with full packs, M-1 rifles, Browning Automatic Rifles (BARS) and heavy bandoleers of ammunition.

"It's the fucking Russians," the Gunny told me *sans* further enlightenment. We boarded the U.S.S. Warhawk at *Qinhuangdao* to leave China. Two years later the communists took over the country and Chiang Kai-shek and his followers fled to Formosa (Taiwan).

The United States had responded initially to the threat of communist aggression with a policy of containment. After World War II the Marshall Plan provided $17 billion for the economic recovery of European nations torn by the war. The initiatives developed by the Marshall Plan addressed the growing problem of communist aggression.

It is interesting to note that United States police assistance to countries ravaged by World War II can be traced to the early Marshall Plan. A man named Hankey had joined the Berkeley Police Department in 1938 when a Bachelor's Degree was a requirement. He later obtained a Ph.D and left the Berkeley Police Force in 1942 to join the U.S. Army.

Hankey, a Major in the U.S. Army, was assigned to work with O.W. Wilson, who was then a U.S. Army Colonel, to reorganize the West German Police. O.W. Wilson, a former professor at Berkeley University and former

Chief of Police of Chicago, is deceased but is known as the foremost authority of modern police administration in the United States.

When World War II ended, an initial effort by the United States to strengthen the police forces in Japan was under the management and administration of the U.S. Army intelligence Corps (G-2) of the headquarters of General Douglas MacArthur and under the command of an Army Colonel named Pulian. A group called the Department of the Army Civilians (DAC), led by a retired Deputy Chief of the Los Angeles Police Department named Henry Eaton, was under Pulian.

It was obvious then that in the aftermath of a war, the police become indispensable to peace and the economic progress and security of nations recovering from any conflict. Experience has clearly demonstrated that law and order is crucial to economic progress and political stability in any nation.

In America, resistance to anti-Communist initiatives during the Cold War and to the Vietnam conflict generated major internal dissent and conflict that threatened the internal security and well-being of the United States. The police played a key role in the maintenance of law and order.

In the 1960s and '70s, ideological differences fueled by the Vietnam War created major disruptions, potential violence and security problems in the United States. Peace movements, anti-war demonstrations and frequent mob action served to spark discord and ignited an extremely difficult political period and threats to public safety in many communities of the United States. The division that threatened to tear the country apart during the Cold War period became a grave challenge for democratic principles and for democracy in America as a whole.

To protest the war in Vietnam, activists organized mass demonstrations that commonly resulted in mob violence. The civil rights movement was also in full bloom with demonstrations and violence that often resulted in violent encounters between the police and activists.

But an interesting anomaly was the resistance to American anti-Communist initiatives during the Cold War by specific groups. The opposition to United States foreign policy became as common as forest fires in a dry summer month, because of what appeared to be mostly Far-Left Radical ideology, misled liberalism, and self-serving morality. Much of it began in the 1960s along with the freedom movements organized by young misguided liberal Americans.

The national controversy about the threat of communism had started much earlier. Henry Wallace, the Vice President of the United States during the third term of Franklin Delano Roosevelt, called President Harry Truman's description of the conflict with communism as being between democracy and dictatorship "pure fiction."

Other ideologues reacted in a similar fashion. United States Congressmen Staughton Lynd and Tom Hayden openly boasted. "We refuse to be Anti-Communist." Hayden had once headed the radical left-wing organization called Students for a Democratic Society (SDS).

After the Korean War, when communist aggression continued inexorably, containment turned into nation building with a hot war in Vietnam. President Kennedy defined the goal in Vietnam as "to create in that country a viable and increasing democratic society through military, political, economic, psychological and covert action." Meanwhile, Nikita Khrushchev publicly threatened Americans with the ominous prediction: **"Your grandchildren will live under communism!"**

Ronald Reagan was President of the United States in the final stages of the Cold War and is credited with driving the Soviet Union into economic bankruptcy. Others, imbued with political surrealism more than reality, insist it was Jimmy Carter's human rights movement that pushed communism down the tubes. The way things developed, communism would probably have collapsed on its own without the Cold War. But if Josef Stalin had lived longer, things might have turned out differently. Human rights were the least of Stalin's concerns.

In 1950, communist North Korea invaded South Korea and the United States committed over half a million troops to a war that resulted in 33,629 Americans killed in combat and thousands of casualties. President Harry Truman had stood up to communist aggression in Korea, but at a price. But Truman's actions may have turned the course of history. The Korean War created a lull in a hot War.

But in Latin America, Fidel Castro took on the leading role of a communist persona in the Western Hemisphere. His insurgent movement of about three dozen men and women traversed the ocean in small boats from Mexico to invade Cuba in 1956, and for three years, after he landed in Cuba, Castro conducted guerrilla warfare against the forces of the Batista regime.

The crippling corruption and ineffectiveness of Batista's government extended all the way to his troops and gave Castro a major advantage. In 1959, with the opposition against him mounting, Fulgencio Batista, the Dictator of Cuba, fled to the Dominican Republic and Castro took over the country. Forty-five years later, at age 75, Castro remains the *"Líder de la Revolución"* in communist Cuba and is still considered by many to be a threat to the national security of the United States.

Throughout the world, people initially rejected the notion that Fidel Castro was a communist and supported his efforts to topple the corrupt Fulgencio Batista regime. The Central Intelligence Agency (CIA) raised uncertainty about Castro, but any doubt about his ideology ended when once he was seated on the throne of power and declared to the world that he was: *"Un comunista hasta la muerte!"* It appeared to me that most CIA officers in WH (Western Hemisphere) could not speak Spanish.

As a Marxist/Leninist, Dr. Ernesto *Che'* Guevara and his trademark black beret helped Fidel Castro became a critical and important ally for the Soviet Union in the hemisphere. Consistently harassed with the problem of Fidel Castro and the threat of communist aggression in Latin America, President John F. Kennedy turned to covert operations and secret armies.

In 1961, short of a broad base of support for U.S. military intervention, President Kennedy approved a secret CIA plan to invade the small island of Cuba with Cuban exiles to overthrow Castro.

Richard Bissell had developed the CIA plan under President Dwight Eisenhower. In March of 1960, President Eisenhower had directed that an adequate paramilitary force of Cuban exiles be organized to overthrow the Castro regime.

The Bissell plan inherited by Kennedy had the support of Allen Dulles, the Director of the CIA. But Kennedy found out that master-spies are capable of serious blunders. Bissell had wrongly assured President Kennedy that the military resources of the United States would not be needed for the invasion. Some people have suggested that the CIA counted on the fact that Kennedy, once the invasion was underway, could not risk defeat and would be forced to send in the Marines if needed.

Major uprisings were expected to happen inside Cuba once the invasion started and would help to overwhelm Castro. But the plan failed to provide for cancellation. In effect, Kennedy was trapped by the plan once it was implemented.

With Richard Bissell being pressured by the Cuban exiles and Kennedy obsessed with the idea of eliminating Fidel Castro, the CIA was given the green light to train a secret army of Cuban exiles in Guatemala and other locations. But the plan to invade Cuba did not remain secret for long. Castro's operatives in the hemisphere knew about the training of the Cuban exiles by American CIA personnel.

The invasion of Cuba planned for April of 1961 drew near and President Kennedy and his Cabinet continued to express misgivings about the CIA plan. The invasion site was changed from a place called Trinidad on the Southern Coast of Cuba to the *Playa de Giron* (Bay of Pigs). Many critics contend that changes made by Kennedy in the invasion plan paved the way for disaster.

But after the Bay of Pigs fiasco, Fidel Castro admitted that he was prepared to resist an invasion at Trinidad and it was his opinion that a blood bath would have occurred if the invasion had taken place at Trinidad. He said that Cuban security forces were prepared for an invasion at Trinidad, but not at the Bay of Pigs. Castro did not have reason to lie.

A CIA plot (called AMLASH) to assassinate Fidel Castro became an integral part of the invasion plan and, albeit fascinating, was doomed to fail. Of course, Castro was expected to rally resistance, and it was a good idea to eliminate him as soon as possible once the invasion started.

The CIA plan was that Fidel Castro was to be assassinated by hired "Mafia" personalities from Chicago. But Cuba had little similarity to Chicago and the assassination plot quickly unraveled. The Americans involved in planning the invasion of Cuba clearly underestimated Fidel Castro's cunning leadership, his military strength, and the popular support he enjoyed in Cuba. The Bay of Pigs turned into a fiasco for Kennedy.

President Kennedy is said to have believed that the invasion would eventually become a mass infiltration of Cuban exiles to fight a guerrilla war from the mountains against the Castro regime. That might have been a better plan. But Castro suggested after the failed Bay of Pigs invasion that the initial air strike made by the Cuban exile air force served to warn him that an invasion was about to take place.

Subsequently, the resistance by Castro's troops to the invasion turned surprising and stronger than expected. Once the invasion started, the Cuban exiles found themselves isolated on the beach, running out of ammunition, and taking heavy losses from Castro's artillery and tanks.

Meanwhile, Kennedy, apparently concerned about an adverse political reaction in America and in other countries, refused to let American military aircraft conduct further air strikes that might have extricated the invading exile force from an untenable position. He had been told initially by Bissell that no American resources would be needed for the invasion and Kennedy stuck to that.

The limited number of World War II B-26 medium bombers flown by Cuban exiles to attack Castro's air force were eventually shot down by Russian MIGs, some reportedly flown by Russian pilots. Without the American air support desperately needed, the Cuban exile invasion force had little chance to survive after taking heavy losses and running out of ammunition. Different sources provide different figures, but about 200 Cuban exiles were killed and 150 wounded; 1,189 exiles were taken prisoner.

Fidel Castro suggested after the Bay of Pigs fiasco that further American air strikes would not have made a difference in the outcome. But we will never know.

When I was posted in Latin America, Latin American friends and high-ranking government officials told me that they were bitterly disappointed to see that President Kennedy lacked the *cojones* (balls) to move forcibly and aggressively against Castro in the Bay of Pigs invasion.

Meanwhile, the plan to assassinate Fidel Castro failed miserably. The massive internal uprising expected when the invasion started also did not happen. The Cubans were aware that Castro's security/intelligence operatives would move against any sign of an internal rebellion. But after the Bay of Pigs landing, Castro's Minister of Internal Security, Ramiro Valdez Melendez, revealed that 20,000 Cubans were arrested after the failed invasion. The American assessment was correct that an internal uprising would take place with the invasion. But that was short-lived.

A CIA report later criticized every aspect of the invasion effort to include: "Misinforming Kennedy Administration officials, poor planning, faulty intelligence, and conducting an overt military operation beyond Agency responsibilities as well as Agency capability." Many Americans watching the scenario develop stepped back to say, "I told you so."

Following the failure of the Bay of Pigs invasion, Fidel Castro ventured into harvesting the growing seeds of social and labor unrest and discontent in Latin America to destabilize countries and to spread communism in the region. Castro openly declared war on non-communist countries.

Assistant Secretary of State for Inter-American Affairs Thomas O. Enders predicted a pattern that became a reality. Enders suggested there was a disagreement over tactics by the radical left in the hemisphere but that some factions opted to set up "*Che'* Guevara style *focos*." That meant putting armed *guerrilleros* into the countryside with the hope that their presence would radicalize the peasants.

Others of the radical left opted for a *guerra prolongada* (the long war). That meant discrediting an existing regime by hitting the economy. Kidnappings and assassinations became common factors.

Fidel Castro reveled in his role of being one of America's most dreaded *bête noirs*—and openly exported violence and revolution to support communist guerrillas in Latin America. He did this from only 90 miles off the Florida coast. Like Lenin in Russia, Castro became the rallying figure for communist movements in the hemisphere.

Castro's totalitarian regime in the beautiful island of Cuba consolidated its power and communist expansionism prospered. Cuba's military forces, strengthened by Russian equipment, technical assistance, training, and a large number of Soviet advisors, gave Castro a military power capable of capturing ground for the communists as far away as Angola. Castro was estimated to have a well-equipped armed force of over 400,000 men and more than 900 tanks, 650 armored vehicles, anti-aircraft guns, missiles, frigates, and submarines.

Meanwhile, Cuban operatives infiltrated Bolivia, El Salvador, Mexico, Guatemala, the Dominican Republic, Grenada, Nicaragua, Panama, Venezuela, and Uruguay on missions of espionage, subversion, and guerrilla warfare.

In 1962, Fidel Castro was aligned with the "defensive interests" of the Soviet Union and, pushed by Ernesto *Che'* Guevara, led the world to a near nuclear war. With a Russian military base established in Cuba, the USSR had clandestinely constructed SAM (Surface to Air Missile) sites throughout the small island. Informed of the threat to the United States developing in Cuba, President Kennedy approved the use of U-2 flights and other military aircraft to fly intelligence missions over the island.

The information subsequently developed by the United States on the Soviet missiles in Cuba was indeed frightening. Besides 500 SS-5 IRBM (Intermediate Range Ballistic Missiles), 21 Russian IL Beagle Bombers, and 101 Soviet fighter aircraft had been introduced to Cuba. The nuclear-tipped IRBM missiles had a range of 2,200 miles and were capable of hitting major cities in the United States. U.S. intelligence further determined that Soviet military personnel in Cuba had been increased to over 23,000 people. The number of Soviet troops in Cuba was almost equivalent to the size of the U.S. military force used in Operation "Just Cause" for the invasion of Panama to get Manuel Noriega. The number of Soviet military personnel in Cuba amounted to a small army.

Based on the reports of the Soviet threat in Cuba, President Kennedy ordered a naval blockade of the Island. The United States prepared for war against the USSR, and the Cuban missile crisis brought the world to a near nuclear catastrophe. Reportedly, *Che'* Guevara argued strongly in favor of a first strike by the Soviet Union and Cuba against the United States.

With the United States and the USSR on a war footing, secret negotiations taking place between President Kennedy, Robert Kennedy, and Soviet Premier Nikita Khrushchev resulted in an agreement deemed acceptable to both nations. Kruschev backed down from a potential nuclear exchange and removed the Soviet missiles from Cuba.

The Time Magazine issue of March 9, 1998, indicated that Khrushchev had sized up Kennedy as a weakling, given to strong talk and timorous action. The U.S. itself, Khrushchev told Poet Robert Frost, was "too liberal to fight." Time suggested that Kennedy obviously shattered those illusions. The negotiations with the Soviet Union were not made totally public but the outcome was a triumph for President John F. Kennedy.

The Cold War pushed on and United States used traditional *raison d'état* to protect national security interests. The collective security of the world continued to be essential to the national security of the United States. At the same time, the communist bloc used insurgencies to continue a policy of expansionism. Soviet Premier Nikita Khrushchev pledged the support of the USSR for "Wars of Liberation." Communist movements, supported by Castro Cuba, attacked what Richard Nixon called "the soft underbelly of the United States," Central America and the Caribbean. The poverty, social injustice, and lack of opportunity in many countries provided solid ground for communist insurgency.

Despite the dismal economic conditions, lack of social progress and zero political reform in Latin American countries, U.S. foreign aid had been severely limited. After his election, President John F. Kennedy approved the creation of the Agency for International Development (AID) and the Alliance for Progress to provide foreign aid to Latin American and other countries. Still, democracies in Latin America continued to vie with military coups and communist insurgencies during the Cold War.

The Cold War included espionage, subversion, guerrilla warfare, terrorism, disinformation, criminal acts, assassinations, kidnappings and clandestine activities. Clandestine operations became the blood and marrow of political movements. A guerrilla force had political power beyond its size.

On the American front, Actress Jane Fonda assailed American troops in Vietnam with rhetoric that supported the communist cause. American POWs held in Hanoi prisons were accused by Fonda of killing babies during bombing raids made on North Vietnam.

On a visit to North Vietnam, she posed on top of North Vietnamese army tanks, frolicked with communist leaders, and visited Ho Lo Prison where the North Vietnamese were torturing American POWs. Jerry Driscoll, a captured American pilot, was ordered by his captors to tell the visiting Peace Activist (Jane Fonda) about the humane treatment he had received at the POW camp. Instead, he spat on Fonda and was brutally beaten.

At the Institute for Policy Studies (IPS), a well-known radical left-wing think tank in Washington, D.C., Karen de Young was heard to tell attendees of a conference, **"western journalists, at least, are very eager to seek out guerrilla groups, leftist groups, because you assume they must be the**

good guys." The implication seemed to be that any anti-Communist action was wrong.

In 1969, Philip Burnett Franklin Agee, a CIA officer motivated by what he called the "wrongdoing of the CIA," defected to the communist side. Agee had emotional problems, was estranged from his wife, and despite warnings not to do so, took their children to Mexico without her permission. Matters for the **Company** worsened after Agee's affair with a Cuban Communist in Mexico. He defected and moved to London to write a book he believed would seriously damage the CIA. Albeit, many still believe that Agee's defection was a dumb CIA ploy.

David Atlee Phillips, a former CIA Station Chief in Caracas, Venezuela, and former Chief of the Western Hemisphere (WH) for the **Company**, observed in a televised interview: "I know that our intelligence services should not do anything which violates our Constitution. That's the way it must be. So now we find ourselves conducting the incredible adventure of trying to determine whether or not it's possible to conduct secret operations in Macy's window." But he found out it was hard to fight the logic of the communists and their supporters in the Cold War.

Phillips said he did not know who pulled the trigger on the pistol that killed Richard Welch (Welch was the CIA Chief of Station in Greece). But in a publication released before Richard Welch was killed, Philip Agee had said that his job was to obtain the names, photographs, and addresses of CIA people throughout the world and to have the information published in local newspapers. The purpose was to expose CIA personnel and have them killed or harassed to a point where they were neutralized.

Over lunch in Washington, D.C., in 1983, Dave Phillips was sympathetic about false allegations made by Roger Morris, an American free lance reporter accusing me in a New Mexico tabloid of heading a **"CIA inspired program"** (OPS) in Uruguay that taught torture to the police. Morris had trained in Moscow, in the Soviet Union, for one year. That alone should have made him suspect. Any allegation is extremely difficult to deal with if it is cloaked in the wiles of a pseudo journalist

David Phillips told me that an American publication had accused him of being involved in the assassination of President John F. Kennedy. I do not recall the name of the publication but Phillips told me that he had sued the publication, but settled out of court. He cited the impossibility of proving "malice." "Don't count on help from the U.S. Government," he said. He was right on both counts.

Before he died, David Phillips founded the **Association of Former Intelligence Officers (AFIO),** a national organization of former intelligence officers who have served in U.S. Government Agencies, the CIA, FBI, etc., or in the U.S. Military Forces.

Roger Morris had also accused my friend Herb Hardin, a former OPS Officer, of the same false allegations he used against me. Hardin filed a libel suit against Morris and a local weekly tabloid from Santa Fe called **The Santa Fe Reporter.** In a trial held, Federal Judge Juan Burciaga subsequently found that the allegations made by Morris were **"patently false"** and that he **"had come perilously close to reckless disregard for the truth."** Malice had to be proven since Hardin was a public official.

Morris had made the same allegations against me in the same Santa Fe tabloid and in a **Playboy Magazine** article written in connection with a bloody New Mexico State Prison uprising in Santa Fe. I was trapped in the middle of the violent morass of the prison riot in New Mexico after my appointment as Secretary of Corrections was announced to the media two days earlier. In his article, Morris reported that I had **"postured as the commander of the troops in the retake of the prison. But (I) seemed practiced, too practiced, in that role."** For Roger Morris, I was a CIA-sponsored terrorist.

The truth is that I had absolutely **no authority** to intervene in the prison riot. Nevertheless, I did intervene to lead the effort to effectively stop the bloody inmate killings and the savage violence that had been ongoing for thirty-six hours without any action by the State. My first visit to the prison was on the day the brutal uprising in the state prison exploded. That is another story.

Roger Morris is an effeminate, nervous individual who likes to wear cravats, and promotes himself as a former assistant to the United States Secretary of State. But U.S. Government records show that his grade in the U.S. Department of State was FSO 6 (equivalent to a GS-9 or -10). At that grade, Morris was obviously a mere horseholder.

He brags that he worked for the National Security Council (NSC) but again the record shows that he was assigned to the NSC from the Department of State on a non-reimbursable detail. Morris resigned eight months later in protest of what he called the "U.S. invasion of Cambodia."

After leaving the NSC, Morris vehemently condemned Henry Kissinger for his role in the Vietnam War and his alleged involvement in the military *coup* led by General Agosto Pinochet in Chile in 1973 to overthrow the communist regime of Salvador Allende. In a book he wrote about Kissinger, Morris focuses on the usual left-wing attacks used in the Cold War during the Vietnam War. His book about Alexander Haig follows the same theme.

On February 12, 2001, on C-Span, Roger Morris, with a panel of ideologues, charged Henry Kissinger with being a war criminal. I wonder if Kissinger really cares?

A former KGB Officer named Yuri Bezmenov, AKA Tomas Schuman, analyzed the articles written by Roger Morris. He concluded: **"The author (Morris) consistently used the same methods of disinformation, the same semantic manipulation, and the same type of propaganda I had been instructed to use during all my years with the KGB."** Was Morris trained in *Novosti*? Well, he was in Moscow, in the USSR, for one year.

On another Cold War front, the dark secrets of the CIA made known by William Colby, the Director Central Intelligence Agency (DCI) alleged that the **Phoenix Program** in South Vietnam had caused the deaths of over 20,000 Vietnamese. The **Phoenix Program** was a CIA initiative and focused on the identification and elimination of Viet Cong cells operating in South Vietnam. It was a common practice of the North Vietnamese military forces to infiltrate South Vietnam villages to carry out espionage missions, sabotage, and guerrilla warfare operations.

Ironically, General Vo Nguyen Giap, one of the most effective North Vietnamese military commanders, was quoted as saying: **"The Phoenix Program was probably the most successful and feared program of my tenure that threatened the Viet Cong infrastructure in South Vietnam."**

Colby was farcically accused of being a KGB Agent behind his back and he explained in hearings held that it was simply his constitutional responsibility to let the American people know the truth about the matter.

Many Americans have asked the following question. So we went from a hot war, called World War II, to the Cold War that included Korea and Vietnam, and then to something called Détente? But the Gulf War dramatically changed things. Osama bin Laden and al Qaeda have declared a terrorist war that will have long-term implications and will bring sheer horror for all Americans. Is that considered another Cold War? It depends on what is meant by is.

Preface

"One of the objectives of the OPS was to counter communist inspired or exploited subversion and insurgency."
—David Bell, AID Administrator

To understand why the United States became involved in assisting foreign police forces beginning shortly after the end of World War II, it is important to examine the role of the civil police in democratic societies and as it is practiced in the U.S.

In any country, the police are considered to be the governmental agency that is responsible for humanely enforcing the law, without bias and strictly in accordance with how the law is written. In pursuing this task the police must prevent crime, control dissent lest violence emerge, and assist each member of society in pursuing their individual rights. Protection of life and property go hand-in-hand with law enforcement. In these ways, the civil police in the United States differ markedly from those in regimes where dictators rule.

For the first time since World War II, the United States responded to requests for assistance from other countries in improving the effectiveness of its civil police forces. Initially, such assistance was provided under the aegis of the U.S. occupation forces in Japan, Germany, and Italy. Advisors were provided in Iran and Turkey. These efforts were unilaterally provided by the United States after the war and were instrumental in recreating civil police forces essential for the reconstruction of those nations reeling from the aftermath of the most major world war that has existed.

In 1954, President Eisenhower recognized the need for helping civil police forces in addition to military forces of foreign nations. He directed and provided leadership for the establishment of a resource within the foreign aid agency at the time, to help civil police forces with advice, training, and commodities. The first such program was in Indonesia in 1954.

President Kennedy provided new impetus for the police assistance program in directing that a new program be established within the Agency for International Development, the foreign aid agency within the State

Department. As a consequence, the Office of Public Safety was established in November 1962.

From the outset, and until the program ended in July 1975, nearly 1,500 civil police advisors were assigned overseas and aid was provided to 56 nations of the free world. Nearly 7,000 police officers were trained in the U.S., mostly at the International Police Academy. The program left a legacy of trained, dedicated police officers throughout the world, and the need for the continued contribution of such officers is evident in daily reports of violence and the frustration of human rights.

The author of this book, Mr. Adolph B. Saenz, was a senior advisor in the Office of Public Safety program. He joined the civil police assistance program in November of 1958 after serving as a police officer in the Albuquerque Police Department. He was assigned as a Police Training Advisor in El Salvador and as Chief of the OPS programs in Uruguay, Panama, and Venezuela, and as Chief Instructor at the police school in the Panama Canal Zone, called the Inter-American Police Academy. He brings a special and personal perspective to the story of OPS as one intimately involved.

Lauren Jack Goin
Former Director, OPS

1

The United States Office of Public Safety
OPS

"The politicians and Marxists may have discontinued our program but no one can diminish the good we accomplished throughout the world and our pride in what we were able to do in the time allotted us. I feel that the world would not be experiencing the current proliferation of international terrorism if we had been permitted to continue our work." **—Byron Engle, OPS Director (May 1986)**

In the 1960s, the tocsin of the communist threat rang loud and motivated new action from President John F. Kennedy. Counterinsurgency became an initiative and a buzzword in United States Cold War planning. The OPS began operations in 1962 as a United States strategy to counter communist aggression. The basic policy for OPS (public safety programs) began with AID Order 1542.1. "It is United States policy to assist less developed friendly countries in achieving internal security."

Since communist takeovers usually started with subversion, the provocation of labor and civil unrest, followed by guerrilla action and a full-blown insurgency, counterinsurgency was a good idea. Stalin lied when he told the Western Allies in 1945 that **"the Soviet Union's peaceful policy does not include attacks on capitalist countries."**

Subversion, mass violence, riots, insurgency, and guerrilla warfare became principal instruments of communist movements to expand their control and hegemony in the Cold War. That strategy proved effective in many countries of the world. The United States looked for ways to counter the threat.

In 1954, in a meeting of the National Security Agency (NSA), President Dwight Eisenhower made the observation that the United States was providing assistance to the military forces of other countries when in many cases a clear military threat to those countries was absent. He expressed concern that the civil forces in those same countries that were responsible for the protection of life and property and for law enforcement had been left out.

As a consequence, the Hoover Commission was tasked to look at the public safety situation and security requirements in select foreign countries. Subsequently, the Hoover Commission recommended U.S. police assistance and programs were initiated in Indonesia, Laos, the Philippines, Cambodia, and Iran. U.S. police assistance programs were also started in Bolivia, Honduras, Ecuador, and El Salvador.

The United States had years of experience after World War II in providing assistance to the civil police forces of other countries. A great deal of the American police assistance provided to other countries after World War II had been under the aegis of the U.S. military occupational forces. In Japan, civil police assistance was under the command of General Douglas MacArthur, the Supreme Commander of the Allied Powers in the Pacific.

Historically, in the early 1950s, United States police assistance was administered under the Foreign Operations Administration (FOA) under the U.S. Department of State, and later by the International Cooperation Administration (ICA) also under the U.S. Department of State. U.S. police professionals, and CIA officers worked as public safety advisors and were assigned to the United States Operations Missions (USOM) in foreign posts.

In terms of the U.S. foreign aid, it was an accepted principle that police assistance, if properly served, would strengthen the internal security of foreign countries and would promote humane law enforcement practices. Both were considered essential precursors for the economic, social, and political progress of any nation.

When the conflict broke out in South Vietnam in the early 1960s, America sought ways to fight that war, and Secretary of Defense Melvin Laird believed Vietnamization was the answer. That meant helping South Vietnam develop a "stronger administration, a stronger economy, stronger military forces, and **stronger police** (emphasis mine) for internal security." The Cold War was heating up when the Kennedy administration initiated consultations with U.S. foreign policy planners to study the issue of police assistance to foreign countries.

In early 1962, Byron Engle, a veteran CIA Officer, was detailed to head a Technical Subcommittee to work with an Inter-Agency Committee appointed by Kennedy and chaired by U. Alexis Johnson, the Deputy Under-Secretary of State for Political Affairs. Engle had played an important role as a civil police advisor under General Douglas MacArthur and as head of the U.S. police assistance effort for the Japanese Police after World War II. A plan developed by Engle to reorganize the Japanese Police had been approved by General Douglas MacArthur in 1946 and served to achieve peace and economic recovery initiatives in Japan after the war.

Engle's report on the need for U.S. police assistance was the basis for the Inter-Agency Committee's memorandum sent to President Kennedy, dated July 20, 1962, and signed by U. Alexis Johnson. That memorandum to President Kennedy concluded that: **"U.S. police aid is essential, along with military and economic assistance, to preserve the freedom and viability of third world countries."** The Inter-Agency Committee with representatives from the Central Intelligence Agency (CIA), U.S. Department of Defense (DOD), U.S. Department of Justice (DOJ), National Security Council (NSC), the Agency for International Development (AID), and other agencies recommended **"a more vigorous management of the existing Public Safety Program."**

It was determined that developing countries needed technical assistance, training, and commodity assistance. A classified National Security Action Memorandum (NSAM177) provided the mandate to expand U.S. police assistance to free world countries.

In 1962, President Kennedy created the United States Office of Public Safety, OPS, and installed the organization under the State Department's Agency for International Development, AID.

Ambassador Frank Coffin, the AID Administrator and a member of the Inter-Agency Committee chaired by U. Alexis Johnson, complied with the NSA memorandum and provided the OPS Director the autonomy to recruit and hire its own people.

Robert Thompson reported in the Los Angeles Times in 1963 that the program was developed **"in large part from the intense interest of Attorney General Robert F. Kennedy, the President's brother, in the urgent need to control communist subversion in Latin America."** Robert Kennedy provided strong support for the OPS, and the program became one of the most important United States initiatives to help other democracies resist communist takeovers. In Robert Kennedy's case, national interests came first in the Cold War politics.

The professionals of OPS were called Public Safety Advisors or Public Safety Officers. In line with the U.S. policy of foreign police assistance, the Kennedy Administration approved a proposal for the establishment of a police academy to train Latin American police officials. The academy was to be installed in the Panama Canal Zone, a location considered ideal for it. Military bases in the Canal Zone were training Latin American military and police officials at the School of the Americas, Ft. Gullick, and at Albrook Air Force Base.

The Inter-American Police Academy (IAPA) began operations at Ft. Davis, in the Canal Zone, on July 2, 1962, but shortly after the vicious Panama riot of early 1964, the IAPA was closed and the training programs were merged with the **International Police Academy (IPA),** Washington, D.C. The IPA was located at the Old Car Barn in Georgetown and opened its doors in 1963 as the first U.S. national training institution to train police executives, commanders, and senior police officials from foreign countries.

The Old Car Barn, the historic trolley car headquarters in Georgetown, had been refurbished as a training facility, complete with an indoor pistol range. The curriculum of the IPA included police administration and management, police operations, criminal investigations, internal defense, police counterinsurgency techniques, and anti-terrorist doctrine.

But in the midst of the Cold War conflict, one controversial media personality, **Washington Post** columnist Jack Anderson, seemingly impulsed by a sense of advocacy, reported that the IPA was "promoting research that led to the use of violence and torture by police."

One of Anderson's staff, armed with French and Spanish interpreters, examined student research papers in an attempt to prove or support his allegations. After an investigation, Anderson finally concluded, **"we have found no evidence that the Academy advocates third degree methods."**

But in the story published, Anderson quoted student research papers out of context, and when challenged by Accuracy in Media, AIM, he was unable to support his facts. The IPA was guilty of spreading anti-Communist doctrine but the real experts on torture were Stalin, Fidel Castro, and the North Vietnamese. But the attacks against the OPS took on a pattern of left-wing opposition.

At the graduations held for foreign police officials at the Georgetown site of the International Police Academy, the United States Marine Corps Band provided inspiring music for the ceremonies. Attorney General Robert Kennedy became the keynote speaker for the first graduation ceremony held.

Other graduation speakers included Averill Harriman and top liberals in the U.S. Government to make the ceremonies held for the foreign police officials at the Georgetown site of the International Police Academy, gala events. Over 7,000 foreign police commanders and officers from over 80 countries were graduated from the International Police Academy. But trouble for the OPS started soon after President Kennedy's assassination and grew vile when Nixon was President.

In 1970, James Abourezk, a notorious left-wing U.S. Senator from South Dakota, was reported as having said in several news items that a 'reliable source' from Guatemala had described to him an enormous number of horror stories about police torture being inflicted on political prisoners in that country. He alleged that the informant had told him that the use of torture was known and condoned by the American public safety advisors assigned to Guatemala.

When questioned by reporters, Abourezk said that he did not get his informer's name. He alleged that the man had simply walked into his office at the U.S. Senate Office Building.

Oddly enough, not one member of Abourezk's staff had remembered to get the man's name. So it appeared that a complete stranger from Guatemala penetrated Abourezk's office, got past the Senator's staff and talked to the Senator without being challenged or identified? More importantly, no one ever corroborated Abourezk's story about Guatemala.

U.S. Senator Abourezk took a more serious political gamble and opportunity to defame OPS when Dan Mitrione was kidnapped and brutally murdered by Marxist guerrillas in Uruguay in August of 1970. Abourezk led an attack against the OPS program on the Senate floor with a speech taken from the communist *Tricontinental* Magazine published in Havana, Cuba. The magazine accused American OPS Officers of much wrongdoing including the involvement in torture.

The Senator was more than a left-wing version of Joseph McCarthy in the Cold War, but must have been aware that the allegations of torture were false. Nonetheless, one U.S. Congressman reported to his colleagues in the U.S. Senate: **"Mr. Abourezk has quoted from an article by Klare (Michael Klare was a well-known radical left-wing activist) which first appeared in Cuba's English language *Tricontinental* Magazine in 1971, entitled, 'USA: Policing the Empire.'"**

Representative Wompat from Guam also made the following observation: **"Whatever the reason behind the Senator from South Dakota's (James Abourezk) actions to kill the International Police**

Academy, it is clear that the Far Left in our country is very much in support of his effort."

Human Events on October 12, 1974, reported in an article, **"Senator Abourezk launched an amendment to the 1975 Foreign Aid Bill based on an article published in *Tricontinental,* a rabidly anti-American Havana-based publication. Abourezk never once mentioned the article or its source. The piece was written by Michael Klare."**

The purpose of the Abourezk amendment was to destroy the OPS. Nevertheless, after two decades of police assistance by the OPS, no valid evidence of American involvement in torture or terrorism was ever produced by Abourezk or anyone else. The organization became a maligned, dark part of Cold War history.

After he left the U.S. Senate, Abourezk quietly joined the Board of Directors of the Institute for Policy Studies (IPS), a radical left-wing think tank in Washington, D.C.

As resistance to the Vietnam War mounted, attacks against the OPS program increased. Allegations by Amnesty International of **possible** involvement of OPS Officers in foreign countries in torture were made public. Yet, Amnesty International had absolutely no evidence or proof of any kind.

In 1970, after Dan Mitrione was kidnapped and murdered by Marxist *Tupamaro* terrorists, the Director of the Catholic Conference in Washington, D.C., called a press conference to demand an "international investigation" of charges that American advisors were instructing the police in Brazil and Uruguay in torture. He mentioned Dan Mitrione by name. Mitrione had replaced me after I had been in Uruguay for almost five years. The effort by the Director of the Catholic Conference appeared to be a direct effort to justify the murder of Dan Mitrione by Marxist terrorists.

I was a Catholic. "But why is the Catholic Conference taking such a position, I asked myself?" I could only deduce the answer: radical leftist ideologues in the administration of the Catholic Church.

Dr Knute Thorpe, a retired Army Colonel and former OPS Officer, accompanied me to meet with the Director of the Catholic Conference in Washington, D.C., and talk about the allegations. The Director (unfortunately, we did not get his name, but the interview was in 1981) was not a church official but was the Conference administrator.

He seemed to presume we were there to support his allegations. (It was interesting to me that the physical security of the building was tougher than the Pentagon's.) The Director of the Catholic Conference quickly grew impatient when we told him that Dan Mitrione was our friend and colleague. He was told that I had been in Uruguay for many years during the *Tupamaro* period and felt very knowledgeable about the situation in that country. I pointed out that the allegations made against Dan Mitrione were clearly false and represented communist propaganda. The Director of the Catholic Conference grew visibly angry by my remarks and proposed that as far as he was concerned the allegations were true, based on reports he had received.

We asked for proof but there was none. Those things happen when Americans intervene in the internal affairs of other countries, the Director told us. Fifteen minutes later, he was obviously upset, angry, and not interested in talking with us.

I posed the following question to the administrator: "What about the repression and torture that takes place in communist countries? **Does that mean anything to you?**"

His response turned very harsh. "Those are allegations that are meaningless and have no absolutely no interest for the Catholic Conference," he responded.

Nevertheless, the Catholic Conference of the United States, with an administration of left-wing advocates, apparently supported communist attacks against OPS **"whether the allegations were true or not!" That was not surprising for me. For some, the Cold War was terra incognita.**

In El Salvador, unknown to most Americans, Monsignor Freddy Delgado of the Catholic Church in that country wrote a book in Spanish titled, *"La Iglesia Popular Nacio en El Salvador"* (The Popular Church was born in El Salvador). In his book, Monsignor Delgado reported that: **"The Catholic Church of El Salvador will be used by communist insurgents to install in the country a Socialist Republic of Workers and Peasants."**

According to Monsignor Delgado, the Catholic Church in El Salvador would be used to support the communist insurgency in that country. Shortly after his book was published the *Farabundo Marti Movimiento de Liberacion Nacional* (FMLN) guerrillas killed Monsignor Delgado. It is a matter of record that Monsignor Freddy Delgado was a loyal priest and legitimate senior official of the Catholic Church in El Salvador. It is not believed that fact can be denied.

As a lifelong Catholic, I personally saw portions of the communist insurgency develop in El Salvador. After reading Monsignor Delgado's book, I realized what he had written was true. Several priests in El

Salvador were not only supporting the FMLN, some were fighting on the side of the communist rebels. The question was, why? Was it to help the poor people of the country? Was communism the only solution to the existing poverty? So far there is no concrete answer.

It was apparently a sin to be anti-Communist in El Salvador during the communist insurgency. I was a Catholic but also anti-Communist. Thus the Cold War put me between a rock and a hard place, or in Spanish, in the position of a *Pendejo*. (The word *Pendejo* was a favorite of General Omar Torrijos, the *Maximo* Leader of Panama, and he used it with oblatory frequency. In the vernacular, *Pendejo* means "stupid," or "dumb ass." In Spanish/English dictionaries, the word is often defined as fine pubic hair.)

No one has ever suggested that the Cold War or any war was fair. It is well documented in the United States Congressional Record that U.S. Senator James Abourezk plagiarized remarks from a communist publication called *"Tricontinental"* to attack the OPS on the Senate floor. **That was not fair.** The publication was obviously anti-American and had its origins in communist Cuba.

Tom Daschle, a former assistant to Senator Abourezk, admitted that the information used to attack OPS on the U.S. Senate floor was derived from Michael Klare, a well-known hard-core, extreme left-wing radical. Both Michael Klare's mother and father were, in fact, card-carrying members of the communist party.

When challenged by Accuracy in Media, AIM, Senator Abourezk rebutted that he would take information from anyone he chose. Daschle was instrumental in obtaining the information for Abourezk to use for his attacks against OPS. He is presently the U.S. Senate Majority Leader and one of the most powerful men in the U.S. Congress. In regard to the current terrorist threat, on September 20, 2001, Senator Tom Daschle said: "We are resolved to work together" to fight the terrorist threat.

Senator William Fulbright also seemed impassive about the truth related to the OPS Program. He had consistently insisted that American foreign policy be legal and moral. Well, we all wanted things legal and moral, but those words were foreign for the communists.

Fulbright reportedly supported President Kennedy in sending troops to Vietnam and Thailand on the premise that it be legal and moral. But on the issue of OPS he pushed the position that **"whether or not the allegations were true the United States should not be in the business of police assistance to other countries."** On the other hand, he did nothing to clarify the communist lies that vilified the men and women of the OPS.

Fulbright was known to be an opponent of United States intervention in the internal affairs of other countries, and eventually sought the withdrawal of U.S. troops from Vietnam and a cutoff of aid to South Vietnam.

The **Washington Star News** of January 26, 1974, quoted an unnamed U.S. Official as saying that **"there was a direct link between the film State of Siege and a series of amendments to a foreign aid Bill signed into law on December 17, 1973, by President Nixon.** (The amendments by Abourezk proposed the elimination of the OPS program.) For reasons unknown, it was never publicized that the film was written by **Francisco Solinas, a card-carrying member of the Italian Communist Party,** and directed by **Costa-Gavras, a card-carrying member of the French Communist Party.** The film depicts the assassination of Daniel Mitrione by the *Tupamaros,* a unit of the communist Southern Guerrilla Command operating in several South American countries."

Human Events reported in April 7, 1973, that **"the chief purpose of State of Siege was to glorify and justify the 1970 kidnapping and cold-blooded assassination of American OPS Officer Dan Mitrione by *Tupamaro* terrorists."** It was more than that.

Dan Mitrione was in charge of the U.S. OPS program of police assistance to the security forces of Uruguay. That is the most valid reason the *Tupamaro* guerrillas assassinated him. Strengthening the security forces of Uruguay made it a major obstacle for the Marxist guerrillas in their quest to take over the country. That seemed to be the real answer to Mitrione's murder.

The politicians shrugged off the tragedy but the vilification of Mitrione by false communist allegations of torture after his assassination was evil and unjustified. For such a good man and patriotic American, it was a hell of a way to be remembered. He was innocent of such terrible allegations. I personally knew Dan Mitrione as a fine human being and a very good Catholic.

Other powerful U.S. Senators joined with Abourezk to push through his amendment to the foreign aid bill concerning U.S. police assistance to other countries. They were J. William Fulbright (D-Ark), Frank Church (D-Idaho), William Proxmire (D-Wis.), James Abourezk (D-S.D.), and Hubert Humphrey (D-Minn.). But as part of the furor these Senators obviously also had in mind the need to further discredit and bring down a seriously politically wounded Republican President, Richard Nixon, who was looking for a way to dodge the **Watergate** fiasco. Moscow-trained Roger Morris called the liberal putsch a bipartisan congressional effort.

The closure of the OPS came after President Richard Nixon, increasingly desperate and occupied with Watergate and possible impeachment, left the organization and the Americans who served, dangling on the gallows. He provided no defense for the OPS against the false communist allegations. Perhaps it is overly blunt on my part, but pushed by self-serving politics and unmotivated for the truth, the United States Congress cowardly yielded to the powerful forces of ideologues.

Senator Birch Baye, a solid American, showed courage and defended the truth about the OPS program. He called **State of Siege, "a cold-blooded piece of communist propaganda."**

Penelope Billiatt of the **New Yorker,** for unknown reasons called **State of Siege** "a thoughtful new political film." It did not take thought, only communist creativity.

Liz Smith of **Cosmopolitan** said the film was "the most important political film of this decade." Is it fair to ask for who?

Archer Winsten of the **New York Post** said that the **State of Siege** was of "inestimable value." It *was* for the communists and Far Left radicals in America. The communists must have been jumping for joy with the misguided American acceptance of the Cold War propaganda of the Soviet Bloc.

Edward Behr of **Newsweek** predicted that, "the film will be greeted with ecstasy wherever the premise that America is the world's No. 1 imperialistic power is accepted without reservation."

Ultimately, the United States Government provided no defense for the men and women of the OPS. The Americans killed or wounded in the service of their country with OPS in the Cold War were never acknowledged. In quiet ceremonies, the OPS Officers killed in the line of duty were called "patriots" and "martyrs for democracy."

Nixon, unable to defend himself in the Watergate fiasco and torn apart by the politicians and forced to resign, shamefully abandoned the Americans who served their country in the Cold War with honor. It was politically expedient under the circumstances.

The Americans who shed their blood and risked their lives serving their country during the Cold War were left vilified by the communist allegations of torture. The patriotic service of OPS Officers in helping the police forces of free world countries resist communist subversion and insurgency was never acknowledged. Without any sign of moral courage, the United States Congress did nothing to find the truth or to defend a program they had approved to defend national security interests.

Politicians flushed the OPS program down the tubes. Americans were left betrayed.

The OPS operated in a sinister and turbulent era of history. Today, a New World Order and *politik* exists. In 1988, Mikhail Gorbachev was elected President of the Soviet Union and awarded the Nobel Peace Prize!

In 1996, Boris Yeltsin defeated his communist rival in the Russian election for President with the help of American political advisors.

In the year 2000, Vladimir Putin, a former KGB officer, was elected President of the Soviet Union. Communism is no longer called a threat to America or to the world.

With the Cold War supposedly over, in the middle of the year 2000, President Clinton proclaimed that the "Soviet Union and the United States are in a period of transition. But they (the Soviets) are not really our allies." Was it the threat of Soviet long-range missiles with nuclear warheads?

In February 2001, Russian officials expressed shock over CIA Director George Tenant's description of Russia as a security threat and his concern that President Vladimir Putin is trying to return the country to its Soviet past.

Perhaps as the saying goes, "can't we just get along." The joke about who won the Cold War continues. For many cynics, Japan won the Cold War.

In the year 1999, President Bill Clinton sent 100 American police advisors to Bosnia and the Balkans to assist the police forces in those countries maintain law and order and internal security after the war. Since the year 1989, the United States Department of Justice has spent over two hundred million dollars to assist the police forces of El Salvador before and after the communist insurgency and to provide technical assistance and training to about a dozen or more Latin American countries.

Many retired FBI and police professionals, including myself and my partner Gene Crickenberger, a retired FBI Special Agent, have provided consultant services to a program called the International Criminal Investigations Training Assistance Program, ICITAP, of the U.S. Department of Justice. For the past eleven years, Crickenberger and I have provided technical assistance and training for the police of El Salvador, Guatemala, Honduras, Costa Rica, Panama, Colombia, Peru, Bolivia, the Dominican Republic, and Jamaica.

In the year 2000, the U.S. Department of State and U.S. Department of Justice established police academies in Budapest to train foreign police officers and in Roswell, New Mexico. The opposition from misguided liberals and from left-wing radicals will soon start. But what is the beef? We are no longer fighting communist aggression. But the battle against insane and fanatic terrorists is real.

The Battle for OPS

The man given the responsibility for the administration and management of the OPS program was Byron Engle, a CIA veteran with impressive law enforcement credentials. As a former advisor to the Japanese Police under the command of General Douglas MacArthur after World War II, Engle brought strong and effective leadership to the organization and surrounded himself with outstanding patriotic professionals to make the OPS program a valuable and successful effort.

As the Director, Engle was a stunning administrator and professional without par. But with so many enemies in the U.S. Government bureaucracy, the administration of OPS consisted of bitter battles with ideologues entrenched in the Agency for International Development (AID), the State Department as a whole, and the U.S. Congress. Engle's fight with bureaucratic fraternities and ideologues in the U.S. Department of State and AID during the Cold War became legendary.

To satisfy complex AID bureaucratic programming requirements, OPS goals were basically defined toward the following: **Provide technical assistance, training, and commodity assistance for foreign police organizations to support economic, social, and political development goals through the maintenance of law and order and internal security.** An objective of less importance for ideologues in the Washington bureaucracy was the development of foreign police capabilities to combat communist subversion and insurgency.

In terms of the OPS assistance, a basic AID policy (Order No. 1541.1 dated December 10, 1963) established the criteria for programs of police assistance to foreign countries: "A. The existence of an active or potential subversive threat beyond the ability of local police forces to handle. B. The existence of serious deficiencies (in the police of foreign countries) in training, management or equipment. C. The absence of a more appropriate free world source of aid or certainty that U.S. aid will complement rather than duplicate such assistance. D. The desirability of seeking to deny the police assistance field to the communist bloc."

Of major concern for the managers and planners of U.S. police assistance was to determine what countries of the free world would receive aid and in what amounts. To this end, a wide spectrum of AID and State Department bureaucrats became involved, bringing to the forefront moral, political, and ideological interests. The situation aroused sensibilities in hard-core activists on the right and left side of the political spectrum.

For example, Anastacio Somoza, the military dictator of Nicaragua, received limited OPS assistance, although it was obvious the country was a prime target for a communist takeover. The ideologues in government repeated their position that "the United States OPS program would support any dictator on the pretext of fighting communism." President Somoza's American friends readily abandoned him, and self-serving bureaucrats in AID and the U.S. Department of State ensured that the level of U.S. assistance and support for Nicaragua remained minimal. *Sandinista* communists, perhaps rightly, overthrew Somoza.

The Cold War seemed far-reaching and many Americans intervened in subtle ways to pursue ideological interests. For example, the struggle in Nicaragua between the *Contra* Freedom Fighters and the communist *Sandinistas* attracted special interest for Bill Richardson, a former U.S. Congressman from New Mexico and Secretary of Energy under the Clinton Administration. Richardson, another darling of the American left wing in the United States calls himself a "Fighter for New Mexico" although he was born either in Mexico or California to a family of wealth. I am Hispanic and also born in New Mexico.

In 1985, New Mexico Congressman Bill Richardson, pushed by a conglomerate of his left-wing followers, arranged for a public forum to be held at the Sweeney Center in Santa Fe to debate the conflict between the *Sandinistas* and the *Contras* in Nicaragua. In a letter signed by Richardson, I was asked by his office to get three people to participate in a political debate on the matter of "U.S. intervention" in Nicaragua. He enlisted three individuals on the left side of the political spectrum for the event. He wrongly assumed that I was automatically on the side of the *Contras.*

But when Richardson was informed that our team consisted of U.S. Army General Gordon Sumners, a man with great experience in Central America, and Geraldine Macias, a former Minister in the communist Government of Daniel Ortega who had defected, he canceled.

In the struggle against communist aggression, the Special Group Counter-Insurgency (SG/CI), an array of powerful U.S. Government officials, directed the effort in the early '60s, and Attorney General Robert Kennedy often chaired the meetings. Robert Kennedy was probably the most important supporter of the OPS police assistance program. He resisted entrenched radical left-wing and misguided liberal bureaucrats in the AID and the U.S. Department of State in their efforts to obstruct U.S. police assistance. The SG/CI played a major role in the formulation of U.S. foreign aid policy and programs designed to combat communist insurgencies. The OPS program was defended by the Special Group against a myriad of opponents during several administrations. But support for the OPS died with the Kennedy legend.

My friend Bill Bartreau, a former OPS Officer, suggested in an OPS newsletter, "I wish news people would tell the truth about OPS. One reason they don't is because no one challenges the left-wing propaganda." Many Americans supported communist causes in the Cold War and many continue to support the socialist/communist ideology. But is that not their right in a democracy?

The counterinsurgency doctrine of the United States during the Cold War involved the use of foreign police as front-line warriors. Teams of OPS police advisors assigned to missions in various countries of the world were accused by the left wing of being CIA-spawned programs used to support repressive regimes and to keep military dictatorships in power.

The resistance to OPS by the left side of the political spectrum in America would have pleased Karl Marx and Lenin. Meanwhile, guerrilla groups supported by communist bloc countries openly attacked many democracies of the world. Communist insurgent movements in Latin America exploited the discontent, poverty, and social injustice that existed for years. The provocation of labor unrest and violence to destabilize a government became a communist militant art.

Under KGB Chief General Yuri Andropov, disinformation practices flourished during the Cold War under a separate entity known as Directorate A. Agents of influence in Western Countries spread false information, provided covert support for terrorists, manipulated the western media, covertly sponsored strikes and demonstrations to destabilize existing governments, and attacked western intelligence services in the press. OPS advisors found themselves pawns in the politics of the Cold War.

Many OPS Officers would be killed combating left-wing or communist terrorists or guerrillas in the politics of the Cold War along with hundreds of police officers and security force personnel around the world. This should not have been surprising.

Lenin once wrote: The first objective of armed struggle is to kill individuals such as high officials and lower ranking members of the police and the army. The violence was certain. In China, Communist leader **Mao Tse-tung proclaimed, "Every communist must grasp the truth. Political power grows out of the barrel of a gun."**

For any communist or left-wing radical movement there were no rules, no morality, values or restrictions that impeded the success of their operations, clandestine or otherwise. A large number of radical left-wing/communist movements existed in the Cold War and continue to exist in Latin America and other places. The people will determine what they want.

2

El Salvador, Central America

"A few days after the final offensive of the FMLN in their attempt to take power (in El Salvador), on January 10, 1981, a group of Catholic priests from the 'popular' church openly declared themselves members of the FMLN." —Monsignor Freddy Delgado, the Catholic Church of El Salvador, 1983

The Republic of El Salvador is the most heavily populated country in Central America but the smallest in size. The country was torn by a communist insurgency for twelve years during the Cold War. El Salvador is a beautiful country with semitropical jungle teeming with wondrous flora and fauna from coast to coast. After the peace agreement was signed between the Salvadoran Government and the *Farabundo Marti Movimiento de Liberacion Nacional* (FMLN), the country continued under a persistent communist hegemony. In the late 1950s and '60s the country had approximately four million people in a geographical area of 8,400 square miles. The country's economy, dependent on coffee cultivation, was affected with the widespread poverty in the Cold War period. As the population grew, coffee exports, ergo the economy, did not increase proportionately.

Historically, El Salvador was a classic example of the poverty that existed in Central America for decades. Poverty was an important factor in the communist insurgencies that took place in Central American countries. El Salvador and Nicaragua became prime targets for a communist takeover in the *Guerra Fria*...Cold War.

Political and social unrest, caused principally by the existing poverty in many countries, provided fertile ground for a communist insurgency. Communism in El Salvador was seen as an opportunity to break the chains of poverty and the politics of the past and achieve political, social and economic change. The portentous volcanoes of *Izálco, Boqueron* and *San Salvador* served to symbolize the boiling cauldron of civil and social unrest in El Salvador.

A little known organization called the International Cooperation Administration (ICA) was responsible for United States foreign aid to other countries in the late 1950s. U.S. police assistance was to support political and economic progress and to improve public safety for growing urban communities.

The communist insurgency and drug trafficking were incipient problems when I was posted to El Salvador. The communist party was quietly growing in strength. Despite the U.S. police assistance provided, action was also needed to improve social justice, to reform outdated laws and to upgrade the quality and administration of the criminal justice system. Those things were not even in the horizon of the '60s. The harsh politics, the weak economy, labor and social unrest made most issues irreconcilable.

Traditionally, Latin American governments depended on their military forces to stay in power, and that continued during the Cold War. For many decades, Latin American military leaders had problems supporting the civilian leadership of a democratically elected government. Many military leaders believed they could do better if they had the power themselves and, as a consequence, installed military dictatorships. With a traditional monopoly on iron technology the military forces had the weapons needed to dominate local politics. But the Cold War brought changes when communist guerrillas and terrorists entered the picture equipped with modern weapons of war.

For centuries, civil police organizations in Latin America had been under the control of the military forces in the country. The control of the police forces by the military in Latin America was considered traditional, legal, and moral. Police organizations were generally under the Minister of Defense or the Minister of Interior and in the direct control of the military forces. One exception was Costa Rica, since that country did not have a military force or army and depended on the *Policia Civil* (Civil Police) and Technical Judicial Police for internal defense and law and order.

Over the years, Panama's police force had developed into a portentous army with U.S. military assistance. With the ambitious guidance of corrupt *politicos,* the *Guardia* eventually overthrew the Government of Panama and brought an era of military control to the country for over a decade. The U.S. invasion of Panama (Operation Just Cause) eventually resulted in the destruction of the Panama National Guard and the arrest of General Manuel Antonio Noriega. But for decades, change in many Latin American countries was characterized by the domination of the country by a few, and changes that came about in the government generally were as a result of military *coups* or revolutions.

The police and military forces in Latin America were perceived as a necessary evil but considered by many citizens to be inept, corrupt and major abusers of human rights. That was a vital issue in the Cold War. Public support for the military and police forces was critical in combating subversion or an insurgency. To defeat an active insurgent movement in any country, the support and cooperation of the populace was considered not only an advantage, it was deemed essential.

The communist guerrillas knew that support of the populace had to be won over to their cause if they were to be successful. The approval of the populace for the cause was necessary and as an analogy, the concept was labeled as "community policing" in the United States and called a new approach to law enforcement.

In El Salvador, the growing discontent and dissatisfaction of the populace deprived the government forces of the cooperation and support needed to resolve internal security problems. The principal recruitment base for communist guerrillas was from the disgruntled factions of the populace. For the police forces, recruitment was not much better. The young men recruited as policemen had enjoyed little opportunity for education or employment and were even less motivated to fight guerrillas.

In Latin America, change did not come easy. In many Latin American countries the practice of appointing military officers as Chiefs of Police and as commanders of police organizations served to militarize the civil police. That practice was rationalized by the military *obiter dictum* that the police are an armed force and civilians did not have the experience or training to command an armed unit. In most cases in Latin America, the police become mere pawns of the military in the dynamics of power politics.

In the '50s and '60s, the aim of left-wing forces was to gain economic and political power in Latin America. The existing social and labor unrest was used as the fuel to drive the cause of communism. In El Salvador, the economically impoverished *campesinos* in the rural areas felt exploited by the oligarchy and were converted to the communist cause by demagogues promising social, economic and political change. But the majority of *campesinos* in El Salvador did not necessarily believe in the

Marxist/Leninist communist doctrine but had nothing to lose by joining a revolution that promised them a better life. The left wing and communist forces actively pursued political and economic power in El Salvador for over four decades without letup.

In 1945, with the country beset by economic problems, General Maximiliano Hernandez Martinez, the President of El Salvador, confronted a formidable communist army of *campesinos* in the vicinity of the small town of *Izalco*. The leaders of the self-proclaimed communist movement had been killing coffee plantation owners to lay claim to the land. In a landmark battle that ensued between the Salvadoran Army and the communists, an estimated 10,000 *campesinos* were killed or executed.

Killed in the battle that took place was a young, Trotskyite by the name of *Farabundo Marti*. The young communist had reportedly fought with *Sándino* against the U.S. Marines in Nicaragua. Three decades later, the communist insurgents in El Salvador took the name of *Farabundo Marti Movimiento de Liberacion Nacional* (FMLN) and *Marti* gained immortality.

The real ruling power, the intransigence of corrupt politics and the unfortunate linkages to U.S. foreign policy, was often a disappointment for me. Political and social unrest, injustice and the lack of opportunity energized the potential violence in an unrelenting manner. In El Salvador, poverty was a powerful source of discontent, especially in the rural communities. That was not easy to fix and required tremendous give and take on the part of the government and the rich oligarchy.

The *campesinos* in the rural areas were hard working and peaceful and depended on the *machete* as an indispensable work tool. But the *machete*, commonly used to cut sugar cane and grass, would become a symbol for rebellion. This large, sharp, curved work tool could be used as a formidable weapon. Even before the insurgency, the *machete* had deadly consequences when combined with *"Tic Tac,"* the local booze, equivalent to the "White Lightning" found in some southern states.

The lethality of the *machete* was horrible and in many conflicts, severed limbs and decapitation were common. Further armed with AK-47s and led by the more educated members of the Salvadoran society, the *campesinos* joined the left-wing insurgency to improve their lives and not necessarily because they believed in communism. The potent *"Tic Tac"* could not numb the pain of oppression and poverty for the indigents forever.

Most Americans in El Salvador made an effort to understand and appreciate the culture and people of the country. The Salvadoran people were certainly deserving of American assistance, friendship and support. But the *Ugly American* often emerged in the United States Foreign Service. "We're all pretty much alike when we get out of town," said Kin Hubbard. I saw a bad example.

The U.S. Marine residence in the capital of San Salvador was located in *Colonia Escalón,* in one of the nicer sections of town. The residence had been burglarized in the dead of night while off duty Marines slept inside. I took pains to explain to the "Jarheads" how it probably happened.

A handkerchief is soaked with chloroform and tossed through an open window into the bedrooms where people are sleeping. Chloroform was readily available in Latin America and bought from any local pharmacy. A handkerchief loaded with the sweet smelling liquid probably placed every Marine in the room into a deep slumber. In this case, the burglars were able to take wristwatches off burly hands, wallets from trousers placed next to their bed and even radios from under the pillows of the sleeping off-duty Marine guards. The burglars were surrealistic shadows in the night.

I reminded the Marines of the biblical story of Saul when he went to the desert of Ziph with three thousand men to find David and destroy him. David hid in the mountains but one night he and a few of his men went quietly into Saul's camp while he was sleeping with his troops inside his barricade. The Lord had put everyone in the camp into a deep slumber. Taking Saul's spear, David left the camp without killing him while he slept. According to the Bible, David refused to kill the Lord's anointed. The Marines stared at me when I suggested they were lucky the intruders did not kill **them** in their sleep.

My friend Alfredo Zapata, the head of the Criminal Investigations Division of the National Police of El Salvador, responded to investigate. Unfortunately, a few days later, still smarting from the embarrassing burglary, three of the Marines, without bothering to question, assaulted two men who were standing in front of the Marine residence and savagely beat them. Both of the men were hospitalized. Ironically one of them happened to be a police investigator from Zapata's division who had been assigned to investigate the robbery.

The word spread quickly in the city and that evening a crowd of about fifty Salvadorans gathered outside the Marine residence and protested the beating of the Salvadorans by the *Gringos.* Agitators in the mob screamed and threatened to burn down the Marine residence. Some individuals in the mob were armed. I called my friend Zapata and the General Consul of the U.S. Embassy. I was surprised when the American General Consul arrived inebriated.

Minutes later, to my dismay, the General Consul of the U.S. Embassy was standing on top of a grassy mound in front of the Marine residence and in a drunken state, traded insults with the leaders of the mob that were assembled in front of the house. The American Consul was threatening to bring the full might of the United States to bear upon the Salvadorans if they did not disperse. The atmosphere grew volatile very fast.

"Gringo borracho, borracho, hijo-de-puta! (*Gringo* drunk, drunk son-of-a-bitch!),"* the crowd screamed angrily at the American Consul. Worried about the situation, Zapata urged me to get the Consul out of there before all hell broke loose.

"Boddy," he told me, "there is going to be big trouble."

The U.S. General Consul stubbornly resisted any effort to remove him from the mound where he arrogantly preached doom to the mob members. But finally, I was obliged to threaten him with violence and to call U.S. Ambassador Kalijarvi. We dragged him into the house and Zapata quickly called police units to disperse the angry crowd. The incident was publicized in local newspapers but did not include the whole story. With Zapata's help the Marines involved in the beatings were not arrested and an amicable solution was reached with the men that were beaten up by giving them money.

The people of El Salvador were admirable in their culture of honest hard work and the majority persevered as pro-American in the struggle against communism. My ability to speak Spanish fluently enabled me to make lasting friendships. Some of my Salvadoran friends rose to powerful positions in the government.

My *compadre* Dr. Tomas Pineda, a compassionate and skilled medical doctor, became the Minister of Public Health. He and his beautiful wife Nena Nieto de Pineda baptized our son Michael who was born in El Salvador. My *compadre* died about fifteen years ago but my family remains in touch with his family in El Salvador.

Another close friend, Colonel Fernando Sigui, was one of the heroes of a war that took place between El Salvador and Honduras over an emotionally charged soccer game. Called the "Soccer War," the conflict erupted over a soccer game held between teams of the two countries. We met when he was a major in the Salvadoran Army and was assigned to the command staff of the National Police. We remain good friends. A source that prefers anonymity told me that Colonel Sigui was selected by the ruling oligarchy of the country to be President of El Salvador in the '70s. Sigui, a handsome, intelligent and charismatic military officer, was allegedly caught in a compromising position with the wrong woman and subsequently exiled to Chile as a military attaché. We met again in Santiago, Chile, in 1971, the week that Salvador Allende was elected President.

In the late 1950s, prior to OPS, United States police assistance was limited to countries with which the U.S. had political and economic interests. Foreign police agencies were helped toward democratization. In El Salvador, the left-wing forces in the country were active and the police commanders denied them any gains. When the communist organizations provoked demonstrations or strikes, the leaders of the political and labor groups involved were arrested. Mass demonstrations organized by the communists often grew violent and had to be dispersed with force.

To help the National Police cope with the violent disturbances, we introduced the 26-inch wood baton for the purpose of riot control and for self-defense. The baton was recommended to replace the use of firearms for riot control and provided an option for the use of non-lethal force.

But in one particularly vicious riot, a young demonstrator by the name of *Liber Arce* was clubbed to death by police officers and many demonstrators were injured. The name *Liber Arce* was ironic in the local scenario of political violence. In English, the name translates to "liberate or to free oneself." The death of *Liber Arce* became an excellent cause for the communists.

The left wing proclaimed *Liber Arce* a 'martyr' for the cause of freedom. His death served to dramatically increase the opposition against the Government of El Salvador. We were between a rock and a hard place. The incident created more urban violence while more serious unrest stirred ominously in the rural communities where communist guerrilla leaders were planting the seeds of insurrection.

The Salvadoran Army, led by Colonel Julio Rivera, with consummate opportunity used the ongoing civil unrest to justify a military *coup d'état* and assumed control of the government. President Jose Maria Lemus and his family were exiled to Nicaragua. John F. Kennedy once said: "Those that make peaceful revolution impossible will make violent revolution inevitable."

Roland Kelly, a former FBI Special Agent and the chief of the police assistance program in El Salvador, was a serene and capable individual who was highly respected by the military officers commanding the National Police units. He encouraged the upgrading of police services to better serve the public and to improve the image of the National Police.

But those efforts did not help much in terms of forestalling the forthcoming insurgency. The communists were promising food, justice, opportunity and an egalitarian society. Those were attractive local issues.

Kelly and I provided technical assistance to the Salvadoran military officers to improve patrol services, investigations, riot control, forensics and the basic police services for the public. Salvadoran military officers were narrowly focused but intelligent, well educated and actually bonded to causes that helped the populace in general. Assuredly, the Salvadoran military officers provided excellent leadership for the police but the economic foundation of the country was crumbling. The payroll roster for the police included "phantom" police officers that in fact did not exist. The extra salaries were divided among the ranking military officers, who were also poorly paid. The extra pay was well deserved in my opinion and was considered an incentive.

Other traditions were also keynote incentives. Salvador *Chamba* Palacios, a Salvadoran Army Major assigned to the National Police of El Salvador, had gained notoriety because of his involvement in several attempts to overthrow the Government of El Salvador. Palacios was known to be one of the most intelligent and toughest military officers assigned to the National Police. Although calm and stable on the outside, his eyes reflected a tough interior.

Palacios was a friend and he and his wife occasionally visited our home in *Colonia Escalon* for drinks and hors d'oeuvres. He was good company and, once exposed to a martini or two, *Chamba* mellowed. Chain-smoking Salem cigarettes, Palacios maintained his stoic character, but with libation acquired an admirable sense of humor.

One dark night I was told that *Chamba* had been arrested for conspiring to pull off a *coup d'état* against the government along with several other military officers. As a prestigious military officer, *Chamba* had held a machine gun to the head of the Commandant of the notorious National Guard of El Salvador during the failed *coup d'état*. Salvadoran military officers loyal to the government prevented the *coup* and the individuals involved in the attempt, including *Chamba,* were arrested and exiled to Nicaragua.

A month later, in a pounding tropical rain, a shadowy visitor arrived at our residence at *Colonia Escalon* with a heavy knock on our front door. Wearing a dark felt hat and a raincoat, the individual looked frightening as any nightmare movie.

The man brought a cryptic message, albeit not heavy in prose. *"Saludos Querido Amigo, estoy bien, por favor, preciso Mártinis y Salems— Chamba."* *Chamba* wanted Beefeater gin and Salem cigarettes. I provided two bottles of gin and a carton of cigarettes to the mysterious visitor, who disappeared into the darkness. *Chamba's* messenger returned monthly until I left El Salvador for the Canal Zone.

Ironically, *Chamba* and I met again twenty-two years later, in the middle of the FMLN insurgency in El Salvador. In the country as a consultant for the U.S. Embassy, I encountered *Chamba* Palacios in the halls of the National Police *Quartel.* He was a full Colonel assigned to the National Police as the *Pagador* (Paymaster). Now he was in charge of who got what.

As the communist insurgency developed, sudden violence became a part of daily life. My Salvadoran friends lived in fear of the future. Despite the political problems and the potential violence of the era, my family and I grew to love El Salvador. The surprise military *coup* against President Jose Lemus was alarming and distressing. But the takeover, reported as "bloodless" (only a few people were killed), was efficiently carried out by the Salvadoran military.

Such were the risks in Central American politics. Although discomfited about the coup, I kept quiet when U.S. military officers assigned to the U.S. Embassy congratulated their Salvadoran military counterparts on their successful overthrow of the government. The new government of El Salvador would be recognized by the United States soon after. It appeared the only reason President Lemus was overthrown was because the channel was changed on him. I knew the Salvadoran officers involved in the *coup* very well.

In viewing the situation objectively, El Salvador was ripe for political change through a military *coup,* a revolution or communist insurgency. Rumors existed for years that fourteen families in El Salvador controlled and enjoyed the country's wealth, while the vast majority of the populace lived in extreme poverty. An illiteracy rate of over 80% kept the poor from participating in economic or political programs. Little dialogue existed between the dissidents, the *campesinos* and the government. But no one could solve all the problems of the country. Despite the volatile ambiance, the people of El Salvador remained strong and pro-American.

My son's godfather, Dr. Tomas Pineda, proposed that the Spaniards that had colonized El Salvador and other countries in Central America were thieves, crooks and murderers taken out of Spanish prisons to make the long voyage to the Americas with the *Conquistadores.* They commingled with Aztec warriors, he said.

"What do Americans expect from Salvadorans?" he asked me. "It is in our blood to be what we are, *compadre.* We work and fight hard. We need a harsh government for our own good." He chuckled but with a serious appearance on his face.

But were *Don Francisco Cuervo y Valdez* who colonized Albuquerque, New Mexico, *Hernando de Soto, Coronado,* and other Spanish colonizers of the United States considered better people?

The training of the civil police to function as a positive force in bolstering democracy in countries like El Salvador amounted to a small grain of hope. Economic improvements, political and social reforms were desperately needed. The strengthening of the Latin American security forces to combat communist guerrillas would not guarantee a democracy. Democracy in El Salvador was in the heart and soul of the people and it was hard to sell more military strength in a climate of injustice and no economic opportunity.

The left-wing guerrillas used propaganda that promised freedom from oppression, a fair redistribution of wealth and a pluralistic democracy. In reality, all that, of course, would be missing under communist rule. But for the poor and oppressed, that was fine propaganda.

In San Salvador, communist agitators incited mob violence and labor unions, student groups and left-wing organizations held mass demonstrations against the Julio Rivera military junta that had deposed President Lemus. The leadership and strength of the communist party in El Salvador was growing and an important factor in terms of the forthcoming insurgency. The proselytization of *campesinos* in the rural areas to the communist cause was also growing.

The country did not have the economic resources or leadership to overcome irreconcilable social and political differences. Unemployment and inflation were growing to a level of 40 percent in the '60s. Seventy percent of the country's wealth was in the hands of less than 15% of the populace.

Eventually, the United States provided massive aid to the government of El Salvador to combat the communist insurgency. As a result, Americans in El Salvador became prime targets for FMLN guerrillas. The communist bloc, including Cuba, openly supported the insurgents in El Salvador and the list of young left-wing ideologues grew.

Young Shafick Handall, a member of the communist party of El Salvador, aspired to have a role with the *Farabundo Márti Movimiento de Liberacion Nacional* (FMLN) and he was not illiterate. He became one of the leaders of the FMLN and provided psychological indoctrination for a unit of Salvadoran children who were trained to fight as guerrillas. One child guerrilla, 8 years old, named Jose Antonio, AKA *Coronel* (Colonel), and another 13-year-old named Marco Tulio Flores, AKA *"Pedro,"* were used on reconnaissance missions and 10-year-old Joaquin Remberto Flores, AKA *"Manuel,"* was a combatant.

The children carried AK-47 or M-16 rifles and some of them participated in suicide missions. The children's unit was named, *"Los Samuelitos,"* after the first child killed fighting against the 3rd Infantry Brigade of the Salvadoran Army in the early days of the FMLN insurgency.

The communists meant serious business in El Salvador. According to Monsignor Freddy Delgado, "the Jesuit priests in the country would establish an *Iglesia Popular* (Popular Church)" to be used by the sans-culottic priests to support the communist guerrillas. The violence would peak with the mindless and brutal murder of Archbishop Romero. That tragedy revealed that people in El Salvador were convinced that the Catholic priests were supporting the FMLN.

There was no way to fight a bloodless war. Before the FMLN guerrillas and the Government of El Salvador signed a peace accord in January of 1992, an estimated 76,000 persons were killed in the twelve-year war. In the year 2001, law and order in El Salvador remains in total chaos despite U.S. assistance. The problem is that ideologues and non-professionals in the U.S. Department of Justice and the U.S. Department of State are the managers of U.S. police assistance.

In Washington, D.C., over two decades after I left El Salvador, an article written by Allen Brownfield for Human Events used a headline: **The National Council of Churches: Advocate for the World's Militant Left.**

3

The Inter-American Police Academy

"As a part of neocolonialist policies and the Alliance for progress in 1962 under President Kennedy's direction, U.S. imperialism established the Inter-American Police Academy." —Gus Hall, Communist Party of America the United States.

The National Police Headquarters (*Quartel*) was a dark gray fortress in a crowded downtown business district of the capital city. Silhouetted against the slate-colored sky the building seemed oppressive with hidden dark secrets of the past. Guards with rifles guarded the entrances to the building. Our office was in that building.

After three years in El Salvador, my wife and I had decided to return home. Our life was less exciting but more predictable in New Mexico. Roland Kelly, the Chief of the police assistance program in El Salvador, was surprised with my decision to resign. He and his family loved life in El Salvador and the U.S. Foreign Service. He tried to change my mind but we looked forward to our return to the "Land of Enchantment." But life was full of surprises. That would not happen for a long, long time.

About one month prior to the effective date of my resignation, my friend Herb Hardin, the head of the Latin American Branch for the OPS, called me. Hardin had been my training officer when I was a fledging police officer with the Albuquerque Police Department and he had helped me get into the business of a police advisor. He suggested with jocularity that he had a new job for me that I couldn't refuse. He also let me know with a subtle chuckle that I had been promoted to a higher grade. The new job he proposed would be in U.S. controlled territory in the Canal Zone, he told me. He was right. It was a job I couldn't refuse.

Weeks later, Jim Brooks, a CIA field officer, arrived to join the police advisory team in El Salvador. Brooks, a former Texaco employee in Venezuela, had friends in the CIA. With communist activities building up in El Salvador, the CIA needed the program.

Hardin suggested that with newly elected President, John F. Kennedy, things were going to change in terms of the Cold War struggle. One change had taken place when Fidel Castro landed in Cuba and had taken over the country to establish a communist regime.

For me, El Salvador had been a new and exciting world with sublime landscapes of mountain and jungle. But the struggle between right- and left-wing factions produced violence that was growing too common. Powerful support was growing for the left wing in El Salvador and Americans seemed in denial. Personal considerations weighed heavily on my heart and mind about my job. I was in my prime as a professional and appreciated by the hierarchy in Washington, D.C. But my wife and I worried about the safety of our young children, although they thrived in the environment of El Salvador. Nevertheless, the country was headed for a long cycle of violence.

For me it seemed that the U.S. was committed to fighting the Cold War and **Camelot** looked good. My assignment would be in the Panama Canal Zone, the home of many generations of Americans who could not speak Spanish. The Canal Zone was supposedly safe territory with none of the political violence and dangerous communist torment of El Salvador. The Zone was considered U.S. territory with its own government, an American police force, an American criminal justice system, and plenty of supermarkets and U.S. military bases. The Commander in Chief of the U.S. Southern Command was based in Quarry Heights, on the Pacific Ocean, on a side of the Panama Canal.

I was informed that my assignment concerned a new police training academy that was to be based in the Canal Zone. Hardin advised me that the project had priority and requested I leave for Panama as soon as possible because the project had the support and interest of the Kennedy Administration. My family would follow in about a month when the children were out of school. My small children were absolutely elated; they were learning Spanish and albeit their life at times was confusing, they loved the fun and excitement of the different countries and cultures.

I was informed by OPS Washington to link up with two other individuals in Panama. We were to locate an appropriate site for the Inter-American Police Academy and initiate operations as soon as possible. The three members of the team would be assigned to the new academy once it was operational. U.S. military officers in the Canal Zone would provide the logistical support and assistance needed to open up the police academy.

March 1962—Panama

David Laughlin, a tall, lanky, soft-spoken former Captain from the Indiana State Police, was appointed the team leader for the project of the Inter-American Police Academy. Laughlin had been the Chief of the OPS Program in Honduras and was an experienced police advisor who spoke Spanish.

The other individual was a young man by the name of Jerome (Jerry) T. French who did not have a police background but would handle administrative matters. French had the appearance of an undergraduate student, with a blonde crew cut and steel rimmed glasses. His experience in military counterinsurgency operations had been honed by working as an aide to U.S. Air Force General Edward Geary Landsdale, known in U.S. Government and military circles as "Mr. Counterinsurgency."

General Landsdale was a key CIA officer and had served as the principal U.S. advisor to President Magsaysay during the Philippine Huk rebellion. (Ironically, in 1981, I participated with General Edward Landsdale in a meeting held with a small group of officials from El Salvador to discuss the communist insurgency in that country. Suggestions were offered on how to fight the war. But El Salvador was not Vietnam or the Philippines. There were no magic solutions. The communist insurgency in El Salvador changed the course of political events in that country. The process involved a draconian U.S. and United Nations *á tout prix*…fix at any cost, political scenario.)

Panama was hot and humid but unlike El Salvador, the Canal Zone was strictly a piece of American-controlled territory. It was the equivalent to a humongous military base. After several visits inside the Canal Zone and meetings with U.S. military officers in several bases, Ft. Davis, an active U.S. Army installation, was suggested as a possible site for the Inter-American Police Academy. Ft. Davis was on the Atlantic side of the Isthmus and considered one of the most attractive military bases in the Canal Zone. The academy at Ft. Davis would be about five miles from the U.S. Army School of the Americas.

Ft. Davis was a beautiful military installation with attractive green lawns and spick-and-span appearance. The base received approval from

OPS headquarters in Washington, D.C., and the U.S. Department of Defense as a site for the Inter-American Police Academy (IAPA).

Work to make IAPA a reality began in earnest. Instructors and staff were selected from a list of individuals recommended by the OPS Office of Personnel. Panamanian employees were hired locally for administrative and support duties. The excitement of building a new academy surged as the work was divided and the installation of the historic IAPA took shape.

With Washington approval, arrangements were made with local CIA officers based in the Canal Zone so that the American instructors assigned to the academy would occupy furnished residences at Ft. Randolph, a CIA "owned" facility located near *Coco Sólo,* a Canal Zone Company community.

The access to Ft. Randolph was restricted and guarded by U.S. Army Military Police. For most people in the local area the base was a "spook" hideout. The CIA maintained the facility and provided a custodian who lived with his family on the installation. An old white horse with short legs and a short disposition had been named J. Edgar Hoofer by the children of the caretaker, and roamed the base freely. The horse showed signs of paranoia and threatened any adult that got near him by lowering his ears and baring yellow teeth. But the horse was partial to the children.

Although somewhat neglected, the base had beaches and trees loaded with coconut, bananas and areas with lush jungle vegetation. The only families living on the base were the American instructors and the staff of the academy.

The work began to hire staff and to construct classrooms, living quarters, a kitchen and a dining room with the assistance of U.S. Army crews. The project moved full steam ahead when we received word from Washington, D.C., that the academy should be inaugurated by July 2, 1962. We learned that Robert Kennedy, the U.S. Attorney General, was pushing for the inauguration to take place by that date because President Kennedy would mention the academy in his forthcoming 4th of July address to the nation. The IAPA was an initiative of the Kennedy Administration to help Latin American countries preserve their democracy in the Cold War.

At the nearby city of Colon, Major Omar Torrijos, the Panama National Guard Officer in charge, assured us of his cooperation to help us resolve any problem involving the apprehension of IAPA students by the Panama National Guard in Colon. Within six years, Torrijos would take over Panama via a coup carried out by the National Guard and declare himself ruler of the country.

I met with Torrijos several times and found him to be a well-liked and respected leader within the Panama National Guard. When he found out we had a special training program in Internal Defense he asked if he could attend the training course. I was in charge of the course and we became friends.

Torrijos was an intelligent and charismatic individual and it was hard not to like him. He liked to talk about the economic and political problems of the country with us over drinks and frequently he focused on the corruption that he said existed in the Government of Panama. The Panama National Guard had to take over, he implied, to correct the problem.

I jokingly suggested to him that corruption was a relative thing in many governments. In the United States, what may appear to be corruption is not real. Politicians who do not have money have tremendous difficulty running for public office. Politicos who want to run for office but do not have money to run, can be bought with large amounts of money by the rich and powerful, I told him. The United States is too large to keep track of all the corruption, I suggested. But that was no reason for our military to take over the country, I told him. He laughed.

Contrary to left-wing critics, *coup d'états* were not included in the training curriculum of the IAPA. But as things stood, it was reasonable to assume that no one could change the political future of Panama anyway, except perhaps the Panamanians.

Meanwhile, the founders of the IAPA had separate visions for a training paradigm. Laughlin focused singularly on making the academy operations as economical as possible, without hubris. In most respects, Laughlin was right, because any publicity could be risky and dangerous in the Cold War.

French was interested in applying military counterinsurgency techniques to police work, but could not define the tactics that would work in a civilian environment. Arguments and near fistfights between French and myself occasionally grew heated enough to distress our wives.

"Quit fighting," they screamed at us. "We're not fighting," French would retort. "We are discussing." Our wives told us we were 'nuts.'

The training would focus on basic police services such as police administration, patrol operations, control of civil disturbances and riots, investigations, command functions and internal defense. Firearms training and subjects on human rights and police management were also needed. Special units were needed to address the terrorist problem.

Of major importance was the matter of joint planning and operations between the police and military to cope with emergencies. Police commanders in Latin America needed training in planning for emergencies, the control of civil disturbances and emergency management to cope with the increasing problems of civil unrest. Use of non-lethal force by the police to control demonstrations and riots was emphasized. The enhancement of the intelligence capabilities of the police in Latin America was a major requirement.

To provide the training needed, instructors were recruited from various U.S. city and state police departments and U.S. Federal Law Enforcement Agencies. Instructors were obtained from the Federal Bureau of Investigation (FBI), the Central Intelligence Agency (CIA), the U.S. Bureau of Narcotics and Dangerous Drugs, the U.S. Border Patrol, the U.S. Customs Service and the U.S. Secret Service. CIA instructors would provide instruction in counterintelligence, threat assessments and on communist ideology and philosophy. Only instructors with fluency in Spanish were selected.

The *esprit de corps* manifested by the instructors was exceptional. The IAPA would have historical implications in the Cold War and the camaraderie among the members of the IAPA staff exceeded any expectations. I was pleased with my assignment.

4

The School of the Americas

"One does not have to invoke the sinister image of the CIA, however, to establish beyond a doubt that the United States is intimately involved in every barbarous act."
—Michael Klare, Students for a Democratic Society

The training of foreign police officers by the United States probably made a difference in the eventual outcome of the macro ideological struggle between communism and democracy. But it would be economic factors that would eventually defeat the Soviet Union in the Cold War. As Henry Kissinger pointed out: "the Soviet Union was a military superpower and at the same time an economic dwarf."

Nevertheless, the communist apparatchik seemed convinced that a strong police force was an obstacle for any local left-wing or communist subversive movement in any country. The U.S. justified police assistance to foreign countries to establish the internal security needed for socioeconomic and political progress but communist aggression was also a factor.

The Inter-American Police Academy (IAPA) was officially inaugurated on July 2nd in time for President Kennedy's 4th of July address. The participant training office of OPS in Washington, D.C., processed thirty-five candidates from sixteen countries for the pilot course. The countries represented were Argentina, Bolivia, Brazil, Chile, Colombia, Costa Rica, the Dominican Republic, Ecuador, El Salvador, Guatemala, Honduras, Mexico, Panama, Peru, Uruguay, and Venezuela.

The immediate problem with the student selection was that the candidates were a mix of military and police officers with ranks that ranged from sergeant to colonel. But a sense of frugality demonstrated by

David Laughlin to provide adequate living accommodations and classrooms appeared headed for trouble. It was hard to believe that IAPA had budget problems.

The students were housed in barracks-style accommodations that provided minimal privacy or comfort. The students were fed in a cafeteria and dining room that generally served good meals. But some students from South American countries were voracious meat eaters and found it difficult to adjust to the spices and gravies provided in the local fare. Also many of the participants were senior officers and managers of police agencies in their countries and would complain about living accommodations.

We were also mixing South American military colonels with much lower-ranking police officers, such as a sergeant from Central America in the pilot course. That was a serious test for us.

But the most glaring problem on the Atlantic side of the Isthmus however, were horrendous bloodsucking sand flies. Wire screens on the windows of the training facility were coated with an oily substance to keep them out. But that did not deter the tiny biting horrors from entering a building. Sealing and air conditioning was the only way to stop them.

From the founding trio, **David Laughlin** was appointed the Director of the Inter-American Police Academy. **Jerome French** was appointed Business Manager and would handle administrative matters. I was assigned as the head instructor for internal defense and firearms training.

Lou Page a former FBI Special Agent, CIA Officer and linguist who spoke Spanish, Italian, French and Portuguese, was appointed Chief Instructor by Laughlin.

Robert (Bob) Melberg, a toothpick-chomping former FBI Special Agent and veteran CIA Officer, taught counterintelligence. Melberg was trying to quit smoking and frequently went through the motions of smoking a toothpick. On occasion a smart aleck staff member would offer a light and Melberg would accept.

Dr. Alfred (Al) Grumwell, a diminutive CIA officer with a Ph.D. from Virginia University, taught international communism. Grumwell, a man with misogamist tendencies, was about five feet even and endowed with a hefty proboscis and mean disposition. "If his *pinga* is as big as his nose he is quite a man," a Bolivian student observed. Grumwell was quickly nicknamed *El Periquito Malo,* "mean little parrot" by the students.

Robert Florstedt was a quiet, mature, likable, nondescript CIA Officer, who rarely had a strong opinion about anything. He taught internal security without complaints.

Joe Santioana the charismatic Special Agent in Charge (SAC) of the FBI office in Tampa, Florida, provided instruction in firearms with me and also taught criminal investigations. He was considered one of the Bureau's best and was personally assigned by J. Edgar Hoover, the FBI Director for the pilot course.

Miguel "Mike" Gutierrez, a young, handsome, personable lieutenant from the Los Angeles County Sheriff's Department, was assigned on loan to teach police administration.

Eddie Chavez, a friend of mine and veteran detective of the Albuquerque Police Department, taught criminal investigations and assisted in riot control training.

Robin Clack, a senior officer from the U.S. Border Patrol, was a bilingual and talented instructor who handled border control training. His extensive police experience was used to help in other areas.

Several U.S. Army Military Police Officers and OPS Officers were assigned on temporary duty to conduct special courses. We were indeed a motley and interesting crew!

Mario Vasquez was an excellent audio-visual expert from Puerto Rico and was dubbed *"Coñito"* by the staff. Vasquez was not quite five feet tall and vocal. He could not express himself in English or Spanish without prefacing his remarks with the word *"coño."* In Puerto Rico and in Caribbean countries, in the vernacular, the word *coño* means vagina. *Coñito*, therefore, in vulgar terms can be literally translated to mean "little vagina or little cunt."

Mario's wife would giggle in embarrassment when members of the IAPA staff knocked on the door of her house and asked for *"coñito."* Mario unassumingly assured everyone that was interested.

"That's okay, *coño,* you all look normal, at least we don't seem to have any *maricones." Maricones* means homosexuals in the Spanish vernacular.

Luis Nentzen-Franco, a Lieutenant with the Panama National Guard, was another willing and capable instructor assigned to the IAPA. The Panama National Guard, originally the police force of Panama, was subsequently named the Panama Defense Force (PDF) by General Omar Torrijos.

In retrospect, Nentzen-Franco was a confident, intelligent man with dreams of a more important role in the politics of Panama. Assigned on loan to the IAPA, he was a diligent, cooperative young officer with an ambition beyond most cops. Within five years, as a PDF Colonel,

Nentzen-Franco would join Colonels Silvera, Sanjur, and Bernal in an attempt to overthrow the *"Máximo"* leader of Panama, General Omar Torrijos. The attempt would fail and in a few years Franco would disappear.

IAPA instructors wore dark trousers and white short sleeved shirts for uniformity and comfort. The students were issued U.S. Air Force khaki uniforms. A patch for the student uniform shirt was designed for identification purposes. The patch displayed a yellow background with a gold and green outline of the Western Hemisphere with the words **"Academia Inter-Americana."** The emblem showed nothing that could be linked to the United States but that was not intentional. Some students were not happy about having to wear surplus American military uniforms.

But on graduation day the students wore their county's military or police uniform. Consequently, the dress uniforms worn by the military and police officers from Argentina, Chile, Uruguay, Colombia, Peru, Venezuela, Brazil and other Latin American countries and the military music provided by a local military band added color, pomp and formality to the graduations held.

Student selection for the first class was of concern for everyone because of the disparity in ranks but the students were eager and motivated. With professional reputations on the line, informal discussions held by the staff regarding the lack of air conditioning often grew heated and affected morale. Pressured by the staff, I agreed to become a spokesperson with Laughlin inspired by the suggestion by a few members of the staff that it was the fault of the original team of "nebbishes" (Laughlin, French and myself) that we had so many problems.

Everyone believed it was a mistake to mix colonels and sergeants in the same course at IAPA because Latin American military colonels would not appreciate lieutenants or enlisted personnel in the same class with them. Laughlin took the position that if OPS Washington had problems with the student selection they would let us know. But the issue was important because it involved respect for Latin American tradition and customs.

"The police sergeant from Central America is going to feel damned uncomfortable sitting in a training course with military and police commanders from Argentina, Brazil, Chile and other South American Countries," I suggested to Laughlin and French.

French went silent with a look of fake solemnity on his face. He suggested that if we made changes at this point, Washington would raise hell!

"Don't forget President Kennedy's July 4th speech," French reminded me. The IAPA's deadline conformed to the President's address to the nation on July 4th. But that was not an issue. French suggested that people in colleges come from all walks of life and I suggested that the IAPA was not the University of California at Berkeley.

Outside, the rain had turned into a deluge. The tropical rain sounded like machine gun bursts hitting the roof. It would rain for at least two hours and normal conversation was now impossible.

I candidly informed the two men that the students and instructors were complaining about the uncomfortable training classrooms and the housing accommodations. The problem was generating distractions. Without air conditioning in the classrooms the sand flies feasted on the students and instructors. High-ranking military and police officers living in a barracks full of bloodthirsty sand flies and in hot and uncomfortable conditions were bound to cause problems. It was suggested that air conditioning would eliminate the problem.

Laughlin was opposed because of the cost and he intended to keep training expenses as low as possible as a measure of cost efficiency. But the sand flies did not know that. Allergic reactions and infections caused by sand fly bites would become indisputable.

"Latin American colonels expect privacy, just as we do," I said. "Wait till they have to take a crap and will sit on open rows of commodes like exhibitions of asses." Many participants were police chiefs or top police commanders in large police organizations. Laughlin was unconvinced and he walked out as the rain continued battering the rooftop. French assumed a cornered look.

"Don't forget, Batista was only a corporal when he took over the Government of Cuba and brought the mob in," he said lightheartedly. "The sergeant in this course may show these guys how to!"

"Don't forget what happened to the bastard," I told him. French laughed and suggested that we had fans for the classrooms. But I felt anger because the living environment would be unduly harsh for no reason at all.

Tiny Cuba under Soviet tutelage was boldly using its resources to destabilize Latin America and to support Marxist guerrilla and terrorist movements. Nothing we had compared to the image and support enjoyed by the Patrice Lumumba Friendship University (PLFU) under the sponsorship of the KGB. The PLFU provided training for **Carlos the Jackal** and other left-wing zealots and terrorists of the world. That was friendship? It was fortunate that **Carlos the Jackal** was all fluff.

For certain, IAPA was not in the business of training terrorists. At least, not many terrorists were on our side. But there was reason for uncertainty. The young police captain from the Dominican Republic sat in my office with a ready smile that was disarming. Trained in guerrilla warfare in Cuba, he explained that it was in the line of duty. His name, Juan De Dios Marin translated to "John of God."

When Lyndon B. Johnson sent the Marines to the Dominican Republic to stop a communist takeover I wondered where "John of God" (Marin) was in the conflict.

The United States Embassy in the Dominican Republic was apparently unaware of the special training he had received in Cuba and selected him as a candidate for IAPA. It was also possible that Marin was a CIA Agent but we did not have a need or a right to know. Students told me about Marin when he bragged about his expertise in guerrilla warfare while drinking Panamanian *Seco Herrerano*. This libation was made locally and commonly imbibed with milk.

When we met, the first thing Marin told me was that he was not a communist.

"There may be officers from other countries attending the *Academia Inter-Americana de Policía* that do not admit to being communist, but are," he said. I had to stifle a laugh. We may have to check all student tushies to see which ones have a hammer and sickle tattooed on their ass, I thought humorously.

According to Marin, the Director of the National Police in the Dominican Republic had been aware of the training he received in Cuba. His face demonstrated concern but the litany he expounded grew worrisome for me.

"I'm sure you understand that communism has popular support in Latin America," he told me. "People in our countries feel the oppression every day," he said with a dramatic stare. "We have a ridiculous gap between the rich and poor that has existed for centuries in Latin America. The people have little hope for justice, especially the poor. The socioeconomic problems in our countries are powerful reasons for an insurgency," he said, his eyes registering an ecclesiastical glint.

"The masses of poor and starving children that die every day in the poor countries of Latin America is not mere communist propaganda," he told me in an impressive display of oratory. "The imperialistic image of the United States is real for many people in Latin America who associate the military forces with repression," he said. I felt cornered. Lenin would have been proud.

"To defeat communist insurgents," he continued, "there will have to be socioeconomic justice and a benevolent sharing by the rich in Latin America or there will be violence." He stared at me for signs of a reaction.

"The poor are caught in the middle of any political struggle and many will join the insurgents." He assumed a thoughtful pose to tell me, "blood will flow before it is over, count on it. The United States, the *colosos del norte,* supports economic development in the hemisphere that benefits the rich but not the poor. There is a dire need for political and social reform in Latin America. The oligarchy must be convinced that economic power must be shared. Otherwise communism will win." Marin was emotionally affected by his own remarks.

"The strengthening of the military establishment in our countries by the United States simply means the continuation of the *status quo,"* he said. I was on the receiving end of a freshman lecture. The fact that many in the world would have agreed with Marin was unsettling for me. I asked him pointedly about the training he received in Cuba and his eyes narrowed.

"One of the basic manuals for students at the guerrilla warfare school at Santiago is a book by General Alberto Bayo, called **150 Questions to a Guerrilla.**" General Bayo, a Spanish revolutionary, was an instructor for Ernesto *Ché* Guevara, Castro's right-hand man.

Outside, students noisily roamed the facility dressed in sports attire eager to compete in basketball and soccer games scheduled by the academy while Marin, with commendable patience, answered my questions.

"We learned to make bombs in Cuba that are simple to construct but effective." He quickly drew a picture of a Molotov cocktail on a flip chart with impressive skill.

"The addition of soap chips and a bit of sawdust to the gasoline and oil in the Molotov cocktail causes the formation of napalm when the bomb explodes," he said. "You have to see it to believe it." He smiled in a nervous way to describe Molotov II used by terrorists to attack at night.

"Molotov II is a simple wine bottle with the usual mixture of gasoline and oil with soap chips added. The fuse consists of ampoules filled with acid that react with small tissue paper envelopes containing potassium chlorate. When the tissue tears and the potassium makes contact with the acid you have ignition." He sketched a picture of the bomb on the chart.

"Molotov II is particularly awesome at night," he added. "You can't see it coming until it hits and explodes in a violent outpouring of fire. The police in Latin America are scared to death of this bomb," he explained. Marin explained other devices and their use in guerrilla warfare. Marin said that communist guerrilla movements preferred to recruit young people, even as young as ten or twelve years old, because it is easier to motivate and train them.

That was precisely what the FMLN did in El Salvador. Castro's followers inspired the various trainees to embrace the communist cause through emotional and charismatic presentations, he said. The simple message to new recruits was that communism was on the side of the oppressed in the fight against Yankee imperialism.

Marin provided information about pipe bombs, incendiary devices, land mines and more complex war artifacts used by Castro in the training of guerrillas. Much of the data was in General Bayo's book, a paperback sold openly in many Latin American and U.S. bookstores. I was surprised to learn that Fidel Castro himself proselytized many young people in Latin America to the communist cause. He was a charmer, Marin said.

Nevertheless, Marin's information on his guerrilla training in Cuba served to enliven counterinsurgency presentations in class. Many of the IAPA students were aware of Castro's homemade bombs. In fact, discussions on Castro's training promoted an enlightened exchange of ideas between students that were already experienced in the matter. Participants from Colombia, El Salvador, Uruguay, Chile, Bolivia, Venezuela and the Dominican Republic had true stories on communist weaponry and tactics to prove that the Cold War was real.

The Cuban Missile Crisis

Early one morning on a weekend at Ft. Randolph, my wife woke me up as I tried to sleep late. "You have to see this," she told me as I put on a pair of pants and hurried to the kitchen. Our kitchen window faced the Atlantic Ocean and I was surprised to see dozens of U.S. Navy Battleships, Destroyers and other American Naval vessels anchored off Colon. Hundreds of U.S. Marines in full combat gear marched by *Cocó Solo* on both sides of the main roads leading to the American military bases.

The Cuban missile crisis had arrived in Panama with the United States on a war footing. Many of the residents of Ft. Randolph speculated that the Panama Canal was a prime target for a nuclear attack and suggested we travel with our families to the interior of Panama. It was finally agreed that traveling to the interior of Panama would do absolutely no good if nuclear bombs were used. Thirteen anxious days passed before we learned that the crisis was over.

IAPA Training

Once the training began, the American instructors at IAPA were surprised by the dissimilitude of law enforcement practices in different police organizations in Latin America. In most countries, the death penalty did not exist, even for the most heinous of crimes. Fidel Castro nevertheless, firmly believed in the death penalty. But why are the liberals in the United States so strongly opposed to the death penalty, some of the students asked? I could not respond properly to the question.

But the subject generated a great deal of discussion. In Latin America, law enforcement was often capricious and prosecution was worse. Surviving in the harsh environment of a Latin American prison was an uncertain possibility, the students suggested. Latin American prisons were loaded with the mentally ill and violent people, I was told. The living conditions are intolerable for the weak, they said.

Law enforcement problems consisted mostly of burglaries, civil unrest, riots, terrorist activity, kidnapping, murders and bank robberies that were increasing in many countries. Narcotics trafficking and terrorist activity was growing. Community policing on foot was a common practice as police officers walked the streets in their countries because vehicles and bicycles were severely limited.

Many of the civil police forces were militarized and military influences inculcated disciplinary policies and procedures that in most cases were unduly harsh and outdated. In many Latin American countries, police operations and administrative practices were unchanged for over ten decades.

The classroom discussions and the exchange of ideas promoted by the instructors of the IAPA brought to the surface various roles, policies, practices and procedures commonly used by the police and paramilitary forces in Latin America. The debates were enlightening.

There was little doubt that the militarization and politicization of the civil police organizations in Latin America inclined the criminal justice systems, based on the Napoleonic Code, to operate as comedian Richard Pryor once observed: "justice means just us."

Respect for human rights often depended on the politics, ephemeral points of view or connections to the self-serving machinations of the individuals in power. It seemed that criminal justice in Latin America, similar to some places in the United States, was idyllic for the rich and the people in power but oftentimes a nightmare for the poor. Legal reforms were urgently needed. A speedy arraignment and trial for anyone arrested was virtually impossible unless the individual involved had *tortazo* or *palanca*—influence or money. Thousands of people spent lengthy and unwarranted time in horrendous jails without due process or without even being charged with a crime.

In Latin American countries, a civil police officer generally could not arrest a military officer even for a criminal act committed in his presence.

Like the United States, justice in Latin America often took many twisted turns. Activists screamed about the violation of human rights by the police but it seemed unlikely that a communist takeover would bring about any positive changes. Human rights had nowhere near the importance of hegemony for the communists.

We found that countries governed by military juntas or dictatorships in Latin America were attractive targets for communist insurgencies in the Cold War. That included the countries of Bolivia, El Salvador, Guatemala, and Nicaragua. Providing U.S. military assistance to the military forces of Latin America amounted to American support for dictators and for maintaining repression at a *status quo* according to the left wing of the world. A much broader and important policy issue was at stake.

If the U.S. did not provide military assistance in Latin America, the Soviet Union and other countries from the communist bloc would eagerly oblige. Peru and Cuba were already receiving significant military assistance from the Soviet Union. Many other Latin American governments were considering military assistance programs offered by the USSR.

The U.S. military establishment saw things from a perspective of allies, influence and the denying to the enemy of important terrain. There was a Cold War going on. The School of the Americas had been training military and police officers from Latin America since 1950 and was growing controversial as attacks by the American political left wing multiplied. The protesters argued that the School was training tyrants and torturers. That was left-wing rhetoric and unfair. Did Stalin, Ho Chi Minh and other mass murderers get training at communist schools?

Nevertheless, coordination between the instructors from the School of the Americas and the Inter-American Police Academy was to ensure we were not in conflict with regard to doctrine, policies and tactics. It was obvious the police and military forces in Latin America had to work together to combat communist insurgencies and terrorist movement. The coordination involved nothing sinister but for the opponents of United States policies, both schools were in the business of training death squads, torturers and tyrants. But tyrants and torturers require no training if you consider Fidel Castro, Joseph Stalin, Adolph Hitler, and many others.

In the air conditioned office of Colonel Edward Schroeder, the Commandant of the School of the Americas, French and I sat in silence surrounded by U.S. military officers. We were there to discuss the production of a training film on joint planning and operations between the police and military forces during emergencies. The film was considered important to the U.S. counterinsurgency training provided to the security forces of other countries.

The idea had been proposed to the White House by Edward R. Murrow, the popular news columnist and head of the U.S. Information Agency (USIA) at the time. Murrow had suggested that a training film be made of a Command Post Exercise (CPX) he witnessed on a visit to both schools. The training film would help train the security forces of other countries in coping with communist-inspired riots and insurgencies. The exercise (CPX) involved Latin American police officers from the IAPA and military officers from the School of the Americas.

The initial script was based on a violent riot situation and ensuing guerrilla action by communist insurgents trying to overthrow the democratic government of a fictitious country called *San Martin*. The general trend of the script developed by the School of the Americas seemed to be that the civil police were incapable of dealing with a crisis and that military force was the solution to any emergency. I had objected to the script.

In the meeting, Colonel Schroeder implied that the experienced instructors from the School of the Americas could do a better job of training Latin American police officials in counterinsurgency than the civilians of the IAPA. His rationale was simple.

"The police forces in Latin America are under the command of the military officers in those countries," the colonel told us. "Most Latin American countries do not have civilians capable of commanding an armed police force." The colonel was correct, military officers generally occupied the top command positions of the police organizations in Latin America.

"Military training and discipline are indispensable to counterinsurgency operations," he said. He became a pithy high-strung preacher pacing the floor.

"For example, rifles with bayonets work for the job of riot control. Policemen employing batons against rioters are useless. Countries in Latin America are experiencing significant civil unrest, fomented by communist militants." The Colonel was dramatic in his lecture.

"Violent riots are caused by and exploited by communist guerrillas as part of the process of an insurgency that permits them to take over a country." He was preaching to the choir, I told myself. He pointed an index finger upward.

"On the other hand, rifles and bayonets are effective in controlling mob violence. Starting riots is simply a communist tactic that helps promote chaos."

It seemed certain we had to convince the colonel that the civil police had the primary role in controlling civil disturbances and in defending against subversion and insurgency in any democracy. But the point at which the military would have to come in and help had to be determined. There had to be a reasonable and logical plan for an escalation of force in any violent situation that threatened the internal security of a country or the safety of any community. The Colonel again pointed his trigger finger.

"Once a riot gets out of control, you have problems. The control of riots and civil unrest by the armed forces works because we know what needs to be done." For a long time, we listened attentively. French grabbed my arm to discourage any response. I tore away.

"Colonel, communist guerrillas and terrorists do not follow rules of war. That is the reason they are successful. They are beating the crap out of the military and police forces in Latin America. It is more political than Vietnam," I suggested. Faces in the room turned to granite.

I suggested that the communists in Latin America wanted a violent response from the security forces during mass demonstrations so they could claim government repression and capitalize on the martyrs that resulted in order to gain the sympathy and support of the populace.

"Left-wing guerrillas are known to kill people during a riot to make them martyrs," I added.

The silence in the room assured me I had crossed the line. I made an effort to explain that the populace is usually caught in the middle in such a crisis and the people fear they can not be protected.

"The populace must be protected from violence and not alienated to the side of the guerrillas. To do this, Latin American civil police forces need police training by civil police experts," I suggested.

"But the police and the military must cooperate and plan and work together to resolve any internal security problem. The British experience in Malaysia is a good example," I pointed out in a hopeful gesture. The Colonel's face darkened.

"The population of any country seems to prefer not having soldiers out on the streets with automatic rifles," I suggested. There was total silence.

An Army Major with gold leaves gleaming on his shirt collar could not contain himself. His face had turned rigid and he appeared frustrated with me.

"You don't have your facts straight," the Major said, staring unwaveringly at me.

"The military forces are crucial to any counterinsurgency effort. Without our help, the Latin American military and police don't have a chance." The police are less prepared than the military to deal with insurgents, he pointed out.

"They don't have the training or resources to combat a communist insurgency. That's why they will lose." He was crisp and cool.

He was partially correct and my attitude placed us in a confrontational position. I resisted the urge to point out that Latin American military officers seemed sufficiently trained with plenty of resources to pull off military *coup d'états* in their own countries to put themselves in power. Was it a matter of sublimating their efforts from gaining power for themselves to fighting communist guerrillas? The meeting raised interesting questions for all of us. What could we do to bring the police and military forces closer together to fight an insurgency? We were working on that.

Lt. Colonel Knute Thorpe and Major Paul Romero were top-notch military officers at the School of the Americas and we worked together on the joint planning and operations concept. Major Paul Romero, a *Chicano* U.S. Army Officer from Texas was important to the project but unfortunately was killed in an automobile accident while he was TDY in Ecuador. Colonel Thorpe, Romero and I had become good friends.

Colonel Thorpe suggested that there was a way to solve our differences in regard to the training film proposed. He was right. It was reasonable compromise and a spirit of professionalism.

French's heavy silence alerted me to a previous agreement that we would not push or shove if polemics developed. A turf war placed us in a confrontational position on the proposed training film. The work ahead was going to be tricky. We had to join forces to fight communist aggression. The IAPA and the School of the Americas were already accused of training military tyrants and torturers by the left wing and their communist advocates. Doing the job as the "bad guys" in the Cold War was tough enough and it was growing tougher.

Cuban operatives in many countries in Latin America were supporting activists in provoking civil unrest and helping guerrilla movements. Portentous resistance to the Vietnam War was growing as Americans became increasingly divided primarily by ideology.

Despite our differences, **"The First Line of Defense,"** a training film on Joint Planning and Operations for Emergencies was written, produced and directed by a genuine professional named Loren McIntyre. The film was a huge success. Students from the IAPA and members of the Panama National Guard performed as actors in the film. The filming was done in Panama, inside the Canal Zone. Lt. Luis Nentzen Franco, the instructor on loan from the Panama National Guard, acted as the commander of the military forces in the film. Another top officer of the Panama National Guard assumed the role of the Chief of Police of San Martin, a fictitious city in a fictitious country. The film was translated to Spanish, Portuguese and French and was used to train the security forces of many countries on joint planning and operations in an emergency.

But it was Loren McIntyre who brought everyone together to make the film a reality. He was a highly talented and unusual man. (I was on active duty as a Captain in the U.S. Air Force Reserve assigned to General O'Meara's Joint Intelligence Command, J-2. A few days later, a frustrated Loren McIntyre showed up at my quarters to find out why I was not available to start work on the film. I explained that I was on active duty in the U.S. Air Force Reserve and he left.

The next day I was astonished when McIntyre showed up wearing the uniform of a Navy Captain. He told me my ass was now his to work on the film. I was obliged to follow his orders and became one of the technical advisors on the film. McIntyre's rank of Navy Captain was equivalent to a full colonel in the U.S. Air Force and he used his rank well. I grew to admire McIntyre.)

5

The CINC

The historic port of the city of Colon, located on the Atlantic Ocean side of the Panama Canal, often has a distinct haze that gives it the appearance of sadness. The climate is hot, but always lively and colorful. The population of the city has a diversity of blithesome people. The students attending courses at the IAPA loved the city of Colon, especially the *"putas,"* according to Mario Vasquez.

French and I traveled from Ft. Randolph to Ft. Davis in the afternoon after lunch, and stopped in Colon to enjoy a cold beer at *El Pito,* a dive by most standards but an interesting place. We sat at an old bar that appeared to have a memorable history.

An attractive young girl with light chocolate skin, wearing a soft white dress clinging to a firm voluptuous body, smiled at us. French smirked when she walked sensuously toward us. Feeling the pressure of a soft pelvic nudge gently into my knee, the girl smiled at me sensuously.

"Cómo estan, mi amor?" she asked. French could not speak Spanish and seemed frustrated.

"Come on, let's get the hell out of here," he said, saying that we would smell like a brewery and whores by the time we got back to the academy.

French was as oppressive as the heat. Pressing a couple of dollars on the bar, I stood to leave.

"Porqué, mi amor?" the young girl asked, stroking my arm. She asked me why we were leaving.

French stared at me, perplexed.

"One beer and you're drunk," he said, pulling at my arm.

"Don't be such a rude bastard," I told him. Walking out of the bar to the street I turned to tell the girl why we were leaving so as not to hurt her feelings.

"Tenemos problemas que atender cariño." I told her we had problems to take care of and she laughed out loud, showing perfect white teeth. Irritated, French asked what I told her.

When I suggested that I was not his interpreter he grew sullen and grouchy, making me laugh. French became irritated, but it was not my fault he could not speak Spanish.

"I told her you were my boyfriend," I finally told him. French's face turned a deep red.

"You're so full of crap!" he said, while I laughed with gusto.

It was amazing to see how Americans were so vulnerable, helpless and stupid when they could not speak the language of the foreign country in which they were assigned to work.

When we reached Ft. Davis, problems at the IAPA had suddenly cropped up like the "Panama Red" marijuana plants growing "wild" at the *Perlas* Islands. Three high-ranking police officials from Uruguay that had just arrived informed us that they returning to their country. In an outraged manner they complained bitterly about the "unacceptable and inferior living conditions" at the IAPA at Ft. Davis. Before departing, dressed in their elegant white military uniforms, they chastised Americans at IAPA for subjecting them to what they called an unconscionable "ridicule and lack of respect."

The Director, Dave Laughlin, had found out that both men had been selected to attend the pilot course at the IAPA by Ned Holman, the CIA Station Chief in Uruguay. Influenced by the Uruguayans, three senior officers of the Chilean *Carabineros* prepared to pack up and leave for the same reason. We met with the Chilean officers and promised changes in the accommodations to convince them not to leave. Laughlin agreed to put stalls in the bathrooms to provide more privacy for the students.

But now, things were growing difficult for me. For weeks, I had worked on a design for a pistol range and had finally found a location for its construction. Since I was in charge of firearms training but there appeared to be no concern by anyone else at the IAPA about the lack of a suitable pistol range that could be used to train Latin American police officers. Training in the use of firearms was essential and important. The program at IAPA included forty hours of instruction in the .38 caliber revolver and the semiautomatic shotgun.

In a small jungle clearing near Ft. Davis, I had located a perfect spot for a small arms range that would permit up to forty students to be trained in a basic course in firearms and combat shooting. French suggested that the U.S. Army Corps of Engineers would construct the range and the IAPA would reimburse them for the cost. The site selected and the design of the range were approved by the Safety Officer at Ft. Davis. Revolvers, shotguns, holsters, ammunition, targets and reloading equipment ordered through the OPS Technical Services Division (TSD) was held in storage at Ft. Davis. The site selected for the construction of the range would displace only a few iguanas.

At the administrative office of the Corps of Engineers, the forms required for the construction of the range were diligently filled out. Requesting that the construction of the range be done as soon as possible, I was told it was up to the colonel. I decided to talk to the colonel.

To my astonishment, the bulky commander of the organization quickly dispelled any doubt about the construction of a pistol range for the IAPA. In a brutal, officious manner he let me know.

"Unfortunately, we have higher priorities than constructing a pistol range at Ft. Davis," he told me. I stood in disbelief, staring at the huge silver metal eagles shining on the colonel's collar. He told me there were several military pistol ranges available that could be used for our purposes. I stayed silent because the good colonel seemed intent on grinding me into the ground. He had all the power.

"We'll get to you eventually," he said cockily. He scribbled on documents, glancing up occasionally while we talked, impatient and anxious to get me out of the way. My plea about the urgency of firearms training at the police academy made the colonel's response even more hectoring.

"In the Army, we call it tough shit. Planning ahead helps. Tell your boss you should use the military ranges available. It'll be easier all around."

The attitude of the colonel from the U.S. Army Corps of Engineers was an obsession. Touring military firearms training ranges in the area, my hunt had grown desperate. The military ranges were too far from the IAPA and would not work for the purpose of the FBI Practical Pistol Course (PPC), even with modifications. I sought help from Laughlin. He sat in his chair cradling documents.

"What's going on? You look worried," he said. I felt a burning sting on my arm. A sand fly had entered pinned to my arm. Noting that the office was air conditioned, I was told that the electric typewriters had to be protected from the humidity. Typewriters are more important than human beings, I thought humorously. I explained the problem with the construction of the firearms training range to Laughlin. It would not be completed in time for the first course at IAPA, I reported.

"The U.S. Army Corps of Engineers believes we have little priority. The fat ass colonel in charge said it may be three months before they can start building a range for the academy," I reported dejectedly and Laughlin seemed disturbed by my disrespectful description of the U.S. Army Colonel.

He inhaled deeply. His face darkened and he stayed momentarily silent, looking at a group of soldiers marching on the parade ground, sweating in the midmorning sun. Smiling patiently, he offered to see what he could do.

"We don't want to piss those guys off," he said, suggesting that arrangements could be made to borrow a military range in the interim.

I explained that military ranges were not set up with what was needed to train civil police officers and that the firearms program approved by OPS included the FBI PPC. Laughlin nodded, stretching his arms above his head to let me know he would try to get the colonel to reconsider.

Three days later, he received a negative response from the colonel and my frustration grew. It was hard to accept that a project approved by the President of the United States had a limited priority. The powerful colonel had to be convinced.

Meanwhile, IAPA instructors and their families had settled into military-type residences at Ft. Randolph with the CIA as their landlord and caretaker. My wife and children were happy in our large furnished home and new surroundings. Al Grunwell, *El Periqito,* became the sole bachelor residing at Ft. Randolph, along with J. Edgar Hoofer, the CIA horse with a mean streak, also unmarried.

When Grunwell's new *Mercedes Benz* arrived from the United States, we discovered he was a very wealthy landowner from Virginia. My wife became the only person at Ft. Randolph allowed to ride in his new *Mercedes,* seemingly to upset me. But other important things were happening.

In the midst of the Cold War, the Soviet Union celebrated Fidel Castro's visit to the USSR. In the United States, a "credibility gap" between official reports and the truth on events in Vietnam and Cuba surfaced. Communist advances in Chile, El Salvador, Nicaragua, Uruguay and other countries ushered in covert CIA action as Salvador Allende, the *Tupamaros* and the *Sandinistas* waited in the wings.

Meanwhile, more esoteric problems developed for the IAPA. An officer who had never been outside his country broke down, hopelessly homesick, and had to be sent home. Three "students" were caught shoplifting at the Ft. Davis Military Post Exchange.

Several students became infected with gonorrhea as a result of visits to prostitutes in Colon. Fortunately for the Latin American police officers attending the IAPA, a charismatic U.S. Army Medical Officer was the equivalent of a protective angel for them. Major Juan Cabezas, the U.S. Army Medical Officer of Ft. Davis, handled student medical problems with extraordinary compassion. He talked to the IAPA students with a Castilian Spanish accent and a special sense of humor to chastise them.

"Lath putas, lath putas!" he would say. Latin American students at the IAPA were lectured by Dr. Cabezas on the dangers of venereal disease in Colon and treated discreetly with antibiotics.

Despite the problems, in training sessions, the exchange of ideas between the students demonstrated an increasing awareness about the tactics of communist subversion and insurgency. Differences in equipment and operations in the various Latin American police agencies were logically affected by the local politics and the state of the country's economy. But since demonstrations, riots, terrorist activity and communist guerrilla movements had challenged internal security and the political stability in many countries, improvements needed in civil police infrastructures were moving faster, aided by the OPS program.

The 26-inch baton used by police organizations in the United States for riot control and for self-defense purposes was recommended to replace military rifles and bayonets. The wooden American police baton and training in its use aroused great interest among Latin American police officers. But it was not an easy sell. Without proper training, the wood baton was a club and could become a lethal weapon. Nevertheless, many Latin American police organizations accepted its use.

The police in Latin America used a variety of equipment and methodology to control civil disturbances and urban violence that included rubber truncheons, firearms, policemen mounted on horseback, police dogs, tear gas, water-throwing cannons and armored vehicles. The Gendarmarie Nacional of Argentina did not hesitate to shoot at rioters on rooftops, especially if they were throwing rocks or Molotov cocktails. A no-nonsense approach by police was an advantage in coping with communist-led civil disturbances.

Colonel Roberto *"Toto"* Quintanilla from the Bolivian *Carabineros* offered humorous advice to the students on the 26-inch wood baton. *"Le sugiero a los señores oficials que no les pase lo que le paso al Oficial Ángulo."* *Ángulo* rhymed with *culo*, which in the Spanish vernacular means ass. He cautioned the officers to "be careful with the wood baton so what happened to Officer *Ángulo,* does not happen to you." The colonel proposed with jocularity that in that case the wood baton was worse than a rubber truncheon.

The polemics and debates in the classroom were exceptional and a real learning process. But at graduations, the speeches and demonstrations of camaraderie were tributes to the staff. Emotional *despedidas*...farewells between the graduates, showed that professional relationships developed at IAPA would make a difference in the fight against communist insurgents and even international criminals. Many friendships developed between the police officers from the various Latin American countries during the course of their training.

With time, the tropical heat, the sand flies and the dynamics of the IAPA training grew oppressive for the instructors and the staff. To escape the heat and sand flies the instructors escaped after work to the air conditioned Officer's Club at Ft. Davis. Happy Hour at the Ft. Davis Officer's Club was paradise in comparison to the IAPA facility where the fight against the vicious wee biting beasts called *"no-see-ums"* never ceased. Only air conditioning could stop the sand fly.

Several staff members threatened to resign or to return to their parent organizations. The wife of Reynaldo Cantu, a Special Agent for the Bureau of Narcotics and Dangerous Drugs (BNDD), had to be medically evacuated as a result of the serious allergic reactions and infections caused by the sand fly bites. Cantu complained bitterly and unfortunately eventually requested to return to the BNDD.

For certain, the sand fly could make life miserable for the instructors, the students and the American families living at Ft. Randolph. Floor fans set up in the facility only made the airworthiness of the sand fly more difficult. By late afternoon, few instructors remained in the sweltering heat of the new academy. My standard gray U.S. Army desk in an open area with the other instructors was hot and uncomfortable. It was a high-risk area for sand flies.

Beads of sweat trickled down my back when I heard a familiar voice ring out.

"Dolphin." French ambled up with his round-rimmed glasses askew and a weary look.

"Dolphin," he repeated. With his hands in his pockets he stood in the corridor with a feeble grin on his face.

"It's Happy Hour!" he announced cheerfully. "What the hell are we doing here? Let's go have a drink. Hell, let's have two drinks. Maybe we can even get drunk!" I glanced at my watch.

"Everyone else is there 'cept us," he reminded me. I did not need to be convinced. Stuffing my paperwork in a desk drawer I grabbed my umbrella and joined French. Torrential rain in Panama had made me a believer. The Club was only a short walk away but on a rainy day, we would be soaked before we made it to the front porch overhang. A Panamanian once said that the people of Panama would rather face bullets than the onslaught of a tropical monsoon rain.

We arrived at the officer's club and heavy libation was underway with music and chatter inside the refrigerated privileged sanctuary. Instructors already there greeted us. The Ft. Davis Officer's Club had a Happy Hour that commonly attracted a sizable crowd of military officers and their wives, joined preemptively by the "civilians" of the IAPA, wrongly lumped together with less affection by some residents of Ft. Davis as "CIA assholes."

Like the *Tivoli* Hotel, the Ft. Davis Officer's Club had the reputation of serving excellent martinis. Amid the din, French and I talked about sand fly problems and training operations at the police academy. Two martinis later, I mentioned my problem with the construction of the range to French, using standard Marine Corps terminology. It seemed to me that former Marines could not express themselves without using the "*F*" word.

I blamed French for not supporting a resolution to the problem of student selection and the problem of air conditioning. I laughed when his scalp turned red under his crew cut as I cut into him.

"Okay, okay, what is the fucking problem?" he asked. I deliberately ignored him. Irritated, French ordered two more martinis and placed one in front of me.

"See what I mean," he said, slurringly. "You don't know what you're talking about." I sipped on the martini and quickly felt its potency.

"I told you, the problem is that we get no respect," I told him with an angry chuckle. I explained the range construction problem and the fat colonel from the Corps of Engineers. He sighed.

"He's your fat ass colonel. I have my own," he said sipping his martini. I suggested that he obviously did not give a crap about the training program and our conversation grew heated. French assumed a pensive, inebriated look.

"Listen, don't blame me! I'm just the business manager. You guys are the thugs!" He grew silent, but in a few minutes he leaned forward with a sly smile.

"Listen, I have an idea. We're going to meet with the Commander in Chief (CINC), U.S. Southern Command. If you're not too drunk to remember, we have a meeting with General Andrew O'Meara tomorrow. Tell Andy about your damn pistol range problem. I'll bet he can help." French threw his arms out to emphasize a point.

"We're talking about a four star General who kicks ass!" He grinned raising his glass to order more drinks. French was right. It was a good idea.

A hand touched my shoulder surprising me. It was Lou Page, the Chief Instructor.

"Dolph, you were sorta late this morning," he told me with a grimace. He was ahead on drinks.

"Yeah, Lou, I know. A whole five minutes. You also know I'm never late for class and work while you guys suck up martinis!" Page stiffened and I grinned. I constantly gave him a hard time.

"Is Page getting on your ass?" French asked.

I ignored his question to ask him what O'Meara could do to help a bunch of pseudo-cops. As far as I was concerned he was all army. I hoped French would convince me otherwise. French made a sucking noise between his teeth to admonish me.

"Listen, I support our boys in uniform and was once in uniform myself. But that fat ass colonel from the Corps of Engineers is a martinet!" I told him. The bar was full of military officers.

"Why would General O'Meara help?" I asked. French shook his head impatiently and grinned.

"O'Meara is a good guy and supports the IAPA. He's been in touch with the Pentagon on this project all along and he likes it." French finished his martini and smacked his lips.

"Besides, this is an opportunity for you to try your charm on the girls at Quarry Heights." He laughed with a giggle.

"I'm serious!" French lifted his glass as if to toast.

"Trust me, Andy can help." His face was flushed with the ingestion of martinis.

General Andrew O'Meara was known by civilians in the Canal Zone as a skinny, strict military man, ramrod straight and mean as the crack of a bullwhip on bare skin. With four stars on the collar of his uniform shirt, Andy O'Meara was a deity in the Canal Zone. He hated fat soldiers and disliked most civilians. But principally because of O'Meara's reputation for being mean, I was not optimistic.

The next day, I arrived early at the academy still feeling the effects of the consumption of martinis with French the night before. A strange nostalgia hit me and drained my energy. My birthday had passed a few days earlier and my wife had thrown a surprise party for me. I felt insecure and middle-aged. My family was growing and I worried about our future. But I needed a job, and liked this one.

French waited for me in a dark navy blue IAPA van to drive us to Panama City. It was a hot, humid day and it would take an hour to drive from the Atlantic to the Pacific Ocean on the transisthmus highway. The van had air conditioning and the scenery was beautiful. Picking up my stride I figured this had to be a good day. Entering the van, French handed me a cold beer. That was a fine start.

By mid morning French parked the navy blue IAPA van at Quarry Heights. Our visit with General Andrew O'Meara, Commander in Chief (CINC), U.S. Southern Command, was already scheduled. Inside, we found the office of the CINC almost empty and quiet except for the shuffling of papers by Army officers in an outer office. They wore khaki summer uniforms, rigidly starched.

A receptionist directed us to O'Meara's secretary, a friendly elegant woman who immediately advised us that the General would see us shortly. She offered coffee and we accepted. A few minutes later, General O'Meara was ready to see us. Standing, French snickered when I spilled a few drops of coffee on my white shirt. The General's secretary smiled as I tried to clean my shirt with a handkerchief.

We entered a bright and sunny room with a large bay window that overlooked beautiful jungle terrain and tropical vegetation and in the distance the Pacific Ocean shimmered in the bright sunshine. Thatcher Ferry Bridge, a beautifully engineered marvel, linked the two portions of land at the entrance of the Panama Canal on the Pacific Ocean side of the Republic of Panama. It was an impressive sight.

General Andrew O'Meara, in khaki summer uniform, stood from behind a mahogany desk piled high with important looking documents.

"Come in, come in," he ordered cheerfully, his four stars glittering like silver ingots on his collar. He shook hands vigorously with us, smiling pleasantly and motioning for us to sit. We were put at ease, tentatively. O'Meara was an old salt and enjoyed casual chitchat occasionally. However, the General wasted little time getting down to business and abruptly his friendly smile froze into a granite frown. He pointedly asked how things were going at the police academy.

"How's Laughlin?" he asked. The General stared at us, glancing from one to the other, clenching his jaw.

"Any problems?" he asked. I looked at French and he smiled in a casual, relaxed way. General O'Meara's face grew serious.

"Things are going just great, General," French reacted cheerfully. My friend was cool, not showing any tension. He would creep up on the range issue. French explained that the excellent cooperation from the military officers at Ft. Davis and Ft. Gullick in setting up the IAPA was much appreciated by Laughlin and everyone. He was self-assured and apparently enjoying himself.

I smiled and tried to appear comfortable and at ease. The General was in a good mood and French, a superb bureaucrat, described in dramatic detail the help provided by Army personnel at Ft. Davis to set up classrooms, living quarters and a dining room for the academy. O'Meara seemed pleased until French moved the conversation hesitantly to the problem of a firearms range.

"We have one minor problem, General." French chuckled and nodded tersely at me as if I was the problem.

"Perhaps Dolph should explain." A grin remained on French's face and the General growled.

"What?" I felt my buttocks grow rigid. With four large stars twinkling on his collar, General O'Meara had transformed into *Darth Vader.* His dark eyes locked on me.

"What's the problem?" the General asked somewhat menacingly, staring at the small coffee stains on my shirt. I explained that coffee had spilled on my clean white shirt and O'Meara grinned.

With my face reflecting serious concern I explained the firearms training at the IAPA and the need for an appropriate range. The decision by Colonel Duncan of the U.S. Army Corps of Engineers made it very difficult for us to meet our training goals and objectives, I suggested. General O'Meara tilted his head slightly, to stare at the carpet.

The construction of a pistol range at Ft. Davis was a serious problem for us I explained in a respectful manner, avoiding any appearance that I was complaining about the U.S. Army. I was on dangerous ground and one did not bullshit the CINC.

"Colonel Duncan informed us we'll have to wait three months or more before construction of the IAPA range can be started," I said in a soft voice and the General nodded. I looked at French wondering if he had anything to add. He stared calmly at his hands. I knew I had to hurry. O'Meara hated long-winded explanations.

I explained that the academy had started operations on July 2 and President Kennedy had mentioned the inauguration of the IAPA in his July 4th speech back home. The General was advised that as a result of the delay in the construction of the range we were late with our firearms training. We had been unable to convince Colonel Duncan about the urgency of our problem.

General O'Meara tilted his head to scratch it, seemingly impatient and puzzled.

"Sir, we were told the range would not be constructed because there appears to be higher priorities." I played the only card available. The General would not like my mention of a low priority. French knew that the mention of priorities was a sensitive issue for the General. The White House had allocated the IAPA top priority.

"We don't have much priority, according to the colonel," I said. The General roared at the wall. French and I impulsively sat up rigidly in our chairs and he gave me an angry stare.

"Why, that sonofabitch!" General O'Meara's face grew stone hard.

"I'll handle *that* problem," he said ominously. Walking briskly behind his desk, he pressed a button on the telephone and his secretary arrived nervously at the door, smiling pleasantly. O'Meara lowered his voice to a normal tone and with a sardonic grin asked her "to get him Colonel Duncan."

The room grew silent and time passed with infinite tediousness. French glanced nervously at me as we waited. Rigid and silent, we watched the General pace the floor. His face was dark and he was extremely piqued. In silence French stared at me accusingly and I mouthed an obscenity at him. He shook his head. Nothing else would work to get our range built.

Time dragged heavily and unconsciously, I drank from an empty cup, sucking air. It was raining outside and French frowned at the wall. The General looked at documents on his desk and stopped pensively to watch the rain striking a large window.

The intercom on O'Meara's desk seemed to explode in a ringing buzz. The CINC picked up the telephone and a mellifluous voice informed him that Colonel Duncan was on the line. We tried to stand but the General angrily motioned that we stay sitting. He softly tapped his fingers on the desk.

"Colonel Duncan, this is General O'Meara," he said. "Listen carefully to what I'm going to tell you." He paused momentarily and raised his voice.

"I want you to get off your fat ass and construct a pistol range for the police academy at Ft. Davis as soon as possible. Do you understand me, Colonel?" His voice rose menacingly and French and I stared at the wall. O'Meara paused.

"Is that clear, Colonel? I mean as soon as possible."

Recalling my Marine Corps experience, it was obvious to me that it was a formidable ass chewing. Suppressing my joy, I visualized the colonel at the other end of the line, at attention, crapping in his shorts. French sat rigid, staring straight ahead.

The General's conversation with Colonel Duncan ended and he slammed the phone down with due purpose. Turning to us he told us with a smile on his face.

"I think that's taken care of. What else can I help with?"

We stood and French glared at me, sensing my intent to raise another issue. If we continued with a miasma of complaints the CINC would find something to give **us** 'a ration of shit' about. We both thanked the General. But he smiled and I took the opportunity.

"There is something personal I would like to raise, sir, if I may," I suggested.

The General visibly stiffened and assumed an impatient truculent look that seemed to say: "Don't bullshit me, son."

"I'm an Air Force Reserve Officer sir, and am greatly interested in working for the CINC, sir, in a reserve capacity." Watching me instinctively assume a military posture, O'Meara smiled.

"I have the highest admiration for the CINC, **sir**," I said emphasizing the sir and French riveted his eyes to the ceiling.

The General narrowed his eyes into thin slits. I was sincere as hell.

"I am an Army General, son, and am not particularly fond of the Air Force," he growled, his jaw jutting out! My heart accelerated but I remained at attention.

"What do you do in the Air Force, son?" he asked. I responded briskly.

"I'm an Intelligence Officer, sir," I told him, still standing at attention.

O'Meara had a staunch reputation as a hands-on Commander-in-Chief but I had the feeling that it was a bad move on my part and that I had imposed on his good will. But the General smiled and pointed at me with his finger.

"Okay. We'll see if we can get you assigned to my J-2 staff here at Quarry Heights. But you better be a damned good Intelligence Officer," he said with a dry grin.

(Within three weeks, I was assigned as a reserve officer to J-2, the Joint Intelligence Command that served the CINC. The unit was composed of Army, Navy, Air Force and Marine personnel.)

Now, the fat ass colonel would not sleep until the IAPA range was completed.

We returned to Ft. Davis and I had three messages from Colonel Duncan waiting for me. He asked that I please call him. He needed to coordinate with me on the construction of the pistol range for the IAPA as soon as possible. He apparently had changed his mind and given us priority. That was a tactical application of power.

Attorney General Robert Kennedy and General Andrew O'Meara visit the Inter-American Police Academy at Ft. Davis, Panama Canal Zone, October 1962

Third graduating class of the U.S. Inter-American Police Academy, Ft. Davis, Canal Zone, 1964. Ted Brown, Director of the Academy, is in front.

Joseph "Joe" Santioana, Special Agent in Charge,
FBI, Tampa, Florida, assisting at the Inter-American
Police Academy, 1964

Latin American police officers who graduated from the first class held at the
Inter-American Police Academy in the Canal Zone

Director Ted Brown (in the dark suit) and members of the Inter-American Police Academy Staff. Adolph Saenz is next to Brown. Lt. Nensen-Franco of the Panama National Guard is in uniform.

6

Bobby Kennedy

"I hope we teach these guys more than how to direct traffic."
—Robert Kennedy, U.S. Attorney General, August 1963

The Inter-American Police Academy generated special interest for top officials from the United States Government and from Latin American countries. John McCone, the Director of the Central Intelligence Agency (DCI), General Maxwell Taylor, the Special Advisor to the President, General Edward Landsdale ("Mr. Counterinsurgency"), and Edward R. Murrow, the head of the United States Information Agency (USIA), each made separate visits to the academy. Attorney General Robert Kennedy brought a special message from his brother, the President of the United States.

We waited for his visit as the early morning fog dissipated languorously on the Atlantic side of the isthmus and the sun cast streamers of bright sunshine across the lush green jungle foliage that surrounded Ft. Davis. For me the plush manicured lawns of Ft. Davis were unlike any found in the rundown ghettos and dirt streets in the nearby city of Colon.

The residences, buildings and roads inside the Canal Zone were in sharp contrast with the poverty of Panamanian communities. The Canal Zone was strictly U.S. territory.

The Panamanians called American employees living in the Canal Zone, "Zonians," and the tranquil jungle surroundings and fine U.S. Government housing were perks. For the special residents of the Canal Zone, the *Hay-Bunau-Varilla* treaty signed by President Theodore Roosevelt in 1903 was an agreement in perpetuity.

Ft. Davis was situated on the Atlantic side of the Republic of Panama and was one of the finest military posts in the Canal Zone. The trunks of beautiful coconut and palm trees that lined the roads of the facility were painted with a white band on the bottom. When the United States took over the construction of the Panama Canal from France, the coconut and palm trees were painted with a colorful white band from the dirt line to a few feet up the trunk. The trees appeared to be in military formation. But the white paint was for more than aesthetic purposes. Mixed with pesticides, the paint prevented insect damage to the trees and served as a protective barrier against destructive vermin.

Nevertheless, the practice enhanced the beautiful jungle surroundings and provided a military columnar look to the dozens of trees. Ft. Davis indeed looked centurion.

Ft. Davis and the military personnel assigned at the base were important to the mission of the Southern Command in the Western Hemisphere and consisted of well-trained combat units. The troops at Ft. Davis, Ft. Clayton and other military bases in the Canal Zone were under the Command of the Southern Command (CINC South). The CINC's Joint Operations Center (JOC) located in an underground tunnel at Quarry Heights coordinated any U.S. military operation in the hemisphere.

For decades, U.S. troops based in the Canal Zone trained in jungle warfare, special operations and anti-guerrilla warfare. Their mission included the protection of the Panama Canal, the most prized strategic jewel in the Southern Hemisphere. But as a result of canal treaty negotiations with Panama by the Carter Administration, the canal was turned over to Panama. Many believe the canal wound up in the hands of the Chinese. That is partially correct. But it is an Israeli married to a Panamanian who has the inside track on the operation of the canal.

In the dry season, the heat from the noon sun and the tropical humidity commonly turned the area into an outdoor sauna and the infamous sand flies, called *chitras* in Panama, attacked with elephantine bites. On the 21st day of August the area swarmed with tiny black dots. We were told that U.S. Army Colonel Chris Olson, the Base Commander of Ft. Davis was waiting patiently outside our large gray building, taking the steamy heat and biting sand flies in stride. A sign at the entrance to our building spelled out in black letters, **"POLICE ACADEMY."**

From the screen window near my office I watched U.S. Army troops as they marched sharply to the cadence of a Non-Commissioned Officer (NCO) who barked out syllables understood by those in the formation.

The troops wore sweaty camouflage fatigues. M-16 rifles handled expertly by the soldiers in the formation indicated to me that they belonged to a special combat unit. A few yards from the formation of elite troops, red colored strips of cloth laid on the ground formed a large "**X**" to mark a landing spot for a helicopter that was due to land there. The NCO shouted cadence for the troops and left no doubt he was in charge.

At about 10:20 a.m., we walked out of the building with Dave Laughlin, the Director of the IAPA, to join Colonel Olson. The likable Base Commander greeted everyone with a warm handshake. We waited outside for what appeared to be about ten to fifteen minutes when a military helicopter approached the area flying low over the jungle terrain. The "whump, whump" of the rotor blades was already audible. David Laughlin as well as the IAPA staff wore dark suits and ties in the hot climate.

The helicopter descended slowly, hovering over the red markers on the grass and finally touching down as the rotors whipped up debris. The contingent of soldiers formed a wide protective circle around the aircraft. The rotor of the helicopter whispered to a stop and three men disembarked. Laughlin and Colonel Olson stepped forward to greet them.

The Attorney General of the United States, General Andrew O'Meara, and another gentleman walked briskly toward us as we watched their arrival in silent interest. Robert F. Kennedy was wearing a white long-sleeved dress shirt with his collar open. He carried a pair of sunglasses in his hand. His shirtsleeves were rolled up and his body was marked with perspiration—about what one might expect for Panama. He flashed a winning smile at the group and ran his hand through an abundant head of dark-red hair.

Accompanied by General O'Meara in his starched khaki summer uniform they paused to shake hands with everyone in the group. Afterwards, Laughlin led the way into the building. Kennedy and General O'Meara entered the police academy and talked with the local Panamanian staff, visited classrooms and other parts of the facility. Later, Kennedy was led into a conference room that had refrigerated air conditioning to meet with the instructors who were already gathered there. The coolness of the room quickly provided relief from the heat.

Kennedy sat nonchalantly at the table looking jaded but alert. He sat in silence and wiped sweat from his face with a battered handkerchief. The civilian with him sat at his side, notebook and pencil at the ready. General O'Meara and Colonel Olson sat together near Kennedy.

Unknown to Kennedy, the OPS men in the room were glad this particular room was air conditioned for the occasion. Luxuriating in the temporary relief from the heat and sand flies, Kennedy glanced around the room with a grin on his face. In the stillness of the room, the pause that ensued seemed out of order. In a soft low voice Laughlin finally spoke.

"Mr. Attorney General, my name is David Laughlin. I'm the Director of the Inter-American Police Academy. We're pleased to have you here with us today and thank you for taking time to visit us." Laughlin chuckled with a touch of uncertainty at this point.

"We're working hard on this historic project," he went on, "and are pleased to say that the Inter-American Police Academy was inaugurated a few weeks ago...and...on schedule." He paused to check the notes held in his hand on a piece of paper.

"We have selected for the first class at IAPA thirty-five police officers representing sixteen Latin American countries, including Mexico, for a three-month general training program." It surprised us when Laughlin looked at Kennedy as if he had a special bit of news.

"Mr. Attorney General, you would be astounded at the major traffic problems that exist in these Latin American countries." That did not sound important for me.

"For that reason we also emphasize traffic control," he said. I wondered if he was preaching the liberal line to placate Kennedy. Kennedy leaned forward with his fist under his chin and stared.

"Things are going very well thanks to Colonel Olson and the U.S. military in the Canal Zone. Those guys have been just great," Laughlin punctuated his remark with a smile and soft chuckle. There was a muted pause. Kennedy's face tightened and he looked stonily around the room. His eyes lingered on the group of men sitting around the table. He sat back and inhaled. There was a moment of silence. Kennedy suddenly interjected with a trace of impatience.

"The President has a lot of interest in this project," he announced testily. "We are here to convince you that this is an important effort." He paused and stared around the room.

"Now, can someone tell us what type of training we are providing in this facility?" There was a dribble of pugnaciousness in his voice, his Boston nasal twang unmistakable. "What the hell are we teaching these people?" It appeared that Kennedy was there to give us a hard time.

Laughlin, momentarily discomfited, remained calm. He looked around the room.

"Dolph Saenz is responsible for teaching non-lethal methods of riot control. He also teaches internal defense," he said matter-of-factly.

Internal defense sounded like strategy for a football game but it was a buzzword in government circles.

"Our training program includes criminal investigations, counterintelligence, police administration, riot control and patrol operations. This is a prime example of the type of training Latin American Police officers need," Laughlin said.

"Dolph also teaches firearms," Laughlin added. My heart rate jumped when I heard my name mentioned again.

"It is hard to believe that veteran police officers in Latin America have never received basic firearms training," he went on to say. He pointed to a distinguished gray-haired Italian sitting at the table.

"Joe Santioana of the FBI is helping with firearms training. Joe is the SAC (Special Agent in Charge) in Tampa and we're sure happy to have him with us." Santioana kept silent. He shifted uneasily in his chair to look grimly at Kennedy. Bobby Kennedy's disdain for Hoover's FBI went almost undetected. Santioana seemed to sense this.

Laughlin looked in my direction to ask that I explain some of the subjects I taught. Caught by surprise I loosened my tie and stood up, expecting a hard time from Kennedy. I was unprepared for any briefing for the Attorney General of the United States but this was not the time to make excuses.

"Mr. Attorney General, the pilot course includes representatives from Mexico, Central America, Panama and South America." I suggested that expectations were high on the part of the participants, but many of them were or wanted to be military officers. Laughlin and several instructors stared at each other with a trace of discomfort. Their eyes said, "dumb shit, that's not relevant." The ominous silence pushed me to get more aggressive.

"We stress in our training sir, that the police forces in a democracy are the first line of defense against any threat to internal security. We encourage a timely response by the police; first, to protect the public, second, to maintain law and order, and third, to counter any communist subversive threat. Our training is hard core in terms of strategy and tactics," I told the Attorney General. My briefing had become a boring lecture but I continued.

"The police forces of Latin America need training and technical assistance to improve basic services such as patrol, investigations and riot control." I emphasized riot control training and the use of non-lethal force. It was difficult to tell whether Kennedy and his group were paying attention to anything I said. My colleagues stared at me mindlessly.

This was not another Kodak moment. My uneasiness increased when I realized I was not prepared to provide any information on IAPA training to the Attorney General of the United States. I focused on the problems of civil unrest and communist-inspired violence taking place in Latin America and mentioned that in some countries in Latin America, terrorist and guerrilla groups were killing a police officer a day. That was intended to destroy the will and spirit of the security forces to fight any communist movement, I suggested. We were training the police to fight back. The hum of the air conditioner grew distracting and Kennedy glanced at me and pulled at his open collar.

"Wait a minute," he said cockily. "We know all that." He grinned and sat back. "Tell us something we don't know. Tell us something about yourself." He turned to people sitting around the room. A frown crossed his face.

"What's your full name and your background?" he asked. "Where the hell are you from?"

The room was cool but for me it was growing hot and uncomfortable. My mind raced with an occasional obscenity. I was in the hot seat, just like Jimmy Hoffa. The similarity between Bobby and his brother Jack was not **Camelot.** The man asking questions was a powerful member of the United States Government and to boot his brother was President. My mind played with jocularity.

He should have stayed in Washington to harass J. Edgar Hoover, I thought. And why wasn't he skinny dipping with his brother and the two broads called Fiddle and Faddle in the White House pool? Al Grunwell, *El Periquito,* had mentioned this to me in jest when we learned of Kennedy's visit.

But I was not sure what Kennedy wanted, perhaps information on IAPA objectives, philosophy, purpose and for some reason, information on my background. Our basic philosophy was to teach cops to combat terrorists without becoming terrorists. My background was far from impressive.

I told him my full name and explained with uneasiness that I was from New Mexico and had served as a police officer in Albuquerque while completing my degree from the University of New Mexico. Kennedy looked blank and unimpressed. I had just over four years of government service.

"I am a veteran and served with the U.S. Marine Corps and U.S. Air Force in two wars," I offered. Kennedy adjusted himself in his chair, his face flushed but showing little reaction.

"I have three years of experience as a police advisor to the National Police of El Salvador," I said with frustration. Bad thoughts crossed my mind. Mr. Kennedy, I am patriotic but unlike you I come from a poor family in New Mexico. But like you, I have a high libido, I thought to myself.

Kennedy stared intently at me and I felt a trace of anger. He nodded and wrote something on a pad. I pretended not to notice his scribbling.

"Latin American Police forces need U.S. assistance in a bad way, sir, if they are to cope with communist-led mass violence and insurgencies." Terrorists and guerrillas are not nice altar boys like you liberals want us to believe, I thought angrily. Kennedy looked at me with bleary eyes.

"You speak Spanish?" he asked abruptly.

"Yes sir," I answered quickly.

"I am bilingual in Spanish." That's all the *bona fides,* I thought, still smarting. A smile lit up Kennedy's florid face. He stared at me with droopy eyes.

"How old are you?" he asked.

"Twenty-nine, sir," I answered stiffly. Kennedy grinned. He was five years older than I was but he couldn't speak Spanish, I mused. He pushed back tousled hair with his hand to glance at his wristwatch. My colleagues stared at each other.

"Very good," he said with emphasis. He apparently liked the fact that I was young and conservative but liberal enough to learn about deception and sinister politics. I was not old enough to be dangerously cynical.

"Let me say something," Kennedy said suddenly raising his voice to underscore his own thoughts in terms of what he perceived we were teaching at the IAPA.

"I hope we <u>teach these guys more than just how to direct traffic!</u>" The room fell ominously silent. Kennedy stared around the room sternly.

"Policemen have to be trained, organized and equipped to take tough action against communist insurgents and terrorists. You have to help provide that training." The men in the room stared at each other. Kennedy seemed to be a conservative/liberal hawk. But his words took on a special meaning for those in the room. We were in the fight to win.

Too many people in Washington insisted that communism posed no threat to the democracies of the world. Left-wing insurgencies were normal political change according to the ideologues of America. It was the police and military forces that violated human rights in the Cold War, according to the communists and their supporters. Kennedy's message was clear. We were to train police officers to win the struggle against communism in their own countries. But we were losing the fight in our country.

Kennedy leaned back and smiled.

"Thanks!" he told me in a low voice. That made me feel better. For the next fifteen minutes he asked hard questions about counterinsurgency doctrine, the material resources needed by the police, and gleaned estimates on the capabilities of the security forces of Latin American to fight urban and rural guerrilla movements. Kennedy mentioned that the IAPA should be in the United States in a civil police environment where Latin American police officers could see how policemen in American cities operate.

Someone expressed a philosophy that any equipment provided should be with caution since Latin American police did not maintain or repair equipment properly. The reality produced cold stares. In many countries in Latin America the police did not have the funds to buy the equipment needed to combat crime and, even less, to fight an organized terrorist group or insurgent movement. That was always a tough call. The police forces of Latin America were in dire need of vehicles, communications equipment and weaponry.

The communists and left-wing reactionaries in the United States were doing everything possible to stop OPS assistance to the security forces of foreign countries based on the fact that it was intervention in the internal affairs of sovereign nations. Left-wing radicals and misguided liberals in the United States were making every effort to put the OPS out of business. Kennedy was right, things had to be balanced out or the communists would win. Yet, Kennedy was supposed to be a liberal. Not all liberals have the same agenda, I thought.

Nevertheless, the President's message brought by Attorney General Robert Kennedy was loud and clear. We had to get tough on communist aggression.

"If the United States is going to be successful in counterinsurgency operations, let's provide the security forces of our allies with the technical assistance, training and equipment that's needed. Let's do it in a timely fashion," he said. Kennedy conveyed the message with no equivocation.

"Assistance to the security forces of friendly countries serves a purpose. First, to help protect a democracy. Second, to help prepare the security forces of friendly countries to defend themselves against communist-inspired violence and subversion. The assistance by the United States to the police forces in Latin America is in the best interests of our national security. It is justifiable and necessary. Let's do what we can to help before chaos takes over in these countries and communism wins."

The message from the President charged the room with energy. When Robert Kennedy stood up, those in the room rose spontaneously.

The Attorney General and General O'Meara walked out of the building with everyone following behind.

Outside, Kennedy waited until everyone was out of the building and General O'Meara joined the group. A grin froze on Kennedy's face as he took time to shake hands with everyone. He reached for my hand and gripped it tightly. He smiled at me crookedly.

"Good luck, Mr. Sanz," he said, mispronouncing my name. He stared momentarily and then walked away briskly with General O'Meara and the other civilian towards the helicopter.

"Thank you, sir, " I hollered. Kennedy waved as he boarded the helicopter. The rotor picked up speed and the aircraft disconnected from the ground, banked toward the sun and the Pacific Ocean and disappeared. I was very impressed with his visit.

The IAPA staff was also impressed with the visit of General Andrew O'Meara and Robert Kennedy and the fact that the President supported our efforts. There was a foreboding uncertainty in our minds about the dank politics of the Cold War. As if an omen, dark rain clouds gathered above as we walked back into the building. French stopped to stare at the rain clouds, his face expressionless, uncertain about what comment might be fitting in this situation. The deluge began.

"Kennedy was kind to us!" I told him, breaking the silence. "That was a damn crappy briefing. I'm surprised he didn't tear our asses apart," I lashed out at French.

"There's no doubt we could have done better," French offered. "Who the hell knows? Perhaps we should have prepared a more solid and organized briefing to push on doctrine, tactics and anti-Communist police strategy to anneal his support."

We walked slowly, ignoring the relentless pounding of the rain on our heads. We were as wet as jumping into the ocean. My anger surged and I suggested to French that we should have organized and prepared a more solid briefing.

"I said that," he said, shaking the rain that had drenched his crew cut.

"Too late," I said. "You need to stop kissing Laughlin's heinie and be candid to help him out!"

French frowned and faked offense to my remarks.

"You're all wet," he said, chuckling, as the rain became a total drench.

"I have to prepare a cable to send to Washington on the Kennedy visit. I can't wait to report to Washington bureaucrats that we had a shitty meeting with Kennedy," French said grinning forcibly.

"I'll have to report the truth." He stopped to stare at me with a fake expression on his face.

"Don't worry. I'll cover up your fuck-ups during our meeting with Kennedy. You're my pal." French walked hurriedly away.

"You blockhead. I don't give a crap what you write," I shouted.

"Just add a ring of truth, for a change." French grinned. How does one intervene in a foreign country without being accused of intervention? If there was one word that aroused repugnance in Latin America, that word was "intervention."

7

Panama Explodes

"The Government of Panama has a long history of corruption. The "Guardia" must take control and get rid of the corruption." —**Major Omar Torrijos Herrera**
Colon, Panama, July 1963

The training of Latin American police officers at the Inter-American Police Academy pushed on while the war in Vietnam expanded from token levels of advisor status in a limited war to more serious levels of combat. For the IAPA the number of applicants from Latin American police agencies increased tremendously. But resistance from left-wing quarters to U.S. training of foreign police also grew. We were both popular and unpopular.

We had completed a pilot course and the IAPA range constructed by the Corps of Engineers at Ft. Davis proved to be excellent to train Latin American police officers on the use of firearms. The range was nestled in a square graveled clearing in the middle of beautiful jungle surroundings. The range became a popular showcase for the Academy, complete with visiting wildlife. Three-toed sloths occasionally entered the training area, moving in slow motion, curious about the noise and early morning activity. Huge green iguanas could also be seen napping on top of trees at any hour of the day and occasionally a snake would scamper by on the gravel.

Joe Santioana, the FBI Special Agent, and I were the instructors, and eventually the firearms training became one of the most popular and enjoyable subjects for the students. Other instructors semijokingly accused us of spending time at the range just having fun. We countered in jest that it was dangerous to train people in the use of firearms and that we faced danger every day.

In reality some of the deadliest critters in the world, the Strawberry Poison-Arrow Frog and the fer-de-lance snake claimed the Panama jungle as their home. We were the intruders. The skin of the Strawberry Frog contained enough poison to kill several human beings. The *Choco* Indians dipped their arrows with the poison of the Strawberry Frog to hunt other animals. But we rarely saw dangerous snakes or animals and found out that the riskiest part of our training was that the IAPA pistol range could be used only in the morning.

By 1300 hours (1 p.m.) in the rainy season the monsoon rains poured nonstop and use of the outdoor range was impossible. The rain could punish a person with gallons of balloon size raindrops.

Joe Santioana had a pleasant, easygoing nature and sense of humor that made him a pleasure to work with. We became good friends and we enjoyed our efforts to train Latin American police officers in the use of firearms.

When the students fired for qualification scores we were obliged to be especially careful. The training included firing the .38 caliber revolver and the police shotgun. The students shot from various distances and positions to qualify in the FBI Practical Pistol Course (PPC). The training was conducted totally in Spanish

The students wore U.S. Air Force khaki uniforms and blue baseball caps. They were issued revolvers, ammunition and holsters at the range. We enjoyed the firearms training and the great majority of students displayed a keen interest in learning how to shoot a handgun under simulated combat conditions. All shooters on the firing line were closely supervised and controlled with strict instructions provided in Spanish. A bullhorn was used to direct live firing.

"*Listos... todo el mundo listo* (Ready. Everybody ready)." That phrase always got the adrenaline going for the students when they shot live ammunition. Their excitement flared when the order to fire was given. Hundreds of .38 caliber wad cutters were fired every day at bullseye and silhouette targets. When the firing intensified, smoke billowed throughout the area. Qualification times were usually contentious because the students competed for high scores. But there were fun times with laughs.

In the pilot course, a Brazilian Federal Police Officer by the name of Augusto Da Costa made the competition exciting. He was an excellent shot and taunted the students from other countries, exclaiming loudly in Portuguese that he was the champion shooter of the world.

"*Campeón da todo mundo, campeón da todo mundo,*" he would scream and punch his fists in the air. Many students would grow angry with

Da Costa, especially the Argentines who were fierce competitors with the Brazilians. Students from Brazil and Argentina argued constantly about anything. But no one could beat Da Costa. He ensured excitement with his practice of punching fists to the sky to shout, *"Campeón, campeón da todo mundo!"*

I was surprised when several students ganged up on me and jokingly accused me of being partial to Captain Luis Bazet M., a Federal Police officer from Mexico, because I was a *"Chicano."* They humorously pointed out that J. Edgar Hoover, the FBI Director, had announced in the media that Mexicans were good with a knife but could not shoot worth a damn. Therefore, Captain Bazet's expert score could not possibly be correct.

They howled in laughter when I suggested that Joe Santioana should be asked about that. Santioana grinned broadly but adamantly declined any comment on Mr. Hoover, despite the exhortations of the students. FBI Director Hoover had handpicked Santioana for the assignment to the IAPA.

The times the students fired for qualification scores, invariably there were protests and cheating occasionally occurred. But any close scores were settled with closely supervised shoot-offs. But many of the students became expert shooters and that was a deep satisfaction for Santioana and myself.

Rain in Panama was highly predictable in terms of scheduling any outdoor training. Rain was rare in the morning but a deluge was certain in the afternoon. One wet afternoon we returned to the Academy, Mario Vasquez, AKA *"Coñito,"* cornered us with the latest gossip. He whispered the news.

"We're getting a new Director for the IAPA! A fellow by the name of Ted Brown," he said. But no one seemed excited about Mario's announcement.

"Do you guys know Ted Brown?" Mario asked nervously. He seemed worried that none of the staff appeared concerned about the change in Directors. But within two weeks after *Coñito* announced the news, David Laughlin was gone, assigned to head the OPS program in Colombia. He had been a good Director of IAPA but his vast field experience and ability to speak Spanish made him a particularly effective and valuable Chief of a Public Safety program in a complex Latin American post. His replacement, Ted Brown, was transferred as Chief of the OPS program in Brazil to take over as the Director of the IAPA.

When Brown arrived, the staff discovered he was a no-nonsense administrator, dynamic, hardworking and with endless energy. Brown's crew cut, demeanor and excellent physical appearance frequently made people mistake him for the local commander of the Special Forces (Green Berets) unit in the Canal Zone. Brown immediately moved offices around and changed policies and programs. For the instructors getting up in the morning at Ft. Randolph, it was a common sight to see Ted Brown up since daybreak doing push-ups or scrubbing down his Volkswagen Beetle outside his residence.

Shortly after Brown's arrival, family and student quarters and classrooms were equipped with air conditioning and other improvements made. New courses were added and new instructors arrived.

Major Larry Santana and **Captain Fernando Bruno,** U.S. Army Military Police Officers, **Paul Gutierrez,** a Lieutenant with the Los Angeles County Sheriff's Department, and **Felipe Sandoval** and **Mel Holguin,** two former police officers from New Mexico, arrived for permanent assignments. **Michael Salseda,** a former Lieutenant from the Los Angeles County Sheriff's Department and Chief of the OPS program in Ecuador, also arrived to help conduct special courses in riot control. The training courses provided at the IAPA were expanded.

Brown was a mover and shaker and full of surprises. Shortly after he arrived he called me abruptly into his office for a meeting. Grinding the palms of his hands, he nervously paced the floor to give me the impression that I was in trouble. He suddenly stopped pacing and stared sternly at me. I was in trouble, I thought

"I want you to take over as Chief Instructor," Ted Brown told me as he fidgeted with energy. He wanted a quick response with no dilly-dallying. He frowned when I hesitated in responding.

"What about Lou Page?" I asked somewhat puzzled. Page was assigned as the Chief Instructor.

"Never mind that," Brown told me angrily. "*Dagnabbit.* Are we in agreement?"

Embarrassed and caught off guard, my response was mindless. But the majority of the staff had more experience and higher grades than I did. But my vacillation upset Ted Brown.

"Yes sir," I answered quickly.

"Okay. It's settled. You take over. Now let's get to work," he told me in a serious tone. "But *dagnabbit,* you need to be more forceful in the future if you're going to be supervising the training conducted at this facility," he told me sternly.

Concerned, I tried to explain my hesitation but Brown cut me off and left me talking to myself. We would soon find out that the only harsh word Ted Brown ever used was *"dagnabbit,"* no matter how angry or upset he was. He would never curse or use obscene language. He was an exemplary and admirable man.

Brown had a great desire to speak Spanish but found it very difficult despite his keen efforts. His efforts to try to speak Spanish murdered the language and cracked up the staff. He called instructor Mel Holguin, "Mel Holcomb," and that name stayed that way forever. Holguin would grin and bear it.

Caught totally by surprise with the responsibility of managing the training provided at the Inter-American Police Academy, I wondered if Bobby Kennedy had anything to do with the changes made.

Lou Page accepted his demotion gracefully and accepted my supervision without question. Actually he was happier being an instructor. As a former FBI Special Agent and CIA Officer, everyone knew that Lou was a nice guy. The staff waited for me to harass Page but they were disappointed.

Joe Santioana and I continued as firearm instructors until replacements were appointed. In the interim, the overall training at IAPA continued smoothly without disruptions as we prepared to train the students in the use of the shotgun.

Our control of the students at the range was tighter with instruction in the short barrel shotgun. Any individual that had never qualified in the use of an automatic shotgun was capable of making very dangerous mistakes during training. Normally only two students were permitted to shoot the shotgun at one time. With 00-buckshot, the shotgun was an awesome weapon and students would get nervous.

The training required close control by us. For safety reasons, we emphasized that the shotgun barrels should always be pointed down range. Any violation of that rule meant a fast ejection from the firing line. The students understood the need for hard rules. But shotgun shooting was always worrisome because of the lethality of the weapon with the use of .00 buckshot.

November 22, 1963

In the hot humidity of the tropics, people can get impatient and often irritable. Two students were shooting the shotgun on the firing line and were stopped from firing when a blue van from the police academy drove inexplicably into the area at a high rate of speed. The student I was supervising on the firing line apparently became distracted and carelessly moved the loaded shotgun barrel to the rear where a group of students were standing.

Angrily, I pushed the shotgun barrel down range and the weapon discharged. A fierce burning on my left hand told me that I was very lucky. A shotgun loaded with .00 buckshot can literally take one's head off at close range.

Taking the weapon from the frightened student I ejected the shotgun rounds left in the weapon and turned my anger to the driver of the van. It was my friend **Alfred Allen.**

He hurriedly dismounted from the vehicle and was immediately surrounded by students, chattering animatedly in Spanish. Allen was with the IAPA administrative support section. Allen, nicknamed *Panchito,* was a popular individual with the staff and students.

"Panchito," I screamed at him as he ran toward to me. "What the hell's wrong with you?"

Panchito shouted something almost incoherently, stumbling as he approached.

"Coño! President Kennedy has been shot!" he shouted. His voice echoed eerily through the jungle clearing. "The President has been shot," he repeated. There was total silence.

The students seemed stunned by the news. *Panchito* was extremely unsettled.

"Come on, they want you guys back at the academy right away," he said nervously. Staring at my hand, red with powder burns, the pain seemed lost in the depth of my despair. President Kennedy had been shot. It was hard to believe. Why, I wondered? Who shot the President? Morbid thoughts crossed my mind. Fidel Castro did it, I thought.

At the academy, students and instructors had gathered quietly in small groups around television sets to watch the reports on the assassination attempt on the President of the United States. Suddenly, a TV newscaster announced that President Kennedy had died of shotgun wounds to the head. Loud cries immediately erupted and then the room suddenly grew quiet. Many students had tears in their eyes. Minutes later, Ted Brown was told that student delegations wanted to convey their condolences to us. Nervously, Brown asked me to go with him to meet with the student representatives.

Together we listened to heart-wrenching speeches from several student delegations. The condolences of the students were expressed with oratory that moved many of the students to tears. Remorse gripped those in the room. I felt stunned as student groups continued to present their condolences.

Colonel Antonio Diaz from the Chilean *Carabineros,* torn by emotion, described the assassination of President Kennedy as a *"malevolent and tragic blow to America and the people of the free world."* Choking back tears, he proclaimed in Spanish, *"Kennedy was a shining beacon of hope for the Americas and now there is only darkness."*

It was dramatic oratory and Ted Brown, unable to speak Spanish, asked what the colonel had said. I told him and he suggested I respond. Feeling emotionally mangled, I struggled to thank the colonel and the other students for their condolences while morbid questions raged through my mind. What was happening to our country? Who had killed the President? Was the death of Kennedy a communist plot? I recalled the assassination plot to kill Fidel Castro. Did he beat Kennedy to the punch? We would never know for sure. Kennedy's assassination would be debated forever.

Mourning for President Kennedy continued for weeks with the American flag flown at half-mast at every military installation in the Canal Zone. The light of Camelot had dimmed forever. Despite rumors about Kennedy and the dark side of Camelot, he was loved and admired. For some Americans, he was a giant among the intellectual crowd and had led a charmed life. He was openly criticized by many as a weak liberal.

Kennedy had initially committed U.S. troops to combat in Southeast Asia but then issued a rescinding order to bring them home after the war grew inexorably. Forty-five days after he issued Executive Order #293 to bring American troops home from Southeast Asia, Kennedy was assassinated in Dallas, Texas. OPS no longer had its champion.

The atmosphere at the police academy grew gloomy after the assassination of the President. Many of us mulled the course of our future in the ever-changing politics of the Cold War. Frustrations lingered and French and I added more golf to our life. The beautiful golf course at Ft. Davis was within walking distance from the Academy and an easy way to shake off bad feelings.

One especially gloomy day French and I marched to the course with our golf bags and he suggested that we tee off on the sixth hole. After playing out the sixth hole we were held back by two men playing on the seventh hole. They stood in the fairway chatting nonchalantly, leaning on their golf clubs and conversing. Growing impatient, French hollered at them.

"Can we play through?" The two glanced up and one of the men ordered brusquely, "No, you fellows wait a minute."

Despite his rudeness, we patiently waited, totally disregarded by the dynamic duo on the fairway.

After a few minutes, bereft of patience, I placed a golf ball on the tee and picked up a driver.

"What the hell are you doing?" French asked with obvious concern.

"Playing golf," I told him. I hit the ball with a loud crack and yelled, **"Fore."** The two men on the fairway ducked as the ball went over their heads.

French chuckled and then grew solemn.

"You're nuts," he said dryly.

Immediately, one of the men who had been standing on the fairway shouted obscenities and walked briskly up an incline headed for us.

"Ah oh," French muttered. "Now what?" The individual looked very angry.

"What the fuck are you doing!" the man asked us as he got close. "Didn't I tell you to wait?"

I walked toward him. "We yelled fore," I suggested. He stared harshly at me, angered by my attitude.

"Who the fuck are you?" he blurted out, pumping his chest out like a horny peacock. French grimaced in a cautious mode.

"What's your name?" the man asked menacingly, growing impatient. I stared at the man but did not answer.

"Who the fuck *are* you?" he asked again. I stared back at him.

"Who the fuck are **you!**" I asked him in a soft voice. He stiffened.

"I'm Colonel Joe Higgins," the man answered quickly with a fierce frown and a best effort to intimidate me. My attitude seriously worried French. He remained silent. The colonel stared daggers.

"I don't give a shit who you are," I told the colonel sharply.

"Besides, I'm a colonel myself!" French's knees seemed to buckle. The colonel grew subdued.

"Damnit," he said. "I can't believe what you did. That was sorry ass behavior. You could have hit us with the fucking golf ball. What you did was irresponsible as hell." I did not respond.

"What did you say your name was?" he asked.

"My name is Saenz," I told him in a harsh tone of voice. The colonel turned away angrily. "You should apologize," he suggested as he walked away.

Instinctively I mastered military protocol. I smiled and apologized with a touch of sarcasm.

"Sorry, Colonel!" French, wide-eyed, was muttering to himself.

"Unbelievable!" he said. The men on the fairway continued playing golf, obviously upset. Colonel Higgins stared in our direction until they were out of sight.

"What if he calls the MPs?" French asked worriedly.

"I'll blame you," I told him, laughing at the thought. We finished playing six holes with French nervously looking over his shoulder.

"You are a candy ass," I told him.

"And you are crazy," he said.

In the ensuing months, when French and I were at the Ft. Davis Officers Club, Colonel Higgins would scrutinize us from a distance, still unsure about us. While we drank martinis at the Ft. Davis Officers' Club during Happy Hour, French and I would bet on the possibility that the colonel would ask us something. I won every time.

French contended it was my mean "Pancho Villa" look that intimidated Colonel Higgins. But now things were growing complicated on another front.

January 9, 1964

The children of school age residing at Ft. Randolph attended schools at *Coco Solo* or *Balboa*, in the larger American communities in the Canal Zone, along with other American students. Their safety was not something that we worried much about. But this time, the bad news spread quickly at Ft. Davis and at other U.S. military installations. Violent riots had erupted in Panama City. Thousands of Panamanians were rioting in the streets burning, looting and shooting on the fringes of the Canal Zone.

We were told that the violence had broken out as a result of a flag-raising incident at *Balboa* High School. A large group of Panamanians had reportedly entered the Canal Zone with the intention of hoisting a Panamanian flag on a flagpole at *Balboa* High School. The American students had resisted and violence had broken out in Panama.

Dinner at my house at Ft. Randolph that evening grew tense and lively. Margo, our Panamanian live-in maid, had prepared an excellent meal for us. My wife Jan and I talked with our children while Margo served delicious fried chicken, prepared Panamanian style, with *"chombo"* sauce, rice, and fried plantains. The cheerful faces at our dinner table were in sharp contrast with the mob violence that was building up in Panama City.

Lori, our oldest daughter, led us in prayer before dinner was served and seemed to be in a hurry.

"Easy, easy," I laughed. Once prayers were finished, she called out to me.

"Dad, Dad!" she insisted, trying to attract my attention. "I have something very important to tell you." She appeared frustrated with me.

The platter of chicken served by Margo disappeared. She brought more and our children cheered for her. She grinned ear to ear.

"Yea, Yea, Margo," they told her, applauding for her and she giggled happily. Lori however grew pouty until we paid attention to her.

"There was big trouble at our school this afternoon," she told us with large worried eyes. Lori was a very beautiful girl, with glamorous brown eyes and long lashes that were stupendous.

"There was a big fight at school," she continued in a low voice. Lori attended school at Cristobal in *Coco Solo.* "A bunch of Panamanians came into the Canal Zone and tried to put up the Panamanian flag at our school. They tried to pull the American flag down from the pole." She recounted the story with a semblance of pride.

"But we didn't let them," she told us. She did not know that rioting had broken out in Panama.

Lori described that the American students had resisted the Panamanians that were trying to hoist up their flag and there was scuffling and fighting. The girls had also resisted with pushing and shoving the intruders, she said proudly. But in the process of the fight, the Panamanian and the American flags were both torn. Lori told us that the Canal Zone police arrived at the scene and had arrested several Panamanians. For me it was certain that the arrests would cause major problems.

Lori was disturbed that the Panamanians would come to the Canal Zone to cause trouble.

"Fortunately the Canal Zone Police showed up right away," she said tremulously. It surprised me to hear my daughter describe the incident that happened. The violence was spreading and Americans in the Republic of Panama were now in serious danger.

My children stared at me in anticipation and Margo hovered near the dinner table. She was a proud Panamanian with Caribbean ancestry and my kids loved her. Like us, she was caught in the middle of a festering political imbroglio. My wife stared at me with a quizzical look on her face.

"The Panamanian flag has a right to fly side by side with the American flag in the Canal Zone," she suggested. I nodded in agreement. "I think this was recently approved by the Canal Zone Governor," she said. "But it's not being done," she added. I nodded again.

Margo paused to stare at me, holding a plate of chicken in her hand. My daughter Lori shook her head in disagreement.

"The Canal Zone is Panamanian territory, sweetheart," I told her. "The Canal Zone is on loan to the United States based on a treaty signed between Panama and the United States a long time ago." Her eyes blinked in surprise as she listened to what I said. We were very proud of her. As our first born, she was a straight "A" student, very responsible and conscientious. At age thirteen she was the conservative-liberal in the family.

"Panamanians are rioting against the Canal Zone because of what happened at *Balboa* High School and *Cristobal*," I explained. "The flag of Panama is a source of pride to Panamanians just as ours is to us." Suddenly, we had a combative discussion going. My children were learning about hegemony. I did not mention to my children that radicals in American cities had spit on, stomped and burned the American Flag on several occasions.

My youngest son Eric stared at me wide eyed. He suspected something bad was happening.

"Fight?" he asked me quizzically. (Six years later, with my assignment to the Republic of Panama, Eric would meet General Omar Torrijos and Colonel Manuel Antonio Noriega when they attended a reception at my house in Panama City. Both lightheartedly admonished him that he was Panamanian because he was born in the Canal Zone. I was pleased when Eric responded without hesitation that he was an American but that he loved Panama.)

Margo listened with silent interest and entered occasionally into the discussion. She and her three-year-old son named Gustavo lived with us at Ft. Randolph. My kids called Gustavo "Cassius Clay" and had laughing fits at my expense when they taught him to call me "Daddy."

After dinner, we watched television and news bulletins on the U.S. Southern Command Network (SCN). Vicious rioting was taking place in the streets of Panama with buildings burning out of control in the background of a dark sky. Local Panamanian television stations showed mobs on a rampage looting stores, shooting and throwing Molotov cocktails and bombs into the Canal Zone. Rioters scattered as the Canal Zone Police used tear gas to keep them from entering U.S. territorial boundaries. Wisps of smoke suddenly visible on top of buildings in Panama City were from the rifles of snipers shooting into the Canal Zone.

U.S. military units from Ft. Clayton and Ft. Amador were deployed on a grass knoll on the boundary of Fourth of July Avenue, near the *Tivoli* Hotel. But the deployment of U.S. troops on the knoll was a mistake. From the top of the Panamanian Legislative Palace across the street snipers were shooting at the *Tivoli* Hotel and several American soldiers deployed on the knoll were shot. We saw two American soldiers fall, hit by gunfire as we watched.

The beautiful *Tivoli* Hotel, located on Fourth of July Avenue on the border of the Canal Zone, became a target. *Avenida Cuatro de Julio* (4th of July Avenue) in Panama City was subsequently named *Avenida de Los Mártires* (Avenue of Martyrs) after the riots. The *Tivoli* Hotel, truly one of the most popular places in the Canal Zone, attracted the violence like a magnet. The elegant white structure with attractive high ceilings, black bellboys and waiters dressed in white uniforms seemed like a throwback to a southern plantation. It was sad to see the *Tivoli* Hotel, one of the finest attractions in the Canal Zone under a vicious attack.

In 1906, President Theodore Roosevelt had visited the Canal Zone to see the construction of Panama Canal and he had stayed at the *Tivoli* Hotel. My daughter Lori and I stayed at the historic hotel when we traveled on a medical emergency from El Salvador to have her appendix removed at Gorgas Hospital. The maids at the hotel helped me dress my daughter and combed her hair before we went to the hospital. It was heartbreaking to see the beautiful *Tivoli* Hotel become a target of violence. (Subsequently, with Canal treaty negotiations underway by the Jimmy Carter administration in the late '70s, the *Tivoli*, a historic monument, was totally torn down and the Smithsonian Tropical Research Institute constructed in its place.

An old giant tropical tree, probably centuries old, was located in the indoor courtyard of the *Tivoli* and received innumerable impacts of rifle fire during the riots. Three decades later, on a visit to Panama, I found the beautiful tropical tree preserved in the back of the Smithsonian building.)

All night long, snipers shot at people in the Canal Zone. Eventually, U.S. Army troops directed .30 and .50 caliber machine gunfire into rooftops in Panama to devastate the shooters. It was an awesome display of firepower, but too close to the image of a total war. Local newscasts revealed that the rioting was spreading throughout the Republic of Panama.

Americans trapped there were now in dire straits. Several Americans caught in Panama had been killed and many injured by rioting mobs. The Panama National Guard, the only police force in the Republic of Panama, did not want to get involved in the miniature war. Rioters in Panama had a proverbial license to kill Americans in the Republic.

The following morning, Ted Brown met with the IAPA staff to discuss the volatile situation existing in Panama. With the problem still growing, I suggested that standard tear-gas supplies used for IAPA training be turned over to the Canal Zone police. They were happy to get the supplies. M-25 military tear-gas bursting grenades were also provided to the police. But an unexpected problem arose for the IAPA.

Three official visitors from the National Police of El Salvador were scheduled to arrive at *Tocumen* Airport that afternoon. The Salvadorans invited to the IAPA were unaware of the ongoing violence in Panama and they expected to be picked up at the airport and taken to Ft. Davis. *Tocumen* Airport was about two hours from Ft. Davis by car, and had to be reached by driving through the Republic of Panama where the rioting was most severe.

One of the visitors from El Salvador was my good friend Alfredo Zapata, the head of the criminal investigation bureau of the country's National Police. Zapata spoke English and had received extensive training in the United States. (As a graduate of the FBI National Academy, he eventually became a target for the FMLN guerrillas and was killed in the throes of the left-wing insurgency.)

I decided to make the trip to *Tocumen* Airport myself but two instructors quickly volunteered to make the trip to *Tocumen* to pick up the Salvadorans. Paul Gutierrez, a tough Lieutenant from the Los Angeles County Sheriff's Department, and U.S. Army Military Police Major, Larry Santana agreed to drive a van to *Tocumen* Airport to pick up our visitors. They knew they would have to go into a war zone. The trip would take them on the Transisthmus Highway inside the Canal Zone until they reached the road that led into the Republic of Panama and *Tocumen* Airport. The Transisthmus Highway stretched from the Pacific to the Atlantic coast in the Canal Zone, and was bordered by magnificent jungle on both sides. Ships traversing through the canal could be seen from the highway in normal times. This was not a normal time.

Once the IAPA instructors reached Panamanian territory they would drive on the *Tumba de Muerte* (Tomb of Death) highway to the airport. Despite the morbid name of the road, the two Americans reached the airport safely. Once the visitors from El Salvador were aboard the van they headed back to the Canal Zone. Within forty minutes they approached the boundary of the Canal Zone, where a Panama National Guard checkpoint loomed ominously in the way.

The checkpoint was a small concrete building with a moveable wooden barricade where all vehicles were required to stop. But instead of Panama National Guard personnel, a mob had gathered at the checkpoint and was blocking the road with large boulders, tree trunks and other debris. Several people in the mob carried clubs and guns. The Panama National Guard personnel that normally operated the checkpoint had obviously abandoned their post, and left the area.

Gutierrez slowed the vehicle down and several people in the mob signaled for him to stop. But stopping the vehicle would indeed place everyone in the car at the mercy of the rioters. Instead, Gutierrez accelerated and smashed through the barricade as the mob attacked the car with rocks and clubs. Almost losing control, Gutierrez drove the van into the charging mob.

"Fuck you!" he screamed as the vehicle plowed on through the barricade careening wildly. Only Zapata knew what "fuck you!" meant.

When the group arrived at the IAPA facility, every window of the van was broken and glass was hanging in shards. Five bullet holes were found in the rear and on the sides of the vehicle. Miraculously, the only injuries sustained by those in the vehicle were lacerations and bruises. My friend Zapata confronted me in a humorous vein when they arrived.

"Hey, *boddy*," he asked jokingly. "Did you arrange that welcome for us? **Condenado** (Damn you)," he told me laughing.

"I bet you did." Zapata and I hugged spontaneously in an *abrazo* (embrace). Paul Gutierrez and Major Larry Santana were very brave men and we were proud of them.

Meanwhile, the Panama National Guard officers who would play a role as future rulers of Panama demonstrated that they were disciplined students. Major Omar Torrijos, Lt. Diaz Herrera, Lt. Florencio Flores, Lt. Armando Contreras, Lt. Amado Sanjur and Lt. Juan Bernal would attend different courses. The officers were attentive and cooperative. Perhaps prophetically, Lt. Manuel Antonio Noriega preferred his training at the School of the Americas. All of our students from Panama would become Colonels or Generals in the National Guard and be called "tyrants" by their countrymen.

Ruben Blades, Sr. (the father of Ruben Blades, the popular movie star), was an Inspector with the Panama *Departamento Nacional de Investigaciónes* (DENI) and one of the most popular students at IAPA. He was a good athlete and we often played basketball on the same team. We remain good friends.

By noon, we were disappointed to see five officers from the *Guardia Nacional* (Panama National Guard) and the *Departamento Nacional de Investigaciones* (DENI) leave the IAPA after Panama broke off diplomatic relations with the United States and they were recalled to Panama by their government.

By early evening, the violence had spread to nearby Colon and other parts of Panama. The city of Colon, very close to Ft. Randolph, was about thirty minutes away by boat. Because of the riots in Colon, U.S. Army military police manning the main gate at Ft. Randolph were reinforced and armed with .30 caliber carbines along with their .45 caliber automatics. Despite the fact that Ft. Randolph was totally surrounded by a chain link security fence, the base was considered vulnerable if hostile intruders made any attempt to penetrate into the facility. Patrols were needed. Every military base in the Canal Zone was on alert because of the riot, with all available personnel mobilized. Several combat units were sent to problem areas on the Pacific Ocean side of the Panama Canal.

My suggestion to Ted Brown that we meet with the American staff to discuss security measures needed at Ft. Randolph because of the violence met with his approval. That night, at Brown's residence, the volatile situation in Panama and the security at Ft. Randolph was discussed with all the staff. The violence had escalated on a countrywide basis increasing the potential danger for Americans. The situation at Ft. Randolph was considered risky because the large facility was near the City of Colon where major rioting was taking place.

The south part of the base faced the Atlantic Ocean and was accessible by boat. A high chain link fence protected the ocean boundary but we had to make sure that any intrusion into the base could be detected. The chain link fence could easily be cut and there was no way for us to know if anyone had penetrated into the facility.

My suggestion to set up watches throughout the night received unanimous approval. We were obliged to develop our own options on security because of the rapid and widespread escalation of violence in the Republic of Panama. Ted Brown was understandably hesitant about the fact that all personnel would carry firearms on their watch. Guns made the situation risky in terms of a possible panic response by less experienced members of our group. Nevertheless, it was agreed that watches of four hours each would be assigned each individual to cover the period of darkness. All personnel on watch were to carry revolvers and shotguns.

I took a first watch sitting on my front porch, watching the ocean glimmer from the reflection of buildings burning in the city of Colon. My wife provided a pot of coffee and waited inside our air-conditioned house. The wire screen mesh on the porch and insect repellent provided some protection from the dreaded sand flies. Crickets, bullfrogs and the scramble of white land crabs on the gravel sporadically broke the silence of the night.

At about 0200 hours, Bob Florstedt raised the alarm from his house situated near the ocean.

"We have visitors," he announced in a low-key voice. The members of the staff were alerted.

I ran to join several others already gathered in the darkness of the fence line near the ocean. We watched in silence as the silhouette of a shrimp boat crept up in the darkness of the inlet, the sound barely perceptible. Going down on one knee I raised my revolver to shoulder level and when the boat was about twenty yards away I shouted. "Put lights on them!"

Immediately, lights from our flashlights lit up the area and the sounds of rounds being cranked into shotguns interrupted the silence. In the sudden brightness of the flashlights, the men on the boat saw our weapons trained on them and they seemed surprised.

"Alto," I shouted at the top of my voice. One of the individuals in the small cabin on the boat immediately raised his hands in the glare of the flashlights and the boat sputtered to a halt. With his hands in the air, he hurriedly issued orders to the others in the small vessel. The other men on the boat stepped out into the light and waved their hands desperately above their heads screaming in Spanish.

"No disparen, no disparen! **(Don't shoot, don't shoot!)"** They kept their hands up.

The men on the boat kept shouting at us **not** to shoot. They were told again to keep their hands above their heads and they complied. The boat was stopped in the water.

"Qué quieren! (What do you want?)" I shouted at them.

"Nada, nada (Nothing, nothing)," one of the men screamed nervously.

"Andamos pescando (We are fishing)!" he shouted in a loud voice, his hands above his head.

"Es mejor que se marchen!" I yelled to tell them in Spanish to go fish somewhere else.

"Está bien, está bien! (Sure, sure, that's fine!)" squealed the apparent leader of the crew. The boat turned slowly in a wide circle and chugged away. It surprised me that the men on the boat did not respond in English. Many Panamanians speak English. The boat disappeared in the darkness. In the distance, buildings could be seen burning in the city of Colon.

The alert in the Canal Zone lasted about three days until the violence in Panama subsided. U.S. territory was finally declared secure. In the wake of the riots, Panama blamed the United States for causing and perpetuating the violence. Twenty-one Panamanians had been killed by

American troops. Snipers had killed four American soldiers and several Americans were killed inside the Republic of Panama by rioting mobs. Nearly five hundred on both sides were wounded or hurt.

The activists claimed that the United States had raped Panama too many times. The riots created another emotional issue that affected the course of events in the Canal Zone forever, culminating with the foolish canal treaty negotiations by the Jimmy Carter administration.

There were more equitable ways to negotiate with the people of Panama on the canal issue. I was later assigned to the Republic of Panama when negotiations on the canal treaty by Americans with fixed ideas gave away the Canal. I knew we had gone *de mal en pis.*

Within six weeks, the decision by Washington to shut down the Inter-American Police Academy reached us. We joined the ranks of the victims. The flag-raising incident at *Balboa* High School and the outbreak of violence that followed created another bleeding political chancre between Panama and the United States. The bloody riots were to plague relations between Panama and the United States for decades. But more political bloodletting lay ahead for Panama, as the era of the "tyrants" emerged. It would become one of the most politically bizarre and complex periods in the history of Panama and the Canal Zone.

Inflammatory rhetoric in the aftermath of the riot increased as the politicians on both sides reacted. There was no doubt in most minds that Panama deserved a better treaty in regard to the canal. But so did the United States. My favorite option was that the canal be operated and defended jointly by Panama and the United States as equal partners. There were many reasons for keeping the presence of the United States in the Canal Zone besides the fact that we built it.

But many in the American government bureaucracy decried the strategic value of the canal. Panama deserved sovereignty in the Canal Zone and if the self-serving politics of the past had not been such a harsh part of Canal Zone history the situation could have been different. It seemed to me that the majority of the Panamanians did not want the Americans to leave. But the bloody violence of 1964 and the history of the Canal Zone would be hard for Panamanians to put behind them.

I would miss Ft. Randolph and the times with my children when we walked the vast expanse and beautiful tropical environment of the CIA/military facility. My two oldest sons, Kurt and Michael, would accompany me on long treks along the coastal waters of the Atlantic Ocean to explore jungle areas. They had discovered huge concrete bunkers on the coastline and many times played on top of rusty World War II cannons pointing toward the Atlantic Ocean and the entrance to the Panama Canal. J. Edgar Hoofer, the CIA-trained horse with paranoia, would follow us on our walks through the isolated jungle areas. My daughter Sisi frequently rode J. Edgar Hoofer without fear and chased white land crabs that scrambled about in large numbers throughout the base.

Occasionally, I would use my revolver to shoot down a stalk of bananas from a tree, and J. Edgar Hoofer would neigh in approval, unperturbed by the gunfire. He was apparently used to war. It commonly took four or five well placed shots to cut the banana stem from the tree. My kids would take the stalk of green bananas home to hang on the front porch until the fruit ripened. Life was rich, different and very private at Ft. Randolph.

The unique and interesting life at the CIA base came to a close. IAPA was ordered to shut down operations and we prepared to move from Ft. Randolph.

In Panama City, Jack Hood Vaughn, the U.S. Ambassador to Panama, was impressed with a Panama National Guard Officer with the fire in his eyes for power. His name was Omar Torrijos Herrera. Within five years, Torrijos would bring to Panama a period of military dictatorships and rout U.S. negotiators in Panama Canal Treaty negotiations.

After Torrijos, Manuel Antonio Noriega, Ruben Paredes, and "Chito" Flores would become Generals in the Panama National Guard and bring a period of military control to the country. I would be assigned to work with the Panama National Guard theoretically in the position of an ally.

8

Assignment to Uruguay

"The real Third World War has been fought and is being fought under our noses, and few people have noticed what was going on." —Brian Crozier, Expert on Guerrilla Warfare

The Inter-American Police Academy had come to a finale after a short-lived history of two years. The training programs were merged with the International Police Academy (IPA) in Washington, D.C., and personnel were assigned there. My wife and I discussed the prospects of our move to Washington with deep concern and uncertainty. My friend Joe Santioana suggested he could process the paperwork for me to join him as a Special Agent with the FBI office in Tampa, Florida, where he was the Special Agent in Charge (SAC). I was still young enough he said. Santioana was a respected veteran of the FBI and I was glad to have him as a friend. Tampa seemed like a fine place to raise our children.

My wife and I agreed to make the move despite the fact that this meant a sizable cut in pay, at that point. But without warning, Ted Brown, Jerry French, and I were ordered to report to Washington, D.C., immediately, without delay. Our families would follow by boat from Panama City to New York City. We were prohibited from any delay in our travel.

A fast-track assignment to the International Police Academy (IPA) was in store for me when I arrived in Washington. My thoughts about the FBI were momentarily deferred. Ted Brown recommended my appointment as Deputy Director of the IPA, but Michael McCann, the Director, preferred an active duty U.S. Army Colonel and military police officer by the name of William Norman.

The IPA complex in Georgetown was luxurious by comparison to the IAPA facility in Panama even with the improvements made there by Ted Brown. The IPA Academy was located next to Georgetown University and its *haute academe* and historic background. The stairs leading to the International Police Academy from 3600 "M" Street in Georgetown had been shown in a scene from the movie, **"The Exorcist."** In the movie, when Father Karris was possessed by the demon and he jumped from a window to kill himself, he landed at the bottom of the metal stairway that led to the entrance of the IPA. Was that a bad omen?

In Washington, our roles were different from the police academy in Panama. I was appointed Chief of the Internal Security Branch. **Al Grunwell, Bob Melberg, Bob Florstedt, Pete Ales** and **Ed Bishop** were assigned to the Branch. Ted Brown was assigned to head the Latin American Branch of the OPS at headquarters, and Jerry French assumed a management position with the Agency for International Development (AID) at the U.S. Department of State.

The daily machinations of the IPA were logically structured and operations closely supervised. Branch Chiefs were responsible for developing doctrine on the role of the police in counterinsurgency operations and the Director or Deputy Director chaired the meetings. It was unfortunate that disagreements with top management often resulted in disfavor because, in general, the disagreements were attributable to the growing cynicism of Cold War politics and not IPA operations

For many OPS officers assigned to the IPA it was the excitement of an overseas assignment that was most attractive. Unless an individual assigned to Washington, D.C., possessed a senior rank, the high cost of living in the area made it a hardship. Nevertheless, the activities of the IPA prospered and kept the staff busy with numerous students from free world countries in attendance. The physical layout of the IPA was attractive and professional albeit the offices of the staff were windowless and devoid of pictures on the walls. But the academy had an excellent professional library and numerous reference materials were available for both the students and instructors.

Full schedules and daily classes kept everyone busy. Police management and operations were primary subjects, although international communism and the characteristics of a communist insurgency were important topics. Ways and means for the police to combat communist terrorists and insurgents was emphasized. I believe that for that reason, the elimination of the IPA became a principal objective for the ideologues that supported communist causes in the Cold War.

Adjustment to life in the Washington, D.C., area and to the frustrations of Cold War madness in the Nation's capital was not easy. A nice home we had purchased in Alexandria, Virginia, made my wife and children happy. For me, the daily travel on the crowded George Washington Parkway and across Key Bridge to reach Georgetown included beautiful scenery. Most of the officers assigned to the International Police Academy lived either in Virginia or Maryland.

But the growing attacks in the media against the Vietnam War and the sinister politics ignored most notions of U.S. national security interests. I thought about the FBI job and prepared my paperwork. In the interim, I met some of my OPS colleagues and was very impressed with them.

John Walton, a former intelligence officer for the U.S. Marine Corps **Black Sheep** Squadron of *'Pappy'* Boyington during World War II, stopped by to say good-bye on his return to Vietnam. Walton, a retired Deputy Chief of the Los Angeles Police Department, was in Washington for consultation. He was in charge of the OPS program in Vietnam operating in a hot war.

Jake Jackson was on his way to Bolivia to head the OPS program in that country. Sadly, within two years, Jake would be shot in the back by Marxist guerrillas in the mountains of Bolivia and left paralyzed for life. Most OPS officers, including me, believed it could never happen to them.

Mitchell (Mike) Mabardy was a top assistant to Byron Engle, the Director of the OPS and a retired U.S. Air Force Colonel, former Provost Marshall and top commander of the Office of Special Investigations (OSI). He used important management glue to keep the various elements of the OPS working together effectively. His visits to the IPA were always welcomed and were beneficial and fun.

Mabardy had a knack for promoting relationships in our business.

"Dolph," he would tell me, "I want you to meet two fellows I know you'll like." He flashed his elfin grin. "You better like them because they're friends of mine," he chuckled.

Mabardy introduced me to Dan Mitrione, a stocky Italian from Indiana. I was one of several people who knew Mitrione intimately, as an outstanding American and a great human being. We did not know that he would eventually replace me in Uruguay and be brutally murdered by Marxist terrorists.

Mabardy introduced me to a young man with bright red hair and a flashy grin.

"This is John McPoland," he told me. Assigned to *Vinh Long* Province in South Vietnam as an advisor to the National Police Field Forces, McPoland would emerge as one of the most decorated civilians of that war.

Mitrione, McPoland and I talked frequently about OPS assignments and the possibility of working together in Latin America. Most OPS officers wanted overseas assignments, not only because crime in the Nation's capital was growing ridiculous but because the Cold War was out there, in Bolivia, El Salvador, the Dominican Republic, Guatemala, Laos, Peru, Thailand, Uruguay, Vietnam and many other parts of the world. The Cold War in Washington, D.C., was a mixed bag of sinister political treachery, intrigue and unpredictable chickenshit. One could not be sure who in the Washington bureaucracy was the enemy.

Beautiful and interesting sights were plentiful in the Washington, D.C., area but life in the city could also be hectic and risky. It was expensive to live in Washington, D.C., and there were risks.

Shortly after he arrived in Washington, D.C., Jack Neely, a former FBI Special Agent and CIA Officer, found himself being mugged in broad daylight a block away from the International Police Academy on "M" Street. Neely graciously accepted our kidding that he looked distinguished and prosperous. He explained that he never had a chance against two orangutans using guns, portable radios and their grandmother as a lookout. Neely was a former member of the Scouts and Raiders in the Second World War, the forerunners of the Navy Seals.

In the throes of the Cold War, the IPA prospered as an American institution capable of training foreign police officers in democratic law enforcement practices. But there was also fun and humor along with the satisfaction of training police officers from other countries.

To prepare for a graduation ceremony with Averell Harriman as the main speaker, the Director, Michael McCann, ordered Branch Chiefs to bring their staffs to the large auditorium to put up a hundred metal chairs that were needed to seat the guests invited to attend the ceremony.

Of my staff, Al Grunwell adamantly refused to participate. With fierce anger in his eyes he informed me that he was not putting up any "flipping chairs" for anybody. He argued that he was not hired to do janitor work and putting up metal chairs was not in his job description, he insisted. He warned me ominously that he had rights.

Fifteen or more individuals including myself were busy putting up metal chairs in the auditorium lining them up in straight rows, when McCann asked where Al Grunwell was. I explained to McCann that Dr. Grunwell, a Ph.D. from the University of Virginia, had taken a position that he was not hired to do "janitor" work.

Unexpectedly, McCann became furious and ordered me to tell Grunwell that he was no different from other OPS officers and to have him report for duty. He threatened to hold me responsible. Confronting Grunwell in his office, I was obliged to force him to help as ordered by McCann. Upstairs, I advised an angry Grunwell that I had to follow orders.

Enraged, Grunwell began to throw chairs violently across the floor of the auditorium. The metal chairs thrown by Grunwell slammed into the floor and careened crazily to hit against anything in the way. One chair thrown in anger by Grunwell hit the leg of Colonel Norman, the Deputy Director. Grunwell was very angry and continued to throw chairs furiously across the hardwood floor. Colonel Norman screamed.

"Dolph, stop that crazy bastard!" he shouted, as people in the auditorium laughed.

"I can't," I shouted back. "He's a killer." Norman simply grew furious with me.

"Stop him. That's an order!" he told me in a harsh military tone. Grunwell continued to hurl chairs across the floor and seemed to be enjoying himself.

"Stop him, stop the son-of-a-bitch! He's gone crazy," Norman shouted.

Grabbing Grunwell in a bear hug, I picked him up and forcibly carried him to his office. He kicked and screamed obscenities but his small size made it easy for me to stifle any resistance. When Grunwell saw me laugh at his enraged florid face, he calmed down.

"Get some coffee," I told him. I went back upstairs to be upbraided by McCann who angrily told me that I could not control my people.

"Grunwell is not my people," I joked with an angry McCann whose anger with me increased. "He's a damn redneck from Virginia," I kidded. "He speaks some Spanish but he is no *Chicano,* that's for sure." It was hard for me to resist being a wise ass. I guess I basically agreed with Grunwell.

Afterwards, discussing the matter in my office, Grunwell apologized behind closed doors. I told him that he was crazier than a CIA psychiatrist testing his own drugs and that McCann was mad at me.

"I'll buy you lunch for a week," he laughed. "At Blackie's."

"That's blackmail," I told him.

"That's right," he said. "But it's better than being on McCann's shit list," he suggested. Grunwell, a wealthy Virginia landowner and CIA Officer, was a very independent man. He was actually an outstanding Intelligence Officer and I admired him.

After eight months in Washington, I had acclimated to the Washington environment. I was now seriously considering the move to go with Joe Santioana and the FBI to Tampa when "Jack" Munroe, the Deputy Director of OPS, caught me by surprise with a phone call. He told me in his best southern drawl to get my butt down to the State Department Building at 21st and Virginia, ASAP.

"The Boss wants to talk to you," he said with a chuckle that gave me the impression that perhaps I was in trouble.

I could not find McCann in his office. Colonel Norman, the Deputy Director, was also not in his office. Engle was waiting, so I decided to go find out what the top Boss wanted.

"Tell Mr. McCann that I'm going to the State Department to meet with Mr. Engle," I told his secretary. "Mr. Engle wants me over there as soon as possible." Nodding, she jotted down the information on a note pad.

The State Department was a mini-Pentagon, only square. I walked through huge metal doors at the East entrance, while outside a large anti-Vietnam war demonstration was on its way to the White House. The noise of the multitude muffled when I entered the building. A large marble counter blocked the entry and I showed my identification badge to a mature but attractive woman who smiled warmly and opened a metal gate. At the elevators, a black woman in uniform asked what floor I wanted.

The State Department building was a frustrating maze if you did not know your way around. She laughed softly when I complimented her on how pretty she looked in her uniform.

I entered a vestibule on the fifth floor that led to a series of offices. **Pete Ellena,** a former cop from Pasadena, California, greeted me when I walked in. Pete, a tall handsome Italian/American with a sharp sense of humor, was one of my best friends. He longed to go abroad but had become too valuable a bureaucrat in Washington.

"What's up, Pete?" I asked him and he shook his head with a grin.

"I'll let the Boss tell you! I can't believe you screwed up again!" he told me with a chortle. Grinning, he walked with me to Engle's office where his secretary, a lovely lady named Ruth Rooney, watched us approach and smiled. She was the epitome of efficiency and professionalism.

"Come in," she said cheerfully. "Mr. Engle is expecting you." I walked in on the plush maroon carpet and Pete held back to mutter.

"You've had it. But when you finish getting your ass chewed by the Boss, I'll buy you lunch." I wondered what I had done wrong.

"It's your negative attitude," Pete told me with a smile. I knew he was kidding.

Engle stood from his desk to shake my hand when I entered his office, forming a weak smile on his face. He asked me to wait while he signed a couple of documents. The smell of cigar smoke permeated the room and it was obvious to me that Jack Munroe had just left Engle's office. Munroe was an avid cigar smoker and was Engle's right hand man. Both had worked together on international police projects most of their lives.

Stacks of classified files and correspondence cluttered Engle's desk. It was a nice comfortable office with wood paneling and plenty of memorabilia on the walls. Pictures of Engle with politicians, dignitaries and while on wild African safaris covered the walls. A large window faced east toward the Washington monument.

My attention instinctively focused on a jungle boot on top of his desk. A vicious looking metal spike penetrated the boot from the sole on the bottom all the way to the top. Copious amounts of dried blood covered the boot. I picked it up to look at it.

"That boot was on the foot of one of our advisors working with the South Vietnamese Police Field Forces in a Province near the Delta when the spike went completely through his foot," Engle advised me placidly. "The spikes are buried in trap holes and are a very common practice for the Viet Cong," he added.

"They bury the damn spikes and cover the holes with branches and leaves so they can't be seen. They smear the spike with human feces or buffalo dung to ensure a serious infection for the poor bastard that steps on it." He asked me to sit on a red leather couch.

"How are things going?" he began. "How are you getting along with Mike McCann?" he asked before I could answer. I wondered if that was an issue.

"Fine, fine," I told him, anxious to learn what he had in mind. Engle was a tough-looking individual but in reality was an unusually kind and compassionate person. He made important decisions with no excuses if anything went wrong. Everyone in OPS looked up to Engle with admiration. He was not a complainer, although we knew about the vicious battles he was experiencing with liberal left-wing advocates and practiced Washington bureaucracy.

With Engle, OPS had a great leader. Everyone appreciated the fact that he was a true patriot and he expected us to keep the faith. I felt very comfortable with him.

"I've been thinking of assigning you to Vietnam," he told me casually. "We need experienced people there. What do you think?" he asked. I stared at him, puzzled but not showing surprise.

"If that's where you think I should be assigned, that's fine," I told him abruptly. Engle looked at me with a strange look and a slight grin on his face.

"You're not thinking of resigning, are you?" he asked. I suspected he was flushing me out.

"Nope," I responded sharply and he laughed out loud, leaving me guessing. But at the time I was not real sure about going to Vietnam. I thought about the bloody boot on Engle's desk as he talked.

"Ted Brown speaks highly of you," Engle told me, openly analyzing my reaction.

"I'm glad," I said, making small talk. "Ted Brown is an outstanding American and one of my favorite people," I told Engle. "I really like and admire him." For me, Ted Brown was the best of the best. I didn't care what he wanted to hear because I was most sincere about that. Suddenly, Engle straightened up in his chair.

"Do you know where Uruguay is?" he asked abruptly. The question caught me by surprise. I wasn't sure but nodded anyway, wondering why he asked. I knew Uruguay was in South America.

"I think I've changed my mind," Engle said with a quick smile. "How would like to go to Uruguay?" he asked. "This will be an opportunity for you to go out as Chief of an OPS program. What do you think?" He stared at me.

"You'll have to start the program." He glued the Engle grin on his face. "Do you think you can handle it?" I nodded in response but he waited for me to say something.

"Absolutely," I told him. "I can handle it." Engle took time to describe the country and the security problems involved. He handed me a copy of a report that described the police forces in the country, the public safety situation and internal security problems. The report was based on a survey conducted by OPS personnel. Engle told me to read it before I departed.

He suggested that I would be one of the youngest Chiefs at any post. I knew it was a chance for a promotion. Enthusiasm hit me but I tried not to show it.

"When do you want me there?" I asked, hoping he would say as soon as possible.

"Within thirty days, we want you there." Engle told me with an attentive look. Then he grew casual and candid with a tight smile on his face.

"Listen, some question your ability to handle the Uruguay program," he said. His grin widened and I listened carefully.

"It's a very tough challenge." Engle was giving me a chance to respond and stared at me.

"I can handle it," I replied without hesitation. "I want the job, Byron." He grinned broadly.

"You got it. But I want you there in thirty days. They have major security problems developing." He stuck his hand out.

"Agreed?" I grabbed his hand firmly.

"Agreed," I told him eagerly. This was considered a plum assignment. Engle placed his arm on my shoulder and walked out with me.

"Thanks, Boss," I told him. "I won't let you down." Engle had a grin on his face.

"I know," he said reassuringly. I thought about my experience.

I rushed out and Pete Ellena met me at the doorway.

"It was not a bad ass chewing," I told him. "And, I still have a negative attitude." Pete smiled and we walked through the maze of the State Department building to the cafeteria to have lunch.

"Lucky bastard," Ellena finally told me with a broad grin. He had known all along. How lucky was I? If urban violence, guerrilla warfare, terrorism, kidnappings and murder counted, I was in luck.

I returned to my office at the IPA and was surprised to see Mike McCann and Colonel Norman standing at the entrance to the building. I thought they would be happy for me. But McCann immediately asked where I was in front of several staff members.

"I went to see Byron," I told him casually and he grew disturbed.

"I didn't know anything about it!" he said irritably.

"He called and wanted me over there ASAP," I said. "He's the Boss!"

"**I'm** your Boss," McCann told me testily.

"Yes, and you are a good Boss," I said. "I tried to tell you, but you were not in your office at eleven o'clock." My temper started to flare. I liked McCann and wanted him on my side.

"What'd he tell you?" McCann asked.

"I'm going to Uruguay," I told him. What's the big deal, I thought.

"I just talked to Byron. You're staying here at the academy. We can't afford to lose anybody." McCann smiled in a half-hearted way. Who could I believe? Well, it was flattering that I was needed, but my plans were to be in Uruguay in thirty days. I did not hear otherwise. McCann understood.

9

Switzerland of the Americas

"Congratulations…you have finally made it on Havana's black list." —Johnson Munroe, Deputy Director OPS, April 23, 1965

January 1965

The State of Virginia had a white Christmas, and the New Year winter continued with more snow for historic Alexandria where we lived. On January 6, Pete Ellena informed me that clearances and approval for my assignment to Uruguay had been received from the United States Embassy in Montevideo. The Government of Uruguay (GOU) had signed the agreement for U.S. assistance to the security forces and had approved the OPS mission and my assignment in that country.

Our household furnishings were packed and shipped to Uruguay. The instructions that I should be in Uruguay within thirty days were a reality. The country faced serious security problems and I was needed there *pronto* according to Jack Munroe, the Deputy Director.

Two weeks later, with airline tickets and passports in hand, on the day of our travel to Montevideo, we woke up with snow on the ground ten inches high. On Cool Spring Drive in Alexandria where we lived, snow covered the area with a gleaming white blanket. Snow on the ground sparkled in the morning sunshine. But it made things difficult for us.

The home we had purchased ten months earlier was warm and comfortable, with the fireplace burning pine logs. Our children had fun sleeping on blankets on the soft carpeting near the fireplace that night. But amid mid-morning grumbling my wife and I pushed them to finish packing for our long journey to Uruguay. Everyone seemed excited.

Snowplows had cleared the George Washington Parkway and National Airport was reported to be operating normally with few flight delays expected despite the snowfall. Our Pan American flight was on schedule and would depart on time. Across the street from our house, Air Force Major Bob White and his wife Marion waited to take us to the airport. White, a copilot on Air Force One, warmed up their station wagon while a taxicab waited to take our large array of suitcases to the airport.

It was not easy packing for a trip with six kids. The new car we had purchased was on the way to New York for shipment to Uruguay by boat. But the thought of leaving our new home filled me with sadness and nostalgia. I would miss the greenery and beautiful scenery of Virginia. Our home would be rented through a real estate company in Alexandria until our return from Uruguay in three years.

My oldest son Kurt helped take our suitcases out to the waiting cab. The snow was a problem but we did not take time to clear the sidewalks. Carrying a heavy load of suitcases, I slipped out of control on the slick sidewalk and landed on my back hard and on the concrete walkway. I felt a stabbing pain. The cab driver muttered, "nice triple axel," and instinctively an expletive left my mouth.

"Flipping redneck," I told him. He grinned and apologized.

"Are you okay, Dad?" my son asked worriedly. An injury would prevent our departure so I was determined to be okay. Sweeping the snow from my topcoat with my hands, my son walked with me nonchalantly into the house. Inside, my face grew hot with anger and pain. In the bathroom I washed my face and glanced in the mirror to chastise myself. This was not the time for me to get hurt. It was near the time to depart for the airport.

In our bedroom I found my wife crying as she packed last minute items such as stuffed toys, snacks and other things needed for the long journey with six youngsters. Sorrow gripped me unexpectedly and instinctively I held my sore back. My wife's mascara had run and her face was a bright red from crying. She looked up startled and her beautiful brown eyes flashed.

"What's wrong?" she asked worriedly. I was in pain.

But it was the thought of leaving our new home to live an uncertain life in another country that really bothered me. Lightheartedly, I told her about falling on the icy sidewalk. With an expletive I told her that I was fine.

"Don't cuss," she admonished me and turned me around to see my back. The doleful look on my face apparently looked funny and she giggled.

"Your ass is all dirty," she said, laughing.

"So it's funny? " I said jokingly, faking anger and she continued laughing. She squealed when I grabbed her in a bear hug and kissed her. She held onto me, afraid to let go. We were both worried about leaving home to go to an unknown place and an uncertain future. I was uprooting my young family again to take them thousands of miles away from their country, perhaps to danger.

My wife reacted to my worried look and hugged me reassuringly.

"We're going with you," she said. "Don't worry, we'll be fine. I've read the Post Report and everything is positive with plenty of healthy vegetables, lots of meat and the water is safe to drink."

The Post Report did not mention the political violence developing. She was not aware of that.

"We'll be back in two or three years," I promised with all sincerity. "If we're not happy we'll come back anyway. But in three years we can save a lot of money." The U.S. Government would provide housing for us. We had already served over five years in Latin America.

The drive to National Airport took us past Alexandria on the George Washington Parkway and our children cried openly when the reality of our departure hit home. At the Pan American ticket counter, the airline agent processed our pile of tickets, passports and checked in about nine bags for us. Hundreds of people skittered through the airport, and we rushed our children directly to the gate where we boarded our flight. It was a different period of history with no airport security checks or searches but the start of a long journey for us.

After stopping in Panama, the flight took most of the night to reach *Azeiza* Airport in Buenos Aires. The plane approached the airport and in the darkness the huge span of city lights seemed unending. Buenos Aires was one of the largest cities in the world.

In the early dawn, the flight took off again across the *Rio de La Plata* and arrived at *Carrasco* Airport in Montevideo in less than an hour. We were proud of our young six children. They had behaved very well on the long tiresome flight. The size of our family had grown out of control. Our son Michael was born in El Salvador and Eric in the Panama Canal Zone. Maybe it was the tropics, I thought humorously.

My oldest daughter Lori, now fourteen, helped entertain and supervise her siblings the entire flight. I called her my beautiful princess. A bright orange sun emerged when we crossed the territorial boundary of Argentina into Uruguay. It was summer in that part of the world when the plane landed at *Carrasco* Airport. We had gone from winter to summer in one day.

It did not take long to clear customs and immigration with the help of a kind and friendly U.S. AID Officer who met our plane. Piling into two U.S. Government vehicles, we were driven by beautiful beaches overrun by happy people until we arrived at the **Cottage Hotel,** a landmark in Montevideo. The Hotel Cottage (pronounced Kot-ahg by Uruguayans) was an attractive family inn situated in an area called *Carrasco,* near the Bay of Montevideo.

The owner and employees of the Cottage made us feel welcome and we were provided four very comfortable rooms. The hotel maids fussed happily over our young children and we looked forward to the wonderful home-cooked meals served in the family dining room of the picturesque inn. Our stay at the Cottage ended on March 8 when we moved to an attractive and spacious residence on *Copacabana* Street in *Carrasco* paid for by the U.S. Government.

It took a while to get settled in beautiful Montevideo but it was worth it. The quality of life was excellent. The City of Montevideo initially looked grim because of the dull cement grey Gothic architecture, but the ambiance had a nice classy European atmosphere with attractive shopping centers, outdoor cafes, and well-dressed men and women. In many areas, *parrilladas* (barbecue places and pizza stands) offered the best steaks and pizza in the world, Italian food, cow udder, bull testicles, and other fine delicacies. Montevideo, the capital city, had a population of about 1.3 million people.

The entire country, about the size of the State of Washington, had nineteen *Departamentos* or Provinces. *Punta del Este,* the beautiful world-famous ocean-side resort, was about an hour's drive by car from Montevideo. The rural areas and the countryside were delightful and unlike any we had ever seen, with attractive green rolling hills and plains called the *Pampas.* The *Pampas* were home to the *Gauchos,* popular and rugged native cowboys with a colorful and historical repertoire. We felt privileged to live in beautiful Uruguay. It was truly a beautiful country with gentle cultured people.

Widely known as the **"Switzerland of the Americas,"** its strength was a strongly united, educated society and of course a democracy. A council of nine men governed the country. A mostly homogeneous population of white European stock dominated the population. Colonizers had killed off the predominant group of Indians in Uruguay called the *Charruas* in the 1700s. Spanish, Italian, British, and German immigrants formed a diverse culture of intelligent people in Uruguay.

The country enjoyed a phenomenal literacy rate of over ninety per cent (90%). Uruguay had one of the highest standards of living in South America. It appeared to me that Uruguay had everything going for it. I was mistaken.

Uruguay's declining economy during the Cold War created serious labor unrest that resulted in urban violence and destruction, especially in Montevideo. Used to a lifestyle probably unmatched in the hemisphere, Uruguayans were now subject to severe austerity measures as a result of the falling world market and prices for beef and wool, the country's two major exports.

To complicate matters, Uruguayans were consummate eaters of beef with a limited affinity for eating pork or fowl. Uruguayan friends made fun of me because I liked and ate *"porotos"* (beans). Uruguayans were truly carnivorous and would perish without a good *"churrasco"* or "baby *bife"* every day.

A shortage of beef or an increase in the price of meat literally created political upheavals and explosions. Higher revenues needed by the government could not come about by increasing the exportation of beef because that meant less meat would be available locally for Uruguayan citizens to enjoy. Meat was a primary political issue.

But there were other economic and political issues in social welfare programs which had been set in concrete many years earlier by Jorge B. de Ordonez, a former President of Uruguay. Uruguayans were entitled to a free college education. The existing labor force in government was thirty percent more than finances could sustain. Government employees could retire at age fifty with full pay.

Meanwhile, inflation was rapidly escalating and tearing at the national economy. It appeared the nine-man Council of Government in Uruguay was lodged firmly between a rock and a hard place.

Meanwhile, the communist party exploited the situation in an attempt to destabilize the government. The communists seemed to have an inordinate interest in Uruguay as a doorway to the rest of South America, while Montevideo was increasingly threatened by a growing civil unrest caused by the declining economy. The country was beset with economic problems that created unrelenting civil unrest, discontent and political turmoil. The situation had all the factors needed for an insurgency.

Two days after we arrived in Uruguay the U.S. Embassy *Chargé d' Affairs,* William (Bill) Briggs, took me to meet with the Uruguayan Minister of the Interior (MOI), Dr. Adolfo Tejera. The United States

Ambassador, Henry Hoyt, was in Washington, but I was supposed to get started in helping Uruguay resist communism.

The MOI was responsible for all police agencies in the country as well as fire departments and the immigration service. The delicate political character of the OPS program in Uruguay was worrisome. I was glad that the Director of AID, Milo Cox, and the U.S. Embassy Political Officer, Jim Cunningham, accompanied us. The OPS program, called the Public Safety Program, was under the Director of AID.

Dr. Adolfo Tejera, a big affable man with dark eyes that often turned wary, was anxious to talk about U.S. assistance for the police and security forces. The Minister explained that the project agreement with the United States for police assistance had been ratified on November 23, 1963, by the Uruguayan National Council of Government (UNCOG). (That was the day after the assassination of President Kennedy.) The action taken by the UNCOG on the agreement was among the fastest ratification in the history of Uruguay, he explained somberly. It was the U.S. bureaucracy that had held up implementation.

The U.S. assistance to the security forces was viewed as highly important to the internal security of the country. The Minister expressed concern about labor and student unrest expected in the coming winter months, and was worried about the ability of the Uruguayan police forces to cope with a potential increase in violence. He emphasized that the police were expected to maintain law and order, but would also be expected to respect the rights of all citizens in accordance with the constitution of Uruguay. This meant all rights, he said. If the police used undue force under any circumstances, this would surely aggravate the problem. The police could not afford to be brutal, he added. The Minister was absolutely sincere and correct in his assessment.

But how do you deal with mindless mob violence and terrorism, without using harsh and forceful tactics, I wondered? We were entering into an alliance with Uruguay that seemed replete with plenty of political pitfalls and dire consequences. Things could only get worse. I walked out of the meeting impressed but keenly aware that Uruguay was a sophisticated society with Cold War problems. The civil unrest was the tip of the iceberg. I felt more like a politician than a police advisor, but adjusted quickly to the work environment. One U.S. Embassy official offered the suggestion that I better hit the ground running because there was no other U.S. program in Uruguay that had more significance than the OPS effort. I assumed he was trying to be funny. He was not.

Ned Holman had the title of First Secretary and Consul at the U.S. Embassy but he was more than that. In his late forties, he came across as a calm, earnest man who preferred to remain very low key. Technically he posed as U.S. Embassy staff, but in reality he was the CIA Chief of Station. As a veteran CIA Officer and a former FBI Special Agent with extensive Latin American experience, Holman recommended that the OPS program be implemented as soon as possible after the growing threat of communism in Uruguay became patently clear. If an exemplary democracy like Uruguay fell to communism, that would indeed be a victory for the Soviets.

I liked and trusted Ned Holman and he reciprocated by providing excellent support for the police assistance program. The program, however, was not under the control of the CIA Station.

Within a matter of days after my arrival, Holman and I stood outside the headquarters of the Montevideo Police Department as he explained the inner workings of the major police organization in the country. The Montevideo police had about over 7,000 men and women and included two quasi-military units called the *Guardia Metropolitana,* an emergency response force, and the *Guardia Republicana,* a mounted police force. Uruguayan Army military officers were in charge of the police organizations.

The building called the *Jefatura* (Headquarters) was a phenomenal structure of grey stone and designed in Gothic architecture. Entering a back door, we walked through tiled corridors until we arrived at the office of the *Jefe de Policia* (Chief of Police). When we were announced by his secretary, the Chief immediately opened his door.

Holman introduced me to the Chief of Police, Colonel Ventura Rodriguez, a handsome man with a cherubic face wearing a mustache. Colonel Ventura Rodriguez was extremely effective and was soon promoted to General. He was one of the most sincere, honest and competent persons I would ever meet. His calm temperament and brilliant charisma belied his tough and strong nature. I was fortunate that General Ventura Rodriguez became my good friend and my counterpart in the Cold War struggle in Uruguay.

My acceptance as a *Gringo asesor* by the various commanders and police personnel and as a representative of the U.S. Government did not come easy with the proud Uruguayans. Nevertheless, U.S. police assistance to deal with the internal security crisis was an important item for political circles in Uruguay as well as for the local Communist Party. The local communist and left-wing newspapers, such as *El Popular, Marcha* and *Epoca,* did not delay in accusing the U.S. Government of intervening in the internal affairs of Uruguay. I was accused of meddling as a spy for the *Yanquis* (Yankees).

Three months after I arrived in Uruguay, I received a letter from Jack Munroe, the Deputy Director of OPS. He informed me that the *Prensa Latina* in Havana, Cuba, on April 23 had issued a press release reporting my presence in Montevideo as causing **"general protests and discontent among the popular segments of said capital."**

Munroe added an interesting comment in his letter. **"Congratulations—you have finally made it on Havana's black list!"** Was it the good news or the bad news?

About five months after my arrival in Uruguay, the President of the National Council of Government, Luis Giannattasio, died. Another member of the governing council, Washington Beltran, assumed the Presidency in a quiet and traditional transition.

But during the changeover of the Presidency, amid national mourning, the communists took direct action. They tested the new President in terms of his resolve to deter any communist *putsch*. In a superbly organized effort and with surprise on their side, a mob of over a hundred persons attacked the U.S. Embassy, pelting it with rocks delivered beforehand and taking numerous potshots at the building. Windows at the Embassy were hit by gunfire.

Ironically, at the same time, American students were demonstrating in Washington, D.C., against U.S. involvement in the war in Vietnam. In Birmingham, Alabama, Bull Conner mowed down civil rights protesters led by Dr. Martin Luther King, Jr., using dogs and water cannon. Facetiously, I pondered whether my role in Uruguay was with the good guys or bad guys in the Cold War struggle.

The attack on the U.S. Embassy in Uruguay also left me wondering whether the country had gone mad. Dozens of young men and women imbued with the communist ideology were throwing rocks, shooting guns, burning cars and trying to hurt anyone that stood in their path.

The struggle in Uruguay represented a complex offensive for the communists. Uruguay had an educated and sophisticated society and the people were not easy to deceive. The communists were well organized and intended to take over the Government of Uruguay. But what was the basis for the unrest and discontent? Uruguay was one of the most democratic countries in the world.

I watched the contingents of the *Guardia Metropolitana* disperse the mob attacking the U.S. Embassy. They responded to gunfire directed at them by members of the mob. Demonstrations and mass violence seemed to be a part of daily life in the politics of the Cold War. The communists apparently knew it was the democratic way.

Despite the violent security situation that frequently erupted in downtown Montevideo, life in Uruguay was great, especially living in *Carrasco,* a popular district with elegant houses, a suburban atmosphere and beautiful beaches. Our children were happy in their new home and attended the British School in *Carrasco* despite the fact that they hated the discipline and uniforms. Our residence was generally secure with fences and wrought iron bars, but we hired a traditional *sereno* (watchman), for protection of our home.

Eventually, the most effective security for us turned out to be a vicious silver colored German Shepherd dog we named *Lobo.* Captain Hervasio Somma of the *Guardia Republicana* gave *Lobo* to me when he was a tiny puppy. *Lobo* matured into the best guard dog possible. He protected our family with an uncommon ferociousness and valor, gaining a reputation in our neighborhood.

My wife and I later surprised our children with a cute charismatic brown pony named *"Puchito."* My children were elated when I rented a lot next door and assembled a corral and stable. We hired *Don Jose,* an old *Gaucho* who loved horses, to feed and to take care of the pony. Another dog the children named "Snoopy" and a short fat horse called *"Chiquito"* was eventually added to our menagerie.

As part of the agreement with the Government of Uruguay, I received a nice car with two police drivers assigned on a 24-hour schedule. I had a car and a chauffeur any time I needed it. Life was good in Uruguay.

In order to determine the funding needed to provide assistance to the security forces, specific goals and objectives were developed in line with AID programming requirements. Despite some resistance by AID liberal bureaucrats, the needs for the police assistance program in Uruguay were defined and the funding approved by Washington under the U.S. Foreign Assistance Act.

The OPS program was an important and a critical part of United States foreign assistance strategy in Uruguay. The primary goal was to improve the internal defense capabilities of the Montevideo police to cope with an expected increase in civil unrest, crime and communist subversion. The United States would provide technical assistance, training and police equipment needed to upgrade administration, emergency management, riot control operations, patrol services, communications, intelligence capabilities and criminal investigations.

An office established at the USAID/U.S. Embassy complex seemed proper for OPS operations but due to the stupid intransigence of a misguided AID Administrative Officer, another office was established at the *Jefatura,* the Montevideo Police Headquarters. The AID officer touted this as a reciprocal contribution by the Government of Uruguay but this move put us deep in the trenches.

The Chief of Police was delighted to provide us an office at the Montevideo Police Headquarters and named it the *Oficina de Asistencia Tecnica* or Office of Technical Assistance. My office was complete with the Uruguayan and American flags standing side by side.

The communist media immediately characterized the presence of Americans at the Montevideo police headquarters as, "*Yanqui* control of the *Jefatura.*" Despite local communist allegations of espionage, the OPS program activities grew positive. Officers in the U.S. Embassy watched with great interest. My ability to speak Spanish became invaluable. Nevertheless, problems were often unpredictable in my role as the top *Gringo Asesor* (American advisor) to the police.

The OPS office at the *Jefatura* was next to the office of the Director of Criminal Investigations occupied by Inspector Guillermo Copello, a thin red-faced veteran cop with an explosive Italian temper and a fondness for Scotch. Everyone was aware that Copello could be real nasty and temperamental. I knew he was in the habit of lambasting *Gringos.*

Copello required special handling and tactful motivation since he was a very proud Uruguayan. The prime motivation was that I became a valued supplier of Scotch for Copello. Despite occasional anti-*Gringo* tirades Copello was cooperative and friendly with me. Besides, I learned that *Gringo* in Uruguay meant any foreigner not just Americans. With Copello, however, things could get difficult.

John Wachter, the FBI Legal *Attaché* based in Buenos Aires, complained that Copello refused to provide important information he needed in connection with the investigation of one of his cases.

According to Wachter, Copello had grossly insulted him, telling him the FBI was *pura mierda* (pure shit). It was his opinion, I told Wachter. Although this was not my problem, it seemed that Copello was not only ungrateful and uncooperative with Americans, he was pushing us around. The incident had an anti-American attitude that was in serious conflict with the OPS mission. I decided we should talk to him.

Wachter and I entered Copello's office unannounced, to the surprise of his secretary. The office had vestiges of a night of serious boozing and the smell of alcohol remained heavy in the air. Copello watched us enter in silence but his face showed a nasty contempt.

In a calm manner, I informed Copello we were disappointed with his treatment of Wachter, especially since we were friends. Copello's bloodshot eyes grew mean and he reacted with belligerence. Raising his voice he yelled obscenities to no one in particular.

"*Si, haci es* (Yes, that's the way it is)," he blurted out. "*A mi no me vengan con mierdas* (Don't come to me with any of your shit)," he added with a touch of arrogance.

"*A mi no me dan ordenes los Gringos.*" (He said that he did not take orders from *Gringos*.)

He grew louder and gestured excitedly with his hands, *a la Italiana*. Many Uruguayan police officials with Italian names and heritage spoke Spanish as well as Italian. The Spanish spoken was similar to the Argentine *Rio Platense* and contained numerous Italian words and gestures that enriched conversations, especially heated arguments.

Copello had to be challenged, otherwise we would look weak and vulnerable. More importantly, I was in a better posture in the political chess game than he was. His eyes grew menacing when I got close to his face and addressed him angrily in Spanish.

"*Té éstas portando como gran hijo-de-puta, Copello!* (You are behaving like a humongous son-of-a-bitch, Copello!)" Impulsively I had insulted him. But it was common slang in Uruguay.

I wondered what Copello would do. What could he do? He could arrest me but the police assistance program and agreements between Uruguay and the United States might go down the tubes. I was easily replaceable but Copello did not know this. It was a risk but I wanted to stand up to Copello.

Copello's face grew florid and he screamed invectives in Spanish. My voice also rose.

"*Muy bien, Copello. Al Jefe de Policia le interesara nuestro conflicto de cooperación* (Fine, Copello, the Chief of Police is going to be interested in the conflict and the matter of your cooperation)." In the nature of an implied threat, I informed Copello that **his** lack of cooperation would be discussed with General Ventura Rodriguez and he was not invited to the meeting.

Copello's face paled when he heard this. He grew pensive. He knew General Ventura Rodriguez was my good friend and high level people in the Uruguayan government counted on our assistance. Copello's eyes widened but Wachter seemed stunned by my brashness. He was probably wondering how he would explain to FBI Director J. Edgar Hoover that Copello had arrested us.

"*Un momento,*" Copello yelped obsequiously. He stared at me.

"*Vamos, que pasa?*" he told me in a low sullen voice. "*No es para tanto.* (Wait a moment. What's wrong? What's the big deal?)" He circled in front of me and chuckled to gauge my reaction.

"*Somos amigos. Que pasa?* (We're friends. What's the problem?)" He grabbed my arm playfully.

"*Mira,*" he told me and pulled me toward his desk. He pulled out a bottle of Johnny Walker Red Label Scotch from a drawer. We laughed when he did this. It was one of the bottles of Scotch I kept him supplied with. He had a whole case. Abruptly he instructed one of his aides to bring him some glasses and ice.

"*Tomemos una copa* (Let's have a drink)," he said jovially, his attitude totally changed. But this was Copello's way. I knew we would have a drink with him and we were friends again. He explained that he was under great stress with the ongoing problems of crime and political unrest. This made him irritable, he said. The business of dealing with cops under stress was not easy for anyone.

Wachter felt obliged to decline the mid-morning drink of Scotch but I urged him to accept or he would offend Copello. J. Edgar Hoover would not be told he was drinking on duty.

After one stiff straight shot of Scotch, Copello turned mellow and hurried his staff to provide Wachter the information he needed. My ability to function as a police advisor in Uruguay had been severely tested. But after all, booze was the basis for many friendships and lubricated the intricacies of any relationship. When booze enters, information comes out, someone once said. My friendship with John Wachter motivated me to intervene. But we could not afford to let Copello get away with anti-American posturing as long as we were there to help. OPS assistance was a complex matter.

At the U.S. Embassy, Ned Holman and I often discussed the ongoing security crisis. Holman agreed with me that an additional input of U.S. assistance would be necessary and he supported me on that. There were no guarantees about the urban unrest and where it was leading. U.S. assistance had to be expanded with additional advisors.

Frank Stewart, the Director of AID, was an attorney and he saw the security problem in Uruguay in terms of OPS objectives and U.S. foreign aid policy and strategy. He was extremely supportive. I grew to greatly admire Frank Stewart. He was a true intellectual with three Vs, vision, valor and value. I felt proud that an intelligent and patriotic American like Frank Stewart was involved with us in the Cold War struggle. His excellent judgment was always invaluable *vis-a-vis* United States interests in Uruguay. He was a solid American and I was happy to call him a friend.

Every pertinent officer in the U.S. Embassy eventually agreed that the security situation was deteriorating rapidly. An expansion of the program of U.S. police assistance to Uruguay was deemed necessary if we were to accomplish our defined objectives. More strikes and mass demonstrations were taking place and more were expected. Communist leaders were busy promoting violence as the demonstrations held by labor and student groups increased. Acts of terrorism were also increasing and banks were being robbed at unprecedented levels in daring daylight assaults. Behind the violence and labor unrest, operatives from the Cuban and Soviet Embassies in Uruguay lurked in the shadows. Holman kept tabs on this.

In preparing an assessment with the U.S. Embassy on the security problems, it was determined that the capacity of the Montevideo police to cope with a further increase in strikes, demonstrations and violence was worrisome. The police and military forces, along with other public employees, had not been paid their wages for the past two months because of the economic problems. The morale and will of the security forces to cope with the civil unrest would eventually be affected.

Colonel Carlos Martin, the Deputy Chief of Police, pointed out a critical problem to me. The tear gas stock for riot control units was nearly depleted. Tear gas was ordered immediately from OPS Washington and I classified our need as an emergency.

The increase in strikes by organized labor, mass demonstrations and the agitation of the civil unrest by communist militants was increasing to serious proportions. As a result, rumors of a military *coup d'état* surfaced. The Government of Uruguay was forced to institute what was called Emergency Security Measures to permit the security forces to cope with increasing civil unrest and urban violence.

OPS assistance was approved by the U.S. Embassy to help the police cope with emergencies such as the control of civil disturbances. Commodities were ordered to upgrade the capabilities of the police for that purpose. Training was provided to the police commanders on the techniques and concept of riot control. As a result, they were convinced to train every man available in the control of civil disturbances. The 26-inch wood baton replaced rifles and sabers.

The credibility of U.S. assistance to the police soared as the morale of police officers stabilized. I spent hours analyzing the big picture and concluded that no matter what we did, Uruguay had major problems.

The communist movement was gaining momentum. The future looked grim for the police and security forces.

Caesar Bernal, an OPS advisor, arrived by the end of the year to help implement training assistance for the Uruguayan police forces. Bernal, a former detective sergeant from the San Antonio Police Department was a good choice. Having played football for Rice University prior to becoming a cop, he was in excellent physical condition. I advised him kiddingly to stay in shape because there were times when we might have to make a run for it! With a Mexican-American background like myself, he spoke fluent Spanish. He reminded me of Karl Malden because of his likeness to the actor. Balding, he liked wearing a fedora. Dalinda, his wife, and his two children adapted smoothly to life in Uruguay. (After OPS, Bernal became a top official in the U.S. Department of State Narcotics Control Assistance.)

An OPS communications technician arrived a few months later, but experienced difficulty adjusting to his role and acclimating to life in Uruguay. His inability to speak Spanish totally frustrated him. Learning a foreign language as an adult was always extremely difficult unless you had the knack for it. The communications technician unexpectedly decided to resign and return to the United States. The communications capabilities of the police needed critical and immediate improvement and the internal security threat was growing ominous.

Allegations of police brutality and repression under the 'control' of U.S. Government agents suddenly appeared in the communist media. There was some truth to the allegation, since we were supporting the police forces to control the violence created by the civil unrest. The stability of the government continued to be threatened by civil unrest and violence in Montevideo. The Communist Party membership in Uruguay, one of the largest in the hemisphere, was very active.

The ongoing urban violence and civil unrest promoted by the communists frustrated economic recovery and exacerbated internal security problems. Urban guerrilla warfare and terrorism would be the final stages for toppling the government. The communist strategy was clear and Dr. Alberto Heber, the President of the Council of Government, urged that Uruguay break diplomatic relations with the Soviet Union. He had information that the Russian and Cuban Embassies had financed and directed the strikes and violence under the guise of the labor unions. The CIA Station provided the proof to Heber.

In retribution, a bomb exploded outside the door of Dr. Heber's home. The communist threat had entered a new dimension in Uruguay.

A Marxist guerrilla group emerged that proved to be the *alter ego* of communist militants in Uruguay.

For me, the United States government was helping Uruguay combat communism in a Cold War life or death struggle for democracy not understood by many in America. In any country, the use of civil police forces against a communist insurgency involved inherent political risks. More importantly, U.S. assistance to the police in such cases placed American advisors in the center of a potentially violent political situation. Communist propagandists developed allegations of human rights abuses and accusations of repression by the police to attack American OPS advisors and the United States. But as Attorney General Robert Kennedy once said, **the police had to be taught more than just how to direct traffic** in order to combat communist subversion and insurgency. But it seemed we were accused of being repressive terrorists and torturers. We were screwed if we did and screwed if we didn't. Debbie Fields was right. **"Good enough, never is."**

Fortunately the *esprit de corps* among the officer corps of the Montevideo police units remained high. The officers were among the best in the hemisphere. Despite the overwhelming problems of maintaining law and order the police units in Uruguay performed admirably and courageously. I felt comfortable being in the hot seat of the U.S. effort to help Uruguay resist a communist takeover. After all, I considered myself anti-Communist.

On May Day, the communists celebrated by attacking targets throughout Montevideo. In Uruguay, the United States Embassy, the Coca Cola Company, Pan American Airlines, the Ford Motor Company, General Electric, the Organization of American States (OAS), local newspaper offices and several police substations were attacked with Molotov cocktails and bombs. The urban war escalated and the police forces of Uruguay remained severely challenged.

My assessment was that we were operating in waters loaded with mines and vicious *tsunami*. The time had arrived for the Uruguayan military to help. We began to plant seeds of joint planning and operations between the police and military forces in Uruguay.

Nevertheless, no matter what they did, the police were falsely accused by the communist media of killing innocent people, of abusing their authority and violating the human rights of the workers and citizens. Ironically, the same allegations were made by ideologically inclined U.S. Government bureaucrats in Washington, D.C., to attack OPS missions anywhere. Any denial of the allegations resulted in accusations of a cover-up and protests that the United States was intervening in the internal affairs of a sovereign nation. We were *Pendejos* lodged precisely between a rock and a hard place. History was a good lesson.

America had had its share of labor unrest in the 1800s and throughout the 1900s with the communists in the United States deeply involved. The Haymarket Riot of Chicago, led by leftists was especially vicious. The American Federation of Labor (AFL), founded in 1886, initiated strikes almost immediately after its inaugural. Violence became common. In 1894, the labor war against George Pullman and Pullmanism resulted in mass violence. Thus labor strife and unrest belonged in a democracy. The bad economy, labor unrest and bank failures in Uruguay were the principal causes of civil unrest. But in Uruguay's case, the communist party used the situation as an opportunity to take over the government. That was not normal political change!

Because of the economic chaos that created the civil unrest, the police forces and the OPS program were accused of repression. As head of the OPS program in Uruguay, my job was to direct U.S. assistance to enable the police to maintain law and order and to combat communist subversion but not legitimate protest.

But who could define what aspect of the violence was subversive? We could not bleed forever. According to police intelligence sources, the communist party had over 20,000 people as members with 50,000 sympathizers and growing. We were not sure of the numbers. The police unit handling intelligence was called *Inteligencia y Enlace* (Intelligence and Liaison) and was under the command of a controversial young man named Alejandro Otero who was more in tune with being a soccer referee than intelligence operations.

In Uruguay, the ideological struggle was shifting to all-out war. The police needed to develop their intelligence capabilities in the Cold War. It was no longer an overt war. The *Tupamaro* guerrillas would soon rear their enigmatic head.

From Artigas, in the interior of Uruguay, hundreds of *cañeros* (sugar cane workers) marched on Montevideo (over four hundred miles away) in a mass demonstration that was organized by the communists. The resolve and leadership of the *cañeros* was impressive.

The man in charge was Raul Sendic Antonaccio. He would be identified as the head of the left-wing *Tupamaro* guerrilla movement, the *Movimiento de Liberacion Nacional* (MLN). The MLN (National

Liberation Movement) brought the *Tupamaro* insurgency to the forefront. The police were advised to prepare for a prolonged crisis and to plan to deal with a glut of civil unrest and violence in Montevideo. The improvement of the communications capabilities and mobility for the Montevideo police remained a critical problem for the security forces as the urban violence increased.

Fortunately, U.S. Ambassador Henry Hoyt and AID Director Frank Stewart strongly supported the OPS objectives of strengthening the police infrastructure in Montevideo and for increasing the preparations needed for the police to handle emergencies. It seemed clear that as long as the economic crisis in Uruguay continued, the prospects for internal stability would be deferred. Other officers in the U.S. AID and U.S. Embassy would address any assistance needed by the Uruguayan Government in order to overcome the economic problems.

Because of the ongoing political struggle and economic crisis in Uruguay, the role of the OPS program attracted uncommon interest in Washington, D.C. Many Washington bureaucrats expressed concern that U.S. intervention in the internal affairs of Uruguay was risky. Because of the criticality of the situation, Byron Engle, the Director of OPS, arrived in Montevideo before the year ended to confer with the U.S. Ambassador and representatives of the Government of Uruguay (GOU). Engle would assess the situation himself, inspired by the reports made to Washington by the Embassy.

When Engle arrived in Uruguay, we visited various police units to talk to the commanders about security problems and to discuss OPS assistance. Visits with the various Uruguayan police officials went very well but there were always surprises. After a meeting with the commanders of the *Guard Metropolitan,* GM (Metropolitan Guard), Byron Engle was challenged by the commander of the unit to shoot with him using a small pistol range located inside the *Quartel.*

Marksmanship was apparently a measure of Engle's worth for the Uruguayan officers. I tried to dissuade Engle but he insisted on taking on the challenge. Surrounded by Uruguayan police officials, he prepared to shoot the .9 millimeter Luger at a bull's-eye target from twenty meters.

"Dolph," he called out. "How do you sight in with this weapon?"

My heart jumped. He was asking how the weapon would shoot if he aimed with the sights precisely balanced on the bulls-eye target. I knew Engle was an expert shot but the wrong information from me would throw him off.

"The weapon shoots slightly high and to the left," I told him. I remembered having shot the Luger before. Engle squeezed off five rounds.

When he finished shooting, the Uruguayan officials rushed to check the target. There were four rounds directly in the bull's-eye and one shot about an eighth of an inch from the others but in the black. The group of hits was impressive and great shooting. Engle winked at me.

"You were right about that gun," he said. I proudly escorted him around the *Quartel.* But I knew Engle was great with firearms. He was on the Board of Directors for the National Rifle Association (NRA) and often competed against the best.

Police officials crowded around us to congratulate Engle on his shooting. Pleased with his visit and satisfied with what we were doing and planning, Engle left the following day. Impressed with our relationships with Uruguayan Police Officials, he suggested we keep doing what we were doing and to work closely with the police commanders. OPS had respectability and credibility in Uruguay and the Boss provided his approval.

A few days later, Colonel Carlos Martin, the Deputy Chief of Police of Montevideo, and I inspected the tear gas stocks and found the inventory almost depleted. Most of the tear gas munitions left were old and the effective date of use had expired. More alarming was that many remaining tear gas grenades contained CN/DM, a chemical mixture of tear gas and vomiting gas. That was a risky combination of chemicals for the police forces to use under any circumstances. The vomiting gas would indiscriminately affect men, women and children in potentially dangerous ways.

I proposed to Colonel Martin that the CN/DM items in stock be immediately destroyed and promised that the U.S. Government would replenish the tear gas stock as soon as possible.

"How soon?" he asked.

"Within forty eight hours," I told him. He agreed.

We advised OPS Washington of the situation by classified telegram. The police needed tear gas that was suitable for use in police emergencies. A new chemical munition called CS used by civil police forces in the United States and Europe for riot control purposes was recommended for Uruguay. The cable explaining our predicament was dispatched to the OPS Technical Services Division (OPS/TSD) in Washington, D.C., and resulted in fast action.

Forty-eight hours later, the CS tear gas arrived in Uruguay. On the same day, labor and political unrest orchestrated by the communists erupted with a vengeance. The delivery of the tear gas to the police units was immediate. In the thirty-day period that followed, seventy-three (73) disturbances and violent incidents provoked by the communists erupted in Montevideo. Prophetically, the CS tear gas caught the communist militants leading the violent strikes and civil disturbances by total surprise. To say that the CS tear gas was effective would be an understatement.

Confrontations between the police and striking workers and demonstrators intensified while propaganda attacks against the United States grew. We were riding the same leaking boat as U.S. troops in South Vietnam. I grew concerned that the United States would abandon the struggle in Uruguay. The security problems were growing. Large quantities of guns and ammunition continued to be stolen from gun stores. That could only mean someone was planning a war. The robberies of gun stores taking place seemed to be a calculated effort and were carried out with excellent timing and skill.

October 1965: The Incident at the International Association of Chiefs of Police (IACP) Conference

General Ventura Rodriguez, the Chief of Police of Montevideo, and Lt. Colonel Pasqual Cirillo, the deputy commander of the *Guardia Metropolitana,* were experienced and intelligent military officers who provided excellent leadership for the police force. We were good friends. But our friendship was severely tested on a trip to Miami Beach to attend the annual International Association of Chiefs of Police (IACP) conference.

In order to expose the Uruguayan military officers to civil police operations in the United States and other countries, I invited them to attend the IACP conference in Miami Beach. They were scheduled to see demonstrations of new technology and police equipment and to attend seminars held to discuss police issues in the United States and other countries. But the trip turned into a nightmare.

Our second night at the IACP Conference at the *Fontainebleau* Hotel in Miami came close to a tragedy. Invited to a reception hosted by Federal Laboratories, a quirky lieutenant from the Miami Beach Police Department followed us to the function after we attended another function held. The inebriated police lieutenant persisted in talking to the Uruguayans who spoke almost no English. He made the off-handed comment that he did not like the fact that the communist party was legal in Uruguay but I paid no attention to this.

Hundreds of Chiefs of Police and top officials from police organizations in the United States and other countries mingled throughout the elegant hotel attending seminars, receptions or visiting the displays of police equipment. General Rodriquez and I momentarily stepped out of the room where the Federal Laboratories reception was being held and left Colonel Cirillo behind. We were told that the lieutenant from the Miami Beach Police Department continued to talk to Colonel Cirillo about Uruguay. Colonel Cirillo patiently responded to the lieutenant's questions in broken English.

But without warning the lieutenant suddenly pulled a gun from a hip holster and pointed it menacingly at Colonel Cirillo. Wild shouts and screams erupted when people in the room saw what was happening. American police officials in the room wrestled the gun from the drunken police lieutenant and were holding him down when General Rodriguez and I entered the room. I was told that Colonel Cirillo had instinctively pushed the gun away and the move probably saved his life.

Later, an astounded Cirillo tried to apologize for the incident. He was the victim of an assault with a deadly weapon and had no reason to apologize. In the confusion, the lieutenant was removed from the conference site by other police officers. I reported the incident to Byron Engle, the Director of OPS, who was also at the IACP conference. He talked to the Chief of Police of Miami Beach.

It was expected that the lieutenant would be charged with assault with a deadly weapon. There were dozens of witnesses.

The following day, Byron Engle and Rocky Pomerance, the Chief of the Miami Beach Police Department, asked me to arrange a meeting with the Uruguayan military officers. At our meeting Rocky Pomerance apologized for the insane behavior of the police lieutenant. But despite our best efforts, the apology was not well received. General Ventura Rodriguez insisted that we return to Uruguay the following day. Our visit to the United States became a near tragedy.

Without Colonel Cirillo's testimony the lieutenant could not possibly be tried and convicted. Colonel Cirillo told me he did not know why the crazy lieutenant had pulled a gun on him, but I knew, and felt rage and embarrassment. The Cold War had violent fanatics on the right as well as the left side of the political spectrum. I urged Rocky Pomerance to fire the lieutenant but he seemed uncertain. The incident went unpublicized in the American media. It was difficult for me to explain to the Uruguayan police officers the motive of the Miami Beach Police officer and U.S. Embassy officials were stunned.

In Uruguay, the most threatening glimpse of the *Tupamaros* probably occurred late in the year, when the delphiniums and roses were starting to bloom and in the spring-like weather, the tranquil beaches of *Punta del Este* and *Pocitos* beckoned. A large bomb exploded at the Bayer Company in Montevideo causing considerable damage to the plant. Leaflets left at the scene displayed a crudely drawn five-point star with a *"T"* in the center and contained an ominous message.

"Death to the yanqui assassins in Vietnam. The nazi-owned Bayer Company helps produce toxic gases for the gringos."
—Viva el Vietcong
—Viva La Revolucion

The frightening announcement left by the *Tupamaros* at the Bayer Company coincided with changes taking place with **'Company'** personnel at the U.S. Embassy. Ned Holman was transferred and replaced by John Horton, an experienced CIA Far East hand. Unpretentious and friendly, John Ryder Horton was eastern establishment with spy qualities sharpened by experience. Rugged looking and handsome, he displayed a confidence coupled with a sense of humor that made him extremely valuable in Uruguay. Because we were in the middle of an internal security crisis, Horton and I often discussed the *Tupamaro* threat and the growing security problems. The emerging terrorist movement of the *Tupamaros* dictated new measures, and that the intelligence capabilities of the police had to be enhanced. What was needed was an expert in the intelligence craft to help strengthen police capabilities.

We agreed that a position for an OPS Investigations Advisor for the program in Uruguay would be requested from Washington, D.C., and an experienced CIA officer would be assigned once it was approved. The individual assigned would work primarily with the unit of *Inteligencia y Enlace* (Intelligence and Liaison) of the Montevideo police to upgrade their capabilities for intelligence. We received expeditious Washington approval.

The Station Chief's office was in back of the Political Section in the Embassy. Horton and I had discussed a scheduled visit to Uruguay by U.S. Secretary of State Dean Rusk. As I walked out he introduced me to a grim young man standing at the door. He appeared to be waiting for someone.

"Dolph," Horton told me, "I want you to meet Philip Agee. He's working liaison with the police and other local matters." I shook hands with the young man and he stared at me.

Agee had a skull-like face, small eyes and a sharp nose. His thick slick black hair enhanced a hard florid face. He had a cold arrogant look about him. (Philip Agee would subsequently defect to the communist cause and would describe Horton as having a perpetual sneer and called me naive.)

"The cops are almost hopeless, aren't they?" he said, seemingly interested in what I had to say.

"They're doing a great job," I responded to his chagrin. He apparently wanted me to say they didn't have a chance. From that point on I disliked Agee and felt uncomfortable with him. For me, Agee was just another anomaly of the CIA.

Within a few weeks, the CIA officer assigned as an OPS Investigations Advisor arrived without fanfare. Bill Cantrell, a round-faced man in the true fashion of spies, was an avid pipe smoker. He was a former Secret Service Agent who had worked briefly on U.S. Presidential protective details. Prior to Uruguay and his selection for assignment in Uruguay, he was with an OPS program in the Middle East. Uruguay was different. Language ability was important but Cantrell did not have fluency in Spanish.

The Chief of Police frequently invited the OPS staff to *parrilladas* (a barbecue). Traditionally, blood sausages *(morcillas)*, sweetbreads, huge steaks and plenty of red wine were always served. The Chief suggested we bring the new advisor *(asesor)* so he could meet key police officials. Inspector Requeirro, the plump, jolly Director of the uniformed police, a connoisseur of good beef, plied Cantrell with *chinchulines* (cow intestines) in an effort to get him to speak Spanish.

Cantrell, like most non-Spanish speakers, could not pronounce the word *churrasco*. The rolling of the R's was tough. The assignment was tough for any CIA officer that could not speak Spanish.

The Urban Struggle in Uruguay Lengthens

In Montevideo, civil disturbances and strikes continued to plague the political, labor and economic environment without letup. Daring daylight robberies and burglaries as well as attacks against the police, public buildings and government offices were now commonplace. Molotov cocktails, bombs and machine guns became the favorite weapons of the attackers.

The police forces were in desperate need of mobility and a reliable communications network and were having a hard time with the growing problem of urban terrorism when a true American hero emerged in the crisis. United States Ambassador Henry Hoyt became the stalwart in the fight against communism in Uruguay and supported OPS assistance to the security forces *con pelotas*. He assured me the United States would not abandon the struggle in Uruguay as long as he was Ambassador. He seized my recommendations *con brio* and *cojones*.

We quickly obtained funding for twenty patrol cars, several large trucks and minimal communications equipment urgently needed by the Montevideo police to control the growing civil disturbances. With glasses askew and a wide grin, Hoyt led Americans as well as Uruguayans in the fight.

"Let's go with it, Dolph," he would say, making me laugh. "But remember, no draconian crap."

"I promise, Mr. Ambassador," I would respond dutifully. But the whole mess was draconian. The police needed one hundred cars and armored tanks. He would wink at me and smile broadly.

With time, the OPS office at the *Jefatura* became the place to meet with police officials. Caesar Bernal, Bill Cantrell and a newly arrived police advisor named Julian Lindenauer shared offices with me in the *Oficinia de Asistencia Tecnica*. We coordinated efforts as often as possible.

Julian Lindenauer was a former cop from the Miami Beach Police Department, was well educated and could speak Spanish fluently. He became a valuable member of the OPS team and concentrated on acquiring the equipment vitally needed by the police. Philip Agee criticized our office as a "hub of sociability." But he was not invited.

In line with Uruguayan tradition, we frequently drank *maté* with the officers of the Montevideo police, and with Danilo Micali, the Director General of the National Police, and our friend called *Pepito* Cantisani. *Maté*, an herb, was consumed daily by Uruguayans in the morning and evening. I drank *maté* from an attractive gourd laced with silver and gold. Once the gourd was filled with *maté* herb, hot water was added to make a tea. A silver and gold *"pipa"* (a metal straw with a strainer) was used to sip the hot liquid. I liked *maté* and consumed it in the morning instead of coffee. Micali told me jokingly that *maté* kept a man alert and, if one cared, hard for hours. He advised me to be careful drinking large amounts.

In Uruguay when you shared your gourd, *"pipa"* and *maté* with anyone, that person was considered a good friend. The idea of drinking moonshine from the same jug was comparable. Micali, a former Uruguayan Air Force pilot, was a political charmer and *"Pepito"* Cantisani was a blonde Italian/Uruguayan who could speak five languages, play the piano, violin, clarinet, and guitar. We frequently drank *maté* together. Both men were in their early thirties and had fears that Uruguay would fall to communism. Micali requested help for the police forces in the interior of Uruguay when the *Tupamaro* attacks started to mount.

He was aware that the police organizations in the *Departamentos* (Provinces) were included in a telecommunications study that would be conducted by OPS technicians **Paul Katz** and **Charles Redlin.** Micali felt enthusiastic about the effort. He suggested we meet with the two OPS Advisors when they arrived in Montevideo. I told him that Katz spoke some Vietnamese and Yiddish but no Spanish. Katz knew one Spanish word, *"huevos"* (eggs). In the vernacular that meant "balls."

Micali had recommended a Cuban national named Manuel Hevia as an interpreter for the survey team. He explained that Hevia, the nephew of a former president of Cuba, was destitute and had asked him for a job. But hiring a non-Uruguayan was impossible for Micali and since Hevia spoke English fluently, he suggested that OPS might be able to use him as an interpreter. Micali was sorry for the poor bastard, who allegedly had a law degree from the University of Cuba but could not find a job in Uruguay. He swore Hevia was a legitimate political exile. But what was he doing in Uruguay? Eventually, I declined to use him on the communications survey but hired him to do translations from Spanish to English of specific articles published in communist newspapers.

But Cantrell would open the door for the man, despite warnings that he could not be trusted. Hevia was too condescending, and ultimately surfaced as another sinister player in the Uruguayan struggle and anti-OPS drama. The CIA had no record on him.

In Montevideo, communist inspired violence grew, but with OPS assistance, the police improved their ability to respond to problems and to control urban violence. The ability of the police to control civil disturbances by the use of horses became legendary.

The *Guardia Republicana* (GR) was an elite mounted police force with over 300 horses. The outfit was disciplined and tough with riders that commonly used sabers for riot control and often with serious consequences. The sabers were replaced with 36-inch wood batons, diminishing what I called dash and macaroni. Colonel Hontu, the commander of the GR, was an effective and innovative leader.

The other paramilitary unit was the *Guardia Metropolitana* (GM), and was commanded by two no-nonsense colonels named Colonel Alfredo Rivero and my friend Colonel Pasqual Cirrillo. The GM was the elite police force used primarily for the control of civil disturbances, anti-terrorist activities and quasi-military operations. Rivero and Colonel Pasqual Cirrillo provided outstanding leadership in the struggle.

To strengthen the police riot control capabilities of the Montevideo Police Units, commodities and training provided by the OPS became a top priority. Large trucks and horse trailers procured with OPS assistance hauled police personnel and their mounts to a riot scene in a quick response, often surprising communist-led mobs.

Radios, gas masks and chemical munitions provided on an urgent basis for the control of communist-inspired disturbances and riots were tremendously helpful. But police operations against communist-led mobs were not facile.

The communist-provoked disturbances were carefully planned and almost always turned violent. To thwart the use of horses in controlling civil disturbances mob leaders threw petards (firecrackers), Molotov-cocktails and rocks to frighten the animals. Marbles were thrown on the street to cause the horses to fall when they stepped on them. Horses were often shot at and stabbed with knives, large pins and other sharp objects. Barricades constructed with planks, debris and automobile tires blocked the main streets in Montevideo and were set on fire during riots.

But the officers of the Republican Guard *(Guardia Republicana)* responded with exceptional skill and valor. The officers would jump their horses over the burning barricades in the finest tradition of the Calvary to reach rioters and the leaders. The Montevideo Police units gained ample respect in the internal war with their excellent performance during civil disturbances.

Many times I watched the GR and the GM in action out on the street and concluded that the paramilitary police units were among the best in the hemisphere. But it was a war with no end in sight.

Training for police riot control units became intense and simulated exercises were frequently held to train personnel and horses. Horses and their riders were exposed to loud noises, explosions, mob action and some amounts of tear gas. The police veterinarian ensured that the horses were not harmed or injured in any way during the training exercises. The main concern of the veterinarian was the frequent exposure of the horses to tear gas.

As a result, the possibility of gas masks made for horses were considered. Tear gas masks made especially for horses could be bought in European countries. But in repeated training exercises it was found that even large amounts of tear gas did not significantly affect the horses. The horses used by the police in Uruguay performed remarkably well despite exposure to tear gas and cruel attacks by rioters. They became the heroes in the urban struggle. Their performance was absolutely impressive.

In nearby Brazil, American Ambassador Charles Burke Elbrick was kidnapped by the MR-8 terrorist group of the *Partido Comunista do Brazil* (Brazilian Communist Party). He was indeed fortunate that the Brazilian Government agreed to meet the demands of the MR-8 terrorists and released fifteen terrorists held in prison. Elbrick was released in exchange. Otherwise, he would have likely been killed.

A. J. Langguth, an American communist *aficionado,* in his book **after** Dan Mitrione was kidnapped and assassinated in Uruguay by the *Tupamaros,* alleged that Angela Camargo Seixas, a member of the MR-8 terrorist group had been tortured by the Brazilian police. Langguth quoted Seixas, a hardcore terrorist as saying "she would never forgive the United States for its role in training and equipping the Brazilian police." But the situation in Brazil had nothing to do with Uruguay or Mitrione. Langguth consistently aggrandized the exploits of the communist terrorists and fabricated allegations of torture in Uruguay in an attempt to justify Mitrione's murder by the *Tupamaros.* That is understandable. Angela Camargo Seixas, Philip Agee and Langguth are known to be friends. They have common interests.

July 29, 1966

A lengthy article appearing in the local communist newspaper, *El Popular,* accused me of installing an FBI office at the police headquarters in Montevideo complete with wiretaps and monitoring devices. The attacks against the OPS program in Uruguay were growing assiduously. But summer approached with warm weather and a brief respite was expected from student violence and demonstrations in Montevideo as the University prepared to shut down. The beaches of *Punta del Este, Pocitos* and elsewhere would be invaded by hundreds of people. In the United States, it would be the start of winter.

In early November, my wife and I attended an official reception at the residence of the CIA Station Chief. Official receptions included standing for long hours drinking booze, eating strange hors d'oeuvres and exchanging gossip with airy diplomats and nosy wives. Shortly after we arrived at the Horton residence, Ambassador Hoyt took me aside to alert me to the fact that I was to be the security coordinator for a scheduled visit by Secretary of State Dean Rusk.

"I want you to ensure the security needed for the Secretary of State while he's here, Dolph," he told me. I was getting pulled more often into security functions for the U.S. Mission. The nearest U.S. Department of

State Regional Security Officer was based in Buenos Aires and covered an immense area of South America. Security for U.S. Embassies worldwide would dramatically change within eight years when the threat of terrorism intensified.

Abruptly, Ambassador Hoyt scrutinized the house full of guests and grew agitated.

"Where the hell is Horton?" he asked abruptly. He was concerned about the CIA Station Chief.

"I don't know, Mr. Ambassador," I told him, unconcerned. "He's around somewhere."

"Find him," the Ambassador told me nervously. "The Minister of Foreign Relations just arrived. Horton should be at the door, greeting people." The Ambassador walked away quickly, to greet the Uruguayan Minister of Foreign relations and his wife who were standing at the door.

Frustrated, I grabbed a drink and wandered through the house asking people if they knew where Horton was. No one knew, but at least four people asked why I asked, adding to my frustration.

I checked the outside of the rear of the Horton residence and in a partially lit back *patio*, John Horton was bending over peering intently into a clump of bushes.

"Here, *Pinqüino,* come here, boy," he called out. What a strange name for a dog, I thought.

"Who the hell are you calling, John?" I asked, startling him. Horton stood up, a drink in his hand and a wry smile on his face. He told me he was looking for his pet penguin and had him cornered. I scanned his face for signs of drunkenness.

Asking me to hold his drink, he pulled a nervous baby penguin out of the bush. The tiny penguin suddenly decided to get away and Horton chased after him as the little fellow made soft squealing sounds. We laughed when he caught the penguin. He explained that the penguin was a pet.

"Hell, yes," I kidded. "I didn't think you were going to eat him."

He stood up holding the penguin, a satisfied smile on his face.

"He's cute, isn't he?" he said. I had to laugh.

"Damn it John, the Ambassador's looking for you," I told him. "He sent me to look for you." The penguin continued to make soft noises and Horton patted his head unconcernedly.

"What the hell does he want me for?" Horton was very unpretentious.

"He wants to talk to you and the flipping penguin," I told him jokingly.

"John, the Foreign Minister just arrived and the Ambassador said you should be at the door, greeting the guests," I explained to him.

"Shit, I guess I better go inside," he turned to tell me. I liked Horton. He was different and made things enjoyable and fun.

The visit of U.S. Secretary of State Dean Rusk was announced later that week, in a Country Team meeting. We were told that the advance party of the State Department Office of Security (O/Sy) would arrive in Uruguay a week before the Secretary. Two officers from the O/Sy would accompany the Secretary of State and provide personal security. The size of the protective detail in terms of the local potential threat for the U.S. Secretary of State left me in dismay. I knew OPS personnel would have to fill the gaps.

One week before the Secretary of State arrived, we met with Inspector Ramiro Requierro and Inspector Guillermo Copello of the Montevideo Police Department to discuss the planning for police protection. Security had to be provided at the airport, the U.S. Embassy, the *Casa de Gobierno* (The Office of the President) and the Plaza *Independencia* where a wreath-laying ceremony was scheduled to take place. Inspector Requierro, the head of the uniformed police, and Inspector Copello, the head of Investigations for the Montevideo Police, responded magnificently to provide the security needed. The two Uruguayan police officers made everything easy and were a pleasure to work with. As veteran police officers they had acquired a unique sense of humor, despite their tough work situations.

On any operation, Requierro and Copello reminded me of New York cops working the Bronx. They joked incessantly with each other, kidding and bickering constantly. But when the crunch came, they were true professionals. They made fun of the O/Sy officers because they did not speak Spanish.

"*Éstos no hablan mierda de Español* (These two can't say shit in Spanish)," Copello told Requierro. "You talk to them, they won't know what the *mierda* you're talking about anyway."

Inspector Alejandro Otero, the Chief of *Inteligencia y Enlace,* provided an assessment of the potential threat against Rusk. The communist party planned to hold demonstrations, he reported.

"We assumed that," I told him. Otero suggested we carry weapons, he had no information on what the *Tupamaros* might try to do.

November 16, 1966, 1530 Hours

United States Secretary of State Dean Rusk arrived at *Carrasco* Airport on schedule. The day was cheerful, sunny and the situation looked good. The large crowd gathered at an upper tier outside the terminal building cheered and waved when Rusk appeared at the door of the U.S. Air Force plane that had brought him to Uruguay. Police personnel had closed off the area and Rusk walked out to be greeted by U.S. Ambassador Henry Hoyt and Vidal Zaglio, the Uruguayan Minister of Foreign Relations.

Following a brief interlude of ceremony and handshaking, Rusk and other dignitaries were escorted to designated cars and Inspector Requierro gave the policeman involved the signal to move. Bernal and I followed in our car behind the caravan as it traveled down the *Rambla* past the area called *Pocitos* and on to the U.S. Embassy. Two police officers were with us.

At the Chancery, police personnel held back a small group of spectators while Rusk and the Uruguayan and American officials with him entered the Chancery. Everything was diplomatically peaceful in the splendor of the bright Uruguayan sun. We disembarked from our cars and entered the Embassy while Rusk met with Uruguayan Ministers Ferreria Aldunante and Dardo Ortiz.

About twenty-five minutes later, Ambassador Hoyt walked out to advise me that they were ready to go. The caravan with Secretary Rusk proceeded to the *Casa de Gobierno* where a large crowd waited outside, controlled by police personnel. The crowd was friendly and cheerful enough, but in the group of spectators, communist agitators waited quietly to make their move. It was expected.

Waiting outside of the *Casa de Gobierno* (Government House), we chatted with the police officers with us and smoked cigarettes. Uruguayans loved to smoke and never turned down a cigarette. In Uruguay, especially among friends, it was considered impolite and uncultured to light up and not offer a cigarette to people around you.

Inside the *Casa de Gobierno,* Rusk met with the President of Uruguay, Washington Beltran, and the incoming President of the Governing Council, Alberto Heber. After the meeting, Rusk and the group with him walked outside the building. Rusk's cherubic smile generated applause when he stopped and waved to the crowd. The group entered cars parked outside the elegant governmental building just as shouts and screams filled the air.

Leaflets thrown in the air by individuals in the crowd littered the street. The police moved in quickly to make arrests. They were young people just having fun. The display was over in two to three minutes and Rusk did not appear to be aware of the incident.

Later, in our car, a solemn-faced police official handed me a leaflet he had picked up from the street. It said: "*Fuera del Uruguay Dean Rusk. Asesino de Vietnam y S. Domingo* (Dean Rusk, out of Uruguay. Assassin of Vietnam and Santo Domingo)." Pictures on the leaflets showed Dean Rusk wearing Nazi insignias and scowling. The police officers were surprised when we laughed at the depiction of Rusk in the leaflet. I explained that it was hard to see Secretary of State Dean Rusk with Nazi insignias and scowling.

A few minutes later, the caravan stopped at the *Plaza Independencia* in front of the *Victoria Plaza* Hotel. In front of the hotel was the site for the wreath-laying ceremony scheduled for the U.S. Secretary of State. The United States Secretary of State would lay a commemorative wreath at the foot of the statue of General Jose Artigas, the hero of Uruguayan Independence. Rusk had received favorable news in the local media. The communist press on the other hand, vehemently condemned his visit.

The crowd assembled to watch the ceremony at the *Plaza Independencia* numbered over 200 persons. A simple ceremony was planned, Ambassador Hoyt told me. But we had to be careful. Inspector Requierro had positioned his uniformed police personnel in a cordon in front of General Artigas's statue where Rusk was to lay a wreath. The police officers formed a tight line and held on to their batons to hold people back. But with their backs to the crowd, the uniformed police officers faced the statue of General Artigas to watch the ceremony. That was a mistake.

Inspector Guillermo Copello had loaded the crowd with his investigators and they were ready to take action if a problem arose. But hidden in the crowd of spectators, and unknown to us, a nineteen-year-old Uruguayan by the name of Jesus Roland Rojas planned to attack the American Secretary of State. He was not very bright, just anxious to advance his popularity and commitment to the communist party. The leading communist newspapers, *El Popular* and *Epoca,* were ready to capture on film the attack by the young Uruguayan patriot against the *Yanqui* imperialist. They waited for Rojas to attack.

A colorful Uruguayan military band played grandiose marching music and at a designated time, they played the Uruguayan national anthem and the American national anthem. There was a solemn silence in the air. I stood behind Ambassador Henry Hoyt and Secretary of State Dean Rusk facing the statue of General Artigas. To my left, Inspector

Alejandro Otero, the head of the police *Inteligencia y Enlace* nodded to let me know he was available if needed.

To the left of U.S. Secretary of State Dean Rusk were the Uruguayan Minister of Foreign Relations, Military *Attachés* and other Uruguayan Government Officials. The band stopped playing and moments later a designated Uruguayan Air Force Officer handed Rusk the commemorative wreath that was to be placed at the foot of the statue of General Artigas.

There was total silence and out of the corner of my right eye, I was surprised to see a human blur dash toward Rusk. The individual had broken through the police cordon. Moving quickly to my right I hit the subject with my shoulder and knocked him a few feet away from what I knew was his intended target, the U.S. Secretary of State. My hand went for the gun in my shoulder holster. I knew there would be only microseconds for me to shoot.

I quickly raised the sights of my gun to his body mass. But in a split second, the man stopped a few feet from Rusk and spit on him. In the blink of an eye, he cowered down and covered his face with his arms. That was no reason to kill him, I thought.

The small figure was obviously frightened and remained crouching, covering his face with his hands. Within seconds, the Uruguayan Air Force Officer next to Rusk jumped on him and other police personnel piled on. The man was beaten with fists and truncheons as he screamed out in fear. Otero reached him and applied a headlock. The young man struggled, provoking more blows from the officers. An Embassy Officer shouted at me with urgency in his voice.

"Dolph, don't let them make him a martyr." The worst thing we could do was to confer the title of martyr on the bastard, I thought. I shouted at the police officers in Spanish.

"*No lo hagan mártir, no lo hagan mártir!* (Don't make him a martyr, don't make him a martyr!)" I screamed at Otero and the police officers in Spanish to stop beating Rojas. The officers stopped and the young communist was removed from the premises.

When Rojas made his move to attack Rusk, agitators in the crowd had thrown leaflets in the air. Some had screamed obscenities and insults at the U.S. Secretary of State but that ploy was short-lived when Copello's men quickly entered the fray and arrested some of the agitators while the less militant fled, in a hurry to get away. The leaflets thrown at the scene were the same as those used at the *Casa de Gobierno* earlier.

Feeling anger I asked Bernal where the O/Sy Officer assigned to protect Rusk was.

"Taking pictures of the ceremony," he said calmly.

Nevertheless, Secretary Rusk remained unperturbed and displayed no sign of anger, fear, or nervousness. He calmly completed the wreath-laying ceremony with impressive dignity and poise and generated a warm round of applause from the crowd that remained. He left smiling, waving to the crowd who applauded even more.

The following day the communist *El Popular* published a touched-up picture of Rojas spitting on Dean Rusk in the front page of their newspaper. The story was replete with rhetoric that described a general disgust of the people of Uruguay in regard to the visit of the U.S. Secretary of State. The story was creative in true communist propaganda fashion and described that young Rojas had been brutally beaten by the police and Uruguayan military officers assisting the Americans on the scene. Despite that, my perception was that we were very lucky.

10

The *Tupamaros*

By early 1967, the Marxist *Tupamaro* guerrillas in Montevideo were in full swing, carrying out attacks throughout the city at opportune times and at different places in an effort to destabilize the government. Assaults on police officers and bank robberies increased and government officials were abducted without any way of preventing it. The kidnapping of Ulises Pereira Reverbel, a close friend of the President of Uruguay, was treated as a joke by the communist press. But his abduction made the point that no one was safe. Jokes abounded that Pereiria Reverbel was gay and that other gay individuals in the city were looking forward to being kidnapped.

The communist media promoted an unlikely "Robin Hood" image for the *Tupamaro* terrorists by using aggrandized stories that the guerrillas stole from the rich to give to the poor. To add to their mystique, the Marxist guerrillas had taken the name of *Tupac Amara,* the name of an Inca Indian Prince, killed in 1780 fighting Spanish rule in Peru. The *Tupamaros* claimed they were the liberators of the oppressed and fighters for freedom from the existing tyranny.

But where could a person get more freedom and liberty than in the country of Uruguay? The country was known as the *Switzerland of the Americas.* But the *Tupamaros* made their objective known: they were going to overthrow the government of Uruguay to establish a socialist/communist state.

In Washington, D.C., misguided ideologues continued to openly resist what they called U.S. intervention in the internal affairs of Uruguay. The internal ideological bureaucratic war within the United States Government was a distinct disadvantage for those Americans fighting communism in the Cold War. Lyndon Baines Johnson was a liberal and President of the United States and Uruguay was a true democracy. Again, where was the beef?

In Uruguay, the war was getting hotter with *Tupamaro* terrorist attacks and mass demonstrations against the government that were growing increasingly violent. I obtained a commitment from the Chief of Police of Montevideo that he would provide the *petrol* or gas needed to operate two dozen patrol cars on a twenty-four-hour basis so that the patrol units on the streets could be increased. Ambassador Hoyt and OPS officers in Washington, D.C., intervened to enable us to purchase the vehicles. The cars were equipped with police radios and emergency equipment. Additional uniformed police officers were trained in patrol techniques, the use of firearms and street survival. The major problem was the training of police officers to drive a car. Caesar Bernal began training that emphasized skills as policemen first and driver abilities after.

A young police official of Italian lineage by the name of Jose Bonaudi had graduated from the International Police Academy (IPA) in Georgetown, Washington, D.C., and was selected by the Chief of Police of Montevideo for a supervisory role in the new mobile patrol force. Bonaudi, a *Sub-Comisario* (Lieutenant), was a promising police official in the Montevideo police department. He would experience the first battle between the Montevideo police and the *Tupamaros,* albeit unknowingly. It was a deadly encounter.

The urban areas of Montevideo were usually crowded with people and busy during the week. Bonaudi and another patrol officer were dispatched to a bank robbery in progress and they responded in their new patrol car. At the location of the reported robbery, the officers saw a pickup truck rush from the scene at a high rate of speed until it reached the *Rambla,* a comely boulevard that stretched for miles along beautiful beaches. Bonaudi and his partner gave pursuit using their emergency equipment, unaware that those in the pickup truck were *Tupamaro* terrorists. The Montevideo police officers were surprised when they saw the tailgate of the pickup drop and two men in the back of the truck fired with automatic weapons at the patrol car and threw several grenades.

Bonaudi and his partner saw the gunmen take cover behind a parapet of reinforced concrete that had been installed in the back of the truck. The *Tupamaros* were prepared for combat.

Despite the automatic weapons fire directed at the police car, the officers continued in their pursuit. Apparently unnerved by the persistence of the Montevideo police officers, the driver of the pickup lost control and crashed into a large tree in the area of *Pocitos.* The police car stopped about 25 yards behind the truck.

The other police officer was wounded and Bonaudi responded frantically with his revolver, hitting one of the terrorists precisely on the forehead, killing him instantly. Seeing this, the other terrorist in the back of the truck dropped his gun and ran desperately through a maze of traffic. The driver of the truck quickly surrendered.

Police investigators found the pickup truck loaded with money, automatic weapons and homemade bombs. The *Tupamaros* had suffered an important blow and the incident was sensationalized in the local media. The new mobile patrol force was seen as a powerful addition to the Montevideo police force. But ten times more police cars were needed out in the street to cope with the security threat

Bonaudi's brave action against the *Tupamaro* guerrillas served to uplift the spirits of the entire police force. We complimented Bonaudi and the Director of the Patrol Force, *Comisario* Silveira Regalado, also a graduate of the International Police Academy. Both men were considered important assets for the police in the fight against the *Tupamaros.*

On the 23rd of December, Regalado and Bonaudi visited the American public safety advisors located at the *Oficina de Asistencia Tecnica,* at the Montevideo Police Headquarters. A bottle of Scotch was opened and we drank a toast for the holidays and to congratulate Bonaudi for his brave action. Bonaudi had killed one of the terrorists with a single shot between the eyes. *Comisario* Silveira Regalado described the weapons and bombs found in the truck. He concluded everyone was lucky.

Pumped up with adrenaline, Regalado told us about raids planned against *Tupamaro* hideouts and safe houses identified after an investigation was made. As American advisors, we were prohibited from participating in actual operations and would watch the war from the sidelines. It was the day before Christmas Eve.

Comisario Silveira Regalado and Bonaudi were cautioned to be very careful against the *Tupamaros* because the terrorists obviously had good armament. Regalado stood up and showed us a classic .45 caliber Thompson submachine gun equipped with a drum. He stroked the weapon jokingly with a paternalistic flair.

"Don't worry," he said. "Tomi will take care of any problem." He was referring to the Thompson. Silveira Regalado, a tall handsome officer, had an Errol Flynn style about him.

In the early evening of Christmas Eve, a small police task force had surrounded a rustic looking house located on *Jose L. Terra* and *Larrañaga* streets. It had been identified as a target for a police task force raid. As the police unit prepared to assault the residence, *Tupamaro* guerrillas inside the house became aware of this. A terrorist lookout had spotted the police and warned those inside the house.

The *Tupamaro* terrorists silently took positions to resist the raid on the innocent-looking abode. They knew it could result in a gunfight to the death. Outside the residence, *Comisario* Silveira Regalado took cover behind a tree. He moved in the darkness, holding his Thompson submachine gun. Police personnel waited for the order to assault the small *finca,* but Regalado unexpectedly ran to the front door of the residence and stopped.

The sudden move by *Comisario* Regalado surprised the other police officers of the task force. In another surprise move, Regalado kicked open the door and entered the house brandishing his .45 caliber Thompson submachine gun. The guerrillas inside the house scattered when Regalado entered. In the dim light, a crucifix was seen hanging upside down on a wall.

But *Comisario* Regalado froze in astonishment when he pulled on the trigger of the Thompson but nothing happened. The gun had inexplicably jammed. As he frantically pulled on the reloading mechanism of the Thompson, *Tupamaro* bullets tore into him. The task force assaulted but Regalado had mortal wounds.

Days later, *Comisario* Silviera Regalado lay in state at the Montevideo Police Headquarters in a coffin draped with the flag of Uruguay. Many people attended a service held to pay their respects to the brave police officer. The men from the Patrol Force provided an honor guard.

We sadly presented our condolences to Regalado's family and to the distressed Chief of Police. The economic hardship on the family would be enormous. It was clear that many good police officers were losing their lives in a senseless ideological conflict that had the capacity for destroying a beautiful country.

The Montevideo Police Headquarters, like most major police centers of the world, was always busy. American advisors with OPS had offices next to the Criminal Investigations Division of the Montevideo Police Department. Philip Agee alleged after his defection from the CIA that he often heard screams when he was in the building to imply that torture was going on inside the police headquarters.

But when Agee was in Uruguay, OPS had four Americans present on a daily basis in the building but not one reported hearing the screams alleged by Agee. Belligerent drunks, brawlers and often the mentally disturbed often cause disturbances, noises and screams common to any police station. The Montevideo Police Headquarters included a jail to hold prisoners. Many visitors were constantly in the building at all times, but no one ever reported hearing what Agee alleged in the five years that I was there. In addition, Uruguayans were not shy about reporting such occurrences.

As expected, Agee never produced proof to back up his allegations. He made the allegations in order to connect American police advisors to torture after he defected. But there were allegations made by the communist media in Uruguay that were difficult to explain.

Mirta Gorban, a pretty German/Uruguayan secretary at the *Oficina de Asistancia Tecnica* (OPS), was a trusted and loyal employee. She was pro-American and sensitive to the local politics and problems that affected the police assistance program. On one occasion she surprised me when she let me know that the communist newspaper, *El Popular*, had a very bad story about OPS.

"The article in the paper alleges this is an office of *espionaje* (espionage)," she explained in Spanish. "You know, *espias* (spies)," she said with uncertainty. She handed me a copy of the communist newspaper.

"You and Mr. Cantrell are mentioned in the article," she told me with a distressed look of concern on her face. She struggled with the English language when she was nervous or upset.

"You're not worried?" she asked, raising two sharp eyebrows above her blue eyes. I told her that I was not concerned about communist propaganda.

"I worry about all of us," she said. "And I like my job very much. I just hate the intrigue," she told me.

I told her not to worry and suggested that she should expect stories in the communist newspapers about Americans in Uruguay that were not true. She accepted that. But where was the truth?

Mirta served me *maté* and suggested worriedly that I be careful. She offered her opinion that the communists knew a great deal about what was going on in the American *"Oficina de Asistencia Tecnica"* at the *Jefatura*. She was right. The *Tupamaro* guerrillas, communists and sympathizers were infiltrated into the police.

The headlines of the communist newspaper *El Popular*, however, reported that the United States had infiltrated the Montevideo Police

Headquarters with an *"Oficina de Espionaje."* Bill Cantrell and I were identified as the prime participants in the "Office of Espionage," along with Juan Noriega, a CIA Officer assigned to the U.S. Embassy Political Section. But Noriega had nothing to do with the OPS in Uruguay.

"Dagnabbit," I thought humorously. "We all look alike."

The Americans assigned to the OPS program in Montevideo were frequently accused in the communist media of being spies and teaching repressive techniques to the police. But the most consistent accusation was that of intervention in the internal affairs of Uruguay. Intervention was known as a dirty word in Uruguay. The Governing Council of Government of Uruguay had voted against United States intervention in the Dominican Republic when President Lyndon Johnson sent U.S. troops to that country to prevent a communist takeover. Now, a similar problem existed in Uruguay, but now we were invited to intervene in the resolution of that threat.

The *Tupamaros* persisted in their attempts to destabilize the existing government and the climate of civil unrest continued. In this regard, the security forces were seriously handicapped by the lack of adequate communications in the urban crisis. **Paul Katz,** an OPS telecommunications engineer, arrived in Montevideo with another OPS technician named **Chuck Redlin.** Short, wiry, with wild red hair, Katz had a perpetually mean look about him. He was considered to be among the best in telecommunications but he also had experience in counterinsurgency operations. He had served with OPS in combat zones in Vietnam. When we first met I suggested to him that he was a shrimp ingrained with a Viet Cong mentality. He responded that he did not give a crap what I thought. Katz became my friend.

One month after his arrival in Montevideo, Katz had completed a design for a nationwide telecommunications system for the police. The system was desperately needed by the security forces to help them cope with the ongoing civil unrest and labor violence and to respond to the *Tupamaro* attacks.

The new communications system linked the police and military forces on a tactical frequency. The Minister of Interior, the Minister of Defense and the heads of the police, Army, Air Force and Navy were linked on an administrative frequency. The design of the system by Katz provided a nationwide capability for police telecommunications. A new operations center for the Montevideo Police was included in the plan. The total system would cost over three million dollars. The Government of Uruguay would help pay most of it.

Danilo Micali, the Director General of Police at the Uruguayan Ministry of the Interior, requested we meet with Katz to discuss the new telecom system and socialize a bit. Micali suggested we meet at *Pepito* Cantisani's bachelor apartment, since he had volunteered to cook *Capelleti al Tuco*…meat-filled pasta in a bacon-flavored white sauce…for us. Cantesani was a great gourmet cook. It would be an informal get together.

Micali and Cantisani were trusted friends. At the meeting Cantisani entertained everyone with jokes and hilarious tales about his love life. The many jokes about a nasty, foul-mouthed Italian kid were in Spanish. Katz did not understand Spanish and merely grunted. I translated a few of the jokes to Katz but told him the foul-mouthed kid was Jewish, like him. Katz said there was nothing wrong with the obscene language used by the kid in Cantisani's jokes. All his friends talked that way when he was growing up in New York, he said.

Cocktail parties and official receptions were part of our job. But Micali and *"Pepito"* were good friends and we had a great deal of trust in our relationship. Micali was very knowledgeable about the political situation and was appointed by the President of Uruguay. He proposed that the civil unrest that was spreading to the interior of Uruguay involved the *Tupamaro* guerrillas. They continued to hit at the economy. Sugar cane fields in Artigas near the Brazilian border were being burned by the terrorists.

The civil unrest was also growing like an evil omen in the major cities in the interior of Uruguay he said. We discussed the violence in Montevideo. In a plant lockout by union employees at FUNSA, a tire factory affiliated with Firestone, the facility was badly damaged when a huge communist-led mob attacked the compound with *Molotov* cocktails and pipe bombs.

Micali said that the communist party in Uruguay was pushing for a united popular front with a "People's Congress" that would unite labor and student groups and inexorably expand the violence. A united communist front had to be considered a grave threat to the Government of Uruguay. The Minister of the Interior would recommend to the Uruguayan Governing Council of Government the prohibition of a Moscow-sponsored Inter-American Congress of Solidarity for Cuba, scheduled to take place in Montevideo.

After that happened, a mob of about 5,000 people assembled at the *Palacio Peñarol,* the stadium of the World Champion Uruguayan soccer team, to protest of the government's decision on the "People's Congress." Led by communist agitators the huge crowd turned violent. Police contingents on the scene were attacked by the mob and tear gas, horses, batons and shields were used to control the violence. Many persons were injured.

The new CS tear gas and equipment provided by the OPS proved extremely helpful in controlling the large mob. But continuing economic woes were adding fuel to the civil unrest and violence. Inflation had increased twenty-six percent (26%) in the first few months of the year and there was no end in sight.

Micali informed us that the Government of Uruguay would "intervene" in the operations of the *Banco Nacional* by six o'clock the next morning and close the National Bank and other banks in Uruguay for an undetermined period. Uruguay had four government banks and sixty-three private banks including five hundred branches. Police and military personnel would surround the banks and forcibly shut them down. The devaluation of the Uruguayan peso would follow with serious economic consequences for the average citizen.

The measure was intended to improve the economy in the long term but would be difficult to explain to the citizens of the country. The U.S. Embassy was not aware this was about to take place. Internal security repercussions would be grave. It was expected that outbreaks of violence would be widespread and immediate.

The U.S. Embassy had to be notified because of the potential political impact and violence that would surely ensue. Late that night I explained the situation to John Topping, the Deputy Chief of Mission (DCM).

"Are you sure, Dolph?" he asked worriedly.

"Count on it, John," I told him without hesitation. He prepared a cable for dispatch to Washington.

At six o'clock the next morning, police and military personnel surrounded the banks and closed them. Shortly after, the *peso* plummeted from 24 *pesos* for one dollar to 60 *pesos* for one dollar.

Violence exploded almost immediately, with huge demonstrations against the Government of Uruguay (GOU) as a result of the devaluation of the peso. The GOU enacted a decree declaring a state of emergency and security measures were implemented. The internal security situation turned grave, with rumors of a military coup. But drastic changes were taking place in the Government.

The Minister of the Interior (MOI), Dr. Adolfo Tejera, and the Chief of the Montevideo Police General Ventura Rodriguez unexpectedly declared they would resign their positions after a public disagreement occurred between them over the release of five communist labor union leaders who had been arrested. Their resignations represented a serious setback for the country at a critical time, leaving a serious gap in the leadership needed for the management of the security crisis.

The entire management staff of the Montevideo Police Department resigned in a show of solidarity with the Chief of Police. There was no way to heal the breach between the two men. It had become a matter of honor. But the violence was growing worse.

Dr. Agosto Legnani, a practiced politician and a former Minister of the Interior, was appointed the new Minister of the Interior, and a veteran Uruguayan Army Colonel, Rogelio Ubach, was appointed Chief of Police. Both officials took the helm to lead the effort of coping with the civil unrest and the *Tupamaro* threat. We quickly established excellent working relationships. Sometimes we were obliged to get intimately involved with the security threats. It was starting to look like part of the job for me.

The Marine House

The neighborhood where we lived in *Carrasco* was generally peaceful and quiet except for occasional visits by burglars looking for an opportunity to steal anything. The noise of the telephone in my bedroom ringing angrily at two o'clock in the morning surprised me and I fumbled sleepily in the darkness to answer. *Lobo* scratched at the door and barked to let me know he was there in case he was needed. The dog was incredible. I let him into the bedroom and he lay quietly on the floor waiting for me to tell him what to do.

Bob Gershensen, the U.S. Embassy Administrative Officer, was on the phone. I knew that meant trouble if he was calling at two o'clock in the morning.

"Dolph," Gershensen said in a calm voice. "You've got to come to the Marine house right away." He said. "One of the Marines at the Embassy called me by radio. Someone placed bombs on the front and back door of the house." He paused, waiting for me to respond.

"What the hell do you want me do?" I asked sleepily. "I'm not a bomb expert!" The fact that the Embassy had not prepared for such an emergency upset me.

"We need **your** help," Gershensen said without explanation. "We've already called the police," he told me impatiently. I immediately suggested that he also call the military bomb squad.

"It's been done," he said. He continued to pressure me.

"The Ambassador suggested I call you." He knew it would be hard for me to say no if the Ambassador wanted me involved. He was not going to let me sleep.

"Okay," I told him. "I'll see you there in a few minutes." My wife woke up and sat up in bed.

"I'll be back in a few minutes. Go back to sleep." I told her, gently patting her.

"You know I won't be able to sleep," she retorted drowsily. I dressed quickly and strapped on my gun. *Lobo* walked out with me but I told him to go back into the house.

The Marine residence was an elegant brick house in *Carrasco* and home to about fifteen men assigned to protect the U.S. Embassy. The Marines had been hosting their Friday night Happy Hour when a late visitor arrived and discovered a cardboard box that had been placed at the front door. Another box had been placed at the back door. He immediately notified the Marines on guard duty at the Embassy.

When I arrived at the Marine residence, a police official outside told me they were waiting for the military bomb squad. The police official in charge recognized me and quickly explained that he knew nothing about handling bombs. A fire truck loaded with firemen dressed in colorful red uniforms also waited indifferently, presumably until the bombs exploded. Cardboard shoeboxes had been placed flush against the front door and back door of the residence. It was obvious that the innocent looking shoeboxes were firebombs.

The police official and a fire department captain cautiously examined the box placed at the back door.

"Son bombas," the captain from the fire department murmured.

The Marine residence had had plenty of guests that evening and several young ladies had remained after the "Happy Hour" party. The Marine Gunny Sergeant talked to us through the wrought iron bars on a window. The bars on all the windows now served to make the house a prison.

"We can't get out, all the windows are secured with wrought iron. The two side doors are also locked tight with wrought iron," the Marine sergeant explained with a face of embarrassment.

"And we don't have the fucking key," he added. It was presumed that if the front or back doors were opened, the bombs could go off. The people inside the Marine house were, in effect, trapped. Gershensen muttered in a deadpan monotone.

"Now what?" We walked to the front to take another look at the shoebox. I let Gershensen know that the firebombs would not provide us much time before they exploded. He stared at me as if to say, "so what are you going to do?" I knew the fuses on the bombs were sulfuric acid and potassium chlorate. The insides of the boxes were loaded with plastic bags of gasoline mixed with oil and explosives. Gershensen stared at me when I suggested the wrought iron bars might be able to be torn from the windows. It would take time.

"With what?" Gershensen responded hurriedly. "We will need explosives to get the wrought iron bars off," he told me worriedly. We knew the *Tupamaro* bombs had a reputation for causing very serious damage. I also knew the military bomb squad would not make it in time. They were home sleeping.

"We haven't much time to do anything," I suggested candidly. The fire department had only small tools and that made it difficult to rip off the wrought iron bars and would take too long. The bombs would explode before the bars could be removed. I explained the makeup of the bombs to the fire department captain and the top police official while Gershensen listened.

"The box has a cardboard cylinder inserted on the top that is loaded with sulfuric acid," I informed them. It was nothing more than a stupid cardboard tube from a roll of toilet paper. It was now used as a detonator. A piece of tissue paper fastened with a rubber band at the bottom was used to hold back the sulfuric acid until it burned through the thin paper. That generally took ten or fifteen minutes, depending on the thickness of the paper. Once the acid burned through the paper and hit a mixture of potassium chlorate, sugar and pulverized carbon, the bomb would ignite and explode. Any movement of the box could also cause it to explode. Cuban-trained guerillas commonly used this type of bomb.

The fire department captain was told to get his men ready to put out fires that would certainly take place. He looked anguished and issued orders to his men.

"Gunny, you better move everyone into the bathrooms," I suggested. He moved his head pensively.

"Are they gonna go?" Smoke-like vapors were already escaping from the cylinders on the boxes. The acid was eating its way through the thin tissue paper holding it. Time was critical.

Using my portable radio, I told the Gunny the firemen would move as fast as possible to put out the fires once the bombs exploded. But the radio volume on that end was too loud and everyone inside the residence heard the transmission. The women inside the house grew hysterical. Gershensen cursed softly.

There was no doubt about the ingredients that made up the bombs and water was an option if we hurried. If the potassium chlorate mixture could be soaked with water, combustion could be neutralized. But I was not sure there was time to do this. It was a serious risk.

The police official in charge was requested in Spanish to move the onlookers gathered at the scene away from the residence. I then convinced the Fire Department official in charge to let me try to get a couple of volunteer firemen to help disarm the bombs with water. He stared at me and nodded. Uruguay was no backwater country, only trained fire fighters were permitted to use their equipment. The man in charge agreed to my request and I addressed the firefighters. I decided my best approach was to challenge their *machismo*.

"*Escuchen, quien tiene suficiente pelotas para echarle aqua a los bombas?* (How many of you have the balls to help us spray water on the bombs?)" I asked in a loud voice, holding back a grin. The immediate reaction of the firefighters was one of indignation.

"*Estan locos los Gringos,*" one of the firemen muttered.

"*Es muy ariesgado!* (The *Gringos* are crazy. It is too risky!)" he repeated. The firemen were attractive in their bright red uniforms but now were mere spectators.

"We know it is risky," I let them know with annoyance.

"*Se precisa cojones* (You need balls to do this)." The firemen grew silent and I felt let down. It was Cold War chickenshit.

Suddenly, two young firemen stepped forward.

"*Yo,*" they told me in unison. I involuntarily broke into a smile. We had a slim chance to neutralize the firebombs, but had to move as quickly as possible, before the detonators worked to explode the bombs. The risk was growing and here I was again, a *Pendejo* and a risk taker.

I instructed the two young firefighters to get the smallest hoses they could find in the fire trucks and I urged them to hurry.

"*Muy bien, muy bien* (Very good, very good)," I encouraged them in a calm voice as we walked to the front door. The two young firefighters were told to stand about five feet from the bomb and to adjust the spray of water from their hoses to a very fine mist. The shoebox had to be saturated with water.

Suddenly, one of the firemen stopped and held back, seemingly scared. Impulsively I cursed in Spanish. We were taking too much time. I told him to let me have the hose and he vigorously shook his head.

I moved to forcibly take the hose from him but his partner, a lean handsome Italian lad, reacted.

"*No seas maricón!* (Don't be a faggot!)" he screamed at the other. The youngster reacted with irritation.

"*Muy bien,*" he said with an embarrassed look. They both moved closer and began to spray the fine mist of water on the bomb. People there broke out in laughter.

Chuckling impulsively, I asked the young firefighter, "*Cómo te llamas?* (What's your name?)" He blinked, hesitating as if he had forgotten what his name was.

"Panagatti," he stuttered out his name shyly.

"*Muy bien, Panagatti, adelante con la aqua, vamos!* (Very good Panagatti, come on, let's spray some water)" I stood by the two young firemen, encouraging, cajoling, and joking with them as they sprayed a fine mist of water on the cardboard box for what appeared to be a long time. But it actually took less than two minutes to completely soak the box with water.

Saturated completely with water, the cardboard box fell apart and revealed two large plastic bags loaded with black powder, gasoline and oil. The bomb could not possibly function at that point. I urged the two young men to hurry to the back door of the house where the other bomb was.

My concern increased by a thousand percent. Smoke was already wafting ominously upward from the miniature funnel formed by the toilet paper roll. There were seconds to go before the bomb exploded. Nervously, the young firemen began to soak the cardboard box with water.

When it was completely soaked, the box with the sulfuric acid and the mixture of explosives fell apart. It took less than fifty seconds. People cheered and the two young firemen jumped up and down in excitement. They had scored a goal.

"It's over, Bob," I announced cheerfully to Gershensen. People around us applauded.

"That's great, Dolph," he told me with a sigh of relief. The Marine residence grew noisy as the young ladies trapped inside became overwhelmed with emotion and cried out loud. I wondered if they would ever attend another "Happy Hour" at the Marine house.

Panagatti and his partner hugged each other happily. Other firemen patted them on the back to congratulate them.

"*Bien hecho, bien hecho* (Well done. Well done)," they told them.

My knees were stiff from bending over, but I hugged them both.

"*Muy bien hecho* (Very well done)," I told them happily. We were fortunate to have their help.

Grabbing Gershensen by the arm I suggested that we owed the two young men something for their fine help. He grinned broadly.

"Don't worry, we'll take care of it," he assured me. "Thanks for **your** help," he said.

"Don't worry, you owe me, too," I told him and he snorted a laugh. Gershensen was obviously not aware of the serious risk we took in taking the time to disarm the bombs. Fortunately, the terrorists had used thick tissue paper to hold back the acid, perhaps to ensure their own safety.

After the incident at the Marine house, we conducted demonstrations to show the police how the bomb was put together and how it worked. The new Deputy Chief of Police, Colonel Juan Morales, attended one of the demonstrations held, along with police forensic personnel. Everyone was impressed by the destructive power of the bombs. It took a simple mixture of chemicals to create them.

The CIA Chief of Station estimated that the *Tupamaros* had less than four hundred hardcore men and women in their organization. My assessment of the *Tupamaro* strength was higher.

For me it was the hidden underground apparatus of the guerrillas that made them so dangerous to the Government of Uruguay. *Comisario* Otero and others in the local intelligence community believed that many of the *Tupamaros* were members of the *Inteligencia*. But many of the *Tupamaros* were university students and young teenagers with a delirium. They used police uniforms, the work clothes of local utility companies, frocks worn by priests and nuns and other creative apparel to carry out terrorist acts and kidnappings. Young teenage girls were used for surveillance and as lookouts.

It seemed obvious to me that *Tupamaros* had infiltrated the police, the armed forces, student and labor groups, the USAID and the U.S. Embassy. Organized into cells, the terrorists had safe houses dispersed throughout the country loaded with guns, food and the materials needed to fabricate grenades and bombs of all types. A few *Tupamaro* hideouts contained human cages—**"the people's prisons"** they were called—with fake walls cleverly constructed that concealed people and weapons. (Six were discovered when the *Tupamaros* were finally dismantled.) The guerrillas had access to hospitals, x-ray equipment and operating tables to care for the wounded. Some of the members of the *Tupamaros* were known to be medical doctors or skilled medical students.

My estimate was that the *Tupamaros* had sufficient money, weapons and resources to support a combat army of over 2,500 men. It crossed my mind that the *Tupamaros* were infiltrated into every segment of society in

Uruguay and unknowingly we were in contact with them. The situation was capable of driving one into paranoia.

The importance of training for the Uruguayan police grew by leaps and bounds. Caesar Bernal provided technical assistance for the firearms training which was desperately needed. The firearms training became popular for many top military officers assigned to the police. But our *machismo* was constantly challenged.

On one occasion a short amicable Uruguayan Army colonel assigned to the Office of the Minister of the Interior asked me to go with him to visit a firearms training session held with OPS assistance. We arrived at the range and about fifty police officers were undergoing training in combat shooting.

It was a beautiful day and the students appeared to be enjoying the training. The left wing called it United States training of death squads. The Colonel unexpectedly pulled out a .45 caliber automatic pistol and suggested that we take a few minutes to shoot a few rounds. I humorously recalled later that for a split second, when he pulled his gun out, the thought occurred to me that the colonel was a *Tupamaro.*

With Bernal's approval, the colonel and I agreed to shoot from the twenty-five yard line at silhouette targets. I would use my .38 caliber S&W Combat Masterpiece. Bernal temporarily suspended student firing and the young police officers gathered behind to watch us shoot. On my right, the colonel braced his .45 caliber automatic pistol on his bare arm and prepared to fire.

"Hold on, Colonel," I asked him placidly. "You're not going to fire that automatic that way, are you?" He smiled, seemingly upset with my question.

"I always shoot this way," he responded with a trace of indignation.

"Muy bien," I told him. "It does not seem to be a good idea to shoot that way."

The first shot fired by the colonel with his automatic singed the hair on his bare arm. I remained silent, pretending not to notice. The colonel, however, apparently changed his mind after the first shot and decided to shoot with his arm extended, off hand.

Amused, I continued to shoot at the silhouette target and my first shot was in circle number ten in the black. The high velocity service rounds I was using instead of wadcutters made it difficult to see the impact of my hits on the black silhouette target from twenty-five yards.

"No pega mierda (He didn't hit shit)," one of the police officers watching from behind us observed sarcastically after my first shot hit the

target. I fired five more rounds, in rapid succession. The young police officers watching us shoot argued about whether or not I was hitting the target.

"I don't seem to be hitting the target," I told them jokingly in Spanish, laughing when one of the police officers standing directly behind me muttered once again.

"No pega mierda!" The group burst into laughter. "The *Gringo* missed every shot," he said again. Another officer rebutted.

"Si pega (He did hit)," the officer told the others.

"He may be right," I told them in Spanish. "I did hit the target."

We had fired six rounds in ideal conditions. There was almost no wind, so my sights were held at six o'clock and every round squeezed off. I knew where my hits were. When the colonel finished shooting, the police officers participating in the training course made a mad scramble to check the targets. I remained on the firing line with my gun holstered and smoking a cigarette.

"Hijo-de-puta," I heard one of the young police students exclaim.

"He hit every one in the bulls-eye!" All my shots were in a tight group and in the center of the bulls-eye. It was easy to impress people that were just learning to shoot. In reality, Bernal, Cantrell, Lindenauer and I were excellent shots and were frequently pressured to prove our shooting ability and *machismo* by the Uruguayan military and police officers.

Trienta y Tres

The Chief of Police of the Department of *Trienta y Tres* invited the officers of OPS to spend a few days at his large *finca* (ranch) in the interior of Uruguay to discuss police training scheduled for his department. The new Minister of Interior, Dr. Jimenez de Arechega, was in full agreement that police courses be held as soon as possible at *Cerro Largo* and *Trienta y Tres,* two border Provinces. The Chief of Police of *Trienta y Tres* was not a military man but a wealthy landowner.

The Departments (Provinces) were charming bountiful areas of green rolling hills and prosperous cattle country in the Northeast part of Uruguay on the Brazilian border and near the Atlantic Ocean. Caesar Bernal, Julian Lindenauer and I accepted the invitation to *Trienta y Tres.* Bill Cantrell declined. He was growing wary and possibly saw the trip as a security risk. The U.S. Embassy Political Officer, Nicholas (Nick) McClausland, asked if he could join us in Cantrell's place.

Trienta y Tres translates in English to Thirty-Three. The province is named in honor of General Artigas and his original thirty-three brave warriors who fought with him to gain independence from Spain. The *finca* or ranch in the province that we visited had hundreds of acres and plenty of fine horses, cattle, green rolling hills and blue skies that seemed picture perfect.

We were told that during our stay at the beautiful *hacienda*, we would be treated to a traditional barbecue called *asado con cuero*. That type of barbecue was commonly prepared in the rural areas of Uruguay. We were told that an entire side of beef would be cooked slowly over hot coals for about seven hours with the hide of the animal left intact. The *Gaucho* chef promised that when he finished cooking the beef, the hide of the animal would not be burned at all and would be untouched by the fire. In explaining the process of cooking an *asado con cuero,* the Chief of Police guaranteed that it was truly a feast for carnivores. He was right.

Festivities at the ranch began with straight shots of Scotch for everybody. No ice was available. Following a period of heavy drinking and socializing, the Americans were challenged to a shooting match and this was to be followed by a horse race. *Gringos* against the Uruguayans, they insisted with loud laughter. It amused me as an American Hispanic from New Mexico to hear people in Latin America call **me** a *Gringo*. Growing up as a kid I called everyone *Gringo* except my friends. When I used it, it was meant to be contentious and derisive.

The shooting match that was held consisted of shooting at bottles and cans. The OPS officers were judged to have won. But the horse race was a different matter. The *Gringos* were matched against the best *Gaucho* rider on the ranch. McClausland and Bernal refused to race. Lindenauer also declined so I was left as the only one willing to ride against the *Gaucho*. The ranch hands kidded me about my *machismo* in order to get me to accept the challenge. What they did not know was that as a westerner raised in New Mexico, I loved horses.

The Chief of Police introduced a stern-looking *Gaucho* named Jose as my opponent. I was assured that the horse chosen for me was a good one, frisky, but a very fast mount. I mounted the horse and it immediately started to buck. I settled the horse down and the Chief of Police kidded that the horse was just not amenable to *Gringos*. With prodding the horse responded and I patted his neck, whispering to him in Spanish. I laughed to tell the Chief that the horse was now confused because I was speaking Spanish.

The rush I felt from the straight shots of Scotch consumed earlier made me happy and eager to compete. I dramatically announced to the *Gauchos*, "it is an honor and a privilege for me to compete in this fine competition between friends." I faked an involuntary hiccup and the

Gauchos erupted in a roar of laughter. They presumed I was drunk. But I was serious as hell.

The race was to start at a far point of the extensive ranch and finish about three miles later near where the meat had been cooking for hours over hot coals. Two of the ranch hands held bandanas up in the air to mark the starting point and two police officers did the same at the point where the race was to finish. My *Gaucho* opponent and I held back our mounts and waited for the Chief of Police to shoot his pistol in the air.

My horse was nervous but when the gun went off I dug my heels into his belly and he took off at a fast gallop. The excitement of the race grew and I rode my horse with pleasure and very comfortably.

The Chief of Police of *Trienta y Tres* was right, my horse was a very fast mount. Both horses ran neck and neck while my opponent and I shouted, using our reins as a whip. Loud screams and shouts filled the air when the horses approached the finish line. It was truly a memorable and exciting race. Amidst the screams of the *Gauchos* and ranch hands I instinctively urged my mount on and the horse surged ahead by at least two lengths to win the race. Reining my horse back, he slowed down. I then pulled hard on the reins to make the animal stand up on his hind legs. The horse did this beautifully, until the other horse and my opponent crashed into us.

My *Gaucho* opponent fell from his horse and rolled out of control into the hot coals of the barbecue that were still smoldering on the ground. Everyone had charged to the finish line after the race. The meat had been removed from the fire and the cooks were already cutting the *Asado con Cuero* to serve the guests. Pandemonium broke loose when Jose rolled into the hot coals on the ground. The ranch hands roared with laughter while he frantically brushed hot coals off his ass and back. Jumping up and down he cursed violently while hot embers continued to smoke and burn on his clothes.

From the top of my horse, I shouted an apology to Jose but the ranch hands erupted in boisterous laughter. They screamed to tell Jose that the *Gringo* had deliberately knocked him into the fire.

Laughingly, the Chief of Police congratulated me on winning the horse race. The *Gauchos* liked the race, and I was presented with a huge piece of meat as a prize. The hide of the animal was still on the enormous steak on my plate and was untouched by the fire. A *Gaucho* deftly cut the large piece of meat away from the hide with a sharp knife. With *Vino tinto* (red wine) and homemade bread, the steak was absolutely delicious and tender. I had never eaten a piece of beef like that in my life. The entire side of beef was consumed.

Our visit to the ranch was very enjoyable and a lot of fun. Before we departed, the Chief of Police gave me a gift that I treasure to this day. It was an antique silver stirrup from the days of the Spanish oligarchy and General Artigas. It was my prize for winning the horse race, he told me. It was an unforgettable trip.

Life seemed full of surprises. Shortly after our trip to *Trienta y Tres,* Nicholas McClausland, the U.S. Embassy Political Officer, traveled to San Francisco, California, for his "home leave." While he was there, he was allegedly arrested in a gay bar in San Francisco and had resigned from the Foreign Service.

McCausland was a very intelligent and effective diplomat. But we found out later that he was a target of the *Tupamaro* guerrillas. A decade later, getting caught in a gay bar was not a problem for anyone. But an American diplomat getting abducted by the *Tupamaros* in Uruguay was.

It soon became clear that many Americans in Uruguay were attractive targets for the *Tupamaro* guerrillas. The guerrillas tried with me one late afternoon in February. Sergeant Emilio Gonzales, my police driver, drove the car home from my office and I sat in the front seat with him. When we entered the driveway to my residence, Gonzales tilted his head in the direction of a truck parked in front of my house.

"*Tupamaros, señor!*" he said tersely. I nodded in agreement. I told him to get out of the car. Immediately after we parked, three young men dressed in blue work clothes walked to us from the truck parked out in the street. All three had jackets on and that caught my attention. One individual had remained sitting in the driver's seat of the truck. The three men came closer and my revolver snapped noisily from my clamshell upside-down shoulder holster.

Gonzales told me later that it was impressive to see the gun appear so quickly in my hand. Pointing my gun at the individual leading the pack, I ordered them to halt in a loud voice.

"*Alto.*" The three men stopped about fifteen yards away. Their faces turned baleful and they glanced at each other with uncertainty. That made it pretty suspicious that they were *Tupamaros.* Gonzales had also raised his gun and was now pointing it at the three men in our yard.

My children's voices were audible inside the house. My mind raced as I cocked the hammer on my revolver. Milliseconds counted in any firefight and with the hammer on my gun cocked it would be hard for me to miss my first shot. I asked the men what they wanted.

"*Somos de OSE,*" one of them said offhandedly. They claimed to be from the government-operated water utility. It was not known as an officious work force. Why four of them, I wondered? I warned the individuals not to come any closer and yelled loudly to our maid inside the house.

"Maria," I shouted. Maria was a tough live-in maid with Brazilian roots and built like a pro linebacker. She had worked for us for over two years. She stuck her head out of the kitchen window and her eyes opened in fear when she saw the spectacle in our front yard.

"Tú llamaste a OSE? (Did you call OSE?)" I asked her. Her response left no doubt in my mind.

"No, Señor!" she told me emphatically, vigorously shaking her head. She let me know that my wife and our oldest daughter Lori had gone to the grocery store.

I told her in a low voice to let *Lobo,* our dog, out of the house. Less than a minute later, to my astonishment, Maria stepped out of the door of the house with a huge knife in her hand and holding *Lobo* at her side. I lost control of the situation.

The men from *OSE* broke and ran desperately to their truck. Gonzales ran after them, threatening to shoot if they did not stop. It would have been easy to drop all three but the congested residential area made it risky. I came very close to using my gun and had to exercise very strong restraint not to shoot.

The men from *OSE* lunged desperately into the back of the truck. *Lobo was* on their heels and I called the dog back angrily. He stopped as the vehicle sped away at a high rate of speed. There was no license plate on the truck.

Gonzales used the radio in the police car to inform the Montevideo Police Operations Center about the situation at my house and provided a description of the truck involved. A few minutes later he let me know that the police officers at the communications center told him that *OSE* supervisors were adamant that they had **not** sent any of their employees to my residence.

Afterwards, lightheartedly, I asked Maria what she intended to do with the huge knife.

"Cortar bolas! (Cut some balls off!)" she told me with a serious face. I believed her.

Ironically, the same Sergeant Emilio Gonzales was Dan Mitrione's driver when the *Tupamaro* guerrillas kidnapped him. Gonzales carried a .38 caliber revolver but Mitrione was unarmed. Gonzales had been hit on the head and knocked unconscious when the kidnapping took place. Mitrione was brutally beaten by the *Tupamaros* for no reason and then shot on his side when the guerrillas panicked.

In discussing the *Tupamaro* visit to my house with Bob Gershensen, the Embassy Administrative Officer, we concluded that things would become riskier for Americans in Uruguay. I already was assigned as a member of the U.S. Embassy Internal Security Subcommittee and helped resolve security problems for the U.S. Mission.

One week later I received some bad news that caught me totally by surprise. My father died unexpectedly from a heart attack and I traveled to Las Cruces, New Mexico, with a heavy heart. Since he was a veteran of World War I, a military funeral was held for him, and as a retired Captain and Deputy Chief of Police, the Las Cruces police force provided an honor guard for him.

Earlier when we visited, my father had told me he liked what the United States was doing with OPS in other countries. After the funeral service, alone at my mother's house I could not help but shed tears for my father, perhaps in an involuntary release of stress. My mother worried to see me so afflicted with grief and asked me to return home to New Mexico. She had no idea what we were doing in Uruguay.

11

The Summit

In Uruguay, the struggle continued unabated for three years, with the *Tupamaros* practicing the art of terrorism and violence. The Cuban and Soviet Embassies continued to support labor unrest, student violence and the guerrillas. As a matter of foreign aid policy, the United States, through the OPS program, provided technical assistance and equipment to upgrade the overall capabilities of the security forces of Uruguay.

The new communications system for the police was now operational and improved police response time and command and control. The training of police personnel was also showing results. The police were fighting back and numerous *Tupamaros* had been killed or arrested.

Violent clashes between the police and the *Tupamaros* invariably resulted in casualties on both sides. There was no way to fight a bloodless war. The guerrillas were growing more aggressive, and the kidnappings of government officials and attacks on police officers increased. The growing strength of the security forces was now a major obstacle for the guerrillas, but the internal war put the members of the local security forces and American OPS advisors in the position of pawns in the deadly ideological conflict in Uruguay. Unfortunately, some would die before the conflict ended.

Police Inspector Moran Charquerro was an intelligent and valued friend of the OPS police advisors. But as a tough, respected police veteran and effective combatant against the *Tupamaros*, he was feared by the guerrillas. He became a coveted target for the *Tupamaros* and was eventually killed. Moran Charquerro was ruthlessly gunned down in cold blood and his body riddled with forty bullets, indicating that the *Tupamaros* were terrified of the Inspector. He did not have a chance to defend himself.

We felt a deep sorrow because Moran Charquerro was a patriot and a good man. He was merely effective in his job of combating the *Tupamaros*. Leaflets left at the scene of his brutal murder provided a threat to other police officers as well as the *Yanqui* Imperialists who were working with the police. It was in effect an ominous warning for all Americans in Uruguay. Sadly, Inspector Moran Charquero had paid with his life in the service of his country, in a senseless and brutal ideological war.

The Chief of Police agreed that OPS advisors should carry their guns and police I.D. cards were provided. I carried my .38 caliber S&W Combat Masterpiece revolver in an upside down shoulder holster and it appeared that became well known to the *Tupamaro* guerrillas and sympathizers infiltrated in the police.

In the communist propaganda film produced by Costa Gavras and Franciso Solinas, titled **State of Siege,** Dan Mitrione was shown carrying a gun in a shoulder holster. The truth is that Dan Mitrione did not carry a gun and was not carrying a gun when the *Tupamaros* kidnapped him. Yves Montand portrayed Dan Mitrione in the movie and wore a shoulder holster and a gun similar to mine in the film. Many Americans who saw the movie were awed by the propaganda film produced by Costa Gavras and Francisco Solinas, card-carrying members of the Communist Party of France and Italy, respectively, and believed the film was based on fact. In essence, the film was pure fabrication.

But the Cold War was often unpredictable. The top leadership of the Communist Party of Uruguay was appalled by Mitrione's cold-blooded murder and denounced the *Tupamaros* as **"insane fanatics!"**

In June 1987, the New York Times reported the following. **"Raul Sendic, the former leader of the *Tupamaro* guerrillas in Uruguay, had said there was no intention to kill Dan Mitrione, the American police advisor whose death became the basis for the film, State of Siege."** The *Tupamaros* had in fact made a terrible mistake in murdering Mitrione because the people of Uruguay turned violently against them.

Raul Sendic had been captured by the police and was in prison, unable to communicate with the *Tupamaro* terrorists holding Mitrione when he was murdered. Sendic had been shot in the jaw in a confrontation with Uruguayan security forces and could not talk. He later said a *Tupamaro* cell **"acted independently to kill Mitrione."** (It was later revealed that an idiot called Antonio Mas Mas had killed Mitrione on his own. But what triggered the assassination was the failure to negotiate an ultimatum that had been set by the terrorists and eventually ignored.)

Under the conditions that existed in Uruguay, many United States policy makers believed that assistance to the security forces of the country was necessary if democracy was to be preserved in the *Switzerland of the Americas*. Albeit, the hard-core Washington ideologues wanted OPS out of Uruguay. We were having trouble identifying the enemy in the politics of the Cold War.

But there were too many people dissatisfied with their lives in many countries and communism seemed an attractive opportunity for change. My own concern was to finish my tour of duty in Uruguay without getting bushwhacked. OPS Officers in overseas posts consistently faced the risk of being royally fustigated on the job and their careers destroyed. Some were being killed. We operated overtly against a hidden enemy.

The Country Team was comprised of the top officers of the U.S. Embassy who met on a weekly basis to discuss matters related to the political situation in Uruguay. They provided advice to the U.S. Ambassador on political and economic issues and on the security situation.

I would walk to the Embassy for those meetings from the *Jefatura* whenever possible. It was a nice walk with plenty of attractions. Gonzales or Ovedo, my police drivers, would follow me in the car. As I walked to the Embassy one day, the bright sun seemed to be a reminder that the beautiful beaches of Uruguay were not far away. But neither were the *Tupamaro* guerrillas. The risks were growing unpredictable.

When I reached the Chancery, a nervous young man in front of the building attempted to take my photo. Reacting instinctively, I knocked the camera from his hands. My hand went for the gun in my shoulder holster and the young man's face turned pale. Desperately pushing his way through people, he ran through a maze of cars until he was out of sight. I considered myself lucky. The young man could have had a gun instead of a camera. I suspected that my photo was needed to complete *Tupamaro* dossiers.

Inside the Embassy, U.S. Air Force Colonel Lorenzo Caliendo was at the door of the conference room. Cal was a New Yorker of Italian descent and the commander of the U.S. Military Assistance Group (U.S. Mil Group) in Uruguay. He was my close friend.

"We're coming over for drinks tonight, Dolph," he told me when he saw me. "Keep that fucking dog or wolf you call *Lobo* inside the house until Dottie and I can get out of the car." Caliendo chuckled and put his arm around my shoulder.

"That son-of-a-bitch doesn't like me," he suggested lightheartedly, making me laugh. Cal and I had been working together with the military commanders to set up joint planning and operations between the police and military forces to combat the *Tupamaros.*

"*Lobo* doesn't like anyone except my son Eric," I told Caliendo. "Eric feeds him big chunks of good raw meat at my expense. *Lobo* doesn't care about anything else except his steaks and getting laid once in awhile." Colonel Caliendo laughed out loud and sat next to me for the meeting. I admired my friend Cal. He was a Senior Command Pilot, pragmatic and an outspoken and tough commander.

Minutes later, Ambassador Henry Hoyt walked in with John Topping, the Deputy Chief of Mission (DCM), and people in the room rose to their feet. Later, the Ambassador asked for reports on the economic, political and security situation. Reports on the continuing civil unrest, the *Tupamaros* and the progress made by the Government of Uruguay on resolving economic issues were made.

After other people reported whatever information they had, I mentioned internal security problems and in the process carelessly described a friendly visit with the Uruguayan Army officer in charge of the Metropolitan Guard *(Guardia Metropolitana).* He was a tough, strong military officer and a fan of General Ongania, the Military dictator of Argentina. He had shown me an autographed picture of the General decked out in his military dress uniform. General Ongania and General Alfredo Stroessner, the Military Dictator of Paraguay, had the type of strong leadership needed in Uruguay, he suggested. To illustrate a point, he suggested that Stroessner did not allow beards in Paraguay in reference to Fidel Castro and *Ché* Guevara who both had full beards. The colonel contended that communism did not flourish with military governments in control. Apparently, a military dictatorship and communist dictatorship were different.

In my visit, he had offered his opinion that a military takeover in Uruguay might eventually become necessary because of the increasing problems of internal security, the growing chaos in the country and the *Tupamaro* threat. My remarks attracted Ambassador Hoyt's attention.

"What did you tell him?" Ambassador Hoyt asked in a voice of concern. Lt. Colonel Rudy Tamez, the U.S. Army *Attaché*, straightened up in his chair. He often added comments on the security situation to show the Ambassador that he was on top of things.

"I told him that a military takeover would worsen the security crisis and create monumental problems for everyone," I responded.

The Ambassador sighed audibly. He would probe the Embassy Political Section, the U.S. Military *Attachés* and CIA Station Chief on the possibility of a military *coup* in Uruguay. Immediately, the representatives of those offices were asked to refute or support the possibility of a military *coup* in Uruguay.

Jim Tull, the new U.S. Embassy Political Officer, stretched information he had available to conclude that a military *coup* was always possible but very unlikely in Uruguay at this time.

John Horton, the CIA Station Chief, stared at me with a puzzled look that indicated I had lost my mind. He reported in a semiserious tone that he was not aware of any activity in connection with a *coup* in Uruguay.

Caliendo smiled and nodded toward Lt. Colonel Rudy Tamez, who had grown pensive. Tamez, a sharp, handsome, ambitious young military officer, was caught by surprise by my report. But he also had a bulging hangover. The Ambassador queried him on the possibility of a military *coup* in Uruguay.

"Yes, sir, Mr. Ambassador," he began. His voice rose to enunciate a firm commitment. "We believe a military *coup* may be imminent!" The Ambassador's face grew dark.

Tamez described Uruguayan military troop movements the day before near *Pando,* a small city near Montevideo. He could not have said a worse thing. The Ambassador immediately tasked everyone present to obtain information on the issue and to report back as soon as possible. Several officers in the meeting including myself tried to allay the U.S. Ambassador's fears about a military takeover. My report was now a problem.

Before the meeting ended, the Ambassador announced a surprise of his own. A Summit Conference was to be held in Uruguay from April 12 to April 14, 1967. The meeting of the Chiefs of State of the Nations of the Inter-American system was an important political event in view of the Cold War.

That meant Uruguay would be swarming with reporters, security personnel and the staffs of twenty or more Presidents from Latin America, including the President of the United States, Lyndon B. Johnson. This was no time for a military *coup* in Uruguay. But the Summit itself could open a window for the *Tupamaro* terrorists to do some serious damage.

John Horton pulled me aside after the meeting with a twisted grin on his face.

"That crap about a *coup* is all bullshit," he told me, chuckling through his teeth. Horton took his job to heart. He did not have any information about a military takeover in Uruguay.

"You heard Tamez," I responded with a laugh. "He said a *coup* is **imminent!**" Horton stared at the wall.

"I think he was led astray." My report was growing worrisome. I suggested to Horton that in my humble opinion a military *coup* in Uruguay was very unlikely at this point in time.

"Hah, humble opinion," he smirked. "It's that damn *tequila* you've been drinking with Caesar Bernal, Rudy Tamez and Juan Noriega. That shit drives all of you plain crazy."

"Now how in the hell did you know we've been drinking *tequila*, John?" I asked, feigning surprise. Bernal, Tamez, Noriega, and I had consumed over a half a gallon of *tequila* two nights before. The *tequila* had been a gift from a Mexican official at a trade fair.

"Have you been spying on us?" I asked cuttingly. Horton laughed out loud.

"I know everything," he said mockingly and walked away.

March 13, 1967

A few days later, a Summit Memorandum signed by U.S. Ambassador Henry Hoyt dated March 13, 1967, assigned John Horton and myself functional responsibilities for security support matters for the Summit Conference. We would support Uruguayan officials with a security system and with the security preparations needed for the Summit. The Summit would be held at *Punta del Este,* an internationally famous and beautiful seaside resort area.

The following week, my wife Jan and I attended a farewell reception for Philip Agee and his wife, also named Jan. Agee's wife was a gracious woman, seemingly unaware of her husband's dark side. Agee was being transferred to Mexico. It was surprising to me because Agee was already vocal about his problems with the CIA.

March 19, 1967

Colonel Raul Barloco, the new Chief of Police of Montevideo, was a noble gentleman, a respected military officer and a man with a kind heart and a delightful sense of humor. He asked that we meet to discuss the security needed for the conference.

At the meeting, it was suggested to the Chief of Police that staff officers be named as soon as possible to manage the planning and security preparations for the conference site at *Punta del Este.* As a result, Colonel Santiago Acuña, the Chief of Staff for the Montevideo Police Department, was appointed to manage the security operations of the police at the Summit.

In early March, Dr. Agosto Legnani, the Uruguayan Minister of the Interior, requested our presence at a meeting held on the Summit Conference and attended by top Uruguayan military and police officials. General Alfonso Gonzales, the head of Army Region 4, Colonel J. Carabajal, the Uruguayan Army Chief of Intelligence, and Colonel Raul Barloco, the Chief of Police of Montevideo, as well as the Chiefs of Police for the Departments of *Maldonado, Canelones* and *Rocha*, attended the meeting. We were told that Uruguayan Army General Alfonso Gonzales would be in charge of the overall security operations at the Summit.

The Summit Conference was important and in terms of organizing a cohesive security system and operation to protect the various Presidents of Latin America and the President of the United States the element of flexibility had to be appreciated by those involved or they would have a mental meltdown. Political, diplomatic and ideological interests defied the formulation of ordinary security plans or systems.

We were surprised in the meeting when a colonel from the Uruguayan Army eloquently proposed that in the interests of security, the Latin American Presidents attending the conference should occupy rooms at the Hotel *San Rafael,* the site of the Summit. In this manner they could all be protected under one roof, he suggested. Nevertheless, this was predictably disastrous for security planning and protective purposes and would be strongly resisted by the U.S. Secret Service as well as the twenty or more delegations of the Presidents attending.

In a quasi-jocular vein I suggested that was equivalent to placing our eggs *(huevos)* in one solitary basket where they could be squashed with one good blow. (In the Spanish vernacular, *huevos* means testicles. My reference to *huevos* caused people in the room to giggle.)

It was suggested that it seemed more prudent that the Presidents and their security contingents be dispersed throughout the peninsula in private residences, to avoid the danger of a huge omelet. Fortunately, the idea of putting all the Presidents in the Hotel *San Rafael* was rejected.

The Hotel *San Rafael* had a capacity of 300 rooms and would be occupied by the numerous Foreign Ministers attending the conference and their staffs. Nevertheless, the President of Uruguay, General Oscar Gestido, and Uruguayan representatives would occupy one entire floor of the hotel.

In line with the United States commitment to help with the security of the conference, it was proposed that a police operations center be installed at *Punta del Este* with the help of the OPS program. Radio communications would be installed in the center to link the police and the Uruguayan military units providing security at the Summit. The center would enable superior officers to exercise command and control and to coordinate operations between the various security units at the conference site. The idea was quickly accepted.

In the middle of the meeting, Dr Legnani, the Minister of the Interior, suggested that the group travel to *Punta del Este* to look at the terrain, and to get a feel for the potential problems that would ultimately have to be faced. While at *Punta del Este,* the Minister of the Interior approved the rental of two apartments located at the *Edificio Uruguay* for the installation of the police operations center. OPS advisors would provide equipment, technical assistance and training.

Additional manpower to help the Uruguayan security forces prepare for the Summit Conference was requested from OPS Washington by cable. Two weeks later, **Brian Quick** and **Joseph C. de Lopez**, veteran OPS police advisors, arrived in Uruguay. **Rene Tetaz,** an OPS telecommunications specialist, arrived soon after.

Rene Tetaz would assist in the installation of the police operations center in the *Edificio Uruguay.* Tetaz, a tall, mature, charming Frenchman, loved *Punta del Este* and consumed fresh seafood and mussels in garlic sauce at every opportunity. With a heavy French accent he would later complain about his "poor *stomako.*" Tetaz spoke fluent Spanish with a heavy French accent and became one of the most popular individuals at the Summit.

U.S. Embassy personnel in *Punta del Este* established their control center at the *Draga* Inn, a popular resort hotel near the Atlantic Ocean. The CIA control center was installed in a *chalet* nearby.

March 21, 1967

The advance party of U.S. Secret Service personnel always created anxiety and anticipation in any U.S. Embassy in any foreign country where the President of the United States was scheduled to visit. U.S. Embassy officers prepared for heartburn and problems with the arrival of the advance Secret Service team.

Special Agent Lem Johns led the advance Secret Service team to Uruguay for the Summit. He was quiet and taciturn. Meeting with Lem Johns and members of the advance group at the residence of John Topping, the DCM, we were surprised by the abruptness of the meeting.

"They seem more interested in partying," Horton speculated.

The date of the Summit Conference drew near, and *Carrasco* Airport grew busy. Local government officials rushed to meet foreign delegations arriving from other countries. Lem Johns also met other

Secret Service Agents arriving at the airport in connection with President Lyndon Johnson's visit. I was told that Rufus Youngblood would accompany LBJ to the Summit with the Presidential Protective Detail. President Johnson had appreciated Youngblood's efforts to protect his life when President John F. Kennedy was assassinated in Dallas, Texas. Secret Service Agents do not have an easy time ensuring protection for the President of the United States anywhere. And in a country with an active terrorist group there were numerous details to attend to, including the coordination of security matters with local police. We were instructed by Ambassador Hoyt to support the Secret Service team in dealing with the police.

I walked with Lem Johns on the airfield tarmac to meet an U.S. Air Force plane bringing security equipment needed for the conference. He stooped down and unknown to him his revolver fell from his hip holster. He walked away unknowingly, as his revolver lay on the asphalt, shining in the bright sunlight.

"Lem," I shouted. "You dropped your gun." The police officers with us looked at the revolver on the tarmac with fascination. Lightheartedly, I told Johns that my policy was never to touch another man's weapon.

He stared at his revolver on the asphalt in frustration, wondering how the hell it got there. He looked at me as if I had played some kind of a trick on him. Picking up his gun he stuffed it pensively into his hip holster. He did not even say thanks.

March 22

The training of the Uruguayan police officers that were assigned to perform security functions at the Summit Conference became a priority. Brian Quick and Joe de Lopez, both fluent Spanish speakers, provided assistance in security analysis and planning and helped to train police personnel in the searches of people and vehicles. Caesar Bernal worked on firearms training, emphasizing revolver training for protective details.

The police units at *Punta del Este* carried beautiful antique Thompson submachine guns and 7mm Mauser rifles. Those weapons were assigned to personnel who patrolled the perimeter of the Hotel *San Rafael*. Uruguayan officials agreed that security personnel inside the hotel should not carry automatic weapons, but if needed, they would be available inside the building.

The *San Rafael* and the conference room where the Presidents of South America, Central America and North America would meet in several sessions would get crowded. To augment firepower, short barrel shotguns were ordered from OPS Washington by Julian Lindenauer for shipment by air.

FM portable radios designed by Paul Katz for the police field forces in South Vietnam were also shipped by air to Uruguay for the use of the twenty individual protective units and police personnel assigned to checkpoints and roadblocks. The operations center installed with OPS assistance had the communications needed to link all security units involved in security functions at the Summit.

Decisions were being made quickly, and we hoped they were right ones. The United States was in an alliance with Uruguay for the security preparations and operations needed for the Summit Conference. It was obvious that an attack against any Chief of State in attendance would be a serious setback for the Summit. We also knew that the *Tupamaro* terrorists were waiting in the wings and we had to plan for any possible contingency.

A few weeks before the Summit Conference opened, the Chief of the Montevideo Police, Colonel Raul Barloco, called for an urgent meeting, and police officials, military officers and other Uruguayan Government officials attended. The Chief of Police quickly made it known that he counted on help from American OPS advisors. He requested that the operations center at *Punta del Este* be made operational as soon as possible. Police personnel were assigned to the facility and would develop maps and data boards to record the number and location of police personnel available and manage all pertinent information on resources, incidents and casualties that might occur.

Colonel Barloco requested that OPS officers periodically inspect the physical security at the Hotel *San Rafael* and provide recommendations on the daily monitoring of the workers and the ongoing construction at the hotel. A system was established to identify and control workmen at the site.

The Chief of Police requested that OPS Officers help in reviewing the routes that would be used by the Presidential Delegations from other countries arriving at *Carrasco* Airport and traveling by car to *Punta del Este*. The checkpoints and roadblocks established would control all access on the roads leading to *Punta del Este*.

Everyone in the room was requested to intensify efforts to identify individuals or groups that would pose any threat to the Presidents of the hemisphere scheduled to participate in the Summit. The *Tupamaros* were a given. Bill Cantrell would coordinate with CIA personnel at the U.S. Embassy, the Montevideo Police Intelligence Section, and with U.S. and Uruguayan Military Intelligence sources.

Before the meeting ended Colonel Barloco assigned other top officials of the Montevideo Police Department to assist Colonel Santiago Acuña in the security operations at the Hotel *San Rafael*. The officers assigned were Inspector Mario Guerrerro (S-1 Personnel); *Comissario* Alejandro Otero (S-2 Intelligence); *Comissario* Lucio Mobillio (S-3 Operations); and Inspector Carlos Grau Saint-Laurent (S-4 Logistics). Three veteran Montevideo police commanders would remain in *Punta del Este* to help manage security operations. They were Inspector Ramiro Requeirro, the head of police uniformed services, Inspector Guillermo Copello, the Chief of Criminal Investigations, and Inspector Lopez Parcharotti, an experienced criminal investigator. The officers were considered *La crème de la crème*. All of them were well known to OPS personnel.

We were surprised when the Chief of Police ordered that all security planning for the Summit Conference be coordinated with the OPS public safety advisors of the *Oficinia de Asistancia Tecnica*. The United States was inexorably in the fray. The Far Left Wing called it intervention in the internal affairs of Uruguay.

The Chief of Police, Colonel Raul Barloco, an experienced military officer and statesman with excellent leadership qualities, stressed the need for full cooperation from everyone involved at the Summit and with an impressive display of oratory touched on the patriotism and emotions of all of the people in the room.

"If we fail to provide a secure climate for the conference," he predicted, "the enemies of democracy will declare themselves a victory. Our enemies lurk in the shadows ready to strike. They will take violent action and we must be prepared for that," he added.

"The struggle in Uruguay means a great deal for democracy," he said. The silence was stunning.

In a gravelly voice Colonel Barloco articulated a concern in an emotional note in eloquent Spanish.

"Everyone has a job to do. Do it right. We **must** not fail," he declared, raising his voice and his hand.

"Por la gloria y honor de nuestra patria (For the glory and honor of our country)," he said raising his voice. The police and military officers in the room stood in unison and snapped their heels with a loud crack. Colonel Barloco admirably provided inspiration for everyone in the room.

For those who did not understand local mores and idiosyncrasies, security preparations for the Summit could be perplexing and frustrating.

An identification system for individuals that were authorized access to *Punta del Este* and to the Hotel *San Rafael* was based on the recommendations of the U.S. Secret Service. The identification system developed by Bill Cantrell became problematic as the date of the conference grew near.

Police and military officials as well as the office of the Uruguayan Foreign Ministry insisted on issuing the I.D. badges that were provided by the Organization of American States (OAS). Different colors had been assigned to Presidential Delegations, to media representatives and to support personnel. The badges were numbered for control, but could easily be duplicated. The system of I.D. Badges had become a potential risk.

For this reason it was decided that security personnel working at the site would be issued metal lapel buttons obtained from the United States by the CIA. The only technology available for the security forces were ultraviolet lamps to check a particular marking on the I.D. badges. But the I.D. badges could be duplicated.

It was understood that the *Tupamaros* were trained terrorists and would exploit any weakness in the overall security system. Fortunately, a tough Uruguayan Army Officer by the name of Colonel Ramiro Chavez assumed the control of the checkpoints on the roads leading to *Punta del Este*. Checkpoint No. 1 at *Laguna del Sauce* was especially important because it controlled the principal access to *Punta del Este.*

The rules and procedures established by Colonel Chavez to control access into the area worked. All individuals were required to have an appropriate I.D. badge and a special pass for vehicles. It is estimated that three possible attempts by the *Tupamaros* to penetrate the area were stopped at the checkpoints.

Colonel Chavez took his job seriously. The Montevideo Police Public Affairs Officer (PAO) had demanded I.D. badges to provide to his colleagues in the media but Colonel Chavez refused because he suspected that the PAO had ties to the *Tupamaros.*

The start of the Summit Conference approached and the United States Secret Service grew more demanding. I compared the situation to the wicked *yetser.* The ancient Rabbi Isaac once warned, **"First it is a wayfarer and a lodger. At last it becomes the master of the house."** So it was with the U.S. Secret Service in Uruguay.

Lem Johns had requested a tour of the conference site at the Hotel *San Rafael* with other Secret Service Agents. John Horton and the Chief of Police of Montevideo, Colonel Raul Barloco, decided to go with us.

The Hotel *San Rafael* was situated near the Atlantic Ocean and bordered by popular and attractive beaches. The hotel was a beautiful structure with ornate furnishings and plush surroundings.

Along a park-like lawn dotted with pine trees and a serene landscape, police personnel patrolled the grounds with automatic weapons. It was obvious that the Government of Uruguay had contributed an enormous amount of time, effort and money to prepare for the conference of Hemispheric Presidents.

Followed by an entourage of Secret Service Agents we entered the Hotel *San Rafael* where the Presidents of the countries attending the Summit conference would meet for three days. The conference room was located in the southeast part of the hotel and was elegantly furnished with smoked glass and antique mirrors on the walls throughout. Twenty-one beautiful maroon leather chairs were spaced out around a massive circular wooden table that was polished by workmen to a fine glow. The sounds of a few workmen laboring inside the room echoed throughout. The conference room had a serene majesty about it and seemed appropriate for a conference of Presidents. I admired the beauty of the room and a large object suspended above the table caught my eye but I made an effort not to dwell on it.

Lem Johns stared at me then lifted his gaze to the beautiful antique circular wood chandelier suspended above the table on enormous metal chains. It was truly an elegant *object de arté* hovering ostentatiously above the conference table from a beamed ceiling. I cursed myself for looking up.

"Uh-uh, that has to come down," Lem Johns said, pointing with his nose in the direction of the chandelier. Ignoring him, I walked away.

Arquitecto Framiñan, the world famous Uruguayan architect, was responsible for the ongoing construction at the site and now had a problem on his hands with the *Gringos.*

We sat in the spacious lobby of the *San Rafael* among a row of fine couches and chairs strewn about plush carpeting to talk. Lem Johns pulled me to one side.

"That monster chandelier in the conference room has to come down," he reiterated in a low, adamant tone of voice. "There is no way that thing can stay."

"What if the chains are reinforced?" I suggested optimistically.

"No way," he said firmly. "No way." Everyone blithely ignored us. I decided to leave.

"Screw this," I thought. Casually I walked up to Horton.

"John, will you please explain to the Chief of Police Lem's problem with the conference room? I have a meeting with Colonel Acuña," I told him, feigning urgency. "I'm late."

"Hah," he blurted out. "Hell, no!" he said, pasting a saturnine grin on his face.

"I can't do that. Your Spanish is better when you're totally drunk than mine will ever be when I'm totally sober." His grin grew wider.

"Besides, the Chief is your counterpart and you're the one who tipped Lem Johns off to the problem. I saw you look up at the chandelier with that strange way of yours. You do the honors," he chuckled.

"I wish you luck in convincing the Chief of Police on this one," Horton chortled, unmoved. It was now a major problem, especially for me.

From a distance, the Chief of Police, Colonel Raul Barloco, watched in silence as we argued. Horton and I tried to convince Lem Johns not to mess with the beautiful chandelier but to no avail. Lem Johns waited steadfastly for one of us to take the action needed to resolve the problem. It seemed it was up to me to tell Colonel Barloco about the problem. He would probably blame me, I thought.

It seemed obvious that it would be extremely difficult to convince the Chief of Police that a chandelier hanging over the conference table to provide light for the gathering of the Hemispheric Presidents during their sessions was a security problem. I had little choice at this point.

"Jefe," I intoned in a soft voice to explain Lem Johns' position on the chandelier and his insistence that it come down for security reasons. The Chief immediately reacted, showing pain and alarm.

"Imposible!" he sputtered angrily in Spanish. "That chandelier was created," he took a deep breath to repeat himself, "created, do you understand me, by one of our foremost artisans especially for the Summit conference." His eyes overflowed with distress.

"The artist did this at the request of the President of Uruguay. The removal of his magnificent work will be a monumental insult to him, the entire art society of Uruguay and to the President of Uruguay." The Chief implied that I should tell the *Gringos* they were out of their fucking minds. He looked worried and the situation made me feel bad. There was no way I could walk away from the problem.

Translating what the Chief said for Lem Johns I added an expletive here and there for his benefit. He stared vacantly at the Chief of Police.

"We are truly sorry," he said in English. "But the President of the United States will not participate in the Summit unless the chandelier comes down." I wanted to tell Lem Johns that he was truly a sorry ass.

The Chief bellowed in disbelief when I translated what Lem Johns said.

"Imposible!" he said. He could not believe what I translated. His eyes grew watery and his face paled. I liked Colonel Barloco a lot and admired

him. The Chief of Police was my counterpart in the pursuit of my already tenuous career in Uruguay and he would probably never speak to me again. Sitting morosely next to him, I tried to show I was on his side.

The Chief of Police brooded momentarily in silence, staring at our group in anger. He was probably sorry he had come with us.

"Jefe," I suggested in a low-key voice. *"Yo se que los Gringos probablemente estan locos!"* I smiled in an attempt to relieve the tension by telling him that the *Gringos* were probably crazy just as he suggested.

"We've been friends a long time," I told him. "And we have to admit that the chandelier, despite being absolutely beautiful, is now a security issue." The Chief shook his head deprecatingly in silence, growing nervous.

"The chandelier will never fall," he said angrily. "It has been installed based on the calculations of professional engineers." I nodded to agree with him.

"Es locura! (This is madness!)" His face grew flushed.

With all the sincerity I could muster I let the Chief know that he was probably right, but the matter was capable of becoming an obstacle for U.S. participation in the conference. I reminded him that the *Gringo* Secret Service Agent would not budge and he was responsible for the security of the President of the United States.

"You are a highly respected superior military officer in every country of the hemisphere, *Jefe,"* I said, chopping at the air with my hand.

"But there is one possible security consideration. From a purely clinical point of view, let's say, the tragedy I can visualize is that during the Summit conference held in *Punta del Este* in 1967, several Latin American Presidents and the President of the United States were killed by an antique chandelier that fell on them." He looked at me with a stunned look.

"And you were the Commander in Chief of the security forces at the Hotel *San Rafael* and were told about the problem," I added in a soft tone. I felt like an asshole, but a convincing asshole. Colonel Barloco was a very patient and compassionate man.

The Chief stared at me with a profound weariness in his eyes and sighed deeply.

"Muy bien," he told me and stood to look dejectedly around the hotel lobby. He talked briefly with Uruguayan military and police officers with him and with a faint attempt at a smile excused himself. He walked to the north end of the elegant hotel as we sat in silence. I felt a lot of anguish. We were not only intervening, we were interfering.

"What is he going to do?" Lem Johns asked. I stared at him in semidisgust.

"He didn't really say. He did mention that he may just put all of our dumb asses under arrest," I told him facetiously. "He told me that he didn't need this shit from dumb-ass *Gringos*." Lem Johns stared at me.

"I need a drink," I said feeling vulnerable and unhappy. Ordering a Scotch and soda from an attentive waiter, Horton and the others followed suit. We sat in silence and waited.

Disgusted with developments, I told Horton that the matter would create a breach in the excellent relationship I had with the Chief of Police. Cradling drinks in our hands, we sat in front of a polished eighteenth century antique table.

"He'll never forgive me for the dumb-ass exercise on the chandelier," I suggested to Horton.

"Well, ordering drinks was a good idea," he said. "So you do have good ideas. Let me give you an idea. Give the Chief a case of Scotch and get drunk with him. You can cry on each other's shoulders." He chuckled when I stared harshly at him. I told him that he was a ruthless bastard.

"Look, blame it on Lem Johns and the Secret Service," he said. "Everybody knows they are a pain in the ass anyway," he said, laughing. Horton was cynical but good for morale. He tipped his glass of Scotch.

"Cheers," he told me with a grin.

A few minutes later, a shrill scream that emanated from the north end of the hotel lobby was surprising.

"Damn, what's that?" one of the Secret Service Agents asked hurriedly. Horton glanced at me. There was another scream.

"No, no, no puede ser (No, no, it can't be)," someone screeched in Spanish.

"Well, I guess the Chief of Police just informed the Uruguayan artist that created that beautiful chandelier in the conference room that it has to come down." At the north end of the hotel an angry and loud dialogue erupted among a group of people. The Chief of Police was in the middle of the heated discussion.

"I don't know the artist, but if anyone other than the Chief of Police walks toward us, I'm leaving," I said jokingly. "You talk to him, Lem." I said, feeling a touch of misanthropy. "You're on your own."

The chandelier came down with a pseudo-human scream heard for miles. The scandalous deed perpetrated by the *Gringos* would be talked about for years to come. *Cretinos* (Cretins) they called us, devoid of culture. Lem Johns did not even say thanks.

The next day, the violence in Montevideo continued. A white phosphorous bomb exploded at the residence of the Paraguayan

Ambassador. The bomb was to protest the presence of General Alfredo Stroessner, the military dictator of Paraguay, in the Summit. White phosphorous would ignite on contact with air or dampness so the bomb was designed to explode if the police used the water-soaking technique that had worked to disarm potassium chlorate and sulfuric acid fuses on the bombs used previously by the terrorists. The *Tupamaros* were trying new things.

The Summit brought more violence to Montevideo. Police guards at the U.S. Chancery and the residence of the U.S. Ambassador were reinforced. Bombs were thrown at vehicles parked at the U.S. Embassy causing serious damage. U.S. companies doing business in the sprawling metropolis became frequent targets for firebombs. The start of the Summit Conference approached and Ambassador Hoyt secretly assigned me as his **anti-graffiti** officer. The assignment felt embarrassing but he asked in a nice desperate way and in confidence.

The routes leading to and from *Punta del Este, Carrasco* Airport and other prominent areas of Montevideo were favorite spots for the communists to display anti-American propaganda. Vile propaganda against President Lyndon B. Johnson suddenly appeared plastered on many walls throughout the city.

Posters of President Johnson wearing a Nazi uniform and a swastika band on his arm had an ugly message. "LBJ is a nazi who rapes women and kills children," it said. That poster was particularly agonizing for the U.S. Ambassador. Because of the Vietnam War, LBJ had lost the propaganda battle at home and abroad. But he was a sensitive man and would be offended by the scurrilous posters. Ambassador Hoyt knew this.

"Dolph, we've got to get rid of those damn posters and signs before President Johnson arrives," he insisted. I could tell the Ambassador was hurting. LBJ would feel hurt if he saw the scurrilous posters. The Ambassador depended on me to stop it and this was an impossible task without help.

Organizing an anti-graffiti team led by Detective Walter Spinelli, the young cop assigned to the *Oficina de Assistencia Tecnica* (OPS) at the *Jefatura,* we waged war on the communist propaganda. I provided money for Spinelli to hire young kids to help fight the graffiti war. The kids were provided a special paint brought from the United States by the CIA. The paint at first glance appeared to be plain water and this baffled the youngsters. They painted over the graffiti with the clear liquid and nothing happened.

Spinelli reported back that the kids thought the *Gringos* were really bananas and were worried about getting paid. I told Spinelli to take them back to where they had painted over the graffiti. He returned laughing and told me the kids were amazed to see the graffiti they had painted with "water" completely blacked out.

The Ambassador was delighted and occasionally pointed out a spot we missed. I could have made a fortune in the United States painting over graffiti in our major cities.

The date of the Summit approached and Bernal and I went to a business district of the city to check out a new tactic used by communist militants to continue their crusade of urban violence. The new tactic was called *manifestaciones relampago* (lightning manifestations or mini-riots). Small groups of ten to twenty rioters would attack various parts of the city simultaneously, breaking windows and wreaking havoc in the crowded urban areas. Some groups attacked with *Molotov* cocktails and bombs to terrify the populace and created the illusion that things were out of control.

The *manifestaciones relampagos* or mini-riots, as many as forty a month, were extremely difficult to control. We recommended the use of small police teams armed with tear gas and shotguns to respond to the problem.

While we were out on the street, a mini-riot exploded and we were caught between the police unit and the rioters. The police used tear gas and suddenly, a short-range tear gas missile was shot directly in our direction. It hit the ground and skipped merrily by us along the pavement spewing CS gas as people scrambled to get out of the way. But shooting suddenly grew indiscriminate and dangerous.

"Let's get the hell outta here," I shouted to Bernal. We ran for about fifty yards until we reached an alcove. Entering, we saw that the inside was crowded with people also taking cover from the violence outside. Three frightened young girls were huddled at the foot of a stairwell, crying hysterically. They were American.

"What the fuck are we going to do?" one of them wailed in a loud voice. She seemed terrified and cried out in a farcical way.

"We're going to get killed. The fuckers are going to kill us," she said, crying out in English. Bernal and I broke out in laughter.

"Tsk, tsk, such language," I laughed, walking up to them.

"Oh, shit!" one of them reacted. "Are you guys American?" they asked excitedly.

"Affirmative," we informed them. "And we don't drink, smoke or cuss." The girls erupted in giggles.

"Yeah, right." They seemed very happy to see us.

We talked and enjoyed their company until the riot outside subsided. They kept asking what we were doing in Uruguay. We kidded them by telling them we were Peace Corps volunteers. All three exploded with immediate questions. The problem outside ended and we went out to the bright sunshine and parted company with three pretty, frightened Peace Corps volunteers wearing tight mini-skirts and enjoying life in Montevideo.

One week remained until the Summit Conference began and all OPS officers remained in *Punta del Este* in a large *chalet* rented by the U.S. Government. The week before the conference started, a large group of military officers representing Uruguayan Army, Navy and Air Force units arrived at the conference site in *Punta del Este* and surprised security personnel there. The military officers had insisted they be given the opportunity to serve their country by helping with security duties inside the hotel during the Summit Conference. General Alfonso Gonzales had approved this but the communication on this new development had faltered. The military officers felt patriotic and we needed all the help we could get. The politics of the Summit were complex and terrorists often used military and police uniforms to carry out attacks. Cantrell, an ex-Secret Service Agent, had already chewed through one pipe stem.

April 12

The Presidents of the Hemisphere went into the first plenary session at the Hotel *San Rafael* without problems. Every Presidential delegation had arrived with its own security detail that was linked up with a security unit provided by the Government of Uruguay. President Johnson arrived the day before the conference started and was taken to a private residence on the peninsula. A special bed was flown in for him.

The U.S. Ambassador, the staff accompanying President Johnson and two U.S. Congressmen occupied 24 rooms in the Hotel *San Rafael* on the second and third floors. Our workday grew to over fourteen hours.

Rene Tetaz was excited when he reached me at the Hotel *San Rafael* by radio.

"Inteligencia y Enlace has information from a citizen in Cordova, Argentina, that an unknown individual flying a small plane intends to crash it on top of the Hotel *San Rafael,"* Tetaz said. "I thought I better pass it on," he told me in his charming French accent.

If the information on the small plane reported by the police intelligence unit was correct the U.S. aircraft carrier parked off the coast of Uruguay along with other U.S. Naval vessels would pick it up on radar.

Meanwhile, *Comissario* Alejandro Otero, the Chief of the Police Intelligence Unit, sent me a message asking that I wait for him at the hotel lobby. He had an intruder in custody.

The Uruguayan Minister of Foreign Relations had detained a man he found inside a dining room where the President of Uruguay General Oscar Gestido was hosting a dinner. The name of the individual was determined to be Juan Jurgensen Romero. He did not have the proper I.D. badge.

But the individual's behavior was bizarre. He could not explain what he was doing in the Hotel *San Rafael*. He did not have weapons on him. The man remained a mystery and he would have to be checked out.

Otero confirmed that a small aircraft reported flying out of Cordova, Argentina, was headed for *Punta del Este*. It was alleged that the pilot intended to bail out and crash the plane on the hotel full of Presidents, he said.

12

Americans in Uruguay

The small Cessna aircraft approached the historic body of water that separated Argentina from Uruguay, called *Rio de La Plata*. If the purpose of the flight as reported by Uruguayan intelligence officers was correct, the small Cessna posed a clear and present danger to the twenty-one Presidents attending the Summit Conference at *Punta del Este*. According to unconfirmed reports, the pilot intended to crash the plane into the Hotel *San Rafael* where the heads of State were in plenary session.

The small plane approached the coast of Uruguay at a low altitude. A flight plan was voluntary in Argentina and detailed information on the flight was not available.

On the river below, Hovercraft transported people back and forth from Argentina to Uruguay skimming over the placid waters of the river. Further inland, at the *Aéropuerto del Este,* Uruguayan Air Force personnel prepared to launch two military aircraft to patrol the sky over *Punta del Este.* Meanwhile, the U.S. aircraft carrier stationed off the Atlantic coast of Uruguay near the Island of *Gorriti* picked up a small blip on their radar screens. Cantrell reported that the CIA could not confirm the information on the aircraft but were aware of the threat. The police *Inteligencia y Enlace* (police intelligence unit) had no other information on the potential threat.

Comissario Alejandro Otero, the Director of the police intelligence unit for the Montevideo police, reported that he passed the information on the Cessna aircraft to Uruguayan Air Force personnel. Air space over *Punta del Este* was supposed to be restricted during the Summit.

"Operación Tango," he said with a trace of amusement.

U.S. Air Force Colonel Lorenzo Caliendo suggested that it would be extremely difficult for the pilot of the Cessna aircraft to hit the Hotel

San Rafael, unless the bastard made it a kamikaze effort and went down with the plane, he said. But the small aircraft could crash into the numerous residences in *Punta del Este* where President Lyndon Johnson and other Latin American Presidents were staying.

The U.S. Secret Service was informed. It was agreed that the evacuation of the Hotel *San Rafael* would be a disaster. The emergency evacuation of twenty-one Presidents from the conference site would mean chaos.

Colonel Acuna and I anxiously discussed the problem and agreed to meet immediately with top Uruguayan Officials. Suddenly, U.S. Navy aircraft appeared with a roar above us. Sky Raiders flew over *Punta del Este* in powerful sweeps across the sky. Everyone felt better.

A worried Inspector Emilio Maximo Guerra of the Montevideo Police, the man in charge of the police security forces at the Hotel *San Rafael,* waved happily at me.

"*Macanudo!* (Great!)" he shouted. We were told that the small Cessna had fled to Argentina.

The third day of the Summit, the communist newspapers *El Popular* and *Epoca* reported numerous demonstrations taking place in Montevideo to protest the presence of the *Yanqui* imperialists, military dictators, and tyrants at the Summit. A protest march led by communist agitators to *Punta del Este* dwindled in number and was peacefully dispersed by police units when the mob reached one of the checkpoints.

The Summit was winding down by the third day and the polemics and debates subsided. The issues of communist aggression and solidarity against Cuba waned as sexy topics. The Cold War was a way of life in the hemisphere and would run its course. Rodney Arosemendi, an elected representative of the Communist Party in the Uruguayan Legislature, in local newspapers, repeatedly condemned the intervention by the United States in the internal affairs of Uruguay.

The *concierge* of the Hotel *San Rafael* prepared for cleanup as the final session grew to a close with impressive final oratory. Pandemonium erupted when the Presidents of the Latin American countries walked out of the conference room and a myriad of people in the hotel gathered to applaud for them. The lobby grew crowded with security personnel as the different Presidents of the hemisphere shook hands with each other and the different groups broke up to leave the premises.

I was told by radio that President Lyndon B. Johnson was headed for the lobby of the hotel. Several members of the U.S. Embassy staff and their wives asked me to let them enter a restricted area where LBJ would pass. It was hard to refuse. Minutes later, the President of the United States walked in, smiling, wearing a dark navy blue suit, sparkling white shirt, and red tie with blue stripes. Surrounded by Secret Service Agents, he seemed surprisingly fit and cheerful. With a John Wayne gait he stopped to shake hands with the Americans in the hotel lobby. Applauded by the crowd, Johnson stopped with a wrinkled grin on his face and waved as he left the hotel. The Summit was officially over.

Outside, in the fresh ocean breeze, an officer from the U.S. Embassy waved from the entrance of the Hotel *San Rafael*.

"It's over," he said. "Let's get the flock outta here."

The Summit had been a mixed success for U.S. resolutions that included the continued isolation of Cuba. Despite the fact that many Latin American countries had severed diplomatic ties with Cuba, Mexico, Chile, Uruguay, and Bolivia did not. On his way out, Ambassador Hoyt told me cheerfully.

"Dolph, the security forces did a great job." We had had a few roisterers and minor problems, but the *Tupamaros* were kept at bay. Terrorists were considered the major threat to the security of the Summit. The Ambassador formed his toothy grin to tell us he needed to rest. The Summit had been especially rough for him. LBJ had brought a huge demanding entourage with him.

In the aftermath of the Summit, any breaches that had occurred in relationships between Americans and Uruguayans in the process of preparing for the Summit now had to be repaired. We passed out cigarette lighters, pens, and other items engraved with the U.S. Presidential seal to Uruguayan officials and the police officers that had worked with us in the Summit. The Chief of Police of Montevideo, Colonel Barloco was a very gracious man and did not appear unhappy with me.

In the months following the Summit, challenges in the political and security climate continued. Civil unrest increased as police forces clashed frequently with hundreds of workers from the *Frigorifico Nacional* (National Meatpacking House) in *Cerro Largo*. The workers received *gratis* five pounds of meat per day but now demanded added incentives for the holidays. Meat continued to be a major cause for rebellion in Uruguay.

In a surprise move, Colonel Zia Fernandez replaced my good friend Colonel Raul Barloco as Chief of the Montevideo Police Department shortly after the Summit. The effort to ensure adequate security for the Summit conference would have been extremely difficult without Colonel

Barloco. It certainly would not have been any fun. Personally, I was unhappy to see Colonel Barloco leave.

Nevertheless, Uruguayan Army Colonel Zia Fernandez quickly took charge and it did not take long for the new Chief of Police of Montevideo to recognize that the lack of mobility was a major problem for the police in coping with the urban violence in the city. After an assessment of police vehicle requirements vis-a-vis the existing security threat, Colonel Zia Fernandez moved expeditiously to buy one hundred new patrol cars. The local GMC representative cinched a sale with a promise of quick delivery of the vehicles needed.

OPS advisor Julian Lindenauer developed the specifications for the police patrol cars and provided technical assistance on the shipment of the cars from the U.S. to Uruguay. The Government of Uruguay paid for the vehicles and the OPS program provided the mobile radios needed for the patrol cars. A plan to put more patrols out on the street was implemented to improve the capabilities of the police to respond to problems and emergencies. The increase in motorized patrols would also help the police to combat the *Tupamaro* terrorists.

Colonel Zia Fernandez was a decisive and aggressive Chief of Police. He frequently made decisions needed to cope with urban violence and directed the police action needed from the new police operations center. Paul Katz, the OPS telecommunications engineer who designed the system, would have been proud to see it in action. With the improved communications system and added mobility, the police forces were in a much stronger posture to cope with the internal security crisis.

Ambassador Henry Hoyt had provided excellent leadership to help Uruguay resolve the economic crisis and the ongoing security threat. But as in all wars, there were always casualties.

"You'll never have a quiet world till you knock patriotism out of the human race," Bernard Shaw once said. Well, Bernard Shaw did not believe in God, either. Ideological convictions divided Americans during the Cold War and especially in regards to the Vietnam War. Patriotism had become an archaic tenet and viewed as dumb by many in the United States.

Holidays always created nostalgia for most Americans in Uruguay. Regardless of how other Americans felt about patriotism, hearing the Marine Corps hymn and the American National Anthem always choked me up.

Despite the dangerous security climate in Montevideo, U.S. Ambassador Henry Hoyt decided that Americans should celebrate

Independence Day with a picnic. The Ambassador had a strong sense of patriotism.

July 4, 1968

More than thirty Americans with their families and friends, assembled on the grounds of the local British School for a Fourth of July picnic, amply blessed with a bright blue radiant sky and plenty of sunshine. This time of the year in Uruguay brought near perfect weather. Our children scattered with their young friends to play on the school grounds of the British preparatory school. The clear lucent skies made it ideal for a July 4th picnic.

"Screw George Bernard Shaw," I told my wife playfully. "No one can feel patriotic on an empty stomach." She patted my belly playfully.

"Yep, it's empty," she kidded. Uruguayan *morcillas* (blood sausage), Bratwurst, plump Italian *salchichas* (sausages), and hamburgers were already cooking on the grill. My wife could not understand that I liked eating blood sausages, bull nuts, sweetbreads, cow intestines, and beef tongue.

"Just don't try to kiss me with any passion," she admonished, "if you eat that *caca.*"

My bite into a blood sausage coincided with the sounds of terrifying screams and shouts coming from the direction of the softball diamond. Frank Stewart, the USAID Director, grabbed my arm and said that something had happened to the Ambassador. We both ran towards the softball diamond and my initial thought was that we faced a possible security problem and my gun was locked in my car.

We reached the softball field and found Ambassador Hoyt prostrate on the ground. He appeared lifeless with a dull pale look on his face. Kathy Cantrell was a registered nurse, and she desperately applied CPR to no avail. The Ambassador was DOA (Dead on Arrival) at the hospital.

Ambassador Hoyt was barely in his fifties and had succumbed to a massive heart attack while playing softball. His death was a terrible blow for Americans in Uruguay. His experience, intellect, and leadership were invaluable in regard to American policy and strategy in the Uruguayan crisis. I personally had grown very fond of Ambassador Hoyt and like many other Americans felt a deep sorrow and loss.

He and his lovely wife Joyce represented the United States with distinction in several countries for many years. He was a compassionate man, loved and admired by Americans as well as Uruguayans.

The church holding the memorial service for the Ambassador in Uruguay was filled to the street as hundreds paid final tribute to a good man and a great American. His contribution to the American Diplomatic Service would go generally unnoticed in the United States.

Standing at the back of the crowded church, I felt a deep sadness. Hoyt's demise meant problems for the growing complexity of the OPS mission in Uruguay. He was a staunch and wise supporter of our efforts.

John Horton stood at a corner of the crowded church and glanced at me with a grave look on his face during the service for the Ambassador.

The United States had lost an excellent Ambassador in the Cold War struggle and he would be hard to replace. His replacement depended on Lyndon B. Johnson, and in view of the political and ideological morass of the Cold War, everyone seemed to feel apprehensive about the future.

But within a few months, President Johnson came through by appointing a true professional as the new Ambassador to Uruguay. Robert (Bob) Sayre, a career diplomat, arrived a few months later to replace Ambassador Henry Hoyt. This was Sayre's first time as an Ambassador of the United States but as an experienced member of the U.S. diplomatic corps, he arrived in a cautious mode. It was difficult for a new Ambassador to totally trust the U.S. Embassy staff in any country, where people were involved in programs that were potentially problematic or affected by politics, ideology or personal agendas. Like most Ambassadors, Sayre seemed aware that things might happen locally that he would not officially hear about.

Robert (Bob) Andrews, a CIA Officer assigned to the Embassy, attempted to slough off the matter of his emotionally disturbed wife slapping my fifteen-year-old daughter Lori because she had made her angry. My daughter's friends were furious with Mrs. Andrews and arrived en masse at our house to complain that my daughter Lori had done nothing wrong. They insisted that we do something. They insisted that the Ambassador be notified. Close friends of my wife urged that we report the matter to the police and have Mrs. Andrews arrested. I was in a powerful position to do that.

My wife had tried to talk to Mrs. Andrews but she refused to answer the door to her house. My wife was furious and cried bitterly, demanding that I tell the Ambassador. Instead, I arranged a meeting with Bob Andrews after giving the matter thought.

Andrews and I talked while sitting on a park bench in a quiet section of Montevideo. My anger soon rose out of control when he rationalized what had happened and suggested that it was unfortunate. I gently asked him to stand.

"What for?" he asked me.

"Because my family's satisfaction and my satisfaction is going to be by my whipping your ass," I told him harshly. "You are plain lucky my wife can't get her hands on your wife." Surprised, he shook his head with instant fear in his eyes.

"But you and I can settle the matter our way," I told him.

My anger was dangerously high and I wanted retribution. Expecting a good fight I waited anxiously for him to stand but it was my turn to be surprised. He absolutely refused to stand; he put his head between his legs and covered it up with his hands. I presumed it was a ploy and prepared for a dirty trick. I waited eagerly for him to try something but Andrews remained sitting and covering his face.

In a fit of rage I told him he was "a yellow-bellied bastard." I was astonished when he refused to stand despite anything said to him. In the barrio we had no such protocol and I would have hit him anyhow.

In a whiny way he turned gracious and apologized for the mistreatment of my daughter. In the United States, his wife would have been arrested. In Uruguay, it was a scandal for the American Embassy if the incident were reported to the police. Only John Topping, the DCM, was aware of what had happened but let me handle things my way. But for years I felt bad and empty because Andrews simply would not let me have retribution. But there were other things that went unreported.

John Horton, the CIA Station Chief, advised me that a Russian officer arriving with a group of Soviets at *Carrasco* Airport had been identified as a potential defector. He requested that I arrange for a phalanx of police officers to be at *Carrasco* Airport when the Soviets arrived for their scheduled visit to Uruguay. The Soviet identified as a potential defector was to be taken from the area by a team of agents while the Uruguayan police contingent held the KGB escorts back. It appeared the potential defector was to be forcibly extracted.

"What if the S.O.B. doesn't want to go?" I asked Horton. "We'll make him go," was the response. The fallout would be widespread not only for me. I prepared to tell Horton that was not my job. Luckily the plan apparently did not fly in Langley and was called off. But there was always excitement in Montevideo.

Inspector Guillermo Copello, the head of the Criminal Investigations Division of the Montevideo police was a temperamental man with a tough countenance. He accepted the presence of American advisors in the *Jefatura*, but as a proud Uruguayan did not want to appear subject to the will of the *Gringos*. He was a smart cop and tolerated the politics. But it seemed he had provided a service for the Soviets and they reciprocated.

"Saenz, you strike me as the type of *Gringo* that is interested in what the Soviets are doing in Uruguay," he told me. His red face indicated he had been imbibing some of the Scotch we kept him supplied with.

"I do not give a crap what the Soviets are doing anywhere," I told him and Copello laughed.

"Listen to me," he said. "The Soviet Embassy invited me to take a few friends to visit a Soviet trawler that's presently docked in port. We're invited to have drinks with the Captain," he continued with a sly grin. "If you *Gringos* are not stupid, you should know those whalers are electronic spy ships." I smiled to let him know it was not taken as an offense.

"Some of us *Gringos* **are** stupid," I told Copello. "Just like **many of you** Uruguayans." He smiled to tell me he did not take that as an offense.

"Que mierda quieres (What the shit do you want, Copello)," I added, faking anger. *"Estoy occupado* (I am busy)," I told him, lightheartedly. Copello and I had developed a friendly relationship; we often kidded each other.

"Well," he retorted, seemingly amused, "I thought you might want to go with us to visit the Soviet trawler. I'm inviting you." He stared at me, waiting for me to answer.

"Tú pasas por Uruguayo," he told me with growing sarcasm.

"Pero un Uruguayo muy feo," he said facetiously, whipping his fingers fiercely in the air trying to irritate me. He suggested I could pass as Uruguayan but a very ugly one. I laughed and Copello patted my shoulder to urge me to go with him to visit the trawler. I kidded Copello.

"Why should I trust you? *Tú me entregas a los Russos hijos-de-puta* (You'll turn me over to the fucking Russians)." He laughed with gusto.

"We're friends. I would never do anything like that to you." He kept trying to convince me.

I asked him how much they had offered him for me and he laughed in an uproar, suggesting that I was very distrustful.

"Vamos, los Russos no sabran que tú eres Norte Americano!" He belched involuntarily to tell me the Russians would not know I was an American.

"What the hell would the Russians want **you** for anyway," he said, laughing. Copello gave me his word for whatever it was worth and I agreed to go with him.

"No mas no abras la boca," he kidded. *"Los Russos no son Pendejos."* He suggested I keep my mouth shut because the Russians were not totally stupid and would be able to tell I was not Uruguayan if I opened my mouth. He continued to irritate me.

"Ché, ponte el lindo traje que compraste en el Uruguay," he added. He suggested I wear a nice suit bought in Uruguay. "And leave your damn

camera at home," he chuckled as he walked away. I agreed, anxious to do something different. But I needed approval from the Embassy.

Consulting with John Topping on my proposed visit with Copello to the Soviet trawler he agreed, and instructed me not to tell anyone. The rationalization was that I was a guest of the Uruguayan Police. That rationale would not fly with the Soviets if they read me wrong and thought I was spying on them.

In the late afternoon Gonzales, my driver, took me to where the Soviet whaler was docked. Copello was waiting. The Soviet vessel was enormous with a huge flat surface on the fantail where the whales that were caught were pulled on board with mammoth winches. Copello had two other persons with him and introduced them by name but not as police officers. I recognized one of the individuals as an officer from the Israeli Embassy. He attended diplomatic functions held at various residences. Copello had connections.

A man on the starboard side of the vessel spoke in fluent Spanish to Copello. The man was a member of the Soviet Embassy and a KGB officer who spoke Spanish, Copello whispered. The man let us know he would be our escort during our visit.

The diplomat from the local Embassy of the USSR was a friendly sort but looked at me with a strange glare that put me on guard. My picture had already appeared in local communist newspapers with propaganda that alleged that I was the *Capó* of the local CIA and the FBI office in Uruguay.

Our group walked up the gangplank to board the vessel and armed personnel in military regalia followed us and watched every move we made. At the fantail the Soviet diplomat stopped to explain how the whales were caught, brought on board and how the whale meat was cut up for storage. An armed escort stayed with us, moving solely on orders from the man from the Soviet Embassy.

Numerous antennas of different varieties littered the top part of the whaler and the top decks. They were obviously linked to electronic spy gear. On every deck, Soviet sailors mingled with women dressed in jeans and loose fitting khaki skirts. A strong smell of fish and whale meat permeated the air, provoking crude remarks from Copello about the crew of Russian women on board. We toured various parts of the vessel, including a spacious dining room for the crew, living quarters for men and women, and refrigerated processing plants for the storage of whale meat. The people on board appeared busy in every part of the huge boat.

A dishwater blonde buxom woman with a pensive, quiet look led our group in silence to an auditorium. We were escorted inside and stood in awe of a huge colored portrait of Lenin staring sternly from the top of the stage. The Russian communists were for real. The place was embraced by a pontifical and religious dead silence. Those in the group instinctively whispered to talk to each other. Copello seemed impressed by the bewitching stare of Lenin's portrait. The blonde's face softened when she told us we were to go to the captain's galley where officers of the crew waited.

One of our companions thanked and complimented the blonde in Spanish.

"Eres uná bella mujer (a pretty woman)," he told her. She smiled modestly as if she understood Spanish. Copello jumped in to add that she also had a *lindo culo* (beautiful ass) in Spanish. She was not offended by Copello's nasty flattery and her comely face brightened momentarily with the lewd remark. She apparently did not understand Spanish.

In a large stateroom, a burly man with a large red face sat alone at a table and was identified as the captain of the ship. Using the interpreter from the Soviet Embassy, he bid us welcome in a rough raspy voice. He chain-smoked foul smelling Russian cigarettes and the entire place reeked of sweat and whale meat. Two waiters suddenly appeared and immediately served a translucent liquid in water glasses to everyone.

"Wodka," the Captain said cheerfully in a flat tone of voice and a smile that was missing a tooth. At close scrutiny, the *"Wodka"* appeared cloudy as if one or two drops of milk had been added. The Captain raised his glass, offered a toast, and licked his lips.

"Vasha Darovye." He swallowed the contents in one Russian gulp and the other officers followed suit.

Taking a swallow I found the *"wodka"* smooth as silk with an impressive fast punch. Copello stared at me, smacking his lips. The vodka was excellent.

For about an hour, we drank heavily, keeping pace with the Russians. Copello transformed into a blithe diplomat, congratulating the Captain for the excellent *"wodka."* Four glasses later I felt drunk but happy, anticipating the next drink with punishing eagerness. The visit had become a drunken brawl. The Soviets joked cheerfully with us, and we laughed spontaneously at Copello's efforts to speak Russian. More vodka was passed around and the Russians tried to converse with us in Spanish.

"Uruguayi," one of them said slapping me on the back. Caught by surprise I instinctively muttered in Spanish, *"hijo-de-puta"* (son-of-a-bitch), and the Russians broke out in loud laughter. The "diplomat" from the local Russian Embassy stared at me with a smirk on his face.

"Tovarishch (Friend)," the Russian told me with a friendly grin. *"Bono,"* he laughed with a slur.

"*Yest* (Eat)," he suggested, "*yest,*" pointing to large amounts of red caviar and black caviar heaped on plates with large chunks of smoked whale meat. The smell and taste of the whale meat lingered on my tongue.

Nevertheless, the excellent vodka made the food tolerable. Eating a glob of black caviar I looked around for crackers. Crackers were nowhere in sight. The Russians ate caviar by the spoonful. The major difference between a *Chicano* capitalist and the Russian communists was crackers for the caviar. The vodka was superb and the food a serious challenge. The black caviar was excellent but the red caviar had a strong fish taste.

Everyone drank copiously, enjoying the party. The Russian Captain sporadically broke into laughter to show teeth black with caviar.

Meanwhile, Copello communicated with the Russians by muttering obscenities in Spanish.

"*Russos hijos-de-puta,*" he snorted. "*Son animales.*" The captain guffawed when Copello cursed drunkenly in Spanish. He proposed another toast.

"*Darovye,*" he belched. Everyone eagerly drank another glass of vodka with the captain. We drank vodka to show solidarity with the Captain and I did not give a crap if he was a communist.

Later, inebriated, the Captain grunted noisily to let us know he was leaving. Waving, he staggered off without a word. Everyone in the room was intoxicated. Shaking hands with the Soviet Officers we were escorted by armed guards to the gangway.

On the way, Copello and his friends tried to harmonize on a tango and two sailors wearing jeans walked by us talking in Russian. They stared at our group with a look of disdain. One of the sailors had a label on the back of his jeans that said in bold lettering: **TEXAN.** I laughed impulsively at the label and the sailors scowled.

Flipping a finger at them I muttered "Texan," and pointed to their ass. Unsure of the meaning, the sailors walked hurriedly away. We reached the bottom of the gangway and Copello stopped me.

"The only reason to be a communist. The excellent vodka," he told me. I was glad my driver, Gonzales, was waiting for me. He was fascinated with my description of the visit.

The visit to the Russian trawler was fun and had been enjoyable. Nevertheless, life was rich and enjoyable in Uruguay but undoubtedly, it had become a dichotomous world for me. It was an opportunity to serve my country and to help protect democracy in Uruguay. But it was also a period of my life loaded with sadness for friends getting killed in the internal war there. We were in the middle of the conflict.

My affection for the people of Uruguay had grown tremendously. The proud tradition of democracy, the bountifulness, and the beautiful green rolling hills, the *Gauchos,* the marvelous beaches, and the people were very special. Besides, I had made many friends in Uruguay.

The internal war in Uruguay heated up and allegations in the communist media of American involvement in torture surfaced. The allegations were totally unfounded and had no credence with the Uruguayan authorities working with American OPS advisors. It seemed logical that if the allegations of torture had any foundation, Uruguayan officials in the police would have taken immediate action against anyone responsible, including Americans. It was not in the nature of the Uruguayans to condone or hide such practices.

The Chief of the Montevideo Police, General Ventura Rodriguez, and I talked occasionally about the allegations of torture at the *Jefatura.* The Chief of Police was sincerely concerned about the allegations and told me that the torture of prisoners, including the *Tupamaros,* would never be tolerated. He said anyone involved in such practices would be arrested. The U.S. police assistance program would be terminated if it were confirmed that torture was taking place in Uruguay and everyone knew this.

General Rodriguez was one of the most honest and honorable men I had ever meet. It was mere communist propaganda, he suggested. He reminded me that Uruguayan officials would expose anyone involved in torture at the police *Jefatura.* That included Americans.

Free-lance Moscow trained reporter Roger Morris wrote in a weekly Santa Fe tabloid and in **Playboy** Magazine that "allegations" of torture followed me from Uruguay.

U.S. Federal Judge Juan Burciaga found in a libel suit filed against Morris in 1981: **"In a free society there will always be those that abuse their freedom. It is regrettable, yet necessary, that innocent individuals ... will from time to time pay a dear price in order that all others enjoy their freedom."** That did not make me feel better. Morris lied amorphously during the libel trial held.

The Terrorist Network, a book written by Clair Sterling, found **"there was no evidence of torture or police mistreatment of prisoners"** in Uruguay. That was after Mitrione's kidnapping and assassination. Who was telling the truth? I am certain that Clair Sterling was truthful. I knew the communists were not.

OPS advisors became pawns in the Cold War struggle. Dan Mitrione replaced me in Uruguay and was kidnapped and brutally assassinated despite the fact that he was totally innocent of the allegations that he was involved in torture. The political environment and security situation created risks and problems for any American living in Uruguay during the *Tupamaro* period.

Bill Cantrell, under the guise of the OPS program in Uruguay, had a beguiling job. But he preferred to operate on his own and secretively, because of his assignment. He had to survive in a very dangerous and uncertain situation. His mission was covert but it was easy to make mistakes in a terrorist environment where Americans are targets. Cantrell had hired Manuel Hevia, the Cuban exile, to be his translator from Spanish to English. But unknown to us, Hevia was a communist who subsequently supported the false allegations made against Mitrione. He later passed himself off as an employee of the OPS and informed the communist media that Cantrell was a CIA officer.

Cantrell reportedly paid Hevia with CIA money and without adequate precautions. Besides, that was not necessary. OPS had a trust fund that could have been used for that purpose but Cantrell did things his way. I had suggested to him that Hevia could not be trusted. To complicate matters, Cantrell hired a fat cop named Nelson Bardesio to help him with intelligence functions and as his driver because he (Bardesio) spoke some English. He was warned that the man was known as a milksop in the police intelligence section *(Inteligencia y Enlace)* of the Montevideo police. A skinny young man named Galan joined Bardesio to form a quirky team under Cantrell. Galan was related to a former President of Uruguay and was politically connected.

The major disadvantage for Cantrell was that, working as a police advisor in a dangerous Latin American terrorist environment, he could not speak fluent Spanish and missed nuances that were extremely important. Galan and Bardesio were too weak in character and experience for the job that had to be done.

After Cantrell was transferred from Uruguay, the *Tupamaro* guerrillas were able to abduct Bardesio. He went down on his knees to confess to anything the guerrillas wanted. The *Tupamaros* obtained a written confession from Bardesio that Cantrell was a CIA Officer and published this in a communist newsletter. Bardesio sang like a bird to confess to the covert activities of Cantrell.

But other American screw-ups took place in Uruguay. The local communist publications, *El Popular* and *Epocha,* always took pleasure in excoriating the U.S. Embassy and the United States for intervention in the internal affairs of Uruguay. Bill Cantrell and Juan Noriega (a CIA officer assigned to the Embassy) were caught in the act of installing telephone taps to the Russian Embassy at the *Pocitos* exchange. It was as bad as Watergate.

As a consequence, a scandal developed and the names of Cantrell and Noriega became front-page news in local non-communist as well as communist newspapers who reported it as an American espionage operation.

The incident cast a shadow over the OPS program. The wiretap effort was a calculated risk by the CIA and Cantrell should have stayed out of it. After a week, the media stories grew banal and boring but problems with top police officials we worked with were growing difficult.

Comissario Alejandro Otero, the head of police intelligence, was a sensitive man, albeit intelligent and capable. Many top officials in the Montevideo police considered Otero a *prima donna* and too emotional for the game of intelligence. He called to ask me if we could meet at the *Jefatura,* and not knowing what he wanted, I agreed. Otero arrived a few minutes later and entered my office without saying a word. He was ominously quiet and his eyes reflected a mesmerizing stress. I knew it was trouble.

There was no doubt Otero could be sinister. He was growing nervous and his work was becoming dangerous because of the *Tupamaro* terrorists.

"*Te puedo hablar en confianza?* (Can I talk to you in confidence?)" he asked in a shaky voice. He checked to see if anyone in the office could hear.

"*Por supuesto, si, Otero,*" I told him we would talk in strict confidence, curious about his strange behavior.

"*Qué pasa?* (What's wrong?)" I asked him. I foresaw complications because Otero was a proud individual but somewhat of a complainer. To my surprise he nervously expressed bad disagreements with Cantrell on ongoing intelligence operations. He candidly told me that he was having serious problems with Cantrell and did not trust him. I quickly suspected that Cantrell had an effort afoot to replace Otero with another officer from the Montevideo police. The more he talked the more distraught Otero became, almost to the point of being incoherent.

Within seconds, the man who held one of the most important and powerful positions in the police department of Montevideo, broke down in tears. What I perceived as a mere disagreement had turned serious.

Otero seemed to be on the verge of a nervous breakdown. He confessed that Cantrell had accused him not only of incompetence, but also the improper use of CIA money.

"Don't tell me you don't know he is See Ah (CIA)," he asked me sullenly. He had complained to the Chief of Police and was told to talk to me. I promised to speak to Cantrell to see if the conflict could be resolved. But I did not comprehend what the conflict was. Otero could not clearly explain. Perhaps Cantrell knows, I thought. Wiping copious tears from his eyes with his handkerchief, Otero thanked me and left with a sad look on his face. I felt disappointment. Were we risking too much working with the police to fight terrorists? Were we too intrusive? I thought about the wicked Yetzer and wondered what Cantrell had in mind. I believed that Otero wanted me to get Cantrell off his ass.

Cantrell was a calm independent sort on the outside but bubbling inside with the stress of his job. When he was angry, his face turned a deep red. His face glistened as he listened carefully to the explanation of my meeting with Otero and my description of his mental state.

Cantrell immediately called Otero a "big baby." He was probably right. But Otero could cause a great deal of damage to all of us with his vindictiveness, I warned. (And he eventually did.) The situation was growing more complex with no end in sight.

In late 1968, John Horton was transferred to Langley to take over the Western Hemisphere Division (WH), and his replacement, Richard (Dick) Sampson, a veteran CIA Officer, arrived shortly after. The new CIA Station Chief did not like the Horton residence, apparently because the house was too large. Security was also a factor. Because of the *Tupamaro* threat, a guarded apartment complex was considered more secure.

Sampson asked me if I wanted the house. The residence we had lived in had been burned in a mysterious fire that happened a week earlier. I was surprised when my wife and children took the matter of the fire that had burned our house down in stride. They were not overly scared and reacted without major complaints. I was the one who was traumatized by the fire and our situation.

The house we lived in previously was beautiful. It was large and elegant with a park-like lawn and many trees surrounded by a high fence. We had held a reception at the house the night before the fire broke out. It was a working get-together attended by the Uruguayan Minister of Interior, the Minister of Defense, the heads of the Uruguayan Army, Navy, and Air Force, the Chief of Police, top police commanders, the U.S. Ambassador, and U.S. Military Officers from the U.S. Embassy. The objective of the reception was to discuss joint planning and operations between the police and military forces in the fight against the *Tupamaros*.

Nevertheless, my family settled comfortably into our new house. But things were growing frustrating for me as head of the OPS program in Uruguay. There were idiosyncrasies we were obliged to deal with.

Jennifer Hyland, a pretty British Uruguayan with long beautiful auburn hair and long legs, worked as a secretary at the OPS office located at the USAID mission. She handled all administrative matters for the public safety advisors. She greeted me at the door of my office at the AID Mission with a message.

"The Ambassador's secretary called to make sure you attend the meeting scheduled for today at the U.S. Embassy. The meeting is scheduled for 9:30." She told me.

I immediately started out the door and she blushed when she saw me frown.

"Excuse me, sir," she said. "I just got the word from the Ambassador's secretary," she said. I faked a serious frown and involuntarily she giggled out loud.

"Stop it, Jenny," I said lightheartedly, making her laugh more. Jennifer was twenty-one years old and a part of the U.S. Embassy crowd. She was a trusted employee, but this time she missed an important detail in regards to U.S. Embassy meetings and nuances of the environment. The Ambassador had never checked to see if I was going to attend a meeting before. It appeared I was in trouble.

When I arrived at the U.S. Embassy, Ambassador Robert (Bob) Sayre, a small handsome man with fine features, tensed when I walked into the conference room. Despite outward calmness, he looked disturbed. The local communist newspaper *El Popular* was on top of the conference table. He picked it up and held it in the air.

"Dolph, have you seen this?" he called out in a loud voice.

The Country Team members, the top officers of the Embassy, sat in silence around the conference table.

"The article in the paper has your picture in it and says you are the *Capo* of the CIA in Uruguay," he said. He seemed to be trying to restrain an overpowering irritability with some difficulty.

"I can't help that, Mr. Ambassador," I responded briskly. *"El Popular* is hardly a credible newspaper. I've already been accused of being *El Capo* for the FBI repressive mission in Uruguay with my picture in the paper. *El Popular* is the leading communist newspaper in Uruguay, Mr. Ambassador," I added.

"I want you to talk to the Minister of Interior and find out what position the Government of Uruguay is taking in regard to the matter," he said. He looked stern. He suggested I do this as soon as possible because he wanted to report on the matter to Washington. That worried me. That had never been done before.

"Don't worry about it, Dolph," John Topping told me after the meeting. "I'll talk to the Ambassador. He can't take stuff like that seriously. Bring **me** the Minister's response after you meet with him." I had to follow orders but did not like it. Was it possible that as a result of the article I would have to leave the country?

Storace Arosa, the Uruguayan Government Minister of Interior, was a dapper handsome man with a remarkable resemblance to Ronald Coleman, the popular movie star of the '30s and '40s. The President of Uruguay had appointed him to his tough position a few months earlier. As Minister of Interior he was responsible for all the police and public safety forces in the country, and fortunately we had an excellent working relationship. Like most top Uruguayan Government officials he was unpretentious and easy to work with. He was most friendly and down to earth.

At seven o'clock at night he was diligently at work. My secretary had called his office and was told to tell me to come over that same evening. His assistant informed him of my arrival and the Minister came out to greet me. He joked about the serious look on my face, suggesting I had lost my *"Novia"* (Girl Friend).

"No te preocupes, en corral pequeño hasta los Gringos enlazan." He laughed to tell me not to worry, in a small corral even a *Gringo* can lasso a heifer. It was an old Uruguayan saying. He asked me to sit.

Sitting in a stuffed chair, I pulled out a bottle of Johnny Walker Black Label Scotch from my briefcase. His valet brought two glasses, ice, and a pitcher of water, and set them down on the coffee table. *Tiqueta negra* (Black Label) was the Minister's favorite, he told me.

The Minister came into the room, sat without a word and grinned as I filled a glass for him.

"Salud," he said, tapping my glass and taking a long swallow. He exhaled deeply.

"Qué pasa?" he asked lazily. I grinned at his laid-back attitude.

"Tengo Problemas! (I have problems!)" I told him.

"Tú no tienes problemas, yo tengo problemas," he laughed. He told me I didn't have any problems, **he** had the problems. Our conversation was entirely in Spanish and informal.

I explained that Ambassador Sayre was concerned about the story that had appeared in *El Popular.* Dr. Storace Arosa stared at the wall and suddenly laughed out loud.

"I thought it was a nice picture of you," he told me. He wasn't taking me seriously.

I explained to the Minister that the U.S. Ambassador wanted to know what position the Government of Uruguay was taking in regard to the matter. I felt uncertainty about my approach. Perhaps I was miscalculating, and diplomatically, it was a serious problem. I candidly suggested that the Ambassador was concerned about the potential political reaction to the story about me that had appeared in *El Popular.*

The Minister seemed to disregard what I told him and stared sullenly at me.

"Hablas en serio? (Are you serious?)" He drew himself back in his chair and chuckled in amusement.

"Your Ambassador has not been in Uruguay very long, has he?" he asked. Before I could answer, he asked for a cigarette and we both lit up.

"I can't believe you *Norté Americanos,"* he said in open frustration. "How can an American Ambassador possibly give a shit what the communists write in their newspapers?" I laughed and he shook his head.

"Tell him not to read the communist papers," he said cheerfully. "That way he won't get heartburn."

"Doesn't your Ambassador know the communists are your enemy?" he asked sarcastically. I took a long drink of Scotch, feeling tired and distressed.

"Puta, no se! (Fuck, I don't know!)" I said impulsively, and he laughed.

Our conversation turned to the problems of internal security and the police. He suggested that since I had been in Uruguay for four years I had a good understanding of the local political environment.

"The United States has helped Uruguay in this economic and security crisis and we count on more help. Until we can resolve the economic crisis, the political and security problems will remain unresolved," he said.

"La efectividad de la policia es crucial en estós tiempos (The effectiveness of the police is crucial at this time)," he suggested placidly. "The fight for democracy in Uruguay will be a long one." His voice indicated that he was weary. "The economy has to improve before we see any letup on the labor unrest and violence. But we need time for economic reforms to show results." He lectured me on the variety of economic improvements made.

"Austerity measures are tough on all Uruguayans so we are not going to be popular for awhile," he said. "But the economy is improving." We continued to drink and talk.

My line of work was going to make me an alcoholic, I thought. The Minister poured two more glasses of Scotch. I tactfully reminded him of the purpose of my visit. I had been there an hour.

"*Mira* Saenz," he said irritably. "Why don't you tell your Ambassador that if he is going to worry about the stories that appear in the communist newspapers, then we are really in deep shit." I laughed impulsively and his eyes crinkled with a smile.

"Tell him he should see the shit *El Popular* and *Epoca* print about the President of Uruguay," he said sarcastically. He took a swig of Scotch to stare at me.

"They print whatever lies they please. The Ambassador should see the *mierda* they print about me." He chuckled and took a long pull on his drink. I joined him in another toast.

"*Salud,*" he said. He continued his lecture in a clear voice, almost an oratorical one.

"We are a true democracy and the communists want to change that. We are in a real-life struggle for survival and the communists capitalize on the fact that Uruguay is a democracy. They enjoy their freedom and run their candidates for public office, even for President. Now the Marxist *Tupamaros* are trying to forcibly overthrow the government." He paused to empty the bottle of Scotch into our glasses.

"I don't believe Uruguay will ever accept communism. Some of our liberal *inteligencia* are communists, but a lot of them don't know why; it is just a fad. They are not prepared to die for it. The communists say they have 20,0000 members in Uruguay. So be it." He took a long drink of Scotch.

"Politically, the *Blancos* and the *Colorados* are like the Democrats and Republicans in the United States. The *Blancos* are elected to power and govern for a period of time, and then the *Colorados* are elected to power and they govern for awhile until things get messy." He looked sternly at me.

"The people choose who will govern in Uruguay. But when the crunch comes, everyone is Uruguayan. Our great concern is losing our freedom and independence. I don't see where communism is going to help the situation in Uruguay," he told me. He grinned slightly.

I felt like applauding. I felt very comfortable with the Minister and was enjoying the visit. We talked for over an hour and in the process polished off the bottle of Scotch. But we were both relaxed and in a cheerful mood. I asked him if that was the position of the Government of Uruguay and he said yes.

"*Vayase por la sombrita,*" he told me as I stood to leave. This was equivalent to telling someone in English "be sure to walk in the shade," or to "take care."

He told me that the majority of Uruguayan officials depended on the support of the OPS program. I personally was satisfied we were in a fight to help a democracy survive communist aggression. But the mystique of communism attracted many people. Even Uruguay, a model democracy, was vulnerable.

Gonzales, my faithful chauffeur, waited patiently to drive me home. The police officers assigned to me were named Gonzales and Ovedo. Both were good people and a pleasure to have around. Gonzales was very serious and dependable. Oveda was a stout sort with pink cheeks and a jolly disposition. They were very loyal and were loved by my children. I had grown extremely fond of them. Both men were discreet and intelligent and always ready to help in every aspect. But I knew they were not assigned as my protective detail albeit they were ready to help. But my security was my problem and could not be assigned to anyone. If I didn't like it, I could resign. That was my perception of my security situation.

Two weeks later I was surprised when I received orders to proceed to *La Paz*, Bolivia, on a temporary assignment. My instructions were to link up in *La Paz* with Jake Longan, the Chief of the OPS program in Venezuela. We were to evaluate the capabilities of the Bolivian *Carabineros* in terms of their ability to cope with civil unrest and a communist insurgency in Bolivia. But the assignment turned out to be a historical event.

Months earlier, Dr. Ernesto *Ché* Guevara had passed through *Carrasco* Airport in Montevideo on his way to Bolivia, but no one had recognized him. *Ché* had cut his long hair and shaved his famous beard and was wearing thick myopic eyeglasses. His black beret was in his suitcase. His eyebrows had been altered.

Hidden CIA cameras had snapped pictures of his passport but *Ché* was unrecognizable. I thought of him disguised as **"a mighty penis rising,"** like Abbie Hoffman described Fidel Castro when it came to light that he was a communist and leader of the *revolución* in Havana.

I had never been to Bolivia, but Longan and I would get caught up in the history of *Ché* Guevara, his insurgency in that country, and his diary.

Jake Longan and Adolph Saenz in La Paz, Bolivia, August 1967

Adolph Saenz in Bolivia during *Ché* Guevara insurgency,
August 1967

13

Ché Guevara and Bolivia

August 1967

My temporary assignment to Bolivia would take me from one unstable political situation to another. I had never been in Bolivia and was told the political climate in Bolivia was capable of becoming volatile and highly uncertain. The situation could become a political labyrinth with Dr. Ernesto *Ché* Guevara in the country trying to take over the government. He was a communist fanatic convinced that a socialist/communist state was the answer to the injustice, poverty and oppression that existed in Latin America. *Ché* was imbued with the fervor and authority of a high priest.

Trying to convert the masses in Bolivia to Marxism/Leninism and the communist faith was not easy. *Ché* reached out to do that and was willing to kill those who did not support communism. He had already participated in dozens of political executions in Cuba.

In Bolivia, things were not going well for *Ché* Guevara. He trekked the desolate area called *La Hiquerra,* a large rural area in the *Santa Cruz* Mountains, trying to get the *campesinos* to join his insurgency. He put up with rugged and difficult terrain, but what depressed him was the attitude of economically deprived *cholos* and *campesinos*. They did not comprehend the importance and the benefits of a communist insurgency. The peasants in the rural villages of Bolivia were unlike most people in Latin America. They were uncommonly stoic and uncommunicative. The peasants in the small villages dispersed throughout the *Santa Cruz* Mountains listened in silence but seemed uninspired.

Despite the many problems that could affect an insurgency in Boliva, *Ché* Guevara appeared unstoppable because of his fame, experience, and popularity. Nonetheless, "how long could Guevara **stay** in power if he proved successful in overthrowing the Government of Bolivia?" people asked. In the past century, Bolivia had experienced a violent change in government almost every two years. But it seemed that for *Ché* Guevara, once a communist government was installed, things would be different.

Ché Guevara excited the left-wing revolutionaries of the world and several outsiders from different countries rallied to his cause. Regis Debray, AKA Danton, an extreme left-wing *afficionado,* delivered his favorite cigars. But Debray brought little in the way of fighting power or knowledge of guerrilla warfare in Bolivia. He was gone by the time the fun started in *La Higuera.*

Ché Guevara was experiencing serious problems in convincing the *cholos* and *campesinos* to join his insurgency. He did not understand the Indian dialect and apparently did not comprehend that the people of the *Santa Cruz* Mountains would likely support **anyone** trying to overthrow the Government of Bolivia. That had been done many times before.

For centuries, the *campesinos* in the rural areas of Bolivia had worked hard for a minimal existence under difficult conditions. *Ché* spent hours preaching to them about government oppression, injustice and the glory of an egalitarian society. But the *campesinos* knew nothing else. Mostly Indian with a few bearing traces of Spanish blood, they remained emotionless when he talked about his *gran revolucion.* They were not impressed that the great *Ché* Guevara was there to lead them in an insurgency. *Ché* was growing impatient.

One *lugar teniente* (trusted deputy) returned from *La Paz* and reported that there was little action from the comrades there in support of his insurgency. But *Ché* complained about something else. "The *campesino bruto* (dumb asses) do not appreciate a communist revolution," Guevara told his men. His efforts to topple the military government of General Juan Barrientos were faltering. His options were narrowing to a point of concern. Bolivia was an unpredictable world. Other countries were far more understandable. But in his first two attempts for a *Ché* Guevara type of insurgency, in Argentina and the Congo, he had experienced total disaster. Obviously, his reputation was also not enough for success in Bolivia.

In Washington, D.C., at the Lincoln Memorial, 50,000 demonstrators gathered to protest U.S. involvement in the Vietnam War. But in New York 700,000 persons marched on Fifth Avenue to demonstrate support for U.S. troops fighting in Vietnam. In local New

York theaters a vaunted play titled *A Man for All Seasons* played to capacity crowds. In Bolivia, stress aggravated *Ché* Guevara's asthma and he lit a Cuban cigar anyway.

In Uruguay as I prepared to leave for *La Paz* with a morbid discomfort about the trip, I recalled that my friend Vic Surface, an AID official who had lived in Bolivia for many years, told me that it was equivalent to visiting another planet. It was unlike any other country in the world, he said. But he loved Bolivia.

The Pan American flight from Montevideo to Lima, Peru, connected with another flight that would cross over the *Andes* Mountains on the way to *La Paz*, Bolivia. There I would link up with Jake Longan, a dead pan, bald headed, tough ex-border patrol officer with many years of experience in Latin America. He was considered one of the most effective officers in OPS.

Dr. John Stanham, the British physician who was the U.S. Embassy doctor in Uruguay, concluded after my physical exam that I was in excellent condition. He warned me to be careful of the altitude but, like *Ché* Guevara, the unique character of Bolivia was totally unfamiliar to me. By noon the flight from Lima to *La Paz* was airborne. The Pan American flight over the majestic *Andes* Mountains was a sublime treat and the vast snow covered mountain ranges below seemed like marmoreal sculptures of white "happy" valleys.

Two hours after our departure from Lima, the Pan American turbo prop descended rapidly over splendid green mountains and valleys. The flight stewardess announced preparations for a landing at *La Paz* International Airport and a few minutes later the wheels of the aircraft hit the runway with a hard jolt. The pilot braked harshly to bring the plane to a complete halt.

He then taxied over a bumpy tarmac until we reached a brown terminal building. People outside the dusty terminal stared at our arrival with wry curiosity. Bolivian *Carabineros* wearing green uniforms watched from a distance.

The passengers disembarked on a metal platform and ladder that led to the ground from the door of the aircraft. I walked down the ladder still disconnected with the reality of Bolivia and reached a *terra cotta*-like surface. Suddenly, a strange light-headedness hit me. Black spots exploded silently in front of my eyes. My heart pounded furiously in my chest and I experienced a strange shortness of breath. Bracing myself against the ladder leading to the door of the airplane, the thought occurred to me that perhaps I was having a heart attack.

Jake Longan suddenly appeared and grabbed my arm. He showed me a pile of six white tablets he had in the palm of his hand. He ordered roughly that I take and swallow them.

"Take them," he ordered again. I felt dizzy but felt concerned about taking pills I knew nothing about.

"If you don't take them, your ass is going to pass out," Longan warned me, laughing. Popping the tablets in my mouth I chewed and swallowed frantically.

"Where's the water?" I asked anxiously.

"No water here. You can drink some Scotch later," Jake chuckled. Incredibly, I felt better quickly.

"What the hell happened to me?" I asked Jake.

"Shit, you were passing out from the lack of oxygen. Didn't anyone tell you?" Longan's face grew intense as he pointed to a large sign in front of the terminal. The sign said: **"Welcome to La Paz, Bolivia. Highest Commercial Airport in the World, 13,358 Feet."** I was glad Jake was handy with the white pills.

Jake had boarded the plane in Caracas and unknown to me, in Lima he had transferred to the Pan American flight I was on. Prepensely armed with *"Soroche"* tablets, Longan was not affected by the altitude as harshly as I was. I learned later that the *"Soroche"* pills are commonly prescribed for high altitude sickness and are considered a must for high mountain climbers. (The common medication currently used is Diamox.) Airport personnel carried small cylinders and administered oxygen to several passengers who had fainted.

The small customs area was crowded and chaotic but we zipped through with the assistance of Hugh Murray, a CIA officer assigned to the OPS program in Bolivia. We walked outside the terminal building and the bright sunshine was immediately warming. To get to *La Paz* Murray drove a car down a long spiraling road into an enormous open pit that overflowed with homes and buildings that seemed to be encrusted on the mountainsides. The long twisting road took us into an awesome valley and the city of *La Paz,* a sprawling metropolis of nearly 800,000 people situated at 12,000 feet altitude. Bolivia was not for sissies.

Murray took us to the Hotel *Crillon,* one of the best hotels in town where we had reservations. Inside the lobby of the hotel, oxygen cylinders were made available for guests having trouble with the altitude. The service in the hotel included daily servings of *Maté de Coca,* a tea made from the coca leaf plant. The *Maté de Coca* was provided gratis three times a day. To those in the cocaine trade, with precursors the coca leaves could be processed into pure cocaine. But the *Maté de Coca* was already processed into a mild herbal tea and could not be converted to cocaine.

Later, the local U.S. Embassy doctor in *La Paz* recommended that we consume *Maté de Coca* no less than twice a day to help us cope with the effects of the high altitude. The *coca* leaf tea was effective and permitted me to sleep soundly at night and wake up refreshed every morning. Many people seemed to experience serious problems with insomnia in *La Paz* because of the high altitude.

The next day at the U.S. Embassy, Hugh Murray, a young man with a cool military style seemed uncertain about Bolivia. He was not at all forthcoming and almost anti-social. Murray was a loner with a quaint personality that belied the atrocities he had experienced as a Green Beret in South Vietnam. The CIA used Green Berets in Vietnam for the tough assignments.

As an advisor to the Montagnards near the border with Cambodia, Murray had escaped the war generally intact and was now a police advisor with OPS, a world away from Vietnam. He had no experience in police work and seemed uncertain about his job in Bolivia. Nonetheless, he was in tune with every other American in Bolivia.

The interior of the Chancery was not a cheerful place, but neither was *La Paz,* a silent city with low overhanging clouds. We discovered that many Americans walking around the Embassy were U.S. military personnel out of uniform.

The U.S. Embassy political officer subsequently briefed us on the local political situation in an abrupt and officious tone. He confirmed that *Ché* Guevara was organizing an insurgency in the *Santa Cruz* mountains. The United States Government was providing assistance to the Bolivian security forces to resist the insurgency, he said. Several U.S. programs were at play, including covert efforts by the CIA and U.S. military assistance.

According to what we were told, Bolivia was one of the most politically unstable countries in the world. There had been over 60 mass changes of key officials in the Bolivian government in *coups* and revolutions during the past 50 years. That did not explain why we were in Bolivia.

We met afterwards with AID Officials in a separate building. The officers there were more enlightening and explained that a survey of the police capabilities in Bolivia was needed to determine the parameters of an expanded OPS assistance program to that country.

Our mission was defined. We were to evaluate existing police capabilities in Bolivia and to provide recommendations on the U.S.

assistance needed to cope with traditional crime and civil unrest, communist subversion and the *Ché* Guevara insurgency.

The President of Bolivia, General Juan Barrientos, a Bolivian Air Force Officer, appeared to be an uncertain ally of the United States in the Cold War and often provided mixed signals on his ideology to American officials in the Embassy. President Barrientos had survived seven known assassination attempts and obviously understood the intricacies, risks and complexities of the political environment in Bolivia. Undaunted, we humorously concluded that he had had a "horseshoe implant" on his ass.

Politically, Barrientos stood moderately to the left but was fearful of a communist takeover in Bolivia. We were told that affiliation with the right wing was unpopular in Bolivia, but many people in the country had German names. After World War II, Nazi exiles had flooded the country. But the Political Officer suggested that Bolivians had disdain for any individual with right wing tendencies.

"What about Klaus Barbie," I asked.

"He is doing O.K." The political officer smiled grimly.

"How about plain ol' shitheads?" Jake asked. The political officer chuckled impulsively.

Bolivia seemed peaceful and innocuous but apparently could be unpredictable and risky. Eight years earlier, Jake Jackson, an OPS officer posted in Bolivia was shot in the back by left-wing guerrillas in a rural area of the country. After he was shot, Jackson was evacuated to the United States for treatment and he survived. But the bullet had severed his spinal cord and left him paralyzed.

The last time I saw my friend Jake Jackson he was a paraplegic and doing research in Central America. We played poker in Panama with some friends from the local U.S. mission and Jake was in a wheelchair. After a few drinks he told me sadly that he often thought about killing himself. One could not underestimate the potential danger of Bolivia.

The terrain in Bolivia was extensive, unique and fascinating. Lake *Titicaca* was a fresh water lake considered the highest in the world. The *Yungas* where the cocaine fields were cultivated involved incredible mountain terrain that seemed to beckon those contemplating suicide. The urban areas were dangerous and replete with the type of individuals interested in the politics, crime, and in the cocaine production. They did not hesitate to kill anyone threatening them or their operations. Terrorist danger was latent in major cities and coupled with labor unrest that was common in the country could become extremely explosive. Now *Ché* Guevara was attempting to overthrow the country in the name of communism.

It was expected that the police would play a major role in combating *Ché* Guevara's insurgent movement. But the police capabilities for this effort required strengthening. The reality was that *Ché* had taken a huge personal risk by starting an insurgency in a country as intractable as Bolivia. As an asthmatic he would have a hard time surviving in the *altiplanos* or in *La Paz.* Thus, he chose the *Santa Cruz* area where a more tolerable altitude existed. The *Yungas,* the beautiful jungle and mountain terrain where cocaine crops prospered, was 8,500 feet altitude at its lowest.

Anyone traveling to the *Yungas* faced a unique and dangerous challenge. The trip was usually undertaken by large buses or 4 x 4 vehicles that were required to drive on a solitary narrow dirt road that snaked for miles through an extraordinarily high mountain range. Hundreds had been killed on the treacherous road leading to the *Yungas.* Any driver with experience driving on that mystical road was in high demand. Upon reaching the top of a very high mountain range, the road spiraled dangerously down into the small villages where the cocaine fields were cultivated.

Landslides frequently blocked the road for days. On the top of the mountain peaks, one could play with the clouds. Many believed they felt a strange overpowering peace on the supernatural mountain peaks prior to reaching the abyss of the *Yungas.* Visitors often felt the overpowering presence of God among the clouds layered on the mountaintops. Chewing coca leaves helped that feeling.

While we were at the Embassy, Jake received a note from U.S. Ambassador Douglas Henderson inviting us for cocktails at the residence that weekend. Jake had served under Henderson in Venezuela.

"His wife is a beautiful person and a lovely lady," he said. "You'll like her."

"You old bastard," I told him in a humorous exchange.

Our days grew immediately busy and by dusk we were both physically exhausted. Our meetings with Bolivian police officials were productive and provided valuable information on the local internal security situation and on the requirements to cope with the problems of the ongoing civil unrest and insurgency. Many Bolivian *Carabineros* from the principal police units were old friends and former students of the Inter-American Police Academy (IAPA) or the International Police Academy (IPA).

Colonel *Toto* Quintanilla was a friend and met often with us to discuss the public safety situation. Toto, a tall, rugged looking individual with a sense of humor, was the head of the Bolivian Police Intelligence Section. He explained that *Ché* Guevara was having problems organizing the *campesinos* in *Santa Cruz* for his insurgency, but that he attracted many visitors to Bolivia, he said.

"El hijo de puta tiene mas visitantes que el Presidente de la Republica (the son-of-a-bitch has more visitors than the President of the Republic)," he told us over *pisco* sours. *Pisco* sours, a tasty but potent drink made with local *chicha* (booze) and egg white, creeps up on you. They were delicious, and I acquired a taste for the local libation. *Piscos* became my favorite drink while I was in Bolivia.

"Ché won't make it," *Toto* told us. "He has tremendous left-wing support in *La Paz* but he can't put it together," he chuckled. *"El Indio Boliviano es muy pueblerino y inasequible* (The Bolivian Indian is very parochial and unapproachable)," he added. The Colonel enlightened us more on the local situation than anyone else.

"What moves the communists and left-wingers in Bolivia is **not** that they have a real keen understanding of Marxism or communism. Their motivation is whatever opportunities it may bring for them. The MNR (*Movimiento Nacionalista Revolucionario*...Nationalist Revolutionary Movement) is a mix of people that cannot agree on what they are or what they represent."

"Ché is a romantic," he concluded. "He is a *Don Quixote.* He will fail with his insurgency in Bolivia," he said.

Toto worked closely with American military and CIA officers trying to track down *Ché* Guevara. "If we can cut off the cycle of visitors who bring him his Cuban cigars, we've got him," he kidded.

"We could also entice him to move his insurgency to the *Chagras.* He wouldn't have to be chased down there."

Toto explained that in the Chagras, a *bicho* (a beetle called a *vincucha*), had an aberrant lethality. The bite of a *vincucha* was an unequivocal death sentence for any individual, according to him.

"However, *Ché* will continue to be a pain in the ass for a few years," he added. He described the matter in a very serious demeanor.

"A person bitten by the *vincucha* dies in about three to five years of heart failure," he explained. He swore that the bite of the beetle never failed to kill.

"Shit, we could use some of them bugs back home," Jake suggested laughing.

I grinned at *Toto* with a look of skepticism. "No cure, eh?"

Quintanilla kept a straight face. "No cure!" he said firmly. Now that was real mystique.

The following day we continued our assessment of the capabilities of the police and concluded that the officer corps of the *Carabineros* were an elite group, among the best trained in the hemisphere. The average cop was another matter. They were poorly selected, poorly paid and poorly motivated. The training was highly militarized. Military personnel were worse off. Training in counterinsurgency was sorely needed.

The use of police dogs to find and to destroy enclaves of guerrillas had been very successful in Bolivia. The use of dogs to fight guerrillas seemed to be a good strategy but the casualty rate for the dogs was always high. The Bolivian *Carabineros* were breeding police dogs and training them for that purpose.

Colonel Juan Lopez, another old friend from the *Carabineros*, worked with us to set up meetings with the various police commanders. But when he was asked to set up a meeting with Arguédes Mendietta, the Minister of Interior (MOI), the Colonel's jaw dropped.

"Para qué diablos quieren reunirse con el hijo de puta? (Why the devil do you want to meet with that son-of-a-bitch?)" he lashed out in unabashed anger. "He is a communist!" Colonel Lopez became visibly disturbed.

"That's why we want to talk to him," I tried to explain.

"Don't expect him to cooperate with you," Lopez responded harshly. "He may not even want to meet with you." He was probably thinking that the dumb *Gringos* did not know who the enemy was. The colonel's deep displeasure was obvious.

"Mi coronel, si se puede, bien," I told him. *"Si no quiere, bien tambien."* I told the colonel that if the Minister would meet with us, that was fine and if he did not want to meet with us, that was fine, too. We were interested in getting a reaction from him in regards to U.S. assistance and *Ché* Guevara. Tired, we broke to eat dinner.

The Hotel *Crillon* served fine international cuisine at the dining room on the top floor of the hotel. We invited Colonel Lopez to have dinner with us and he accepted. We sat and talked over drinks before eating dinner. Jake said he was losing his appetite and complained about being unable to sleep at night.

Lopez suggested that the problem was the altitude. He recommended that despite the cold air, Longan keep the windows in his room wide open to maximize the amount of oxygen coming into his room at night. Jake drank heavily, apparently in hopes of overcoming his persistent insomnia. The Colonel and I drank with him. But Jake was growing morose and unhappy.

"Saenz," Colonel Lopez told me lightheartedly. "Tell your friend not to despair about not being able to sleep. What he needs is a nice young *chica* to help him relax." Longan understood what he said and looked at us with a lecherous grin on his face.

"Did you know," Lopez continued in a light vein, "in *La Paz*, you can have the most glorious orgasms you have ever experienced because of the high altitude? However, that is also the cause of the high rate of heart attacks in *La Paz*," he chuckled. We were being lectured on the good things of Bolivia.

"*Las mujeres se enamoran con una pingá loca,*" Colonel Lopez suggested with a broad smile. "The women fall in love with a perpetual erection driven by *Maté de Coca*. Women go crazy when they get screwed at this altitude. *Maté de Coca* gives a man a perpetual hard-on," he told us.

"It's true," Lopez insisted. "It is a proven fact that the high altitude provides the most prolonged and intense orgasms any person can possibly have." We laughed spontaneously.

"Well, that certainly is a good reason for us to get laid, Jake," I quipped. Jake smiled and Lopez raised his glass in a toast. He offered more good advice.

"And, Saenz," he said, "it is a universal custom in Bolivia. *Tomar maté de coca para mantener la pingá loca.*" In more vulgar terms, Lopez suggested with a lecherous gleam that we "drink coca leaf tea to keep our penis *loca* and in a frenzy for sex!"

After an hour of heavy imbibing Longan stared bleakly at a full moon hanging brightly outside the large window. He had a twisted grin on his rugged face. We had been in Bolivia for over five weeks and had experienced one bout with intestinal problems but otherwise we were in good shape. That week we had one social commitment we could not avoid.

The residence of the U.S. Ambassador in Bolivia was an elegant house with the usual perks, marble floors, beautiful patios, terraces and fountains surrounded by begonias and geraniums and blue and white tiles. At the residence an Indian-looking maid in a black uniform and white apron led us to a small living room where Ambassador Henderson and his wife waited.

The Ambassador, a typical diplomat, greeted us warmly and introduced his wife, a charming effervescent lady with alert hazel eyes. I was impressed with the friendly warmth of the American Ambassador and his wife. We talked informally and were made to feel at ease. A maid served drinks and hors d'oeuvres consisting of small sandwiches and hard-boiled quail eggs in a reddish sauce.

The Ambassador mentioned *Ché* Guevara briefly, more in frustration than concern.

"Why would the communists want to take over a poor country like Bolivia with an insurgency?" he asked. He pointed out that the communist party in Bolivia had the large worker's union on their side and plenty of left-wing support. But Bolivia had extensive divisiveness, with right wing and left-wing groups attempting to organize their loyalists and with the *Quécha* and *Aymara* Indians inassimilable.

For certain, the police and military forces had to prepare for a guerrilla movement led by an expert and dedicated communist insurgent, *Ché* Guevara. But the Ambassador was more concerned about losing track of the CIA and Special Forces that were working with the Bolivian military and police forces trying to find and destroy *Ché* Guevara's guerrilla force. He would be held responsible for any fuck-ups.

A telephone call took the Ambassador away momentarily and left us alone with his wife.

"While he's gone, let me play some of the latest music craze in the United States," she said. "I love this music." She turned on the record player and offered us another drink.

"This is Herb Alpert's music," she said with a burst of excitement. "I love his music," she repeated. I took a long sip of Scotch and Jake looked bored.

Music filled the room and the Ambassador's wife swayed with the brassy Latin tempo of Herb Alpert's band. I had been out of the U.S. too long. I had not heard of Herb Alpert.

"Makes you want to dance," I told Jake. He let off a derisive snort.

The Ambassador returned shortly after and Jake looked pallid. I had been enjoying the music.

"Dolph, let's go," he told me with a worried glance. I nodded. Longan obviously had a reason for leaving. But we had been there for over an hour.

"We have to get up early, Mr. Ambassador." He said. "We have several meetings and may go to *Santa Cruz.*" I wondered if it was a good idea to go to *Santa Cruz.* Ambassador Henderson smiled graciously.

"It is good to see you, Jake," he said. He turned to face me with a friendly grin.

"And you too, Mr. Saenz," he added politely, shaking my hand. We walked out to the car waiting for us.

"Ambassador Henderson is a hell of a nice person," I told Jake. Not many U.S. Ambassadors were as candid and down to earth.

"And he is a damn good Ambassador," Jake said and slouched into a deep silence.

"I don't feel so hot," he said in a low voice. I glanced at him and he looked beat.

"We meet with the Minister of Interior tomorrow. Right?" I reminded him.

"Oh, yeah," he said absent-mindedly.

"Are you up to it?" I asked. He stared at me.

"Yep," he said. I was worried about my friend Jake.

Colonel Lopez picked us up at the hotel the next morning wearing the full dress military uniform of the *Carabineros*. He continued to be concerned about our meeting with the Minister of Interior, Arquédes Mendiettta.

"Don't tell him too much," he said. "Don't forget, he is a communist." He stared, a grin on his face.

"It is also rumored that he is a *maricón,*" Lopez said, making us laugh.

The old Ministry building had guards at the door when we arrived. Lopez talked to the armed sentinels and they signaled for us to enter. The Colonel led the way to the Minister's office where an attractive woman in a dark suit sat stoically at a desk. Lopez told her in Spanish that the *Americanos* had an appointment with the Minister and she told him in Spanish that she would let the Minister know we were there. She offered small demitasses of black coffee and asked us to wait.

Various people in the building passed the area and stared at us but did not stop. We waited patiently for about twenty-five minutes without a word. In the interim I read the local newspaper.

"We won't make *Santa Cruz* today, Jake," I suggested.

"I guess not," he responded with little interest. "I'm tired anyway," he said. His face was flushed. Actually the trip was more for the purpose of looking at the terrain, but I looked forward to breathing more oxygen in the lower levels of *Santa Cruz*. Lopez leaned over with a sullen look.

"*El hijo de puta nos hace esperar a propósito* (The son-of-a-bitch is deliberately keeping us waiting)." The Colonel was right. The time grew to thirty minutes.

"Fuck him, let's go," Jake said suddenly, anger in his face.

I nodded and told Lopez in Spanish that were leaving. As if on a signal, the secretary informed us the Minister was ready to see us. Lopez shook his head in disgust and we entered the Minister's office, a non-officious Spartan environment with a solitary desk on a raised platform surrounded by chairs. A short, balding dumpy man with a dark stern look waited for us. Arguédes Mendietta, the Minister of Interior (MOI) for Bolivia was a known communist and was responsible for all the police forces in the country.

The military forces were under the Minister of Defense, but a communist in control of the police forces was a major conflict of interest, especially with *Ché* Guevara running loose in the country. We were flirting with wolves.

The Minister shook hands with a small limp hand hesitantly when Lopez introduced us.

"*Éste es el Señor* Jake Longan," he said, pronouncing Jake's name with an accent. It was a surprise when Lopez introduced me as Hugh Murray. "*Y esté es el Señor Hugo Murray,*" he said. For some unknown reason the colonel had introduced me to Mendietta as Hugh Murray. I smiled and said nothing while the Minister stared at us with wary eyes. Hugh Murray was the CIA officer assigned to OPS in Bolivia. For some reason Lopez did not want the Minister to know my name or what Hugh Murray looked like.

The Minister asked the colonel to spell our names and he wrote them down on a pad. He asked us to sit with an unfriendly gesture. We talked cursorily about United States assistance for the police in terms of the current security situation and he asked us why we were in Bolivia.

"We don't know, *Señor Ministro,*" I wanted to say. The adversarial tip came when the Minister bluntly suggested that it appeared that the United States was intervening in the internal affairs of Bolivia. The Minister made his communist affiliation obvious and made no attempt to hide it. It amused me to be face to face with a communist enemy but no one made any moves to kill. We were dancing with the enemy, I thought jokingly

The Minister conceded that President Barrientos apparently appreciated the assistance from the United States. He said he did not. Colonel Lopez reminded him that the President of Bolivia had requested assistance from the United States and Arguédes Mendietta grunted in displeasure.

"*Y Ché Guevara?* (What about *Ché* Guevara?)" He asked the question sullenly in an abrupt manner. It appeared he was interested in finding out what we knew. Jake nodded for me to respond.

"*Bueno, Señor Ministro,*" I asked him in Spanish. I stared into his dark eyes.

"*Dónde esta?*" I asked him to tell **us** where *Ché* Guevara was.

He smirked. I looked at him with a smile on my face and Jake frowned. The Minister had open contempt in his eyes. I felt angry and wanted to tell the bastard something nasty.

"*Ché esta bien,*" he told us. (*Ché* was fine.) He was playing games with us.

"*Bueno, Señor Ministro,*" I finally told him in a semigracious tone.

"*Muchas gracias, pero nos vamos a retirar para no quitarle mas tiempo.*" I told him we would not take up more of his time. He laughed throatily with a sneer. I squeezed his small hand hard as hard as I could when he offered a limp handshake. His face grew darker and he rapidly blinked watery eyes but he said nothing. I smiled in satisfaction as the Minister stared at me with a sneer on his pudgy face and held on to his hand. He would not forget *Hugo Murray,* I thought.

"Fuck him," Jake muttered loudly. I wondered if the Minister understood English.

In the police car I immediately asked Colonel Lopez to tell me why he had introduced me as *Hugo Murray* to the Minister. I felt there was something sinister in that act.

"*Para confundir al comunista hijo-de-puta* (to lead the communist son-of-a-bitch astray on who you are and to keep him confused about Murray)," he said.

Lopez suggested that the Minister knew about *Hugo* Murray's assignment to Bolivia as an OPS advisor. But Arguédes Mendietta had never met Hugh Murray and now would look for me instead.

"That will confuse the bastard when he can't find you," he said. "He delights in calling Americans CIA *Pendejos.* Mendietta has his own dossiers on most Americans in Bolivia." Lopez had me confused. I remained uncertain about the matter.

"*Ché* Guevara and his men killed two *campesino* leaders in *Santa Cruz,*" the colonel told us unexpectedly. "We're not sure why." His eyes glistened while he pensively scratched his full head of hair.

"I think he is having problems with his insurgency," he said. Jake lowered his eyes tiredly.

"That son-of-a-bitch won't hesitate to kill anyone that doesn't cooperate with him," he said wearily.

The following night, we attended a reception at the Embassy and talked to several U.S. Army officers that were training Bolivian Rangers in anti-guerrilla warfare. A U.S. Army Major there confirmed that *Ché* was traipsing around the *Santa Cruz* area and that the Bolivian security forces were having trouble finding him. Colonel *Toto* Quintanilla was with the Army Major at the reception and joined us for a drink. His mission, along with the Americans involved, was to find *Ché* Guevara.

"The bastard spawns followers that are bound to create problems for a long time," *Toto* suggested. "He must be killed quickly if he is captured." Jake glanced at me.

"Another fuck up for the Company," he said softly.

"Do you know an American by the name of Felix Rodriguez?" *Toto* asked me. I shook my head wondering why he had asked.

"Es de la See Ah," he told me hesitantly. He meant CIA.

"Do you want to come to *Santa Cruz* with us?" my friend *Toto* asked. Jake and I had agreed *Santa Cruz* was not our problem. The potential for screw-ups for us increased if we went to find *Ché*. For us, the only attraction in *Santa Cruz* was that it was at a lower altitude. Too many people were already involved in *Santa Cruz*.

Jake suggested he might be able to sleep if he got drunk so we indulged at the Embassy reception. We did not worry about drinking too much since a policeman was our designated driver. We drank and talked about Guevara's insurgency and U.S. OPS assistance to the *Carabineros* until past midnight.

It was agreed that the strategy we would propose was joint planning and operations between the police and Bolivian military forces to combat *Ché's* guerrilla force. *Toto* was already working with CIA and military intelligence units. The *Carabineros* needed equipment, weaponry, vehicles and communications. Joint training would have to be implemented. The fight against *Ché* was expected to be a protracted one. Long drawn-out wars are acceptable to the communist guerrilla mentality. But that would not be good for us or for Bolivia.

August 26, 1967

We walked out in the bright mid morning sun to search for souvenirs on a long stretch of a main avenue in front of the hotel known as the *Calle Central* or *Calle Principal*. The street was crowded with Indian women carrying pudgy babies strapped on their backs. The avenue was divided into two streets, one headed north and one street headed south separated by a large cement divider in the center. Indian women wore brown Bowler hats and colorful ribbons in their braids as they laid their wares on the sidewalks to sell *alpaca* sweaters, caps, cigarettes, candy, watches, jewelry and trinkets of all kinds.

Small wooden carts also lined the avenue with all kinds of items for sale. Benches and statues were strewn along a wide divider where the Indian women sold their goods from dawn to dusk. The Indian ladies were persistent in negotiating sales but did this in a serious vein and without smiling.

We shopped leisurely at outdoor markets and indoor bazaars located along the boulevard and picked up magnificently carved silver and gold jewelry, gold nuggets, *alpaca* sweaters and fossils hustled by *Quecha* Indians. Tea bags of *Maté de Coca* were sold for about fifteen cents a box. Fresh green *coca* leaf plants cost about five cents a bunch. Barrel-chested Indian men chewed the leaves with a touch of lime (calcium oxide) for a strong stimulating effect. A teen-aged lad, obviously an American, walked by us holding a bouquet of *coca* leaves in his hand, his eyes at half-lights.

The police driver had been instructed to wait for us at a Catholic Church located at a point north of the boulevard. Jake and I walked slowly, enjoying the bright sunshine and an environment unlike any other in the world. The physical effects of the altitude slowed us down as we walked up a slight incline leading to the church. The altitude of about 12,000 feet made the oxygen pretty thin. The driver waited near the church. The street was overrun with ladies wearing Bowler hats, hustling their goods and souvenirs.

When we stopped on the south side of the church we suddenly heard automobile tires screech roughly on the pavement. An early sixties vintage Chevy pulled up about forty yards away from us and two men stepped out holding automatic weapons. One of them pointed excitedly at us and exclaimed loudly in Spanish.

"*Si, estos son.*" I knew they were talking about Jake and me.

"Jake," I hollered. "Watch it, those guys have guns." People at the church scattered in all directions, screaming. There were a lot of people all around us.

"*Cuidado, cuidado!* (Look out!)" the people running were screaming. I hit the ground when I heard gunshots. I saw Jake duck behind the thick walls of the church. The automatic weapons fire was unmistakable. Bullets hit the south wall of the church and on the ground spitting up debris violently. The thought unexpectedly occurred to me that we were pretty stupid to walk around like two dumb-ass *Gringos* buying local crafts.

I laid flat behind a portion of the cement road that had curled up and felt bullets pass over my head. The hair on the back of my head seemed to move on a will of its own. I felt that phenomenon before in the Marine Corps. Fifteen or twenty rounds were fired in about three seconds. I desperately hugged the ground.

The shooting momentarily stopped. I shouted to Jake to make a run for an indoor bazaar behind us. We were both unarmed. I had made up my mind that I would not wait to be shot at close range. With bullets flying I could run a hundred yards in ten seconds flat. With my heart pounding through my chest I took a couple of deep steady breaths and prepared to run. Jake was leaning on the wall of the church, quietly scanning the area.

"Jake, let's run for it. Head for the bazaar!" I screamed at him.

"We can't run! They'll get us," he shouted back. They'll get us if we don't run, I thought angrily. I cussed at Jake and suddenly heard the car drive off.

The noise of the car speeding away was baffling. But I recalled that was generally the case in assassination attempts by terrorists in Latin America. They would approach their target by surprise, shoot as much lead as possible as quickly as possible, and then get the hell out. I just could not believe it.

Seconds later, the driver of our police car ran up to where we were. As was customary in most Latin American countries he was more of a chauffeur than a police officer.

"*Esta bien, Señor?*" he asked. He asked if I was O.K.

"*Si, estamos bien* (We're fine)," I told him.

"*Está sangrando de la frente, arriba del ojo* (You are bleeding from a cut over your eye)," he said worriedly.

"*No es nada* (It's nothing)," I told him. I had a tiny cut over my right eye.

"*Tenemos que informarle al Colonel Lopez* (We have to inform Colonel Lopez)," he suggested.

"We go to the hotel first," I told the police driver hurriedly in Spanish.

"Are you O.K.?" Jake asked nonchalantly. I told him I was fine as I could be.

"Let's get the hell out of here," Jake said grinning. "Shit, we were lucky," he said.

My souvenirs were scattered on the ground but a nice gold nugget I had bought for my first grandchild was in my pocket. My grandson, Billy Krachman, would lose it by the time he became a teenager.

The small nick on my forehead continued to bleed. A doctor summoned by the hotel examined me and put a Band-Aid over the cut. (In the years to come, when my head was x-rayed for any reason, the doctor would invariably rush in to let me know I had a piece of metal in my head.)

Later at the hotel Jake and I talked about the incident over *pisco* sours. We had to report the attack to the U.S. Embassy but Jake suggested we say nothing. An official report of the incident would only increase security concerns and alarm the Embassy. What could the Embassy do? Send us home? Every American in Bolivia was preoccupied with their security. The shooting of the attackers was so bad that perhaps it could be considered that we were not the targets. Colonel Lopez reported the shooting to the police and several .45 caliber shells were picked up at the scene. Witnesses had fled the area, scared of problems.

"Maybe *Ché* isn't pissed off at us," I suggested to Longan. "His people are armed with AK-47's." Then again, maybe the guerrillas have Thompson sub-machine guns, Jake suggested with a grin.

Colonel Lopez arrived soon after at the hotel. He had reported the incident to his *Jefes*. I was interested in knowing who the hell was mad at us. Lopez did not know, but the Colonel provided an interesting insight.

"Why were Fidel Castro and *Ché* Guevara interested in taking over a poor country like Bolivia?" he asked. He explained that the United States provided over thirty-five per cent of Bolivia's national budget every year. It was doubtful that Fidel Castro could do that. The Colonel suggested it was not necessarily communist expansionism. And it was more than the fact that Bolivia was vulnerable with a military government, he said.

He suggested that Fidel Castro and *Ché* Guevara were interested in the production of *coca* leaves. He suggested that the cocaine trade was an incredible source of wealth for the people involved. In addition, Fidel Castro and *Ché* Guevara had no love for the United States, the best market in the world for cocaine. Flooding the United States with cocaine was better than fighting a war and more profitable, Colonel Lopez suggested.

Bolivia was already a principal producer of *coca* leaves used to process into pure cocaine. With a bit of effort the production could easily be tripled. Lopez believed that the people who shot at us might have mistaken us for Agents of the U.S. Bureau of Narcotics and Dangerous Drugs (BNDD). The BNDD was the forerunner of the Drug Enforcement Administration (DEA).

"Even the drug traffickers are concerned about *Ché* Guevara taking over the cocaine market," he said.

That evening I reminded Jake that we had an invitation for *enchiladas* at the home of Joe Baca, an American from New Mexico posted in *La Paz* with the Agency for International Development (AID). After many years of working on the U.S. Mexican border, my friend Jake loved Mexican cuisine.

Red Chile *enchiladas* prepared by Joe Baca's wife Mary Jane were great. Mexican food, like cocaine, was addictive. The Bacas had smuggled the ingredients for the *enchiladas* all the way from New Mexico. Over drinks Baca insisted that Longan and I were there in connection with the *Ché* Guevara problem. We told him we were there to make recommendations on police assistance. Albeit his guests were satisfied with our explanation, Baca was not. **(Twelve years later, Joe Baca pushed hard to convince me to take the job of Secretary of Corrections for the State of New Mexico. As a senior state official in the State, Baca convinced me to accept the top position in one of the most volatile and troubled corrections systems in the United States. Two days after my appointment was announced, the State Penitentiary erupted in the bloodiest prison uprising ever recorded in U.S. penal history. He figured I was used to uprisings.)**

Jake and I had been in Bolivia for over seven weeks, but the end of our mission seemed elusive. In meetings with *Toto* Quintanilla he confirmed that *Ché* Guevara was having problems getting support from the villagers. But the Bolivian security forces could not find the guerrillas.

"*Es muy audaz y arrogante* (*Ché* is bold and arrogant)," *Toto* told us with a touch of respect. *Ché* Guevara was an experienced guerrilla and would not be easily caught. His insurgency could last a long time. He had all the time in the world.

Bolivia was a fascinating country with plenty of mystique, *coca* leaf production, a history of revolutions, excellent *pisco* sours and dynamite for terrorists that could be bought at a cheap price. But it was not easy to assess the politics. The officers of the Bolivian *Carabineros* were cultured, friendly and a pleasure to work with, but it was tough to figure out where their interests lay. We reached agreements with the Bolivian *Carabineros* to define specific objectives regarding the U.S. police assistance needed to pressure *Ché's* forces until he was defeated. OPS advisors would be recommended for the police assistance program in Bolivia.

The following night, in the early morning, I was in a deep slumber when a loud knock on the door to my room brusquely awakened me. Anyone knocking on my door at this time of the night could only mean trouble. Taking my revolver from under my pillow I stepped quietly to the door.

It suddenly occurred to me that perhaps Colonel Lopez had sent over a couple of *Chicas* ...young girls, to take care of our *nececidades humanas* (human needs), he called it and I was overreacting. After almost eight weeks he figured we had to be horny. I stood at the door with my gun in hand.

"*Quién es?*" I asked.

It's me," Jake answered hoarsely. "Open the fucking door." I opened the door and Longan walked in without a word, wearing only his pajama bottoms. He headed straight for a chair and sat in silence. He looked terrible, with dark circles under his eyes. He asked if I had any Scotch. We had several bottles bought at the U.S. Embassy commissary, and I served us both a stiff drink. Jake's eyes looked watery, and desperate.

"What's wrong?" I asked apprehensively.

"I can't sleep," he replied with a groan. He massaged his face with his hands.

"I'm going nuts not being able to sleep. We've got to get out of here. I need to go home," he said in a desperate tone of voice.

"Damn," I muttered. "We can't. We're not finished. We need to finish our mission."

Jake looked decidedly sick and pale. Unsure of himself, he stood up to gaze at the wall.

"Fuck the mission," he said angrily. "I promise to draft a written report in Caracas and hand carry it to Washington myself. I just can't take not being able to sleep. It is sheer torture. I have to get the fuck outta here," he said firmly. I stayed silent, wondering what to do. We drank Scotch in silence without talking.

"Shit, Jake," I finally broke the silence. "You want to leave just when we're starting to have fun," I kidded. His face grew dark. He was serious as hell about leaving. I asked what he suggested.

"We both leave the country on the same day," he said. It would look bad if he left and I stayed.

"Look, we have enough data to write our report and to provide recommendations on what needs to be done," he suggested. "We agree the U.S. has to support the police and armed forces with *Ché* fucking around with his insurgency." Jake paced the floor rubbing his balding pate with his hand.

"The problem in Bolivia will continue whether we are here or not. *Toto* knows what to do!"

I felt bad about the situation and was caught by total surprise by Jake's suggestion.

"*Ché* will never come to *La Paz*. The son-of-a-bitch will die here from the altitude. Our own reputations are intact," he said. "Let's get out now. *Toto* can work with the U.S. Special Forces advisors. We are in the way now, anyhow." Jake stopped to look at me plaintively.

"We know what to recommend on the OPS program and on the advisors needed. Okay?" he asked with a worried look. I nodded in agreement. Jake was my partner and my friend.

We agreed he would finalize our report and hand carry it to Washington, D.C. We would leave a preliminary report for the U.S. mission. Bolivia was a most interesting country and a challenge but we had reached a down side. We left Bolivia before OPS Washington could react to stop us.

Returning to Uruguay, I faced other problems. The matter of Bolivia and *Ché* Guevara were behind me. I had only caught a mere glimpse of his shadow anyway.

According to my kids, their mom was happier with me home again, but while I was gone she had bought a couple of antique grandfather clocks. They giggled when I frowned. But in thirty days there was important news about *Ché* Guevara.

October 1967

Ché Guevara was killed by Bolivian troops in *Vado del Yeso,* an isolated area in the interior of the country. The *campesinos* had pinpointed his location for government troops in *La Higuera.* The village leaders he had ordered killed because they refused to join his insurgency proved to be his downfall. *Ché* simply did not understand the cautious and simple nature of the indigenous people. Their parochial spirit and sense of family was deep rooted and required patience and understanding. Besides, the rural poor of Bolivia did not readily assimilate with strangers.

The villagers simply could not understand how Guevara's insurgency could change the poverty and deprivation they had experienced for centuries. The hardworking *campesinos* in the *Santa Cruz* Mountains were used to their particular style of poverty. Life in the *Santa Cruz* Mountains was more predictable than the political violence, upheavals and military *coups* that characterized the City of *La Paz*. Strife and politics dominated lifestyles in the Capital City but in the *Santa Cruz* Mountains the indigents generally were at peace and able to be close to their families. With the basic necessities of corn, chickens, llamas, chicha, and *Maté de Coca* they survived semicontentedly in the poor environment. There were no television sets in the *Santa Cruz* Mountains to put other alternatives in the minds of the *campesinos*. Simon Reyes, a popular communist leader in Bolivia, once observed that the peasants *(campesinos)* alone do not make a revolution, they have to be taught how to make it.

After *Ché* Guevara killed several of the *campesino* leaders from villages in the *Santa Cruz* Mountains the villagers told the President of Bolivia where *Ché* and his forces were hiding. The story told to me by Colonel *Toto* Quintanilla was confirmed by other sources.

President Barrientos received reports that *Ché* Guevara had murdered several village leaders with "extreme prejudice" because they were not actively supporting his insurgent movement. Sensing an opportunity, Barrientos flew by helicopter to *La Higuerra* and met with the villagers to find out what had happened. After he heard the story, President Barrientos convinced the *campesinos* to help him bring *Ché* Guevara to justice for killing their *Jefes*. He just did not tell them what justice.

The President of Bolivia, with emotional overtones, told the villagers that the small children left as orphans because *Ché* had killed their fathers would now be raised as his own family. With brilliant oratory he won the hearts and minds of the *campesinos*. They told him where the guerrilla forces were hiding and within hours, Bolivian security forces surrounded *Ché* and the members of his guerrilla group.

Guevara told the Bolivian military commander that he was surrendering as a prisoner of war and was entitled to be treated as such. He suggested that he was more valuable alive than dead.

But *Ché* Guevara and several of his men were soon taken to *Vallegrande,* where they were summarily executed. The bodies were secretly buried in a remote area. Guevara's hands were cut off and kept in a jar to prove he was in fact dead. I recalled what *Toto* had predicted to Longan and myself earlier.

In August of 1967, *Toto* Quintanilla had suggested that *Ché* Guevara could not be taken alive. I presumed he meant that communist idol would fight to the death. But what he meant was that *Ché* could not be taken alive because with the guerrilla idol incarcerated, he would be a problem for life.

Ché Guevara and his men were executed under Bolivian rules of war. A Bolivian official described to me that he died with a cigar in his mouth. *Ché* had once said that cigars were the only vice he had, suggesting that "the smoke from a cigar will expel the dragon sleeping in my chest." Guevara's life as a guerrilla was complicated by the fact that he was asthmatic. After his death it was reported that he had left a diary.

Toto Quintanilla's *raison d'etre* for not taking *Ché* Guevara alive sufficed for many minds. With Guevara taken prisoner by the Bolivian Government, the worldwide reaction would predictably be formidable, and create major security problems. Fanatics from all over the world would pressure, fight and perhaps die to free *Ché*. People all over the world, even non-communists, mourned his death. Despite the fact that he was responsible for the execution of over fifty individuals in Cuba, *Ché* was called a saint by many in Latin America.

T-shirts with a picture of his bearded face and wearing a black beret circulated in Bolivia, Uruguay and in many countries of Latin America and Europe. The words *"Viva Ché"* emblazoned on placards with Guevara's picture appeared in Bolivia, France, Spain, Greece and the Western Hemisphere.

Thirty years after his death, *Ché* Guevara is the hero of the **17 November** Marxist/Leninist Group operating in Greece since 1975 and similar movements in other countries. The symbol of the **17 November** terrorist group is a star identical to the Marxist *Tupamaros* of Uruguay.

U.S. Embassy reports from Bolivia indicated that *Ché* Guevara had left a diary but that it had mysteriously disappeared. Jake Longan called me urgently from Caracas, Venezuela with interesting news.

"Hey, *Hugo Murray,*" he kidded. "You're famous." He explained that the Minister of Interior, Arguédes Mendietta, had somehow obtained the diary and in a surprise move had flown secretly to Cuba.

In Havana, in an emotional ceremony held before a huge throng of Cubans and members of the worldwide media, Fidel Castro proudly displayed *Ché* Guevara's famous diary. With Arguédes Mendietta, the Bolivian Minister of Interior at his side, Fidel Castro vehemently condemned those he considered responsible for the "murder" of *Ché* Guevara, American CIA mercenaries and Bolivian traitors he said. For bringing Guevara's diary to him, Castro was generous in his praise for comrade, Arguédes Mendietta.

The story appeared in the *Tricontinental* Magazine published in Cuba in October of 1967.

With visible emotion shaking him, Arguédes Mendietta erroneously told a large array of people and news media representatives at the ceremony held in Cuba that day, that two Americans, described as CIA Officers, had been in Bolivia trying to find *Ché* Guevara. Mendietta identified the two Americans as Jake Longan and *Hugo Murray.* (When Jake and I were in Bolivia, Colonel Lopez had introduced me to Mendietta as *"Hugo Murray,"* to "confuse the communist bastard," he said. I wish he had used my real name. People in my *Barrio* would have been impressed).

Within a year, Colonel *Toto* Quintanilla was assassinated in Vienna allegedly for his role in *Ché* Guevara's death. Assigned to the Bolivian Embassy in Austria as an *Attaché,* an unknown woman entered his office, shot him and escaped. He was the same age as *Ché* Guevara when he was killed, 39.

14

The Replacement

In Montevideo things seemed the same yet different. The city looked peaceful, yet terrorist activity had increased and the situation was growing even more dangerous. Leaving my family alone until my return from special assignments was a concern. If anything happened to me while I was gone, my wife and children would be left isolated over 3,000 miles from home. The U.S. Embassy would help get my wife and young children home to New Mexico, but my family's security was my responsibility.

Personal problems had occurred while I was gone. My five-year-old son Eric and his six-year-old friend Eric Johnston had purchased a large bottle of beer from the local neighborhood grocery store claiming it was for me. They drank most of it. Our maid discovered them sitting on a curb near our house drinking beer, giggling, and getting inebriated.

Our dog *Lobo* had killed a large dog in a fight that had ensued when the other animal tried to enter our enclosed yard. Our dogs, Snoopy and *Lobo,* were invaluable guardians and permitted no one in our fenced yard.

My wife had had sleepless nights as urban violence in Montevideo continued. Uruguay, one of the great democracies of the world, was in the throes of a mindless insurgency. The *Tupamaros* believed that the economic and social problems of the country would be resolved under a socialist/communist government.

But despite the urban violence, Uruguay's President, Pacheco Areco, surprised the nation by partially lifting the emergency security measures that had been in effect for nine months. The President's action was seen as an expression of confidence in the police and the ability of the armed forces to maintain order. It was also a gesture of reconciliation with political groups and organized labor. But the President's action did not help the political/economic crisis. Economic and political issues were not easy to fix, especially in a security crisis.

The communist putsch in Uruguay, driven by ongoing civil unrest, served to exacerbate the economic crisis. Demonstrations and strikes by labor groups against the government continued without letup, and impeded normal economic trade and commerce. Stores and business establishments closed.

It didn't take long for me to get immersed in the internal security problems of Uruguay again. Official meetings with a new Minister of Interior, Dr. Alfredo Lepro, and the new Under Secretary, Jorge Suarez, focused on formidable public order problems that would not let up. The Uruguayan Officials expressed their view that United States assistance for the police was extremely important during this critical period. The police had been severely challenged by the increase in labor and civil unrest. The *Tupamaros* were another matter. The Marxist guerrillas had declared war.

After almost five years as Chief of the OPS program in Uruguay my assignment was officially over, but Ambassador Sayre asked that I extend for another year. I agreed to do it although the *Tupamaro* threat in Uruguay made the job risky and complex. Political problems, urban violence, and potential security threats continued in the background. Like the Americans fighting in Vietnam, we were damned to hell by ideologues in the United States for our intervention in the internal affairs of other countries.

In the interim, the United States Government used our services in a serious political gamble in Uruguay. There was little doubt we were on the hot front lines of the Cold War. Although worried about the increasing risk, I liked my job in Uruguay and was committed to helping out in the public safety sector and in resolving internal security problems.

My children loved life in the *Switzerland of the Americas* and my wife took things in stride, working part-time at the U.S. Embassy and often shopping for antiques. The good things about Uruguay, its temperate climate, the delightful beaches, pure clean air, and beautiful buxom women in bikinis, remained the same despite the fact that the security and economic crisis did bring some change to lifestyles in Uruguay. But the fabulous *churrascos* and the European cuisine continued to be the best in the hemisphere. Yet, police officers earned as little as a hundred dollars a month risking their lives in an unrelenting ideological war. Too many lives had already been lost in the senseless struggle.

The OPS program had succeeded in upgrading the mobility, communications, weaponry, training, intelligence operations, and crisis management for the police in Uruguay. That helped to improve police effectiveness in coping with the urban violence and the *Tupamaro* terrorist threat. Despite the advantage of surprise attacks, the guerrillas took losses. When I returned from Bolivia, two hundred terrorists languished in *Punta Carreta* prison, including top guerrilla leaders. But Americans continued to sour our credibility.

In the midst of internal security problems in Uruguay, allegations of OPS involvement in torture had surfaced in the communist media of Brazil, and Senator Frank Church (D-Idaho) had traveled to that country with a large entourage of Americans to investigate the charges. Left-wing groups and representatives of the Communist Party in Brazil met with Church and his staff. The local representatives of the Brazilian Government also met with Church and his group to discuss the charges. Ultimately no concrete proof surfaced that could legitimately support the allegations that Americans were involved in torture. Meetings held with the U.S. Ambassador and Embassy officials also proved negative in regard to the allegations. Church found no evidence that Americans were involved in teaching torture or advocating torture in Brazil.

Other American journalists came to Uruguay to pursue similar allegations and to write sensational stories on United States intervention in the internal affairs of the country. I met Julian Lindenauer at the hotel and he cautioned me about an interview I had scheduled with Georgie Ann Geyer. He explained that when he was in Guatemala, Bill Leary, one of his friends from the Miami Beach Police, sent an issue of **Saga** Magazine to him that featured a story by Geyer.

She claimed in that story that there were 1,000 Green Berets in Guatemala fighting the Revolutionary Armed Forces (FAR), a Cuban trained guerrilla movement led by Luis Turcios. Lindenauer suggested that story was not true. Jokingly, I expressed confidence there were no Green Berets in Uruguay. Ironically, Costa Gavras and Franciso Solinas, the two communists who produced the propaganda film, **State of Siege,** had portrayed me as a Colonel in the Green Berets.

Georgie Ann Geyer tried hard to find out if the OPS advisors were involved in torture. In an interview with me over drinks at the Victoria Plaza Hotel, she pressed hard, interrogating me to find out what we were doing wrong. My integrity and values were questioned at length. She seemed sincere about her wrong perception in regard to United States intervention in the internal affairs of Uruguay.

Meanwhile, documents taken from captured *Tupamaro* terrorists by the police revealed they planned an escalation of violence in Montevideo. Reports and plans drafted in proper intelligent Spanish showed strategic planning for a continuation of terrorist attacks that increased the danger for Americans in Uruguay.

Comissario Alejandro Otero, the head of the Intelligence Section of the police, summarized the contents.

"The violence will grow more desperate, intransigent and potentially more dangerous for all of us." Cantrell described the documents with a caveat.

"They may be an effort to put the fear of God in us," he said.

"They're wasting their time. I already have the fear of God in me without them," I told him, feeling anger. After reviewing the documents I understood what Cantrell meant. The *Tupamaros* had compiled dossiers on several Americans assigned to the United States Mission in Uruguay, including myself.

I was highlighted in one document as a praetorian ruffian, leading repressive Uruguayan forces to kill and oppress the innocent citizens of Uruguay. We were denounced as spies. My home telephone number and address in *Carrasco* were accurately listed. A narrative in a document alleged I was having an affair with the wife of a Mexican diplomat whom I did not know. I was also credited with having an affair with the daughter of an Uruguayan Army Colonel that I had never met. Nevertheless, the documents did not accuse Americans of involvement in torture.

My name was second on the list of names. It appeared I was on the top of a "hit list for the *Tupamaros*." The names of the U.S. Ambassador and the CIA Chief of Station Dick Sampson were also on the list along with Bill Cantrell and Caesar Bernal. Americans were now prime targets of the *Tupamaros*.

A few days later a cable arrived instructing me to report to OPS Washington for consultation. My wife had to be convinced that the trip would take two to three days at most. She expressed concern about her safety and suggested she quit her part-time job at the CIA office at the U.S. Embassy. The travel time from our home in *Carrasco* to the U.S. Embassy was over forty minutes on a good day. I agreed. Danger had become an incessant part of our daily lives.

My travel from Montevideo to Washington, D.C., included a thirty-minute *Aerolinas* flight across the *Rio de La Plata* to *Aereo Parque* Airport in Buenos Aires. From there I would have to go to *Azeiza* Airport to connect with a Pan American flight to Washington National Airport. The first leg of my flight was uneventful, and after going through Argentine Customs, I grabbed a taxi to take me to *Azeiza* Airport. The forty-minute drive to *Azeiza* was pure adventure.

My cab driver, a typical Argentine with a *Rio Platense* accent and an oversized topcoat, was terse and taciturn but nonetheless helpful. I saw his jaw tighten as he sat behind the wheel of the car and nodded reassuringly to let me know we were ready to go. He drove rapidly into the street honking madly at other cars and weaving brusquely in and out of traffic.

"Cuidado! (Look out!)" I shouted impulsively. He paid little attention as he plunged in and out of traffic forcing his way into crowded intersections without slowing down. We barely avoided colliding with several cars at intersections as their drivers screamed obscenities at us a *La Italiana.* Obscene gestures and words filled the air as drivers screamed at each other. The traffic grew incredibly heavy but it seemed every car drove quickly into crowded intersections, stopping inches from each other. The drivers appeared to be playing a game of "chicken" with their cars.

When the cab reached a curve in a residential area the driver finally slowed down. He turned to mumble that it was a *"redondel"* (circle) and *"mucho tráfico"* (much traffic). We waited behind a line of cars in silence, but without warning, our cab was suddenly surrounded by men in khaki military uniforms and carrying automatic rifles.

"Alto, Alto!" they screamed hysterically. *"Manos arriba!* (Hands up!)".

Men in uniforms pointed rifles at us. It appeared we were under attack. I sat rigidly inside the cab when the driver was forcibly removed from his seat and I was told not to move.

"Esta bien, esta bien! (All right, all right!)" he pleaded and held his hands up in the air.

"No me maten, no me maten." He begged the soldiers not to kill him. My heart pounded in my chest and I thought about options in the crazy situation.

The rear door of the cab was suddenly jerked open and a soldier pointed a rifle at me.

"Afuera! (Get out!)" he said brusquely. I stepped out of the vehicle and was hit with a rifle butt on my back.

"Manos arriba, hijo de puta (Put your hands up, you son-of-a-bitch)," someone ordered. Holding my hands in the air I scanned the area. The soldiers wore the uniform of the Argentine *Gendarmarie Nacional,* a quasi-military border patrol force. They had a reputation for being abusive and tough. But if they were real, there was nothing for me to fear.

I had many friends in the *Gendarmarie*. The organization was considered an elite force used by the government of Argentina to combat guerrillas in the rural areas.

But now things were getting out of control. A soldier threw me roughly against the cab and another individual in a wrinkled uniform and a dour looking, unshaven face prepared to search me.

"Un momento," I told the soldier and stepped away from him. The soldier tried again to put his hands under my coat to search me and I stepped back again.

"Soy Norte Americano!" I told him in a loud voice. That was risky but the soldier suddenly grew stiff and aborted his search. He pushed his face close to me, his breath reeking of alcohol. I smiled involuntarily as he stepped back and stared at me with a dumbfounded look.

"Qué dijo, qué dijo," the soldier muttered, asking me to repeat what I had said. He was slightly cross-eyed and constantly clenching his jaw.

"Soy Diplomatico Norte Americano," I said in Spanish.

"Quiero hablar con la Embajada Norte Americana! (I want to talk to the United States Embassy!)" I told them with a trace of anger in my voice. I had a maroon Official Passport but it looked important enough. There was a dead silence. The individual's reaction was a good sign. The soldiers were unsure of themselves.

"Mi Capitan, mi Capitan," one of them called out in a loud high-pitched voice. A small young man wearing tight riding breeches and polished leather boots looked scornfully at us. He had three silver stars on his shoulder. I recognized it as the rank of a Captain in the *Gendarmarie.*

He approached us and spit brown matter spitefully to one side as the soldiers snapped stiffly to attention, clicking their leather heels. The Captain's round face and thin mustache gave him a murky look that reminded me of a martinet in a grade B movie.

He stood in momentary silence, glaring arrogantly at me and then spit again.

"Su pasaporte por favor, Señor (Your passport, please, Sir)," he told me. Reaching inside my coat pocket I handed my passport over to him. The Captain leafed impassively through the passport, occasionally looking at me through half-closed eyes. He narrowed his dark eyes to ask where I was coming from and where I was headed. I told him and he abruptly brought the heels of his riding boots together with a loud snap.

"Perdóne Señor," he said in Spanish. *"Nos equivocamos.* (It was a mistake)." He looked away quickly.

He told me I was free to go and added that it was a case of mistaken identity. When I did not move, the cab driver in the oversized topcoat stepped forward nervously.

"*Gracias, mi Capitan, gracias!*" he said, cupping his hands and staring anxiously at me with frightened eyes that said, "Don't mess with these guys." The cab driver became nervous with my vacillation.

"*Señor?*" he told me in a sharp fluctuating voice.

"*Podemos irnos!* (We can go now!)" His eyes pleaded for me to get in the cab. In my best Spanish I addressed the Captain in a loud voice.

"*Usted conoce al Commandante Hector Yemmi de la Gendarmarie, mi Capitan?* (Do you know Commander Hector Yemmi, Captain?)" His eyes widened in surprise.

"*Si, es uno do mis Jefes,*" he responded quickly. My friend Yemmi was one of his superior officers, he told me. Smiling to put the Captain at ease, I informed him that *Commandante* Yemmi was a former student of mine and also my very good friend. The captain grew solemn.

He kept staring at the ground to explain that the *Gendamarie* was after "*dos locos*" that had killed a police officer earlier. The description of one of the crazy terrorists fit me "*muy bien,*" he suggested nervously.

"*Gracias, mi Capitan,*" I responded in a joking manner and he grew embarrassed. He explained he did not mean it in derogatory sense. When I walked away, the Captain snapped his heels.

On the way to *Azeiza* Airport, the cab driver muttered obscenities at the police, calling them abusive *cornudos*. It did not take long for him to metamorph into an errant knight competing against some of the worst vehicular dragons in the world. We were running short of time to connect with my other flight anyway, so I asked him to hurry. He did and enjoyed himself.

The flight back to the United States was uneventful. At Washington National Airport a myriad of people flooded the main terminal. I had already gone through customs in Miami and searched for my luggage in a pile of bags. Finding a cab we drove out of the airport and traveled north on the George Washington Parkway until we crossed Memorial Bridge. It was summer and the weather was hot and humid. The cab dropped me off at the Burlington Hotel.

In my room, tiredness and remorse hit me. My job was becoming too unhappy. I prepared a few notes for my meeting with Byron Engle, the Director of OPS, scheduled for the next morning. Geraldine Jelsh, an attractive CIA officer, was scheduled to talk to me after my meeting with Engle. It was no surprise to any of us when she and Engle were married a few years later.

The following day, my meeting with Engle developed expeditiously. Ruth Rooney, his secretary, led me immediately to his office. Pete Ellena and Ted Brown, two of my best friends in OPS, were in the office. Brown was the head of the Latin American Branch and Pete worked for him. I was delighted to see them both and promised to buy lunch. Both seemed in excellent physical condition.

"Hey, Pete, why don't you grow a mustache?" I kidded. "You'd look good with a mustache."

Ted Brown laughed heartily and Pete Ellena chuckled.

"Bullshit," he said cheerfully. "Engle would have my balls." Engle strongly disliked beards or mustaches on OPS advisors. This was an ongoing joke at OPS Headquarters. Officers that were returning from Vietnam with a beard, after meeting with Engle, would return the next day sans beards.

Engle invited me to sit on a maroon leather couch to talk about the situation in Uruguay. He alerted me to the fact that the OPS program was under heavy attack by left-wing U.S. Congressmen and misguided liberals in the Washington, D.C., bureaucracy. I wondered what we were doing wrong. Implementing United States anti-Communist policy and initiatives? Engle immediately asked for my assessment of the *Tupamaro* threat.

"The *Tupamaros* are a tough Marxist terrorist group and not a passing fancy," I told him. I suggested that the guerrillas were a very dangerous threat to the Government of Uruguay. Engle frowned and studied me.

Ambassador Sayre had requested my assessment of the *Tupamaro* threat in Uruguay months earlier. My estimate that at least two thousand or more left-wing guerrillas were operating in Uruguay had caused some dismay. Dick Sampson, the CIA Station Chief, provided his assessment to the Ambassador that the *Tupamaro* strength consisted of about five hundred guerrillas.

The Ambassador did not reject my assessment, but probed me to find out why my assessment was so high. The correct number of *Tupamaros* would probably never be known but my assessment was close. There were too many of them underground. Engle apparently knew more than he let on.

"Do you think the *Tupamaros* have the capacity to overthrow the Government of Uruguay?" he asked casually. I was certain the same question had been asked of Sampson, the U.S. Ambassador, and other U.S. government officials assigned to Uruguay. The Country Assistance Strategy Paper (CASP) developed by the U.S. Embassy had addressed that question, but hedged on the possibility.

"Yes, I think they do." I told him without hesitation. Engle stared at me seemingly in frustration.

"Why in hell would you think that?" Engle probed, to make sense of my position in regard to the *Tupamaro* threat.

"Well, Fidel Castro took over Cuba with about three dozen men and women," I suggested lightheartedly. "Communist guerrillas are more serious than we are and they are intransigent. They apparently make very good fighters." Engle's face grew dark.

"Guerrilla hit and run tactics in an urban area are almost impossible to stop." I added. The *Tupamaros* appear to have significant support in Uruguay, I suggested. I explained that a great deal would depend on the security forces and the will of the people of Uruguay to hold onto their democracy.

"Right now, the security forces are holding their own, but the guerrillas do not fight fair."

Engle stared as I loosened my tie, glad that it was a solid blue color. Like J. Edgar Hoover of the FBI, Engle had quirks. He was vocal about his aversion to people working for him who wore yellow ties or had mustaches. It irked Engle to see men with beards or wearing yellow ties.

I explained that communist newspapers fabricated stories about Americans in Uruguay and the lies were repeated in the worldwide media and especially in the United States. The OPS, *ergo* the United States, was the favorite target of the communist press in Uruguay. Engle stared at me, his eyes telling me he wanted more substance. He already knew a lot of what I told him. My briefing was low-key because Engle was no fool.

"The left-wing activists in Uruguay exploit labor unions, radical student groups, and the folks who are disenchanted with the economy to organize demonstrations against the government that generally become violent. That helps their cause." Engle stayed silent, letting me talk.

"The police intervene to stop the violence and are often obliged to use force. The local communists call it U.S. Government-sponsored repression." Engle listened carefully, nodding occasionally.

"The OPS is helping the security forces of Uruguay and therefore is in the way. The United States is accused of intervention in the internal affairs of Uruguay by the communists and far-left radicals," I told him. We discussed the Robin Hood image of the *Tupamaros* and I made the observation that the terrorist acts carried out by the guerrillas had killed and hurt many innocent people.

"Despite what the left-wing press says, the police are doing a good job of combating the terrorists under the circumstances. There is no abuse or torture. The capabilities of the police for riot control, patrol operations, intelligence, and emergency management has improved immeasurably," I told him.

"With Paul Katz's help the Uruguayan security forces now have better communications. The Montevideo police have purchased 100 patrol cars and this has made a big difference in the urban struggle." Engle stared at me with a twisted grin.

"We are emphasizing the importance of joint planning and operations between the military and police forces to combat the *Tupamaros.*" Engle broke into a smile.

"The training film, **The First Line of Defense,** produced by Loren McIntyre, has been seen by the heads of the Uruguayan Army, Navy, and Air Force, as well as most police commanders," I said.

"The left-wing media excoriates the Government of Uruguay daily for police repression, human rights abuse, and violation of civil rights. But that is not true. Albeit, as police advisors, we are caught in the middle."

"Boy, it makes our left-wing friends here in Washington very happy when we are under the gun," he said. I wondered if it would do any good for the United States to get out of the business of police assistance and let the communists win. Would that permit 'normal' political change?

The consultation was almost over. Engle did not seem unhappy with what I told him.

"Well, you're doing a good job. I hear good comments about our program in Uruguay from Ambassador Sayre and other folks," he said. The other folks probably meant reports from the **Company.**

"The police in Uruguay need our help. There's no question about that. The GOU (Government of Uruguay) counts on our help." I felt like smoking a cigarette, but Engle would not like it. He was an avid nonsmoker. Engle wrote something on a tablet, waiting for me to continue.

"The GOU views United States assistance as extremely important." I paused. I was not sure how he would take my next statement.

"As a matter of fact, General Oscar Gestido, the elected President of Uruguay, personally called me at my office to thank us for our help and asked that we expand our assistance to other cities in the interior of the country." Engle glanced at me and his eyes shone in satisfaction. The OPS was a strong and positive impact in Uruguay despite the objections of the communists.

"I sure did not encourage any calls from the President of Uruguay but I did ask him to let Ambassador Sayre know he was satisfied with our help and he sure did. I understand he did call Sayre."

"What about Ambassador Sayre? Has he been supportive?" Engle relaxed a bit and leaned back on the couch. I wondered what Engle wanted me to say about Sayre. I was sure they had talked.

"Thank God Sayre has been supportive," I told him. I felt my face wrinkle and get hot describing one concern about Sayre.

"It took a while for him to recognize that the attacks against OPS by the left-wing and communist media in Uruguay are nothing more than propaganda," I suggested. Engle's tired eyes brightened.

"Henry Hoyt was always supportive of OPS when he was Ambassador," I told him. Engle straightened up and interjected with a question.

"What happened to Hoyt? I liked him. He was gutsy." Sadness hammered me with unpleasant flashbacks. For me, Henry Hoyt was a true American hero. He had been an outstanding Ambassador.

"The U.S. Embassy was celebrating a Fourth of July picnic at the British School. Hoyt was playing softball with the staff and ran from second base to third base on a hit and suddenly collapsed. He had a heart attack," I told him. Two years after his death I still felt sadness.

"He died shortly after. He was a damn good Ambassador," I added, feeling a touch of nostalgia.

We talked more about the *Tupamaro* problem and the assistance we were providing to help the police forces cope with that threat. Engle appeared pleased that planning for joint operations was taking place between the police and military commanders in Uruguay in order to combat the *Tupamaro* guerrillas. He seemed happy with the close working relationships we enjoyed with police and military officers in Uruguay. We were considered valued advisors despite our limited rules of engagement. Engle stood with a smile on his face.

"Keep up the good work. Now I believe Gerry Jelsh is waiting to talk to you," he said offhandedly.

"Have a safe trip back," he said and offered a handshake with a typical Engle satisfied grin. Engle was the Boss, much respected and very much needed.

Outside of Engle's office, Gerry Jelsh and two other CIA officers waited. We sat in a corner office and their efforts to set me at ease with small talk made me feel uneasy.

"How is Bill Cantrell doing?" I was eventually pointedly asked. My only concern was that Cantrell's cover was blown and that created problems. It was obvious the group was not there to talk about the beautiful beaches or the huge variety of roses in Uruguay.

"He is doing fine," I told them. But they pressed and prodded until I explained that the word was out that Cantrell was a CIA officer doing more than advising the Uruguayan police on criminal investigations. It was unfortunate that Alejandro Otero, the head of the police intelligence section in the country and Cantrell's counterpart, was probably his worst enemy in Uruguay. Otero had a bad grudge against Cantrell and was damn vocal about it. As a result, both men had been neutralized in terms of their effectiveness.

I proposed that Cantrell's recruitment of Nelson Bardesio and Manuel Hevia as compatriots was a mistake that would come back to haunt the police assistance program. The two men spread the word that Cantrell was CIA and that made us a more attractive target for the *Tupamaros.*

My own assessment was that Manuel Hevia was a Cuban communist, in Uruguay for a purpose. Too many people in Uruguay knew that Cantrell was a CIA Officer. The reaction of the group was defensive.

"Dolph, you know that some of the locals have to be told about Cantrell's role," Gerry Jelsh explained. "Besides, locals usually think all Americans assigned to the U.S. Mission are CIA Officers." Well, that did not help matters in Uruguay, I thought.

But things were bound to get dangerous when an individual used a cover in a legitimate U.S. program, in a terrorist environment, and it was made known that he was an American CIA Officer.

The meeting left me looking like a bungler, but I had legitimate concerns about the problem. It seemed strange to me that in the intelligence game, some individuals have so much power yet at the same time they could be so vulnerable. I was glad to leave Washington. But things were not getting easier in Uruguay.

Back in Montevideo, the *Tupamaro* attacks continued without letup. Americans would soon be targets for attempted assassination or kidnapping. I knew it was only a matter of time. My two drivers, Gonzales and Ovedo, were instructed to pick me up at my residence at different times and to change their routes into the city every day. It amused me to see my drivers get nervous when I drove the car and they would sit next to me in the hot seat. Returning home from my office at night, I would often lie down and catnap on the back seat of the car. This gave the impression no one else was in the vehicle. I believe those practices may have saved me some serious headaches.

For me it seemed obvious that personal security was a major problem for Americans as well as other people in Uruguay. My revolver and portable radio were always with me. But subjecting my family to a potentially dangerous situation was a constant worry and every American in Uruguay was in the same boat. It bothered me to think that the United States would abandon the struggle for democracy in Uruguay because of the persistent and controversial Cold War politics in Washington. I personally was extremely fond of Uruguay and despite the danger felt right about being there.

It appeared that many Americans back home did not know what was happening in Uruguay or in other places of the world during the Cold War. One had to accept that some folks in America were rooting for left-wing causes. This was called living in a democracy. But the Cold War created tremendous political risks for other countries. For many, it was either democracy or communism and the choices were narrowing.

The terrorist problem affected all Americans in Uruguay and the threat was getting worse. Americans stuck together to protect each other, but the Ambassador was obviously the most attractive target for the *Tupamaros*. He was pleased when I tightened security measures and safeguards at his official residence.

United States Ambassador Elbrick had been kidnapped in Brazil by the MR-8 left-wing terrorist group and almost killed. The U.S. Ambassador to Guatemala, Gordon Mein, and the U.S. Army military attaché were not so lucky. They were both killed in separate kidnappings attempts. The danger was real and growing.

I arranged for police dogs and handlers to patrol the grounds of the Ambassador's residence twenty-four hours a day. The police guards posted at the residence were provided with automatic shotguns loaded with .00 buckshot. Radio communications provided to the guards linked them with the police operations center.

It was impossible to assure total protection for the Ambassador, but we could sure make him a very tough target for anyone. The Marine guards were needed to protect the Embassy, so the Montevideo police helped with other aspects of the physical security. We could only hope that not many cops were *Tupamaros*.

The problems of labor and civil unrest continued in Montevideo as workers from the National Slaughterhouse *(Frigorifico Nacional)* and meat packers union in *Cerro Largo* went on strike and provoked violence. The ability of the GOU to pull out of the economic decline was obstructed by the persistent civil unrest. The communists continued to exert efforts to hamper economic recovery and the OPS continued to provide assistance to the police forces in order for them to cope with the never-ending problem of labor violence. It was a vicious cycle, and training for the police had become a top priority.

The Minister of Interior had requested that OPS advisors help provide training courses for police officers assigned to cities in the interior of Uruguay. The violence was spreading to the interior of the country. The training would concentrate on the *Tupamaro* terrorist threat, the control of civil and labor disturbances, combat shooting, mobile and foot patrol techniques, and internal defense measures.

Caesar Bernal, the OPS police training advisor, had assembled a mobile training team consisting of instructors from the Montevideo police to conduct training for the various *Departamentos* or States. The Under Secretary of the Ministry of Interior, Jorge Suarez, anxious for the training to be accomplished, provided the funding needed. The Sixth Regional Training Course planned for the Department of *Maldonado* would train about sixty police officers. Bernal and I would attend the opening ceremony at the request of the Chief of Police and the Mayor of the city.

The scenery on the way to the training site had lush green hills and pastures reminiscent of Southern California. Uruguay was great for raising cattle. Our caravan of unmarked police vehicles stayed close together. The training equipment needed and the instructors for the course were in the two front cars. Bernal and I were in the last car. A police *Comissario* by the name of Luis A. Lovato capably led the mobile training team of eight instructors.

On the road, a slight rain turned the weather cooler, and about 45 minutes from our destination we reached a flat piece of terrain that was surrounded by many trees. The lead vehicle unexpectedly stopped. Police officers dismounted and pointed excitedly at the road ahead. Pessimistically I suspected an *ambuscade*. Bernal quickly asked the driver why we had stopped.

"*No* se (I don't know)," he reported hurriedly. Several officers that had left their cars pointed excitedly at the road to shout.

"*Miren! Miren!* (Look! Look!)"

On the road, hundreds of huge hairy black Tarantulas blanketed a large area of the road. The asphalt highway was literally covered with the big spiders, some as large as baseballs. The Tarantulas swarmed on top of the road like a science fiction movie. Several officers drew their guns and shot the huge spiders with .38 caliber bullets, driving them into the air like furry flying saucers.

We continued on the road with the drivers driving slowly in an effort to avoid the spiders covering the road. But that proved impossible and the tires ran over the Goliath spiders with an audible sound. Such a large number of Tarantulas was apparently not uncommon in some parts of the interior of Uruguay.

Six weeks later, the police training in the Departament of *Maldonado* was completed and at the urging of the Chief of Police we returned for the graduation. Uruguayan Government officials as well as the communist media attended the ceremony held.

The following day, communist newspapers reported the training as: **"The Art of United States Terrorism and Repression."** Our names were used in the stories that were published and the Americans involved were described as expert advisors in the art of terror and repression.

A few days later, in Montevideo, the *Tupamaros,* under the flag of the National Liberation Movement (MLN), carried out simultaneous attacks against police officers throughout the city, killing a young policeman and wounding several. The Chief of Police met with us to discuss the attacks and we suggested that well-armed, four-man teams be used to patrol the city. The morale of the police stabilized. It seemed obvious that the *Tupamaro* attacks had the purpose of intimidating the police and demoralizing the security forces.

But the escalation of terrorist action was predictable. The terrorists were losing too many of their people. They had to show they were well and strong enough to continue the fight and were capable of retribution.

May 22, 1969

John Topping, the DCM, called urgently to tell me he needed to see me as soon as possible. Ambassador Sayre had dispatched a cable from Washington, D.C., and he wanted me to see it. Topping smiled grimly when I entered his office and he handed me a copy of the telegram. It was from Ambassador Sayre to Topping as *Charge' d' Affaires* of the U.S. Embassy.

"Read it, Dolph," he said. "Maybe we can both respond to it."

The telegram from Sayre was dispatched from Washington, D.C., on May 22, my birthday. I was surprised to read it. It said:

"I have discussed here extension Saenz assignment until latter part 1969. Have reluctantly agreed on August 1 departure date for Saenz. Sayre." My assignment was over.

"I'm truly sorry to see you go, Dolph," Topping told me. Washington knew I was number two on the *Tupamaro* assassination list. I was ready to leave but it was more than an act of fate. The *Tupamaros* would kidnap and brutally murder my replacement, Dan Mitrione, ten months after my departure from Uruguay.

Topping suggested with prescient instinct that my replacement would have a very hard time. We drank coffee and chatted. His son Monk and my daughter Lori were very good friends. Topping asked what OPS had in mind for me, where my next assignment might be. I laughed impulsively.

"Maybe Vietnam," I suggested jokingly. "The 'Boss' told me I needed experience with the Viet Cong."

Topping broke into laughter. "I might see you there soon," he said.

The walk to the *Jefatura* (police headquarters) from the Embassy was about nine blocks. It was enjoyable for me to walk, as long as my gun was handy. There was a lot about Uruguay I would miss. The flower shops with hundreds of varieties of beautiful roses and the Italian restaurants and pizza parlors where pasta, dough, and everything else was made from scratch.

The *parrilladas* were the most unique. Almost every part of the animal was barbecued on a grill over slow-burning coals. I delighted in eating delicious *morcillas*...blood sausages, golf ball-sized bull testicles, sweet breads, *chinchulines* (intestines), and cow brains sprinkled with *fines herbs*.

I would miss Uruguay with all my passion. I had grown to love the *Switzerland of the Americas*. I had been very happy living in Uruguay and I would never forget all my friends there. I was entitled to forty-five days of 'home leave' with my family, and we planned to go to New Mexico to wait for my next assignment.

June 10, 1969

A few days later I received a letter from Byron Engle, the Director of OPS. He told me in his letter: **"We appreciate the thought you gave the matter of your replacement and have discussed this with Ambassador Sayre. We think Dan Mitrione was well chosen and fulfills your requirements as you related them in your letter.**

Dan Mitrione will arrive on or about July 15. We are depending on you to help him get his feet firmly on the ground before you leave. Byron Engle."

So my friend Dan Mitrione was going to replace me. He was a topnotch officer, a real gentleman, and an American Italian from Indiana who spoke Spanish. He would be at home in Uruguay because of the large population of Italians who spoke Italian.

Governor Nelson Rockefeller scheduled a visit to Montevideo and *Punta del Este* before Mitrione arrived and we prepared for trouble. The communists reacted with demonstrations to protest Rockefeller's visit. The demonstrations quickly became violent. Two days before Rockefeller arrived in Montevideo, the administrative offices of the General Motors Corporation automobile plant were burned to the ground by *Tupamaro* terrorists. In an impressive coordinated attack, the guerrillas gained entry by using police uniforms and then overpowered the armed guards. Mitrione would have his hands full.

When he arrived, Mitrione and I enjoyed our time together, and we spent long hours talking about the local security crisis and life in Uruguay. As a noble and gracious good friend, he told me not to be concerned about his safety because he had been in tough situations before. He told me he did not believe in carrying a gun. He believed a revolver was useless against the automatic weapons used by terrorists.

I cautioned him about being too trusting and to be alert for nuances in the environment. It was hard to tell who the enemy was. And there was much danger from the *Tupamaros* in the political and volatile unrest. The Uruguayan police officials looked forward to working with him, but the *Tupamaros* would not give him a chance.

News of my departure traveled fast. Invitations to receptions and dinner parties multiplied. On the day before my departure, Uruguayan police officials held a *despedida* (farewell) and *bienvenida* (a welcome) for Dan Mitrione that was packed with the top officials of the Uruguayan military and police forces that had worked closely with me for almost five years.

I felt proud but humbled that every Uruguayan military officer that had served as Chief of Police of Montevideo during my time in Uruguay attended the function.

Colonel Rogelio Ubach, Colonel Raul Barloco (the Chief of Police who sweated out the Summit Conference), and my close friend, General Ventura Rodriguez (the Chief of Police at the inception of the US OPS police assistance program), attended and I felt very proud of that fact.

Colonel Zia Fernandez, the current Chief of Police of Montevideo, hosted the event. All of the Deputy Chiefs of Police and top police and military officers attended the function as well as my old friends,

Inspectors Guillermo Copello and Ramiro Requierro. It was a formidable and very special occasion.

All of the Uruguayan police and military officers with whom I had shared almost five years of very challenging police work were there. Several of the officers spoke eloquently to describe the Cold War struggle in Uruguay and my role in leading the United States police assistance effort during a difficult period for the country. Oratory skills were appreciated in Uruguay.

The encomiums were articulated with impressive oratory concerning my work with the security forces of Uruguay and were indeed flattering. It was an emotional event, replete with many *abrazos* (hugs) from *amigos* that night. It was a great honor for me. But, in essence, I was leaving many good friends that I would never forget.

In a surprise, emotional and symbolic gesture, my good friend Colonel Pasqual Cirillo presented me with the sword he had received when he graduated from the Military Academy of Uruguay. He told me that we had **"fought the good fight"** together. Colonel Cirrillo's gift gave me enormous pride, but some day, I will return the sword to my good friend. It belongs with him. He earned it.

Another good friend, Lt. Colonel Carlos Legnani, the Deputy Chief of Staff for the police force of Montevideo, presented me with a *Gaucho* knife and enclosed a card. The inscription on the card said: **"Perhaps there will be an occasion to defend similar causes like the one we worked on together."** He added humorously: *"No aprete boton* **(Don't push the panic button)."**

As the last round of speeches ended, the current Chief of Police of Montevideo, Colonel Zina Fernandez, presented me with a plaque that contained the various emblems and badges of the police forces of Uruguay. It was finale for me, but for Dan Mitrione, it was the beginning of a tough assignment.

I was touched when Miss Jennifer Hyland, Mirta Gorban, and Mavorneen Ellis, the beautiful secretaries of the OPS office, cried when we said good-bye. Teary eyed they hugged me in a spontaneous embrace. It was sad for me to leave Uruguay but it was by the Grace of God.

Albuquerque, New Mexico

I was on home leave in Albuquerque, New Mexico, when David Powell of the OPS Latin American Desk called. He informed me that I had been selected for a temporary assignment in Colombia that involved kidnappings. He mentioned that it was a classified matter.

"It will be better if you find somebody else," I told him. "I don't have much experience in kidnapping investigations." But Powell did not let up. "The Boss (Byron Engle) wants **you** on this assignment," he insisted.

I continued to disagree with the assignment. Finally I heard from Jack Munroe, the Deputy Director of OPS, and that settled the matter. He told me I would now be an "expert" on kidnapping problems and not to be concerned. "You can handle the assignment," he told me cheerfully.

Republican Guard—Riot Control Unit

Metropolitan Guard—Riot Control Unit

Riot Scene in Montevideo—1967

Police Officers from Uruguay receiving firearms training with OPS assistance.
Caesar Bernal and Adolph Saenz, OPS—Uruguay 1967

Adolph Saenz with the Chief of Police of *Cerro Largo* and other top officials in Uruguay, 1967

Adolph Saenz with Uruguayan police officials after a horse race in *Trienta y Tres*, 1967

U.S. Ambassador Henry Hoyt with Astronauts Armstrong and Gordon on their visit to Montevideo, Uruguay 1968

Astronauts Armstrong and Gordon with OPS Officers, Montevideo, Uruguay 1968

Adolph Saenz, Chief OPS Uruguay, with his replacement Dan Mitrione, August 1969. In August of 1970, Dan Mitrione was kidnapped and murdered by the Marxist *Tupamaro* terrorists.

Caesar Bernal, Bill Cantrell, Adolph Saenz—Montevideo, 1966

Adolph Saenz with U.S. Embassy officials
Frank Stewart, Director AID; Colonel Lorenzo Caliendo, USAF
Milgroup Commander; Allen Claxton, Deputy AID Director;
Richard Sampson, CIA Station Chief; Caesar Bernal, OPS; and U.S.
Military Attachés, Montevideo, Uruguay 1968

Caesar Bernal and Julian Linenauer, OPS,
with officers of the Republican Guard
Montevideo, Uruguay 1968

Adolph Saenz with General Ventura Rodriguez,
Chief of Police, Montevideo, and Nicolas McClausland,
U.S. Embassy Political Officer,
Uruguay 1966

Adolph Saenz with Colonel Raul Barloco, Chief of Police, Montevideo. Colonel Barloco was head of Security Forces for the Summit Conference at *Punta Del Este, 1967.*

William Briggs, Chargé d'Affairs, U.S. Embassy, Montevideo
Adolph Saenz, Chief OPS, Montevideo
Joseph Livornese, U.S. Consul General, Uruguay

OPS officers in Montevideo
John Horton, CIA Station Chief, Montevideo
Colonel O. Hontu, Commander, Republican Guard
General Ventura Rodriguez, Chief of Police, Montevideo
Dr. Adolfo Tejera, Minister of Interior, Uruguay
Adolph Saenz and Ron Holko, 1965

Dr. Agosto Legnani, Minister of Interior,
and his wife talk to Adolph Saenz
Montevideo, Uruguay 1967

15

Bogota, Columbia

October 18, 1969

The classified assignment to Colombia interrupted my "home leave" in New Mexico but there was no way to get out of it. I was enjoying being home and visiting with our parents, family, and friends. In Washington, D.C., I was told that my mission was to function as an advisor to the *Departamento Administrativo de Seguridad* (DAS), the Colombian equivalent of the FBI, on a complex kidnapping problem that was taking place, mostly in Cali.

After being briefed by OPS personnel in Washington, I was on my way, headed for Bogota. My biggest concern was a classified cable sent from Washington to the U.S. Embassy in Bogota describing me as an "expert" on kidnappings. But despite what the FBI public relations people or anyone else believes, there are no "experts" on kidnappings. The only "experts" on kidnappings are people that have been abducted.

I was told that Byron Engle, the Director of OPS, had specifically named me for the assignment. But many people in OPS had far more experience than I had on kidnapping cases. The FBI also claimed to have "experts." Why me? I wondered. I had been robbed of my vacation, I thought in jest.

The Pan American flight approached Bogota, and above the city lights, a lumpy row of cumulus clouds reflected a bizarre orange streak in the twilight evening sky. Below us, the city looked peaceful, serene, and beautiful. But on the ground, things could turn dangerous for certain people and guys like me.

The plane flew over bright green hilly terrain on the outskirts of the city and banked gently to start the descent for a landing at *El Dorado*

International Airport. In Spanish, the word *El Dorado* translates to 'gilded,' but in the larger sense, the word meant gold. In the moonlight the aerodrome reflected a shiny gold glint. The plane approached the runway and on the *Autopisto del Norte,* the principal highway leading to the airport from Bogota, the cars below us looked like little toys probing the night fog with tiny streams of light.

On the side of the North/South runway, on the tarmac, other planes waited in line to take off as our Pan American flight touched the ground with a loud surge of engine noise. From my window I saw an airfoil flare out for our landing. Passengers inside the plane suddenly erupted in cheers, applauding when the landing gear hit the concrete runway. People were apparently happy to get home safely.

When my "home leave" in New Mexico was rudely interrupted with my assignment to Colombia, Jack Munroe, the Deputy Director of OPS, suggested lightheartedly that it would be a nice vacation for me. The good news was that my wife and children were safe with our parents in New Mexico.

I knew that my temporary duty in Colombia would not be facile or quick. For years, Colombia had experienced major problems with left-wing guerrillas in the rural areas and with a bloody enigma called *La Violencia.* The kidnapping crisis was another threat to the security of the country while the guerrillas and drug cartels waited in the wings. The fact that the top boss of OPS personally wanted me on the assignment worked as a stimulant to my ego. Working on kidnappings in Colombia was not exactly a routine assignment. It was real life "balls to the wall."

The plane taxied to the terminal and passengers were provided immigration forms to fill out. Miniature lights on the airfoils continued to blink until the aircraft stopped and the engines shut down. Minutes later the front door of the aircraft opened and a flight stewardess peered out into the night fog covering the area. Men in blue coveralls pushed a metal ladder flush to the door of the aircraft.

Beyond the slim figure of a stewardess silhouetted in the dim light of the doorway, I saw soldiers armed with automatic weapons surround the aircraft. The stewardess seemed undisturbed about that and continued her preparations to disembark the passengers. Everything was apparently normal for our arrival.

Passengers descended on a metal ladder leading to the ground, and a few steps behind me, a beautiful young woman smiled at me. She wore a tight miniskirt that displayed awesome legs and a great body. Her light brown hair blew gently across her pretty face. She was openly coquettish. I smiled at her.

The disembarking passengers were instructed to form two lines for a search of personal effects prior to entering the terminal. Several men in green police uniforms milled about, watching the passengers disembark. I recognized the uniform as that of the National Police of Colombia and a volley of adrenaline hit me.

My Smith & Wesson Combat Masterpiece and a box of high velocity ammunition were locked in one of my suitcases. But I knew that Colombian authorities would not search my luggage unless they had good reason to do so. My suitcases were locked and my passport entitled me to diplomatic privileges in Colombia. I presumed someone from the OPS program in Colombia would meet me and assist in getting me through Customs at the airport. If it were to become necessary for me to explain why I was bringing a gun into the country...that would be a serious problem!

People in line underwent fast searches, and passports and I.D. pictures were closely examined. Presumably false passports were in fashion and, as a consequence, passengers with diplomatic passports were closely examined. But the picture was the easy part to fake in a passport.

A commotion erupted among the passengers waiting to be searched. The young *señorita* in the tight miniskirt was resisting a body search. Her voluptuous body looked tempting for a search by horny cops hoping to find something hot. She relented to a search by a woman, and passengers waiting in line broke out in laughter.

In the line of passengers, a police officer singled me out and asked me in Spanish to open my coat so he could search me. I raised my arms and the officer conducted a pat down search from my waist to my ankles but was careful not to touch my crotch. That was precisely where something could be hidden.

He finished his search and pointed in the direction of the airport complex.

"Muy bien, Señor," he told me. At the entrance to the terminal, I recognized a tall familiar figure dressed in a dark suit. From the doorway, Roy Bill Driggers shouted a greeting. He was at least six feet five inches tall and weighed a muscular 250 pounds. His size and round florid face towered over the large crowd of people waiting inside the terminal. I entered the terminal and Driggers stuck his hand out.

"Bien venido a Bogota, partner," he told me, gripping my hand tightly. I tightened my grip and he squeezed. "Okay, okay! Let go, you big bastard," I complained impulsively and he broke out in laughter.

"How've you been, Dolph? We haven't seen you in ages, partner," he said with a chuckle.

We were both suddenly distracted when the beautiful girl with the great body and tight miniskirt approached and smiled at us. When she ambled by, her hips swung provocatively, her firm round buttocks sharply outlined by the tight skirt. She smiled warmly at us.

"Up to your old tricks, huh?" Driggers muttered with a crooked grin.

"Hell, I don't know who she is," I told him wistfully. "For all I know she could be the Station Chief's moll." Driggers shook his head laughing and continued to stare at the girl's ass.

"Naw, the Company has a policy of recruiting ugly agents in these countries," Driggers retorted. The young beauty turned and smiled one last time before entering the Immigration Section.

"Shit, out of sight, out of mind," Driggers sighed. We went inside the immigration area and discovered she was a former Miss Colombia and the media and an array of cameras were waiting for her. She was being aggressively stalked and interviewed by reporters.

The Immigration Section was extremely crowded with passengers. A tiled corridor led into the building and Driggers was silent as he led the way inside. Anxious to find out if Driggers knew any more about my assignment, I suggested in jest that I really did not know what I was doing in Colombia. Driggers merely laughed and we continued walking through the corridor with ceramic tile on the floor.

Driggers was a fairly good Spanish speaker and a former captain in the New Mexico State Police. He had been in Colombia for almost two years and had replaced my good friend Herb Hardin as Chief of the OPS program in Colombia. He was Hardin's handpicked successor.

Passengers formed two lines to wait their turn to process through immigration. For any visitor to Colombia the immigration process was especially important because the clearance needed to get into the country was the same clearance needed to leave. We stopped and a line had formed in front of four booths enclosed with glass. One booth had a large sign on the top with the words, **Diplomatico y Oficial.**

"Let's see your passport," Driggers told me sticking out a large hand. He handed my passport to the Immigration Officer in the booth where the man closely studied the passport. He placed the passport on a glass counter and furiously stamped the pages with official looking seals. Driggers glanced at me.

I thought about the hidden camera at the immigration counter at *Carrasco* Airport in Montevideo. *Ché* Guevara's passport had been photographed when he passed through Uruguay on his way to Bolivia to start his communist insurgency. *Ché's* long curly locks were trimmed and his famous beard shaved. He had also shaved his eyebrow lines. With a weak chin exposed, it was difficult to recognize him. *Ché* had worn extra thick myopic glasses and looked like a schmuck.

"*Bien venido, Señor,*" the man in the Immigration booth nodded to tell me. Driggers gave him a friendly wave. We entered the Customs area where a hundred passengers searched frantically for their luggage. The final step was for passengers to pass through Customs before leaving the terminal. International travel was not glamorous and was getting tougher. Driggers led me to a small office located inside the terminal and a young man at a desk stood when he saw us.

"This is Carlos," Driggers told me. "Give him the claim checks to your baggage and your passport." He pointed a stubby finger at Carlos. Carlos took my passport and claim checks and left.

We waited, and Driggers picked up a local newspaper and handed it to me.

"This is what it's all about," he told me. I scanned the headline: **"*Amenaza de Secuestros en Cali.*"** The local newspaper *La Nacion* displayed a dramatic headline: **"The Kidnapping Threat in Cali."** There was a lengthy story about the kidnapping problem. There was nothing specific about the kidnappings, but because of the threat, a State of Siege had been declared in the province of *Valle de Cauca,* placing the area under military control. Cali was the capital of the province of *Valle del Cauca.*

According to the account in *La Nacion,* a leading newspaper in the country, two Swiss diplomats kidnapped a few weeks earlier had totally disappeared. The Swiss Ambassador refused any comment to the local media and declared in effect, "we don't know nutting." The fact that I could read Spanish was enormously helpful. There were no English newspapers available.

A short time later, young Carlos appeared with my two suitcases. Pleased to see my bags intact, I offered him five dollars. He was glad to help, he told me in Spanish. I insisted and the youngster accepted the money.

"*Gracias, gracias,*" he told me. Five dollars could buy almost fifty *Colombianos.*

"Come on," Driggers told me abruptly. "Let's go." He picked up my heaviest suitcase and led the way through long corridors until we reached the outside of the building and a parking area. The place was deserted except for a few cars parked in spaces marked **Reservado.** Driggers pointed to a dark blue Wagoneer and opened the trunk to put my bags in it. It would be hard for me in Colombia without Driggers.

This was actually my second time in Bogota, but at this point it could just as well be Fantasy Island. I was not familiar with the city. Bogota was a city with a population of over a million people spread out almost evenly in an urban area assailed by special problems of crime and violence.

We entered the car in silence and drove out of the parking lot into a main road called the *Autopista del Norte*. Dim streetlights illuminated the Colombian equivalent of a freeway as we snaked through open and desolate terrain, headed for Bogota.

"You have reservations at the Hotel *Tequendama*," Driggers said breaking the silence. "It's one of the best hotels in Bogota. You'll like it." He scanned the rear view mirror for traffic. "It's an active place and within walking distance to the Embassy." Driggers glanced at me with a puzzling smile.

"By the way, you have a meeting with U.S. Ambassador Jack Vaughn Monday morning." I nodded in the darkness.

"Now I know," I told him. Driggers looked at me with an inquisitive look.

"You remember Jack Hood Vaughn? He headed the Peace Corps under John F. Kennedy and was U.S. Ambassador to Panama. He's part of the Kennedy clan." I was learning about my assignment in bits and pieces.

"Who's going to be at the meeting, Bill?" I asked. Drigger's big hands on the steering wheel tightened. (Few people called Driggers by his given name, Roy. Everyone who knew him well called him Bill.)

"I still don't know why I'm here?" I suggested and we both laughed.

"I'll bet," he muttered. I was serious.

"I don't know the details," Driggers said. "I know that top Colombian officials asked Ambassador Vaughn for help in dealing with the kidnapping crisis in Cali. I understand it was the President of Colombia who asked for U.S. assistance, but I don't know for sure." Driggers laughed when he thought of something else.

"The U.S. Embassy requested help from the FBI to help the DAS with the problem, but the Bureau wants no part of it. Ol' J. Edgar Hoover told the State Department to go to hell," he snorted.

"You know J. Edgar and the State Department don't get along too good." He clenched his jaw and his face looked enormous.

"Hoover says the State Department is loaded with left-wingers, commies and faggots. So you're it," Driggers suggested with a friendly smile.

"What do you mean, I'm it?" I asked him laughing. Driggers kept his eyes on the road and the dim light showed a trace of uncertainty on his face. The assistance by OPS seemed to be purely political and intended to placate the President of Colombia and to keep him on our side in the Cold War.

Driggers seemed hesitant about the political situation, so I bluntly explained my own misgivings on my assignment for him. It seemed to me that a hundred OPS advisors were needed to help resolve the kidnapping problem in Colombia, especially if the kidnappers and left-wing guerrillas were in cahoots. It seemed I was to provide an outside view on the kidnapping investigations conducted by Colombian police officials. But at this point I did not know much about the kidnapping problem. It seemed like mission impossible with a likelihood of getting whacked by kidnappers if I was not careful. Driggers seemed to read my mind and reacted.

"Don't worry. If you need help, you'll get it. Personally, I think you're better off working by yourself. I think Byron Engle thinks the same way." He grinned sympathetically.

"If you fuck up, you will probably be the only one who knows it besides the Colombians." Driggers laughed. I shifted in my seat feeling a touch of discomfort about the situation.

"Thanks for the Presbyterian assessment," I told him as he chuckled away. He laughed when he saw the frown on my face. Driggers was a nice guy. I was glad he was candid and that he felt comfortable with me.

"Look at it this way. Byron must have confidence in you," he suggested. Impulsively I reached in my coat pocket for cigarettes and Driggers' lips twitched in alarm. He acted like I was pulling a gun on him.

"Yo, give that shit up," he said. I had found one of his weaknesses. He had an aversion to cigarettes.

"So it's okay for me to fuck up, eh?" I told him and lit a cigarette anyway, rolling the window down. The cigarette had Driggers on the defensive.

"What else, Driggers?" I asked dryly and puffed away.

He told me with a disgusted look at my cigarette that the Country Team would be at Monday's meeting.

"They want to see what a trained killer looks like," he said, laughing with gusto. The Country Team was the common description of the top officers of the U.S. Embassy who worked with the Ambassador on the broad spectrum of local problems and politics. Driggers squirmed, bothered by the cigarette smoke.

"Just for the hell of it, ask for the classified cables received by the Embassy announcing the arrival of the U.S. kidnapping investigations expert. It's impressive." He grinned and faked a cough.

"You're an important guy, *Dolphi*," he chuckled hoarsely, making me laugh. I liked Driggers. Faking solemnity, I blew cigarette smoke in the direction of his grinning face. He reacted like it was mustard gas.

"Yect!" he said, waving the smoke away with his hand.

"Come on, Driggers, cut the crap. This is risky business," I suggested. "I don't know why Byron sent me here alone. I'm no kidnapping expert."

Driggers laughed vigorously. He was enjoying himself.

"Hey, you're the Lone Ranger. Byron Engle always said, 'one kidnapping problem, one Ranger.' You know Byron." The exercise helped me sort things out.

"Okay, what about you? Are you going to be at the meeting on Monday?" I asked. His face turned a craggy red. He puffed up his chest and scratched his chin.

"Hell no, I haven't been invited. The meeting is for a few chosen people. You're the expert advisor," he said. It was hard to believe. Driggers' reaction was semiwounded pride. What he was telling me was strange, since my work was not covert. He would have to help.

"Bullshit, Bill Driggers," I kidded. The large man behind the wheel stayed silent. I suggested he wasn't invited because he had told people in Washington that he wanted no part of the mess.

"I know you told Washington you didn't know crap about kidnappings," I said. Driggers laughed.

"Besides being a *schmaltz,* just because you speak a little Spanish I hear you call yourself Rodriguez here in Colombia." The big man laughed out loud.

"Roy Driggers is close, but you look just like another flipping *Gringo* cowboy to me!" We both laughed. Laughing made me feel better and it would not be good if the big guy was negative on the situation while I had my back to the wall and needed him.

I crushed the remainder of the cigarette in the car ashtray. He grinned happily.

"OK, I won't smoke. I just hope you don't have any other quirks," I told him dryly.

Drigger's aversion to cigarettes was hard to understand. Smoking cigarettes was in fashion. The majority snorted, smoked pot, cigarettes or some type of hemp or weed, even Republicans and Democrats. Of course, some did not inhale.

The passing terrain zipped by the window. Colombia was a beautiful country with a rich history and culture. Why was there so much violence? *Montaigne* was right when he said, *"one should always have one's boots on and be ready to leave."* Driggers was my friend, easygoing and helpful.

My thoughts kept changing channels like with a T.V. remote; a **clacker,** my kids called it.

I apologized to Driggers for calling him a *schmaltz* and he grinned.

"I don't know what the hell it is," he said. "But you better not be saying bad things about me." We both laughed in good spirits.

"Seriously, I need your help and count on it," I told him. He looked back at me with a tight grin.

"You got it, partner," he snapped back in a serious mode. I checked the rear view mirror. The *autopista* was almost deserted. I wondered where I could start in terms of my assignment.

Driggers' eyes squinted almost imperceptibly to tell me that the FBI did not want to get involved in the problem for obvious reasons.

"We could be on the edge of an explosive situation if the crooks find out we're helping the police with the kidnapping problem." He pointed a stubby finger to tell me it could get damn dangerous. His analysis made me uncomfortable.

"Byron may like me, but he's not doing me any favor with this assignment. He told me to be very low profile and to be careful not to cause reprisals against the U.S. Embassy," I told Driggers. He listened with a smile on his face.

"I feel like a damn *Mafioso* trigger man," I told him humorously.

"The FBI has people that are experienced in kidnapping investigations," he chuckled. "They could help but they know this is a no-win situation." I watched the darkness rushing by. Driggers turned to me with a thoughtful expression on his face.

"I just remembered, Ben Stotts is here. He wants to talk to you." Ben Stotts was one of the FBI Legal *Attachés* stationed in South America. I had met him before.

"He's a nice guy and may be helpful," Driggers suggested. "We're meeting with him tomorrow afternoon if that's O.K. Don't forget, tomorrow is Sunday and we plan to have you over to our house for dinner."

I nodded in agreement, but was not sure about Stotts. The FBI knew about our involvement with kidnapping investigations in Colombia but they were not interested in helping the police. Stotts wanted to talk to me about it. Maybe he was trying to be helpful. Driggers seemed to grow thoughtful.

"The FBI really doesn't have many Spanish speakers with any talent for complex cases. Hoover has no confidence in Hispanics so they are rare in the Bureau. You know that, Dolph." Driggers seemed to grow pensive and was being honest.

"I don't know what you've been told, but I understand this is a very sensitive mission. No one is supposed to know you're here to help the DAS with kidnapping investigations." Driggers looked serious.

"The U.S. Embassy is concerned about retaliation by the bad guys," he said.

"That is plain bullshit. There is no guarantee there will not be any reprisals against anybody," I told Driggers. I asked about the DAS, the *Departamento Administrativo de Seguridad.*

"The DAS is the Colombian FBI?" I asked. Driggers glanced at the signs on the freeway.

"Yep, you got it. It's the FBI equivalent, but DAS Agents are not prone to foppishness. The Director is a fellow by the name of Luis Etilio Leyva, an Army General. He's smart, honest, and pro-American. He speaks some English and looks forward to meeting you." He grinned smugly.

"He said he never met a kidnapping expert before. He said you must be a real *macho.*" Laughing, he emphasized the word *macho.* Driggers enjoyed spoofing me and I was pleased with his soft shots.

"After your conference with the Ambassador Monday morning, I'm to take you to DAS headquarters to meet General Leyva and his staff and get you started." Driggers seemed to have an agenda ready.

"They expect us at the DAS at eleven o'clock. After that, you're on your own." He seemed anxious to disengage from the problem.

The *autopista* straightened when we reached the outskirts of the city. I was satisfied that Driggers didn't know much about the kidnapping problem either. The Wagoneer sped unencumbered by traffic through dark narrow streets, but close to the Hotel *Tequendama,* the traffic grew heavier. In the damp night air, thoughts about my shadowy role occupied my mind. Scrutiny could be expected from several quarters, including the media and those in the U.S. Embassy who had their own agenda. Colombians would be a challenge because they were proud and independent and would not easily trust an American, even one who spoke fluent Spanish. The reception waiting for me at the DAS was unpredictable. I would have to gain acceptance in my role as an advisor before getting involved in any kidnapping case. There were many problems inherent in the assignment, but I vowed to remain positive despite the uncertainty. There was little choice, anyway.

Near the Hotel *Tequendama,* the city was very much alive. The streets were full of seemingly carefree people. The environment exuded a European flavor, with warm and tangible signs of Spanish architecture. The spirit of Simon Bolivar infused the air with large statues of the great

Libertador on horseback visible in city parks. Simon Bolivar, the noble wars of antiquity, and the glorious military campaigns of old contrasted with the existing violence in the *Llanos* where guerrilla and bandit groups competed with each other to terrorize the populace.

Horrible mutilations were a nightmarish part of *La Violencia* (The Violence). I had studied reports on the violence in Colombia prior to my arrival. Thousands of people had been victims of *La Violencia* in the country. One popular method used by the practitioners of *La Violencia* to dehumanize people was to slit a victim's throat with a sharp knife and pull the tongue out through the incision to grotesquely hang outside of the neck. This primordial mode of killing was called *La Corbata,* or "the necktie."

In other cases, the skin on the outer part of some poor bastard's thighs would be slit with a sharp knife and his hands would be inserted inside in the bloody incisions. That atrocity was called *"Las Bolsas,"* or "The Pockets," in English. In many cases, male genitals were severed and stuffed grotesquely into the rectums or in the mouths of the victims. The mangled corpses were displayed out on the street to terrify and intimidate the populace. The chilling realization hit my mind that it could happen to me.

La Violencia seemed to serve the purpose of the communists in destabilizing the country, according to local assessments. But the left wing blamed *La Violencia* on the Colombian security forces. I was glad to have my gun with me.

Driggers announced our arrival at the Hotel *Tequendama* and I felt the unique rush of excitement of my new assignment. It had already crossed my mind that some people would find it ironic and amusing if I were to be kidnapped while in Colombia. I thought about media headlines.

American Kidnapping Expert Kidnapped in Colombia. It would not be amusing for me. That was one reason why being described as an 'expert' on kidnappings bothered me. My job was to function as an expert advisor to the Colombian police on kidnapping investigations and **not** get operationally involved, I was told. As bait for human sharks, the situation made me a moron. No one could work in a kidnapping environment without getting operational. Operational was an ambiguous term and my gun would go with me even to the bathroom.

Ironically, the U.S. Embassy bureaucrats who would be scrutinizing me for wrong moves tended to put me on the defensive. I could only go from dumb to *Pendejo*. More ominously, I would be in deep sewage if the kidnappers discovered that an American was helping the police in the investigation of kidnappings. Engle had suggested I make sure this did not happen. He did not tell me how.

If I were to be abducted, the kidnappers would demand a ransom and the United States Government would refuse to pay. I would pay with my life. That was the latest policy of the United States Government. We would not yield to terrorist demands, we were told. I was only a pawn.

Byron Engle seemed to believe my willingness to take the assignment was because it was my job. That was partially correct, because we were in the middle of a Cold War. But I needed a job and liked the excitement. The FBI would have none of the headache because failure was a sure thing. Driggers suddenly pulled into the driveway of the hotel and suggested I check in. He would meet me in my room.

The Hotel *Tequendama* was crowded with people and the lobby looked bright and elegant, with high ceilings and sparkling mirrors in antique gold frames. Beautiful ladies dressed in modish clothes and well-groomed men milled about. Small wonder people were being kidnapped.

A young girl with dark flashing eyes at the hotel reception desk found a reservation in my name made by someone in the U.S. Embassy. Cordial and professional, she gave me a message to call a number at the U.S. Embassy. The message had my name and room number. I realized that it was Saturday and only the Marine Guards were working. I was in no mood to talk about work.

A bellboy with my luggage led the way to the elevator. We met Driggers carrying a bottle of Scotch.

"We need to talk some more, partner," he said. Inside the elevator, Driggers towered over the bellhop, who stared at him in wonder. A low profile with Driggers was impossible.

The hotel was clean and comfortable with perfect room temperature, around 70 degrees. The room was plush and furnished with large polished antique oak tables and chairs. The beautiful Italian marble tile on the floor was shiny clean. The bellboy brought ice, glasses, and a pitcher of potable water, staring occasionally at Driggers who ignored him. I tipped him in dollars and he left happy.

Driggers seemed anxious to relax, and poured two strong drinks of Scotch in crystal glasses. Handing me one, he tipped the top of my glass.

"*Salud,*" he said. I took a long swallow and the Scotch was smooth and comforting. We sat in momentary silence at the antique oak table, enjoying the Scotch.

"What do you think I can expect from the meeting Monday?" I asked Driggers. He looked dimly at me and grew pensive. He took a long pull of Scotch and exhaled loudly.

"Well, there have been numerous classified cables exchanged between the Embassy and Washington on the Colombian Government's request for assistance on the kidnappings," he said. "You are identified by name as an expert on the investigation of kidnapping cases."

"Well, that's bullshit," I responded. "I'm no expert. There are **no** experts on kidnapping investigations anyway. Especially in Colombia." Driggers smiled.

"Many people at the Embassy question your background. Some question your experience. You know how it is at the Embassy." He smiled placidly.

"Too damn many people already know about this. Some say you'll be reckless, take chances and expose the U.S. Embassy and staff to serious danger. Some argue that if the kidnappers find out that an American is helping the police, the kidnappers will retaliate against the U.S Embassy. You know how that crap goes." I listened attentively, feeling a surge of anger.

"Did anybody mention that it might get dangerous for **me**?" I asked sarcastically. Driggers grinned.

"You are expendable," he said chuckling. "Anyway, Ambassador Vaughn is anxious to talk to you. He's uptight, but supportive." Driggers took another sip of Scotch and smacked his lips.

"There's a lot of speculation and concern at the Embassy about getting involved in this type of situation. You have the usual assholes that don't like TDY (Temporary Duty) people, spooks, or cops," he suggested with a trace of cynicism.

"The top Embassy crew will be at the meeting tomorrow, including Dino Pionzio, the CIA Station Chief, and the military attachés. You may want to meet with them later, but at the moment, Pionzio is playing coy and is not resisting the Ambassador."

Driggers was matter-of-fact about the situation and knew local players and personalities very well. Pausing, he reflected candidly on his own concerns.

"I don't think Pionzio believes we should help." Driggers seemed to be a skeptic himself in the matter. He seemed anxious to get the hell out of the way, perhaps out of the possible line of fire. I stayed silent to encourage him to talk and poured two more drinks.

"If that much speculation and concern exists at the Embassy about us getting involved, what the hell do they want? What am I expected to do?" I asked sharply. Driggers shrugged.

I had not told Driggers that when the U.S. Embassy requested assistance from Washington on the kidnapping problem and Hoover rejected the Embassy's request with a few choice words, my own experience on kidnappings was embellished so the Ambassador would accept my nomination for the assignment. For some reason, the Director of OPS wanted me to take the assignment. He believed in no pain, no gain, and no glory.

Engle had told me it was up to me to make sure that my role in Colombia was not compromised. If word got out that the United States was helping Colombia with the kidnapping problem, that could result in retaliation against the U.S. Embassy and Americans in the country, he had said. I told him it was a hell of a way to make a living and he laughed. Driggers stood up and placed ice cubes in his glass.

"By the way, there's a fellow here with AID from New Mexico. He claims to know you from a TDY you pulled in Bolivia during *Ché* Guevara's time." Driggers paced the floor.

"The guy's name is Joe Baca. He's sort of a braggart and claims to be a close friend of Little Joe Montoya, the U.S. Senator from New Mexico. He's been asking a lot of questions about you coming here and has told people that he knows you very well." Driggers was trying not to be critical.

"I think he's just nosy and likes to bullshit people. He says he wants to have you over for *enchiladas*."

I laughed spontaneously. Baca's wife made delicious *enchiladas*.

"I'd be careful with him if I was you. He is known to brag a lot, and it'll be out in the streets quickly if he finds out why you're here," Driggers suggested.

Tired from sitting, I ambled over to look out the window. The assignment was replete with potential problems, danger, and chickenshit. But there were more serious risks besides gossip.

I poured another stiff drink, enjoying Drigger's company. What the hell, the woods were going to get a lot darker. Now it was apparent that with his size, Driggers could drink the whole bottle of Scotch and wouldn't feel much effect. I was getting drunk, but needed more information from Driggers.

"The U.S. Embassy is one block from here. I'd walk, if I were you," Driggers suggested dutifully, raising his glass to emphasize his point. "Your arrival with anyone from the Embassy will be quickly noted. I don't know how you can hide yourself, anyway," he said. Driggers stood with his face red from the ingestion of booze.

"I better let you get some rest," he said. "It's getting late and you've got a lot to think about." He paused to drink the rest of the Scotch in his glass.

"I figure your meeting at the Embassy will be over by ten on Monday. I'll pick you up here at the hotel at eleven to go to DAS Headquarters."

I agreed. Driggers grunted and picked up the bottle of Scotch to pour himself one for the road. Raising his glass in a half-ass *salud,* he emptied it in one swallow.

"Good luck, partner," he said. "Don't forget the meeting with Stotts tomorrow and dinner afterwards at my house," he reminded me as he headed for the door. "I'll pick you up around three."

After Driggers left, a strange vacuous feeling hit me. In the silence, the elegant mix of Spanish and French Colonial furniture made me think about my wife, Jan. She loved antiques. With a touch of optimism, I figured to be on my way home in six weeks. What could I do about a kidnapping problem in Colombia anyway?

Unpacking my gun and shoulder holster, I opened the cylinder to check the super velocity rounds loaded inside. I placed the .38 S&W Combat Masterpiece under my pillow. I was on U.S. time, and my somnolence was primed by the Scotch. Exhausted, it did not take long for me to doze off on the comfortable bed.

16

The Country Team

October 19, 1969

Colombia's history of left-wing guerrillas and *Violencia* could not be ignored by anyone in the country. My assignment to assist the *Departamento Administrativo de Seguridad* (DAS) on kidnappings was complicated because I was told to keep United States assistance a secret. But my presence in Colombia could not be kept a secret. The Boss counted on my ability as an American *"Chicano"* (Hispanic) to speak the local language fluently enough to pass as Colombian. But my Spanish was New Mexican-oriented and tainted with an occasional smattering of Central American and Uruguayan. I was to be low-key in a high profile assignment.

The morning noise of urban traffic and movement of people out in the street awakened me. Instinctively I reached under the pillow for my revolver and placed it on the nightstand, resisting an urge to pat it. Under the circumstances, I felt more comfort from my gun than anything else. The booze from the night before was affecting my senses, I thought sleepily.

The glow of first light entered my room at the Hotel *Tequendama* through an open curtain and I felt the soporific effects of a hangover. I did a few push-ups to pick up my heart rate. After shaving and a shower, I had room service deliver a Creole breakfast of three fried eggs, thick bacon, black spicy beans, freshly squeezed orange juice and excellent Colombian coffee. I recalled happily that Jack Munroe, the Deputy Director of OPS, had humorously suggested that the assignment would be a vacation for me after my tour in Uruguay.

By mid-morning, after exploring the premises and tourist shops in the hotel, a church with beautiful gleaming white towers near the hotel had a noon mass, so I decided to attend. After the service, the church entrance teemed with worshipers and a myriad of mendicants begging for handouts. It seemed many of the local folks who had money attended the noon mass and the beggars knew this. After mass I walked back to the hotel. Bogota was peaceful on a Sunday and any risks were imperceptible to me. Walking alone in the street provoked stares from unsavory looking types but the revolver under my coat felt reassuring. I took mental notes of the surroundings on my way to the hotel.

By 2:30 p.m., Bill Driggers arrived at the hotel to take me to the meeting scheduled with Ben Stotts, the FBI Legal *Attaché*. After a short drive, we stopped next to an attractive apartment complex and Driggers nodded his head in the direction of the building.

"That's where Ben Stotts lives," he informed me. Americans assigned by the U.S. Government abroad received rental allowances that permitted them to live in nice comfortable residences. Stotts was no exception and his apartment was large and attractive. He greeted us warmly when we saw him and invited us into his house.

It was obvious that Stotts knew many of the DAS Officers and he provided valuable insights on the personnel involved in the kidnapping investigations. According to Stotts, the Colombian Government had responded to the kidnapping problem with separate investigative teams from the DAS, the military forces, and the National Police. Thus far, not one suspect that had been apprehended that could be linked to any of the 22 kidnapping cases that had occurred in the past year. (The Swiss kidnapping case still remained active and a mystery. The Swiss Embassy would not talk to anyone about that kidnapping.)

Stotts suggested that the police and military units involved in the kidnapping cases were anxious to make arrests, but so far had been extraordinarily unsuccessful. He suggested that I link up with a Branch Chief from the DAS named Gordillo. The man was reportedly in charge of the investigations.

Stotts was interested in what I intended to do in regards to the kidnapping cases. When I told him I had no idea, he glanced at me with a puzzled look. It was funny for me and I laughed. But Stotts grew serious and warned me that things could get dangerous for me personally. I asked him what he thought could be done about it. He shrugged and suggested that I be low-key. I had to laugh again. I had no training in being low-key.

Stotts had high praise for the Director of the DAS, General Luis Etilio Leyva. But there was a perceivable touch of disenchantment when I did not talk about my own plans. But realistically, I had no plan. Later,

Driggers agreed that Stotts had seemed interested in what my plans were and was disappointed that I did not talk more about that. I told Driggers I had no idea what could be done to help the police on kidnappings. Everyone in Colombia knew more about the kidnapping problem than I did. He thought that was funny.

After a couple of hours we left Stotts, and in the car, Driggers leaned over to tell me that he had invited a few friends to join us for dinner at his house. He seemed to want a reaction from me. I suggested in jest that it was his house and he had to pay the tab.

Smiling, he let me know that Joe Baca, the fellow from New Mexico that had met me in Bolivia, and his wife Mary Jane, plus two other friends had been invited. Driggers suggested it was strictly social and included a home cooked meal. I told him that laughingly that I hoped his wife Betty was cooking.

At Drigger's residence, Joe Baca greeted me with special homeboy familiarity.

"Hey *cabrón,* I know why you're here," he told me in a loud voice, hugging me. People in the house laughed. *Cabrón* in Spanish commonly means "bastard" or the equivalent. The word is an insult unless a friend uses it. Baca used *Barrio* lingo comfortably with me and we joked like old buddies.

He finally asked what I was doing in Colombia. In a serious vein, I told him that it was a classified matter and if I told him anything I'd have to kill him. People erupted in laughter, but Baca grew frustrated.

"*Cabrón,* you **are** good at the bullshit," he smiled to tell me.

Joe Baca was a friendly, charismatic person and fun to be with. Drinks before dinner helped put everyone in a warm relaxed mood and the evening was enjoyable. Baca made everyone laugh by telling us about New Mexico's stiff-necked politicians and his close personal relationship with U.S. Senator Joseph Montoya.

He recounted a story about President Lyndon Johnson and Senator Montoya being together at a dedication ceremony of some sort on the U.S./Mexican border, near El Paso. Beer was served during the reception and the time arrived when both men had a desperate urge to urinate. They walked together, followed by U.S. Secret Service Agents, to an isolated part of the mesa and stood next to each other to piss.

The desert night was cold and as they pulled out their penises to urinate, President Johnson turned somberly to tell Senator Montoya, "pretty chilly, Joe." According to Baca, Montoya spontaneously thanked Johnson. ("Chile" is pronounced "chilly" in New Mexico and vulgarians use the word "Chile" to describe their penises.) Of course there was no truth to the story but it was funny. (I found out that Joe Baca and U.S. Senator Joseph Montoya, a popular and beloved United States Hispanic Congressman from the State of New Mexico, were very good friends.)

October 20, 1969, 0830 Hours

I prepared to go to the Embassy, and placed my revolver inside my briefcase. I dressed in a dark wool navy blue suit, white shirt, and blue tie, jokingly thinking that perhaps this was not the time to spike my hair, put on earrings or large medallions to go to this meeting. Driggers had warned my visit would spark curiosity and I mused that by wearing hippie paraphernalia, no one could associate me as being an 'expert' on kidnappings. My experience and training for "hidden terrors" was zilch.

It would not take long for people in Colombia to know an *Americano* was helping the police with the kidnapping problem. If the kidnappers retaliated by blowing up the U.S. Embassy, I would be in the limelight. My friend Pete Ellena suggested with a grin that we wait and see.

The hotel was a short distance from *Calle 26 Carrera Decima* where the *Tequendama* was located to the U.S. Embassy. Walking through the hotel, many corridors had stores with show windows loaded with sparkling beautiful green emeralds, gold necklaces, and bright, colorful *ruanas*. *Ruanas* were classy and attractive wool cloaks that warded off the cold for the rich as well as the poor of Colombia. Reaching the street I headed west for the U.S. Embassy. The streets were extremely crowded.

The revolver in my briefcase felt heavy but leaving a gun in my hotel room was not a good idea. But if the diplomatic sweethearts at the U.S. Embassy knew I was carrying a gun they would certainly object. Most U.S. Foreign Service Officers considered people carrying guns to be low class. But diplomatic protocol does not help if a terrorist has you by the throat and is trying to disembowel you! FBI Agents assigned in Latin America walked the streets for months unarmed because country permits to carry a gun took forever for the Embassy to process. Despite the image portrayed by the movie industry, CIA Officers in U.S. Embassies rarely carried a weapon.

American career diplomats were considered to be the most insipid among the Foreign Service Officers of the world. Despite the fact that the terrorist threat was growing, American diplomats did not feel safer carrying a gun. In fact, many believed that carrying a gun increased the risk of potential violence.

I walked to the Embassy and two men in black leather jackets followed me. I picked up the pace and they hurried. There were no guards outside the Chancery, so access to the U.S. Embassy in Bogota was generally unrestricted in the 1960s and '70s. Marine guards protecting the American Mission were more concerned with pomp and circumstance than security. That would soon change.

The Chancery in Bogota was a huge gray stone building with a large ornate metal door and black wrought iron bars on the windows. In the lobby of the Embassy, an attractive girl with long dark silky hair sat at a desk. The sign on her desk said: **RECEPCIÓN.** Visitors stopped at her desk to inquire about appointments with U.S. Embassy officials. A Marine Gunny Sergeant wearing dress blue pants with a red stripe running down the sides of his trousers watched from a doorway when I entered.

The receptionist, a pretty girl with flashing beautiful brown eyes, was courteous. She had a delectable Latin accent and wore a pair of tight slacks that displayed firm round buttocks and a great figure.

"Hóla Recepción, yo tengo una cita con el Señor Embajador," I told her in Spanish. She asked what my name was and I told her Adolpho. She turned serious to fake a pout.

"Qué lástima, el Señor habla Español!" With an impish look she pretended to be disappointed that I spoke Spanish so fluently.

"I speak English, too," I told her lightheartedly. Picking up the telephone, she dialed the number for the Ambassador's secretary and leaned toward me coquettishly. The Marine Gunny Sergeant quietly approached to interrupt my tête-à-tête with the pretty receptionist.

"Are you Mr. Sanz?" he asked stiffly, mispronouncing my name. When I nodded, he quickly took charge and asked me to follow him.

"The Ambassador is waiting for you," he said in a tight voice. Winking at the receptionist, I fell in step with the Marine. Smiling, she winked back.

The Marine Sergeant led me to the U.S. Ambassador's office on the third floor where a pretty woman with short blonde hair and clothes that glozed a voluptuous figure stood at a large desk. The Marine left without saying a word. The pretty blonde came close to my face. She told me in a soft voice that the Ambassador was in a meeting, but was expecting me, she said.

"He left instructions that if you arrived by 9:00 o'clock he would like for you to join the Embassy staff in the meeting in the conference room." She paused dramatically.

"But if you arrived after nine to please wait. It is now 9:05." She smiled demurely.

"In the meantime, can I get you some coffee?" I shook my head absentmindedly, distracted by her sexy smell. When I gazed into her eyes she stared back without blinking. She had to be from Los Angeles, sexually dramatic, liberal, and independent. Sitting in an overstuffed chair, I tried to hide feelings of intimidation. Within minutes I regretted not accepting the blonde sexpot's offer for coffee. A delicious aroma of coffee permeated the room and it was obviously good Colombian stuff.

While I pondered questions for the meeting ahead, a young man with long frizzy blonde hair and a fuzzy mustache passed by, closely scrutinizing me. I glared at him and he loped off seemingly offended. The *hippies* were invading the United States Foreign Service.

The room was amazingly quiet except for the rustle of silk and sounds made by the Ambassador's attractive secretary. The place seemed almost ecclesiastical and reminded me of the times people waited for the priest to hear confessions at Saint Genevieve's Church in Las Cruces, New Mexico.

"Bless me, Father. My last confession was terrible and this one may be terrible also," I recalled.

A clock ticked softly on the wall indicating it was fifteen minutes past nine. A man in a dark suit and wearing a glued-on smile on his face quietly approached from a nearby door and greeted me in a low voice. He had a friendly look and shook my hand warmly to tell me the Ambassador was waiting. Leading me into a conference room with the palm of his right hand upturned, he invited me to go in.

Ten stone-faced men sat at a long polished table with documents. Two of the men wore military uniforms so I surmised they were U.S. Army and Air Force Military *Attachés*. The faces in the room were mostly deadpan and not overly friendly.

"This is Ambassador Jack Vaughn," the diplomat said, gesturing to a man dressed in a dark blue suit and wearing a rust-colored tie. Jack Hood Vaughn had a full head of red hair and a trim mustache. He reached to shake my hand.

"Come in, come in, Mr. Saenz," he told me amicably. When he invited me to sit near him, I recalled that Jack Vaughn was a former Marine like myself.

"Before we start, let me introduce the people here," he said. The Ambassador wasted little time getting down to business. He introduced Robert Stevenson, the DCM (Deputy Chief of Mission); Earl Lubinsky, Chief of the Political Section; Colonel Harold Lowman, a Military *Attaché*; and Marvin Weismann, the Director of AID. The Ambassador then introduced special members of the Country Team.

"Mr. Dino Pionzio is a Political Officer," he said. Pol 2, he called it. Recognizing the CIA Chief of Station, I humorously pictured him as East

Coast establishment and Shakespearean actor. The CIA Station Chief smiled circumspectly. I felt negative vibrations from the group and went into a cautious mode.

"Mr. Saenz, we're glad to have you here," he began. "This is a very important mission and Washington tells me you're one of the best." I wondered what individual he had spoken to in Washington. Someone had given me a favorable reputation. The Ambassador continued his discourse in a clear strong voice while I merely nodded. It was early for praise as far as I was concerned, but it was more appreciated than condolences.

"Mr. Lubinsky will brief us on what's happening since he knows the situation," the Ambassador said pleasantly. "He is probably the best to begin with." The Ambassador nodded toward a young man with stern, confident eyes. Instinctively, I mistrusted anyone assigned to the U.S. Embassy Political Section. They were considered the *inteligencia* of the Embassy crowd, but they seemed to have the same agenda: power.

In a prevenient display worthy of an experienced U.S. Embassy Political Officer, Lubinsky was articulate.

"Welcome to Bogota, Mr. Saenz," he began in a confident tone, pronouncing my name correctly. "We have learned that most of the kidnappings have occurred in Cali, in the Province of *Valle del Cauca.*" He spoke without reference to notes, seemingly sure of what he was going to say.

"There have been, as far as we know, more than twenty-two kidnappings this year. Two of the victims were killed when the military and police authorities intervened to apprehend the kidnappers and the ransom was not paid." His voice was crisp and clear. He paused to emphasize his next comment.

"It appears the Colombians **have not** been able to resolve one single kidnapping thus far," he reported. Clearing his throat, Lubinsky grew slightly tense, then sanctimonious.

"The Colombians have requested our help," he stated dryly. "The Ambassador has responded on a positive note as we all know. That's why you are here, Mr. Saenz." He looked stiffly at me.

"However, there are some things about the situation that greatly bother me." Lubinsky paused dramatically and inhaled deeply.

"How can we help? That is the tough part. I don't want to discourage or disparage anyone," he suggested, assuming a serious face. I knew what he was leading up to.

"But it is difficult to expect that someone like you, Mr. Saenz, can come to Colombia for a few weeks and succeed in resolving any aspect of the kidnapping problem. The police and military forces have not been able to accomplish anything for over a year despite their experience and all the resources at their disposal." That comment made me smile impulsively.

Lubinsky paused to deliver more wisdom and I looked at him without any appearance of concern on my part. The implacable Political Officer glanced at me occasionally, apparently to seek my reaction. Smiling, I kept silent. I knew Mr. Lubinsky was not finished.

"The National Police, the DAS, and the Colombian Army are all involved in kidnapping investigations," he continued. "Hundreds of men," he emphasized.

"But it seems the most critical issue in this matter is the possibility of retaliation against the American Mission in Colombia by the kidnappers if they find out the United States is helping the police with the problem."

I stayed silent. Lubinsky sounded like a cloned U.S. diplomat, trained and experienced in the intricacies of foreign affairs. What he meant was that if the kidnappers or terrorists found out that the United States was helping the Colombian Police investigate kidnappings, their special action groups would retaliate against Americans in Colombia, bomb the U.S. Embassy, shoot the American Ambassador, kidnap the Political Officer, etc., etc. Left-wing guerrillas in other countries were already doing all that, but so far the security environment for the U.S. Embassy in Colombia was relatively peaceful. Until I had arrived.

My appearance on the scene increased security concerns and made me the proverbial turd in the diplomatic punch bowl. But Lubinsky made the meeting interesting.

In the end, the Political Officer ceremoniously covered all bases and concluded with an ominous warning that attracted the attention of everyone in the meeting.

"Perhaps we are at more risk because of the United States intervention to assist the security forces in the kidnapping problem, than we are in terms of the kidnapping problem." The Country Team members in the room were strangely quiet and this added to the intrigue.

The Ambassador's voice suddenly rang out, rigid and dismissive. He was obviously prepared for Lubinsky's comments and was ready with a response.

"I understand Mr. Lubinsky's concern," he honed in. "But I believe a low key, low profile approach in assisting the Colombian security forces with the kidnapping problem will be of value. I believe Mr. Saenz can and should do it. I consider it necessary." It seemed I was put on trial.

"We are committed to providing the Colombians with help on the kidnapping problem and an expert like Mr. Saenz will be extremely useful," the Ambassador emphasized. I remained silent but felt the tension. There are no "experts" in this business, Mr. Ambassador, just self-serving politicians, I thought sarcastically.

Colonel Harold Lowman spoke up to tell the group that the Colombian military forces actually controlled the action on the kidnapping crisis in *Valle del Cauca*. A recent decree issued by the President of Colombia had established a State of Siege in that province, he reported. The Colonel glanced at the Ambassador.

"General Bernardo Sanchez Salazar, the Commander of the Third Army Brigade in Cali, is in charge of the Colombian Government effort during the state of emergency in *Valle del Cauca.*" He turned to face me.

"I can help you link up with those folks anytime you like," he said. As a Military *Attaché*, U.S. Air Force Colonel Harold Lowman seemed helpful and sincere.

"That's very interesting, Colonel," I told him. "Thank you very much." I needed his help and suggested we get together after the meeting. I didn't know where to start, anyway. Lowman quickly agreed. I looked around the room to scan grim faces. The CIA Station Chief was mum and not talking.

I felt my face tighten and knew the controls on my temper were down and the floodgates to my contentiousness were now open.

"Mr. Ambassador, I thank all of you for your indulgence. There is something I would like to mention quite candidly if I may, since Mr. Lubinsky is so divulgent," I suggested. "One, if I stay, I count on talking with some of you later on. Right now I really don't know much about what's going on in Colombia in regard to the kidnappings." I looked up to see a lot of attention focused on me.

"So far, I have not learned much. Washington did not provide much information and I was told the information would be provided here." I looked directly at the Ambassador.

"It seems we need more facts before we reach any conclusions about how to deal with the problem," I suggested dryly. "But **if** I stay on this assignment, it will be strictly as an advisor to anyone who will listen. I am willing to help wherever possible in regard to the kidnapping problem." I leaned back to stare at Lubinsky.

"Be that as it may, I just want to say that we can't have it both ways. Either I stay and help or go back to Washington tomorrow and avoid any risks for the U.S. Embassy **and** for myself." Lubinsky looked up with a surprised look on his face.

"Any risks involved either way must be accepted and whether I stay or return to Washington depends on what the Ambassador decides."

I raised my voice slightly, to intone with some degree of emphasis that I had **not** solicited the assignment.

Expletives in Spanish I learned as a kid crossed my mind, *"coman caca cabrones."* I looked around the room, holding back a grin. I waited for a response from someone, but none came. The heavy silence in the room pushed me to continue.

"The kidnapping problem in Colombia will affect U.S. interests if it isn't neutralized. Politically, that's the risk the Embassy has to assess," I suggested. My comments generated attention.

"Personally, I don't like the idea of putting myself or the U.S. Embassy at risk. But that's the key issue the Embassy has to face before we do anything else." There was a brief dead silence.

I candidly reiterated that one option available would be for me to grab a flight back to Washington and not waste more time on the problem. The statement was deliberately non-diplomatic. The group in the room stared at me. There were no guarantees on anything in regard to any U.S. intervention, including the threat of reprisals against Americans. Answers regarding a potential backlash or on screw-ups were not available. Nevertheless, for me, the potential for mishaps was real. Driggers had humorously suggested no one would know my "fuck ups" except myself. Maybe he was right. The Ambassador turned sullen.

"That is not an option. I approved the assignment and expect you to stay and do the best job possible." Ambassador Vaughn grew direct. Actually, it felt good to find an Ambassador who was not easily manipulated by the Political Section of the Embassy.

"Good, Mr. Ambassador," I responded optimistically. "Everyone knows I'm not here on a religious mission or goodwill tour. I expect to be low key and will probably have minimal contact with people in the U.S. Embassy. I intend to integrate into the Colombian effort as discreetly as possible." I looked directly at Lubinsky and Pionzio.

"I must emphasize that this is not a covert operation, but I'm not here to do missionary work either. I am an American advisor working with the Colombian police on kidnappings." It was a surprise for me that there was no dissension in regard to any of my comments.

"Under the circumstances, the international media might speculate on our assistance at any time. There is nothing I can do about that," I suggested placidly. "I do not want to be held responsible for any reprisals against the Embassy. I can only try to keep my mission as clandestine as possible." I stared at Lubinsky to propose there were no guarantees that the kidnappers or the media would not find out the U.S. Government was helping the police with the problem.

I felt it necessary to show independence and sort out the insidiousness early. U.S. Embassy officers appeared to have made up their minds on the matter, and several pensive faces nodded agreement. The Ambassador seemed pleased but the Political Officer stared at me with cool eyes.

My stomach grumbled and I reached nonchalantly for a cup of coffee and took a sweet roll from a tray on the conference table. Lubinsky watched me from the corner of his eye. The tension in the room made me hungry. The room was momentarily quiet while I sipped coffee. The Ambassador leaned over to whisper something to the DCM. But my next question garnered special attention.

"There is something that perhaps someone can clarify," I said. "Are there any left-wing or communist guerrillas involved in the kidnappings?" The Ambassador reacted immediately.

"Dino, can you answer that question?"

The short, husky CIA Station Chief sat quietly, stroking a face full of dark beard. He leaned forward with elbows on the table, studying documents held in his hand.

"As far as we know, there is a possibility some of the people involved in the kidnappings are members of the FARC *(Fuerzas Armadas Revolucionarias Colombianas)* or the MOIR," he said. "Both are communist organizations with a militant arm. The MOIR is the *Movimiento Obrero Independiente Revolucionario* (Workers Independent Revolutionary Movement), a labor union." He looked up with wary eyes. He was hedging his bets.

"Both groups have the capacity and interest to pull off kidnappings for ransom. Both organizations are hurting for money. However, there may be others, but their involvement has not been confirmed," he cautioned.

The comments of the CIA Station Chief were cryptically cautious. He was not really saying much. No one really seemed to know much. There were probably political facets to the problem because I sensed an indefinable anomaly. The people in the room did not want to know anything about the problem or else they really did not know what the hell was going on. The risk of retaliation against the U.S. Embassy by the kidnappers or by the guerrillas was a serious concern. The men in the room would soon start to appraise and second-guess me if I remained longer. My hand went up in explanation, hoping it would not be offensive.

"Mr. Ambassador. Everyone is busy and there is no sense taking up any more of your valuable time," I told them. "I have a meeting with

DAS Officials this morning and will get more information on the kidnappings. If agreeable, I'd like to meet individually with some officers later. If you can provide me the opportunity to talk to you or the DCM while I am here, Mr. Ambassador, that will be most appreciated." Ambassador Vaughn nodded quickly.

"Of course," he told me. Dino Pionzio nodded and suggested we meet right after the meeting.

"If you like, we can meet for a few minutes before you meet with Colonel Lowman," he offered. Despite frustrations, the meeting ended on a positive note.

"Good luck, Mr. Saenz," the Ambassador told me as the meeting broke up.

The office of the CIA Station Chief in Bogota was located in the back of the U.S. Embassy Political Section and buried in an enclave of offices, with access to the area restricted. Pionzio led the way and sat behind a mahogany desk stacked with classified documents. He looked pensive and the full beard on his face gave him a scholarly look with a rugged appearance. Pionzio was cautious about the kidnapping problem in Colombia.

"It's a tough problem for Colombia," he said, pulling gently on his dark beard as he spoke. "But I don't believe the kidnappings taking place have political implications. The kidnappers don't appear to have any firm linkages to left-wing or radical movements in Colombia." If this were true, I wondered why the Government of Colombia declared the kidnappings a threat to its national security?

Dino offered his help, including running name checks through CIA files of individuals suspected of having connections with the kidnappers. I kidded that the name checks of local cops might be of interest.

"But it ain't New York or Los Angeles yet," I joked.

Pionzio grinned to suggest that suspicions did exist about the police. He provided the names of possible left-wing groups and their leaders.

"Be careful about publicity," he cautioned. "The media is out en masse. If the kidnappers or bad guys find out about you being here, this may result in serious consequences for you personally," he predicted ominously. "And for the U.S. Embassy," he added.

Smiling, I told him cuttingly. "I have a hellish situation. Everyone here is determined to give me the good news first." Pionzio smiled almost involuntarily. We finished talking and he escorted me to the office of Colonel Harold Lowman. The colonel seemed to know the situation well.

He described the communist and left-wing organizations active in Colombia, but concluded that the kidnappings did not have political implications. That was in line with the CIA Station Chief's assessment.

The *Fuerzas Armadas Revolucionarias Colombianas* (FARC), the *Ejercito de Liberacion Nacional* (ELN), and the *Ejercito Popular de Liberacion* (EPL), the more important communist and left-wing organizations in Colombia were apparently not talking to each other.

Colonel Lowman was of the opinion that in Colombia, kidnapping was a minor offense by law. The crime was equivalent to a misdemeanor in the United States, he suggested. He was absolutely right. Kidnapping in Colombia was a misdemeanor punishable by a few months in jail but the rewards were absolutely great. But the plight in store for any victim of a kidnapping certainly had deadly consequences.

Reaching the lobby of the Embassy, I concluded that talking to U.S. Embassy officers was not much fun. It was almost funereal. The pretty receptionist in the lobby glowed when she saw me. At least she was friendly. Escorted out of the Chancery by the Marine sergeant without delay, I smiled at the receptionist and shrugged. I wondered if she believed I was just another visitor.

Outside, the two men in leather jackets continued to follow me from a distance. I walked slowly toward the Hotel *Tequendama*, wondering why they were interested in me so soon. But more importantly, who the hell were they? Why were they following me? I was new in the country.

17

The Cali Kidnapping Cartel

Bogota sits in the central highlands of Colombia on the Cordillera Oriental and is considered one of the largest and most cosmopolitan cities in Latin America. The city was experiencing serious problems of urban crime, violence, kidnappings, and the drug trafficking problem was growing worse. For decades, *La Violencia* in the rural areas was known as a cultural enigma that baffled historians. The phenomenon of unbelievable violence and bloodletting was taking place in the rural areas but frequently overflowed into the urban areas.

No previous government had been able to control *La Violencia,* and many left-wing advocates and activists attributed the problem to the Colombian security forces. But it was the *"bandidos"* and left-wing guerrillas who were responsible. The problems were a part of the crazy world of the Cold War, intermingled with bloody long-term social and political conflicts.

As I walked back to the hotel from the U.S. Embassy, my mission appeared almost impossible after meeting with the Country Team and the U.S. Ambassador. An army of fully armed people had been unable to resolve the kidnapping problem in Colombia. I was alone in my mission, and if the kidnappers retaliated against the U.S. Embassy, it would be my fault. What explanation could I use, I wondered.

Meanwhile, downtown Bogota bustled with people walking hurriedly in all directions, a la New York. In front of me two long-legged girls showed off large buns wrapped in tight mini-skirts. Ahead on the street, an ambulance and a police car were stopped with emergency lights flashing. A car appeared to have run into a curb. But the two mangled bodies on the sidewalk were shot full of holes. Bright red blood flowed uninterrupted into a gutter as gawkers gathered at the scene to look at the bodies, and the policemen made no effort to control them. It seemed every passing citizen wanted to view the bloody spectacle.

From behind me an old man pushed a small cart that released an aromatic smell of garlic. The "old timer" smiled pleasantly and offered me a small oily paper sack. Looking inside the bag I saw several large black beetles that appeared to have been cooked in oil. Smiling at my reaction, the old man told me that they were *"deliciosos bichos"*...suggesting the beetles were tasty and good to eat. Taking the sack I handed him five Colombian pesos. He offered change and I took the opportunity to see where the two men in leather jackets were.

Near the Hotel *Tequendama*, a light haze and the smell of exhaust fumes permeated the air. Nevertheless, Bogota was a big, attractive city. When I arrived at the hotel, Driggers was inside the lobby calmly reading a newspaper. He saw me and raised his large frame from a hapless chair.

"So, how did it go?" he asked anxiously as we walked to chairs in the lobby.

"Fine," I told him holding out the small paper sack with black beetles.

"I bought something for you." Driggers looked carefully inside.

"Shit, that's gross," he exclaimed, sticking out his tongue.

Sarcastically I suggested that any guy that went by the name of Rodriguez would certainly appreciate the gift. He dumped the contents of the sack into an ashtray and the dark beetles rolled out intact. Once roasted and salted, Colombians eat them like popcorn. I faked popping one in my mouth and Driggers made a face.

"The taste is great and they are excellent protein," I said, urging him to try one.

"Open your mouth and let me see," he insisted. I opened my mouth and showed him a masticated mass of dark chocolate. Driggers thought I had eaten one of the beetles and his face turned red. He stared at me.

"Hot damn, you're nasty," he said with a twisted smile on his face.

"It's an aphrodisiac," I kidded, trying to convince him. "This stuff really helps you get great erections."

"Try one," I insisted. Driggers picked up one of the beetles, looked at it and made a face.

"I'll bet. What about the meeting?" he asked.

"Vaughn is definitely a dashing fellow with more guts than the average Ambassador," I suggested. Driggers listened attentively as I described the people in the meeting and the proceedings.

"There was the usual political bullshit with resistance to U.S. involvement in helping the Colombian police." I explained Lubinsky's position on my presence to Driggers and he nodded.

"I told you," Driggers reminded me. He was suddenly anxious to go. "Hey, we're late, we better get moving." He walked out hurriedly.

"By the way, the newspapers say the Government of Colombia is powerless against the kidnapping threat," he said. He handed me a copy of *El Espectador,* a local newspaper, and headed for the door of the hotel. I pulled at his arm. I needed to tell him about the two men following me to the Embassy.

"Hold on, I wanna show you something." At a window I pointed out to the street with my chin.

"See those two guys in dark leather jackets? They followed me to the Embassy and back to the hotel." The two men were standing across the street from the hotel. Driggers glared out the window.

"Son-of-a-gun, I'd swear they're DAS Agents," Driggers told me in his best western drawl. "The old General probably put them on your tail to keep an eye on your butt!" He showed a thin smile and his face looked intense as he explained that perhaps the General figured I might turn out to be a valuable asset after all. He suggested he could find out if those were the General's men.

"Maybe he figures if something bad happens to you this soon, the impact on his ass won't be good." He smirked and flashed his hand across his face.

"I can see it already, the headlines in the New York Times. **U.S. Kidnapping Expert Kidnapped in Colombia,**" he told me. He grinned broadly, watching my reaction.

I feigned anger and plunked down in a soft chair with a loud grunt.

"Thanks for the cheerful early morning thought!" I told him, faking concern. Driggers snorted a laugh and pulled me out of the chair.

"Let's go, the General's waiting," he said. He told me he had just been kidding, and continued to laugh.

He did not stop laughing until we entered the blue Wagoneer. A short distance away, the men in leather jackets talked to a man waiting in a car. Driggers wriggled his large frame behind the driver's seat, adjusted the rear view mirror and drove away. The two men watched our departure without moving. In the heavy traffic, Driggers used the rear view mirror to scan behind us.

"Well, it doesn't look like anyone's following," he concluded in a serious tone of voice. Laughing at his gyrations I suggested that he was the one who was afraid of getting kidnapped. He grinned as a wave of pedestrians and heavy traffic surrounded us. Smoke from the exhaust of numerous buses and cars in the slow moving traffic intensified the gray haze.

"They won't mess with me," Driggers contended.

"You're the expert." Drigger's concern was growing funny.

"They don't know that," I told him. The kidnappers will probably be looking for a *Gringo* like you and they might just like **your** big-ass **Gringo** look." He chuckled and grew silent. I laughed at his reaction.

A few minutes later, he parked the car across the street from a sprawling brick structure that showed remnants of Spanish architecture with additions here and there. Driggers continued to pull on my strings. A bomb had recently blown away part of the DAS Headquarters, he told me.

"That's just great." I faked my reaction with a concerned and serious tone. "I'm glad it happened before I got here." Driggers gleefully laughed out loud.

Men in civilian clothes guarded the entrance to the building and held automatic weapons at the ready. Walking in, Driggers signaled to a guard and showed him an I.D. card. The guard waved us in. Entering, we walked down a tiled corridor and passed through several offices until we reached a foyer deep inside the building. A comely woman sitting behind a desk jumped up when she saw us and ran to Driggers.

"Buenos Dias, Señor Ro' Driggers! Como esta usted?" She twitted enthusiastically, as she hugged him.

"That's sweet, Señor Rodriguez," I said to him, faking heavy sarcasm. Driggers turned a light pink.

"I hope there's no hanky panky involved," I kidded. He glanced shyly at me and looked away.

"Este es el Señor Saenz," he told the woman. She smiled sweetly.

"Si, si, the General is expecting you," she said in Spanish, nodding vigorously. "He is in a meeting, but I'll tell him you're here!" Her Spanish was warm and formal.

"Yo me llamo Carmen," she said, smiling sweetly. Driggers blushed when she opened a door marked Director General and entered. He grew visibly annoyed when I stared at him. I pointed at the sign on the door.

"Look, the General has his title on the door in English," I told Driggers. "What do you think of that, Rodriguez?" Driggers squinted and took a deep breath.

"Shit, you know it's one of those words that's spelled the same and means the same in Spanish and English," he said irritably. I laughed at his indignation and patted his shoulder.

"Pretty good, maybe you **could** make it as Rodriguez, " I told him. Carmen opened the door.

"Adelante, por favor, pase, pase!" We entered a room heavily saturated with smoke and the smell of burning cigarettes. Driggers wrinkled his nose in dismay and I whispered sarcastically to him that he should complain to the Director General. He mumbled. Inside, three men sitting at a small conference table stood to greet us.

"Bueno," a short handsome man walked to us with a grin on his face. He had a perfectly round balding head kept trimmed on the sides. Short and wiry, his twinkling eyes missed very little. He hugged Driggers in a hearty Latin American style *abrazo.*

"I'm General Luis Etilio Leyva," he said softly, shaking my hand. *"Mucho gusto, Señor* Adolph Saenz." A bantam sized Yul Bryner, I thought. The General was totally unpretentious and friendly, speaking in a mixture of English and Spanish.

"What do they call you?" he asked with a friendly smile.

"Dolph," I responded and the smile on his face faded slightly. He would have preferred Adolpho.

"I hope you speak Spanish, *Señor* Dolph," he said. "We have a lot to talk about." I cleared my throat.

"Si, mi General, yo hablo Español," I told him lightheartedly. *"Y también entiendo Espanol y puedo leer Espanol."* I told him I spoke, read and understood Spanish. He seemed amused. From that point on, he called me Dolph.

"Por favor, join us. You too, Rodriguez. The gentlemen with me are Señor Espasmodillo Gordillo, Chief of the Public Order Section, and Dr. Eduardo Leon, a criminologist." The two men shook hands with us as we joined them at the table. Gordillo was the man FBI Agent Stotts had mentioned.

"We are discussing the most recent kidnapping in *Valle del Cauca,"* General Leyva explained. *"Vamos,* we need to get you involved." The General was extremely likable and personable. If he had not accepted me it would be tough to buy a cup of good Colombian coffee in the police cafeteria.

"Mucho gusto tenerte aqui (We are happy to have you here)." The General led the conversation to more familiar Spanish. "We are discussing the Straessle and Buff kidnapping case. The case involves two Swiss diplomats abducted in *Valle del Cauca* about two weeks ago. Thus far, there are no *pistas. Pistas!* You know, clues," he explained.

"Entiendo," I answered with a grin. The General showed me pictures of two men.

"Mira, estos son los dos tipos," he told me. I examined the faces in the pictures and was astonished.

"Pero uno es un jovensito, Mi General," I exclaimed in surprise. One of the victims was a young boy. The General looked up.

"Si, tiene sólo quince años," he said dryly. One of the victims was fifteen years old, he said. The local media described the two victims as two Swiss Diplomats. I thought about the parents of the young lad. They had to be traumatized. Driggers stared with doleful eyes at the pictures.

We sat, and the General informed us that Inspector Gordillo was in charge of the kidnapping investigation and gestured at the stout young man with slick dark hair sitting next to him. He pointed at the other man with an easygoing smile.

"Dr. Leon is helping analyze evidence collected on the kidnapping of the Swiss Diplomats. He is a criminologist," he explained. *"Un professional,"* he added with a smile.

It appeared that everyone was too nice to be dealing with pathological killers and kidnappers. I was wrong. The General continued to tell us about the Straessle and Buff case. He suddenly glanced at me with a puzzled expression on his face to ask me if I had any questions. Caught by surprise, I surmised he was thinking of me as an "expert" and possibly a clairvoyant. But I did not even know where the bathroom was.

"I don't know much about the Swiss kidnapping. I would like to learn more about that case. Are there any similar clues or patterns in that case that match patterns found in previous cases?" I asked innocuously. Gordillo shifted uncomfortably in his chair and grew rigid.

"We have a serious problem," he explained with a tight face. "The families or the victims kidnapped will not cooperate with the DAS or the police." Gordillo arched thick eyebrows, showing signs of fatigue. "As long as the ransom is paid to the kidnappers and the police do not intervene in the matter, the victims are released unharmed." He appeared to be reciting from a text and seemed frustrated.

"The victims will absolutely not cooperate with any police investigation! They are scared to death of any contact with the police!" He reached for reading glasses and calmly scratched his head.

"In one case, the victim was killed after military personnel tried to apprehend the kidnappers." He scrutinized documents on the table impassively.

"Fabio Gomez Salazar, that was the victim killed when the military intervened," Dr. Leon interjected. "It was this year, in September, I believe." Dr. Leon sported a trim mustache and round rim glasses that gave him a scholarly look. Wearing a hound's tooth sport coat, he looked like a university professor. Gordillo nodded his head in agreement with Dr. Leon. Suddenly, Roy Driggers shifted noisily to rise from the table.

"*Mi General, perdóne me.* This is interesting but I have to go to my office. Mr. Saenz has been delivered to you and now, *con su permiso,* I leave." General Leyva stood next to Driggers and they shook hands.

"*Muy bien. Gracias Rodriguez, hasta luego.*" There appeared to be an understanding of sorts.

Driggers headed for the door and stopped. "Dolph, call me when you want me to pick you up," he said in a clear voice. "You have my number." The General raised his arm stiffly.

"No! He stays with us. We have work to do. We'll provide any transportation he needs. Don't worry. *Adios, Rodriguez. Hasta luego.*" He waved his hand in a gesture of good-bye.

"Don't worry about *Señor* Saenz. We'll take good care of him." Driggers grinned. He squinted and stood at the door with a slight frown on his face.

"By the way, *Mi General.* Two men in dark leather jackets outside the *Tequendama* hotel are following Mr. Saenz. Are they yours?" The General remained quiet, then looked calmly at me.

"*Si, Hombre!* We are on top of things! They've been there since you picked him up at the airport." Driggers snorted a laugh.

"*Muy bien, mi General,* just curious." Chuckling, he waved at me as he walked out the door. "Good luck!" he said. "*Hasta luego.*"

The discussion continued nonstop. I found out that most of the kidnappings had taken place in Bogota and *Valle del Cauca,* a place known as the wild west of Colombia. Cali was the capital of *Valle del Cauca* and a favorite operating ground for kidnappers and narco traffickers. A ransom had been paid in every kidnapping case except two. In one case, a guerrilla group had kidnapped fourteen *campesinos* in the rural area of *Huila* to persuade the villagers not to vote in a local election. The *campesinos* were released when the election was over. Scared to death, the villagers did not vote in subsequent elections.

Another victim, Fabio Gomez Salazar, was brutally executed when military forces intervened to stop the delivery of the ransom. It was tough, living in a democracy.

According to General Leyva, the kidnapping threat in *Valle del Cauca* was terrorizing the populace, and on October 9, the President of Colombia had declared a State of Siege in the Province. The State of Siege placed the Province under military control and in the hands of the Army Third Brigade Commander, General Bernardo Sanchez. But the DAS remained responsible for conducting criminal investigations of the kidnappings. Meanwhile, the Governor of the Province of *Valle del Cauca,* Rodrigo Lloreda Caicedo, pushed for police and military cooperation to cope with the kidnapping crisis.

It seemed that a climate of fear had settled over the Province as a result of the kidnapping threat. It was easy to comprehend why DAS personnel were frustrated with the situation. Thus far, the kidnappers appeared to simply vanish and were impossible to find. The abductions were planned and carried out very much like a terrorist operation, with surprise, excellent planning and timing. Ransoms were negotiated the same way, with a great deal of creativity and secrecy. The kidnappers took incredibly detailed measures to ensure the ransoms were collected without police interference. If a ransom went unpaid, the kidnappers always delivered on their promise to kill the victims. This served to put untold fear in the victim(s) and the families involved.

The kidnappers had effectively neutralized police action with their pay-or-die policy. The policy showed there were no soft bellies in the organization. The people involved in kidnappings were a ganglion of killers.

The families of the victims knew the kidnappers would kill those abducted if the police got close. It was an extremely complex and dangerous game. There were no rules for the game. Anything to win. Feeling a need to lighten up the atmosphere, I impulsively suggested an analogy.

"*Los tipos saben que tiene que quebrar algunos huevos para hacer el omelet* (These guys know you have to break a few eggs to make an omelet)." The General blinked in surprise and burst into laughter. *Huevos* (eggs), similar to the word *cojónes,* translated to testicles or 'balls' in the Spanish vernacular. My remark turned amusing.

"You comprehend the problem," the General said in good spirits.

"*Hasta el momento los unicos huevos que se estan quebrando son los de nosotros* (Up to this time the only eggs getting broken belong to us)." He chuckled and everyone laughed. It seemed that the kidnappers were the only ones breaking any *huevos* (balls).

Gordillo was a cigar smoker and placidly lit a small cigar to take a long drag, blowing smoke upward and following it with his eyes.

"What about Straessle and Buff?" I asked.

Gordillo crossed his arms to stare intently at me. I was beginning to feel like a pain in the ass.

"Good question," he said, pouring coffee in his cup before answering. "The media refers to them as Swiss diplomats. Herman Buff is 28 years old. He is a Swiss Diplomat assigned to the Swiss Consulate in Cali. Werner Jose Straessle is 15 years old and is the son of Eric Straessle, the Swiss Consul in Cali."

Being kidnapped by these characters had to be tough and extremely dangerous for the young lad. I felt a sudden helplessness for him. Gordillo's face wrinkled and tightened instinctively when he spoke.

"The media does not have all the details, but on October 5, Straessle and Buff were kidnapped at gunpoint approximately seven miles south of Cali in *Valle Del Cauca.*" He examined documents on the table, shifting pages noisily, the cigar balanced precariously on his lips. He quoted from official DAS reports.

"At 1830 hours, on October 5, 1969, Werner Straessle and Herman Buff were passengers in a car driven by Eric Straessle, Werner's father." Gordillo looked up momentarily. "His wife and daughter were also in the car. The car was stopped by five men dressed in military uniforms as the group returned to Cali from Eric Straessle's farm in Pance." He pointed to a dot on a map.

"The place where they were abducted is called *Callejón de Las Chuchas.*" That meant, "Valley or Corridor of the Dog Bitches." *Chucha* in Spanish is a female dog. Gordillo straightened the reading glasses perched on his nose and sat back. He didn't remove the cigar from his lips even as he talked.

"Señor Eric Straessle, the Swiss Consul, apparently tried to stop the kidnappers from taking his son Werner. As a consequence, he was shot on the left side with a 7.65 caliber pistol." I pulled out a note pad to take notes. "Young Straessle and Herman Buff were forced into a jeep and taken away. The wounded Eric Straessle and his wife were left in the car." General Leyva and Dr. Leon remained silent, occasionally murmuring and shaking their heads as Gordillo continued.

"*Son audaz y muy vivos* (They are bold and smart)," General Leyva remarked in a low voice. Gordillo looked up at the wall.

"Whoever they are," he said. I wrote down some of the information.

"Could they be military personnel?" I asked. There was a dead silence and quiet glances. Was it a bad question, I wondered?

"Straessle and Buff were transferred from the jeep they were in to a military-type ambulance," Gordillo explained. He looked at me pensively. "It could be. Who knows? They use military uniforms as well as police uniforms to abduct their victims. The bastards are very creative." He looked at the papers in his hands with a tight smile, his lips holding onto the cigar.

"They had good information on how to kidnap Straessle and Buff." Gordillo's face turned dark. I thought about my assignment as an advisor to the DAS. It could lead to an exciting life, paranoia, or a quick exit.

"Straessle is a tough old bird," Gordillo observed. "The area where the kidnappings took place is pretty isolated. But after he was shot, Straessle, his wife and daughter walked over a mile to a house nearby to seek help. He is at a hospital in Cali, recovering from the gunshot wound."

Suddenly, the General's secretary interrupted and, begging everyone's pardon, told General Leyva that General Bernardo Sanchez, Commander of the Third Brigade in *Valle del Cauca*, was on the telephone. I asked if Straessle had been interviewed at the hospital in Cali and Gordillo nodded slowly.

"I have given orders to that effect," he said. I wanted to suggest that any interview accomplished be as discreet as possible, but presumed Gordillo understood the danger.

General Leyva excused himself to use the telephone on his desk. A deep silence fell over the group momentarily. Dr. Leon removed his glasses and leaned forward to whisper to me.

"*Señor* Saenz," he said. "'The Swiss Embassy has taken the position in the Straessle and Buff kidnapping that they do not want the police to intervene in the case. The Swiss Ambassador informed us that they prefer to pay the ransom. The primary concern of the Swiss is that the police do not intervene." He glanced at Gordillo, who grinned wryly.

"The whereabouts of the two victims is unknown. We have no idea where they are. They could be held in *Valle de Cauca*, but we don't know with any certainty." Leon's face grew stern.

"The Swiss Ambassador is afraid the kidnappers will kill Straessle and Buff if the police are involved. The Swiss Embassy won't talk to us." He stood to get more coffee.

"*Es una mierda,*" he muttered in a disappointed tone of voice. He poured cream into his coffee and stirred it. "How do you like that shit. Does that happen in your country?" he asked and raised two fingers.

"In Colombia, two things count and make a difference. Money and the fear of death." The two men laughed in frustration while I nodded, unsure of myself.

"In the United States, it is three things: money, death and taxes," I suggested in Spanish. They stared at me but no one laughed. My humor was meaningless in Colombia.

The families of the victims who had been kidnapped were apparently too terrified to talk to the police, even after the people who had been abducted were released unharmed. Thus, any investigation would not be a short walk in the park. Without cooperation from the victims and information on the kidnappings, things were bound to be extremely difficult. It was certain that if the police intervened in any kidnapping, the death of the victim was guaranteed. It was part of the kidnapping ritual. There was more risk for the families of the victims to talk to the police, than to talk to the kidnappers. The kidnappers had given the matter a lot of serious thought.

It was easy to see that one of the major problems in the kidnapping crisis was the collision of jurisdictions in conducting investigations by the various security forces involved. Who was in charge of these investigations? It was hard to tell. The overall investigative effort was in a state of confusion. The Colombian Army, the National Police, and the DAS were each pursuing separate investigations and competing with each other.

The investigations conducted thus far had been unsuccessful in resolving any of the kidnappings that had occurred. The kidnappers seemed to possess a veritable license to ply their lucrative trade. Kidnapping, like the drug trade in Colombia, had become a profitable business.

I read an Official DAS report that concluded as follows: **"Kidnappings in Colombia have reached an intimidating proportion and established a character that requires the immediate attention of the Government of Colombia (GOC) to prevent chaos from setting in."**

The DAS Intelligence Unit described the kidnapping crisis as **"a priority that needs to be immediately addressed and neutralized, otherwise panic created in the populace by the crisis could result in a violent reaction against Colombian authorities and the existing government structure."**

The implication was that the Colombian government was faced with a clear threat to internal security. The United States Embassy in Bogota had no knowledge of that assessment or I would have been briefed on it. I would try to get it to Lubinsky.

My mind shifted back and forth, recalling the situation in Uruguay and the kidnappings carried out by the *Tupamaro* guerrillas. The impact was the same: it served to terrorize the populace. But the purpose of kidnappings in Colombia differed in a political way from Uruguay. The kidnappings in Colombia had the objective of making money for the participants, but for those kidnapped, it was a deadly game. The planning and operations used by the kidnappers was impressive. The terrorists and kidnappers possessed similar traits.

General Leyva finished his conversation with the Third Brigade Army Commander and returned somber-faced. He sat momentarily silent, and emulated a slow mournful shake of the head. Reaching for his cup of coffee, he told us in a low voice that General Bernardo Sanchez was having a meeting in Cali with all the agency heads involved in the kidnapping problem. He paused tensely.

"The General wants us to be there." He smiled stonily and slowly lifted the palms of his hands.

"Dolph, I informed General Sanchez about your presence in Colombia and he definitely wants you there. I hope this will not be an inconvenience." I expected something more serious. The General gave me a look of concern while I mentally visualized the two Colombian Army Generals talking facetiously about the '*Gringo* kidnapping expert,' now in the country.

"*Si, es el gran pendejo,*" I felt like telling him. But I was quick to show my cooperation.

"*Estoy a sus ordenes, Mi General* (I am at your service, General)." The General clapped his hands, grinning at my response. The three men smiled at each other.

"*Bravo. El Señor Dolph Saenz no tiene miedo meterse al agua* (Mr. Dolph Saenz is not afraid to get wet)." Dr. Leon chuckled approvingly. He placed his hand on my shoulder.

"Let's see if he is willing to get down in the mud and get dirty, too!" Laughter erupted in a spontaneous manner, making me feel silly. Smiling, I thought to myself. Well, at least they're happy. But I wasn't sure what they meant about getting in the mud and getting dirty. I had a good idea about that, but my reputation as a pseudo 'expert' on kidnappings was at stake and OPS counted on me to figure something out.

"Dolph," the compendious General said. He had the winsome habit of rubbing his baldness vigorously with his left hand. He glanced at the ceiling.

"What do you think about the Swiss kidnapping? You are supposed to be a good investigator," he said. "What should we do, as a priority?" He glanced at the two DAS men, then looked directly at me.

"Do you have any comments or suggestions? I don't believe you are afflicted with temerity," he told me in a jovial tone. I knew things would get complex. I wished they would stop referring to me as an 'expert.'

"*Mi General,* this is my first day," I suggested in a friendly tone. I'm mostly a cop and not yet clairvoyant, I mused. "I appreciate your *confianza* in me. I presume you have tapped some telephones." The General glanced at me with a slight grin and nodded. Wiretaps were none of my business, yet.

"No suggestions at this point!" I emphasized. "I would like to stay close to all of you on the Straessle and Buff investigation, that's all." The General nodded briskly.

"However, there is a favor I would like to ask," I added and was surprised by the dead silence and eyebrows going up. I asked to review the files on other kidnappings. General Leyva winked at me.

"*Astuto,*" he said, clasping his hands in front of his face as if to pray.

"*Absolutamente.* Dr. Leon will provide whatever information we have on the other cases thus far. We'll discuss them when you finish looking at them." I recalled there were a large number of kidnapping cases. I planned to scan through as many as possible.

"*Modus Operandi,*" he said in a low voice. "You will find many similarities," he told me. Excusing himself, he left the room, saying he would return in a minute. The General was either being kind or it was easy to impress a Colombian Army General about criminal investigations, I thought. I wanted to tell him to tap every telephone in Cali. I presumed that had already been done.

With the General out of the room, Gordillo ordered the case files to be brought to me and Carmen, the amicable secretary, served coffee and delicious sweet rolls laced with powdered sugar and cinnamon. I ate sweet rolls and drank coffee while Gordillo briefed me on the investigation of the kidnapping of the Swiss diplomats.

"There is a strong need for analysis," he said. "Everyone wants a quick solution, but there is none." He told me that Dr. Eduardo Leon was in charge of the analysis of the information and evidence on the investigation of the Swiss kidnapping.

"We have to concentrate on resolving that case," Gordillo insisted. I nodded in agreement. General Leyva and I would be provided all reports and new leads on the investigation, he said. Gordillo suggested my participation as I saw fit, and for me, that was a great idea. I read the kidnapping cases with a great deal of interest. My ability to read Spanish made it easy.

Active Kidnapping Cases—DAS Jurisdiction 1969
Victim: Lara Olivero
Summary: Victim was 25 years old when he was kidnapped at 7:55 a.m. on July 6, 1969, en route to the University of Colombia. In the early morning, he walked to his car parked in front of his residence and a man wearing the traditional black frock of a Catholic priest called out to him. The "priest," burdened by the weight of an old typewriter held in his hands, asked him for a ride to the University. Olivero acceded, since that

was his destination. En route, they talked about local politics. A few minutes later, apparently at a predetermined spot, the priest drew a revolver from his cassock, pointed it at Olivero and ordered him to stop the car. Two other men boarded the vehicle.

Olivero was told to keep quiet or he would die. His abductors rubbed Mentholatum on his eyes and placed a pair of opaque sunglasses over his eyes. The vehicle was driven for about three hours on a paved road and then for a half-hour on a dirt road until they reached a farmhouse. Five days later after the ransom was paid to the kidnappers Olivero was released. The amount of money paid to the kidnappers was not disclosed. Olivero's vehicle was never found. He refused to talk to DAS investigators for fear of retaliation.

Victim: <u>Dr. Eden Harold</u>

Summary: At approximately 1100 hours, Dr. Eden Harold received a call at his medical office in Cali from a man who told him that his mother was gravely ill and needed immediate medical attention. The man asked Dr. Harold to come to his mother's residence as soon as possible, because she was deathly ill. According to the caller, his mother was too sick to be brought to the doctor's office. An urgent medical diagnosis was needed. The individual grew distraught and pleaded with Dr. Harold when he refused. Eventually the man convinced Dr. Harold that he would send his car and chauffeur to bring him to his sick mother's home. The doctor was told that if he deemed it necessary, arrangements would be made to hospitalize the sick woman, but a medical diagnosis and immediate medical treatment by the doctor was needed.

Within the hour, a young man with a dark round chubby face and stocky build arrived at the clinic to pick up the doctor. With Dr Harold in the car, a stop was made at the intersection of La Paz and 4th Street where a man pointed a revolver at him and got into the car. Dr. Harold was hit on the head with a hard object, presumably the revolver, and knocked unconscious. Eventually he found himself inside a large hole in the ground. When he was fed he saw that he was being held on a chicken farm guarded by men carrying guns. Later, one of Dr. Harold's friends left the ransom demanded for his release in a parked car near a movie theater in Cali. When the kidnappers released Dr. Harold they rubbed Mentholatum on his eyes and blindfolded him. He was taken out in a truck and after traveling for a short time, was released in a small town called Buga.

Victim: <u>Dr. Manuel Juan Mejia</u>

Summary: At approximately 1800 hours, Dr. Manuel Juan Mejia left the medical building in Cali where he worked to drive home. He stopped at a roadblock where four police officers were checking cars. One of the officers told him to get out of his car and he was forced into the front seat of a blue car, told to remain silent and face straight ahead. Mentholatum was rubbed on his eyes.

Mejia recalled being taken on an asphalt road for approximately one hour and then the car a turned on a dirt road to travel for a few minutes. He recalled the place where he was held was a farmhouse. He was kept in a hole in the ground for seven days and was released after the payment of a ransom of 200,000 Colombian pesos ($120,000). Mejia refused to provide other details because he was afraid the kidnappers would kill him.

Victim: Elias Jimenez
Summary: At approximately 1600 hours on May 21, 1969, Elias Jimenez drove his car from his clothing factory in Cali to his residence. On Avenida de Las Americas, a vehicle in front of him suddenly stopped on the road and obstructed his passage. When Jimenez slowed down to go around the vehicle, an individual approached and pointed a revolver at him. He was ordered to move to the passenger side of his vehicle and two men got into the car. Opaque glasses were placed on his eyes and he was instructed not to make a sound. Driven in his car for a short distance, he was repeatedly threatened with death if he did not cooperate. Transferred to another vehicle, he was driven in circles for about an hour. A blindfold was put over the opaque glasses and he ended up in a house somewhere near Cali. Jimenez was released after the payment of a ransom but he refused to say how much money was paid or how it was paid. Following his release by the kidnappers, his father forced him to leave Colombia for his own safety and go to Los Angeles. The DAS did not obtain details.

Victim: Fulgencio Valencia Arbolera
Summary: At about 1630 hours, July 21, 1969, Fulgencio Valencia Arbolera left his office in Cali to drive home. He arrived at the intersection of 44th Street and Carretera de Norte where men in military uniforms had set up a roadblock and were checking cars. When Arbolera approached the soldiers one of them pointed a rifle at him and ordered him to stop. The soldier opened the door of the car and pushed Arbolera to the passenger side. His car was driven to an unknown destination followed by what appeared to be a military vehicle.

Military authorities tapped the telephone lines to Arbolera's residence and learned the family was negotiating the payment of a ransom with the kidnappers. Later a family friend on the way to pay the ransom for Arbolera was stopped at a military roadblock. A military officer took the place of the man delivering the ransom. The military officer confronted the kidnappers and a gunfight ensued. One kidnapper was killed, and the military officer wounded. The following day, Arbolera was found dead in a small village in Valle del Cauca with a gunshot wound to the head. The incident created severe criticism of the security forces and reinforced the fact that the kidnappers would not hesitate to kill the victim if government forces intervened.

I read other reports. Ernesto Gonzales Caicedo, a Medical Doctor kidnapped in Cali on July 21, 1969, paid a ransom of 500,000 pesos, about $250,000. Another doctor by the name of Joaquin Lozada Torres, kidnapped in August 22, 1969, in Bogota, was released when he paid a million *pesos* in ransom. A large amount of detail was missing from the investigation reports, but there were obvious patterns.

Tired, I made the observation that was academic for the group.

"It appears the same gang is responsible for most of the kidnappings. The *modus operandi* used in the kidnappings almost comes from a single mind." Gordillo and Dr. Leon stared at me with blank looks. At that point, the General returned to the office.

"The use of police and military uniforms, the frock of a priest, the schemes, and the planning is the same in most cases. The use of Mentholatum and opaque glasses on the victims to prevent them from seeing anything after they are kidnapped is the same. These guys are damn good." My offhand stupid comment was impulsively tainted with respect.

"They paint the sunglasses with dark nail polish," Gordillo explained. "When the glasses are placed over the eyes of the victim, they are legally blind," he chuckled. The General scratched his baldness vigorously.

"*Si, es verdad.*"... "*Son muy vivos y audaces* (They are very clever and bold)," he said wistfully.

"But they are also cold-blooded killers. We need to figure out how to break a few of their *huevos,*" he said with a grin. The discussion continued for another hour.

18

Cali

We ate dinner at the DAS, a small steak and rice, brought in from outside. No one was really hungry. After a review of the reports on previous kidnapping cases and a lively discussion on the Straessle and Buff kidnapping, we had no firm leads. For certain the kidnappers were effective, organized people.

To get anywhere on the kidnapping problem, leads on the Swiss kidnapping had to be developed and followed up with action, but in an organized and logical fashion. Like other victims before them, the kidnapped Swiss had simply vanished. Before breaking up, we agreed to meet at the Hotel *Aristi* in Cali and go from there to the meeting with General Bernardo Sanchez at the Third Army Brigade *Quartel.* I would travel alone to Cali.

By ten o'clock in the evening General Leyva took me in a DAS vehicle to the Hotel *Tequendama.* At the hotel, sleek Jaguars and Mercedes Benzes transporting members of the Colombian upper class to local festivities lined the entrance. The driver of the DAS vehicle stopped at a cul-de-sac in front of the glittering hotel and an agent stepped out of the car to flash DAS credentials at a bellhop. The DAS Agent stood outside the car while the General and I sat inside and talked in Spanish. Two men in dark leather jackets moved out of the shadows and received a nod and a signal from the DAS Agent standing guard. We were under friendly police surveillance.

General Leyva discussed the Straessle and Buff case in a quiet tone, his round head silhouetted in the dim light. Fortunately, we had established a mutual feeling of trust and I felt very comfortable with him. The General's subtle sense of humor was enjoyable and we talked entirely in Spanish.

"You have to be careful in Cali," he cautioned. "Cali is an unusual place, both endearing and dangerous." He stared out the window pensively. *"Cómo el gran amor* (Like a great love)," he chuckled.

"Te desespera (It makes a fellow desperate)," he said. People attired in fine clothes gathered at the hotel entrance while we talked.

"Cali is an exciting place with plenty of crooked moves going on that are not easy to spot," General Leyva suggested. Lighting a Colombian cigarette, he inhaled the smoke with a sucking sound. He continued to tell me that people in Cali went about their dirty business quietly, in a businesslike fashion. The corruption extended from the police to the politicos in power, including prominent citizens, he said.

"Like many other cities of the world," I suggested.

"But Cali is at the heart of the drug trafficking and kidnapping trade in Colombia," he said wistfully. With twinkling eyes, he suggested that my presence would attract a lot of interest in Cali without my knowing it.

"Make no mistake about it. You will be noticed by certain people in Cali," he said. *"Tienes que tener mucho cuidado."* He emphasized that I had to be very careful.

"Do not expect National Police officials and DAS personnel to readily cooperate. Some may not feel comfortable with you. He suggested that I might not like how some of the officers operated.

"No puedes confiar en esa gente (You may not want to trust some of those folks)." I listened in silence, appreciative of the advice. It was difficult working as a police advisor on kidnappings in Colombia when people you were supposed to advise knew more about the kidnappings than you did.

Reaching into his coat pocket, General Leyva pulled out a small leather packet and handed it to me.

"This might help keep you out of trouble," he said. With a halfhearted smile he warned, "Or it may cause problems for you, depending on how and when you use it." Inspecting the small wallet-sized packet in the dim light, I recognized it as a set of DAS credentials. I had been designated as Investigator No. 20 in the DAS, and my picture and various official seals were affixed to the I.D. card.

"Remember, your *Nom de Guerre* is twenty, *viente, no más,"* the General told me cheerfully.

Prior to leaving the DAS headquarters, General Leyva had asked the I.D. Bureau to take my photograph. At the time it seemed puzzling to me but I remained unconcerned.

"So we don't forget what you look like and for our Rogue's Gallery," he had told me jokingly. In my cynical way of thinking, I also thought it was possible that my picture could be provided to the media in the event that I was kidnapped.

It appeared that my credibility and acceptance as an advisor with the DAS was good. Now it was up to me to get more involved.

"Gracias, mi General, I'll use them *con cuidado* (Thanks General, I'll be careful how I use the credentials)," I let him know. General Leyva obviously wanted me to get involved. I had agreed without hesitation to meet with General Bernardo Sanchez in Cali, and he liked this. It would not do much good for me to hide in an office at the U.S. Embassy. The General and Dr. Leon were to travel to Cali in the late morning, and I would link up with them at the Hotel *Aristi*.

"Have a good trip," the General told me. He provided the name of a contact person at the DAS Headquarters at Cali and a telephone number to call if I had problems. That individual would know how to get hold of him, he said. I entered the hotel lobby of the *Tequendama* and the place teemed with elegantly dressed men and women. Despite crime and violence, the gala life was booming in cosmopolitan Bogota. The displays of green emeralds and brilliant diamond jewelry adorned beautiful ladies and sparkled in the bright lights.

Feeling lonely, I thought dimly about a fast drink in the crowded hotel bar but quickly changed my mind. I headed for my room and my *camita* (bed). Tomorrow the day would start early and I had to be ready to operate in a totally foreign place and a risky environment. That would not be a vacation for me.

Checking at the reception desk of the hotel to get my key, I found three urgent messages for me from Earl Lubinsky, the U.S. Embassy Political Officer. Lubinsky strongly suggested that we get together early the next morning, no later than 8:30 a.m. He did not say what he had in mind, but that it was important.

October 21

I arose at 0600 hours to make the early morning meeting requested by Lubinsky. Roy Driggers had breakfast with me at the hotel and let me know that the rumor was out at the Embassy that an American was working with the Colombian police on the kidnapping problem. I wondered if that was what Lubinsky wanted to talk to me about. I wondered what I could do about that.

On my arrival at the Chancery the pretty dark haired receptionist made me feel welcome, telling me it was nice to see me again. But there was no time to chitchat. She called Lubinsky and a Marine guard escorted me to the Political Section. My plane was scheduled to depart for Cali at 10:30 a.m. I wondered what Lubinsky had in mind that was so damn important? My trip to Cali was my priority and my departure could not be delayed.

Lubinsky came out and greeted me in a cheerful manner. He ushered me immediately into his office and offered me coffee but I declined, anxious to find out what he wanted. A man dressed in a dark business suit waited inside. He appeared to be an American, but Lubinsky introduced him as Armin Kamer, the First Secretary of the Swiss Embassy in Bogota. At last, a Swiss connection, I thought. Lubinsky turned serious to ask if I had learned anything about the kidnapping of Straessle and Buff.

"The most important thing I learned is that there is grave danger in store for them," I told him. "Especially if the ransom is not paid." Both men stared at me.

In a surprise move, Lubinsky asked Kamer to tell me the position of the Swiss Embassy in regard to the kidnapping of Straessle and Buff. Kamer expressed surprise to hear that the United States Government was assisting the Colombian authorities on the kidnapping problem. He said he had not been aware of this and in a sanguine spirit, proposed that the Swiss Embassy was clearly hesitant about any contact with Colombian police authorities in regard to the kidnapping of Straessle and Buff. Using precise terms, Kamer voiced clear concern that the Swiss Embassy would not talk to **any** representative of the Colombian police about the kidnapping of Straessle and Buff. He said they feared that the two victims would be killed if the police intervened. In a cordial and sincere way, Kamer expressed his belief that the Colombian Police would not be able to accomplish anything in connection with the kidnapping of Straessle and Buff, anyway. Then why was he there, I wondered?

Past experience had showed that the Colombian authorities were powerless against the kidnappers, Kamer said. It was surprising when Kamer asked me if I knew why the kidnappers had selected Straessle and Buff to kidnap. Candidly I suggested that the reason was that a ransom would predictably be paid by the Swiss Embassy. He grinned dryly at my comments and countered that the police were ineffective against the left-wing guerrilla cartel involved.

To my amazement, Lubinsky agreed with Kamer that hard core members of Colombian communist organizations were involved with the kidnappers. Both believed the problem had political implications and that the FARC was the organization involved. (The FARC was the

Fuerzas Armadas Revolucionarias Colombianas and for years had operated in rural areas and in the fringes of *Valle del Cauca*.)

Dino Pionzio, the CIA Station Chief, and Colonel Lowman, the U.S. Air Force Attaché, did not agree with Kamer and Lubinsky in regard to that assessment. Pionzio and Lowman did not believe that the kidnappings were connected to any left-wing guerrillas. Who the hell was right?

My instinct told me that there were some issues Kamer and Lubinsky were holding back on. The abrupt silence and momentary brooding looks bothered me. I asked a question that caught him totally off guard.

"When will the ransom be paid?" I asked in a direct question. Both men were surprised by the question. Lubinsky glanced quizzically at Kamer without saying a word.

"The ransom will be paid the day after tomorrow," Kamer replied, his right eyebrow raising a tad. I cursed impulsively and then apologized.

"It's just that things are moving awfully fast," I explained. Kamer became concerned with what he said.

"If the police try to stop the payment of the ransom, Straessle and Buff will likely be killed," he proclaimed with a reedy sound. Nodding to agree, it was not hard for me to appear sympathetic.

"I understand," I told him. "So you have been negotiating the payment of a ransom with the kidnappers all this time," I suggested. Kamer stared at the wall and nodded.

"How much are you paying?" I asked placidly. Kamer shifted his feet and his face grew granite serious.

"Three million *pesos*," he said dryly. "And we do not want police interference," he added. "If the police interfere, it will make it extremely dangerous for Buff and the boy," he said, his face growing florid.

"I can't tell you much more." I smiled. Under the circumstances, the kidnappers were in total control.

Kamer and Lubinsky remained calm and impassive but gave me the impression that they wanted more information from me. But I had no information. Instead I asked more questions.

"Where will the ransom be paid?" Both men stayed silent.

"I can't tell you," Kamer replied, almost fretfully. "We do not want the police to do anything. The situation is very risky and complicated." Instinctively, I realized that Kamer did not know the details of how the ransom payment would take place. Lubinsky had a tense smile but appeared calm.

"The boys are not in Cali, then?" I asked, holding back frustration. Kamer stood facing the wall.

"We don't know." He clasped his hands behind his back and stared out the window. "I wish we could be of more help," he said in a soft voice. He reiterated concern for Straessle and Buff.

"They are in grave danger if the ransom is not paid to the kidnappers," he said. He offered there was nothing anyone could do to help. I agreed that the two Swiss would be killed if the ransom were not paid.

I stood to leave and surprised Lubinsky. He looked at me quizzically, wondering where I was going.

"Cali." I told him before he could ask. "I hope we can stay in touch, Mr. Kamer," I suggested. He stared at me momentarily and nodded.

"We'll see," he responded airily. Mr. Kamer was understandably hesitant about further contact with anyone on the matter. Lubinsky had tried to help, but the situation made me uncomfortable. Thanking both of them on my way out, I wondered what they expected from me in terms of the important information they had provided. I suspected that Kamer was from the Swiss Intelligence Service. Outside the Embassy, I hailed a cab.

The trip to *El Dorado* Airport by taxi was a wild ride, but the excitement of the kidnapping case accelerated my mind. One of the victims was a fifteen-year-old male, but the media referred to him as a Swiss diplomat. The other victim was a Swiss diplomat assigned to Cali.

There was no doubt that the kidnappers would kill the two victims if the ransom were not paid. Kamer was serious as hell that the Swiss intended to pay the ransom, regardless of any police investigation. General Leyva had rightly suspected that the Swiss would pay the ransom for Straessle and Buff. The problem now was to ensure that the ransom was paid to the kidnappers. In my situation, there were two major problems I had to face head on. Should I tell General Leyva about the information provided by Kamer? What would he do? If the police stopped the ransom, there was no doubt that the kidnappers would kill Straessle and Buff.

I had to be low-key in Cali as Stotts had suggested, I thought humorously. The media was already speculating about FBI assistance to the DAS. It would be difficult to keep out of the range of the media, especially if I worked openly with DAS personnel. It would be difficult for General Leyva to avoid protocol matters and the public limelight in Cali, and it would do no good if I were with him when he arrived. There was no guarantee that I could pass as a Colombian. I would have to wing it, when the crunch came.

We would travel within the province by car. First on the agenda was the meeting with General Bernardo Sanchez at the Third Brigade headquarters. But people in the meeting would wonder who I was. General Leyva had told me that he was not concerned. I would be identified as the *"experto en secuestros"* (expert on kidnapping investigations), and not as an *Oficial Americano*.

He let me know that after the meeting with General Sanchez, we would visit the site where Straessle and Buff had been kidnapped. Perhaps something could be learned. We would also talk to DAS personnel in Cali about the case. I kept cryptic notes on what I had learned. Kidnapping was a dangerous business in Colombia.

The *El Dorado* International Airport was always crowded with passengers. With prior reservations for Cali, I checked in and boarded an *Avianca* turbo-prop at around ten-thirty. The plane was loaded with people bound for Cali and then to Quito, Ecuador. Most of the passengers appeared to be businessmen.

The plane zipped easily into a landing pattern and the aircraft touched down, braking to a halt in front of a long two-story beige building. The pilots were obvious veterans of these flight routes and airfields. The plane stopped and men in forest green police uniforms surrounded the aircraft. National Police officers were searching all arriving passengers.

In frustration, I recalled that *Valle del Cauca* was presently under a "State of Siege," and the S&W Combat Masterpiece in my shoulder holster now felt heavy and conspicuous. Passengers disembarking from the plane formed a line while police officers kept a close watch. There did not appear to be any way for me to avoid a search. My "ace in the hole" was to use the DAS credentials and pose as a DAS Agent. No matter what happened, it might be necessary for me to explain why an *Americano* was carrying DAS credentials and a gun. Soldiers with automatic weapons watched as the passengers underwent a search.

The situation churned in my mind. It was early for me to be in trouble. But in the bright sunny day in Cali, I would try to pass as a Colombian. The other possibility was my arrest by the National Police for carrying a gun in Cali, the kidnapping and narco-trafficking center of Colombia. That was sure to be a scandal.

The sun felt warm and toasty and I patiently waited with other passengers to be searched. The situation had caught me by surprise and that part made me angry. Hiding the brand new DAS credentials given to me by General Leyva in my left hand, I made up my mind to use them.

It was certain that the police would react violently when they found my gun. There was absolutely no way the gun under my coat would not be found and any wrong move on my part would be dangerous.

Colombian National Police Officers searched briefcases and packages on top of a table. I took my sunglasses off to place them in my coat pocket and a young police officer stared at me with discomforting officiousness. He approached and suddenly ordered me to put my arms up.

"*Por favor, Señor, levante las manos,*" he ordered briskly. Raising my arms put me in a difficult position and the gun in my shoulder holster was now a serious problem.

"*Un momento* (One moment)," I told the police officer.

"Pick up your arms," he insisted sternly in Spanish. Attempting to show him my DAS credentials, the National Police Officer ordered me with arrogant authority that I keep my arms up. The stripling Colombian lawman rummaged under my coat and quickly found the fully loaded Combat Masterpiece hanging butt down in an upside down shoulder holster. He went from surprise to fear, his color rapidly turning ashen. To my astonishment, he dropped to his haunches without a word and his eyes closed in fear. No one paid attention to the police officer overcome with fear, waiting for me to shoot him. I hissed extemporaneously through my teeth.

"**Soy del DAS—Soy del DAS.**" I shoved the DAS credentials in his face. The officer went from fear to bewilderment. He looked in dismay at the DAS credentials and mumbled softly in Spanish.

"*Qué! Qué! Por que no me lo dijo?*" Regaining control of himself, he looked around with a face of embarrassment. In a low voice, he asked why I had not identified myself immediately instead of scaring the crap out of him. Apologizing in a semiofficious tone, I asked him **not** to identify me as a DAS Agent.

"*Por favor, no digas nada, no digas nada de que soy del DAS.*" Blinking rapidly, he nodded in agreement.

"*Gracias hermano* (Thanks brother)," I told him, shaking his hand as he stared with a bewildered look.

I walked to the terminal and heard him mutter, "*hijo de puta.*" He stared until I reached the door of the terminal. I waved with a smile and impulsively mouthed, "the same to you, asshole."

At the baggage area, a small leather suitcase purchased at a shop near the hotel was easy to find. There was no time to dilly-dally after the search and gun problem. When I flashed a *peso* note equivalent to about three dollars, a baggage carrier grinned and quickly carried my bag to the first cab available.

The scenic drive through the city of Cali was uncommonly quiet and the streets were abstemiously clean, with cobblestone covering narrow roads, probably since the days of Simon Bolivar. We passed several attractive and picturesque houses. The city seemed smaller than Albuquerque and likely had similar stories of murder, narcotic deals, sinister politics and kidnappings in its historic past. Within a few minutes, the cab driver grew talkative and friendly and apparently recognized me as an American.

"Qué hacen los Americanos en Cali? (What does an American do in Cali?)" the driver asked me in a casual tone. "Same thing Colombians do in Cali," I answered nonchalantly in Spanish. He laughed, surprised by my fluency in Spanish.

The taxi stopped in front of a bright white building surrounded by a tall wall and the driver cheerfully announced, "Hotel *Aristi.*" The hotel's attractive red tile on the roof gave it a Spanish charm similar to houses in northern New Mexico and California. At the entrance, an alert bellhop offered to carry my small bag and I refused by thanking him. White walls in the lobby reflected the sunlight and greatly enhanced the interior. A polished mosaic red tile floor accented the clean white interior.

People chatting animatedly in the lobby paid little attention to my arrival. Discreetly scrutinizing me, the hotel clerk turned courteous when I told him my name.

"Buenas Tardes, Señor Saenz. Bien venido." He advised me that a room had been reserved for me. I filled out the paperwork and he directed me to the second floor and gave me the key to my room. Our conversation was entirely in Spanish. The hotel was attractive inside with an oak polished staircase that led to the second floor. A bright patio with beautiful floral arrangements and lush elephant ear plants growing in large pots adorned the area. On the floor, in my room, I found a note written in Spanish from Dr. Leon. He advised me that he and the General were in room 120. They would call me after my arrival.

In my room, after I unpacked, I sat in a chair and began to feel disconnected with my role of advising the DAS on kidnapping cases. There were limited guidelines for me, no written rules of engagement on what I could do and not do. I was merely told not to get operational. Any mishaps were part of the job.

I was provided leeway, but the thought of my posing as a DAS Agent worried me. That was a potentially dangerous political development. I decided this was no time to worry about technicalities. It was already a complex situation. As a lonely American advisor with no authority in Colombia, my role could not be worse.

If I were investigating the case, where would be a good place to start? Tapping the phone lines of the victims and their families was a good start. The General had implied that there were wiretaps on those lines. I wondered if the DAS had learned that the Swiss Embassy was preparing to deliver the ransom in less than twenty hours? Would he tell me if he knew? I had to maintain a low profile in Cali, but had to mix it up with the police and get involved. I was damned if I did and screwed if I didn't!

It was expected that things could get risky in a place that was known to often be dangerous. I removed coins and other objects and placed six bullets with super velocity loads in my right pocket. Six shiny rounds were in the cylinder of my revolver. The six rounds in my pocket would be available to reload if needed. That was the best I could do. The matter of reloading was moot if automatic weapons were used against me.

The hotel was attractive and very comfortable. It was hard to tell how long I would be in Cali, so I had retained my room at the Hotel *Tequendama* in Bogota and left some clothes there. My wristwatch indicated that it was 1300 hours and the city streets were deserted. It was the traditional *"tiempo de siesta."* Everything closed in Latin American countries from twelve to two o'clock in the afternoon for lunch. It was easy to get used to the idea and for many it was an opportunity for a nooner. Nooners were popular in Washington, D.C., I recalled.

Suddenly the telephone rang, and the soft resonance caught me by surprise. It was Dr. Leon.

"Saenz," he said abruptly. "Can you meet with us downstairs in the lobby in thirty minutes?" He faked a whisper to ask if that gave me enough time.

"By the way, how do you like Cali?" Dr. Leon asked.

"I like it fine, except for searches conducted at the airport," I told him. Dr. Leon's voice grew loud.

"Qué? Coño, es verdad!" His voice sounded agitated. "The National Police search everyone at the airport for weapons, drugs, and anything that looks suspicious." His sigh was audible.

"And you were probably armed. Your ability to speak Spanish probably helped avoid serious trouble." It was more of a question than a fact.

"It helped," I answered lightheartedly. Dr. Leon's response was cheerful.

"Of course, the fact that you speak Spanish fluently is a lot of help. But I'm sure your experience and deceptive skills helped," he suggested in Spanish. His chuckle was hollow on the telephone.

What deceptive skills, I thought humorously after he hung up. Not being honest with General Leyva and other DAS officials would eventually create problems between us. We had not discussed the fact that I would carry a gun. The General must have suspected I carried a gun, but Dr. Leon would confirm it now. However, I did not have the authority to carry a gun in Colombia.

I walked downstairs at 1330 hours and General Leyva and Dr. Leon waited at the entrance to the hotel.

"Buenas tardes, mi amigo," General Leyva told me and gave me a Latin American style *abrazo*. It seemed certain the General had felt my gun in the shoulder holster under my coat. It is a common joke in Latin America that an *abrazo* provides one the opportunity to determine if an individual is carrying a handgun. A shoulder holster makes it harder to detect a gun with the *abrazo*. Colonel *Chele* Medrano of the Army of El Salvador once pulled a nice pearl-handled revolver out in the middle of a cocktail party to show me when I detected the gun with an *abrazo*. He created quite a stir at the reception and scared the fun out of everyone.

The General led me outside and was cheerful as we walked to a parked car. He whispered conspiratorially that Dr. Leon had told him what had happened at the airport. He seemed calm and undisturbed.

"No importa (Don't worry about that). We'll get you out of jail," he chuckled. Patting me on the back, he suggested the DAS credentials covered any problem with my carrying a gun. He was in good humor and said it was possible that we might run into some *"malos tipos"* (bad guys), so carrying a gun was a good idea.

The General and I sat in the back of the car and Dr. Leon sat in front with the driver. The driver waited patiently until the General told him to go. The vehicle headed east, the driver apparently knowing where we were going. The payment of the ransom for the Swiss churned through my mind. For certain, Kamer was truthful about that fact. I thought about telling the General that the ransom for the Swiss would be paid tomorrow, but decided to wait. I needed to come up with a workable plan if I divulged the information on the ransom.

The weather turned warm and Dr. Leon removed his coat. I was not uncomfortable and kept my coat on. The shoulder holster and gun made me feel conspicuous.

"Some of our military officials want the telephone lines of the Swiss Embassy tapped." General Leyva told me, with obvious worry on his face. I could tell from the look on his face that the issue was of concern for him. He passed his hand slowly over his smooth head, seemingly in thought.

"I guess I'm old fashioned," he said in a low tone of voice. "I believe in doing things legally if we can. A court order is needed before we tap anybody's telephone." His voice grew lower. The Swiss Embassy was sovereign territory with diplomatic immunity. He stared out the window pensively.

"We could try to justify it on the basis of national security, but that will be resisted." I felt like telling him to tap every phone possible. It was a matter of the national security of Colombia.

I asked if a court order could be obtained and he grew thoughtful for a moment. Apparently he had tried. It seemed doubtful that the judicial system of Colombia would take the chance of violating the Swiss Embassy's sovereignty and risk being found out. It would be an international scandal.

Plush farmland rushed by as the car moved swiftly on a lonely paved road. General Leyva's smooth round head went from side to side to indicate a negative response to my question.

"General Bernardo Sanchez is growing frustrated with the lack of progress in resolving kidnapping cases," he said with obvious dismay. "He plans to use military personnel to set up road blocks and to increase patrols on all the main roads in *Valle del Cauca.*"

When he said that, my heart rate accelerated. That was the worst possible undertaking at this time. If the payment of the ransom for the Swiss were obstructed for any reason, the kidnappers would kill them. Panic and helplessness hit me simultaneously. According to what Kamer had told me, the ransom for the Swiss would be paid sometime tomorrow. My first impulse was to tell the General, but I decided to take time to think about the consequences. I kept quiet and General Leyva kept the conversation going.

"General Sanchez wants to organize a series of raids on residences and business establishments that have been targeted. The raids and roadblocks will continue until we get a break in the Straessle and Buff case." He sighed audibly. "Raids and searches are legal without a court order and legitimate under the "State of Siege" that has been decreed in *Valle del Cauca,*" the General explained.

It was perfectly clear to me that the military plan would create very serious problems for the payment of the ransom for the Swiss. Any police activity would be extremely dangerous for Straessle and Buff at this time. The kidnappers were cold-blooded killers and any interference by the security forces meant death for the victims.

After about an hour, the car reached a dirt road and headed for open country. We seemed to be on the scenic route, but the driver obviously knew the destination. Using his mobile radio, he made contact with local DAS centers en route, speaking in cryptic radio terminology. I fretted about the idea of the Colombian military forces conducting raids and roadblocks at this critical time. They had to be stopped for at least 24 hours, if the ransom was to be paid to the kidnappers without any screw-ups.

In the distance, a barricade manned by soldiers blocked the road. General Leyva glanced at me.

"Those are real soldiers," he said. "We're almost there." A faint smile crossed his clean-shaven face.

"*Qué piensas, Dolph?* (What are you thinking?)" he asked. Instinctively I flipped my knuckles under my chin. It was an Italian gesture from Uruguay that often surfaced involuntarily. It dismayed my bosses in Washington. The General, however, understood the meaning.

"*Quién sabe?* (Who knows?)" He grinned, and leaned back to light his favorite Colombian cigarette. He wanted input from me as an advisor.

"Give me your own opinion," he insisted. "What do you think about General Sanchez's plan?" I recalled my meeting with Kamer, and being told about the payment of the ransom. The raids and roadblocks were a serious problem and jeopardized the safety of Straessle and Buff if the ransom was stopped.

"Where I come from, *mi General,* opinions are easy to come by." The General stared at me waiting for me to provide something more meaningful. It was tough being an 'expert' on kidnappings.

"Well, Colombia faces a terrible kidnapping problem. At this time, we are looking for two Swiss diplomats who have been kidnapped." The General gave me a blank stare. "Nevertheless, the Swiss Embassy does not want to cooperate in any way that will permit the DAS or the police to resolve the kidnapping of Straessle and Buff. They are adamant about that."

I lit a cigarette, and Dr. Leon turned from his seat to face us. There was a need for me to be diplomatic, yet candid. But I could not afford to be ambiguous.

"What is more important to you, *mi General,* the national security of Colombia, or aggravating the Swiss Ambassador's bile ducts and disposition? You **must** tap the telephone line of any individual that may be in contact with the kidnappers." I paused to think, dragging on my cigarette.

"That includes anyone that may be negotiating a ransom with kidnappers."

General Leyva nodded and his eyes brightened. That was bad advice yet good advice. But he had to protect the national security of Colombia.

"Dolph, *tienes cojónes y razón,*" the General Leyva replied with a grin. "You're right." Dr. Leon smiled and nodded in silence. I took the opportunity to offer more advice.

"Telephones must be tapped very discreetly. They are an important source of information in any kidnapping case. One has little choice, if you want to solve the kidnapping problem. You must find out the identities of the people who are co-workers or friends of Straessle and Buff, and tap those lines as soon as possible." It was never too late to tap phone lines in a kidnapping case. I suspected the ransom was probably already on its way to the kidnappers by someone close to the Swiss.

"Raids and roadblocks are dramatic and only create a lot of attention in the media that doesn't help at this point," I suggested. The way had to be clear for the ransom to be paid for the Swiss, or there would be serious danger for them.

"It is better that the ransom be paid and the Swiss get out alive. Then we can go after the kidnappers." I told him, planting some seeds.

"Roadblocks can be very dangerous for the victims. Unless people conducting the raids and setting up roadblocks know what to look for, the effort will be a disaster for the Swiss." I paused to pick my words.

"Raids and roadblocks are bound to piss people off, anyway, and you need the cooperation of the public to get information that can be useful to your investigation. The media will sensationalize and speculate on the events that are happening anyway, and the kidnappers will know what you're doing by reading the newspapers and watching television. The media will only serve to complicate matters."

I tried to convince the General that the police should not interfere with the payment of the ransom without arousing suspicion that I knew this was to take place within a matter of hours. If the police knew what I knew, it was certain they would set up roadblocks, implement heavy patrols, conduct raids, and attempt to follow any suspicious vehicle that could be involved in paying a ransom. That would result in a sure death sentence for the Swiss, if the police stopped the ransom. The General stayed silent.

"Some of the information put out by the media will create problems for the management of the investigation. One of the most complex problems in working on these cases is the media," I told General Leyva. "It is impossible to satisfy a calculating, self-righteous reporter," I suggested.

I tried to control the edge caused by smoking. Smoking made me hyper, but I enjoyed lighting up.

"The kidnappers will read the local newspapers to find out what you are doing." General Leyva glanced at his watch, a nice Benrus bought in the United States.

"We are on schedule," he said. "Dolph, we need to talk more." He slapped my knee.

"*Llegamos* (We have arrived)." The car stopped at a military barrier complete with a guard shack. Soldiers in khaki uniforms snapped to attention and clicked their heels when they recognized General Leyva.

"*Buenas tardes, mi General. Pase por favor,*" the one in charge told him. Very fleetingly, a look of concern crossed the General Leyva's face. Military uniforms and military vehicles had been commonly used to pull off past kidnappings. This could be the lion's den, I thought.

The military *Quartel* of the Third Brigade was neat, clean, and very busy. Men in military uniform and in civilian dress milled about inside a small patio. Several individuals greeted the DAS Director with deference. A distinguished looking man in military uniform was introduced as General Bernardo Sanchez, the Commander of the Third Brigade. I was introduced to Colonel Filippo Villareal Revelo, the Chief of the National Police in Cali. The Governor of *Valle del Cauca,* Señor Rodrigo Lloreda Caicedo, a clean-cut, balding young man, greeted people. In an informal and friendly tone, Governor Coicedo told me that most of the Chiefs of Police in the *Departamento* (Province) of *Valle del Cauca* were present for the meeting. The tough question was whether any of the people in the room knew anything about a kidnapping cartel? The kidnapping expert could be in the room.

The acropolitic Third Brigade *Quartel* resembled an old fort that could have been erected in the days of Simon Bolivar. Inside, a complex of buildings and new construction gave it a modern appearance. Armed guards stationed behind concrete parapets observed the arrival of people for the meeting. Soldiers armed with Madsen rifles and automatics patrolled the corridors inside the *Quartel,* and acknowledged the presence of superior officers with a loud snap of boot heels. Several men wore the green uniform of the National Police of Colombia. Others were wearing civilian clothes or Colombian Army uniforms.

General Sanchez opened the session with admirable oratory to introduce the individuals present, including General Leyva. With painful candor, he described the Straessle and Buff kidnapping as the twenty-second one to occur in Colombia. The situation was challenging the integrity of the Colombian security forces, he said. The tone of the meeting turned conciliatory when General Sanchez suggested that the security environment in the Province of *Valle del Cauca* was one of fear and widespread consternation for the populace.

General Sanchez's comments were eloquent, politically correct, and dramatic in the use of cultured Spanish. General Leyva glanced at me with twinkling eyes and a subtle grin. He made me feel comfortable in my role as an outsider. My concern for Straessle and Buff increased when General Sanchez recommended that mobile patrols, raids, and investigative efforts be augmented to comb the province for the kidnappers. That would help allay the rising fears of the public in *Valle del Cauca,* he added.

In a jocular vein, the General suggested that in a dramatic turn of events, the populace of the province demanded tough action by the government against the kidnappers. The State of Siege in *Valle del Cauca* was now acceptable to people who generally protested such measures, the General reported.

19

Ransom

In the meeting held at the Third Brigade *Quartel*, I listened to what was being said in silence, but felt the discomfort of being an intruder into the sensitive political machinations of a sovereign nation. The advisability of my being there was doubtful. Colonel Villareal, the National Police Commander in Cali, stared at me from behind morbid black sunglasses as General Leyva observed my reaction. Be low-key, I told myself humorously.

"The State of Siege measures in *Valle del Cauca* gives the security forces a great deal of power," General Bernardo Sanchez said. "That power can be abused if we are not careful. That must not happen." General Sanchez was right. The bad guys and the communists in Colombia would benefit from any abuses of human rights by the police and military forces.

"The cooperation and coordination of all units involved in raids, roadblocks, and in the investigative process is imperative," he insisted. "We need to improve the way we work together." General Leyva gave me a bleak look as General Sanchez proposed that sharing of any intelligence information on the kidnappings was vital. There appeared to be political problems and operational misgivings with police officials that I was not aware of. The meeting continued with a discussion of the problems and the action taken by the representatives of the security forces. Nothing outstanding was reported on new leads or developments.

General Leyva reported to the group that a team of nine DAS Agents had been assigned to *Valle del Cauca* to work on the kidnapping case of Straessle and Buff. That was intended to augment the investigative effort in Cali, he said. More than a hundred investigators were needed in Cali, I thought to myself. The FBI would have saturated the place with Special Agents.

General Leyva requested that Gordillo be informed of any apprehensions made, since the DAS had the expertise and forensics personnel needed to analyze any physical evidence found. He emphasized that physical evidence would be very important to the successful prosecution of any individual arrested for kidnapping. General Leyva's comments appeared well received. He was right.

It seemed obvious that planning, coordination and control were only abstractions in the hunt for the kidnappers. Eager and inexperienced investigators of the Third Brigade B-2 (Brigade Intelligence Section), the investigative and intelligence section, F-2 of the National Police, and the DAS conducted separate investigations inspired mostly by Artemis, the mythological goddess of the hunt.

As the meeting of the top Colombian officials working on the kidnapping crisis moved to culmination, I thought about the payment of the ransom for the Swiss. The head of the Colombian security forces had addressed his deep concern about cooperation and the sharing of intelligence information, and here I was, **an outsider, sitting on the hottest information on one of the hottest cases, totally silent.**

Remorse suddenly hit me. I decided to keep quiet about what I knew about the payment of the ransom for the Swiss. The uncertainty of the action that could be taken by the police motivated me to keep silent. There were dire consequences either way and I would be responsible.

Armin Kamer, the First Secretary of the Swiss Embassy, denied that he knew where the ransom was to be paid, but I knew it had to be in Cali. Cali was preferable for the kidnappers for the payment of a ransom. They knew their way around *Valle del Cauca*. The information in my possession regarding the payment of the ransom made the situation aggravating for me.

I asked myself what would the commanders of the security forces do if they knew the ransom for the Swiss would be paid within 24 hours? How would they react to the information? If the police or military forces took any type of action to apprehend the kidnappers, that could mean certain death for the Swiss. If the ransom was paid, the Swiss might be released alive. I continued to believe that with good leads, the kidnappers could be tracked down and apprehended **after** the Swiss were released.

But it was certain the Colombian police and military officers involved would not accept that idea. As Driggers facetiously suggested, I was on the verge of "fucking up and nobody knowing it."

"Mi General Leyva," the Commander of the Third Brigade called out briskly. "Would you and Señor Saenz get together with us for a few minutes after the meeting?"

"Of course, *mi General,*" the director of DAS responded, waving pleasantly. The meeting ended and the Commander of the Third Brigade assigned tasks for intelligence analysis, logistics, and planning to implement surveillances, roadblocks, and raids on targeted residences and business establishments. The anti-kidnapping group broke up amid lamentations about their lack of mobility and portable communications equipment. But the most urgent requirement was the need for centralized command and control.

After the meeting, we met with General Bernardo Sanchez. Rodrigo L. Caicedo, the Governor of *Valle del Cauca,* and Colonel Filippo Villareal of the National Police were in the office. Military memorabilia, diplomas, and awards were prominent on the wall. We sat on attractive wrought iron chairs with beautiful polished leather. A valet served us strong black coffee in demitasses.

"Me alegro de verlos (I'm happy to see you)," General Sanchez told us. The General was pleasant and friendly. He struck me as a sharp military leader and well respected in the community.

"We need to talk," the General said in Spanish. The tone of the discussion was open and straightforward, setting me at ease.

"We are happy to have you with us," the General told me. "We understand you are an expert on kidnapping problems." *Dagnabbit,* I thought, there we go again, the bull crap about the *Americano* 'expert' on kidnappings. The kidnappers are the real experts, I thought to myself, with a touch of cynicism.

"Yesterday, we learned that the Swiss Ambassador has been told by the kidnappers in no uncertain terms they will kill Straessle and Buff if the Embassy has *anything* to do with the police," he added. The General sipped from the demitasse in his hand, pursing his lips. I felt privileged to be accepted by the group.

"The Swiss Ambassador insists on paying the ransom. It seems pretty obvious that the Swiss have been in touch with the person or persons responsible for the kidnapping of Straessle and Buff." He paused thoughtfully. The General grew pensive and rubbed his face with his hands in frustration.

"We need equipment to tap the telephone lines of the Swiss Embassy and the residence of *El Viejo* Straessle," he suggested wearily. I smiled politely and nodded in agreement. He was right.

Perhaps Pionzio would lend them equipment, I thought lightheartedly. But U.S. Government agencies would not help foreign countries with wiretap or eavesdropping equipment unless there was a clear threat to our own security. That was beyond my role.

Military officers in an adjoining office moved about hurriedly, opening file cabinets and talking in hushed tones. I glanced at General Leyva and he nodded for me to speak. I had been in Colombia for over three days now and surely, by this time, I could contribute **something** since I was the 'expert.'

"*Mi General* Sanchez," I said, making an effort to avoid any sign of *Gringo* insolence.

"The line of any person who has a telephone in Colombia can be *interceptado* at the main terminals of the Colombian Telephone Company. This should be done as soon as possible," I suggested.

"The telephone lines of close friends or associates of Straessle and Buff should be tapped as a priority," I added. "They will be used by the kidnappers as a bridge or as a link to the families of the victims to negotiate the payment of a ransom. Those folks should be identified as soon as possible." General Sanchez stared at me. I deferred in responding to his request for wiretaps. That effort would be a problem for me.

I explained to General Sanchez that the effort at the telephone company terminals could be compromised, but that the operation could be controlled.

"Only a few trusted individuals should know what you are doing." It was always a calculated risk to tap phones at the telephone company terminals. I knew the DAS had equipment to tap telephones.

"But I believe the DAS has the equipment to tap the telephone lines of individuals," I said. But General Leyva would not confirm or deny this for his own reasons. General Sanchez frowned, seeming frustrated.

"Well, we _need_ to buy wiretap equipment for our own use," he said, with urgency perceptible in his voice. He obviously wanted to develop his own electronic monitoring capabilities and I was on the spot. He wanted fast and easy solutions. The military were apparently into the kidnapping problem for the long haul.

"You will also need portable radios, tape recorders and surveillance equipment," I added. He nodded. That was a long list of commodities, but I had not been allotted any money to buy equipment.

For me, things would change dramatically if I became involved in acquiring commodities for the Colombian military forces, even if they paid for it. There was no doubt that some equipment was needed to help in resolving the kidnappings that were taking place in Colombia, but commodities were not part of my mission.

Fortunately, dissatisfied with my response, General Sanchez abruptly changed the subject to planning, personnel needs, and roadblocks. I suggested that thus far the roadblocks had produced no results.

"The roadblocks must be planned out and a purpose defined," I insisted. "The media often appears to know more about the kidnappings than anyone else. But they often fabricate or speculate on the news in order to sell newspapers," I said.

"After any abduction, the kidnappers will be glued to the television set to find out what the security forces are doing," I continued. There were wry smiles on several faces. What was my point, they seemed to say?

General Sanchez subsequently identified the essential elements and activities needed to deal with the overall kidnapping problem, but he acknowledged a lack of experience in the management of kidnapping investigations. I was surprised by his honesty.

"There is never enough experience in kidnapping investigations, *mi General,*" I told him bluntly. "But command and control in regard to the overall operation will be helpful." The commander of the National Police in Cali stared at me, seemingly in contemplation. He seemed to agree with my comments.

"You need an operations center to centralize all the activities connected to the Straessle and Buff case, *mi General.* That will help you to control the important decisions that are needed to respond to important developments in that case." I also suggested that there were investigative techniques that applied, but someone had to be ready to take advantage of any lucky break and take immediate action. My comments produced vacant stares from the officers. They seemed puzzled by my remarks; it seemed the *Gringo* 'expert' did not have any magical solutions to the problem.

"*Señores,*" I suggested in a low-key preamble. "If the Swiss Ambassador wants to pay a ransom to the kidnappers for Straessle and Buff, why not let him do it without any interference? We don't know when and how the Swiss Ambassador plans to pay the ransom anyway." There was dire silence in the room and unhappy looks.

"*Qué se pagé el rescate* (Let the ransom be paid)," I insisted. "We are not in any position to do otherwise anyway. The kidnappers can be apprehended later, after the victims are released," I told them.

The room turned silent and slow dissenting murmurs grew louder. My proposal was grossly simplistic and unrealistic for the Colombian officers.

"Let them collect the ransom and we'll get them later," I reiterated.

But for months the security forces had worked hard, diligently turning the place upside down in an effort to find the kidnappers. Roadblocks, searches, and raids were used to beat the bushes without success. Now the *Gringo* 'expert' was suggesting that the kidnappers be permitted to collect the ransom without interference by the security forces. "The *Gringo* is crazy!" the eyes of the men in the room seemed to say angrily. The fitful reaction to my remarks grew audible and General Leyva asked for silence.

"*Por favor, un momento,* let him finish." He nodded for me to continue.

"*Mi General* Sanchez, money is **not** as important as the lives of the Swiss," I suggested candidly to the group. "I hope we can all agree that that approach is valid." Smiling, I made an effort to appear sincere.

"Let the kidnappers have the money for now, since the Swiss are so determined to pay and they have no desire to cooperate." I paused to observe the reaction. This was no fragrant early morning walk in the beautiful autumn sunrise, but I tried to make it sound like it. The reaction of the group was not favorable. The word *Pendejo* formed in my mind but I was only a pseudo 'expert.'

"With a good investigation, we can capitalize on informants, follow up on leads and use wiretaps. In most cases the kidnappers will make contact by telephone and will call close friends of the victims whose names will be provided by the people who have been abducted." People in the room stared at me as I spoke in Spanish. It was suggested that if this was done correctly, we could find out through wiretaps how the ransom was paid, to whom it was paid and other vital information that would lead to arrests. General Leyva nodded in agreement. Colonel Villareal stared at the floor with a wooden grin.

"*Son buenas ideas* (Those are good ideas)," General Sanchez said, perplexed and unconvinced. "But we need results as soon as possible." The kidnappers are the only ones in a position to do that, I thought cynically.

I nodded and suggested in a firm voice that if the security forces intervened to stop the payment of the ransom and the Swiss diplomats were killed, the problem would become a very ugly international incident in which we would all look bad.

"If that happens it will degrade your efforts and complicate the investigation of other kidnappings," I told the group placidly. General Leyva raised his head in surprise and I received ugly stares. The kidnappers had already complicated any investigation. Despite the reaction, I continued.

"*Mi General,* you need the descriptions of people, hideouts, vehicles, roads used, and other information so that apprehensions can be made. The information can be obtained from the victims themselves if they are released alive." General Leyva fixed a smile on his face.

"The problem in Colombia is that the victims will not talk to the police once they are released," he said, using his hands for emphasis. He had an excellent point.

"But the victims will also not be able to cooperate if they wind up dead," I suggested with a grin. "It is better for everyone if the victims are released alive." General Leyva nodded to signal that I continue.

"Even if the victims will not cooperate once they are released, at least they will be alive." The officers in the room stayed silent, staring at me. I was trying to stir up new thinking, but was not very successful.

I suggested that a basic strategy be developed to guide the efforts of all Colombian authorities until a successful resolution to the problem could be achieved. Perhaps the bureaucracy will be slow enough to provide time for the ransom to be paid for the Swiss, I thought.

"Your officers need to know what you want done and how it will be done, *mi General,* especially in the case of Straessle and Buff, *para que no se cometan deslizes!*" I wondered what the Spanish word for "fuck-ups" was.

My discomfort grew when the men in the room went silent. General Leyva calmly stood up to put more coffee in his cup and poured some in my cup.

"What Señor Saenz is saying, I believe, is that a policy that will apply to everyone involved in the Straessle and Buff case and in other kidnappings should be developed and properly disseminated, **especially on the handling of a payment of a ransom**." He raised his index finger to emphasize the latter statement.

"Otherwise, many officers will go off on their own and create grave problems, perhaps even get themselves and the victims killed." General Leyva sat and scratched his bald head. General Sanchez paced the floor, nervously massaging the back of his neck.

"Without cooperation from those kidnapped, we will continue to operate in the darkness. We need information and leads from the victims," I suggested.

"General Leyva, I want you and Señor Saenz to meet with me as often as possible. We must coordinate our efforts. Whatever we do, let's put our heads together and avoid mistakes and unnecessary violence." The men in the room nodded in agreement.

"In the meantime, nothing will be done to stop the payment of the ransom without my authorization," he said firmly. I felt a sense of relief.

"Absolutamente!" General Leyva responded with a friendly smile.

"Muy bien, mi General," I offered happily. We now seemed to have a rational direction to take in regard to payment of the ransoms. But what direction could we take to resolve the kidnappings?

The meeting ended amidst hearty handshakes. I had mixed feelings about my role, but the situation provided me the opportunity to see where the problems were and to get more involved. Contrary to the assessment of the U.S. Embassy CIA Station Chief that the kidnappings did not have political motives or implications, the miasma of kidnappings in Colombia seemed to be part of the same old Cold War. The destabilization of a government by left-wing forces was known communist strategy.

General Leyva had helped to integrate my role into the overall effort and I was accepted as an advisor in the kidnapping crisis, albeit a *Gringo* advisor with a bittersweet candor. But the main concern at this point was that nothing interfere with the payment of the ransom for the Swiss. It seemed difficult to convince the Colombian military and police officials to do nothing if they knew the ransom for the Swiss was to be paid within a few hours. The representatives of the Swiss Embassy remained adamant that they would not talk to the police about the kidnapping of Straessle and Buff.

The United States Government through the U.S. Embassy would have to convince the Swiss to cooperate with the police or the problem had no end. Lubinsky was a boon in terms of his help, but thus far no one at the Embassy had considered asking the Swiss to cooperate. Meanwhile, in terms of past experience, the specter of death loomed large for the victims. It was a Catch-22.

On the road back to Cali with General Leyva and Dr. Leon, the beauty and vastness of the agro-terrain was impressive. Farmland abounded in the area and numerous hiding places seemed available to the kidnappers and to the guerrillas in hundreds of small farms dispersed throughout the Province.

"Hiciste muy bien," General Leyva told me abruptly, nudging me with his elbow. Apparently noting a trace of anguish on my part, he was trying to cheer me up by telling me that I did well in the meeting with General Sanchez. I told him jokingly that there seemed to be little information for the police on which to base any course of direct action. It seemed to be up to the kidnappers to make it any fun.

I thanked General Leyva for his support and thought about the situation. In the Straessle and Buff case, security force personnel continued to operate independently. Despite this, the top Colombian officials were efficient, genuine gentlemen, intelligent, and unpretentious. What more could a *Gringo* advisor want? I was intervening in the internal affairs of Colombia but was treated with respect. I had not accomplished a damn thing on the kidnapping problem and had been in Colombia three whole days.

"I wasn't much help," I told the General and let him know that my intransigence for not stopping the ransom was due to my concern for the safety of the Swiss and was from the heart more than logic.

"You were excellent," he said, smiling to boost my spirits. The night grew cooler when we approached the city of Cali. General Leyva cheerfully suggested we stop and eat.

"*Qué les parece? "Algo para tomar y algo para comer?* (Something to drink and something to eat?)" Everyone was in agreement. The General provided instructions to the driver and in a few minutes we stopped at a small restaurant located on the outskirts of Cali. Inside, the rustic ambiance was warm, comfortable, and clean. A delectable aroma emanated from a pot cooking in the small kitchen and smiling, General Leyva pointed to it.

"*Una recompensa,"* he explained. It was a treat, he said, and ordered large bowls of soup for everyone. He also ordered Scotch for us but none for the driver, who shrugged his shoulders when he was told, "no booze." The General called the soup, *"Zurek,* delicious Polish soup. The owners are Polish," he explained.

Inside the restaurant, relaxing and sipping on Scotch, I mentioned a visit to Quito, Ecuador, seven years earlier where I was exposed to another treat, called *Cuyes* but pronounced Quees. General Leyva and Dr. Leon asked me to tell them the story while we waited for the soup.

The story involved Ernest Lancini, a CIA officer working as an OPS police advisor in Ecuador. But there was no need to mention his role.

In a visit I made to Quito, Lancini held a cocktail party at his residence, and Captain S. V. Arteaga, Inspector Carlos Castro, and Inspector Luis Rueda, National Police Officers and graduates of the Inter-American Police Academy (IAPA) at Ft. Davis, were there. I was the Chief Instructor at the IAPA when they had attended a training course. They insisted on showing me the sights of Quito but Lancini suggested he would not join us because his wife was not feeling well. He handed me a bottle of Scotch and said the Ecuadorian Police officers had a surprise for me. With coy overtones he implied that I was going to enjoy an exotic Ecuadorian dish.

Dr. Leon suggested it was a piece of tail and everyone laughed. We needed a good laugh. I continued the story.

The Ecuadorean National Police Officers drove their police car around the picturesque city with a radio continuously playing melancholy *Andean* music until we stopped at a quaint restaurant located on the top of a hill in the center of the historic city. The small restaurant was family-owned, clean and tidy despite dirt floors.

"No se preocupé," one of the officers assured me. "This is one of the few places in Quito that can expertly prepare a *Cuyes* that is delicious." The Ecuadorian dish was not a woman.

At the restaurant in Quito, we were seated at a large square table with a bright red-checkered tablecloth while the owner and his young wife hovered nearby, attentively catering to us. The owner hugged Captain Arteaga and shook hands with me with cortege deference. Arteaga introduced me with a loud proclamation that I was one of the best police instructors in the world. Filling four glasses with Scotch, the captain, a slim sunburned red faced man with thick black hair and a gnashing look, proposed a toast.

"A nuestro buen amigo, Adolphi Saenz, instructor excepcional." Arteaga visibly choked up. "To the *Americanos* of the *Academia Inter-Americana de Policia,* who enlightened us on the good things of our profession, *servicio, compasión, patriotismo, camaraderia y cariño."* Affected by alcohol, I felt inspired by the Captain's kind words.

The owner of the Ecuadorian restaurant, pleased with our visit, approached Arteaga and rubbed the palms of his hands vigorously to announce, *"primero, una tortilla."*

"Si, no?" with a beaming smile he asked the captain hesitantly. Captain Arteaga grunted and with a smile nodded his approval. Visualizing a tortilla similar to those in the Southwestern United States, Mexico, and Central America I was surprised when the tortillas turned out to be potato omelets. We consumed the Ecuadorian tortillas with a tasty reddish sauce.

Our senses numbed by Scotch, toast after toast was proposed and everyone applauded happily. Arteaga abruptly scrambled to his feet and raised his glass.

"Arriba! (Above!)" Another officer stood, raised his glass to shout.

"Abajo! (Below!)" The group looked at me until I stood and added happily.

"Al centro! (In the center!)"

Everyone turned to the owner's pretty maidenly wife who broke into uncontrollable laughter. Egged on by Arteaga, she screamed excitedly.

"*Y adentro!* (And in, to the hilt!)" Red-faced, she covered her mouth demurely while other clients joined the fun, clapping their hands in approval. The oral exercise in Spanish was purely sexual.

The owner of the restaurant grew anxious, patting his rotund apron covered belly to announce loudly.

"*Ahora, el Cuyes!*" The Ecuadorean officers clapped, urging him to bring the Ecuadorian delicacy.

The owner returned from the kitchen with a metal platter and placed it in front of me as my friends muttered words of approbation.

"*Bien, muy bien, ah qué bien, el Cuyes.*" I lifted my glass for a drink of Scotch, looked down and saw the *Cuyes* on the metal platter. The Scotch helped me control an overwhelming urge to jump in surprise. The *Cuyes* on the metal platter looked like a large rodent, cooked whole, the small head crisp with the mouth open and sharp teeth still intact. The critter stared at me with cold beady eyes and for a moment I thought it was a joke.

"I'm your dinner, asshole," it seemed to say.

The Ecuadorian officers pushed me to eat. Hesitant, I was not sure what to do. Was this a real dinner? The owner quickly placed metal trays on the table with a *Cuyes* for each of the officers who attacked with expedient relish, tearing off legs and other parts of the little animal, eating and enjoying the meal. Reinforced by the Scotch I tore a small leg from the roasted *Cuyes* and ate, fascinated by the little head of the roasted critter, still intact, hollow eyes staring at me.

"What did it taste like?" Dr. Leon asked. The small portion of the *Cuyes* I consumed had excellent condiments and a distinct taste not unlike pork. In Ecuador, at the restaurant, I told the officers. "*No más!* (No more!)" They did not hesitate to eat the portion of the dinner *(Cuyes)* left on my plate. After dinner, we marched through the kitchen to unravel the mystery of the *Cuyes*. Dozens of small furry animals ran freely on the kitchen floor with others housed in wire cages. The animals were guinea pigs, bred for consumption, and considered a delicacy in Ecuador. The *Cuyes* was very popular in Ecuador.

At the restaurant in Cali, the Polish sour-bread soup turned out to be delicious and satisfying. The Scotch awakened our appetites and without warning the waitress served a second bowl of rich soup for everyone. The soup was savory and tasted homemade, with rich portions of barley and hearty beef. Dr. Leon ordered a third bowl and General Leyva and I drank Colombian coffee and talked about the Straessle and Buff case.

I fought the urge to tell the General that the ransom for Straessle and Buff was probably on its way. It was certain to me that if the ransom were not paid, we would be looking for two corpses. If the Swiss were released, we had to move fast to get information from them.

"Tomorrow we'll go look at the site where Straessle and Buff were kidnapped, just to see what the area looks like," General Leyva said wearily. "There may not be much to see. We'll have to get up fairly early," he said. He seemed disturbed that we had not accomplished much thus far. By eight o'clock we returned to the Hotel *Aristi,* and agreed to meet at eight in the morning.

Daylight arrived with bright vivid sunshine and noisy people moving about the hotel. In the hotel restaurant I found General Leyva sitting at a table alone, eating a Continental breakfast.

"*Buenos Dias,* Dolph," he greeted me cheerfully. The General was alert and in good spirits. "I hope you slept well," he told me. The General asked me to sit.

"I know you're hungry," he proclaimed with a smile.

I poured myself "*café con leche.*" In France or Georgetown, Washington, D.C., it would be *latte.* The Creole breakfast of scrambled eggs, black beans and bacon was delicious. The restaurant was crowded in the morning and it seemed that the drug trade and kidnapping business was booming with people making deals.

I ate while General Leyva explained that most of the kidnappings happened either in *Valle del Cauca, Antioga* or Bogota. All of the cases were unsolved. The three places were areas where the FARC, the EPL and ELN operated. (*Antioga* was actually *Medellin.*) The FARC was the Revolutionary Armed Forces of Colombia (*Fuerzas Armadas Revolucionarias de Colombia),* the EPL, the Popular Liberation Army (*Ejercito Popular de Liberacion),* and the ELN, the National Liberation Army (*Ejercito Nacional de Liberacion).*

"I'll bet you some of those *bastardos* are involved," the General said. The differences in the guerrilla groups as explained by General Leyva was that the EPL was pro-Peking, the ELN was pro-Castro, and the FARC was the main action arm of the communist party in Colombia. I ate my breakfast, happy to learn that the different factions of communist guerrillas in Colombia distrusted each other.

"Any suspects in any of the kidnappings?" I asked.

"There is a *tipo* (guy) by the name of Luis Fernando Tamayo Garcia, an individual trained in guerrilla warfare in Peking, Prague, and Cuba. He is a suspect in many of the kidnappings.

"*Ése tipo es malo* (That guy is bad news)," the General suggested without hesitation. He lit a cigarette but put it out on his plate after a few drags. General Leyva seemed calm but he was very concerned about the Swiss.

Hopefully the ransom would be paid soon but the way had to be clear so that the security forces would not interfere. I decided to tell the General what I knew. I would ask him to help me convince the security force commanders to hold up on the roadblocks and patrols for at least twenty-four hours.

Before I opened my mouth, Dr. Leon approached the table with a peevish look on his face. "I'm not going to eat," he told us. *"No me siento bien* (I don't feel that good)." The General and I laughed spontaneously. "Thank you for your sympathy," Dr. Leon said dejectedly. With an elfish grin, the General advised him that his *"mal estado"* was the result of too much booze and *Zurek* soup.

We finished eating and the General grew impatient to go.

"Are you ready?" he asked Dr. Leon. He gulped his coffee and nodded. *"Vamos pues."* The General scratched his head in deep thought. "We have much to do before we return to Bogota."

Outside, after the driver of the car was provided instructions on our destination by Dr. Leon, we went south from Cali for nearly thirty minutes, past the local airport until the car turned west on a dirt road. The area had dark green vegetation with brown spots on flat terrain.

"Callejón de Las Chuchas," General Leyva pointed to a narrow valley between rolling mountains. "Straessle and Buff were taken from there," he said. We walked down a curved dirt road. "That was two weeks ago. The Swiss are probably somewhere in *Valle del Cauca."* General Leyva stopped again and pointed to a hill.

"Around that curve is where the kidnappers hid the military vehicle used to kidnap Straessle and Buff." We scanned the red brown terrain spotted intermittently with colorful green patches and the area appeared innocuous and serene. There was dead silence. The anguished sounds of Straessle and Buff during the kidnapping and the shooting of Don Eric Straessle could only be imagined. Nothing was left in the area except perhaps some of Don Eric Straessle's blood. I thought about the name of the place—*Callejón de Las Chuchas* (Corridor of the Dog Bitches). But there were no dogs in sight.

On the way to Cali, General Leyva explained that Don Eric Straessle had resisted his son's abduction and had been shot. With the help of his wife, he was able to reach a doctor and was treated for a gunshot wound. From there he called his attorney but did not call the DAS or the National Police to report the kidnapping. With obvious irritation,

General Leyva pointed out that Straessle's attorney finally elected to call General Bernardo Sanchez to report what had happened only after several hours had passed.

"Sanchez set up roadblocks and patrols but it was too late," General Leyva concluded. "The DAS was advised about the kidnapping much later." He seemed frustrated.

On the outskirts of Cali, the traffic became more intense. General Leyva expressed portentous thoughts about the safety of the Swiss.

"I hope young Straessle will survive this ordeal," he said with obvious dismay. The General wanted me to say something positive about the matter, despite the circumstances. It was hard for me.

"Being kidnapped by deadly killers at age fifteen is not an invitation to a diplomatic dinner," I observed to the General. "If the Swiss are to survive, the ransom has to be paid without interference." He nodded.

"We're going to the *Jefatura* of the DAS in Cali," the General explained. He suggested I might want to spend time in Cali and DAS personnel should know about me. With a mischievous grin he told me he had told them I was a *gran colaborador* and *asesor* (a great collaborator and advisor) but a *malo hombre* (tough guy).

"They will cooperate," he told me with conviction. "Most of them are young agents but they will listen to you. *Pero ten cuidado* (But be careful)," he cautioned. "Some of the younger agents are inexperienced but eager and aggressive." He paused thoughtfully.

"The media may also pick up on your presence," he told me. "We don't want that." I certainly agreed with him on that part. General Leyva recognized the potential danger for me in Cali.

I did **not** know the terrain and was totally unfamiliar with people, places, and faces. It was possible I could wind up as an attractive target for kidnappers. Roy Driggers treated the matter as a joke that I could be kidnapped, but if that happened, it would create more problems for the Government of Colombian than any help the United States Government could possibly provide. I pondered the idea. No one had thought of that.

The risk of being kidnapped made me think of my family. They would never forgive me if I were kidnapped, I thought jokingly. My ten-year-old son Michael asked me ingenuously before I left, "You're not going to a bad place, are you, Dad? Let someone else go. We need you for gripe night." Gripe night was a weekly event at our house and gave our children a chance to complain about anything they wished. Everyone would then agree to solutions to any gripe. My kids liked it. I thought about home and my wife Jan. I would call home when I returned to Bogota. I felt suddenly distracted from my job.

We stood outside DAS Headquarters in Cali and the General leaned close to whisper as men approached the car. They seemed to be friendly.

"*Tienes tu arma?* (Are you carrying your weapon?)" he asked. I grinned and nodded. The General smiled and gestured with his arm. He asked me to let him know if I needed more firepower and smiled.

"*No te preoccupes* (Don't worry), those fellows are DAS," he told me hurriedly. For a fleeting moment, I thought of asking him for a sawed-off shotgun.

At the entrance to the DAS headquarters in Cali, several men exchanged handshakes with the General and greeted him effusively. Cesar Tenorio, a DAS Supervisory Agent, walked up behind me and unexpectedly grabbed me in a bear hug. It was a total surprise for me, but I was delighted to see him. He was one of my former students at the Inter-American Police Academy. It seemed he was aware of my presence in Colombia and suggested we work together in Cali. I quickly agreed. Tenorio was young, intelligent and tough.

Meanwhile, the payment of the ransom for the Swiss plagued my mind. I prayed in silence that the ransom had been paid. I wondered if anyone in the DAS knew. I would find out afterwards from DAS Agents and other folks that the kidnappers and someone in the National Police knew about the payment of the ransom.

Unknown to us at the time, in a dark room of a building near the National Police Headquarters in Cali, two men talked about kidnappings while smoking strong Colombian cigarettes. Gonzalo Cordova Satizabal, a rugged looking individual in his mid-thirties, had straight black hair, a mustache, and a menacing look. He was reportedly a police informant. Even in the shadows, the other individual appeared to have authority. He was a National Police Officer.

"*Cuándo se paga el rescate?* (When will the ransom be paid?)" he calmly asked his informant.

I also learned later after the investigation was over that in another part of the province of *Valle del Cauca,* in a rustic countryside farmhouse called *"El Eden,"* two leaders of the kidnapping group talked in informal tones while drinking beer. Luis Fernando Tamayo Garcia, a trained terrorist, sat in quiet displeasure in a leather-backed wrought iron chair as he listened to a mean looking individual named Sabas Calderon Castro explain his notion of scruples among kidnappers. He talked to Tamayo in angry overtones.

"Mira, Nelly has complained that Juan Rizo did not pay her the sixty thousand pesos she was promised for feeding Eduardo Varon," he told Tamayo. Varon had been kidnapped previously and was released when the ransom was paid. Nelly was the pseudonym for Luz M. Rengifo Acevedo, and she and Celedonia Rodriguez de Calderon, Sabas' wife, were responsible for feeding the victims who were kidnapped until the ransom was paid. It was not intended to be an elaborate cuisine.

Tamayo sucked air through his throat to laugh derisively at Saba's remarks. Small, sparse, with trousers that flapped around skinny legs, he was a trained terrorist and among the most ruthless of the kidnappers. Tamayo wore a large white turtleneck sweater. With a dark crewcut and beady eyes, he looked like a cornered ferret. He blinked bloodshot eyes as he smoked a cigarette and stared coldly at Sabas Calderon.

"I understand you gave him forty-eight hours to pay her the money," he told Sabas who nodded angrily.

"I told Rizo that if he did not pay the women the money, he was a dead man!" Sabas spat the words out. Tamayo's eyes blinked rapidly and his slim face grew darker, but he listened to the angry comments from Sabas without saying a word.

"Ese hijo de puta no trabaja más con nosotros." Sabas sputtered contemptuously that the son-of-a-bitch was out of the cartel. Tamayo held back his irritation to inquire about the Swiss.

"Bien, y los Suizzos?" Sabas glared at the large yard in back of the farmhouse where men moved about and women fed farm animals. The men had guns strapped to their waist and some carried automatic weapons.

"Hay están! (There they are!)" Sabas told Tamayo, his right eye drooping abnormally. His chin pointed to a piece of cement on the ground.

"I'll pick up the ransom?" Tamayo asked Sabas offhandedly, and he nodded.

"It better be three million *pesos,*" Sabas suggested harshly. He stood up to face Tamayo contentiously.

"If the police interfere or if the Swiss do not pay every *centavo* of the ransom, *matamos a los tipos* (we kill them)! Sabas picked his hand up and pointed at Tamayo menacingly. "I don't want to hear any *mierda* about the ransom. If they don't pay, they die. If they pay, we divide the money as agreed!"

In a deep hole covered with a piece of concrete that fit in place like a puzzle, young Werner Jose Straessle and Herman Buff waited fearfully. They were unable to sit comfortably in the dark, cramped, foul-smelling dungeon. Mentholatum that had been rubbed on their eyes made their tears flow freely. The young boy's silent anguish was unmistakable. He felt like he was experiencing a horrible nightmare.

The only air coming into the hole was from a bicycle tire tube that had been inserted into the top of the piece of cement covering the small dungeon. The air in the hole was stale and putrid.

A sudden noise on the concrete slab above their hole startled Straessle and Buff. A woman moved the piece of cement to feed them black beans and rice. Young Straessle could not believe what was happening to him was real. Each passing day was more grievous and tormenting for him. He was not sure his father was alive after seeing him get shot when he and Buff were kidnapped. Was his nightmare real?

At the Hotel *Aristi,* the afternoon crowd dwindled to a few persons wandering through the lobby and a gift shop. The bright sunlight filled the entrance of the hotel as I waited for my friend Cesar Tenorio to pick me up to take me to the DAS Headquarters. Waiting in the peaceful surroundings of the hotel lobby, I thought about Straessle and Buff. They were in grave danger. Police and military patrols seemed sparse and no roadblocks were visible. My proposal to hold up on roadblocks until a strategy was developed had been resisted by some security force commanders, who thought the *Gringo* advisor was too obtuse. It was hard to convince security force personnel to back off from doing what they saw was their job in order to capture the kidnappers. The *Gringo* advisor had merely tried to make their job of catching kidnappers more difficult.

The speaker system of the hotel suddenly blared out with a melodious female voice calling out.

"Doctor Saenz, Doctor Saenz. *Lo esperan afuera del hotel* (Someone is waiting for you at the entrance to the hotel)." She repeated the announcement. Someone outside the entrance of the hotel was waiting for Doctor Saenz. It had to be Tenorio, I thought. In Latin America, attorneys, professional people, and college graduates are commonly called *"licenciado* or *doctor."* I mused that Tenorio had me classified as a doctor.

Because of the bright sunlight, I put on my sunglasses to walk outside. A solitary jeep parked at the entrance had the motor running and two male silhouettes inside. Ingenuously, I approached the passenger side of the vehicle to look for Tenorio and quickly spotted an automatic weapon cradled in the arms of a man sitting in the jeep. Uncertain about the situation, I impulsively unholstered my gun and held it in my hand.

"Ustedes buscan al Sr. Saenz?" I asked. Both men turned in utter surprise. Cursing violently, the driver of the jeep pulled out at a high rate of speed and made a wide turn while the individual on the passenger side turned to fire his weapon. I went to the ground as gunshots echoed loudly and bullets hit the gleaming white wall a few feet from me. The vehicle was gone in seconds.

The street emptied quickly and a man inside the hotel ran out into the street. Too late I realized he was probably connected to the men in the jeep. Angry with myself, I walked inside the hotel and the lobby was almost devoid of people. The hotel desk clerk called the police, but no one talked to me. I remained in my room to wait for Tenorio. For me it was an isolated incident.

Tenorio arrived about fifteen minutes later and was surprised when he heard what had happened. *"Tal vez era algun pinchi pendejo enojado con algun medico,"* I told him. He laughed when I suggested facetiously in Spanish that it was some dumb asshole pissed off at some doctor.

But there was no easy explanation available. It seemed impossible that anyone outside of the DAS or the top Colombian military and police officials would know I was the *Gringo* kidnapping 'expert.'

"I can't let you out of my sight," Tenorio chuckled, "and you get in trouble."

20

El Eden

The following events were reconstructed based on interviews I conducted of the two men who paid the ransom for the victims, from information obtained by the Swiss Ambassador from Straessle and Buff on their kidnapping, from police reports, and my own personal participation in the investigation of kidnappings in Colombia.

Cali, Colombia, October 21, 1969, mid-morning

The Tropicana Drive-in was a popular and attractive place in Cali with a nice pitched roof and an outdoor patio with large white umbrellas on the tables. There was always plenty of parking space around the building and in front of the service counter that faced out. By late morning, the popular eating establishment teemed with customers from the surrounding *vecindad* (the local neighborhood). Many of the clients knew each other and commonly met there to drink coffee and talk. The drive-in served excellent Colombian cuisine, spicy *carne mechada*, fried plantains, black beans, as well as hamburgers and milkshakes.

The people who had congregated at the drive-in paid little attention to two men who had driven up in separate cars. One of the men was named Max Lupin. He locked his car and joined another man named Manuel Cuestas in his vehicle parked at the drive-in. The men appeared to be local businessmen.

Max Lupin and Manuel Cuestas were at the Tropicana Drive-in to complete a very important mission concerning the kidnapping of Straessle and Buff. They were there to pick up the final instructions for the payment of the ransom for the two Swiss victims. The kidnappers were waiting for them to deliver the ransom and were less than eight miles away.

Cuestas and Lupin were employees of the Croyden Automobile Company in Cali, a company owned by Don Eric Straessle, Werner's father. The two men, Cuestas and Lupin, had been cast into the dangerous role of paying the ransom to the kidnappers by the kidnappers themselves. Cuestas had been told that he would be killed if he went to the police and he knew that it was no idle threat. The kidnappers would not hesitate to kill him as well as Straessle and Buff if anything went wrong. The selection of the two men to pay the ransom was a *faits accomplis* and they were grateful that this was the final leg of their dangerous journey.

To initiate the negotiations needed for the payment of a ransom, the kidnappers had obtained the names of several employees at the Croyden plant from Straessle and Buff. A top supervisor at the plant by the name of Bravo was called and told by the kidnappers to let them talk to Cuestas.

"If you are as smart as they say you are, you will keep your mouth shut," he was warned.

Once the kidnappers made contact with Cuestas, he was provided with precise instructions on what he was supposed to do and consistently threatened with death. He was told when and where ransom notes would be left at different times and locations in Cali. Cuestas picked the notes up without the knowledge of the police or the DAS. The kidnappers avoided calling the telephones of the Swiss Embassy or Straessle's residence, believing they were bugged.

Lupin and Cuestas were made keenly aware that the ransom had to be paid to the kidnappers without fail in order to save the lives of Werner Straessle and Herman Buff. If the two hundred thousand dollars in Colombian *pesos* were not delivered in time as demanded by the kidnappers, the victims would surely be killed. The two men struggled emotionally with the awesome responsibility that had been imposed on them.

Two paper sacks holding the ransom money were sitting behind the passenger seat of Lupin's car. The difficult part ahead was to deliver the ransom money to the kidnappers without the knowledge of the Colombian security forces. The kidnappers informed Cuestas and Lupin that the final instructions for the delivery of the ransom would be found at the Tropicana Drive-in. It was now up to them, they were told.

For the past three weeks the two men kept their involvement in the matter a secret and only a few individuals in the Swiss Embassy knew they were in touch with the kidnappers. Cuestas and Lupin knew that finding the final instructions for the payment of the ransom was indispensable to their mission but not the end of the problem. The tricky part was for them to avoid the roadblocks and the patrols of the Colombian security forces and reach the kidnappers in time to pay the ransom.

According to what Irwin Kamer, the First Secretary of the Swiss Embassy, told me, the ransom payment for Straessle and Buff was to be three million Colombian *pesos*. That was equivalent to nearly two hundred thousand dollars ($200,000, and in 1969 dollars, that was a tidy sum).

The payment of the ransom had the blessing of the Swiss Embassy in Bogota and would be paid clandestinely to avoid interference by the police. The bottom line was that the ransom had to be paid in order to give the victims a chance to get out alive. The pay or die policy of the kidnappers was no joke. If the ransom were not paid, the victims would be killed.

The procedures developed by the kidnappers to negotiate the payment of a ransom was impressive and creative. Lupin and Cuestas had been warned early on by the kidnappers that they had to operate in total secrecy or they would pay with their lives if anything went wrong.

Initially, the kidnappers left several ransom notes at a local cemetery in Cali and at the *Teatro Calima*, a theatre located in a busy business district. The notes left by the kidnappers eventually led Lupin and Cuestas to the Tropicana to pick up the final instructions.

On one occasion, a frightening ending added to a note left by the kidnappers at a local cemetery in Cali helped convince Cuestas of the terrible danger faced by the victims if the ransom was not paid. In a few emotional written words young Werner Straessle, the fifteen-year-old victim, warned Cuestas to do **exactly** as he was told by the kidnappers or he and Buff would be killed.

The contacts between the kidnappers and Cuestas and Lupin had been ongoing for a period of seventeen days. Cuestas had received several messages via cryptic ads placed in Cali newspapers. Messages were also included in the broadcasts of two local radio stations called *Eco* and *Reloj*. The instructions were always communicated at specific times and in code. On many occasions, Cuestas was warned that he would be killed along with Straessle and Buff if he contacted the police. It was certain that his life was also on the line.

At the Tropicana Drive-in restaurant, Cuestas left Lupin's car and walked in front of the drive-in. He stopped momentarily to light a cigarette and looked up at the large Canada Dry sign above the walk-up counter. There were a few people standing at the counter. Once inside the restaurant, Cuestas headed for the restroom. He found the odor inside the restroom stifling with the smell of ammonia and urine.

He paused to urinate and looked around to make sure he was alone. He reached under a commode and removed an envelope glued to the wall. He was surprised to find that the glue on the envelope was still wet. That was frightening enough. The kidnappers had apparently been there minutes earlier. He read the message on the face of the envelope written in Spanish.

Do not open the envelope. Go to your car. Remain inside your car for ten minutes and then open the envelope. The instructions from the kidnappers intimidated him.

In the car, Lupin read the message written on the envelope and said nothing. Both men waited in silence. They felt certain they were being watched. Exactly ten minutes passed and Lupin nodded at Cuestas to open the envelope. To their surprise they found another envelope inside. The second envelope was sealed and had another message written on it.

Go to Carrera 15. Wait there for five minutes. Then open this envelope. Nervously they started the car and drove away.

At *Carrera* 15, as instructed by the kidnappers, the two men stopped and waited in their car for five minutes. They nervously opened the second envelope and found the final instructions for the payment of the ransom *sui generis.* They were instructed to follow a circuitous route in their car until one of the kidnappers would signal them. The individual would use a handkerchief and a code.

At the DAS Headquarters in Cali, Cesar Tenorio and I talked about the kidnapped Swiss and possible suspects. Things looked grim for Straessle and Buff. Tenorio seemed to have a portentous feeling about the bad guys who were kidnapping people and agreed with me that the kidnappers would kill the Swiss if anything went wrong with the payment of the ransom.

Tenorio's experience with so much violence had served to harden him. He had seen a great deal of bloodshed in his lifetime. The sinister effect of a vicious war was in his eyes. Like me, he wanted to be in on the fight. Tenorio was a handsome young man barely past thirty. He was an experienced DAS Agent responsible for the supervision of investigations related to kidnapping cases in *Valle del Cauca.* He patiently contended with the serious disconnection between National Police F-2 units and military personnel working independently on their own investigations. The problem of coordination and cooperation between the security forces made the potential for problems and disaster for the victims a foreboding reality.

But more troubling for me were the numerous roadblocks manned by police and military personnel, at a time when I knew the ransom for Straessle and Buff was to be delivered to the kidnappers. Police action was the last thing needed at this point. I had failed to convince the military to forego the roadblocks and raids until after the ransom for the Swiss was paid and the victims were released. There was a widely-held belief among the top officials of the police and military forces that stopping the payment of ransoms would eventually defeat the kidnapping cartel.

The Government of Colombia had taken the position that if authorities permitted the payment of a ransom for the release of a kidnapped victim that would amount to *corrupcion de la autoridad* (the corruption of authority). Consequently, the police were instructed to stop the payment of any ransom at all costs. The theory seemed logical, but the victims of kidnappers would surely be killed under those circumstances.

"If the ransom for the Swiss is not paid, the kidnappers will kill them. All hell will break loose," I complained bitterly to Tenorio. He sipped his coffee and stared bleakly at me. He sensed an unusual anxiety on my part. My agitation had increased because I knew the delivery of the ransom for the Swiss was imminent. The risk was growing portentously.

"I hope the Swiss are not paying the ransom today," Tenorio remarked with a satirical smile. He searched my eyes for signs of a reaction and then grew dejected.

"*Muy bien.* Let's go check around," he suggested. "Perhaps we can convince some of these people to stop the roadblocks at least for a few days." I patted his shoulder.

"*Gracias Tenorio. Vamos,*" I told him. I had a queasy feeling in my stomach that we might be too late. It appeared there was no way the ransom could be paid without the police knowing.

1230 Hours

Max Lupin and Manuel Cuestas drove their car to the *Plaza de Los Toros* in downtown Cali, following the instructions provided by the kidnappers. They drove slowly, watching to see if anyone followed them. The instructions provided by the kidnappers had to be strictly adhered to, or there would be serious danger. Transporting three million Colombian *pesos* in two large paper sacks was part of the dangerous mission. But the money had to be delivered to the kidnappers in time, as scheduled, and without problems, if Straessle and Buff were to be saved.

The kidnappers had originally demanded a ransom of five million pesos, but Don Eric Straessle convinced them to accept three million in five hundred and one hundred Colombian *peso* notes, the favorite denomination of the kidnappers. Don Eric Straessle had promised the kidnappers that he would make absolutely certain that the *Banco Francois-Italiano* in Cali provided only unmarked bills. The kidnappers warned Straessle that they were negotiating in good faith and were not worried that he would provide marked money.

"You're the one to worry, Don Eric Straessle, if that happens," they told him.

At *Calle 6a,* Lupin and Cuestas drove nervously to *Carrera 15,* driving slowly so as not to arouse any suspicion from police or military personnel in the area. It was up to them to ensure that the payment of the ransom for Straessle and Buff was successfully accomplished or they too could be killed.

They turned into *Carrera 15* and were shocked to find a roadblock manned by military personnel loom ominously on the road in front of them. There was no time to discuss options. The two men quickly agreed to stay on course. If they tried to avoid the roadblock it would attract the attention of security force personnel. They remained in the line of traffic.

Up ahead, a soldier with an upturned arm signaled for them to stop. The two men waited in their car while the paper sacks with the money remained in plain sight behind the passenger seat of the vehicle. If the authorities found the money they would know immediately that it represented the ransom for the Swiss. The ransom would be confiscated and the Swiss would be killed. With their hearts pounding in their chests, Lupin and Cuestas waited.

To accelerate the car and get away from the military roadblock was extremely risky and they were liable to get shot. The soldier that had stopped their car was polite and briefly peeked through the rear window to see inside the car. The two men waited for a miracle.

Cesar Tenorio drove the DAS car to the roadblock, and military personnel behind wooden barricades holding automatic rifles focused their attention on our arrival. Two DAS Agents with us stepped out of the car and I followed. The soldier holding the two men in a dark vehicle suddenly looked up, flashing a face of mean irritation.

"Qué pasa?" he yelled. Flashing his DAS credentials, Tenorio shouted at the soldiers behind the barricade. They held their rifles in their hands.

"Somos del DAS," Tenorio yelled at the soldiers. The soldier holding the dark vehicle seemed distracted by our arrival and waved the car he was holding through the roadblock. He walked immediately toward us. The two men in the car that had been stopped stared stiffly ahead and drove away slowly.

I listened as Tenorio talked to the soldiers. The soldier that had stopped the car with the two men was the NCO (Non-Commissioned Officer) in charge. He informed us in an officious manner that his superior officers had ordered that all vehicles traveling on that road be checked. But he was not clear on what they were supposed to look for.

"Anything suspicious," he advised Tenorio. "There are other roadblocks on roads leading into the city," he said. *"Por orden superior* (by Superior Order),"* he said. The roadblocks were in accordance with a military plan developed to apprehend anyone connected to the kidnappings, he told us. Tenorio glanced at me for my reaction. It would do little good to try to convince the sergeant to remove the roadblocks.

Max Lupin and Manuel Cuestas had carefully followed the instructions provided by the kidnappers and drove to the ***Plaza de Los Toros.*** When they reached *Calle 8a,* they turned on Roosevelt Avenue and then headed back to *Carrera 15* and from there to *Calle 7a.* The route followed by Cuestas and Lupin was a myriad of turns and circles. Cuestas and Lupin had been told to be precise in following the instructions provided to them or matters would get risky. The circuitous route driven by Cuestas and Lupin was to give the kidnappers the opportunity to see if the car was being followed by anyone. The two men followed the same route three times.

Meanwhile, at a small restaurant situated at *Calle 12 Sur,* Luis Fernando Tamayo Garcia, one of the leaders of the kidnapping group, patiently waited. Wearing a white turtleneck sweater and an oversized jacket he sat drinking coffee and conversing with two men in the restaurant. An eye infection caused him to blink in irritation. An automatic weapon hidden under his long jacket made it difficult for him to enjoy his *cafe con leche.* Like most terrorists, Tamayo did not look menacing at all and appeared frail. But he had a slim muscular frame.

At approximately 1325 hours, Tamayo stood to pull a cloth cap low over his forehead. He left without saying a word and walked calmly to a cement divider located at *Carrera 20,* near the intersection of Roosevelt Avenue and *Calle 12 Sur.* He stood impassively on the cement mound.

After a few minutes, he signaled abruptly with a white handkerchief at a car that slowly approached the intersection. The vehicle stopped and Tamayo deftly used the handkerchief held in his hand to conceal the lower part of his face. He fixed hard florid eyes on Cuestas.

"Dos por dos son cinco (Two plus two is five)," he said. Coughing softly behind the handkerchief, Tamayo suddenly erupted in an outraged manner.

"Dónde esta el dinero? (Where is the money?)" he hissed. He waited for the men in the car to react.

The code used by the individual standing on the divider had been described in the written instructions provided by the kidnappers to Cuestas. But the men reacted slowly and Tamayo sputtered out in a fierce tone.

"Qué diablos esperan? (What the hell are you waiting for?)"

"El rescate! (The ransom!)" A nervous move by Tamayo revealed the automatic weapon hidden under his jacket. "Give me the ransom," he instructed the two men scornfully in Spanish. Jolted by the sight of the gun, Cuestas quickly handed Tamayo the two paper sacks loaded with the money. The bags were an armful and Tamayo almost dropped the gun hidden under his coat.

"Se marchan y no miren para atrás," he ordered in a menacing manner. Holding the paper sacks, he ordered the two men to leave and not to look back. Tamayo stepped back cautiously to the rear of the car and then walked hurriedly across the street to disappear behind a building. Cuestas and Lupin drove slowly away.

At the DAS, Tenorio was restless and unhappy. We talked about possible suspects and the sparse leads that had been developed. The kidnappings appeared to affect everyone with a sense of helplessness. Several suspects and houses were under surveillance and the military units involved continued with their raids and roadblocks. As yet, nothing positive had been achieved.

Tenorio had told me about a few suspects in the kidnappings and suggested he knew some of their hangouts. The suspects he identified were Miguel Angel Rincon, AKA *Carino* (Love), and Nestor Hurtado, AKA *Suicidio* (Suicide). In jest, I suggested to Tenorio that they sounded like two nice homeboys.

"Puedes creerlo (You better believe it)," he chuckled. Bored, I agreed to go with him to check out a few places. We had nothing else going. I trusted Tenorio and he was a good investigator.

We arrived at a string of bars located in a poor district of Cali and entered a *cantina* (a bar) that looked like a remnant of the days of the old 'Wild West.' We received nasty stares from nasty looking characters that filled the place to capacity. We were the intruders in a friary, I thought sarcastically. The place was considered by Tenorio to be a favorite watering hole for hoodlums, whores, town drunks, roisterers, narco-traffickers, and kidnappers. He scrutinized several of the characters looking at us and they turned away. Tenorio seemed to be well known as a tough DAS Agent.

We sat at a table and ordered beer. Tenorio said the lower echelon members liked to hang out in dives.

"Con las putas (with the whores)," he explained. He said that kidnappers were held in high esteem by the clientele that frequented the bar. They usually had money to spend, he said.

"Anyone involved in kidnapping people has to be a cold-blooded killer," he observed dryly. "The *chicos* (boys) are known to be mean bastards with a unique relationship with their compeers." Some of the kidnappers were hardcore criminals and homosexuals who did not relate well to Marxists and leftists, he said.

"They tolerate each other, but some of the hardcore bastards are killers, not ideologues," he said of the characters involved in kidnappings.

"They do not believe in the communist bullshit, although sometimes they do get political." It seemed clear that Tenorio had given the kidnapping problem a lot of thought.

"Dr. Ernesto Gonzales Caicedo, the son of a prominent politico, was abducted early this year," Tenorio recounted. "The people who abducted Caicedo were members of the same group that has pulled off many other kidnappings. Anyway, the kidnappers demanded two million *pesos* ransom for Caicedo." He paused to take a drink of his beer.

"The father of the victim, an ex-minister of government, was able to renegotiate the ransom with the kidnappers to five hundred thousand *pesos*. One of the Marxist leaders of the cartel protested vehemently and pissed off other top dogs. The Marxists threatened to split from the group." He laughed ruefully.

"So now we have the possibility of more than one kidnapping group. This is a miserable job," he said. "And the pay is lousy. *Los secuestradores son mucho mejor pagados que nosotros y se divierten mas* (The kidnappers are better paid than we are and have a lot more fun)," he said laughing.

By eight o'clock that evening my thoughts turned to the Swiss, and I prayed that the ransom for them had been paid. It did not feel right for me to hold back information on the payment of the ransom from the

DAS, but I knew the danger to the Swiss would not possibly decrease because of anything the security forces could do. In fact, any action by the security forces at this point made matters extremely dangerous for Straessle and Buff. The kidnapped Swiss were helpless victims at the complete mercy of very ruthless people. Young Werner Straessle was probably a brave lad but was in grave danger.

No one could help at this point. His father was lucky to have survived after being shot by the kidnappers. The grief and sadness gripping young Straessle's parents had to be enormous. Even a chance attempt by the police or security forces to stop the payment of the ransom could result in the two victims getting killed. If the ransom was paid to the kidnappers, Straessle and Buff had a chance to get out alive.

I would regret the Swiss getting killed by kidnappers more than having the DAS and General Leyva mad at me for holding back information on them. I admired the General and hoped he would forgive me. But my best judgment told me to wait. I stayed silent about what I knew about the ransom being paid.

Tenorio suddenly stood up to say he had to make a telephone call. The DAS Agent with us followed suggesting he was going to check the premises to see if he could see anything of interest. I laughed when the DAS Agent moved in tune to the *cumbia*. Fortunately it was no *Tarantella*. I drank my beer and ordered three more. I asked the barmaid where the *baño* was and she pointed tiredly to the back with her chin.

"*Allá,*" she told me. The beer seemed to flow right through me. Getting old was tough, and Colombian beer was good but moved anyone to piss.

The rear of the establishment was crowded and smelly. Weaving through a conglomerate of noisy drinkers I heard someone call out in an angry hoarse voice.

"*Eh, culo apestoso.*" The words were equivalent to "smelly asshole." Someone suddenly struck me from behind with his fist. It was more than a tap and served to sober me up. I turned to face two Neanderthal-looking thugs, who stood menacingly, blocking my way.

One was a bio-negative dark lardy man and the other sized me up like a ferocious Doberman. I searched for Tenorio but could not see him anywhere. I realized this was trouble for me.

"*Quién eres tú?* (Who are you?)" the Philistine asked. His breath reeked with the stink of cheap liquor. The *cumbia* music seemed to grow louder because trouble was brewing. The thought occurred to me, what did the U.S. Government expect a guy like me to do in a case like this? The pair of cretins had singled me out probably because of the clothes

I wore. The rule was, you wear clothes that comport with the local environment. 'Experts' should not go to places where their clothes were known to be in bad taste, I thought jokingly.

Nevertheless, it angered me to be the victim of a pair of unknown drunks. The situation was growing critical because of my urgency to urinate. In desperation, my response came out in Mexican-American slang. **"*Porqué chingaos preguntan? Qué chingaos quieren?* (Why the fuck do you ask? What the fuck do you want?)"** Colombians would know that was not local vernacular.

My spontaneous response was in obscene *Chicano* slang and surprised the two thugs. Meanwhile, my anxious bladder told me an emergency existed and impulsively I held onto my crotch with one hand.

"Hijo e puta, eres policia?" the dark lardy one hissed. He called me a bad name and then asked if I was a cop. I thought of options. I had the DAS credentials on me but I did not respond to the question. My urge to urinate increased tremendously. My single priority was to reach the bathroom as soon as possible, I thought.

The philistine with a thick mustache and straight black hair glared at me and with a snarl moved his hand to his jacket pocket. With my adrenaline flowing out of control, my gun snapped out of the clamshell upside-down holster like an angry piece of steel, surprising the two thugs. But my bladder was about to explode. The thought occurred to me that I was in one hell of a crazy predicament.

"Quieren dormir con los gusanos, hijos-de-puta? (Do you two sons-of-bitches want to sleep with the worms?)"* I told the two men angrily. They shifted back and forth as I held my gun in my right hand and my other hand on my crotch. My mind played tricks on me.

I thought with jocularity that perhaps they might be more afraid of my 'dick' and my pissing on them than my gun. Where the hell was Tenorio, I wondered? I was about to shoot in desperation or ask the two thugs for a break so I could go urinate first. I would promise to come back, I kidded with myself.

In the brief pause that ensued, the *cumbia* music seemed to be an unusual match for the lively ambiance of violence developing. The philistine moved his hand to his pocket and it was unlikely he was reaching for his comb. At this point I realized that using my gun would mean I would have to leave the country. The publicity would be a scandal of sizable proportions.

The U.S. Embassy would do me a favor and send me home, probably in disgrace. I hadn't been much help anyway. My immediate concern was to end this problem so I could go pee.

Suddenly without warning, the head of one of the men was jerked back violently and a gun was pressed hard against his head. He squealed noisily.

"*Ésta bien, ésta bien!*" he said. His partner's face was smashed against the wall, splattering blood from his nose on my good coat. Tenorio and the other DAS Agent had arrived just in time. I had about 30 seconds to reach the bathroom and rushed desperately, my gun in one hand and my other hand holding onto my crotch. *Puta* music filled the place and no one paid much attention to the hostilities taking place between the two drunks and us. Tenorio and his partner pulled the two men toward the door while I charged for the bathroom, pushing people aside. With my gun in my hand, I was given top priority.

The inside of the men's room was suffocating, and the pungent smell of ammonia was powerful enough to choke off my breath. My time in the bathroom lasted an eternity and I cursed my penis for taking so long. After finishing, I holstered my gun and rushed out of the bathroom, desperately holding my breath. I had never experienced such a terrible smell and the people in the bar wondered what the devil was wrong with me. Bumping into walls and tables to escape the murderous stink, I reached the door and took a deep breath.

The fresh air felt marvelous, but Tenorio was nowhere around. I stepped outside and took another gulp of the fresh air. Low voices emanated from the darkness. Tenorio and his partner had the two *cretinos* on the ground and were interrogating them in a dark alley behind the bar. I heard Tenorio ask pointedly about *secuestros* (kidnappings) and heard him mention *Cariño* and *Suicidio,* two of the kidnapping suspects he had mentioned before. The two men on the ground were face down in the dirt and silent. But they cursed out loud when Tenorio kicked their asses. That was a hell of a way to investigate, I thought.

Surprisingly, a search of the men produced two .9 millimeter automatics.

"These two are real *matones* (killers)," Tenorio turned to tell me. One of them whimpered in pain when the DAS Agent stepped brutally on his hand.

"Is it *Cariño* and *Suicidio?*" I asked. Tenorio shook his head in silence.

General Leyva had told me that I might not like how some DAS Agents operated. In this case, this was a real war. I presumed Tenorio would arrest them. But the DAS Agent abruptly drew his weapon and placed it against the head of the fat man.

"*Habla, hijo-de-puta* (Talk, you son-of-a-bitch)," he ordered. Growing concerned, I stepped back. It was pretty certain the man would not admit to being a kidnapper. A threat to blow the man's brains out had to be a bluff, I thought. The threats and obscenities intensified as the DAS Agent pulling on the hair of the fat man demanded answers to questions. I grew anxious. My role as an advisor was now nebulous. I was in the position of being directly involved.

From a kneeling position, the DAS Agent pulled the hair of the individual, tilting his head at an angle.

"*Espera* (Wait)," I asked the agent. But seconds later, the hollow discharge of the .38 caliber revolver jolted me and left me with a tinny ring in my ears. Good grief, I thought, he shot him in the head. But that was impossible, the man was screaming like a banshee and holding onto both ears. The agent looked up.

"*Está marcado* (He's marked)," he said softly in Spanish.

The man held his right ear with both hands while blood spurted on the ground. His face contorted in pain and his cries of pain turned to a low moan. He was "marked" just as if he had been branded. The bastard was probably deaf too, I thought. The two *matones* were told to leave and hesitated. Tenorio screamed at them.

"*Qué esperan?* (What are you waiting for?)" They ran for their lives. I looked at Tenorio and he turned away nervously. He sensed that the incident created problems for me.

"*Vamos,*" he said abruptly. It was close to nine o'clock.

We drove to the Hotel *Aristi* in silence. Stopping at the entrance Tenorio stepped out of the car with me. He became angry when I told him I could not participate in that kind of *mierda*. His face twisted in frustration. I hoped he would not tell me to go screw myself. It was my business yet none of my business.

"*Mira* Saenz," he told me with clear resentment. "Those two would have been happy to kill you without hesitation, especially if they had found out you are an *Americano* advising the Colombian police on kidnappings." He paused to contain rising anger. "These two are very vicious hoodlums," he spat out angrily.

"These hyenas will not only kill you, they will torture and dehumanize you **before** they kill you." Tenorio was clearly agitated.

I recalled stories about *La Violencia* and the technique called "*La Corbata*" (The necktie) where the victim's throat is cut and the tongue is pulled outside the throat to make it resemble a necktie, and sex organs being cut off and stuffed in the mouth or anus.

"I just don't have the time to arrest them," he said. "We are after kidnappers." Tenorio was right.

"**No te preoccupes!** (Don't worry about it!)" I told him.

"Entiendo (I understand)," I told him. He grew sullen.

"Somos amigos verdad? (We're friends, right?)" I told him, putting my arm around his shoulder.

He nodded to tell me he would pick me up in the morning. There was a touch of sadness in his eyes. We were caught up in a deadly game that would throw anyone's emotions off balance.

I trusted Tenorio and he was my *amigo.* I recalled that Pope John XXIII once had said. **"See everything: Overlook a great deal: Improve a little."** In this case, I hoped Pope John was referring to me.

The events of the night before were sharp and vivid in my mind the following morning. I wondered why the kidnappers were like part of a scary movie. The fellow that lost a small part of his ear was called *Pesadilla* (Nightmare) and he was apparitional, with rough dark skin and angry fire in his eyes. Tenorio told me that he found it strange that some of the nastiest members of the cartel were homosexual.

"Maricones," he called them. They liked to frolic and get bawdy, he said. Nevertheless, they were damn tough and dangerous, he added with a trace of respect. Well, there are no secrets to success, I told him kiddingly.

Tenorio and two of his men picked me up at the hotel at ten o'clock in the morning. I had met earlier with the U.S. Consular Officer in Cali, John De Witt. His office was a block from the hotel. De Witt was about my age and provided help in identifying prominent people and personalities in Cali. I thought about how De Witt felt about his assignment in Cali and his own security. He lived and worked in a high profile job in Cali where Americans were targets for terrorists, kidnappers, and narco-traffickers in a city overloaded with potential danger. As a professional Foreign Service Officer, he rarely displayed concern about his safety.

But strange people had also worked in the Consular Office in Cali. I met one by the name of Charles Marquez, an American from Santa Fe, New Mexico, who claimed to have worked in the Consular Office in Cali.

In his campaign for the New Mexico State Legislature, Charles Marquez opted for free publicity when he tried to confirm in a local New Mexico tabloid the false allegations made by Roger Morris, Moscow trained and free lance reporter, in regards to torture in Colombia involving OPS Officers. Marquez alleged that he was assigned to the U.S. Consular office in Cali when OPS torture was taking place.

But Federal Judge Juan Burciaga concluded that Marquez had lied in a hearing held because of a libel suit filed by my friend Herb Hardin against Roger Morris. The opinion of the Judge was unequivocal.

"Marquez's statements were clearly not based on fact. They were misguided and made for the purpose of self-aggrandizement. Marquez did not have 'close liaison' with the American Embassy in Bogota as reported in the (Morris) article. Marquez had never seen or reviewed intelligence reports as reported in the article. Marquez was hardly an American diplomat, as reported in the article, but was merely a low-level employee of the United States Government."

I found out later that Marquez was investigated by the Office of the Inspector General of the U.S. Department of State for selling visas in Cali and forced to resign. That was the type of weird detractor willing to falsely accuse OPS Officers of involvement in torture in the Cold War. Morris merely exploited Marquez.

October 23, 1969

General Leyva, the Director of the DAS, was unusually calm on the telephone and measured his words carefully as we talked. "When are you coming back to Bogota?" he asked calmly.

"Mi General," I told him as coolly as possible, "I believe the ransom for the Swiss was paid in Cali." I heard an audible pause.

"Where did you get that information?" he demanded. I knew he would ask that question.

"From the U.S. Embassy," I told him in a quick lie. He would accept the answer because he knew CIA officers in the U.S. Embassy in Bogota. If he asked Dino Pionzio, the Station Chief, he would not know what to tell him. Luckily, the General did not probe further.

"I'm returning to Bogota today. If the Swiss are released, you need to talk to them as soon as possible," I suggested urgently. "They must be interrogated." General Leyva agreed without hesitation.

"Absolutamente," he said. "I'll have a DAS vehicle pick you up. You and I need to talk," he said.

"We have completed an analysis of all the kidnappings that have occurred in *Valle de Cauca* and I want you to see it." The General seemed glad about my return to Bogota.

Tenorio suggested that he go with me to Bogota to review the General's analysis, but I convinced him that it was important that he be available in Cali if the Swiss were released by the kidnappers unharmed.

"You must debrief them as soon as you can," I suggested. Tenorio stared at me in apprehension.

"What do you mean, **if** the Swiss are released?" He asked the question with a quizzical look on his face. He waited for me to answer.

"The ransom has been paid," I told him poignantly. "They will either release the Swiss or kill them." His reaction was understandable. He wondered how the hell I knew.

"Hijo-de-puta," he muttered softly, growing pensive. He did not ask any more questions.

The two Swiss "diplomats" were released that day in Buga, a small town northeast of Cali. The media went berserk with speculation. Young Werner Straessle and Herman Buff were unharmed, except in spirit. But their ordeal had been traumatizing. The Swiss Embassy immediately announced to the media in Bogota that the two men would travel to Switzerland as soon as possible, for their own safety. I knew if that happened, the DAS would not be able to question the victims.

It shocked me to learn that the Swiss Ambassador reported that no information whatsoever would be provided to the media or to the police about the kidnapping. The information that the Swiss had was vital to the DAS investigation.

Tenorio took me to the airport in Cali. I had grown to respect and understand him. I told him I'd be back as soon as possible.

"Cuidado (Be careful)," he told me.

"Tú tambien (You too)," I suggested.

The flight to Bogota was hot and crowded and I was lucky to get a seat. The General had told the driver from the DAS to have me proceed directly to the DAS Headquarters since my arrival in Bogota was at noon. But I decided to go to the Hotel *Tequendama* to shower and change clothes. There was little to report to the U.S. Embassy that had not been reported in the media. My concern was to get to the DAS. But there was no reason to hurry. The Cali kidnapping group had pulled off another *coup.*

October 24, 1969, 1400 Hours

The DAS Headquarters in Bogota was busy as reporters swarmed to gain access to the facility. At a press conference, General Leyva was hounded by the press about the release of the two Swiss diplomats in Buga. Calm and stoic, he responded to a myriad of questions. Later, we met with Dr. Leon to talk about the Swiss kidnapping case. Gordillo was frustrated because he had learned about the release of the Swiss from the media. But more importantly, he could not get access to the victims.

"The Swiss Embassy refuses to talk to us," General Leyva said angrily. "They refuse to cooperate!" He seemed more agitated than usual. An interview with the Swiss was extremely important. I suggested that without information on the Swiss kidnapping, the DAS would continue to be frustrated in resolving any of the kidnapping cases. The General and Dr. Leon nodded with an anxious look. Dr. Leon told me that some suspects had been identified and DAS personnel were searching for them in Cali. One was Sabas Calderon Castro, AKA *El Negro.*

I was informed that an analysis of other kidnappings and some leads on the investigation of the Straessle and Buff kidnapping case had been developed. The airports and exit routes from Colombia were under close surveillance. The vehicle of a previous kidnap victim was found at a parking lot with the acronym GAR in Bogota, and another was found at *El Dorado* Airport. DAS Agents were trying to determine who abandoned the cars. That should have been done sooner, I told myself.

"It is imperative that the Swiss be interviewed," I insisted, to the chagrin of the General. My intransigence had become a bad habit. General Leyva shook his head.

"The Swiss Ambassador is adamant," he said, distress visible in his face. "They will **not** talk to us."

The Swiss Embassy claimed diplomatic immunity and there was little anyone could do under the circumstances. I felt like an asshole. But it was the politics of kidnappings in Colombia.

The analysis of the kidnapping cases and profiling completed by Dr. Leon and other DAS personnel provided strong indicators that a single organized group was responsible for the kidnappings. Leads developed included a suspect with a badly injured arm, a subject with an eye infection, and an ex-army sergeant.

I probed the CIA Station and the FBI *Legat* Stotts for any information they had on the Swiss kidnapping. Only what they read in the local newspapers, they told me.

At the U.S. Embassy, the pretty, dark-eyed receptionist tempted me with flirtatiousness. It seemed certain she knew why I was a frequent visitor to the Chancery. After several meetings with the Political Section, Lubinsky, the Military *Attachés,* and the CIA Station Chief, Dino Pionzio, I decided there was no other recourse but to talk to the U.S. Ambassador to see if he would talk to the Swiss Ambassador. Help was needed at the highest level of the U.S. Embassy to get the Swiss to cooperate.

I had already suggested to General Leyva that he seek help from the President of Colombia, Carlos Restrepo, to convince the Swiss Ambassador to let DAS Agents talk to Straessle and Buff.

"Ask President Restrepo to stop the Swiss from leaving the country," I told him facetiously. "He can do it in the interests of national security." The General smiled, deep in thought. The politics were frustrating.

U.S. Ambassador Jack Vaughn and Robert Stevenson, the Deputy Chief of Mission, were wary about my proposal but they listened carefully as I explained the grave need to convince the Swiss Ambassador to cooperate with the police. DAS Agents needed to talk to Straessle and Buff to get information from them.

"This can be done clandestinely," I suggested. "If it becomes impossible to convince the Swiss Ambassador to let DAS Agents interview Straessle and Buff, perhaps he can be convinced to let me talk to them. Kamer and Lubinsky can meet with me and Straessle and Buff." I pleaded with Vaughn to intervene.

"A request from the U.S. Ambassador to the Swiss Ambassador might work," I insisted. "Without cooperation, the kidnapping problem in Colombia will never end." The Ambassador promised to try.

Later, I found solace at the bar of the Hotel *Tequendama,* drinking Scotch and meditating my bad fortune. But if the security forces had stopped the ransom payment, the Swiss would have been killed. It was a Catch-22. There was nothing easy about the situation.

Roy Driggers had invited me to a reception at his residence that evening and I decided to attend. It would be a welcome reprieve. Kidnapping was one of the most difficult mazes any investigator could experience. There were too many elements in the situation beyond reach and out of control. As an advisor I was frustrated.

Marvin Weisman, the local AID Director, queried me at the Driggers reception about the current Cali kidnapping fiasco and I grew angry. With more than a few drinks under his belt, he took the opportunity to criticize the OPS program. OPS was of no value to the economic progress of Colombia and had no business in the Cold War, he told me. My presence in Colombia was of political value to the Ambassador, he suggested, but had no value in apprehending kidnappers.

"No offense to you," he said. "No one is going to stop the political change needed in these countries." We were back to that crap, I mused, the liberal left-wing point of view. If his fat ass were kidnapped, Weisman would think differently about the OPS, I philosophized humorously with Driggers. I realized this could be arranged.

The politics of the Cold War was demoralizing. Many Americans resisted anti-communist initiatives and supported communist causes. I had trouble determining the reason for that.

October 27, 1969

Ambassador Jack Vaughn was upbeat when he talked to me on the telephone. He had talked to the Swiss Ambassador that same day and had news for me. He suggested that we needed to talk as soon as possible. I rushed over to the Embassy. Ambassador Vaughn and Bob Stevenson, the DCM, waited for me.

"We have convinced the Swiss Ambassador to meet with you this afternoon," he told me immediately. "Bob Stevenson will go with you to the meeting," he said. I wondered if Stevenson was CIA? What did he know about kidnappings? I was surprised but puzzled by that move. Perhaps it was a question of protocol.

"Will Straessle and Buff be there?" I asked Ambassador Vaughn. He replied that the meeting would be with the Swiss Ambassador. That upset me. The meeting would be a half-assed effort and an obstruction of justice, except in the obtuse world of diplomacy. I felt discontented about the situation. Americans needed *cojones* to fight the Cold War. Small wonder we were getting our ass whipped in Vietnam. In most cases we were obliged to operate under rules of engagement and constraints imposed by American friends of the communists.

"I don't need to talk to the Swiss Ambassador," I told the American Ambassador. "We need to talk to the guys who were kidnapped!" I grew angry and informal. The Ambassador stared at me with droopy eyes.

"That's the best we can do," he told me. "The Swiss Ambassador refuses to do anything else." He drew back in his chair in silence. I could hear my heart beating hard and I controlled my temper.

That afternoon Bob Stevenson and I met with the Swiss Ambassador. At the Swiss Embassy, the Ambassador was alone and made every effort to be gracious. I was not enthusiastic about talking to anyone but the victims of the Cali kidnapping group.

The Swiss Ambassador explained that he had debriefed Straessle and Buff and had obtained information that he thought might be useful. The two victims were traumatized by their ordeal and under medical care, he said. But he had interesting information on the kidnapping, he suggested. Stevenson stayed silent and let me do the talking. It was only fair. He knew nothing about kidnapping investigations, but he supported my efforts.

I initially took notes while the Swiss Ambassador talked, but that appeared to make him nervous. Presumably if the notes fell into the wrong hands, the kidnappers might retaliate against the Swiss Embassy. I put my notepad aside. I would jot down only the most important details such as times, names, and other items.

The Swiss Ambassador was cool and collected. He provided information on how the kidnapping occurred and a description of the kidnappers, the place where the two victims were held, and what Straessle and Buff recalled about their abduction.

The session had lasted over an hour and the Ambassador answered every question in detail. The more we talked, the more comfortable and helpful he became. It occurred to me that he was a pretty smart man. The information he provided was invaluable. The Swiss Ambassador had made the big difference in the kidnapping problem in Colombia, and Stevenson and I departed the Embassy on a cheerful note. We had good information.

The Swiss Ambassador was rightly relieved that Straessle and Buff were safe. They were on their way to their homeland. But the Swiss Ambassador did not know how close Lupin and Cuestas had come to losing the ransom to the security forces. I did not tell him.

I requested an interview with Lupin and Cuestas, the two men who delivered the ransom to the kidnappers, and the Swiss Ambassador agreed for me to do this. This would be done very discreetly.

November 2, 1969

For several hours I analyzed the information obtained from the Swiss Ambassador and from Lupin and Cuestas. I used maps and an overlay to reconstruct the events and it became astonishing to see how simple it was to pinpoint the hideout where Straessle and Buff had been held. There was no doubt in my mind that I had located the kidnapper's hideout.

In his office at the DAS, General Leyva's dark eyes widened considerably when I told him I knew where the hideout of the kidnappers was. He rubbed his head vigorously, apparently to stave off nervousness. As I explained the information obtained from the Swiss Ambassador in detail, item by item, he grew excited. I explained that the only option we had was for me to meet with the Swiss Ambassador in secrecy because he refused to meet with anyone else. He said he understood.

"But I know where Straessle and Buff were held," I told the surprised General. "I believe this is the same hideout used to hold the other victims." Dr. Leon joined us and they both listened in rapt attention.

"The same modus operandi and the same hideout were used in many other kidnappings besides the Swiss kidnapping, *mi General,*" I told him. "The kidnappers wore military or police uniforms, rubbed Mentholatum on the victim's eyes, etc. etc." I pointed at locations on a map on the table.

"When the Swiss were kidnapped at the *Callejón de la Chuchas*, they were transported in a military ambulance by men in military uniform." The General nodded wearily. "The Swiss calculated that the ambulance traveled approximately one hour and thirty minutes on a paved road after they were abducted at the *Callejón de Las Chucas*. Before they arrived at their destination, the kidnapper's vehicle turned left on a dirt road and traveled about fifteen minutes." Both men stared at me. General Leyva suspected I was on the hunt with a fervor he had not seen before.

"Their destination was a farmhouse that had plenty of people and chickens." A chicken farm, I explained. The General grew momentarily amused.

"Muchos huevos," he kidded in a deadpan.

"Por cierto," I said. This was our chance to break some of their *huevos*, I told him jokingly.

"After the ransom was paid, the Swiss were blindfolded and taken in a truck to Buga and released. When the truck left the farm where the two men were held, they distinctly recalled that it turned left on a dirt road. The Swiss Ambassador reported that Straessle and Buff were certain that it took only about fifteen minutes to reach the point where they were turned loose in Buga." I was absolutely certain we had uncovered the lair of the kidnappers.

"The Swiss heard a jet airplane fly overhead every evening and a train whistle during the morning and evening. I have plotted this information on the overlay." Gordillo quietly joined us.

"Straessle and Buff were kept in a hole in the ground during the entire period of captivity. We have heard descriptions from other victims about the same type of accommodations." I lit a cigarette and offered one to the others. Everyone lit up. The case was a puzzle and we had to put it together.

"Mi General, this overlay shows the location of the hideout used by the kidnappers." I pointed to a map of the Department of *Valle del Cauca* and placed the overlay over it.

"Beginning with the point after Straessle and Buff were kidnapped in *Callejón de Las Chucas* (Corridor of the Dog Bitches), the kidnappers used a military ambulance to transport them. The ambulance traveled for approximately an hour and a half on a paved road. The Swiss estimated the speed of the Ambulance at about sixty-five to seventy kilometers per hour." I divided 70 by 1.6.

"That's about forty-four miles per hour." That means the kidnappers could travel approximately ninety-five to one hundred kilometers in one hour and a half. That's about sixty-six miles of distance if they traveled at that speed." General Leyva and Dr. Leon listened with what I surmised was a bored look.

"Me entienden?" I asked harshly.

"Si, si," they responded urgently. I'm not all that boring, I thought humorously.

"You follow what I'm saying?" I asked again in Spanish.

"Yes, yes," they replied in English, prompting me to laugh. The General seemed to visualize other problems while I did the math.

"If we draw a circle using the scale for distance printed on the map, we can determine how far they could have traveled in any given direction. But we know it was a **paved** road." I explained.

"Now, using the point where the Swiss were kidnapped, the *Callejón de Las Chuchas,* we draw a circle." I drew a circle on the map with a red pen. "Call that Circle A," I suggested.

"Using Buga, where the Swiss were released as the center point, we mark the distance the kidnappers could have traveled at the speed and time reported by the victims. That's about fifteen kilometers in any direction from Buga," I explained.

"We know that was a dirt road." I took the red pen and drew another circle on the map.

"Call this Circle B." I hit the map on the table hard with the pen.

"Here, *mi General.* Where the circles overlap, that's where the cartel's hideout is." I felt energized. Thanks to the Swiss, we finally had something concrete.

"Muy bien, muy bien," the General told me with a trace of anticipation.

"Muy impressionante." He glanced at Dr. Leon. "We need to organize a raid." Dr. Leon stared at the General with a cryptic look.

"Don't forget Villareal," he said stonily. They were talking about the Commandant of the National Police force in Cali. Where in the hell does Colonel Villareal fit into the picture, I wondered?

"Mi General, look at the map overlay." I pointed at a line on the map.

"See that line, that's the Avianca flight from Cali to Bogota. (I had checked the flights earlier.) The Swiss described a plane flying overhead every afternoon. Look where it passes. It passes right over the spot where the circles overlap." The General was in deep thought. His brain was processing the information.

"The hideout is right here," I said pointing firmly at a site called *Guacari.*

"Mi General, we've got to move fast," I suggested enthusiastically. He nodded slowly, gazing at me.

"Muy interesante," he stroked his bald head thoughtfully. He paused and stared at me with a pleading look.

"I want you to reach deep into your heart and mind," he told me with a quizzical glance. "The DAS, under my command, is going to ask you as our advisor to take this information to Colonel Villareal, the Commandant of the National Police in Cali." He seemed to be asking for understanding, but I could not understand what or why. My temper began to flare. What is he talking about? I thought.

I did not understand why the General was hedging, but he was my trusted friend. He was trying to tell me something that for them was academic. He was asking me to accept the shadowy realm and perfidiousness of local politics, the hidden interests, concerns and agendas.

"I ask you as a loyal friend," he said with a touch of remorse. "Meet with Colonel Villareal and give him the complete details that you just explained to us." General Leyva lit a cigarette and gave me one of his strong Colombian ones. I felt obliged to light up.

"Tell him that if he does not act on the important information you have provided him, that you will inform General Bernardo Sanchez and myself of the situation." He winked at me with a knowing smile. If I could not trust General Leyva, then there was not one single person in Colombia to be trusted.

"But you must let me know what transpires as soon as possible, Dolph. *Por favor,* bear with me," he said. I was obliged to do it.

November 3, 1969

Tenorio picked me up at the airport in Cali and took me directly to the National Police *Quartel.* He was anxious to know what was going on. I explained briefly and he grew quiet. Men in forest green police uniforms guarded the entrance. An officer in the *Guardia* recognized me and escorted us to the office of the Commandant. Tenorio surprised me when he insisted I talk with Colonel Villareal alone.

The Colonel was formal and standoffish initially, but soon became more at ease as I briefed him on my findings. With glassy eyes he stared at me. The Colonel listened attentively while I explained my analysis and hypothesis in regards to the location of the kidnapper's hideout by using a large map on the wall of his office. I finished my explanation and pointed to a spot on the map.

"Éste es el escondite (This is where the hideout is)," I told him pointedly. There was no doubt in my mind.

"*Mi Coronel,*" I continued. "The Swiss heard a helicopter flying near them on the last few days of their captivity. I checked with the military units in *Valle del Cauca.* It was confirmed that military personnel under General Bernardo Sanchez were flying a helicopter in the area in the week when the Swiss were released." I explained the daily Avianca flight described by the Swiss. The Colonel sat at his desk, his face growing stiff and weary.

"It's a nice theory," he said, "but that area has been searched and nothing was found." He slapped the desk with the palm of his hand. "It's also loaded with farmhouses," he pointed out.

"Which farmhouse are we talking about?" he said. I recalled what General Leyva told me. The Colonel was not going to move on the information I provided to him. It was hard to understand, but it was intriguing.

Suspicion swelled inside of me but I could not afford to lose control of my temper. Sitting close to the Colonel, I looked directly into his black wary eyes.

"*Mi Coronel,* you will have only a small area and a few farmhouses to check. You will not be disappointed. I assure you that you will look good if you take action. Believe me, it will be worth your while." He remained silent and stared at me.

"If you do not take any action within the next twenty-four hours, *mi Coronel,* I will provide General Bernardo Sanchez and General Leyva with the same information you just received. They will also be advised that you did not take any action on the information I personally provided to you," I suggested with a smile that was friendly and low-key. The Colonel looked up at me sharply.

"Leave that overlay with me," he said sullenly. "I need to study it."

I grinned impulsively. The colonel seemed agreeable. He suggested that the National Police would plan a sweep and search the area we had pinpointed. Colonel Villareal continued to look at me with a brooding look.

"*Gracias,* Saenz," he told me and shook my hand. The key players puzzled me. But I would never learn the reason for the cryptic chess moves.

November 4, 1996

I was elated. The news spread fast and the event was an exciting development in local police circles. General Leyva had a perpetual smile on his face. The National Police F-2, searching near a small village called

Guacari, based precisely on my analysis, found the farmhouse described by the Swiss. The farmhouse called *El Eden* was about twenty-three kilometers from Buga.

The National Police engaged the kidnappers in a firefight, but the members of the cartel at the hideout surrendered. (I presumed that resistance was expected.) Special units of the National Police were involved.

On a visit to the farmhouse, it was not hard for me to visualize what the kidnapped victims must have endured. The hole in the ground where the victims were held was as inhumane as they described. Bicycle tire tubes provided a limited amount of fresh air for the victims who were confined in a small dungeon buried in the ground. A search of the farmhouse by the National Police produced weapons of all types, various military and police uniforms, apparel used by priests and nuns, maps, addresses, and telephone numbers. An interesting item found was medication for an eye infection. Tamayo had an eye infection.

A large array of communist literature and books found in a small bookcase at the hideout included *Mao Tse Tung, With the Vietcong Guerrillas, Manual for Marxism-Leninism, Havana Declaration,* and others. Were the communists involved in the kidnapping gang just a few *aficionados* (enthusiasts)?

November 5, 1969

Information developed after the raid on the hideout of the kidnapping cartel grew enticing. The exchange of data between DAS Agents and National Police officers could have been better, but cooperation and coordination improved with the excitement of resolving the kidnapping cases. After the arrests made at *El Eden,* other arrests followed that were histrionic and fun.

We watched from a structure near a middle-class residence in Cali where National Police officers took tactical positions inside and outside. The residence belonged to Elias Vega Arango, a kidnapper. Two individuals and a maid had been arrested in the house earlier. In the residence, the police set up what we called a *Ratonera* (Rattrap). A single light remained inside the house, providing minimal illumination. Police personnel waited in the semidarkness with their weapons at the ready.

At approximately nine-thirty that night, two cars drove up quietly. A group of happy men and women stepped out of the vehicles, heading noisily for the house. No one in the group was aware that inside the house were uninvited guests. One of the individuals paused to open the door to the house with a key. The celebrants entered the house carrying bags with bottles of liquor and scrumptious things to eat.

But the man in front of the group, a skinny squinty-eyed man with a crew cut, stopped at the doorway, his eyes darting in alarm as the group entered.

"Un momento," he said. *"Por que esta tan oscuro?* (Why is it so dark?)"* Quickly, a National Police Major stepped out of the shadows to provide a sardonic greeting.

"Bien Venidos, señores y señoras," he announced in a loud voice. *"Quedan todos detenidos."* (Welcome ladies and gentlemen. You are all under arrest.)" The man with the crewcut went for his gun but stopped when dozens of police officers appeared from the darkness to fill the room. Police personnel disarmed the group and weapons clanged noisily on the tile floor.

Luis Fernando Tamayo Garcia, the trained communist terrorist and a top leader of the kidnapping cartel, was caught in a rattrap. After all, he was a rat. With the whites of his eyes bright red from an infection, he blinked rapidly, obviously dismayed by the situation.

Once identified, he grew quiet and despondent about getting caught in such a stupid manner. In a low stiff voice, he asked to speak to the National Police Major in charge of the operation. With utmost discretion, he hissed in a low whisper to the young Major to let him know that he had a proposition for him. The officer listened in silence. Tamayo offered to give him a large sum of money if he would let him go. The young National Police Major nodded, and asked Tamayo for the money.

"First, if you accept my offer, you must give me your word as a gentleman that you will not arrest me," Tamayo insisted. He trusted no one and especially police officers.

"Tienes mi palabra, como caballero (You have my word, as a gentleman),"* the Major told him. Tamayo led the National Police Officer to a large plant and pointed at it.

"Hay está." The Major pulled the large plant out of the pot and saw one hundred and sixteen thousand (116,000) Colombia *pesos* stacked at the bottom. He grew momentarily silent, then called out loudly, *"Teniente, recoja el dinero!* (Lieutenant, come get this money!)"

A young officer approached, surprised to see so much money. Carefully he packed the money in a bag.

"Y nuestro trato? (What about our deal?)" Tamayo asked the Major anxiously.

"No hay trato! (No deal!)" the Major told him in a low voice. "As a National Police officer, I momentarily forgot the deal was illegal. For that part, I am sorry. But I am a gentleman."

"Hijo de Puta!" Tamayo exclaimed with fury in his eyes. **"Eres caballero hijo de puta!** (You are a gentleman all right, you son-of-a-bitch!)" he screamed.

"Un caballero hijo de puta! (A gentleman son of a whore!)" Tamayo continued to shriek. The Major stared tersely at Tamayo.

Jose Sabas Calderon Castro

**Top Members
of the Cali
Kidnapping
Cartel
"Los Invisibles"**

Luis Fernando Tamayo Garcia

Ricaurte Solarte Gomez

Hubo Beniecio Canabal

Isidro Bahas Vega

Hugo Leon Quijano Yacup

Actual overlay used to find the hideout of the Cali kidnapping cartel

21

Ley de Fuga

The arrest of the kidnappers of Straessle and Buff made front-page news in Bogota. The Americans at the United States Embassy were surprised by developments in the kidnapping crisis, and gossip resurfaced about FBI assistance on the problem. The folks at the U.S. Embassy were intrigued. Frankly, so was I.

The Cali Kidnapping Cartel had collected over two million dollars in ransoms within a period of about eighteen months. The drug cartels would later make 50 times that amount of money in a year. Nevertheless, the kidnapping organization had been a horrifying but successful enterprise. The pay or die policy of the kidnappers terrified the victims and stymied any cooperation with the police. For that reason, the kidnapping cartel's credibility was important. Death was a certainty for the victims if the government security forces intervened. The kidnappers used terrorist tactics to ply their deadly trade and abductions were carried out with precise planning, efficiency and surprise. Secrecy and their willingness to kill were their main weapons.

When the kidnappers' hideout was found, vital information on the members of the organization was uncovered and, based on their investigation, the DAS and the National Police were able to identify over thirty members of the Cali Kidnapping Cartel. It was determined that the kidnapping organization operated with a Board of Directors (upper level managers), mid level supervisors, and a lower echelon of operational personnel. The combination of terrorists, killers, and enterprising thinkers made it a deadly business.

Names, pseudonyms, addresses, and telephone numbers found at the kidnappers' hideout permitted an unraveling of the organization. Apprehensions made by the police at the hideout called *El Eden* included police officers, known criminals, left-wing ideologues and several women. Many met their death when they resisted arrest or tried to escape from the security forces.

One of the first cartel members to die was Gerardo Antonio Montoya Herrera. The man had broken free from police officers that were holding him. He ran wildly into the street and was killed when he was mangled under the wheels of a speeding bus. The left wing alleged that the police had pushed Montoya into the path of the speeding bus.

A few days later, Colombian authorities summarily shot and killed two other cartel members, Argemiro Perez Castrillon and Juan Diego, when they resisted arrest. DAS attorneys assured me the killings were justified under Colombian law and the State of Siege decreed in *Valle del Cauca*. Under Colombian law, the **Ley de Fuga** (The Law of Escape) provided the Colombian police the authority to shoot any individual trying to escape from their custody. Kidnapping was a misdemeanor in terms of Colombian law, but trying to escape from the custody of the police was a more serious crime.

The police action was legal and met the standard set by Senator William Fulbright for U.S. involvement in the war in Vietnam.

The kidnappers were considered *bona fide* killers but in accordance with the constitution of Colombia they were entitled to due process. Nevertheless, gunfights between the kidnappers trying to avoid arrest and the security forces became frequent. The situation had become a war. General Leyva surprised me by telling me not to worry about getting operational. Besides, he did not want me to get bored, he told me jokingly.

"*Vamos*, I want you to meet with two very interesting characters. You know about them. They are Sabas Calderon Castro and Luis Fernando Tamayo Garcia, two of the top leaders of the kidnapping cartel." I told him that it would be a pleasure to meet the two most dangerous men of the kidnapping organization.

"But they may not like me," I kidded. Smiling, he nodded.

"We don't like them either," he chuckled. "You know Tamayo Garcia, the communist. And you know he was the one who collected the ransom for the Swiss." He smiled pensively.

"Seeing them up close and talking to them will give you a pretty good idea of the type of deadly character we were up against. Tamayo and Sabas are very interesting and unique people. They are presently undergoing interrogation. It is extremely frustrating for us because they are absolutely vicious and refuse to talk. These *tipos* are real *matones* that not only kill, they eat people," he said jokingly.

"*Gracias, mi General,* I wondered what those killers ate," I told him in jest. We stopped at a closed door, and he suggested that it was not a good idea to let the two kidnappers see my face.

"We don't want them to know who you are," he said. He handed me a black hood similar to a ski mask and gestured for me to put it over my head. The hood had holes cut out for my eyes.

"It fits fine and you look nice," he told me with a grin. My appearance would attract attention. I looked like a terrorist or an executioner. Well, I would be in good company with the kidnappers in terms of my appearance.

General Leyva was certain the two kidnappers would recognize me as a foreigner and possibly as an *Americano* if they saw my face. I did not argue. Speculation about U.S. involvement in the kidnapping investigation had surfaced briefly in the media. Possible retaliation by the kidnappers against the U.S. Embassy or Americans in Colombia continued to be of concern.

General Leyva led me to a room and stopped at the door. Two DAS Agents stood guard.

"Sabas Calderon Castro was wearing a nice Rolex watch when he was arrested," he told me with a tired look on his face.

"I can't afford a Rolex watch," he said with a chuckle. We entered a semidarkened room crowded with people and the black hood over my head felt hot and uncomfortable.

Tamayo and Sabas were in a corner of the room, their hands tightly handcuffed behind their backs. They stared at us with menacing eyes when they saw us enter. Sabas had on a tight-fitting shirt that showed a packed muscular frame and a bull neck. Short and stocky, with one eye that drooped malevolently, he looked sternly at my hood.

Tamayo sized us up in silence. The infection in his eyes made them flare like infrared buttons. Tamayo was aloof, sullen, while Sabas was calm and talkative. He greeted us cheerfully.

"*Buenas noches,*" he said and stood up with a grin on his round face when we approached him.

"Sabas," Inspector Gordillo was asking questions in a calm low voice.

"*Quién cobro el rescate?* (Who collected the ransom?)" Sabas shifted his large frame in obvious disgust.

"Not me," he responded angrily in Spanish. "I don't understand why you keep asking **me** that question." His voice remained calm but indignant.

"I did not collect any ransom. I have no money."

"We know Tamayo collected the ransom for the Swiss," Inspector Gordillo told him.

"*Yo no se mierda!* (I don't know shit!)" Sabas answered curtly. Gordillo got close to his face.

"Are you the *Jefe* of the kidnapping cartel?" Sabas scowled fiercely and shook his head.

"*Quién es el Jefe?*" Gordillo asked. He asked Sabas to tell him who the 'Boss' of the Cartel was. Sabas stayed silent and stared at the hood on my head inquisitively.

"*Coño, por que diablos me preguntan a mi?* (Why in hell do you ask me those questions?)" He smiled mischievously and repeated his position.

"*Yo no se mierda!* (I don't know shit!)" With a solicitous voice he asked Gordillo to give him a cigarette and his request was denied. He shrugged and muttered an obscenity. General Leyva gestured that I follow him.

"Sabas," the General said, priming his question in an amicable manner. "Who kidnapped the Swiss?" The man called *El Negro* exhaled a loud sigh and frowned like a dark angry cherub. He almost seemed to be enjoying the interrogation.

"*No sé,*" he responded with a grin, and shrugged gorilla shoulders.

"Who do you think kidnapped Straessle and Buff; Dr. Rebeiz, Baron; Gonzales Caicedo, and all those other gentlemen?" The General was polite and non-intimidating.

Sabas stared at the wall and abruptly broke into a broad grin. His eyes suddenly brightened.

"*No sé. Parece que los tipos son de Marté* (It looks as if those guys are from Mars)," he suggested sarcastically. He had a definitive twinkle in his eyes.

"*Tal vez son Marcianos. Tal vez son invisibles* (Maybe they're Martians. Maybe they're invisible)," he chuckled. A sneer formed on his dark chubby face.

"*Sí, parecen invisibles* (They seem to be invisible)," he answered with a sardonic grin. General Leyva glanced sideways at me.

"*Los invisibles,* eh," he said.

"*Qué les parese?* (What do you think of that?)" he said with a smile. His eyes told me that the kidnapping cartel had been baptized. The Invisibles Ones *(Los Invisibles)* was a name that seemed appropriate for the Cartel. But *Los Invisibles* were undergoing their last rites. Sabas stood with an arrogant grin on his face, then grew sullen.

"*Los Invisibles,*" the General repeated thoughtfully. "*Gracias,* Sabas," he told the kidnapper and nodded imperceptibly at DAS Agents in the room. Sabas was led to a door and he stopped momentarily to stare at us in bewilderment and fear. A DAS Agent yanked him outside.

The General immediately turned his attention to Tamayo, sulking in a corner, his red infected eyes looking fierce. He refused to respond to any question and glared at Inspector Gordillo and General Leyva. He finally responded with a taciturn *"no sé"* (I don't know) to every question. He stared at me with a threat of death in his angry bloodshot eyes.

"Quién es el tipo con la capucha? (Who is the guy with the hood?) Why is he afraid to show his face?" he snarled. He kept staring at my hood.

"Don't worry about him," the General replied harshly. "He knows all about you." Tamayo smirked.

"Then who the hell is he?" he asked in Spanish. Tamayo seemed intrigued with my presence.

"Oh, one of the Swiss, eh?" he countered angrily, ferret eyes narrowing. "Or is it somebody who thinks I was involved in **his** kidnapping?" He examined my eyes and peered intently through the holes on the hood over my head. I kept silent.

"I'd like to know who he is," Tamayo muttered menacingly. *"Parece buen tipo* (He seems like a nice guy)."

I smiled under the hood. The bastard had a sense of humor.

General Leyva continued talking to Tamayo and the noise of machine gun fire suddenly erupted outside the building catching me completely off guard. The gunshots exploded noisily in a loud tandem and Tamayo stepped back with panic in his eyes. Instinctively I went for my gun but General Leyva stopped me.

"No té preoccupes (It's okay)," General Leyva told me quickly.

"Trust me, everything is under control," he whispered in Spanish. I held back from asking questions in front of Tamayo but my curiosity was overwhelming. At least twenty rounds were fired. I wondered if Sabas had been killed.

Minutes later, the door opened and Sabas Calderon Castro was ushered brusquely into the room by DAS Agents. His face was pale and his eyes darted desperately around the room. Breathing hard, he was bathed in sweat. He stared at me as if I was the executioner with the hood on my head.

"Everything is okay!" General Leyva told me in Spanish. He signaled for me to follow him to another room where I removed my hood.

"Qué diablos paso, mi General?" I asked worriedly. He grinned at my expressive Spanish vocabulary.

"Don't worry. Nothing happened. The agents were just trying to scare Sabas in order to get him to talk." He walked calmly to a table set up with cups and saucers and served both of us a cup of black coffee. He offered me a cigarette and lit one himself.

"It's over," he said. "There is nothing we can do now. The agents were already angry and got a little carried away." He placidly blew cigarette smoke into the air.

"We have to supervise the agents more closely," he said. "Some of them tend to get carried away," he said. But it was a tough battle; the *Invisibles* were cold-blooded killers, unlike any I had seen.

"*Sabas es un hombre es muy fuerte* (The man is very tough)," General Leyva told me in a mixture of English and Spanish. "We found a gun on Sabas when he was arrested. We discovered he used that gun to kill Edgar Montenegro, a former DAS Agent." I was surprised to hear about Montenegro. He was one of my students at the Inter-American Police Academy at Ft. Davis.

In bits and pieces I learned what had happened to Sabas outside the building. The DAS Agents had told Sabas he was free to go, placed him on a small mound, and gave him a head start.

"*El cabrón de Sabas no es pendejo* (The bastard is too smart to fall for something like that)," one of the agents explained.

I visualized what had happened. Given the opportunity to escape Sabas knew that under the **Ley de Fuga,** the DAS Agents were within the law to shoot his fat ass. He stubbornly refused to run and resisted the insulting exhortations of police personnel who encouraged him to escape. Sabas heard metal slam against metal to drive rounds of ammunition into gun chambers while police personnel taunted him.

"*Corre Sabas, corre cabrón.*" He refused to move one inch. The dust and debris flew furiously as machine gun bursts exploded at Saba's feet. He jumped occasionally to perform an *entrechat.* Police personnel told Sabas that he was a *"gallina"* (chicken).

I was told Sabas stared upwards as if in a daze. Machine gun fire does that to a man, I mused. Sabas was crapping in his shorts, I thought. But he not only looked tough, he was tough.

Sabas was very smart not to run. Ironically, in less than two months, his smarts as well as his luck ran out. While Sabas waited trial, Lauren Menses Gabon, his attorney had filed a motion before the Colombian Courts that his client be incarcerated at the *Cárcel de Villanueva,* the prison facility specified by the law in such cases. The court granted Sabas's petition.

On February 8, 1970, Sabas Calderon Castro, one of the most dangerous leaders of *Los Invisibles,* was shot and killed. At a street called *Calle 34,* near *Carrera 25,* in Cali, he reportedly made an attempt to escape the custody of military personnel. Military authorities explained that a group of armed men had attacked the unit transporting Sabas Calderon Castro to the *Cárcel de Villanueva*. Sabas had tried to escape and was shot to death by security force personnel. Sabas' attorney protested vehemently in the media that the **Ley de Fuga** had been applied to his client. The court determined that the action taken by the security forces was legal and justified.

The Colombian Government in an agreement with the judicial system decided that a military tribunal would be used to try eight of the thirty men and women identified as members of the Cali kidnapping cartel. Military justice was known to be a stricter venue than the civil criminal justice system in Colombia. Not surprisingly, communist attorneys took up the defense of the cartel members that were to be tried by the Colombian military tribunals.

In the end, the top leaders of the cartel were identified as Sabas Calderon Castro, Luis Fernando Tamayo, Santa Cruz Londoño, Juan Fernandez Dominguez, Gonzalo Cordova Satizabal, and Gilberto Rodriguez Orejuela. All were eventually apprehended, including Celedonia Rodriguez de Calderon, Sabas' wife.

Juan Ramon Rizo was also captured. He was one of the original masterminds in the kidnapping of Carlos Eduardo Varon and had been expelled from *Los Invisibles* after a spat with Sabas Calderon. With all of the leadership of *Los Invisibles* seemingly apprehended by the security forces, the kidnapping cartel was crushed.

DAS Agents assigned to follow up on leads and to apprehend the remaining members of the cartel performed with valor and effectiveness. My friend Cesar Tenorio became a *valeroso colega* (valuable colleague) and I kidded him about being a veritable 'Rambo.'

Tenorio had engaged the kidnappers in gunfights with uncommon valor and had killed several. He warned me that information obtained from one of the cartel members indicated that *Los Invisibles* had been planning to kidnap an American. The American was unidentified but the ransom was to be one million dollars. He laughed when I told him, "I've got fifty bucks." But the members of *Los Invisibles* still on the loose were heavily armed with Madsen rifles and automatic weapons, making confrontations with the police extremely dangerous. Firefights had become common and almost inevitable. Several kidnapping suspects had escaped capture using tremendous firepower against the DAS Agents killing several.

Because of the firefights, Tenorio asked me to get him a .357 magnum from the United States. He was worried about his firepower, he said. I promised to do that as soon as possible.

Meanwhile, as the local *Gringo* expert, I was *persona grata* with DAS Agents and was accepted as one of them. I was part of the DAS anti-kidnapping team. I felt privileged as an American to work with the security forces of Colombia in eliminating one of the deadliest kidnapping groups in the world. Under the circumstances, my feeling of pride was esoteric, confined to my colleagues. My difficult mission to Colombia had been successfully accomplished and I looked forward to telling my grandkids about it some day.

The progress made on the investigation of the kidnapping cartel was discussed daily with General Leyva and other officials from the DAS and it seemed certain that *Los Invisibles* were on their way to oblivion. General Leyva did not want to talk about my departure, but I knew Byron Engle would soon be asking when I would return to Washington.

My thoughts turned to Vietnam and my friend John McPoland. Vietnam was a lost cause. The South Vietnamese people were bogged down with American largess and the military forces of South Vietnam were no match for the military power of the North Vietnamese. The communists were winning the war in Vietnam, cheered on by some American ideologues. That wasn't the case in Colombia, Uruguay, and other places.

My assignment to Colombia had been an extremely satisfying adventure. General Leyva was pleased with the resolution of the kidnapping problem. There was no doubt his excellent leadership during the crisis was invaluable. It had been a very complex problem and he was instrumental in resolving the crisis. General Leyva and my friends in the DAS were very generous in their friendship with me and I felt fortunate to be accepted as part of their team. I contemplated my departure but General Leyva was interested in keeping me busy.

"Vamos," he told me one day in a cheerful mood. "We have a lead on *Los Invisibles."* DAS Agents under my friend Tenorio had an operation going at a locale called *Barrio Restrepó.* The DAS had the kidnapping cartel on the run. At this point, six members of *Los Invisibles* were dead and fifteen were in jail.

We stopped at an area where apartments and stores abounded near a busy business district. General Leyva pointed to a spot about fifty yards away, telling me that some members of the *Invisibles* had been spotted at that location. The place was crowded with a great deal of pedestrian and vehicular traffic but Tenorio was nowhere in sight. I waited patiently with General Leyva.

People moved about at the busy intersection and things looked normal. Suddenly, terrifying screams and shouts pierced the air, as people out on the street scattered frantically. The gunshots sounded like firecrackers, but the dull sound of lead hitting the metal of cars parked out on the street was unmistakable.

General Leyva held my arm as the two DAS Agents with us jumped from the car with their guns drawn and moved cautiously out to the street. My heart pounded in my chest when I saw Tenorio on the sidewalk about forty yards away, with his gun drawn. He fired quick bursts from shoulder level and I saw two men go down. More shots rang out and Tenorio slumped, then fell to the ground. Instinctively I made a move to get out of the car and General Leyva clenched my arm.

"*No! Olvidalo* (Forget it)," he cautioned. "Don't go out there." The General shouted at me in frustration. Tenorio was face up on the pavement and there was no movement to help him. Already out in the street, I had taken a sizable and stupid risk, but it was obvious that Tenorio needed help. The shooting stopped and the place suddenly grew deserted. I walked slowly and cautiously toward Tenorio.

"*Cuidado,*" I heard a DAS Agent call out. A man lying on the ground in front of a car was bleeding from gunshot wounds. He stared stonily at me while he groped for an automatic on the pavement.

"*No es DAS* (He's not DAS)," the DAS Agent hollered anxiously to warn me. Fueled by fear and instinct, I kicked his head hard. He hit the pavement and did not move. Considering the circumstances, there was not much else I could have done! I could have shot him! That would have been a more serious screw-up for me. Involuntarily, words came out of my mouth in Spanish.

"*Hijo-de-puta!*" A DAS Agent nearby heard me and chuckled out loud.

"*Bien hecho,*" he told me, grinning. Pointing his gun at the man on the ground, he would take care of him.

People crowded around Tenorio as he lay on the sidewalk. He had been shot several times and was bleeding heavily on the ground. Two other bloodied bodies nearby appeared dead. Tenorio needed medical help quickly, but there were no mobile medical teams in Bogota at this time.

Feeling a surge of helplessness I remembered the .357 revolver Tenorio had asked for me to get for him. There was nothing I could do now. General Leyva watched with a rigid look on his face.

"He's going to be okay," he told me. One of the supervising officers ordered the DAS Agents to take Tenorio and a wounded National Police Officer to the hospital in police cars. There was no time to lose. When they left, I heard the wail of a siren in the distance.

The stupidity of my actions suddenly hit me and I felt lightheaded. General Leyva did not say anything. He suggested we leave and go have coffee. I hoped nothing would be said about the matter. If anyone reported what I had done, that would create major problems for me. OPS personnel in Vietnam were having problems with the same rules of engagement that prohibited us from getting operational. But, OPS officers kept getting killed by the Viet Cong, I thought in frustration.

I was not sure what made me do what I did. Maybe I just lost it.

Later, I was happy to learn that Tenorio would recover from his wounds. He had taken three bullets. Several front-page headlines with pictures and stories about the DAS shootout with the kidnappers appeared in local papers the following day. Tenorio's brave action and valor was prominently acknowledged in *El Tiempo*, a popular newspaper in Bogota. ***"DAS AGENT CESAR TENORIO AGAIN DEMONSTRATED HIS GREAT VALOR IN THE FIREFIGHT THAT OCCURRED AGAINST THE KIDNAPPERS,"*** the headline said. I was proud of my friend and was glad that he would recover.

He had the scars to go along with his valor. Tenorio was a graduate of the Inter-American Police Academy. The left wing would not like that.

The two gunmen killed by Tenorio were definitively identified as members of the kidnapping cartel called *Los Invisibles*. One was Nestor Hurtado, AKA *"El Suicido,"* a twenty-nine year old man considered to be a psychopathic killer. The other gunman killed was Alfonso Montoya Arroyane, a known international killer. Both died at the scene. *Los Invisibles* continued to be killed in confrontations with the security forces.

In less than a month, the Colombian security forces had killed nine members of the Cali kidnapping cartel. Sixty-five percent of the kidnapping cartel's membership (eighteen people) would eventually be killed. Many of the *Invisibles* were killed under the **Ley de Fuga,** resisting arrest or trying to escape police custody. That was legal under the laws of Colombia.

The list of the members of *Los Invisibles* arrested continued to grow. Elias Vega Arango, AKA *"El Pollo Elias";* Isidro Bahas Vega; Pedro Nel Suescum Hernandez; Hubo Benecio Canabal; Argemiro Perez Castrillon; Hugo Leon Quijano Yacup (a known communist, arrested with a large sum of money), and Fabio Moncada Pelaez, a former National Police Officer were in custody. I was provided with a picture of every member of *Los Invisibles* arrested or killed by the DAS or National Police. For my scrapbook, I was told.

Bitter gun battles between DAS Agents and *Los Invisibles* continued to happen. On a bright November afternoon, in a harrowing exchange of gunfire between DAS Agents and six members of *Los Invisibles,* more people were killed. On *Avenida Carrácas* and *Calle 4 Sur* in Cali, four more cartel members were killed and two DAS Agents wounded.

The members of *Los Invisibles* killed included Evelio Pastrana Montoya, AKA **El Bombero** (The Fireman); Miguel Gonzalo Rincon, AKA **Carino** (Love); Teofilo Rojas, AKA **Chispas** (Sparky); and Celimo Alzate Caro, AKA **El Diablo** (The Devil). Using intense automatic weapons fire, two of the cartel members tore holes in walls to escape. One of the cartel members killed wore the uniform of a traffic cop, complete with riding boots and britches. DAS Agents found weapons, police badges, false I.D. cards, and large sums of money in the kidnappers' car. The total number of kidnappers killed reached thirteen. For me, it was time to go.

I bid my friend Tenorio a sad *"adiós."* He seemed in good spirits, as well as could be expected after taking three gunshots. He was the real expert on kidnappings and one of the bravest men I had ever met. The situation made me feel bad. When I told Tenorio that I owed him he laughed, nodding vigorously. I will be back, I told him.

"Don't forget my gun next time," he responded with an owlish stare, making us laugh.

I had been blessed with much good fortune in my assignment in Colombia, but for many Embassy officers, I was an enigma. My job was finished and arrangements were made for me to depart Bogota. FBI Agent Ben Stotts was inadvertently left out of my exit briefings. He would get the story later from General Leyva and Bill Driggers. The complete story on the politics, the near fuck-ups, and chickenshit would never be reported.

At the U.S. Embassy, Bob Stevenson, the DCM, informed me that the U.S. Ambassador had scheduled an exit briefing from me for three o'clock that afternoon. That gave me the morning to prepare a preliminary report on the kidnapping problem prior to my departure from Colombia. I would leave the following morning for Washington, D.C. Driggers agreed to come to breakfast and take me to the airport. With one night left to celebrate, General Leyva insisted that he and I would have dinner the night before my departure.

Stevenson provided an office at the Embassy for me to sort out the details on the kidnapping problem and write the preliminary report. A final classified report on the kidnapping problem in Colombia would be finalized in Washington for consumption by other U.S. Government agencies as well as the U.S. Embassy. I felt melancholy about leaving Colombia, but was happy to be going home intact. It had been a fascinating adventure. Driggers chuckled to suggest that my "fuck-ups" would probably never be known.

Later, working on my report at an office at the U.S. Embassy, I was surprised when a young woman entered and walked quietly toward me. She wore a thin blue dress that flowed smoothly over a firm sexy body. Her blonde hair was combed neatly in a bun and enhanced a beautiful face.

"Are you Mr. Saenz?" she asked politely. She told me her name and that she was assigned to help me with any typing needed. As a professional Foreign Service secretary, she was competent, smart, and also beautiful. I wondered if the DCM had decided to test my *machismo*. She carefully typed my preliminary report on the kidnapping cartel and completely ignored me.

I had been in the dark jungle of loneliness and intrigue too long and instinctively sought interest in blue eyes that reflected only indifference. Despite an inner warning, my search for a spark of passion or flicker of excitement in her demeanor distracted me. Uncontrollable concupiscent thoughts entered my mind and, impatiently, I cast them aside.

I told her that it was time for me to brief the Ambassador, hoping she would not leave. She smiled sweetly and asked if there was anything else she could do. Hesitantly, I suggested there was something. She stared at me with a puzzled frown, making me feel immature and foolish.

"Have dinner with me tonight," I rasped impulsively. "It's my last night in Bogota and I would like to celebrate a bit." Her eyes brightened and she laughed out loud seemingly amused.

"I can't," she told me in a soft voice. I mentally tried to convince myself that rebuff was all to the better in my case. I was growing weaker to temptation in my middle age.

"I'm grateful for your help, that's all," I said, feeling embarrassed and stupid. She came close, her female smell sensuous and enticing.

"I can have a drink with you later this evening, though," she told me in a soft voice.

"If you promise to tell me the details on the kidnappings," she added. I laughed and agreed to tell her the entire story about *Los Invisibles*. She explained that she had accepted a previous invitation for dinner at the home of one of the officers from AID. I suggested we meet at the bar of the Hotel *Tequendama* at nine o'clock that night, and she agreed.

I recalled that General Leyva and I were to have dinner at seven that evening at the hotel. He preferred not to stay out late. But I felt like celebrating.

At the U.S. Ambassador's office, his attractive secretary was friendly, and cheerfully, we chatted. She suddenly crossed her legs and her skirt moved up an inch or two above her knee and she smiled in delight when she caught me gawking. I must have a horny look about me, I thought in worried amusement. I had been away from home for two months. In a husky voice, she told me the Ambassador was ready to see me.

Ambassador Jack Hood Vaughn was in good spirits when his secretary ushered me into his spacious government office. The DCM, Robert Anderson, was with him. My briefing for the two senior officers in the U.S. Embassy would be low-key, I thought humorously. But I started with the blunt suggestion that the kidnapping problem in Colombia had been neutralized.

When Alexander Dumas said, *"nothing succeeds like success,"* he was onto something. The Cali kidnapping cartel had been dismantled, I cheerfully reported. Within the inner circles of government, OPS would get credit for our success and silence some of our critics, I thought. Philip Agee, the CIA defector, had once suggested that I was naive. He was probably right in this case.

Both men listened attentively as I explained the importance of the information provided by the Swiss Ambassador and how it helped to resolve the problem. I was aware that the CIA Station Chief, Dino Pionzo, and Earl Lubinsky, the Political Officer, had already briefed the Ambassador. But with satisfaction, I described the outstanding work performed by the DAS and General Leyva, the National Police, and the Colombian Armed Forces. Reports in the media praised the work of the DAS, the National Police, and Military Forces.

It was my assessment, I suggested, that there would be future threats to the security of Colombia that would affect U.S. interests. Narco-trafficking was growing portentously and the FARC, EPL, and ELN guerrillas were growing stronger. The guerrillas needed money to survive and kidnappings and narco-trafficking were big money-makers. The Cold War was not over and left-wing guerrilla groups like the FARC would get involved.

Feeling a strong sense of pride, I let Vaughn know that it had been a unique privilege for me to serve my country in Colombia. Working with the Security Forces of Colombia to eliminate a dangerous kidnapping threat was very satisfying for me. He smiled broadly, seemingly in agreement. I had been in a position that seemed tilted inexorably toward failure and defeat, but nonetheless was successful. Realistically, under the circumstances there had been little chance for me to accomplish anything. It seemed obvious that Vaughn had shown courage in making the decisions that turned out very well indeed.

The Ambassador surprised me when he stood up and with an emotional gesture, he gripped my hand tightly in both of his hands.

"Son, you've done your country a great service," he told me with a broad grin. The Ambassador's words provided a flood of satisfaction for me. Jack Vaughn, a prominent member of the Kennedy clan, expressed appreciation to the man from OPS for his work in Colombia. Would he pass that on to other people who counted? I was only a poor *Chicano* from New Mexico with a strong antipathy for eastern establishment liberals. But I was in denial about being a liberal on some issues myself. The Ambassador's face sparkled with satisfaction. I told him of my departure the next day, and he wished me a good trip home.

General Leyva met me for dinner at the Hotel *Tequendama* in the early evening. He was a true friend and a fine and noble gentleman. He explained that his wife Cecilia did not like to go out at night, so he came alone. That way we could talk without constraints, he said. I had met his wife earlier and she was a most lovely and gracious lady. She and the General were very close and much in love. He would say good-bye to her for me.

General Leyva's eyes brightened when he informed me that he was recommending me for a decoration from the Government of Colombia. Caught by surprise, I mentioned unintelligently that the matter might get publicity. If the wrong people found out about U.S. assistance in the kidnapping problem, it could result in reprisals against the Embassy and Americans in Colombia, I suggested.

The anguish that grew immediately visible on the General's face dismayed me. He was obviously hurt by my position. There was no way for me to recover once I made such a stupid suggestion. The damage had been done. The issue grew worse when I tried to explain the matter. I had too much credibility with General Leyva. He told me with sadness in his eyes that he understood.

The General and I did not say, *"Adios."* *"Hasta luego"* was more appropriate. (*"Hasta luego"* meant until we meet again.) Hugging in a traditional *abrazo,* we both got misty eyed. I felt privileged and honored to have his friendship. But my sheer stupidity in stopping a decoration from the Government of Colombia would haunt me for the rest of my life. I felt strangely saddened. The General must have concluded I was an ungrateful *Pendejo.*

"Next time we see each other, it will be different," he said. I would miss Colombia with all my heart and never forget my friend General Luis Attilo Leyva and the friends I made in the DAS.

By nine o'clock that evening, waiting in the cocktail lounge of the Hotel *Tequendama,* I felt disgusted with myself. The bar was empty but the night crowd would fill the place after ten o'clock. I thought about my departure in the morning and loneliness gripped me. It was almost 9:30 and there was no sign of the beauty from the Embassy. I ordered another drink and smiled impulsively with the thought that I had been one lucky fellow in my assignment. But I could have had a decoration from the Government of Colombia and I messed that up.

Minutes later, a man and his young libidinous girlfriend entered the bar, hugging and caressing each other. She had her hand slyly on his crotch.

"Si papi, lo quiero todo," she whispered to him. I watched them kiss and clutch in sporadic fits of hot uncontrolled passion. What the hell, they're young, I thought. Lighting a cigarette, I scanned the empty bar. I was very happy with the results of my assignment to Colombia and that I was going home in one piece. I deserved to celebrate and maybe get drunk, I told myself

A soft mellifluous voice behind me whispered: "Hi." I smelled her and my molecules went rocketing. For some reason, she appeared much younger and prettier. Wearing a tight red dress, she displayed a shapely figure with firm round buttocks and strong thighs. Her blonde hair was up in braids and made her face look innocent and beautiful. I stumbled off my stool, surprised to see her.

We sat and she ordered a vodka tonic. She eagerly asked about the kidnapping of Straessle and Buff.

"Wasn't it dangerous for you?" she asked ingenuously. I recounted parts of the story and she listened attentively, seemingly caught up in the drama. My description of Sabas Calderon and Tamayo made her laugh. We enjoyed talking and time zipped by as I happily kept ordering more drinks. It was almost twelve o'clock when she looked at her watch.

"I'm sorry," she whispered wistfully. "I didn't realize it was so late. I've got to go home." It had to end. She was driving her own car and was frightened to be out alone at night, she explained. We walked to the front of the hotel where her car was parked and our bodies bumped twice, causing her to giggle.

I opened the door to her car with her key and held it open. She sat in the driver's seat and turned to me.

"Bye," she said in a dulcet voice. "I really enjoyed meeting you." Bending down, I kissed her cheek.

"Good-bye, beautiful," I whispered, my mouth a fraction of an inch from her full, sensuous lips.

"Thanks for your help," I told her, and her eyes seemed to grow sad.

"Damn," I blurted out impulsively. "I wish I was going with you." It was awkward but could be blamed on drunkenness and a lot of loneliness. Her beautiful blue eyes widened in surprise and she stared at me.

"Why don't you?" she said sweetly. My legs turned to fettuccini as I held onto the door of the car.

"Should I bring my toothbrush?" I asked nonchalantly, in an attempt to be funny.

"Yes," she retorted with a funny laugh. Running up the stairs of the hotel to my room to grab my shaving kit and toothbrush, I did not know what to believe. Where did my good fortune come from, I thought.

En route to her apartment, we were both strangely silent. She glanced occasionally at me with a twinkle in her eye and giggled for no reason. We reached her apartment and I felt uneasy. Was I going to sleep there? When we arrived, I found that she had a splendid apartment with a formal dining room and an indoor garage. We entered and she told me to make myself at home. But I was nervous.

"Want a drink?" she shouted from the kitchen. Ordering a Scotch and soda, she served me a strong drink. We stood close together and lifted our glasses in a toast.

"Salud," I told her. We tapped the tops of our glasses and she giggled to say, "chin chin." She stared at me with a bright smile on her face, her full red lips glistening with excitement. Impulsively I kissed her gently and her warm, soft lips parted. I did not know what to expect but our instincts and passion led the way. I kissed her deeply and she leaned her lithe body against the wall as I slid her dress up with my hands to feel her firm round buttocks. She was wearing soft silken bikini panties. Our kisses grew arduous and strong.

"Let's go to bed," she suggested huskily. "It's going to be a short night." She put on a short white nightgown that enhanced her long beautiful blonde hair and then removed it as I undressed. A pair of black silk bikini panties clung seductively to her hips. A strange fear suddenly enveloped me and overpowering shame and guilt depressed me. But I had a ravenous hunger for her. Lord Byron once said: **"The love of women? It is known to be a lovely and fearful thing!"**

We kissed passionately and I explored her body with my hand. Two dimples above her firm and lovely round buttocks were like velvet jewels on her soft skin. She moaned softly as my mouth moved to pink erect nipples. Lost in lust, my hands went under her hips but stopped when the shocking reality hit me that she could get pregnant.

"What's wrong," she asked in a soft voice. She reached for me and arched her back. "I want you," she whispered. Nothing mattered, our bodies rose and fell together.

We were both spellbound. Our moves grew stronger and in a wild frenzy, she rode astride me with her head back, eyes closed and her long beautiful hair loose, whipping around her face. Reaching with her hands to hold my face, she kissed me feverishly. She shuddered crying out softly while I succumbed to an enormous ecstasy of release. It had been a long, long, time for me.

We slept peacefully through the night and, in the morning, made love again in a strong erotic lust that evoked strange feelings for me. I was in an unreal world of dreams. Tearfully, she told me it was not fair, I made her happy and now it was time for me to leave. I promised it would be hard to forget her.

A cab took me to the Hotel *Tequendama* early that morning. I felt a rush of happiness but there was no doubt I was a risk taker. Feeling tense and remorseful, it was too late for me to repent. My plane was scheduled to leave from *El Dorado* Airport in three hours. I asked the hotel clerk for the key to my room and he seemed very surprised to see me.

"We have gotten many calls for you, sir," he told me worriedly. "General Leyva called many times and the U.S. Ambassador called you numerous times. We simply could not locate you," he added, handing me a stack of messages on slips of paper. Most of the messages said to call the U.S. Ambassador.

Everyone would know I had spent the night out. General Leyva would think I had been kidnapped. But one of the DAS Agents stationed at the hotel had informed him that I left that evening with a pretty blonde woman. The word would get out that the *Gringo* expert on kidnappings was a *"puto."* I felt worried and embarrassed. But what happened next was the most astonishing.

22

Gringo Abduction

The night with the blonde beauty from the U.S. Embassy had left me with an uncomfortable feeling and spectral sense of guilt. I had promised to call her before I left for the airport. But my immiscible existence and disconnection with the normal world had primed me for an *affair de coeur*. The reality of what happened wasn't a matter of succumbing to local mores, it was wrong.

It had been a night of contradictions. Initially shy and innocent, her carnal lust soared during our lovemaking. She had been completely giving and wanting. I felt privileged, but gloom pervaded my feelings. I am only human, Lord, and you are too kind to this poor sinner, I thought.

I showered, relaxed, and prepared for my trip to Washington. My mind was occupied with thoughts of the many events that happened in the past few months. As I grew older, my memory would probably not recall where my house was, but it would be hard to forget Colombia and Uruguay. Within three hours I would leave for Washington, D.C., and Colombia and Uruguay would be only memories.

I finished packing and relaxed momentarily. The messages left for me at the desk of the hotel bothered me. The Ambassador knew my itinerary at this point and it surprised me when I called and his secretary told me he **had** to see me right away. It was most urgent, she said.

My flight to Washington would be in the air in less than three hours. It occurred to me that I might have to leave despite the Ambassador's instructions that he needed to talk to me. My job was finished. But I decided to be a good soldier and took a quick walk to the Embassy.

At the Chancery, the Ambassador's secretary ushered me into his office without delay. Jack Vaughn was alone and appeared disturbed and frustrated. My laid-back attitude seemed to annoy him. We remained standing while we talked.

"We've been trying to locate you since late yesterday afternoon," he told me in a sullen manner. His abruptness and air of chastisement angered me. I wondered if the problem had to do with my night out? Ambassador Vaughn was a liberal and a Democrat. Surely he understood human weaknesses!

"I don't understand, Mr. Ambassador," I responded, feeling a rising anger. "Why are you looking for me?" I felt my eyes narrow involuntarily. It was a habit of mine when I felt combative.

"I leave for Washington in about two hours," I told him.

Vaughn stared at the wall seemingly upset, his face strained and florid. He looked at me to tell me in a deep solemn voice.

"An American has been kidnapped." A stony look grew fixed on his face. I was caught totally by surprise. Damn it! I'm leaving, Mr. Ambassador, don't you understand, I thought impulsively. Morbid thoughts crossed my mind. What was I supposed to do? Risk my ass every time there was a kidnapping in Colombia? The Ambassador's face grew dark and pensive. *Los Invisibles* were more powerful than we thought. My inner mind told me to stay cool.

"We presumed the problem was over," the Ambassador said worriedly. "You have to stay and help with this new problem," he said sullenly.

"The victim this time is an American. I'll call Washington and get approval for an extension of your time here." I went inside my head again.

Good grief, don't I have anything to say about the matter? Kidnappings in Colombia had become my responsibility, I thought in angry humor. I had already decided not to volunteer for Vietnam and it amused me that I was thinking like a true liberal. But it was no fun being a target for ideologues.

Tenorio warned me that *Los Invisibles* had plans to kidnap an American and the ransom would be one million dollars. That information was passed on to Dino Pionzio, the CIA Station Chief, and Earl Lubinsky of "Pol 1," but that was negative forecasting and frustrated the two men. They were just grateful if they were not kidnapped. Both were considered prime targets for the local kidnapping trade. If the kidnappers could get one million dollars for the kidnapping of an American, they were sitting on a gold mine. The kidnappers apparently did not know that any American kidnapped would be a sacrificial goat or a dead duck under President Richard Nixon's new policy. The United

States would not pay a ransom or negotiate with crooks or terrorists. My full doctorate in Cold War madness had instilled a fear in me that the policy was a death sentence for any American caught in the clutches of terrorists or kidnappers.

Kidnappings were in style and growing common in Latin America. Communist guerrillas and terrorists were assassinating and kidnapping American officials anywhere in the world. CIA Station Chiefs were being assassinated in foreign countries to prove that the United States was powerless against terrorists.

Earlier that year, John Gordon Mein, the U.S. Ambassador to Guatemala, was killed when he resisted being abducted by left-wing terrorists. The U.S. Army Military *Attaché* to Guatemala had been gunned down and killed by terrorists the same year. Charles Burke Elbrick, the U.S. Ambassador to Brazil, was kidnapped by the communist terrorist group called the MR-8 and was fortunate to be alive.

The *Movimento Revolucionario do Brazil, Outubro 8* (named in honor of *Ché* Guevara) had threatened to execute him if the Brazilians did not release communist terrorists held in prison. (*Ché* had been killed before October 8 but that was a technicality.) Thousands in the hemisphere and in the world mourned *Ché* Guevara's death. The MR-8, the armed militant group of the communist party of Brazil, was deadly, but the Colombian FARC and the MR19 were just as deadly.

Communist guerrilla groups did not hesitate to kill. When Elbrick was kidnapped, he was clubbed savagely on the head. He was fortunate that the Military Triumvirate governing Brazil at the time, with unusual compassion, released the fifteen left-wing terrorists with President Nixon's blessings. The terrorists were taken to Mexico and released there as part of the deal.

After Elbrick's kidnapping, President Nixon expressed to his staff that the United States had to get tough on terrorists. His new policy was tougher on terrorists but was tougher on any American taken by terrorists. The policy meant certain death for any American in the hands of terrorists.

My mind focused on what the Ambassador had told me. It seemed certain to me that *Los Invisibles* had been completely destroyed. The security forces had terminated most of the organization's top leadership under the *Ley de Fuga*. How many could still be operative? If the *Invisibles* had kidnapped an American at this point, they were indeed formidable.

"I'll call Byron Engle to get his approval for you stay to help with this new problem," the Ambassador suggested nervously. I felt manipulated and expendable, like a low-paid mercenary.

"Let **me** talk to Byron Engle, Mr. Ambassador," I proposed testily. "If he has a problem with it, then you talk to him." The Boss would prefer to hear the story from me. There was no certainty yet that there had been a kidnapping. Although disturbed by my attitude, Ambassador Vaughn agreed and seemed to grow sympathetic about my situation. I had been away from my family for two months risking my ass against kidnappers. It was not easy being a pawn.

"George Phelan is waiting for you in his office. He has other people involved in the matter with him. Please go see him right away," the Ambassador asked. "The victim's father is there with him." He seemed happy to see me go. He was tired of kidnapping problems, but so was I.

Phelan was the General Consul for the Embassy, and his secretary immediately ushered me into a large elegant office, furnished in the finest tradition of American diplomacy. The office had polished oak furniture, memorabilia, the American flag, and government-issued paintings, along with a large framed picture of President Richard Nixon on the walls. I walked in and was surprised to hear General Leyva's voice ring out with a spring of soft laughter.

"This *Gringo* is not going home!" he called out cheerfully.

I did not expect to see General Leyva there. Phelan was duly impressed and seemed glad to see me. He rose from his desk to shake my hand and politely invited me to sit. The General and I hugged in a Latin American style *abrazo*. The excitement in his eyes was infectious and he told me hurriedly.

"We have a new problem. *Te vas a quedar para ayudar, no?* (You're going to stay and help, right?)" Nodding, I asked him what had occurred.

"*Otro secuestro* (Another kidnapping)," he said. Help would be needed from the highest level of government in Colombia if an American had been kidnapped, I thought.

An older man with a beautiful woman at his side stood stiffly at Phelan's desk, watching quietly.

"*Este es el Señor* Hermidez Padilla," the General said. "And this is his daughter, Anita," he told me in English. Both of them greeted me in English.

"It appears Mr. Padilla's son has been kidnapped," Phelan told me with uncertainty.

We sat around Phelan's desk and he explained that Jaime Padilla Convers, an American citizen living in Bogota, had not returned from a trip to the United States. During the past week, his sister Anita and her husband, as well as several employees of a company owned by the family, had received telephone calls from a man in regard to a ransom for Jaime. George Phelan had taken copious notes and handed them to me.

When Mr. Hermidez Padilla met with the Ambassador and informed him of the problem involving his son, Phelan was told by Vaughn to call General Leyva for help. Unknown to me, both the Ambassador and General Leyva had called Byron Engle, the Director of OPS in Washington, to get his approval for me to stay and help with the new kidnapping problem. I was not aware of that.

"Where's a phone I can use?" I asked Phelan. He led me to a small office and with the help of his secretary called Washington. In a few minutes, Engle's secretary, Ruth, had him on the line.

Engle and I exchanged perfunctory greetings and immediately he shot a query at me in a harsh tone of voice. I was not expecting that.

"What the hell is going on, Dolph?" he asked, seemingly irritated. "Ambassador Vaughn and General Leyva both called me to ask that you stay to help with some **new** kidnapping problem!" He paused in silence while I visualized what had happened.

"They are both very excited and adamant that you stay." Engle seemed disturbed. My own insides were building up like a can of beer being shaken.

"You reported that the kidnapping problem in Colombia had been neutralized and you were on the way to Washington," he chided.

"Was that a mistake?" he asked as I kept my anger in check.

My report on the Cali kidnapping cartel had been an interim one, based on the best data available. I felt very comfortable that the conclusions outlined in my report were valid and proper. But I felt like the Prophet Amos must have felt when he protested he was not a prophet. I took a few deep breaths.

"Byron," I told him in a calm low voice. " I do not want to stay. I have been here a long time away from my family." I paused as if to deliberate the matter.

"As far as this new situation is concerned, apparently an American was kidnapped a few days ago in Bogota. That's all I know." I muttered an expletive so Engle could hear.

"As far we can tell, the Cali kidnapping cartel has been eliminated. The members of the cartel are *hors' de combat,* " I kidded.

"Speak English," Engle muttered impatiently. He was not a linguist.

"Well, the Ambassador and General Leyva want me to stay to help with the kidnapping of the American. That's all I know." I felt an angry flush creep up my neck. Engle became silent.

"Listen to me, Byron," I intoned dryly and my voice seemed to echo and rebound eerily on the telephone. "My flight for Washington leaves in about two hours. I'm already packed and am ready to leave. I have my ticket. If I hurry, I'll make that flight," I explained in a furtive tone, chuckling involuntarily. Engle muttered something but I continued in the same vein.

"As far as I am concerned, the job I was sent to do in Colombia has been completed and I would like to go home," I insisted. Being kicked about in the ambivalent role of hero and knave was *pura caca*. But Engle would never agree that I go home under the existing circumstances. His response was not surprising.

"No, no," he told me hurriedly. "The Ambassador wants you to stay." He chuckled to relieve the tension building between us.

"General Leyva thinks you can walk on water." He kidded in a way to uplift my spirits. "He is highly complimentary about you and feels very strongly that you stay and help." Engle suddenly became reassuring.

"You're doing a great job," he said. "You better stay and try to help on the new case. Maybe for a couple of weeks." It would take a miracle to do anything in two weeks.

"It may be longer," I countered. He quickly told me to stay as long as necessary.

"Good luck," he told me and hung up. But it was easy to see that he was pleased. His OPS officers were in demand. But the guys on the left side of the political spectrum wanted to destroy us in the Cold War.

Back at Phelan's office, Mr. Padilla and his daughter waited patiently with anguished looks on their faces. General Leyva and Phelan had obtained additional information from them on the disappearance of Jaime Padilla Convers. Everything indicated that he had just disappeared from the face of the planet. But there was still an uncertainty about it being a kidnapping.

The father of the victim, a handsome ruddy-faced man with a gentle look, pink cheeks, and kind blue eyes, seemed desperate. Although wealthy by any standards, he seemed helpless now. His face was sharply drawn with grief for his only son. He suggested he would pay any ransom demanded by the kidnappers. Nevertheless, we did not know what that was. In his late sixties, Mr. Hermidez Padilla seemed to be a person of immense strength and courage. General Leyva called him

Don Hermidez. I liked him immediately and felt a deep sympathy for him in regard to his son's kidnapping. The thought of having one of my sons kidnapped by pathological killers gave me the shivers. It was hard to believe his son was in the hands of the Cali kidnapping cartel. It was something else.

The victim, Jaime Padilla Convers, a graduate of Harvard with a degree in Business Administration, was known in Bogota as *El Pelirojo*...the Redhead. As a popular entrepreneur in Bogota, he traveled frequently to Puerto Rico, Brazil, Miami, and New York in connection with family business interests. His principal office was at *Pomicol,* a mineral processing plant on the outskirts of the city. He had a good life in Bogota and lived in a nice apartment house with maids, a *Mercedes Benz*, and a chauffeur.

On October 24, he had sent a telegram to his office to inform his secretary that he would arrive in Bogota on Sunday, October 26, 1969, on Braniff flight No. 911 from Miami. He instructed her in the telegram to send his chauffeur to meet him at the *El Dorado* International Airport.

I recalled that that was a few days after the ransom for Straessle and Buff had been paid to Fernando Tamayo, of the Cali Kidnapping Cartel. Fortunately, the Swiss had been released unharmed after the ransom was paid. The events were still fresh in my mind.

By this time, DAS Agents and the security forces had killed thirteen members of the Kidnapping Cartel and at least ten others were under arrest. I felt sure the organization had been destroyed unless the bastards all had nine lives and had resurrected.

But the Jaime Padilla Convers case was different. His original travel to Bogota from Miami had been changed because of a telegram he allegedly sent to his sister, Anita Carreño. The telegram sent to his sister changed Jaime Padilla Conver's arrival in Bogota from October 26 to October 29, three days later than his original scheduled travel. The telegram indicated he would arrive on Avianca flight No. 71 from Caracas, Venezuela.

Jaime's secretary provided new instructions to the chauffeur on his *Jefe's* arrival. He was told to pick up his *Jefe* (boss) on October 29 instead of October 26 and that he was arriving on a different airline. The chauffeur had searched desperately for his *Jefe* at the airport the night of October 29 but could not find him.

He reported to Jaime's secretary at *Pomicol* that the *Jefe* had not arrived on Avianca flight No. 71 or any other flight on that day. The staff at *Pomicol* grew worried. Jaime had never done that before. Five days passed and no word from Jaime Padilla Convers. Queries on Jaime's whereabouts from managers at *Pomicol* sent to business contacts in the U.S. proved negative.

Six days had passed and Jaime Padilla Convers was still missing when Helen Escobar, the secretary to the plant manager, received a telephone call from an unidentified man. He addressed her in clipped tones.

"La vida de Jaime vale cinco millónes de pesos," he said. (Jaime's life is worth five million pesos.) That was nearly a million dollars. A similar call was made the next day. But the police were not notified. Jaime's father, Mr. Hermidez Padilla, was subsequently informed of the situation and he decided something was terribly wrong. He made arrangements to travel to Bogota from his home in San Juan, Puerto Rico, and made a few phone calls to powerful U.S. Congressmen to get their help. They owed him. He was told the U.S. Ambassador to Colombia would help him and for him not to worry. That was politician's talk.

After his arrival in Bogota, Mr. Hermidez Padilla contacted Ambassador Jack Vaughn and made clear his grave concern for his son. He requested that the U.S. Ambassador get the FBI involved. That proved difficult. J. Edgar Hoover, the powerful FBI Director, would not participate. The request from the U.S. Department of State to provide assistance to the Colombian government in coping with the kidnapping problem in Cali had been turned down by the FBI. That was why I was on the assignment. But I worried about jurisdictions in Jaime's case. The investigation of any American kidnapped, even overseas, was the FBI's job. I was strictly an advisor and non-operational.

That night I called my wife, Jan. She and the children were fine and enjoying their stay in New Mexico. The kids were doing great in school and my son Kurt was having fun with the motorbike I bought him before I left. (To my great sorrow, my son Kurt would get hit by a car while riding his motorbike and suffer severe injury to his leg. A local doctor was preparing to amputate his leg when I stopped him. The accident would happen the day I returned to Washington, D.C., from Colombia.) I told my wife about the change in my plans and she tried to understand. When I promised to be home soon, she awakened a fear in me when she added a harsh slant to her response. "You better," she said. Women had a knack for scaring men.

The Hotel *Tequendama* was beginning to feel like home. General Leyva advised me that the DAS had officially opened a case on Jaime Padilla Convers for an investigation. We agreed that the first thing that needed to be done was to retrace or reconstruct Jaime's travel. The question that needed a quick answer was whether or not he had actually arrived in Bogota. It was possible that Jaime, a nice looking, 25-year-old, rich young bachelor, was holed up with some nice *chica*. A possible kidnapping was more mysterious.

The calls made to the mineral plant called *Pomicol* by an unidentified man to propose a ransom for Jaime did not make sense. The General suggested that if the kidnappers were *"legitimo,"* they would make every effort to contact friends or members of the victim's family with clear instructions on how to pay a ransom. We laughed at his use of the word, *"legitimo"* (legitimate).

We agreed the DAS would tap the telephone lines to *Pomicol* as soon as possible. The telephone lines to Jaime's apartment and the residences of his friends would also be monitored. We needed to move fast on telephone interceptions. General Leyva had suggested that we work closely together on this case.

"Don't worry about getting operational," he told me with a funny grin. "Here in Colombia, we are in charge. You are one of us." He smiled slyly. "Who would report you anyway?" he told me with a grin. "Let's not worry about technicalities." We ordered dinner in my room.

"Don" Hermidez Padilla wants to meet with us every evening," he said. "He is a fine man and is very concerned about his son." It was easy to like and admire *Don* Hermidez Padilla. I nodded impulsively.

"If you agree, we can meet here every night for dinner and talk about any new developments on the case," the General suggested. "The situation looks bad and *Don* Hermidez is torn up by his son's kidnapping. But maybe he can provide us with ideas on possible leads." I agreed without giving it a thought. I liked *Don* Hermidez Padilla and felt bad about his son.

"We can eat here in your room at night and talk," General Leyva suggested with a glint in his eye. I realized my assignment was going to cost me money. Now I would sacrifice monetarily for my country. I was naïve anyway, according to CIA defector, Philip Agee. But screw Agee, I thought. I needed a job with excitement to it. Maybe I was a Crusader or maybe I was just an American *Chicano* patriot.

It was great to work with General Leyva again. His intellect, energy, and humor were terrific assets.

"The DAS vehicle will pick you up every morning," he told me with a sly grin. "Tell your pretty *rubia* (blonde) you'll see her on weekends. We need your room and don't want you to be *agotado*...tired." He laughed when he saw the surprised look on my face.

The General and I met with Inspector Gordillo and Dr. Leon at DAS Headquarters every day. It did not seem to me that *Los Invisibles* were involved in the Jaime Padilla Convers kidnapping. The kidnappers in this case operated differently, and I told that to General Leyva. Gordillo's men were to obtain the airline passenger lists and check the name of every individual on board the Braniff and Avianca flights that had arrived at *El Dorado* Airport October 26 through October 30. We had to confirm whether Jaime made it to Bogota. That was a priority.

It felt comfortable working at the DAS Headquarters. People were friendly, making me feel special, like a politician shaking hands with constituents after their re-election. The General's secretary served breakfast for us every day in his office. The *creole* breakfast of eggs, black beans, and bacon could not be better. The General was amused to see me eat with a hearty appetite and kidded me about it.

Within 24 hours, DAS investigators had obtained and analyzed the passenger lists for the airline flights that had arrived in Bogota during the past two weeks from the United States and Venezuela. The passenger list for Braniff flight 911, a flight that had arrived on October 26, clearly showed that Jaime Padilla Convers was a passenger. The question was—what happened to him?

DAS Agents were instructed to interview the passengers from Braniff flight 911 as soon as possible. Airport personnel and employees at airport bars and restaurants were to be interviewed, as well as Colombian Customs Officers at *El Dorado* Airport. Someone had to have seen Jaime.

I reminded General Leyva that the telephone at Anita's residence should be tapped and monitored.

"It's already done," he told me with a wink. I acted surprised.

"Just don't put a tap on my phone at the hotel," I kidded. "I'll be checking my phone." General Leyva and Gordillo broke out in guffaws. *Puta,* I thought, maybe they already have. Laughing, they assured me that my telephone was not tapped.

"Jaime's friends in Bogota may be contacted by the kidnappers," I suggested in a more serious vein. "Those phones must be tapped and monitored." Gordillo, still chuckling at my suggestion that my telephone was tapped, nodded and wrote something down on a pad. He grinned at me and shook his head. I knew Gordillo was an honorable man. I was the one with paranoia. But what if my room **is** bugged, I thought humorously.

"I hope you don't have plans for Thursday night," General Leyva told me with an amused look on his face. "I guess you are anxious to see your *rubia,"* he suggested with a smile.

"But on Thursday night, you and I are invited to dinner at Anita's house. Her father arranged this and he is very interested that we make it." He sighed wistfully.

"There must be a reason why *Don* Hermidez wants us there. Maybe Gonzalo will be there." He looked at me for my reaction. Gonzalo Carreño was Jaime's brother-in-law and Anita's husband.

"*Parese bicho raro.*" He interpreted what he said for me. "He is, you know, like some weird insect."

After Gordillo examined the passenger list for Braniff flight 911, he confirmed that Jaime had arrived in Bogota at *El Dorado* Airport.

"The results of the passenger interviews will be available tomorrow," he reported. "Nevertheless, it seems very certain that Jaime Padilla Convers **was** on the plane when it landed in Bogota," Gordillo said. "Braniff employees swear by it."

"Maybe Jaime is faking his kidnapping," Dr. Leon suggested unexpectedly. "To get money from his Papa." His comment surprised everyone. It was an interesting theory.

"What do you think of that, Dolph?" the General asked, deep in thought.

"Anything is possible, *mi General,*" I responded. "There are a lot of strange things going on in this case. The kidnappers are not behaving as they normally do, especially in regard to negotiating a ransom."

"Maybe it is an *auto-sequestro,*" the General said. "Maybe Jaime faked his own kidnapping." It was something to ponder. Things just did not seem right for a kidnapping.

"Anita and her husband must know something," Gordillo suggested. "They are very sinister."

"*A propósito, mi General,*" I said. "Anita left a message at the hotel that she wants to talk to me. Hopefully that will not be misinterpreted," I chuckled. General Leyva stared at me pensively.

"*Muy interesante,*" he said. "This may be our chance to interrogate her. I think she knows something and perhaps Anita will respond to your questions easier than anyone else," he explained with amusement.

"You should meet with her alone. We will develop questions to ask her," the General's voice grew low. "This should prove to be very interesting," he said in a conspiratorial tone and with a grin on his face. "Maybe you should ask her directly if she is involved in an *auto-sequestro* with Jaime."

I nodded in agreement. We had nothing else at this point.

Sure enough, Anita suggested we meet alone in my room at the Hotel *Tequendama.* We were all convinced she knew more than she was telling us. Nevertheless, I had to be careful about my meeting with Anita because we could be mistaken. In addition, the General probably had my room bugged, I thought facetiously. Nevertheless, Anita could very well turn out to be a key link in the case, I thought.

The following evening I waited for Anita in my room with uneasiness. The soft knock on my door got my adrenaline going. I opened the door and Anita stood waiting, a hesitant look on her beautiful face. Her dark hair flowed in curls around her face in a flattering way. She wore satin that seemed to cling provocatively to a sexy body. The situation was not only on the edge of being operational, it was wickedly sinister. She was definitely a pretty woman.

I offered her a chair and she sat and crossed her legs demurely and waited for me to speak.

"You wanted to talk to me," I told her. She became nervous and immediately asked what the DAS had found out about her brother. She was cool as a cucumber.

"Nothing," I said. "Absolutely nothing." She smiled softly, making me feel uncomfortable.

"We were hoping you could tell us something about the message you received from Jaime that changed his travel plans." I noted a slight tangible nervousness on her part.

"Jaime arrived in Bogota as he originally said in the telegram dispatched to his secretary. The passenger list for Braniff flight 911 shows he arrived on that flight." Her eyes did not register any surprise.

"Jaime disappeared after he arrived in Bogota. Does that surprise you?" I asked. She nodded softly and stared at the floor in silence.

"You told Jaime's secretary that you received a cable from him changing his travel plans. Do you still have the telegram that Jaime sent you?" I asked. Her eyes suddenly welled up with tears. She **was** involved in something sinister, I thought. She opened her mouth to speak and then closed it without saying anything. She shook her head and I could smell a trace of perfume in her hair.

"I threw it away," she said hesitantly. She was cool and every move seemed calculated.

"Where is your husband Gonzalo, Anita?" I asked. Her eyes grew serious.

"He's out of the country. In Puerto Rico," she answered sharply. It seemed she did not like that question and was holding back something. She appeared bewildered with a full range of emotions affecting her, including fear and passionate anger. She was momentarily silent and looked plaintively at me. There was no doubt she was a very appealing young lady, but I had to get her to talk.

"Jaime was not what you think," she hissed abruptly with fire gushing from her pretty dark eyes. "He was a cruel selfish man who dominated my father. He was only interested in my father's money." She suddenly burst into tears.

"He hated me and my husband." Surprised, I forced myself to keep quiet and listen. She had used the past tense when referring to Jaime. Was he dead? The solution to the case could be Anita, I thought. It did not appear the father knew of the serious personal conflicts between brother and sister. I listened, confident and very sure that Anita knew something about her brother's disappearance. She cried openly.

She rambled in a belligerent tone of voice that showed a clear loathing for Jaime. Her eyes glistened with a rage that was unmistakable. But what could she be involved in?

"Anita, I think you know what happened to your brother," I said, feeling heat rise to my face. "I want you to tell me. You must tell me before it is too late," I insisted, staring harshly at her.

"Is it some type of conspiracy?" I raised my voice a notch.

"Is your husband involved?" She lowered her eyes and shook her head. I had underestimated Anita. She was a smart calculating woman.

"Look, maybe it's not too late. Anita, tell me what happened to Jaime. Why did you say he was not what we think he was? Why did you refer to him in the past tense? Is Jaime dead?" I asked gently. She stared at the floor and did not answer.

"Damnit, tell me what happened. Was it an *auto-sequestro*? Did you and Jaime fake a kidnapping?" I asked in an angry voice. "To get money from your father. Was that it? An *auto-sequestro*?" That was a terribly wrong question to ask. She listened avidly because she realized that we were on the wrong track. Not knowing this, I pushed on for answers, feeling uncertainty because we had no physical evidence.

Anita stood slowly, her face red and her eyes filling with tears. She stared at me and suddenly threw her arms around my neck. She wants consolation, I thought, and instinctively I held her as she cried softly. Sobbing, she nuzzled my face and neck, her smell sexy and sensuous, while she pressed her soft body erotically against me and moved her body in soft but persistent undulating waves in all the right places. My growing passion was a serious problem. She turned to face me with her full moist red lips dangerously close. I panicked and pushed away.

She had deliberately manipulated me and my carelessness had blown any chance of finding out anything of value. There was no doubt she had effectively neutralized me. She continued to cry with a look of sincere concern on her lovely face. If General Leyva did have my room bugged, he and Gordillo were probably rolling on the floor, laughing out of control.

"Anita, we're going to find out what happened to your brother," I told her with anger. "If you are involved in any stupid scheme, you will wind up in jail." She stared sullenly at me. I had no idea how close I was to the real story. Anita left in tears, obviously disturbed. But I had become a liability to the investigation.

General Leyva and Gordillo listened attentively when I recounted what had happened in my meeting with Anita. I made it sound humorous, but they did not laugh much. Maybe my room was not bugged; otherwise, they would know how ridiculous it had gotten for me. I had to be more careful. This was a different type of risk. There was no doubt in my mind that Anita knew what had happened to her brother.

Gordillo's men had interviewed passengers who arrived on Braniff flight 911 on October 26 and were able to find a person who was a close friend of the Padilla Convers family.

An American by the name of Kitty Kiellen Kirby reported to DAS Agents that she had arrived at *El Dorado* Airport on Braniff flight 911 on October 26, 1969, and that Jaime was definitely on the same plane. Jaime had helped carry her bags into Colombian Customs, she said. After Jaime cleared Customs, he had left the building, she said. She did not see him again. But more surprisingly, she also saw Gonzalo Carreño, Jaime's brother-in-law, inside the terminal and had actually conversed with him. But he left in a hurry after telling Mrs. Kirby that his wife Anita was not feeling well. Gonzalo had kept his visit to the airport on that night to himself.

General Leyva and I subsequently talked to Mrs. Kirby and found she spoke fluent Spanish. She was sharp and attentive and answered our questions. But she suddenly focused on me.

"You're an American, aren't you?" she asked abruptly. "I know you are." I shook my head in dismay. "You're from the FBI," she persisted. She came closer, after me with a vengeance.

"You're from the FBI, aren't you?" she insisted in a loud voice. Mrs. Kirby, a vivacious, elegantly dressed young woman, was intent on interrogating me. I answered her solely in Spanish.

"*Está equivocada, Señora Kirby* (You are mistaken, Mrs. Kirby)," I told her. She continued talking to me in English but I refused to respond. General Leyva chuckled at my discomfort.

1900 Hours

I waited at the entrance of the Hotel *Tequendama,* and General Leyva picked me up to go to Anita's house for dinner. He arrived late in his five-year-old, beige *Mercedes Benz.* The General was proud of his car and he called it *Merceedees.* He kept his car immaculately clean. He opened the car door to tell me *"vamos pues!"* The inside of the car was spotless.

On the way to Anita's, we talked about the kidnapping. It seemed strange that if Jaime had been abducted, the kidnappers were not pursuing firm negotiations for the payment of a ransom. Telephone taps on some of Jaime's friends were unproductive thus far. There were no firm leads on Jaime. He had arrived in Bogota from Miami and then disappeared at the *El Dorado* Airport.

We arrived at Anita's house within twenty minutes and it was no surprise that the house was spacious and elegant, surrounded by a high wall and the classy residences of affluent neighbors. General Leyva parked his car and we walked to the house on an attractive walkway laced with a variety of beautiful plants and trees. Three cars parked on a large driveway immediately caught our attention. They were all new *Mercedes Benz* automobiles. Each car had a driver or chauffeur, buffing car exteriors or interiors with soft rags as they watched us approach. It appeared other people besides us were invited to Anita's for dinner.

"Mire, mi General," I suggested in jest. "You need to get yourself one of those new *Mercedes Benz."*

"Me encantaría, pero no tengo ningún grano o frijole," he chuckled. He told me he would love to get a new *Mercedes Benz* but he didn't have a bean. Yet we were dealing with kidnappers making hundreds of thousands of dollars per abduction.

"Me either," I said laughing. *"Lo siento* (Sorry)," I told him.

One of the chauffeurs suddenly exclaimed in a loud voice as we approached.

"Mi General Leyva, éste auto esta de venta (General Leyva, this car is for sale)." He pointed at a shiny black *Mercedes.* He smiled amicably to let us know the car he drove was for sale and emphasized that it was new. He obviously knew about the General coming to Anita's for dinner and had overheard us kidding about buying a *Mercedes.* My curiosity clicked in hard. That was probably Gonzalo Carreño's car.

We stopped to look at the car and the chauffeur opened the door so we could see inside.

"*Ésta nuevo,*" he repeated. The elegant interior appeared new. Not a single mark was visible on the seats and dark maroon carpeting. Not even a sign of use was apparent.

"*El Señor Carreño lo vende* (Mr. Carreño is selling it)," the chauffeur told us. The chauffeur watched our reaction with eyes of curiosity.

"*Cómo te llamas?*" I asked him. Latin Americans like to make friends.

"Jose," he told us. It appeared to me that Jose was very anxious to show us the car. Was he doing that to help his boss? In Spanish, I asked Jose if there was anything wrong with the car. He explained there was nothing wrong with the car and insisted the car was new. The right window had been broken but was replaced, he said. General Leyva stared at me with a puzzled look.

"What happened to the window?" he asked him in Spanish. Jose explained that *Señor* Carreño told him that a thief had broken into the car to steal his topcoat when he left it on the front seat of the locked car. The thief broke the window on the right side to steal the coat, he said. We let him talk.

"The car has new carpeting and new seat covers," Jose told us in Spanish. He stared at our faces and continued to talk. "The car is in excellent shape and almost new. I don't know why he wants to sell it." If Jose did know, he wasn't telling us.

"*Jose, podemos ver el baúl?*" I asked. The chauffeur immediately opened the trunk of the car. The inside of the trunk was very clean with nothing in it. On close inspection I noticed tiny pieces of glass scattered on the maroon carpet in the trunk. I picked up several pieces and showed them to the General. He made a face and examined the glass nodding with a puzzled look on his face. I placed several pieces in a small envelope.

"*Muy bien,*" he told the chauffeur.

"*Muchas gracias, Jose!*" He looked at me and said, "*muy interesante.*"

At Anita's house, a maid in a white uniform and pink apron answered the door when we rang the doorbell. She led us into an attractive living room. A man and a woman waited with *Don* Hermidez Padilla, holding drinks in their hands. *Don* Hermidez Padilla greeted us with a warm handshake and introduced us to the man and the woman with him as Dr. Pedro Maria Carreño and his wife, Olga Carreño. They were Gonzalo Carreño's mother and father. We learned later that Anita's husband's parents were distinguished members of the *Sociedad Colombiana*. Dr. Carreño served as a diplomat and consul representing Colombia in Japan for several years.

Anita walked up and pecked me on the cheek. Her sexy smell lingered. We were served cocktails and sat in the living room to chat before dinner. The conversation seemed laborious and reserved as everyone skirted around any serious discussion about Jaime's kidnapping. Any discussion about the whereabouts of Anita's husband, Gonzalo Carreño, seemed to be avoided. *Don* Hermidez Padilla sat quietly, carefully observing and listening. His eyes were heavy with sadness and worry for his son.

"Well, Anita, is your husband still gone?" I asked casually. There was a momentary silence and Anita stared at me. My lack of tact did not go unnoticed and the General smiled. We needed to get a conversation going about Gonzalo Carreño. Her father-in-law also stared at me, deep in thought.

"Oh," Anita responded indulgently. "Gonzalo is in San Juan with our three children. They are staying with my mother." In reality, the three children were from Anita's previous marriage.

"This tragedy has really affected poor Gonzalo. As you know, he was threatened with death by the kidnappers," she said in a soft voice. Her nervousness was barely perceptible.

"He feared for the children and, of course, for their safety took them to Puerto Rico," she explained in a strained voice. Finely wrought and beautifully curvaceous, Anita became silent. Why didn't **she** take them to Puerto Rico, instead of Gonzalo, if there was any danger involved for the children, I thought.

Gonzalo was an enigma, a dark figure in the case that preferred to remain in the shadows. Mr. Padilla told me that when he arrived in Bogota, he was anguished about the disappearance of his son and begged Gonzalo Carreño to stay and help him find Jaime. Gonzalo refused by making vague excuses and left the same day, reportedly to spend some time in Medellin. General Leyva glanced briefly at me.

"We understand he is selling his *Mercedes Benz,*" he said dispassionately.

"I'm interested." He looked at me and grinned. Perhaps I could lend him some *frijoles*. But I knew where he was headed. The car was a suspicious item.

"It's had some repairs, hasn't it?" I asked. Dr. Carreño, Gonzalo's father, reacted immediately.

"It's a very good car," he said in Spanish. "It is actually my car. It belongs to me. I have two *Mercedes Benz.*" Gonzalo borrowed the car often, the father told us.

"It has very low mileage," he said and explained that the car had a broken right window that had recently been fixed and repeated the story told to us by the chauffeur that a thief had broken the window of the car to steal Gonzalo's coat. But Dr. Carreño also explained that the car had new carpeting and seat covers installed and added that the engine and undercarriage had been steam cleaned. That seemed to be a lot of work on a new *Mercedes Benz*.

Dr. Carreño was openly talkative and surprised us when he pulled out a bill for the work performed on the car in question when we asked him where he had had the repairs done. He said his son Gonzalo had suggested that the *Mercedes Benz* be sold to buy a new BMW. The General nonchalantly reached for the repair bill to see what work was done to the car. Dr Carreño kept talking and General Leyva passed the statement on the repairs to me. He did not have his reading glasses with him.

"Gonzalo is a car enthusiast and does the maintenance needed for the car. It's in a very good condition," Dr. Carreño said. The name of the local repair shop, the address, and the date of the work on the *Mercedes Benz* were plainly indicated on the statement. The date of the repairs was October 27. That was one day after Jaime arrived in Bogota and disappeared.

After that, dinner went slowly, but it was a scrumptious meal. Anita knew how to entertain and having a cook helped. We prepared to leave and she squeezed my hand in a friendly gesture. She must have suspected that we were suspicious of her husband, but she seemed to ignore this and did not ask questions.

The General and I left Anita's house excited about possible linkages between the *Mercedes Benz* and Jaime's disappearance. We stayed up late, talking and developing a list of things that had to be done as soon as possible. If Jaime had been kidnapped, Gonzalo Carreño probably knew something about it. The General and I met with *Don* Hermidez the following night at the hotel and talked about Gonzalo and Jaime's relationship. He did not see the relationship as very friendly, but he saw no open hostilities between the two.

Don Hermidez surprised us with the information that Gonzalo Carreño had received instructions from the kidnappers on the payment of a ransom for his son, Jaime. He said that Gonzalo had called his daughter Anita from Puerto Rico. According to Anita, a man named Raul had talked to Gonzalo on the telephone and had given him instructions for the payment of the ransom for Jaime. Gonzalo also told Anita that Raul had warned him not to go to the police or that he and the children would be killed.

According to what Gonzalo had told Anita, the ransom was to be paid at a small border town by the name of Cucuta, located near the

Venezuelan border. The kidnappers were to make contact at the Hotel *Tonchala* in Cucuta and provide the final instructions for the payment of the ransom on Sunday, November 9. But if Anita's phone was tapped, how did Gonzalo pass the information to her without the DAS knowing? The General was more than puzzled. So was I.

Don Hermidez Padilla insisted on paying any ransom demanded for the release of his son. But for unknown reasons, the ransom demands had changed to less than half a million dollars. General Leyva agreed with me that Gonzalo was preparing to make his move. Nevertheless, we had just three days to plan on the basis of the information provided by Anita. We were obliged to go to Cucuta.

The next day DAS Agents invaded the garage where Gonzalo Carreño's *Mercedes Benz* had been repaired. What they found was incredibly fortuitous. The pieces of carpeting that had been removed from the *Mercedes* automobile were in trash barrels and were recovered, along with seat covers that were removed. The workmen that had performed the work on the *Mercedes Benz* reported to the DAS Investigators that they found traces of blood under the rubber floor mats in the front of the car.

When the workmen had confronted Gonzalo about the blood found on the floor of the car, he explained that he had gone dove hunting the day before and had carelessly placed over 200 birds on newspapers in the trunk and in the front of the car. Blood from the dead birds had stained the carpeting, he said. He told them not to worry. That was the reason he had decided to replace the carpeting on the car. Gonzalo had promised to bring some of the white wing doves he had killed for the people that worked on his car. But they were still waiting to savor the little wild delicacies.

Small traces of blood that was found in the carpeting and upholstery removed from the *Mercedes Benz* was analyzed by DAS laboratory technicians and was found to be human blood. The question was, was it Jaime's blood? The seizure of the car was held in abeyance until the results of the tests made on Gonzalo's car could be completed. We needed to develop more information.

It was agreed that DAS Investigators would interview the chauffeurs employed by Anita and Dr. Carreño as well as the maids employed at both residences. The hospitals in Bogota would be checked for people fitting Jaime's description and reports on any unidentified dead bodies found in the city during the past month would be compiled and analyzed. All information developed would be funneled to General Leyva, Inspector Gordillo, and myself. We had no idea to what end the evidence found was leading us but things did not look good for Jaime. I suggested to General Leyva that our dinner with Mr. Padilla that evening be postponed so that the information developed would not be revealed to him until we had more concrete facts. In the interim, I would brief George Phelan. He agreed with a funny look on his face.

At the Embassy, the pretty receptionist with long dark hair, and I remained on good terms. She continued to flirt with me. Reluctantly, she told me where my blonde friend worked when I asked her, but she was curious.

"I have a message for her from an old friend," I told her. Her eyes revealed she did not believe me. The spectral sense of guilt returned. I was on dangerous grounds but took the risk.

She sat quietly at her desk. As I walked up, she looked up to stare in disbelief, her eyes growing teary.

"Hi, beautiful," I told her softly and she jumped up to hug me. I held her in a tight embrace.

"What are you doing here?" She grew nervous. "I thought you were gone." I explained the new kidnapping case and that quickly settled her mind. She seemed surprised but pleased.

"I'm glad," she said softly. "I missed you, damn you." She seemed to grow sad and that worried me.

She wanted to know how long I had been in Bogota and why I had not called her.

"I'll tell you later," I told her urgently. "I've got to go." She blushed in anger but looked lovelier. My rush to go made her very mad and she showed it.

"I'm baking cherry *flambé* tonight," she said snappishly. "Would you like to come to dinner?"

"Tonight and every night," I told her. She giggled happily. "I betta," I thought humorously.

"Seven," she said. I nodded and kissed her cheek to leave. People in the Embassy watched, wondering who I was. I finally had a low profile.

I got back to the DAS and reviewed the plan to travel to Cucuta. When I finished, General Leyva asked what I was doing that evening. I was going to rest, I told him. He laughed mirthfully.

"Not with your *rubia,* you won't." he told me. "Be careful," he said chuckling.

She was dressed in a beautiful shift dress that outlined her beautiful body. After serving drinks, she grew cheerful and talkative, poking around in the kitchen preparing our meal. She carefully opened the oven to show me the *flambé.* I congratulated her on her cooking and pulled her to me. We kissed and with eyes closed we hugged passionately and then she reached for me. I was pleasantly surprised.

"The *flambé* can wait," she murmured softly. Half dressed, we made love with a fervor that astounded me. We seemed overcome by passion. Our lovemaking grew fiercely and she shuddered, crying out several times in ecstasy. We made love until exhausted; she fell asleep in my arms. I was the teacher and she my eager pupil. But it was more than the surreal and mystifying world of sensuality. It was unreal, just like the Cold War.

The next day, planning for the operation in Cucuta to pay the ransom for Jaime Padilla Convers was finalized. The Hotel *Tonchala* would be filled with DAS Agents working as waiters, at the reception desk, at the swimming pool, and in the kitchen. DAS personnel would form two security rings around the perimeter of the hotel and watch from strategic positions ready to move at a moment's notice.

General Leyva and I would travel on the same plane with Mr. Padilla to Cucuta, but all of us in separate seats, apart from each other. We would not talk to each other during the flight or in public. We would stay in touch with old portable radios owned by the DAS or by telephone when we were in our rooms.

Don Hermidez Padilla was unyielding in his determination to pay the ransom in order to save his son. He insisted on carrying over two hundred thousand dollars in Colombian pesos in a bag to pay the ransom needed. A certain Mr. Parra, the manager of *Pomicol,* would accompany *Don* Hermidez to Cucuta. In his heart, Mr. Hermidez Padilla was determined to pay the ransom and save his son's life. We did not believe that would happen. We suspected that Gonzalo was playing games with us.

The day before our trip to Cucuta, General Leyva and I paid a visit to Anita to ask her if her husband Gonzalo had any guns.

"For self protection," the General emphasized. We said nothing about our trip to Cucuta. Mrs. Olga Carreño, Gonzalo's mother, was visiting with Anita. She let us know in very strong terms that Gonzalo did not like guns, did not own any guns, and did not like to hunt. He was incapable of killing anything, she said.

"*Es muy sensible, el pobrecito,*" Gonzalo's mother said. But poor sensitive Gonzalo had told a story to the men that worked on his *Mercedes Benz* that he had killed 200 white wing doves on a hunting trip. It was time to find Gonzalo, I thought. The bastard was too deceiving.

I suggested to General Leyva that we locate Gonzalo in Puerto Rico and have him picked up.

"He's not there," the General told me. "We don't know where he is." He turned to reassure me. "Don't worry, we'll find him." I knew that it was unlikely that Gonzalo was in Puerto Rico.

The following few days we reviewed all reports on dead bodies found by the police in Bogota and in the surrounding areas of the city in the last week of October. There were several reports on bodies found during that period. Suddenly, Gordillo raised a report in his hand excitedly.

"Look at this one," he said. "This is a report of a an unidentified man found dead near the *autopista.*" The *autopista* was the main road that led to the airport. "Initially, we thought the body belonged to a Nazi officer by the name of Rafael Von Steinbeck." But it was not the Nazi, he said. The body was unidentified.

We eagerly read the report. The body of the man had been found on October 27, one day after Jaime's arrival at *El Dorado* Airport. The hands and face of the corpse had been horribly burned. Because the police were unable to identify the body, it was buried in a common grave at the *Cementerio Central.* Three other bodies were buried on top. The report indicated that the man had been shot on the left side of the head and the body burned with gasoline. All possible identification had been removed. The hands were obviously burned to remove fingerprints. Whoever did it knew what they were doing, and like a terrorist killing, it was deliberate and in cold blood.

The DAS Agents had taken pictures of the body at the scene and I examined them. The report indicated that a tie pin, a partially burned tie, a set of keys, a coin purse, and a pair of partially burned maroon, size 8-1/2 E shoes had been removed from the scene as evidence.

"Are the items that were removed from the body available?" I asked Gordillo. He nodded and left to go to the evidence room. He returned a few minutes later with a plastic bag and dumped the contents of the bag on the table. I instinctively picked a burned shoe and looked inside.

"Florsheim," I muttered automatically. The tie was burned in half, but there was no doubt it was the type of quality silk tie that would be worn by a man who dressed well.

"Me parese que cuerpo quemado es de Jaime! (It appears that the burned body found at the *autopista* belongs to Jaime!)" the General Leyva suggested in a low tone. Gordillo and I nodded at the same time.

"We have to try the keys at his apartment, to see if they fit any of the doors," he suggested. There was little doubt in my mind that we had found Jaime. Now we had to get his killer.

23

Resolution of a Murder

"We found Gonzalo," General Leyva told me with a surge of excitement in his voice. "You'll never guess where he is." I simulated closing my eyes and looked up for a few seconds, placing my hand on my forehead in deep concentration.

"Spain," I told the astonished General. He stared at me with a look of surprise.

"Damn, you are good," he said in a half smile. He grew momentarily silent and thoughtful.

"How did you know?" he finally asked, showing a continence of annoyance. I laughed and his eyes showed a touch of impatience. He continued to stare at me until I answered.

"Gordillo told me," I finally answered. He chuckled cheerfully.

"You're still good." He was glad there was nothing strange about me, he said, laughing. So Gonzalo Carreño was in Spain, I thought. He was not collecting the ransom for Jaime.

"Who do you think will collect the ransom in Cucuta?" I asked. The General stared into open space.

"We'll soon find out," he told me in good spirits. But we had to go to Cucuta to find out, he said.

The Avianca flight from Bogota to Cucuta took about one hour. The plane continued on to Caracas, Venezuela. It was agreed we would remain in Cucuta for a minimum period of 24 hours to provide the kidnappers time to make contact with *Don* Hermidez for the payment of the ransom.

It was understood that the information provided to Anita by Gonzalo about the payment of a ransom appeared to be a red herring, but we had to make sure. If there **were** kidnappers involved, they had to be provided with the opportunity to collect their ransom. It was up to them to make contact. *Don* Hermidez was willing to pay the ransom to get his son back. On the airplane, he looked sad and vulnerable, but there was no doubt about his spunk. I sat behind him, three rows back, with the General and Gordillo in separate seats behind us. Once in the air, *Don* Hermidez turned around several times to look at me. I had to smile when he did that because he had been told not to look at us on the trip to Cucuta. Sadness hit me when I realized we would not find his son alive. It was pretty certain to me that Jaime was dead.

In reality we did not know what to expect in Cucuta. If the kidnappers were anything like the Cali kidnapping cartel, things could get plenty tough. I carried my S&W Combat Masterpiece in my shoulder holster and two extra loads of super velocity ammunition. General Leyva carried an automatic. Nine DAS Agents traveled with us and would be reinforced by six other DAS Agents assigned to the local office in Cucuta. Inspector Gordillo was in charge of all planning and had made the assignments. It was necessary to centralize control of the operation at Cucuta.

We had agreed that our arrival at the Hotel *Tonchala* would be at separate times and contact with each other would be via the phones in our rooms. The General's room would be our meeting point. Two separate rings of agents were in position around the perimeter of the hotel, ready to move quickly to make apprehensions if needed. Personnel had been assigned to keep an ongoing surveillance on Mr. Padilla and his companion, Mr. Parra, at all times. Some DAS Agents were disguised as tourists, with one dressed as a priest. I had suggested to the General that we also use female agents, but none were employed by the DAS. Gordillo let me know that the DAS Agents knew each other and knew who I was. He let me know that Mr. Padilla and Mr. Parra's rooms were tapped and monitored. Now, we waited.

Sunday, November 9

Mr. Hermidez Padilla was told to walk the hotel premises alone at different intervals, to provide the kidnappers the opportunity to make contact with him. He was to check frequently with the hotel desk to see if he had any messages. If he received the expected telephone call from the kidnappers, he would talk as long as possible to ensure he understood the instructions provided by the kidnappers for the payment of a ransom. We had no way to trace the call. He was eager to comply with any instructions in order to save his son.

Sunday was sunny and clear, with one or two spume-like clouds in the sky. At the hotel swimming pool, numerous tourists from Venezuela luxuriated in the semitropical climate. Dressed in swimming trunks, I mingled with the tourists at the pool. At a small table nearby, I had my gun inside a small bag. DAS Agents posted throughout the hotel knew my location among the heavy collection of hotel guests. I recalled being told my assignment would be a vacation for me.

At a window of the hotel facing the swimming pool, on a top floor where Mr. Padilla's room was located, a DAS Agent would signal with a handkerchief if the kidnappers made contact. The window where the agent was located was easy to spot if one knew about it. Every effort would be made to let *Don* Hermidez Padilla pay the ransom, and despite the fact that everyone wanted his son out of the mess alive, we were all aware that might not happen. Every DAS Agent involved was told that the priority was not to let the money or Don Hermidez out of our sight. We had no idea how the kidnappers intended to make contact.

By late afternoon, a DAS Agent dressed as a waiter advised me that General Leyva needed to talk to me. I went to my room and called him. Contact had not been made with *Don* Hermidez by the kidnappers.

"*Don* Hermidez is going to take a long walk around the hotel within the next thirty minutes," the General told me. "We must be on top of the situation. He insists on carrying the money with him in case he has to pay the ransom," he chuckled. We agreed that the worst-case scenario would be if someone else jumped *Don* Hermidez and took the ransom money.

"But it will be very difficult to follow him without arousing suspicion. He wants to pay the ransom in a bad way and get his son back," General Leyva told me worriedly.

"I wish that was possible," he said. "If contact is made by anyone, we can't wait. We must move in on them immediately." I agreed. He suggested I meet him in a secluded spot in the north end of the lobby and we could watch *Don* Hermidez. Dressing, I strapped my gun on in a hip holster under a sport shirt.

Dusk approached and the sky to the west changed to a splendid orange tint. At approximately six o'clock, Mr. Padilla walked slowly out of the hotel with a small straw hat perched on his head. He looked like a genuine tourist, except that he kept glancing over his shoulder.

My concern abruptly turned to fear. Mr. Padilla was a mellow, charismatic man with a dulcet temperament. But in this case, he was naïve...like me. He could be in serious danger. Kidnappers were not normal people. They would kill him without any hesitation. But he insisted on being used as bait and was determined to pay the ransom for his son. I was sure that his son was not alive.

About thirty yards away from the hotel entrance, standing at the doorway of a building, a squinty-eyed, thin looking man stared at *Don* Hermidez Padilla with intense interest. With a dark crew cut, he resembled Fernando Tamayo, one of the leaders of *Los Invisibles,* the Cali kidnapping cartel. But that was impossible. Tamayo had been arrested by the DAS and was supposed to be in prison. He was one of the few members of the cartel that were still alive. If that was Tamayo, we had serious problems. Tamayo was a trained terrorist, ruthless and smart. *Los Invisibles* were very dangerous people.

General Leyva pointed to alert me and my adrenaline surged. The stranger scanned the area and then began to walk slowly and deliberately towards *Don* Hermidez. Held in suspense by the uncertainty of the man's intentions, we watched and prepared for the worst. I felt sweat running down my back as *Don* Hermidez walked slowly towards the man, holding onto the bag of money in one hand. Ingenuously, he stopped and waited for the stranger to reach him. It was as if he hoped the stranger was the kidnapper and he would merely hand him the ransom money and his son would be saved.

"*Esto es muy raro* (This is very strange)," General Leyva turned to tell me. We watched as the stranger picked up his pace. Reaching *Don* Hermidez, he appeared to whisper something to him in subdued tones. The man looked at *Don* Hermidez in anger when he stepped back. General Leyva looked at me.

"*Mejor movernos hora que nunca* (Now or never)," he suggested calmly. There was little noise in the area. I nodded and the General ordered in a loud voice.

"*Bueno.*" Immediately, DAS Agents poured into the street from different directions with guns drawn and headed for *Don* Hermidez and the subject with him. They quickly reached the stranger and knocked him to the ground and searched him as he looked up in astonishment. Grappled to the ground, the man screamed obscenities. Worried about unforeseen contingencies, I unholstered my gun and walked out of the hotel. There had to be others involved. Screaming expletives in Spanish, the man in custody covered his head with his hands.

"*Puta madre, puta madre, qué pasa,*" he repeated in a shrill scream. He was spread out roughly on the ground and handcuffed. It did not look right for me. The man was no kidnapper.

"Está bien, está bien!" he screamed. DAS Agents spread out to search the surrounding area and premises. The man on the ground tried to sit up and was roughly pushed back down.

I wondered who he was. It was not Tamayo. *Don* Hermidez remained perfectly calm, holding onto his bag with both hands. With a look of surprise, he turned to me.

"He only asked if I could give him a couple of pesos so he could get something to eat," he said, with a look of surprise on his face. I looked up at the brilliant sky and, overcome by frustration, broke out laughing. *Don* Hermidez stared at me, seemingly puzzled.

The area was silent except for the protests from the man on the ground. Several hotel guests stopped to see the spectacle of DAS Agents swarming through the area.

Thanks to Gonzalo, we had participated in a wild goose chase. I grabbed one of the DAS Agents and told him what *Don* Hermidez had said. He stared at me in disbelief and then turned to look at the man lying on the ground, still in handcuffs.

"Hijo-de-puta!" he said as he walked to the man on the ground. A few minutes later, he removed the handcuffs from our alleged kidnapper.

"Pendejo," the DAS Agent told him. *"No te metas en mierdas* (Don't get mixed up in shit)," he told him in a voice of disgust. The stranger looked up at him with mournful eyes.

"Ustedes me dieron verga (You guys beat the crap out of me)," he said impassively.

"Yo no tengo mierda (I don't have shit)." He stared at me with sorrowful eyes. Taking fifty pesos out of my pocket I handed it to him. His face immediately broke out in a bemused smile. He did not know how close he was to a bag full of thousand peso notes. He walked away smiling, wondering what he had done to merit getting the crap beat out of him and then being given fifty *Colombianos*.

I turned to see General Leyva walking with Mr. Padilla back to the hotel. His face showed a sad disappointment. We had been tricked into playing a sinister game. But we suspected that would happen. We now had to focus on Gonzalo Carreno's arrest as soon as possible. The next day we returned to Bogota.

November 10

A local judge approved a court order that was requested by the DAS to disinter the unidentified body found burned near the *autopista*. An effort would be made to determine the identity of the body. A positive identification was absolutely necessary before *Don* Hermidez Padilla could be told that his son was dead. We agreed that an autopsy was needed as soon as possible. A comparison could be made of the teeth of the victim and hopefully, a mold or even x-rays of the teeth belonging to Jaime were available.

In the interim, the General and I visited Jaime's residence with forensics personnel to check for other evidence. A key found on the unidentified body from the *autopista* fit the door to Jaime's apartment perfectly. The remainder of the keys opened locked doors inside the plush apartment where Jaime lived. One of the keys opened a wall safe containing money, documents and pictures. DAS personnel gathered up the evidence found and marked it. Rows of fine three-piece suits and English wool jackets lined large closets, along with dozens of pairs of top quality shoes, Florsheim, size 8 1/2 E.

The maid at the apartment was frightened by our visit. When interviewed by DAS Agents she told them her *Amo*...Master (actually her boss) had not come home for over three weeks. Shown the burned shoe and the tie pin taken from the body at the *autopista*, she became terrified and broke down crying. Although distraught, she identified the items as belonging to her *Amo*... Jaime.

The evidence compiled by the DAS investigation continued to implicate Gonzalo Carreño in Jaime's disappearance. A man by the name of Guillermo Richard informed DAS investigators that he had several drinks with Gonzalo Carreño at the bar at *El Dorado* Airport on the night Jaime arrived from Miami. He even described the drinks they had consumed. Gonzalo did not tell Richard anything about meeting Jaime that night.

A maid employed at the home of Dr. Pedro Carreño, Gonzalo's father, by the name of Carmen Rosa Rodriquez, reported to investigators that she had seen Gonzalo frantically cleaning the inside of the *Mercedes Benz* in the late evening of October 26. She presumed he was using gasoline to clean the car because of the smell. She had offered to help Gonzalo but he told her not to bother. The car had a shattered right window, she said.

"It appears Jaime was murdered immediately after he arrived in Bogota," General Leyva suggested. "Two things are interesting in regard to Gonzalo's character and possible motive. We found pictures inside Jaime's safe that tell a sad but interesting story," he said.

"Gonzalo Carreño was either a homosexual or bisexual and also a coke head." The General continued to explain that pictures were found in Jaime's safe that showed Gonzalo in compromising positions with other males. He asked me if I wanted to see the pictures and I shook my head to tell him no.

"A substance that appears to be cocaine appeared in several pictures. One picture shows him with some guy's *picha* up his ass," he said rubbing his head with the palm of his hand.

"I think Jaime set him up," he told me with a compelling look.

"Apparently Jaime threatened to show the pictures to Anita and to *Don* Hermidez," the General suggested. The situation involved human frailties that had resulted in murder. "We may have to use the pictures in the presentation of the case to the prosecutors and the judge," the General implied sadly.

"I wish we did not have to show them to *Don* Hermidez." He appeared distressed. I suggested that he not show him the pictures. It seemed we had all gotten personally involved in the case. Everyone admired Jaime's father, *Don* Hermidez.

"After he murdered Jaime, the effort needed to burn the body the way he did was an ordeal for poor sensitive Gonzalo," he said. "Reports indicate that he vomited at the scene of the crime, apparently overcome by the ugliness of the scene and brutality of what he had done."

"But how can such a sensitive man be such a cold-blooded killer?" General Leyva observed.

November 15

The disinterment of the body from the cemetery was a pathetic undertaking. Three other bodies had to be displaced in order to reach Jaime's corpse. A local dentist by the name of Dr. Estephen positively identified Jaime from a previous mold taken of his teeth. The blood analysis conducted by DAS laboratory technicians confirmed that the blood found in the *Mercedes Benz* was Jaime's blood type.

"Forensics should check for glass particles on the body, *mi General,*" I offered helpfully. "A comparison should be made with glass particles we found in the trunk of the car." He readily agreed. The particles I had removed from the trunk of the *Mercedes* could not be used, since it required an authorized investigator and a need for the chain of evidence to be protected. Nevertheless, DAS forensics personnel concluded that small pieces of glass found on Jaime's body matched bits of glass found in the trunk of the car and matched the remains of the broken window of the *Mercedes Benz.*

That showed that Gonzalo shot Jaime inside the car and pieces of the shattered window fell on his clothes. When his body was placed in the trunk of the car, small pieces of the glass that had fallen on his clothes were left there.

I was surprised but proud when General Leyva asked me to join him in presenting the case to Dr. Aida Rangel Quintero, the Colombian Judge who had jurisdiction in the case. I felt honored by his trust. Dr. Quintero was an intelligent and lovely podesta and she listened carefully and with an open mind as we carefully explained the case and described the physical evidence that had been found in several locations. Like other countries, Colombian justice often functioned within a cautious, legalistic, bureaucratic framework and often in slow motion.

I personally was very pleased when Judge Quintero quickly found that there was sufficient evidence for the arrest of Gonzalo Carreño. She issued a warrant for his immediate arrest. Now, Gonzalo Carreño had to be found, and *Don* Hermidez Padilla told the sad news.

At the U.S. Embassy George Phelan, the General Consul, made the arrangements needed to inform *Don* Hermidez Padilla about the circumstances that surrounded his son's death. General Leyva and I attended the meeting to assist Phelan, although he had been provided all of the information on the case. He had requested that we be at the meeting. Anita was not invited. At the request of *Don* Hermidez Padilla, an old friend of his, Mr. Hernando Herrera, would join us at the meeting. It would not be a happy gathering.

Phelan's job was not an easy one, and often extremely difficult and emotionally complex. He was hesitant and understandably uncomfortable in explaining what happened to Mr. Padilla's son. We had let him have all the facts, but Phelan was having trouble getting to the point.

Mr. Padilla grew increasingly anguished and tormented as a result of Phelan's caution and reticence in explaining what happened. He wanted to know as clearly as possible and without any doubt, what had happened to his son. He turned to look at me.

"Dolph," he said with a heavy sadness in his voice. "What happened? Tell me. Is Jaime dead?" I glanced at General Leyva and he nodded slowly. Phelan stared at me.

"Jaime is dead," I told *Don* Hermidez as clearly as possible. The evidence found in the case and the linkages to Gonzalo were explained. It was suggested that there was no way to get into Gonzalo's head to determine his motive. Money and greed were possible motives, I told him.

"Evidence shows that Gonzalo killed Jaime after he picked him up at the *El Dorado* Airport when he arrived in Bogota from Miami. Gonzalo apparently planned to kill him." I found it difficult to look him in the eye to tell him that.

"The telegram Anita allegedly received from Jaime changed his arrival date in Bogota and may have been bogus. As a consequence, Jaime's arrival date was changed and his chauffeur did not pick him up at the airport when he was supposed to. It appears that was the plan. Gonzalo was at the airport when Jaime arrived." There was total silence in the room. I continued, trying to be as brief but as concise as possible.

"His chauffeur did not pick Jaime up because his instructions were changed by the telegram received by Anita. The night Jaime arrived, Gonzalo was at the airport and talked Jaime into accepting a ride home with him. That was a fatal mistake by Jaime. But there was no way he could know."

"As a result of the telegram Jaime allegedly sent Anita, his arrival date was changed to October 29, on Avianca flight number 71 from Caracas. But Jaime actually arrived October 26 on Braniff flight 911 as he told his office he would." I looked at the General and he offered me a cigarette. He lit mine and then lit his. The nicotine felt comforting but *Don* Hermidez Padilla stared at me with sad eyes and I grew uneasy.

"Kitty Kiellen Kirby arrived on the same flight from Miami as Jaime did on October 26, on Braniff flight 911. Jaime actually helped carry her bags into customs. But she told us she also saw and talked to Gonzalo Carreño that same night as he wandered around the airport," I continued. When I told *Don* Hermidez that Kitty Kiellen Kirby knew the family very well, he nodded.

"It appears that Gonzalo gave Jaime a ride from the airport that night in Dr. Carreño's *Mercedes Benz*. On the way, it appears that he shot Jaime on the left side of the head with a .45 caliber gun as they drove on the *autopista*. The gun has not been found." I paused to get Phelan's approval. He signaled with his head for me to continue.

"The bullet shattered the right front window of the *Mercedes* and Gonzalo replaced it the following day. He concocted a story about a thief breaking into his car to steal his coat." That was not true.

Don Hermidez Padilla stared at me with sad doleful eyes. It was extremely hard for him to hear what had happened to his only son. I wanted to tell him how sorry I was.

"After he shot Jaime, Gonzalo stopped and placed the body in the trunk of the car. He then drove off the *autopista* to an isolated spot off the highway and tried to burn the body. Blood found on the carpeting removed from the *Mercedes Benz* matched Jaime's blood. Pieces of glass from the broken window of the car found on Jaime's body after he was disinterred matched other glass particles found in the trunk of the *Mercedes."* The room continued to be totally still. Not even the telephone had jiggled.

"Forensics technicians from the DAS found that the glass found in the trunk and those removed from Jaime's body came from the same broken right window of the Mercedes," I said.

Mr. Padilla's face was drawn and terribly distressed. I did not feel like continuing and asked General Leyva to continue.

"Your hypothesis is excellent and I want to hear the rest of it," the General told me in a firm voice. "You are doing just fine," he added peremptorily.

"There was no kidnapping," I emphasized. "Gonzalo planned Jaime's murder. After he drove off the *autopista,* he tried to destroy any possible identification by burning the body with gasoline. But he was only partially successful."

Mr. Padilla seemed to realize that his son was gone forever. His blue eyes overflowed with tears.

"Gonzalo burned Jaime's hands to remove the fingerprints and burned part of his face. He did not want Jaime identified. He did it in a cruel, calculating, and cold-blooded manner." Phelan looked bereaved and pale. Like all of us, he had grown fond of *Don* Hermidez Padilla.

"When the police found the body and were unable to identify it, Jaime was buried in a common grave, at the *Cementerio Central* in Bogota." I lit a cigarette and passed one to the General.

"Why did he do this?" Mr. Padilla asked in a voice that echoed with sorrow. No one spoke up.

"We have not talked to Gonzalo," I told him sadly. General Leyva looked at me and nodded.

"Gonzalo was apparently jealous of Jaime and believed that he was responsible for his being deprived of economic opportunities with your companies," General Leyva said. "Gonzalo wanted a piece of your business interests and money. Jaime told Gonzalo that he did not want him within five miles of *Pomicol,* or any of your companies. It appears he believed that Gonzalo was a homosexual. Jaime did not like Gonzalo and kept him from working with your company in Brazil." *Don* Hermidez sighed audibly.

"Gonzalo wanted a share of your money, *Don* Hermidez. But he was greedy and deranged," General Leyva said. In the dead silence of the room, Hermidez Padilla stood without saying a word. He turned to us.

"I want to see the body," he announced stonily. The General and I looked at each other. It would certainly not be a pleasant sight.

"Are you sure, *Don* Hermidez?" General Leyva asked.

"I am very sure," *Don* Hermidez announced firmly. "I want to give my son a decent burial."

The General and I went with Mr. Padilla to view Jaime's body. With a heavy heart, he positively identified his son from the remains. At last it was over and he was sure. That following day, in a simple ceremony, Jaime Padilla Convers was buried in the family plot in Bogota. We felt a deep pain and sorrow for his father. He had lost his only son to greed. It was very sad and depressing for me. I did not know Jaime, but his father was a remarkable and noble man.

In the end, George Phelan was probably offended by my strident and harsh approach. What could I say? I just did not want Mr. Padilla to suffer from the uncertainty of what had happened to his son. We needed to tell him the whole story and get the tragedy behind us.

The case made headlines in Bogota newspapers for weeks and the stories reported were very favorable for the DAS and General Leyva. I was proud of my friends in the DAS. It had been an honor and privilege for me to work with General Luis Atilio Leyva again. He was a loyal and valued friend.

Ambassador Jack Vaughn was pleased and in a good mood when I briefed him. My reputation as a kidnapping investigation "expert" was intact.

"I'm leaving before another kidnapping occurs, Mr. Ambassador," I told him lightheartedly. He laughed. U.S. Embassy officers were impressed. Driggers congratulated me in a jocular vein.

"It seems you manage to keep your fuck-ups to yourself," he told me. Lubinsky congratulated me, but Dino Pionzo was out of town. Joe Baca, my political friend from New Mexico, was impressed when he heard the news about the kidnappings.

"I knew it," he told Driggers. "The son-of-bitch was in Bolivia in connection with *Ché* Guevara." Driggers told him he was crazy.

November 16

General Leyva called urgently and asked me to meet him for breakfast at the DAS.

"You look good," he kidded when I arrived. "You look *de pecho* (breast fed)," he said jokingly. I felt like it, I told him, and he laughed. He invited me to walk through the corridors of the DAS building.

"Gordillo has apprehended Gonzalo in Spain. The Spanish Police helped us get him." He lit a cigarette and offered me one. "Gordillo is bringing Gonzalo back to Colombia. He will be tried and sent to prison," he said emphatically.

"Es muy difícil sobrevivir la prisión en Colombia," he told me. He suggested that it would be difficult for Gonzalo to survive his imprisonment in Colombia. We continued walking in silence and he suddenly stopped. He took a long drag on his cigarette and blew the smoke upwards, in deep thought.

"I have a court order to arrest Anita. That will be done tomorrow," he said complacently. "That will break the old man's heart. But we have no choice."

"It appears that Anita conspired with Gonzalo to kill Jaime." The General looked depressed.

"I thought you should know," he told me. I felt my face tighten up like leather. "I tell you this in confidence," the General told me with sadness in his eyes.

The day before I left Colombia, General Leyva met with me and thanked me for my help in a flattering manner. He said I had left an indelible mark and many friends in the DAS. I kidded him, telling him that I was at his service. We hugged and wished each other all the best.

"Mucho cuidado (Be careful)," he said. *"Qué Dios lo Bendiga* (God Bless you)."* I will never forget my good friend General Luis Etilio Leyva.

November 17

I called Washington, D.C., and Byron Engle had already heard the news about the successful resolution of the new kidnapping case. The U.S. Embassy in Colombia had reported the situation with undisguised pleasure regarding OPS assistance in the matter. I had discouraged Ambassador Jack Vaughn from writing any encomiums about my role in resolving the kidnappings. The credit totally belonged to General Leyva and the DAS, I told him. If Jack Vaughn is alive, he will likely remember. Engle was delighted with the favorable official report from the U.S. Embassy. He listened attentively to my story and asked many questions about the case.

"Congratulations," he told me cheerfully. "You did a good job." Unknown to me, he considered me a genuine kidnapping investigation "expert" with more of the same in store for me.

Engle agreed that my report would be completed on my return to Washington. Lauren "Jack" Goin, his assistant and future OPS Director, would provide me with assistance in finalizing the report. Other U.S.

agencies had requested a copy of the report on **The Kidnapping Problem in Colombia.**

"Bob Sayre was named Ambassador to Panama," Engle told me casually. "He suggested your assignment to Panama as Chief of the OPS program there." He was probing for my reaction.

"What do you think?" What happened to my assignment to Vietnam, I thought humorously.

"I'm glad," I told Engle. "I like Panama and Sayre is an excellent Ambassador. He did a great job as Ambassador in Uruguay when we were there during the *Tupamaro* problem." I chuckled almost instinctively.

"But I thought he was pissed off at me," I told him.

"Naw, he seems to like you," Engle said. "But he did say that you were very direct." He chuckled. "The political atmosphere in Panama is totally different now," he said.

"Your old friend, Omar Torrijos, has overthrown the government and is now in charge. He made himself a General and is Commandant of the Panama National Guard," Engle explained. He had emphasized "your friend Torrijos," expecting a response from me, but I stayed silent.

"We want you there as soon as possible," he said in a minatory way. I grinned to myself—what else is new? "Jack Neely will wait until you get there." I was glad. Former FBI Agent and CIA Officer Jack Neely was a friend and top-notch officer.

November 18

The day before I left Colombia, *Don* Hermidez Padilla unexpectedly invited me to dinner.

"We will eat at my house," he said, "so we can talk without interruptions." I did not have the heart to make excuses. He was in pain and grieving the loss of his only son. My beautiful blonde friend from the Embassy was hurt more than angry when I told her we would see each other after my dinner with Mr. Padilla.

"I may not wait up for you," she told me petulantly. She reminded me with tears in her eyes that it was my very last night in Colombia.

"How could I forget?" I told her. "I will be back as soon as I can."

Mr. Padilla's residence was large and elegant, with maids and a cook that took care of the place. The house was apparently unoccupied except when he and his wife visited Bogota. He was waiting nervously for me and broke into a smile when I arrived. It was easy to admire him.

He plied me with *Tiqueta Negra* (Black Label) Scotch until I felt totally relaxed. Later, the maids served an outstanding *vino tinto* with veal medallions and creamy pasta for dinner. Afterwards, we sat in the library near a fireplace to chat. I felt bad about his son's death but was glad we were able to find his killer and bring him back to face Colombian justice.

Don Hermidez seemed at ease with me and we talked candidly about the tragic events that had occurred in Jaime's case. It was clear that he was still in shock with his son's death. He had been unaware of the serious problems that had developed between Jaime and Gonzalo Carreño. Now he was concerned about what he would tell his wife in Puerto Rico. She did not know the whole story behind Jaime's death. She had remained at home in San Juan because she was not well. *Don* Hermidez did not mention Anita.

A shiver ran through me when I thought about Jaime and Anita playing together in the house when they were small children. What had occurred was a true real-life tragedy.

"I'm going to open a bottle of cognac that I have been saving for a special occasion," *Don* Hermidez told me in a soft voice. "The bottle is quite a few years old." His voice was laced with a trace of deep emotion. He showed me a ten-year-old bottle of fine French Cognac and smiled wistfully.

"You are my special occasion," he told me softly and his eyes grew misty. I felt sadness.

We drank cognac in beautiful crystal snifters, warming the glass over a candle. I felt the rush immediately. His eyes brightened when I told him the cognac was absolutely the best I had ever tasted. It was a privilege for me to enjoy it in his company, I told him. The cognac was unbelievably smooth, with a strong potency and a delicate taste that lingered sensuously on the tongue. But *Don* Hermidez had something else on his mind.

"Dolph," he began to tell me with gentle tact. "You're wasting your time in government." He looked at me with a slight grin.

"There is no money in the work you do. I think there is only danger and treachery for you in your job." He studied my face. "I bet there is plenty of sadness too," he added.

I nodded thoughtfully and stayed silent. I should have listened.

"Let me set you up in business," he suggested. He had plenty of sorrow to take back with him to Puerto Rico and I could not believe he was concerned about me.

"Well," I chuckled, feeling uncertainty. "I'm flattered. But I can't retire from the U.S. Government with fourteen years of service, Mr. Padilla," I told him.

"But you are very kind and I certainly appreciate the offer." Sadness and nostalgia hit me. What other competency did I have? For misguided ideologues in America, OPS officers were CIA terrorists teaching torture to the police of other counties. That was a lie. I was a mere cop who liked what I was doing with OPS. Why was it so difficult for people to believe that?

It was past ten o'clock and my thoughts turned to my departure for Washington, D.C., the following morning. Mr. Padilla saw me looking at my watch.

"Dolph," he asked me with a look of despair. "What do you think I should do?" He had a look of supplication.

"What do you advise me?" he asked. We had avoided talking about Anita and her possible involvement in Jaime's death.

"I will have to remain in Bogota for awhile," he said in a soft voice. "But I must go home soon. My wife needs me." He paused sadly.

"She doesn't know the whole story," he told me, looking sad.

I felt troubled that he had asked for my advice. I wanted to help. I felt fortunate to have met him despite the tragic circumstances of his son's murder. *Don* Hermidez had gone through a great deal of pain and sorrow and was obviously stunned by what had happened to his son. He was a good man and had endured a lot of grief. General Leyva had told me in confidence about the court order he had to arrest Anita. Don Hermidez was unaware of this. I had to tell him.

"You did everything that could possibly be done, Mr. Padilla," I told him. "Most importantly, you were able to determine what had happened to Jaime and gave him a proper burial." I paused to control my own emotions. "God knows it has been very hard for you. Don't worry about Gonzalo, he will get what he deserves." *Don* Hermidez looked sadly at me as I struggled with what I was about to tell him.

"I suggest you get the best lawyer you can find in Colombia for Anita," I said plainly. "She will be arrested tomorrow as an accomplice in the case." His blue eyes blinked and his face grew florid. He must have suspected this. He stayed silent for a long moment and I felt lost.

"You have suffered enough, *Don* Hermidez," I told him. "Try to hang on to what is left. Help Anita fight any charge that may be levied against her. Then go home." He looked at me and his eyes welled up with tears. I felt a deep remorse and sadness as he wiped his eyes with a handkerchief.

"I want you to call me in Puerto Rico in one month," he said, handing me his card with his address and telephone number.

"I want you to come visit me. I appreciate what you have done and want us to be friends." I nodded in agreement. I smiled at the thought.

"It will be my pleasure," I promised. "I want to know how things turn out for you." We hugged and we both grew teary eyed. He was one unforgettable and noble person that I will never forget.

Sadness gripped me as I walked to my car. One more night with the beautiful blonde from the Embassy would help assuage my beastly feelings. She was waiting.

Epilogue

Gonzalo Carreno was arrested in Spain by Inspector Gordillo of the DAS with the help of the Spanish Police and returned to Bogota. He was tried for murder, convicted, and sentenced to 15 years in prison.

I learned later from General Leyva that he had lost his mind while in a Colombian prison and died a few years later. Anita escaped conviction and prison.

Straessle and Buff eventually returned to Colombia. Kidnappings continued as a major threat and political issue in Colombia with the *Fuerzas Armadas Revolucionarias de Colombia* (FARC), the *Ejercito Popular de Liberacion Nacional* (EPN), the *Ejercito de Liberacion Nacional* (ELN), carrying out numerous abductions along with the drug cartels. *La Violencia* continues.

In terms of my future, sorrow, heartbreak, more violence, and kidnappings waited for me. Mr. Hermidez Padilla was right about my life. I should have accepted his offer.

Shortly after I left Colombia, I was on my way to Panama to work with General Torrijos and Colonel Manuel Noriega, theoretically in a role of an ally. My replacement in Uruguay, Dan Mitrione, would be kidnapped by the *Tupamaros* and brutally murdered. I pleaded with Washington to let me go help my friend but was denied. I was told it was too dangerous for me. I told folks in Washington, D.C., that Mitrione would be assassinated unless we negotiated with the *Tupamaros*. They did not believe me. That is another story.

In his book, **Hidden Terrors**, A.J. Langguth proposed that Costa Gavras' aim in producing the communist propaganda film, **State of Siege**, was a "a composite indictment of U.S. policy throughout Latin America." He was referring to the OPS program and the U.S. assistance provided to help the police forces of the hemisphere resist communist subversion and insurgency. Costa Gavras was a card-carrying member of the French communist party, so he was biased. Several undisclosed sources told me that Langguth had been a far left-wing advocate for many years.

Langguth mentioned in his book with obvious glee that Philip Agee, the CIA defector, would have his book, **Inside the Company,** published in London. Agee was to move to Paris to live with Angela Camargo Seixas, the MR-8 terrorist from Brazil, Langguth reported. He proclaimed that the publication of Agee's book and his love affair with Angela Camargo Seixas were two happy endings to the Philip Agee story. In 2001, Agee is operating an online travel agency in Havana, Cuba.

I have often wondered how A.J. Langguth, Philip Agee, Roger Morris, Michael Klare, James Abourezk, and others of the same ilk, feel about communism going down the tubes in the Soviet Union. Is it over for them? Does the Cold War go on? I have often seen glimpses of it in the past ten years.

In Uruguay, with the help of the OPS program, the security forces eventually defeated the *Tupamaros.* Over 37 members of the security forces, eight innocent citizens and 50 *Tupamaros* were killed in the senseless struggle.

OPS Cold Warriors

The important contributions made by OPS cold warriors in the fight against communist aggression in many countries remains unknown to most Americans. The OPS program helped combat communist subversion and insurgency in many countries during the Cold War. United States assistance also improved the capabilities of police forces of Free World countries to fight crime, international terrorism and drug trafficking. In many countries of the world, U.S. police assistance helped preserve democracy. Contrary to far-left critics, American advisors emphasized the importance of human rights in law enforcement. OPS Officers often risked their lives to do the job their government entrusted them to do in the conflict with communism. Many lost their lives and careers in the process. Bryron Engle called his OPS Officers, "Superfuzz."

Nevertheless, the men and women of the OPS saw their lives and careers crumble and fall apart as communist propagandists attacked the organization with false allegations of torture and involvement in terrorism. Like the Americans fighting in Vietnam, OPS personnel have reason to believe that many of their countrymen supported the "enemy" in the Cold War. The Americans who served were caught in the crossfire of the corrupt politics, ideologues and politicians.

The record shows that police assistance provided by the United States after World War II involved the Office of Strategic Services (OSS) and later the Central Intelligence Agency (CIA). In 1958, 16 countries received United States police assistance and about sixty public safety advisors were involved.

The objective was to support economic progress, viability and political stability. Later, police assistance was based on the policy of the United States to promote democratization, economic and political progress, and to contain communist aggression. But under the circumstances of the Cold War, the OPS operated in a hostile environment dominated by treachery and faithless politics.

An extensive research of the records available and my own recollection of the individuals I knew, showed with absolute certainty that the men and women who served to carry out U.S. policy concerning police assistance missions were outstanding Americans and superior professionals with impressive credentials and backgrounds. In excess of a thousand served over a period of twenty years, including some not mentioned in this book.

Colonel Arthur Kimberling headed police assistance programs under the FOA and ICA in the early 1950s. After World War II, Kimberling served as an advisor to the Japanese Police during the U.S. military occupation of that country. He served with Byron Engle in the Japanese program. Kimberling, a former Chief of Police of Louisville, Kentucky, brought a tremendous wealth of knowledge, prestige, and leadership for U.S. police assistance efforts. He died on May 5, 1994, after a lifelong contribution to American initiatives for world peace. He was an exemplary American, a patriot, and I am very happy to have had the opportunity to meet him.

Theo Hall was a man with a magnificent personality, great wisdom, and incredible experience. He was a professional Foreign Service Officer detailed as Chief of the ICA police division in 1957. But he had extensive police experience. Hall had served with O.W. Wilson with the Wichita Police Department, and as Chief of Police at Two Rivers, Wisconsin, and Wilmette, Illinois. As a civilian under General Lucius Clay in Berlin after World War II, he headed the public safety branch. Hall was actually a high-ranking American Foreign Service Officer who served his country with great skill and dedication in regards to the police assistance program. Posted in Saigon during the Vietnam War, he met and married his wife Mary Ellen. OPS Officer Herb Hardin accurately described the man. **"Theo Hall was a person**

to admire." Hall died on March 15, 1994. I am happy that I had the opportunity to meet such a great American.

Byron Engle was an extraordinary individual who served his country for many years with a profound regard for loyalty and devotion to duty. His vast police experience began in the Kansas City Police Department where he moved up in the ranks to the position of Director of Personnel and Training. He subsequently served as a civilian police administrator under General Douglas MacArthur, the Supreme Commander, Allied Powers, in Tokyo. Engle developed a plan to reorganize the Japanese police that was approved by General Douglas MacArthur, and subsequently implemented. His U.S. Government assignments, domestic as well as abroad, were important to national security interests.

He was Chief of the ICA Civil Police Administration Branch from 1955 to 1957. Shortly after his appointment as the Director of OPS in 1962, he married Geraldine Jelsh, a veteran CIA Officer who supported the purpose of police assistance to foreign countries throughout her career.

Byron Engle died on January 10, 1990, greatly admired and respected by the men and women of OPS. Mitchell Mabardy, a top aide to Engle, expressed appropriate sentiments in a final eulogy to the Boss. **"He was loyal to members of his team: He loved, protected, and promoted them, and made every effort to learn about each of them and their families.** Mabardy closed by telling the OPS Officers present: **"We can all go on with uplifted spirits and draw strength from having worked for and known such an outstanding, gentlemanly, and especially fine human being."** Engle inspired his OPS personnel. The President of the United States wrote many fine things about Engle when he retired, but the most important was the following. **"You have my deep appreciation for a difficult job exceedingly well done."** But above all, Byron Engle was a great American Patriot. Ultimately, he was my mentor as well as for many others.

Johnson F. "Jack" Munroe started as a police officer in the Nashville Police Department. Educated at Vanderbilt University, he worked briefly as a reporter for the **Nashville Tennesseean.** After a stint in the USAF from 1943 to 1945, Jack Munroe worked as an investigator in Japan for the War Crimes Tribunal in 1947. Byron Engle talked him into transferring to the civilian police administration group working with the Japanese police under General MacArthur. Munroe was with the ICA police group in 1955 and served in Cambodia and Washington, D.C. He was appointed Deputy Director of the OPS in 1961 and retired in 1972.

When he died on April 16, 1984, Byron Engle, the Director of OPS, provided a fitting final eulogy: **"Jack Munroe was intellectually**

honest, completely unselfish, a true gentleman, and a great human being."

Lauren "Jack" Goin, a former Director of the Pittsburgh and Allegheny Crime Laboratory, was a leading American criminalist and forensics expert when he was recruited by the FOA in April of 1954. As a young man, he took on complex police assistance assignments in Indonesia, Turkey, and Brazil. Jack Goin went on home leave from Brazil on "Return to Post Orders" and on reporting to Washington on January 8, 1963, the Director of OPS asked Goin to choose between two positions. The positions were as Chief of the OPS program in El Salvador or as the head of a new division called the Technical Services Division (TSD). He chose the latter and spent eleven years at OPS headquarters in Washington.

Byron Engle appointed him Chief of the Operations Division in June of 1964 where he served for seven more years. Goin succeeded "Jack" Munroe as Deputy Director of OPS in 1972 and was appointed the Director of OPS on April 1, 1973, replacing Byron Engle. He assumed the sad task of closing down the program and fought bitterly to the end to defend the OPS.

Ted Brown, a former Chief of Police of Eugene, Oregon, and Director of Public Safety for the Island of Guam, was a man with deep-rooted values of integrity, compassion, and loyalty. He served with singular distinction as the Chief of U.S. police assistance programs in Liberia, Greece, Libya, El Salvador, Brazil, and Vietnam. Brown also served as the Director of the Inter-American Police Academy and as Chief of the OPS Latin American Branch until he retired.

He was greatly admired and respected by anyone who served with OPS. Ted Brown was truly a great American and I feel very grateful that he was my friend. He was an exceptional individual. It was with a sad heart that I learned that Ted Brown had passed away on April 20, 2001.

Frank Jessup, a former Superintendent of the Indiana State Police, was the head of the overall ICA police assistance effort in 1961. He was considered one of the foremost police administrators in the United States and the best in his field. Jessup was greatly admired by all the people who knew him. I recall he was intelligent, totally unpretentious, patient, and helpful to anyone who worked for him even in the toughest of times. Jessup was a superior police advisor and served in Iran as head of the complex ICA police assistance program in that country, and as Chief of OPS in Brazil, and in many other assignments. He served his country with loyalty and performed exceedingly well.

Michael (Mike) McCann was a veteran of United States police assistance efforts and, at a young age, led public safety programs in several countries. McCann served in Iran, Brazil, and later as the founder and Director of the International Police Academy. His impressive background included experience as a State Trooper in Indiana, as a professor of criminal justice at Indiana State University, and as a Special Agent of the FBI. McCann led the large OPS effort in the hot war in Vietnam during the tough and complex final stages of that conflict. He was considered one of the most effective professionals and leaders in the OPS program.

The information provided on the individuals mentioned above and on others that follow should help any reader comprehend the background, personality, and the type of American that served with OPS. Their record as loyal Americans, their service and accomplishments are indisputable. I am proud to have known them.

Herb Hardin is a recognized expert of the U.S. police assistance effort. He is a calm, intelligent individual, and considered the best of the OPS professionals. After graduating from the University of California at Berkeley with a degree in criminology, he was a key commander in the Albuquerque Police Department when I met him. He recruited me and I am very pleased to call him one of my best friends.

Hardin served as the Chief of the ICA and OPS Latin American Branch for many years and headed the OPS program in Colombia. He completed many difficult assignments, conducting studies and surveys of foreign police organizations. Hardin was one of the few *Gringos* I knew who spoke fluent Spanish and was able to maneuver smoothly in Latin America. He is retired and currently lives in Arizona.

John (Jack) Neely, a former FBI Special Agent and CIA Officer, was assigned to Latin America for many years, including during World War II. He survived hairy episodes, but among the most intriguing was dancing with Eva Peron in Argentina as General Juan Peron watched. Neely says it was strictly business. In World War II, he volunteered for the Scouts and Raiders (currently Navy Seals) and is called Granddad by the Navy Seals when he visits. Neely was Chief of the OPS program in Panama when I replaced him.

Roy (Bill) Driggers, previously a State Police Captain from New Mexico, spoke fluent Spanish and served with OPS in Colombia, Uruguay, and Guatemala. Driggers provided valuable help to me when I was assigned to Colombia to work with the security forces of the country on a deadly kidnapping problem. Driggers replaced Dan Mitrione after his kidnapping and brutal murder by the Marxist *Tupamaros* in Uruguay.

Driggers returned home to New Mexico and was appointed as the first Sheriff of Cibola County and was re-elected twice. He died in April of 2000.

Colonel Mitchell Mabardy, a former U.S. Air Force Far East Provost Marshal and top officer with the U.S. Air Force Office of Special Investigations (OSI), served as a senior advisor to Byron Engle, the Director of the OPS. Mabardy brought admirable experience, professional integrity and leadership skills to the OPS Washington bureaucracy. He took on the sad task of closing down the International Police Academy.

Julian Lindenauer was a young Spanish-speaking Miami Beach police officer when he joined OPS to serve in Guatemala and Uruguay, countries beset by terrorist problems. Shortly before the closure of the OPS, he wound up as a Special Agent with the U.S. Drug Enforcement Administration (DEA). In a vicious shootout with very dangerous Class I traffickers in *Los Mochis,* Mexico, he saved the life of his supervisor, Special Agent Tony Celaya. Lindenauer was subsequently decorated by the DEA for this heroic action. He served many more years in Latin America. He is presently retired and lives in Florida. He and I remain very close friends.

Frank Walton was a Deputy Chief of Police for the Los Angeles Police Department. During World War II, he had served as an Intelligence Officer for the famous U.S. Marine Corps Black Sheep Squadron of "Pappy" Boyington in the Pacific. Walton wrote a book about the exploits of the Black Sheep Squadron called, **"Once they were Eagles."** No one can dispute his record as a patriot. With OPS, he led the police assistance effort in Vietnam during the hot war in the early '60s. Walton was a member of the U.S. Olympic Water Polo Team of 1948. He died November 20, 1994.

Phil Batson was a professional police administrator who had worked his way up the ladder of the Seattle Police Department to become Deputy Chief. He later served as a police advisor for the U.S. Office of the Secretary of Defense, and joined OPS in 1963. He completed assignments as Chief of the OPS program in Indonesia, in Bangkok, Thailand, and as Deputy Chief of the OPS program during the war in Vietnam. Batson died on May 12, 1994. His knowledge of police operations and administration was considered among the best.

Don Bordenkircher was a young man when he worked his way up to the position of warden at San Quentin. There he met and married his wife Shirley who also worked at the prison. Bordenkircher volunteered to serve in Vietnam with the OPS program and experienced the American left-wing conspiracy regarding the *Con Son* prison, on a first-hand basis. The American left-wing conspirators falsely alleged that Americans were using "Tiger Cages" in Vietnam. The cages had been in Vietnam since the French. The allegations were a ploy used by left-wing radicals to condemn American involvement in the Vietnam War.

Bordenkircher's book, called **A Different Order of Battle,** describes the false allegations and identifies the Americans involved in the sinister affair. Bordenkircher is currently considered among the best in American Corrections. He lives in West Virginia.

Colonel Knute Thorpe came to OPS on loan from the Office of the U.S. Army Provost Marshal to serve in the Dominican Republic in 1967 when a communist insurgent movement attempted to take over the country. Thorpe, born in Norway, came to the United States at a young age. He enlisted in the U.S. Army during World War II, was commissioned as an Artillery Officer, and served in combat with the 90th Division, fighting from Normandy to Czechoslovakia.

He was later in charge of all police training at the School of the Americas and served as Provost Marshal of Ft. Belvoir, Virginia. We worked together to develop the ideas that served as the basis for the production of the training film called "The First Line of Defense." Thorpe often discounts that he has a Ph.D. in economics.

Pete Ellena was a young man when he joined OPS after serving with the Pasadena Police Department. After serving in the Korean War, he earned a degree in Police Administration. He served a tour in Brazil and was the Deputy Chief of the OPS Latin-American Branch for many years. When Dan Mitrione was kidnapped by the *Tupamaros* in Uruguay, Pete Ellena and OPS Officer David Arroyo were immediately sent by Washington, D.C., to help the local U.S. Mission. When the two men arrived in Montevideo, Uruguay, the local communist media reported that 200 FBI Agents had landed in the country. Arroyo, a former cop from the Los Angeles Police Department, got sick and the more credible local news media jokingly reported that 100 of the FBI Agents were sick as hell. Many times Pete Ellena and I agonized about Mitrione's cold-blooded murder and the communist allegations of torture. Ellena died of cancer onNovember 25, 1993. He was a patriotic American and a valuable member of the OPS program. I considered him my good friend.

Anthony (Tony) Ruiz was a retired Captain of the Los Angeles Police Department and a law school graduate when he joined the OPS program in the early '60s. He took on the tough assignments without a problem. As a typical *Chicano* cop from Los Angles, he spoke Spanish fluently. He was Chief of the OPS program in the Dominican Republic and did everything possible to help the security forces resist an outbreak of communist subversion and insurgency during a very difficult period. He served as Chief of OPS programs in other assignments and served his country to the best of his ability and without recognition.

Nickolas (Nick) Yantsin, known affectionately as the "Russian Bear," was born in Russia and immigrated to America with his parents over fifty decades ago. He joined the State Troopers of Alaska and volunteered with OPS to serve in Venezuela, Vietnam, and other places, where he received several commendations. Yantsin was a tough-looking man, but in effect was kind and compassionate. He was one of the founders of the **Public Safety Newsletter,** a news bulletin that has served to bond former OPS personnel and keep them advised of the activities and news about their former colleagues. Yantsin died in 1999 and Reg Davis, a former colonel in the USAF Reserve and OPS Officer, picked up the torch to keep the newsletter alive.

Lee Echols was one of the best trick shooters in the world. His admirable sense of humor and funny story telling ability belied the valuable work he accomplished for his country. Echols served in the U.S. Border Patrol, U.S. Customs, as a CIA Officer, as a Sheriff in Arizona, and with OPS in the Dominican Republic, Bolivia, and Uruguay. After he retired he was elected to the Board of Directors for the **Association of Former Intelligence Officers (AFIO),** and, despite my resistance, convinced me to start the New Mexico Chapter. Lee Echols, a true patriot, died in early 1999.

In 1955, when the FOA changed to ICA, the public safety group was under **Byron Engle** with **Colonel Kimberling** assigned as the Deputy of the program. **Jack Munroe, Ed Bishop,** and **Theo Hall** were assigned to the ICA public safety group. In the early '50s, the people who provided oversight and management of the ICA group in Washington, D.C., were **Daniel Van Buskirk,** Training; **Bill Bateman,** Personnel; **Robert Lowe,** Far East Affairs; **Herb Hardin,** Latin American Affairs; and **Ed Kennelly,** Near East/Africa Affairs. **Harry Hahn** handled administrative functions and served as the key assistant to the Chief of the small ICA group.

There were many outstanding police professionals who served with the ICA and subsequently in top positions with OPS. **Carl Betsch,** a former Special Agent of the FBI, **Glenn McClung,** a former Chief of Police of Glendale, California, and **Michael (Mike) McCann** were some of the top professionals in OPS.

The majority of police advisors assigned to the ICA program saw action with the OPS. In the early days of FOA and ICA, **Jim McMahon,** a graduate of Michigan State University in Police Administration, served in South Korea and Indonesia, along with **Bob Janus,** a former U.S. Coast Guard Officer, and **Reg Davis,** a former Far East Command Air Force Staff Officer. Davis survived twelve years of service in Vietnam. **Bob Lowe,** a former FBI Special Agent, **Robert Broughham,** a former Navy pilot, **Charles Nesbitt,** and **Scotty Caplan,** former military officers, and **Paul Katz,** a telecommunications engineer, served in the Far East in the early days of ICA. In 1954, serving in Vietnam as police advisors were **Ralph Turner, John Manopoli, Elmer "Tommy" Adkins, Charles Sloan, Ray Landgren** and **Dick Rogers. Frank Walton,** a retired Deputy Chief of the Los Angeles Police Department, **Michael McCann** and **Robert "Nate" Bush** subsequently headed the OPS program in Vietnam at different times. **Sam Pesacreta** and **David Sheppard** were both retired, decorated military colonels, and assigned to the OPS program in Vietnam. **Chuck Trout,** attorney, professional boxer, and criminal investigator, also served with OPS in Vietnam. In Jordan, **Roy Carlson** and **Charlie Nesbitt** rotated as Chief of the OPS program. **Frank Jessup** was Chief of the complex ICA police assistance program in Iran and was replaced by **Weyland Williams** and later **Dick Rogers** as Chief of the program. **Michael McCann** and former FBI Agent **Tom Finn** were also assigned in that country. **Garland Williams** served as a colonel in the U.S. Army in World War II and trained the first paratroop unit used in the war. He also served at the executive level in the old U.S. Bureau of Narcotics and U.S. Customs and was assigned as a narcotics advisor with the police assistance program in Iran. **Jeter Williamson,** former Chief of the Greensboro, North Carolina Police Department, headed the ICA police assistance program in the Philippines, and later in Saudi Arabia. **Harry Hambleton,** Major, U.S. Army Military Police, served in the Philippines with OPS. In Somalia, **Clyde Phelps** was Chief of the ICA police assistance program. In Thailand, **Albert Dubois,** a former police commissioner from Philadelphia, was in charge of the program. **Ray Foreacker,** a former Chief of the Oakland Police Department, took over as Chief of the police assistance program in South Korea. In Laos, Burma, and Cambodia, **Jack Munroe** and **Paul Skuse,** a former police administrator in Okinawa, alternated as Chief of the Public Safety program. **Ed Bishop,** a former U.S. Army Officer and an expert in internal defense, worked with them. **Ray Landgren,** a former police officer from La Grange Park, Illinois, and Korean War C.I.D. veteran, was Chief of the public safety program in

Laos. **Landgren** also served in Zaire and Vietnam. **Del Speir,** a former Lieutenant with the Aurora, Colorado, Police Department, was Chief of the OPS program in Laos, and later served in Vietnam. **John Wiess,** formerly of the Las Vegas, Nevada, Police Department, headed the public safety program in Nepal. **Charlie O'Brien** became a Chief of the Public Safety Division in Turkey assisted by **Jack Goin. Roy Carlson** served in Jordan and **Clyde Phelps** in Somalia. In Zaire, **John Manopoli, Roy Carlson, Tommy Adkins,** and **Art Garza** alternated tours in that country. **Stan Sheldon** and **Robert "Nate" Bush** managed U.S. police assistance for East and West Pakistan in the 1960s. OPS personnel have interesting and sometimes incredible stories to tell.

Many other Americans served with OPS in Latin America. In Brazil, **Joe Lingo,** a former Director of Public Safety for the State of Indiana, was Chief of the police assistance program assisted by **Jack Goin. Jim McMahon, Jake Jackson, Morris Grodsky, Bob Clark,** and **Dan Mitrione** were assigned as police advisors. **Ray Baca,** a former Director of Public Safety of Albuquerque and police lieutenant with the Albuquerque Police Department, served a tumultuous period in *Minas Gerais* in Brazil. In Bolivia, **Michael Salseda,** a veteran police lieutenant with the Los Angeles County Sheriff's Department, headed the ICA program along with **Lee Echols. Herb Hardin** assessed public safety needs in the Dominican Republic during the period of volatile communist unrest, and arranged for police officers from the Los Angeles Police Department to be assigned as advisors for a short term. **Jake Jackson** served as Chief in the Dominican Republic initially, and was replaced by **Anthony "Tony" Ruiz.** Jackson also served in Bolivia and was shot in the back by leftist guerrillas. **Richard Raugi, Knute Thorpe,** and **Mel Holguin** were assigned as public safety advisors in the Dominican Republic. **David Laughlin,** a former Captain with the Indiana State Police, started the program for ICA in Honduras, and was assisted by police advisors **Earl Sears, Joe Cisneros, Rex Morris,** and **Art Russell. Cleo Baca,** an experienced and veteran *Chicano* Federal Agent, was fluent in Spanish and served as the first Chief of the U.S. police assistance program in Ecuador. **Michael Salceda, Fred Zumwalt, Ernest Lancini,** and **John Doney** were assigned as police advisors in Ecuador at different times. **Desederio Crisostimo,** a former Deputy Director of Public Safety in Guam, served in Guatemala as Chief of the OPS program, followed by **Pete Costello,** a former Inspector with the New York City Police Department. **Julian Lindenauer** and **Felipe Sandoval** served with Costello in Guatemala as police advisors. In Venezuela, **Jake Longan,** a former U.S. Border Patrol Supervisor, was Chief of the police assistance program, assisted by police advisors **Nick Yantsin, David Arroyo, Felipe Sandoval, Robert Cavanaugh,** and **Richard Raugi.** I replaced Longan as Chief of the OPS program in Venezuela in 1973. **George Miller,** a retired Captain of the Pennsylvania State Police, started the Public Safety Program in Peru. In Panama, **Jack Neely,** a former FBI Agent and CIA Officer, headed the police assistance effort for the Panama National Guard assisted by **Richard Biava.** I replaced Neely as Chief of OPS in Panama, with **Robert Mann** and **Paul Hoffey** assigned there. In Costa Rica, **David Powell, Bill Bartreau,** and **Andrew Best** were assigned as Chief of the OPS program in different periods of time. **Bill Bartreau** also served in Colombia as Chief during a period of turmoil in that country. **James Scoggin** and **Thomas Guffain** were assigned as police advisors in Costa Rica. **Roland Kelly,** a former Chief of Police of Fort Lauderdale, Florida, and former FBI Special Agent, was the Chief of the ICA Police Program in El Salvador. **Jim Brooks** and I were police advisors. In 1965, I was assigned to start the OPS Program in Uruguay, and was replaced five years later by **Dan Mitrione. Caesar Bernal, Bill Cantrell, Julian Lindenauer, Lee Echols, Richard Martinez,** and **Dick Biava** served in Uruguay. **Bill Driggers** replaced **Mitrione** after his assassination by the *Tupamaros.*

There were less than 70 police advisors who served early on with the FOA and ICA. One was **Art Thurston,** a retired Superintendent of the Indiana State Police. Others were **Lauren "Jack" Goin** and **Melvin "Buck" Fruit,** a retired Air Force officer from Oregon with police assistance experience. **"Buck" Fruit** became a recruiter for OPS. **Herb Hardin,** an admired and respected veteran of ICA and OPS, served as Chief of the ICA and the OPS Latin-American Branch for many years, and as Chief of the OPS program in Colombia. **John Doney,** a former FBI Special Agent with language fluency, was assigned to Honduras.

In terms of the organizational culture of OPS, the assignment of CIA Officers as police advisors was based on an agreement between the Central Intelligence Agency (CIA) and Bryon Engle, the Director of OPS. The same was true of FBI Special Agents and other Federal Law Enforcement Officers.

Engle was a masterful and consummate CIA Officer, but reportedly had resigned from the **"Company"** when he accepted the position of Director, OPS. Nevertheless, a majority of OPS police professionals were leery about the CIA officers assigned to the organization to perform other than overt police advisory functions. Many OPS officers were former CIA Officers working legitimately as police advisors. Covert intelligence missions in OPS were potentially risky because the practice placed the mission and integrity of the U.S. police assistance program at risk. But when a foreign nation requested United States police assistance, a thorough study of its needs was conducted, and professional officers were recruited from all domestic police agencies and Federal Agencies, including the CIA. Nevertheless, intervention by top officials from the CIA in the OPS program was often inescapable.

In the early '60s when David Laughlin was the Chief of the OPS program in Peru working with the 40,000 men Civil Guard (*Guardia Civil,* National Police), the CIA intervened more capriciously than judiciously. Desmond "Des" Fitzgerald, a senior CIA Officer with powerful ties to the Kennedy Administration, insisted on organizing, training, and equipping a 150-man special police group to combat left-wing guerrillas operating in rural areas. The guerrillas were the original *Sendero Luminoso* (Shining Path) movement.

To compete, in essence, with Peruvian military forces, the Special Police Unit (SPU) was provided with a paratroop capability, special weapons and equipment. The effort was viewed as a covert operation of a flamboyant variety. Laughlin unsuccessfully resisted the effort on the basis that (1) The Peruvian Army, much stronger both politically and militarily, would not like the idea of the police being given a military operations mission and capability. (2) Millions of dollars were put into the budget of U.S. police assistance for the SPU project, and that became obvious for other Peruvian police units who requested similar U.S. assistance. (3) The Civil Guard simply did not have the budget or financial resources to continue to operate and maintain the equipment needed for the Special Police Unit.

Laughlin got a great deal of heat from Washington when he resisted the project. The arrangements made by "Des" Desmond were that the Peruvian Air Force would service and maintain several aircraft and landing strips for the Special Police Unit. But problems soon arose when an expensive aircraft carrying eight senior police officials crashed into the jungle, killing everyone on board.

Later, a C-47 provided to the Special Police Unit also crashed, this time killing 24 policemen who were on board. Things grew worse without a consistent supply of resources and money to maintain and repair equipment. Thirty expensive vehicles provided to the SPU unit went out of service due to lack of upkeep. The operation eventually was obliged to shut down.

Afterwards, the Director General of the Civil Guard posed a question to Laughlin. "If you give us a Cadillac and the battery dies and we do not have the money to buy a battery, what good is the Cadillac?" The cost was three million dollars down the drain and thirty police officers killed in Peru.

To accomplish its mission, the OPS used police professionals, CIA officers, U.S. Military personnel and support personnel for administrative functions, and in the areas of forensics and telecommunications. Initially the organization of OPS included three main divisions: an Operations Division, a Training Division, and a Technical Services Division. Like others involved in the Cold War, OPS personnel became known as "cold warriors."

Many OPS Officers found that the role of cold warrior was not easy. As Charles Krauthammer observed in his syndicated column, **"liberalism reviled the 'cold warriors' and opposed their nearly every step to topple the Soviet empire."** Ultimately, in the Cold War, the men and women of OPS were an amalgamation of patriotic Americans committed to the fulfillment of police assistance missions. But the people of the OPS eventually became an undifferentiated mass of trouble for communist and left-wing forces.

Perhaps it could be conceded that some OPS officers drank too much and perhaps some were toady, hypocritical, cynical, aggressive, horny, and/or tough. But the officers I knew were top-notch professionals and patriotic Americans. The record does not show a single case of **any** OPS officer who was officially reprimanded, indicted, or charged with condoning torture, practicing torture, or teaching or practicing terrorism. The communist and left-wing allegations are plain lies.

The history of OPS shows that many officers became silent victims of the Cold War. Many were wounded or killed in the service of their country. The organization and the Americans who served their country to fight communist aggression in the Cold War were ultimately vilified by the false allegations of torture used by communist propagandists and activists. Following the elimination of the OPS program by ideologically inclined politicians, many young officers, unable to retire, were left without a job. Some were shunted in their careers.

The OPS program has no monument, no wall of names, or any recognition for the officers who died in the service of their country in the period President Richard Nixon called World War III.

Al Farkas, Adolph Owens, Norman Clovers, Jack Wells, Michael "Mike" Murphy, John McCarthy, George Miller, and **Dan Mitrione** were loyal Americans killed serving with OPS in the Cold War. **John**

McCabe, Wyman W. Vernon, Brooks Anderson, Carl Alexander, Duke Guraux, Charlie O'Brien, and **Edward H Forney** (a retired Marine Brigadier General) died or were killed in Vietnam. Nine other OPS officers were wounded serving their country.

Peter T. Chew, a war correspondent assigned to cover the Vietnam War, had befriended OPS Officer Norman Clowers. Clowers was considered to be a non-operational civilian, but was obliged to fight alongside his Vietnamese police counterparts when they were attacked. He was killed in a Viet Cong ambush. Peter Chew saw the valor of the young OPS Officer and grieved his death. He wrote a letter to Byron Engle, the Director of OPS, with the following tribute: *"Norman Clowers was the bravest man I've ever seen."*

OPS Officers who served in the Cold War share untold sad memories, tales of treachery, of danger, and petty chickenshit. It is right to expect that the Americans who were killed serving their country in the Cold War should not be forgotten. General Eisenhower once said about soldiers killed in action: **"He who is forgotten, indeed has died in vain."** Under the circumstances, **the Americans of OPS should not be forgotten.**

George Miller lost his life in an airplane crash in Vietnam after taking heavy Viet Cong fire. He lost his life serving his country, defending our national security interests in a controversial war.

Jack Wells met death unexpectedly, killed in a skirmish with the Viet Cong. A Viet Cong sniper in a province of Vietnam where he worked as an OPS police field forces advisor shot him. He had volunteered to serve his country in an inglorious war and had been in Vietnam three months when he was killed.

Michael Murphy, a former British Officer, served under Sir Robert Thompson in Malaya during the left-wing insurgency in that country. After Malaya, Murphy became an American and a State Trooper in Alaska. After a few years as a policeman in Alaska, he volunteered to serve with OPS as a police advisor in Vietnam. In 1968, the Viet Cong killed Mike Murphy in a firefight in the Delta.

Jake Jackson is a brave American who sacrificed a great deal for his country. He was in his early 40s when he was assigned as an OPS police advisor in Bolivia. On a trip to a left-wing guerrilla infested area, he and several Bolivian police officers were caught in an ambush. Jackson took a bullet in the back and was left a paraplegic. Several Bolivian police officers were killed. My friend Jake had already served his country in World War II, flying B-25s and A-20s in combat. He is a brave and loyal American who remains in a wheelchair.

Dan Mitrione served as Chief of Police of Richmond, Indiana, prior to OPS. He was truly a gentleman and patriot admired by all who knew and worked with him, especially myself. Mitrione is a particularly sad story about OPS. He was kidnapped and brutally murdered by Marxist guerrillas eleven months after he replaced me in Uruguay. After his cold-blooded murder by the Marxist *Tupamaro* guerrillas, communist and left-wing radicals shamefully accused Mitrione of teaching torture to the police.

He died in the service of his country helping a democratic government resist a Marxist takeover. Mitrione was called a "martyr for democracy" by the President of Uruguay and decorated posthumously by the United States Government. A commemorative stamp was issued for Mitrione in Uruguay with the inscription: **"Servant of Freedom."** He left nine children and a young wife. The Dan Mitrione story continues to be defiled by false communist allegations of torture. It is fair to ask what "witness" of the torture can testify under oath that Mitrone was involved in such a practice? There are none and none have ever been produced by anyone.

Al Farkas, a former Chief of police of Lancaster, Pennsylvania, was buried February 29, 1968, at Conestoga Cemetery in Lancaster, after he was killed in Vietnam. A Resolution by the House of Representatives of Pennsylvania issued on March 6, 1968, posthumously praises and commends Al Farkas for, among other things: **"A distinguished career as a policeman, an athlete, a gentleman, and a patriot."** Al Farkas was a real American patriot who served his country with honor and valor. Yet his service is generally unrecognized in America because of the politics. Anyone who knew Farkas will never forget him.

The OPS was an aberration for the communists in the Cold War, but the honest to God truth about the Americans who served their country with uncommon valor and loyalty should be told. There were no "hidden terrors" as alleged by left-wing activist A. J. Langguth, and others of the same ilk.

A.J. Langguth, a former New York Times reporter, wrote a book called **"Hidden Terrors"** and, similar to the film produced by the two card-carrying communists, Costa Gavras and Franciso Solinas, is nothing more than a vile attempt to justify the brutal murder of Dan Mitrione by Marxist guerillas. Langguth wrote in his book: **"After Mitrione's murder, male and female prisoners at Uruguay's jails traded stories about his participation in torture. Usually those were secondhand accounts repeated to convince a doubter that the *Tupamaros* had been justified in killing Mitrione."**

But even this vile effort by Langguth will not justify the murder of an innocent man for the sake of the communist cause. Like other left-wing accusers, Langguth has never been able to provide the names of real people, especially those who were allegedly tortured by Mitrione.

Uruguayan Officials told me unequivocally that Langguth did not talk to any prisoner in their jails. Langguth, a well known left-wing personality, consistently wrote with subtle praise for the *Tupamaros,* CIA defector Philip Agee, and Angela Camargo Seixas, a communist terrorist of the MR-8 group in Brazil who participated in kidnapping U.S. Ambassador Charles Elbrick.

In Brazil, a man suspected of lying is asked, **"Mata Cobra, Muestra Pau!"** I ask the same of Mr. Langguth. He will know what that means. Langguth conveniently alleges that he cannot name his sources because it could mean "prison, torture, or even death" for them.

More on OPS

There were many good men in OPS and too many for me to mention all of them here. **Dave Powell** was a well-educated former police officer from Oakland, California, became a Presbyterian Minister and police chaplain after OPS. **John Lindquist** had a Doctorate of Criminology from the University of California and was a retired Deputy Chief of Police from Berkeley. Linquist was considered one of the best professional criminologists in the United States. He served as Chief of OPS in Jamaica and in the OPS Training Division. His wife Evelyn was employed with him at the Wichita Police Department. **Ellis Lea,** a former West Virginia State Trooper, retired Army Colonel, and former Captain of the U.S. Pistol Team and U.S. Olympic pistol coach, brought tremendous talent to OPS in the area of firearms. **Joanmarie Derenzo,** the first female police advisor in OPS, saw many interesting assignments, including Vietnam. After OPS she went to the U.S. Department of State. **Gunther Wagner,** a German-born naturalized American with exceptional leadership qualities and police skills, served in Nicaragua and Vietnam and, after OPS, gained a reputation of being among the best in American corrections. **Jim Brooks** was a young man when he arrived in El Salvador and I was departing for the Canal Zone. Brooks, a CIA Officer, was selected as the Assistant Deputy Chief of Staff for Intelligence in the Office of the Deputy Chief for Intelligence, U.S. Department of the Army. The position made Brooks a general officer in the U.S. Army Reserve at the Pentagon. Brooks became the security manager for Exxon worldwide. **Robert "Bob" Cavanaugh** studied to be a Catholic priest but became a San Diego cop, Special Agent of the FBI, and former Deputy Director of the Illinois Bureau of Investigation. He was with OPS in Venezuela when I was there. **Loren McIntyre,** a talented photographer, writer, and movie producer, wrote, produced, and directed a training film called the **"First Line of Defense."** The film is used to train people on joint planning and operations by the police and military during emergencies. The film trained police and military officers throughout the world. I was one of the technical advisors on the film. After OPS, McIntyre worked as the point man for National Geographic in Latin America, and has written about and photographed the geographic wonders of South America. His books **The Incredible Incas** and **Exploring South America** are best sellers.

The many Americans who served with OPS during the complex period of the Cold War have faded away but are fully deserving of praise, appreciation and commendation for a job well done. The individuals listed below were police advisors in various assignments, and in different periods of the Cold War:

Don Ackerman, Benton Adcock, Bill Adams, Tommy Adkins, Pete Ales, Carl Alexander, Brooks Anderson, Bob Angrisani, David Arroyo, Cleo Baca, Ray Baca, Jim Bannister, James E. Barrick, Bill Bartreau, Bill Bateman, Phil Batson, Bill Bauman, Don Bennet, Bill Benson, Caesar Bernal, Randolph "Berk" Berkeley, Andrew Best, Carl Betsch, Richard Biava, Edward Bishop, Jack Boors, Don Bordenkircher, Frank Borsody, Glenn Boyce, Walt Boyling, Richard Braaten, Leigh Brilliant, Dudley Britton, Jim Broder, Jim Brooks, Theodore "Ted" Brown, Jerry Brown, Bob Broughham, Robert Broyles, Harry Bruno, Albert Bryant, Wally Burmester, Ken Burns, Robert "Nate" Bush, Oscar Bueno, John Caldwell, Clyde Call, Scotty Caplan, Bill Cantrell, Truman Carr, Roy Carlson, Al Carpenter, Joe Carpenter, Carlos Cassavantes, Robert Cavanaugh, Lyon Chapman, Elliot Chan, Eddie Chavez, Joe Cisneros, Bob Clark, Leon Clements, Norman Clowers, Frank Cohn, Marion Dale Collier, Bob Conner, Joe Corr, Pete Costello, Ashton Craig, Frank Craig, Horace Virgil Crank, Desderido Crisostimo, Ted Curtis, Reg Davis, David De Latorre, Marty Denker, Joanmarie Derenzo, Lowell Diamond, Mike Dobrichan, Drexal Doolin, John Doney, Stephen Donnelly, Jim Donohue, Roy "Bill" Driggers, Albert Dubois, Lee Echols, Carlos Eckert, Art Elder, Pete Ellena, Lloyd Emerson, Gerard Engert, Byron Engle, Albert Farkas, Martin Faul, Bill Fellers, Tom Feeney, Tom Finn, Bob Florstedt, Jack Forcey, Ray Foreacker, Edward Forney, David Fowler, Paul Franklin, Jerome T. French, Buck Fruit, Miles

Furlong, Robert Galli, Art Garza, Guy Gibson, Gilbert Gilmore, Everett Gleason, Lauren "Jack" Goin, Billy Goodman, Earl Goodwin, Frank Gorham, Lucian Gormont, Glenn Gray, Herb Gray, Jerry Greeley, Jack Gregory, William "Pappy" Grieves, Morris Grodsky, Howard Groom, Al Grunwell, Tom Guffain, Duke Guraux, Paul Gutierrez, Mike Gutierrez, Stan Guth, Charles Guzman, Harry Hahn, Rudy Hall, Theo Hall, Harry Hambleton, Paul Hannigan, William E. Hanscom, Herb Hardin, Mike Harpold, Harry Harris, Roy Hatem, Elliot Hensell, Robert "Bob" Hernandez, Vince Herz, John Herczeg, Bob Hildebrandt, James Hoban, Melquides Holguin, Paul Hoffey, Larry Hoffman, John Howard, Harvey Howell, Peter Hurst, Harry Houck, William Bill Ikerd, Jacob "Jake" Jackson, Henry James, Bob Janus, Arlen Jee, Frank Jeffers, Frank Jessup, Chester Jew, Joe Jenkins, Jack Jimick, Bob Joerg, Marvin Jones, Herb Johnson, Marvin Jones, William Jones, Paul Katz, Richard Keatly, Roland Kelly, Ed Kennelly, Harold Kent, John T. Kessler, Jon Kindice, Walter Kreutzer, Louis Labruzza, Chuck La Falce, Ernest Lancini, Ray Landgren, Jack Larrimore, David Laughlin, Ellis Lea, John Lee, Charles Leister, Roy Leonard, Jim Lewis, Harry Lindell, Julian Lindenauer, John Lindquist, Harold Lockhart, Jake Longan, Morris Looney, Joseph C. de Lopez, Robert "Bob" Lowe, Harry Lindell, Joe Lingo, Jake Longan, Otto Ludwig, Mitchell Mabardy, John Manopli, Bob Mann, Hans Manz, Donlad Marion, Richard Martinez, Eugene Mas, Jorge Matos, Steve Mayfield, Major McBee, John McCabe, John McCarthy, Michael McCann, Glenn McClung, Doug McCollum, Edward McCune, Martin McFaul, Loren McIntyre, Sam McKinney, Jim McMahon, John McPoland, John Means, Robert "Bob" Melberg, Bill "the Dutchman" Merghart, Charles Meshlo, Frank Miller, George Miller, Hersh Miller, Arthur Miller, Dan Mitrione, Charles Molfetto, Bill Moody, Robert Mooney, Dave Morgan, Rex Morris, John Moseley, Wendell Motter, John Moxley, Christy Moyers, Lauren "Moon" Mullins, Johnson "Jack" Munroe, Hugh Murray, Michael Murphy, Don Muse, John Myers, Alfred Naurock, Jack Neeley, Jack Nelson, Charlie Nesbitt, Charlie O'Brien, Jess Ojeda, Dolph Owens, Beryl Pace, Louis Page, Bill Parriott, F.H. Reggie Pell, Francis Perry, Pete Peterson, Sam Pesacreta, Bill Peters, Richard "Dick" Peters, Clyde Phelps, Michael Picini, Alfred "Al" Pickles, Bill Spurgon Phillips, Charles Posner, Lou Poudre, David Powell, Brian Quick, Dan Queen, Charles "Chuck" Radmer, Alex Ralli, Gordon Ransom, Richard Raugi, Jack Ryan, Charles Redlin, David Reinhart, Jim Reinhart, Bob Reynolds,

Otto Rhoades, Stephen H. Rimmer, George Roberts, Keith Roberts, Richard Rogers, Al Robinson, Roger Robinson, Dick Rogers, Carlton Rood, Jess Rose, Norm Rosner, Anthony Ruiz, Art Russell, Jack Ryan, Paul Sabol, Adolph Saenz, Michael Salceda, Bob Sanders, William Sanders, Felipe Sandoval, Robert Sauve, Ed Schlachter, Jim Schlosser, Jim Scroggins, Monroe Scott, Bill Searcy, Earl Sears, Mark Seaton, Stan Sheldon, William Bill Simmler Jr., David Sheppard, Paul Skuse, Charlie Sloan, Bob Slonger, Duke Snyder, Charles Smith, Chuck Sothan, Del Spier, Alson Staley, Tom Staley, Horton Steel, Al Stetz, Bill Steeves, Dick Sutton, Walt Swarthout, Rene Tetaz, Knute Thorpe, Art Thurston, Al Turner, Sam Turner, Ralph Turner, Homer "Chuck" Trout, John Valerio, Charles Van, Daniel Van Buskirk, Joe Vasili, Mario Vasquez, Charles Vayhinger, Wyman W. Vernon, Charlie Vopat, Gunther Wagner, Ken Waldrop, Glenn Walters, Frank Walton, Oakley Warren, Robert Weatherwax, Bob Weidner, Jack Wells, John Wiess, Walter Weyland, Garland Williams, Ray Williams, Jeter Williamson, Richard Willig, Bill Winn, Ray Winn, Harry Wynn, Ed Woodmansee, Orval Wooner, Dave Wright, Walt Wyrod, Nicolas Yantsin, Gordon Young, Ken Youngs, John C. Zeigler, John Zorack and Fred Zumwalt. There were others.

The OPS police advisors who served in Vietnam deserve special mention.

Jim Schlosser came to OPS on loan from the United States Bureau of Alcohol, Tobacco and Firearms (BATF) and was assigned to *Ben Tre,* IV Corps in Vietnam. Schlosser demonstrated his mettle when *Ben Tre* came under vicious attacks by the Viet Cong. He took charge of the effort to fight off the guerrillas and provided much-needed leadership for other Americans and for the South Vietnamese. Risking his life, he moved from point to point as bullets barely missed him and mortar rounds pounded the area while he assisted the wounded. Viet Cong mortars nearly demolished the town and, after several near misses, Schlosser found that his hearing was permanently impaired. He received several commendations for gallantry, but prior to leaving Vietnam he submitted the paperwork for the damage to his hearing under combat conditions. The documents were lost three times. He submitted the paperwork a fourth time and Washington Bureaucrats eventually concluded his injury was not service-connected. A dedicated OPS Officer injured in combat was shafted.

Bill Spurgeon Phillips was a Virginia State Trooper when he joined OPS and volunteered for Vietnam. He had previously served in the U.S.

Coast Guard and later with the U.S. Marine Corps during the Korean War. With OPS in Vietnam, Phillips was decorated for bravery by the United States Government and received the Vietnamese Cross of Gallantry with a Bronze Star and the Vietnamese National Police Medal of Honor from the South Vietnamese Government. After OPS, he became Chief of Police for Abingdon, Virginia. He died in May of 1990, still a young man and always a patriot.

Sam Turner was a cop from Dodge City, Kansas, and recruited by OPS from the Los Angeles County Sheriff's Department. He had served previously in the U.S. Marine Corps during the Korean War and was assigned to *Kien Phong* Province as an OPS Police Field Forces (PFF) advisor. He was the only American working with the South Vietnamese PFF in that area. When *Cao Lahn* came under siege during the *Tet* Offensive, Turner and other American and South Vietnamese military personnel prepared to fight off attacks. With the city completely surrounded by the Viet Cong, fierce firefights took place and numerous casualties resulted. The Americans and South Vietnamese wounded had to be evacuated for medical treatment as soon as possible. But a serious danger was that the Viet Cong guerrillas had zeroed in with their mortars on the helicopter pad normally used to evacuate the wounded.

Turner proposed a dangerous scheme that was put into action. He and Army Warrant Officer Don Hadley drove an Army ambulance at a high rate of speed to the helicopter pad. The ploy was that they would serve as decoy and draw the Viet Cong mortar fire. They were not disappointed. When Turner and Hadley drove the ambulance to the helicopter pad, mortar rounds descended on them like fire ants on a honeybee. In the interim, the Medivac helicopters were told by radio to land at a new site and the wounded were evacuated. The Viet Cong were unable to react in time to aim their mortars on the new landing site. Turner received the U.S. State Department's top award for heroism, America's second highest civilian decoration, and the South Vietnamese Police Medal of Honor, in 1968. In the year 2001, Sam Turner was on his way to Kosovo to work as a police advisor with a private company under contract to the U.S. Department of State.

The OPS officers assigned to Vietnam performed courageously in a hot war that killed many of them. **Al Farkas, Sam Turner, John C. Zeigler, William Saunders, John McPoland, Stephen H. Rimmer, William E. Hanscom,** and many others were American heroes and received decorations from the United States Government and the Vietnamese Government for valor and heroism.

John C. Zeigler, a senior OPS advisor in *Bien Hoa* Province, led the effort during the *Tet* Offensive to repulse a protracted enemy sapper attack on the provincial National Police headquarters in February 1969. He killed many of the Viet Cong and risked his life several times during the attack. He received a citation for bravery.

William Saunders provided invaluable leadership to fight off savage Viet Cong attacks in *Phong Dinh* province during the *Tet* Offensive and was cited for bravery. He risked his life several times during the Viet Cong attacks, and his courage and spirit inspired his fellow Americans in the battle. He was credited with killing several of the attacking guerrillas himself. As an OPS police advisor, he was supposedly "non-operational."

Stephen H. Rimmer, an OPS Officer assigned to *Quang Ngai* province, despite heavy Viet Cong fire risked his life to save another American who had been hit and badly wounded in a firefight. Fighting his way to help his fellow American, he killed Viet Cong in the process. He was decorated for bravery.

William (Bill) Hanscom, a Marine in World War II and an Airborne Ranger during the Korean War, served in Vietnam as an OPS officer when his country needed him. He was a genuine hero to those who knew him, not only in Vietnam but also in other assignments. He received little credit until he was buried with full military honors and a plethora of commendations in the funeral service held for him at the Immaculate Conception Cemetery in Fairbault, Minnesota, in May of 2000.

Individuals providing eulogies at the funeral called Hanscom a warrior, a hero, and a patriot. The stories of OPS are true sagas of a real war, heroism, sacrifice, and brave performance in the face of danger.

In 1971, U.S. Ambassador Ellsworth Bunker held a ceremony in Saigon to decorate the American civilians who had served in Vietnam. He declared at the start of the ceremony: **"It is indeed a privilege for me to preside over this ceremony today. Such an occasion is long overdue and—it is appropriate to pay tribute to these men"**... He awarded medals for valor to the OPS Officers mentioned above and to several other American civilians.

He finished by saying: **"Let me conclude by offering my personal feeling that the men we decorate today should be a source of pride to us in another sense. They represent a generation of Americans whose character and accomplishments have not been given their proper due in the eyes of the public. I am proud to present these awards to them."**

But without due recourse or justification, the Americans who served with the OPS program were callously terminated from U.S. Government service. The great majority had families to support. The men and women of the OPS, who often risked their lives in the service of their country, were in the end relegated to the status of dishonored cold warriors by the politicians in Washington, D.C.

The active duty Military Police Officers and Green Berets who served with the OPS were among the best of the U.S. Army and Special Forces. **Colonel William Norman, Colonel Len Becika, Colonel Knute Thorpe, Colonel Tom Guffain, Major Harry Harris, Major Frank Cohn, Major Larry Santana, Captain Charles Gooch, Captain Fernando Bruno,** and many others deserve a special tribute. They performed with excellence and above all served their country with honor.

I took time to write the OPS story because it should be told. Too many friends who served have passed on. My own reputation in the OPS is best illustrated by quoting remarks in an official U.S. Government document and the remarks of an evaluation panel in 1971. The document is quoted verbatim. **"Mr. Saenz, a Chief Public Safety Advisor, has a superior/outstanding performance record and is considered to be one of the best in his field. His advice is eagerly sought by Country Team members and his work is known to be dangerous."** The document states I had **"a bright future with the Agency."** That is OPS history. Personal information is provided on myself in the **Appendix** to make public my background, since I was also accused of involvement in torture by left-wing activist Roger Morris. The details provided will hopefully clear up any doubt about the mission of OPS and that there were no "hidden terrors."

Details are provided on John McPoland and Al Farkas, two OPS Officers who served with uncommon valor in Vietnam. Their story is one of many well-documented brave exploits of OPS Officers in the Cold War and offers truthful insights on the individuals involved. **The OPS Story** is non-fiction with exciting real-life drama that represents unpublished historical facts and events. I am convinced that the generations of Americans who served with OPS had strong moral convictions and values and the ideologues on the side of communism say the same thing about themselves. But there was no torture by Americans, only vile communist propaganda.

John McPoland

My friend John McPoland had bright red hair and an Irish temper. Born in Newport, Rhode Island, in 1935, he returned home again in 1999 for good when he died of a heart attack. Newport is a small, attractive resort town and in the early 1900s, the Rockefellers, Vanderbilts, and other affluent Americans built huge mansions in the community.

The McPolands had been pioneers in the area. Grandpa, a large handsome man with shiny black hair and a pink porcelain complexion, brought black Irish genes to the family. John's father was easygoing but strict and taught his five children how not to have bad dreams. He provided his nightly blessing with a curt suggestion. **"Say your prayers and go to bed."** McPoland swore he never had bad dreams when he was young. His real nightmare was with OPS in South Vietnam.

McPoland played center for the local high school football team and alternated in the position with his friend, Jackie. In one particularly rough game, Jackie got walloped hard in the face and lost two front teeth. That upset Jackie because it should have happened to McPoland and not to him. They grew into adulthood and Jackie became a fireman. To remind McPoland, Jackie would occasionally roll a fire truck noisily into the neighborhood, honk and wave eagerly when he saw McPoland. He would remove his fire helmet and with his tongue displace the dental plate on his front teeth to grin at McPoland with a wide dark gap showing in his mouth instead of his front teeth.

After high school, during the last part of the Korean War, McPoland joined the U.S. Marine Corps. After his discharge, he returned to Newport to enter Providence College on the GI Bill and graduated with a Bachelor of Science degree. Later, he took the United States Treasury Department Law Enforcement examination and was hired as a Special Agent with the Bureau of Alcohol, Tobacco and Firearms (BATF). He was assigned to Boston and to New Bedford, Massachusetts.

In 1966, an advertisement in the *Police Chief Magazine* (of the International Association of Chiefs of Police) for police advisors to serve in South Vietnam caught his attention. McPoland applied and was accepted for an assignment as an advisor to the South Vietnamese Police Field Forces (PFF) in *Vinh Long,* in the *Mekong Delta.* Before the war ended in 1973, John McPoland and his partner Al Farkas were among the most decorated American civilians of the Vietnam War. McPoland was 31 years old.

Albert "Al" Farkas

Al Farkas resigned his job as Chief of Police of Lancaster, Pennsylvania, to serve his country in Vietnam. Farkas was highly regarded as a Chief of Police in Lancaster and was willing to serve his country in a hot war in Vietnam that was resisted by many Americans. He believed he could make a difference in Vietnam as a police advisor. He had served in the Seabees in the Pacific Theatre in World War II but he would be a civilian in South Vietnam in a hot war during the Cold War.

An avid pistol shooter, Farkas was a Master Shooter qualified by the National Rifle Association (NRA) and would be credited with killing dozens of Vietcong guerrillas during his tour of duty. Despite a right lung that had a tendency to collapse, Farkas agreed to serve in one of the most dangerous places in Vietnam, *Vinh Long*. He epitomized the American OPS cold warrior. We took pride that he was one of us.

0315 hours—January 31, 1968—*Tet* Offensive, Chinese Lunar New Year, *Vinh Long*

The *Tet* Offensive began with heavy mortar barrages that seemed endless for the American and South Vietnamese forces in *Vinh Long* Province. From a balcony in their quarters, Farkas and McPoland saw the battle shape up with vicious explosions in the area. At the bottom of the balcony, the South Vietnamese police intelligence chief shouted to tell them that the Viet Cong were attacking in force throughout the country. He suggested that they follow him to the Police Field Forces (PFF) compound located a few blocks away.

Driving separate vehicles Farkas and McPoland followed the Chief of Police Intelligence to the PFF compound as machine gun fire and rockets exploded around their vehicles. When they reached a bridge that crossed over a small canal, automatic weapons fire suddenly tore the entire roof from Farkas' vehicle. Despite that, miraculously the three men reached the South Vietnamese PFF station, surprised they made it without being hit by the heavy Viet Cong automatic weapons fire, mortars, and rockets.

On the way to the PFF Station, McPoland recounted that they saw an old C-47 dropping flares all over the city and lighting up areas of darkness where Viet Cong guerrillas scrambled about in large numbers. They were astonished when South Vietnamese citizens ran out to the streets amidst the violent explosions and gunfire and risked their lives to pick up the small nylon parachutes used to drop the flares. The nylon used to make the small parachutes apparently had value for the South Vietnamese.

McPoland and Farkas took refuge inside the police compound with about forty South Vietnamese police officers and prepared to fight off the Viet Cong attackers. All night long, the Police Field Forces (PFF) compound took heavy machine gun and rocket fire. The attacking hordes of Viet Cong were repeatedly beaten back. No one slept. The Viet Cong launched attack after attack throughout the night as rockets hit the walls of the building and destroyed a section of the roof. Climbing up on the battered roof, Farkas and McPoland watched Viet Cong guerrillas move about in large numbers as flares, bombs, and tracers from automatic weapons lit up the sky.

In the midst of the battle, for one brief moment in the middle of the night, McPoland heard an old man huddled in a corner of a building, whimpering and crying out in a soft voice. He repeatedly called out in pitiful sounds for his 'Mama San' in the terrifying roar of the vicious attacks.

Viet Cong guerrillas stormed the police compound in wave after wave but were beaten back. McPoland and Farkas, armed with 12 gauge shotguns loaded with .04 and .00 buckshot, killed dozens of Viet Cong guerrillas, shooting them from the roof as they tried to penetrate into the PFF compound. The battle greatly intensified and they alternatively used M-16 rifles, hand grenades, and M-79 grenade launchers to kill numerous attackers.

When early morning arrived, dead Viet Cong bodies piled up outside the police compound were in unbelievable numbers. McPoland later recounted to me that the smell of death and cordite remained in his nostrils for days. Both men were credited with killing over fifty Viet Cong that first night.

By dusk the attacks abated sporadically and several police officers caught outside the compound during the *Tet* Offensive finally reached the police station, increasing the number of police personnel there to fifty-two men. Two police officers had been killed and seven others wounded in the initial assaults. The second night, a few police officers were assigned to dig in outside the compound in foxholes. They later reported that the Viet Cong forces were massing to the north and to the northeast part of the city in preparation for a full-scale assault.

The Viet Cong were presumed to be preparing to attack the Provincial Palace, and the South Vietnamese Army Tactical Operations Center (TOC) in *Vinh Long*. The TOC controlled most of the military activity in *Vinh Long*. An ammunition storage depot was also nearby the TOC.

But it appeared that the PFF station would be in the way of any attack on the TOC or Provincial Palace by the Viet Cong. The facility would have to be overrun by the guerrillas to reach the TOC.

The next ten hours brought increased assaults against the police compound. As the Viet Cong mass assault on the TOC and other targets in the area appeared imminent, a tremendous number of rockets and mortars hit the PFF compound and killed fifteen police officers and wounded five others.

In the dim light of dawn, a South Vietnamese Armored Personnel Carrier (ARVN APC) stopped near the PFF Station and dropped off more police personnel and mortar ammunition. The APC was loaded with mortar ammunition and continued to be unloaded. The total number of police officers killed by the third day was twenty. By that time, South Vietnamese Army tanks had moved into the area and one of the armored vehicles stopped and trained its cannon on the bridge that sat astride the canal.

1600 Hours—Fourth Day

By the fourth day, Viet Cong attacks continued and were beaten back. The battle intensified, with furious firefights taking place between Viet Cong guerrillas and South Vietnamese military units and the police. In the devastating battle, the telecommunications system that linked the South Vietnamese Army and the Police Field Forces was knocked out.

February 6,1968

After six days of battle, Al Farkas wrote a letter to his wife dated February 6, 1968, 8:30 p.m.
"My Dearest,

If this turns out to be a strange letter, please forgive me. Don't know where to start. (Farkas describes the *Tet* Offensive and the battle that ensued.) By 0900 Wed. morning, there was no doubt that a full-scale attack on *Vinh Long* City was underway. At 1600 (4 p.m.) the Chief got a radio call from one of his intelligence officers, saying that a new large group of Viet Cong were massing across from the bridge. (The bridge near the PFF Station would have to be crossed by the Viet Cong to attack the TOC.) The only way we could get the info to the TOC was to hand carry it. (The Viet Cong had destroyed radio communications.) John and I hadn't had a chance to let anybody know where we were, so he and I agreed to try to get through to the TOC with the intelligence chief. We drew sniper fire but made the two blocks O.K. The colonel was glad to see us and to get the intelligence info. The colonel went to *Can Tho* to request help from the Americans because he didn't think we could hold out another night."

After a long letter, Farkas closed by telling his wife: (I) "left a lot of little things out but I do want to assure you that I am o.k. You know I damned well would not write this much if I weren't."

The *Tet* in *Vinh Long*—February 7, 1968

By 1630 Farkas and McPoland returned to the TOC and minutes later a tremendous blast occurred and a fluorescent light and debris hit McPoland on the head knocking him to the floor. Miraculously, both he and Farkas were not seriously hurt. It was determined that the explosion was the result of a rocket hitting the South Vietnamese Army tank parked near the PFF Station. The blast tore an entire wall from the PFF Station and caved in the roof. Several police officers inside were killed and many were wounded.

The PFF Station was immediately evacuated and all personnel moved to the Provincial Palace. The Provincial Palace was a complex of several buildings and grounds that were surrounded by a high wall.

Meanwhile, Farkas and McPoland were surprised to find three other Americans located at the TOC. Presumably, they were intelligence officers.

By this time, the situation had greatly deteriorated, and the U.S. Army Province Senior Advisor Lt./Colonel Ron Roberge warned all Americans that it might be necessary to drop all gear and equipment and swim down the river nearby or risk being killed or taken prisoner by the Viet Cong.

The TOC was eventually evacuated and military and police personnel were moved to the Provincial Palace. For days the Viet Cong made repeated attacks but were beaten back. Farkas, McPoland, and the others slept intermittently and, in early dawn, American helicopters arrived and launched attacks against Viet Cong forces with rockets and .50 caliber machine guns. The attacks against the Viet Cong by the helicopters continued nonstop for six days.

By the seventh day, American civilians in the area were evacuated by helicopter. Farkas, McPoland, and the three Americans from the TOC were unknowingly left behind.

In the next three days, attacks by Viet Cong guerrillas continued but were beaten back. On the tenth day, an American gunboat brought supplies of ammunition and rations for the American and South Vietnamese forces in the area. Unknown to McPoland and Farkas, the gunboat evacuated the three American civilians assigned to the TOC, but in the chaotic situation, they were left behind.

On day eleven, two battalions of U.S. Army troops were airlifted into the Province to engage the Viet Cong forces in the area. McPoland and Farkas accompanied PFF personnel to eliminate Viet Cong guerrillas in searches and house to house combat. The *Tet* Offensive finally waned, and the two men were able to get some rest, eat C-rations, and take a first class sponge bath, courtesy of the U.S. Army.

February 10, 1968

Farkas and McPoland were fighting with their South Vietnamese counterparts in a field operation that was undertaken to clear out Viet Cong guerrillas remaining in the area. The PFF forces were suddenly attacked and pinned down. The two OPS Officers had been separated and were with their counterparts at different locations during the firefight. Later that day, McPoland received word by radio that his partner, Al Farkas, had been seriously wounded when a grenade thrown by the Viet Cong exploded near him.

McPoland immediately tried to find Farkas, but he had been taken to an aide center. The information McPoland received was that Farkas was wounded when a grenade thrown by a Viet Cong guerrilla exploded and fragments penetrated under his flak jacket. Farkas had been taken to the rear of the embattled area for treatment. After the situation stabilized, McPoland desperately searched for Farkas and found out that he had been taken to a field hospital at *Dong Tam.*

Flying to *Dong Tam* by helicopter McPoland found Farkas in a medical treatment center. He was in good spirits and resting comfortably. The two men chatted cheerfully, glad they had made it through the *Tet.* Farkas had been hit in the chest and kidded that he was glad that it was not in a more sensitive area. The next day Farkas was evacuated to the U.S. Army Third Field Hospital in Saigon.

February 15, 1968

Nine days after he wrote his last letter to his wife, on February 15, 1968, Al Farkas died from his wounds while at the Third Army U.S. Military Hospital in Saigon. He gave up his life serving his country in a strange war and in a strange land. His body was returned home, to Lancaster, Pennsylvania, for burial.

McPoland was devastated with the death of his partner, but remained in *Vinh Long* with a price on his head. The Viet Cong had offered a reward for every OPS officer killed in Vietnam. But the reward for killing McPoland, the American with *Poc Bo'* (red hair), was doubled. Al Farkas' killer was paid in taels of gold.

In *Vinh Long* after Farkas was killed, a beautiful South Vietnamese girl by the name of *Tu Thanh* warned McPoland one dark night that the Viet Cong were coming for him around midnight. She told him that the Viet Cong intended to drag him out to the street with his hands tied behind his back and execute him with a bullet in the back of his head. The villagers would be rounded up and forced to watch his execution. McPoland left the area before the Viet Cong arrived and shortly afterwards was evacuated to Saigon.

After the *Tet* Offensive, the South Vietnamese Government awarded John McPoland the **Military Cross of Gallantry** with a star. That decoration was normally awarded only to South Vietnamese military personnel but was awarded to McPoland and several OPS officers because they had in fact fought as infantry alongside the Vietnamese Police Field Forces. McPoland also received a meritorious award from the U.S. Government and the **Police Medal of Honor** and **Medal of High Merit** *(Chuong My)* from South Vietnamese President Thieu. Al Farkas was awarded the same decorations posthumously.

Prior to leaving *Vinh Long,* McPoland obtained employment for Miss *Tu Thanh* at an American Army Officer's club at a nearby base. She later recounted to me that during a Viet Cong mortar attack she went under a table to take cover and met an American civilian named Ross Rigby who had dived under the same table. Rigby and *Tu* were subsequently married and now live in Albuquerque, New Mexico. I had the pleasure of visiting with them to talk about McPoland.

In 1968, it was my great satisfaction to recommend John McPoland for a promotion when I served on the OPS evaluation panel. After OPS and a successful career in the U.S. Department of State, Office of Diplomatic Security, John McPoland died from a heart attack in the month of April 2000.

Appendix

The Career of Adolph Saenz

The above headline appeared in a weekly Santa Fe Tabloid on March 6, 1980, in a story written by Roger Morris and with a picture of my face hiding in the shadows. Morris obviously intended to make it appear sinister. The beginning paragraph of a long article started with the following. **"New Criminal Justice Secretary Adolph B. Saenz, the man expected to rebuild New Mexico's reputation after the most horrifying prison riot in American history, spent most of his previous career in an overseas U.S. agency closely linked to the systematic torture of political prisoners in Latin America and elsewhere."** Morris accused me of involvement in a CIA-inspired program that taught torture to the police in Latin America. The story was part of the same communist propaganda used by far left-wing ideologues in the American political arena and in the media during the Cold War. Federal Judge Juan Burciaga, after a long hearing held in Albuquerque, found the allegations made by Roger Morris to be **"patently false"** and that the article had come **"perilously close to reckless disregard for the truth."**

No one has or had at any time accused me of involvement in torture. I retired from the United States Government service after twenty-five years without a blemish on my record.

I was born in Las Cruces, New Mexico, a small thriving community in the southwestern part of the United States where many close friends and neighbors went off to fight and were killed or wounded during World War II, the Korean War, or the Vietnam War. My father served in the U.S. Army during World War I and was in combat in France with Company M, 109th Infantry. My adopted brother, Leo Saenz, was in combat in Europe with the U.S. Army during World War II. All the males in our family served in the U.S. Armed Forces.

Many of my childhood buddies and close friends, Sammy Burke, Richard Armijo, Eddy Gamboa and Arthur (Tudy) Bernal, earned Purple Hearts serving with the U.S. Marine Corps in the Korean War. My friend Tony Barncastle was wounded and another friend by the name of Harry Bradley was killed in action serving in the Korean War with the U.S. Army. We were school chums and were commissioned as Second Lieutenants in the armed services in the same ceremony.

My close friends and neighbors, the Trujillos (Fred, Art, Lambert, Jr., and Philip), Rudy Camunez, Ray Chavez, Felipe "Pito" Roybal, a decorated combat paratrooper, Sammy Chavez, the Carabajals, the Barrios, the Bacas, and the Medinas all served in the armed forces during World War II or the Korean War. Lencho Banegas and Ruben Flores are survivors of the Bataan Death March in World War II. Many of those mentioned were decorated for valor or wounded in combat but have never sought, or now seek, any recognition.

The small city of Las Cruces snuggles up to the foothills of the beautiful Organ Mountains. The place can be hot and parchy in the summer months and damned cold in winter. The population was less than 21,000 people in 1945. The area has beautiful surrounding desert, farmland, and sublime mountainous areas. World travelers compare the pure blue sky and arid environment of Las Cruces to Madrid, Spain. Las Cruces is not far from White Sands Proving Grounds and Trinity Site, where the first atomic bomb was exploded.

Farmers in the Mesilla Valley cultivate cotton, pecans, and large hot chile peppers called "Big Jim," a name coined by researchers at New Mexico State University. Roasted, peeled, and cooked, the "Big Jim" peppers are popular in the southwestern United States, including Texas, Arizona, and California. With the annual chile harvest, when the chile crops turn red, local residents celebrate the "Whole Enchilada" *fiesta.*

My mother and father sacrificed to raise nine children in a small adobe home on Bowman Street in Las Cruces following the Great Depression. Fortunately for my parents, most of their children got married or left home at a young age. Like many other families in this great country, we withstood serious poverty. At the age of ten, I hunted rabbits in the mesa near the "A" mountain with my .22 rifle for food, and chopped and picked cotton for less than a dollar a day. As a youngster, my friends and family called me "Dolphi." My real name was Adolpho.

Our neighborhood was far from being affluent but *Barrio* residents were close. The parents of the former Governor of New Mexico, Jerry Apodaca, lived across the street from us. Rudy Camunez, a local football star in high school and college, was my football coach in high school. The Camunez were a pioneer family of the first order. The family of Pablo Roybal, a chief of the famous *Tortugas* Indians, lived a block away. Sam Medina, a three-time All State High School halfback, Ray Apodaca, Jr., an all conference college athlete, and basketball star Eli Baca were friends of mine. We were rowdy, but no one had the motivation to do drugs or drive-by shootings.

Harmony prevailed in our neighborhood and the diversity was part of the small community. Mexican, Spanish and German Jew cultures formed my heritage, but I considered myself a *Chicano* (Mexican American).

My uncles, aunts, and cousins form a large family tree consisting of Bernal, Nevarez, Barela, Fitch, and Saenz. The prime colonizers who followed the Spaniards into the State were Mexican, Basque, German, Jew, Welsh, Italian, British, and Irish. We had a "typical" American community! But racism and bigotry were always in the background.

Years ago, Las Cruces was quiet and uncomplicated and folks were respectful and friendly. There were few roisterers in town before World War II. Las Cruces was my entire world and as cosmopolitan as I ever wanted to be. Uruguay, Colombia, Panama, terrorists, kidnappings, drug dealers, Ambassadors, Ministers of Government, and men like Omar Torrijos, Manuel Noriega, and *Ché* Guevara were mere abstractions of people and places for me. The problems of other countries had little interest for me. I was unaware that Latin America would be my home and operating ground for seventeen years.

When I was growing up, I had a powerful antipathy and fear of racists and bigots even at a young age. The population of New Mexico grew and so did the number of racists. Since I had the features of a Spaniard or Italian, my adopted brother Leo called me a *Gachupin,* a true Spaniard.

My father, a Captain and Deputy Chief of the Las Cruces Police Department, saw plenty of combat in France with the U.S. Army during World War I. The patriarch of the Carabajal family lived on a street behind our house and, as a kid, I often watched him struggle to walk down our street. He had been gassed and left disabled fighting the Germans in France during World War I. Those were Americans of Hispanic heritage who were in the trenches and saw the devastation of their buddies when the German Army used mustard and chlorine gas on them. Occasionally my father would talk about the atrocities of that world conflict but not often. With our large family, my father was happy in Las Cruces eking out a living working as a cop and as a carpenter on the side. My father was of Mexican ancestry and my mother was the daughter of a tough German Jew/Spanish pioneer family. She never complained about the hardship of raising so many children. For her, life meant sacrifice, but in Las Cruces, life was simple, the past easily forgotten and the future non-foreboding.

With the cultural environment of the southwest, many Mexican/Americans lived in the area, and denigrating prejudices surfaced at inauspicious moments. I saw displays of racism at an early age. The emotional impact of racism often attacked my self-esteem in brutal and humiliating ways. But I was blessed with chutzpah and pride, and racism merely made me angry and ready to fight.

In the red brick school building called "Central" one early morning at the age of ten, the torment of prejudice hit me in a way that only *"a minority"* in America can understand. The loud voice of an angry schoolteacher named Mrs. Hill reverberated through the schoolhouse and a thin scrawny kid nicknamed *Diablito* stood next to me while we were being subjected to a bad scolding. We were scared, embarrassed, and made to feel inferior.

"Shut up! Shut up!" Mrs. Hill screeched. "There are **no** pyramids in Mexico!" she told us. "Once again, Bryan is correct. If you **Mexicans** read your textbook, you will see the pyramids are in Egypt!" Flushed with anger, our geography teacher vented her wrath on us, in particular those who appeared to be of Mexican descent. This was a time when racism was ennobled and, like other places in the United States, Negroes were segregated and had their own schools. There were no Blacks in the school.

In my heart I knew Mrs. Hill was prejudiced because she constantly berated anyone with a brown face or looked Mexican. Perhaps there were students in class who were children of Mexican citizens living illegally in the area and that upset her. Nevertheless, the local cultural chasm kept Mrs. Hill in a constant state of biliousness. Why she chose to live in Las Cruces where she was surrounded by "pseudo" Mexicans she considered of less worth was the question. The Mexican border was about 55 to 60 miles away.

According to the information my mother received periodically, I was disrespectful and accused of "undermining Mrs. Hill's teaching philosophy." My own philosophy was, "I got no respect, I give no respect." In fact the *pinchi Gringa* schoolteacher was the top bigot in our school. As far as I was concerned, she was a noxious, cross-eyed, prejudiced witch. Mrs. Hill had one blue eye and one brown eye that looked in opposite directions. When reprimanded for insolence, I tried hard not to "look her in the eye" because that made me giggle. This was extremely offensive to Mrs. Hill and, as a result, I became a favorite target for her vitriolic upbraiding. Her round mastiff face and bulldog appearance intimidated most students. She often scolded us for speaking Spanish to each other, but that was our way of "maintaining secrecy."

One morning was particularly upsetting for Mrs. Hill because some students exchanged remarks in Spanish during class. Sudden as a stomach cramp, she poured out tenebrous fury against the Spanish speakers.

"You will NOT speak Mexican in this class! Is that clear? You deliberately demonstrate your ignorance. If you do not want to speak English, why don't you go back to Mexico where you belong!"

The heavy cloak of silence that fell on the small group of young children stifled the air. They stared at each other in disbelief. I personally felt betrayed by the *Gringa* schoolteacher. The voices in the classroom grew louder and Mrs. Hill sensed the rising anger of the young students. The atmosphere turned hostile and several students shouted angrily at the schoolteacher. My own anger grew overwhelming and impulsively I stood to scream vulgarities in Spanish.

"*Vieja Cabrona, Vieja Cabrona,* ... you old bitch, you old bitch, you have no right to tell us that!" I had lost control. "We are Americans, you *pinchi bruja!*" I shouted at her.

Frightened beyond description, Mrs. Hill moved cautiously toward the door, her eyes wide with fear as I continued my tirade in Spanish joined by other students.

"Dolphi, sit down, sit down, or I will call the Principal!" she screamed at me and her voice turned threatening. "Shut up and sit down! Dolphi, I will not tolerate your ugly behavior!" She stood with fists on her large hips and her face showing ugly contempt.

A dull momentary silence filled the room and suddenly someone in the back shouted in anger.

"*Vieja pinchi.*" A blackboard eraser hurtled like a shot straight for Mrs. Hill's ample bosom. With a violent "splunk" the eraser smashed into her chest and she uttered a loud gasp, falling to her knees screaming. Her hands held her chest as she cried out in pain.

"God! Oh, God!" Numb with surprise and disbelief, I stood terrified. Never had I seen such a sight. *Diablito! Diablito! Cabrón!* I knew it had to be *Diablito* who had thrown the eraser. He ran by me and in three leaps was out of the classroom.

"Vamos, Pendejo!" he hollered, slapping my head on his way out.

Pandemonium erupted and students ran wildly out to the hall and took off in all directions. Frightened, I bolted outside to the grass-covered ballpark and froze in the bright New Mexico sun to shake my fist in the air in utter frustration.

"That stupid *Diablito! Cabron!"* I cursed to myself. *Diablito* did not care about school. I was in serious trouble and might be expelled. My mother would likely kill me. She had warned me not to cause any problems. It seemed certain that *Diablito* had killed the cross-eyed teacher. He was the spawn of the devil, but the world was crashing down on me.

I survived the incident, was expelled from school for a few days and my mother threatened to disown me. *Diablito* never returned to school. Mrs. Hill passed me with a "C" to get me out of her class.

My world was Las Cruces with all its backwardness. I grew up with a parochial outlook on life with Harvard, Yale, the U.S. Military Academy, and similar achievements far from my universe and reserved for the wealthy Anglo population. But with athletic ability developed through neighborhood sandlot competition in our *Barrio,* I was named Co-Captain of the Las Cruces Union High School football team and played left halfback for the New Mexico State Aggies on a football scholarship. As a "homeboy" I strived to excel against racial prejudice and the poverty that was a harsh part of my daily life. I tried being a racist against "White Boys" and a bigot against the "Blacks," but gave up. It felt stupid and unpleasant being a bigot. Ironically, in later years, I would be called a *Gringo* in Latin America. But as a child I did not escape the pernicious discrimination that often bubbled up to the surface in America. Well, after all, I was an American.

Adolph Saenz—Chief OPS Program, Colonel Manuel Antonio Noriega—G2-Panama National Guard,
Joe Kyonaga—CIA Station Chief, Panama—1972

Averell Harriman is Keynote Speaker at the International Police Academy, Washington, D.C., October 1964
Byron Engle, Director of OPS, is at left of Harriman.

The Director of the United States Office of Public Safety, Byron Engle, and
Top Officials of OPS, Washington, D.C., 1966

Index

A

Abourezk, James G., 5; quotes from *Tricontinental,* 6, 8, 9, 384, and 423

Acuña, Santiago, 161, 166, 177

Agee, Philip Burnet, 123-125, Agee in Uruguay, 138-139, the *Jefatura;* Agee allegations and, 161, 391, 423

Accuracy in Media, AIM, 4

AID, Agency for International Development, 3, 4,

Aldunante, Ferreria, 131

Ales, Peter, 94

Alexander, Carl, 436

Allen, Alfred, 80

Allende, Salvador, 22

Amnesty International, 6; regarding OPS allegations of possible torture

Anderson, Brooks, 436

Andrews, Robert, 181, 182

Andropov, Yuri, KGB General, 14

Antonio, Jose, AKA "*Coronel,*" 25; child guerrilla operating in El Salvador

Arango, Elias Vega, 359

Arbolera, Fulgencio Valencia, 299

Arce, Liber, 22

Arechega, Jimenez de, MOI, Uruguay, 150

Areco, Pacheco, President, Uruguay, 222

Arosa, Storace, MOI, Uruguay, 192-195; meeting held regarding article in *El Popular*

Arosemendi, Rodney, 177

Arteaga, S.V., N.P., Ecuador, 325-327; story on Quees

B

Baca, Joe, 215, 216, 270-274; Driggers description, 416

Balboa High School, 83, 91

Barloco, Raul, Col., Army of Uruguay, 161, 165, 166; meeting with police officials on the Summit, 167-171; Lem Johns incident regarding chandelier, 1967; Summit Conference, 178-179; replacement as Chief of Police and, 238

Bardesio, Nelson, 188, 233

Barrientos, Juan, Gen. Pres. of Bolivia, 199, 203; the politics, 210-219; President Barrientos convinces the *campesinos* to help find *Ché* Guevara

Bartreau, William, 14

Batson, Phil, 428

Baye, Birch, 10

Bayo, Alberto, General, 39; guerilla warfare instructor in Cuba

Bazet, Luis Marin, Fed. Police, Mexico, 77

Becika, Len, Col., USA 444

Behr, Edward, 10

Beltran, Washington, President, Uruguay 131

Bernal, Caesar, 116, 125, 133, 136, 149, 150, 151, 161, 163, 173, 225, 235

Bernal, Juan, Col., PNG, 88

Billiatt, Penelope, 10

Bishop, Ed, 94

Blades, Ruben, Sr., 89

Bonaudi, Jose Evans, Comisario, police of Uruguay, 136-137; shootout with *Tupamaros*

Bordenkircher, Don, 429

Briggs, William (Bill), 107

Brooks, James, Jim, 28

Brown, Theodore (Ted), 77-79; changes in IAPA staff and administration, 81, 89, 93, 94, 100, 229, 426

Brownfield, Allen, 26

Bruno, Fernando, Capt., USA, 78, 444

Buff, Herman, 289; kidnapping case, 289, 290, 293, 294, 305-307; meeting at U. S. Embassy, Lubinsky, Kramer and Saenz on Swiss kidnapping, 313, 316, 319, 321, 323, 324, 328, 329, 333, 335-337; ransom payment for, 340, 344, 350-355; meeting with Swiss Embassador, and, 368

Burciaga, Juan, U.S. Fed. Judge, 187; Roger Morris allegations of OPS torture, 348

C

Cabezas, Juan, Major, USA, 51

Caicedo, Ernesto Gonzales, kidnapping victim, 300, 343

Caicedo, Rodrigo Lloreda, Gov., *Valle del Cauca*, 292, 315, 319

Calderon, Celedonia Rodriguez de, 332, 371

Calderon, Castro, Sabas, 331-332; chat with Tamayo about ransom for the Swiss, 351, and 366-370; interrogation by DAS officials in Cali, 371; Sabas is killed

Cantisani, Jose "*Pepito*," 125, 141

Cantrell, William (Bill), 124-126; arrival in country, 139-140; article in communist newspaper, *El Popular*, 150, 165, 167, 174, 176, 188-190; local problems with Otero, Hevia, and, 225, 232-233; Saenz meeting with CIA Officers on Cantrell

Cantu, Reynaldo, 52

Carreño, Anita Padilla, 386, 389; telegram from Jaime, 393-396; meeting with Saenz at Hotel *Tequendama*

Carreño, Gonzalo, 393, 396, 399, 401; evidence found in Mercedes during repairs, 406; hiding in Spain, 411-412; motive for murder, 414, 416; arrest in Spain, 422

Carreño, Pedro, Maria, 398, 411

Carreño, Olga, 398, 403

Castrillon, Argemiro Perez, 366

Carter, Jimmy, 91

Castro, Fidel, 40, 50, 80, 195, 215, 220, 230

Castro, Carlos, Inspector, NP,
Ecuador, 325
Catholic Conference of Bishops, 6
Charquerro, Moran, Inspector,
Uruguay Police 156
Chavez, Eddie, 35, 52
Chavez, Ramiro, Col., Army of
Uruguay, 167
Chew, Peter, 436
Church, Frank, 9, 224
Cirillo, Pasqual, Col., Army of
Uruguay, 121-122; incident at
the IACP Convention, 126, 239
Clack, Robin, 35
Clinton, William, Bill, 11
Clowers, Norman, 435
Coffin, Frank, 3
Cohn, Frank, Maj., USA, 444
Copello, Guillermo, Inspector,
police of Uruguay, 112-114;
incident with FBI *Attaché*, 130,
132, 182-186; visit to Soviet
trawler
Crickenberger, Gene, 11
Cuestas, Manuel, 335-342;
payment of ransom for Straessle
and Buff and, 354

D

Da Costa, Augusto, Inspector,
Brazilian police, 76, 77
Daschle, Tom, 8; Michael Klare as
source
DAS, *Departamento Administrativo
de Seguridad,* 257-330;
investigations and activities on
the kidnapping problem in
Colombia

DeBray, Regis, 199
Delgado, Freddy, Monsignor, El
Savador, 7, 8 and 26; *"La Iglesia
Popular Nacio en"*
Diaz, Antonio, Col., *Carabineros,*
Chile, 81
Diego, Juan, 366
Dominguez, Juan Fernandez, 371
Driggers, Roy Bill, 259-266; with
Saenz enroute from *El Dorado* to
Bogota, 268-271; discussion at
Hotel *Tequendama,* 273, 274,
286-291; meeting at DAS
Headquarters after Saenz's arrival,
and, 303, 318, 352, 375, 416

E

Echols, Lee, 430
Eisenhower, Dwight, 2
Ellena, Pete, 98, 101, 103, 229,
275, 429
Ellis, Mavorneen, 239
Elbrick, Charles Burke, 128, 234,
385
ELN, *Ejercito de Liberacion
Nacional,* 284, 328, 422
El Popular, Communist Newspaper,
Uruguay, 191, 193, 194
Engle, Byron, 1, 3, 12, and as
Director of OPS starting on 95
EPL, Ejercito Popular de
Liberacion, 284, 328, 422
Epoca, Leftist Newspaper, Uruguay,
194

F

FMLN, *Farabundo Marti
Movimiento de Liberacion
Nacional,* El Salvador, 16, 19

FARC, *Fuerzas Armadas Revolucionarias Colombianas,* 282, 284, 328, 422

Farkas, Albert, 435, 437; his background, 446-451; fighting *Tet* in Vietnam and his death

Fernandez, Zia, Col., Army of Uruguay, 178-179; new Chief of Police of Montevideo gears up to fight, 238, 239

Fields, Debbie, 117

Flores, Joaquin Remberto, AKA *"Manuel,"* 26; child guerrilla in El Salvador

Flores, Marco Tulio, AKA *"Pedro,"* 26; child guerrilla in El Salvador

Forney, Edward, General, USMC Ret, 436

Flores, Florencio, Gen., PNG, 88, 92

Florstedt, Robert, 37, 90, 94

French, Jerome (Jerry), 33, 36; appointed Business Manager, IAPA, 38, 39, 48, 49, 54-60; planning and meeting with General O'Meara, 73-74; reaction to Bobby Kennedy visit, 93-94; assignment to Washington

Fulbright, William, 8, 9, 366

G

Gabon, Lauren, Menses, 370

Gavras, Costa, C.P., Italy, producer "State of Siege" film, 9, 157, 224, 422

Gershensen, Robert (Bob), 143-148; bomb placed at the Marine House, Montevideo, and, 154

Gestido, Oscar, Gen., Pres. of Uruguay, 162, 175, 231

Geyer, Georgia Ann, 224; visit to Uruguay

Giannattasio, Luis, former Pres., Uruguay, 110

Goin, Lauren (Jack), 417, 426

Gonzales, Alfonso, General, Uruguay, 162, 174

Gonzales, Emilio, Sgt., Police of Uruguay, 153-154 *Tupamaro* attempt at Saenz's residence, 158, 195

Gooch, Charles, Capt., USA, 444

Gorbachev, Mikhail, former Premier, USSR, 11

Gorban, Mirta, 139, 239

Gordillo, Espasmodillo, DAS, Chief, Public Order, 289, 290, 292-294; meeting at DAS Headquarters on 10/20/69, 297, 300, 350, 355, 367-369; interrogation of Sabas and Tamayo in Cali, 396, 416, and 422

Grau, Saint-Laurent, Carlos, Inspector, Uruguay Police, 166

Grunwell, Alfred, Dr., 34, 50, 70, 94, 96-98; incident at IPA with chairs

Guevara, Dr. Ernesto, *Ché,* 39, 195, 198, 203-206; factors of an insurgency in Bolivia, and, 208, 215-221; action by General Barrientos, *Ché's* capture and demise

Guraux, Duke, 436

Gutierrez, Miguel, Mike, 35

Gutierrez, Paul, 78, 87-88; risking the wrath of the Panama riot

H

Hadley, Don, 442; at the *Tet*

Hall, Gus, Pres. CP, USA, 27

Hall, Theo, 424

Handell, Shafick, FMLN, 25

Hanscom, William E., 442, 443

Hardin, Herbert, 27, 260, 348, 427

Harold, Eden, Dr., kidnapping victim, 298

Harriman, Averill, 5

Harris, Harry, Maj., USA, 444

Heber, Alberto, President of Uruguay, 116, 131

Hevia, Manuel, 126, 188, 233

Henderson, Douglas, 204, 208, 209

Herrera, Diaz T., PNG, 88

Herrera, Hernado, 413

Hoffman, Abbie, 195

Holman, Ned, 109, 114, 123

Holquin, Melquides, 78, 79

Hontu, R., Uruguay G.M. Commander, 126

Horton, John Ryder, 123, 124, 129-130; search for penguin, 160, 161; the Summit, 167-171; incident at Hotel *San Rafael* regarding chandelier and U.S. Secret Service, 182, 190; transfer

Hoyt, Henry, 108, 119,124, 125, 128, 129, 131, 132, 136, 159-161; Summit Conference, 172, 173, 178-181; contributions to the struggle in Uruguay and his demise.

Hoover, J. Edgar, 77, 113, 114, 230, 262, 390

Human Events, 6; "Chief purpose of *State of Siege* film was"

Humphrey, Hubert, 9

Hurtado, Nestor, AKA *"Suicidio,"* 342

I

ICITAP, International Criminal Investigations Training Assistance Program, 11, 12

IPS, Institute for Policy Studies, 6

IAPA, Inter-American Police Academy, 4, 27–32 installation in Canal Zone, and, 47-60, operations and closure

ICA, International Cooperation Administration, 2, 17

J

Jackson, Jake, 95, 203; shot in Bolivia and, 436

Jelsh, Geraldine, 228, 232-233; meeting on Cantrell

Jessup, Frank, 426

Jimenez, Elias, kidnapping victim, 299

Johns, Lem, 163, 164, in Uruguay, 167–171; chandelier incident at Summit Conference, Hotel *San Rafael, Punta del Este*

Johnson, Lyndon B., 38, 135, 140, 172, 177-178; shaking hands with Americans at Summit Conference, 274

Johnson, Alexis U, 3

K

Kamer, Armin, 304-306; meeting with Lubinsky and Saenz on payment of ransom for kidnapped Swiss, 311, 318, 337, 352

Katz, Paul, 124, 140-141; meeting with Micali and Cantisani, 165, 231

Kelly, Roland, 22, 27

Kennedy, John F., 1, 3, 5, 9, 28, 80, 81, 164

Kennedy, Robert, 3, 4, 5, 14, 30, 65-72; meeting with IAPA staff at Ft. Davis, 117

Kimberling, Arthur, 424

King, Martin Luther, 110

Kirby, Kitty Kiellen, 396, 414

Kissinger, Henry, 33

Klare, Michael, 5, 8, 33, 423

Krachman, Billy, 214

Krauthammer, Charles, 435

L

Laird, Melvin, 2

Lancini, Ernest, 325

Landsdale, Edward Geary, 29, 65

Langguth, A. J., 126, 422-423; regarding purpose of *State of Siege* film and 439

La Nacion, Colombian Newspaper, 261

Laughlin, David, 29, 34, 37, 48, 50, 67, 69, 77

La Violencia, 267; description of and, 285

Leary, Bill, 224

Legnani, Agosto, Dr., MOI, Uruguay 142, 162, 163

Legnani, Carlos, Army of Uruguay, 239

Lemos, Jose Maria, former President, El Salvador, 22

Lenin, Ilich Vladimir, 15

Leon, Eduardo, Dr., 289-297; meeting held 10/20 at DAS, 303, 310-312; in Cali, 314; meeting at 3rd Brigade, *Valle del Cauca,* 350, 351, 353, 355, 393

Lepro, Alfredo, Dr., former MOI, Uruguay, 223

Leyva, Luis Etilio, Gen., Director DAS, 266 273, 289-291; meeting at DAS on 10/20/69, 301-330; introduction to kidnapping problem and politics, 349, 350, 354-358; analysis of Swiss kidnapping case, 359; the *Invisibles,* their hideout, 366-370; interview of Sabas and Tamayo, 371-375; DAS action against cartel, 377, 378-379; proposed decoration from GOC, 386-391; Jaime Padilla Convers, 393 and 413-417; resolution

Lindenauer, Julian, 125, 150, 151, 165, 179, 224, 428

Lopez Joseph de, 163

Londoño, Santa Cruz, 371

Longan, Jake, 195, 200, 201, 205-207; Col. Quintanilla on the *vincucha* and Col. Lopez on *maté de coca,* 209-210; meeting with Arguedes Mendietta, 213-215; shooting on the Plaza, 217, 218; departure, and, 220, 221; call to Saenz on *Ché's* diary

Los Invisibles, Cali Kidnapping Cartel, 368

Los Samuelitos, Child Guerrillas of El Salvador, 26

Lowman, Harold, 277, 280, 283-284; meeting with Saenz at U.S. Embassy, 305

Lovato, Luis, Comisario, Uruguay, 235

Lupin, Max, 335-342; negotiations and payment of the ransom for Straessle and Buff in Cali, 354

Lubinsky, Earl, 277-282 first meeting held at U.S. Embassy on kidnappings, 303-306; meeting with Kamer, 1st Secretary, Swiss Embassy, and Saenz, and, 377

M

Mabardy, Michael, 95, 428

MacArthur, Douglas, Gen., USA 2, 3,

Macias, Geraldine, 14

Marin Juan de Dios, Capt., Dom. Rep., NP, 38-40; description of guerrilla training received in Cuba

Martin, Carlos, Col., Army of Uruguay, 115, 120

Martinez, Hernadez, Maximiliano, President of El Salvador, 19; communist uprising

Marquez, Charles, 348, 349

Mas Mas, Antonio, 157; "acted independently to kill Mitrione"

McCabe, John, 435, 436

McCarthy, Joseph, 5

McCann, Michael, 93, 96-101, 427

McCarthy, John, 435

McClausland, Nicolas, Nick, 150, 151, 153

McIntyre, Loren, 46, 231, 236

McCone, John, 65

McPoland, John, 95, 96, 372, 442-451

Medrano, *"Chele,"* Col., Army of El Salvador, 311

Mein, John Gordon, 234, 385

Mejia, Manuel Juan, kidnap victim, 298

Melberg, Robert, 34, 94

Mendietta, Arquedes, MOI, Bolivia, 209-211; meeting with Longan and Saenz in his office, 220-221; *Ché* Guevara's diary to Fidel Castro

Micali, Danilo, Uruguay Police Director General, 125, 126, 141, 141

Miller, George, 435, 436

Mitrione, Dan, 5-7; allegations made 9, 10, 95, 96, 154, 157, 187, 237-238; nomination as Chief, OPS, Uruguay, 422, 435, 437; background

MOIR, *Movimiento Obrero Independiente Revolucionario,* Colombia, 282

Montand, Yves, 157

Montenegro, Edgar, 370

Montoya, Gerardo Antonio Herrera, member of *Los Invisibles,* 366

Montoya, Joseph, U.S. Senator from New Mexico, 274, 275

Morales, Juan, Col., Army of Uruguay, 148

Morris, Roger, 10, 187, 349, 423

Munroe, Johnson "Jack," 97, 98, 103; "Congratulations, you have made the black list," 110, 240, 258, 272, 425

Murphey, Michael, 435, 436

Murray, Hugh, 201, 202, 210, 211, 219

Murrow, Edward R., 45, 65

N

Neely, Jack, 96, 418, 427

Nentzen-Franco, Luis, Col., PNG, 35, 46

Nixon, Richard, 9, 10, 385

Noriega, Juan, 140, 161, 188-189; wire taps on the Soviet Embassy

Noriega, Manuel Antonio, Gen., PNG, 18, 85, 88, 92, 422

Norman, William, Col., USA, 93, 97; incident at IPA auditorium, 98, 101, 444

NSAM 179, National Security Action Memorandum on OPS, 3

O

O'Brien, Charlie, 436

OPS, United States Office of Public Safety, 1-15; creation of the program, officers involved, and 27; operations and 421-451; cold warriors

Olivero, Laro, kidnapping victim, 297

Olson, Chris, Colonel USA, 66, 67

O'Meara, Andrew, General, CINC South, 46, 54-58; meeting with French and Saenz on range for IAPA, 67; visit to IAPA with Robert Kennedy and 73

Orejuela, Gilberto Rodriguez, *Los Invisibles,* 371

Ordoñez, Jorge B. de, former President of Uruguay, 107

Ortega, Daniel, 14

Ortiz, Dardo, MOG Uruguay, 131

Otero, Alejandro, I&E, Uruguay, 118, 130, 133; visit of Dean Rusk, 148; Otero's assessment of *Tupamaros,* 166, 175-176; at the Summit, 189-190; dispute with Cantrell and 232, 2331

Ovedo, A. 158, 195

Owens, Adolph (Dolph), 435

P

Padilla, Hermidez, 386-391; circumstances regarding the kidnapping of his son, 401, 403, 404, 407, 412-417; details of a murder; identifying Jaime and arrest of a killer, 418-421; final meeting with Saenz

Padilla, Jaime Convers, 387-395; kidnapping alleged, 393, 403, 404-416; and resolution of his murder

Page, Louis (Lou), 34, 54, 78, 79

Palacios, Salvador *"Chamba,"* 23, 24

Parcherotti, Lopez, Inspector, Uruguay Police, 166

Paredes, Ruben, General, PNG, 92

Phelan, George, 386, 413, 416

Pineda, Tomas, 21, 24

Pionzo, Dino, 269, 277, 281 283, 305, 349, 351, 376, 384, 416

Pomerance, Rocky, 122

Powell, David, 239, 240

Proxmire, William, 9

Pullman, George, 118

Putin, Vladimir, President, USSR, 11

Q

Quick, Brian, 163, 164

Quintanilla, Roberto *"Toto,"* Col., Bolivian *Carabineros,* 51, 205-207; explanation of the *vincucha,* 211, 216, and 219-221; *Ché* Guevara's capture and Quintanilla's assassination in Austria

Quintero, Aida Rangel, Dr., 413

R

Redlin, Charles, 126, 140

Regalado, Silveira, Comisario, Uruguay Police, 137, 138

Restrepo, Carlos, President of Colombia, 351

Requierro, Ramiro, Chief, Uniform Police, Uruguay, 130, 132, 166, 239

Reverbel, Ulises Pereira, 135

Reyes, Simon, CP, Bolivia, 219

Richard, Guillermo, 411

Richardson, Bill, 13

Rimmer, Stephen, 442, 443

Rincon, Miguel Angel, AKA *"Cariño,"* 342

Rivero, Alfredo, Col., Metro Guard, Uruguay, 126

Rivero, Julio, former President, El Salvador, 22, 25

Rizo, Juan, 332, 371

Rockefeller, Nelson, 238

Rodriguez, Carmen Rosa, 411

Rodriguez, Felix, 212

Rodriguez, Ventura, General Army of Uruguay; 109, 113, 120-122; incident at IACP Convention in Miami, 142; resignation, 187; discussions with Saenz on allegations of torture and 238

Rojas, Jesus Roland, 132, 133, 134

Romero, Paul, Maj., USA, 45

Romero Juan Jergensen, 175

Rooney, Ruth, 98, 229

Ruiz, Anthony "Tony," 430

Rueda, Luis, Inspector, NP, Ecuador, 325

Rusk, Dean, 123, 128, 130-134; attack by Roland Rojas at wreath laying ceremony, Montevideo

S

Salazar, Fabio, Gomez, kidnapping victim, 290, 291

Salceda, Michael, 78

Sampson, Richard, 190, 225, 229

Sanchez, Bernardo Salazar, General 3rd Brigade, Colombia, Cali, 280, 291, 294, 296, 301, 303, 316-323; meeting held at 3rd Brigade Quartel, *Valle del Cauca,* on kidnapping problem, 330, 357, 358

Sandoval, Felipe, 78

Sanjur, Amado, Col., PNG Officer, 88

Santana, Larry, Maj., USA, 78, 87-88; risking the wrath of the Panama riot, 444

Santioana, Joseph (Joe), 35, 69, 75, 77, 79, 93, 98

Santizabal, Gonzalo Cordova, 331, 371

Sayre, Robert (Bob), 181, 191, 223, 229, 231, 236; telegram regarding Saenz's replacement, 418; Ambassador to Panama

Saunders, William, 443, 444

Schroeder, Edward, Col., USA, 43

Seixas, Angela Camargo, 423

Sendic, Raul Antonaccio, MLN Leader, 118, 157

Shaw, Bernard, 179, 180

Sigui, Fernando, Col., Army of El Salvador, 21

Smith, Liz, 10; "*State of Siege* most important political film of the decade"

Solinas, Francisco, director, "State of Siege" film, 9, 157, 224

Somma, Gervasio, Col., Army of Uruguay Republican Guard, 111

Somoza, Anastacio, Pres., Nicaragua, 13

Spinelli, Walter, 172

Stalin, Joseph, former Prem., USSR, 1

Stanham, John, Dr., 200

Sterling, Clair, 187

Stevenson, Robert, 277, 352-354; U.S. Ambassador meeting with the Swiss, 377, 378; exit briefing by Saenz for Ambassador Vaughn

Stewart, Frank, 114, 119, 180

Stotts, Ben, 265, 273, 274, 289, 375

Straessle, Eric, 293, 294 329, 330, 355

Straessle, Werner, 289; kidnapped, 293-294; held captive 313, 316-319; investigation of his kidnapping by Colombian security forces, 323, 328, 329, 332-333; in captivity, 335-338, 344, 354-356; info provided by Straessle and Buff on their kidnapping and, 368

Stroessner, Alfredo, Gen. and former Pres., Paraguay, 159, 172

Suarez, Jorge, Under Secretary of MOI, Uruguay, 223

Summers, Gordon, Gen., USA, 13

Surface, Vic, 200

Switzerland of the Americas, 106

T

Tamayo, Luis Fernando Garcia, 329; suspected kidnapper, 331-332; chat with Sabas Calderon Castro, 332, 341-342; collecting the ransom, 360, 361; caught in a rat-trap, 366-369; Saenz meets

Tamez, Rudy, 159-161; U.S. Embassy Country Team meeting and coup rumors

Taylor, Maxwell, 65

Tejera, Adolfo, Dr. 107-108; meeting with Saenz in Uruguay re: U.S. assistance, 142

Tenant, George, 11

Tenorio, Cesar, 331, 333; shooting at the Hotel *Aristi,* 334, 340-348; visit to roadblock, Saenz incident at bar in Cali, 371-375; Tenorio wounded in action during shootout at Barrio Restrepo, 384

Tetaz, Rene, 163, 174

Thompson, Robert, 3

Thorpe, Knute, Col., USA, 6, 45, 429, 444

Topping, John, 142, 159, 182, 184, 192, 236-237; Saenz meeting on Sayre telegram

Torres, Joaquin, Lozada, kidnapping victim, 300

Torrigos, Omar, Gen., PNG, 8, 30, 36, 75; "the Guardia must take control," 85, 88, 92, 418, 422

Tricontinental Magazine, Cuban Publication, 5

Tull, Jim, 160

Tupamaros, Marxist Guerrillas, 9, 123, 135, 157, 225, 236; terrorist attacks continue

Tse-Tung, Mao, 15; "every communist must grasp the truth"

Tivoli Hotel, 86

Turcios, Luis, 224

Turner, Sam, 442

U

Ubach, Rogelio, Col., Army of Uruguay, 143, 238

V

Vado Del Yeso, 218; *Ché* Guevara killed in Bolivia

Valle del Cauca, Colombia, 261, 278

Varon, Eduardo, kidnapping victim, 332, 371

Vasquez, Mario, 35, 77

Vaughn, Jack Hood, 92, 262, 277-282; C.T. meeting on kidnapping

problem held after arrival of Saenz, 286, 352, 353, 376-378; exit briefing on kidnapping problem in Colombia, 383-384; meeting with Saenz on kidnapping of American 384, 390, 416

Vernon, Wyman W., 436

Villareal, Filippo, Revelo, Commander, NP, Cali, 315, 317, 319, 356-358; meeting with Saenz on location of the kidnappers hideout

Von Steinbech, Rafael, 404

W

Wachter, John, 112, 114

Walton, Frank, 95, 428

Wells, Jack, 435, 436

Weisman, Marvin, 277, 352

White, Bob, 104

Winston, Archer, 10

Witt, John de, 348

Y

Yanstin, Nicolas (Nick), 430

Yemmi, Hector, Col., Gendarmarie, Argentina, 228

Youngblood, Rufus, 164

Z

Zaglio, Vidal, Min. Exterior, Uruguay, 131

Zapata, Alfredo, El Salvador, 20, 87, 88

Zeigler, John C., 442, 443

Notes:

1. A listing of OPS cold warriors and their accomplishments can be found on pages 424-445.
2. The Foreword, Epilogue, and Appendix were not indexed.